American Ethnicity

American Ethnicity

2ND EDITION

JOSEPH HRABA
Iowa State University

F.E. Peacock Publishers, Inc.
Itasca, Illinois

In memory of Josef Hraba,
my grandfather and an immigrant

Cover photo by Liaison International/Barbara Campbell

Photo credits:

Page 1	Brown Brothers
27	Minnesota Historical Society
43	Chicago Historical Society
77	David Young-Wolff/PhotoEdit
96	Reuters/Bettmann Newsphotos
116	Ulli Steltzer from her book THE NEW AMERICANS
132	The Granger Collection
199	UPI/Bettmann Newsphotos
211	National Archives #111-SC-83744
242	Monty Roessell/Black Star
254	Official U.S. Immigration and Naturalization Service Photo. Washington, D.C.
284	UPI/Bettmann Newsphotos
291	Wide World Photos
333 & 354	Chicago Historical Society
375	Culver Pictures, Inc.
394	Chicago Historical Society
411	Reuters/Bettmann Newsphotos
431	Library of Congress
469	National Archives #210-G2-C153
485	The Bettmann Archive
518 & 523	Ulli Steltzer from her book THE NEW AMERICANS

Copyright © 1994 by F. E. Peacock Publishers, Inc.
All rights reserved.
Library of Congress Catalog Card No. 92-61958
ISBN 0-87581-370-4
Printed in the United States of America
Printing: 10   9   8   7   6   5   4   3   2   1
Year: 99   98   97   96   95   94

CONTENTS

PREFACE TO THE SECOND EDITION

Ethnic relations in America have changed since the first edition of this book, and this edition hopefully reflects that reality. The book has been expanded to fifteen chapters to better capture the increasing ethnic diversity in our society. Its basic theme remains, however: ethnic relations in a changing American society.

Many people have contributed to this second edition. The publisher and critics, Harvey M. Choldin, John Pease, and Lionel A. Maldonado, have made significant contributions. I am also grateful to colleagues at Iowa State University, especially Willis Goudy, for help in this project. Three typists, Rachel Burlingame, Karen Larrew, and Cynthia Gaunt, have been particularly helpful in the preparation of this manuscript. My appreciation is again extended to the social scientists whose works are represented in this book—which is dedicated to ethnic Americans of all races and nationalities.

THE PLAN OF THE BOOK

American Ethnicity consists of fifteen chapters in four parts. The first chapter introduces the book's theme and alone comprises the first part of the book. Sociological and psychological perspectives on race and ethnic relations in American society are surveyed in Part II, Chapters 2 through 6. Chapters 2, 3, and 4 examine the sociological lore on ethnic groups and societal change, which includes assimilationism, pluralism, and ethnic conflict theory. The psychology of prejudice and discrimination is analyzed in Chapter 5. The complementarity of these theories is stressed in Chapter 6.

The perspective of theoretical complementarity is then applied to America's indigenous and immigrant groups in Chapters 7 through

14, which comprise Part III. The theme is that these groups have exchanged land, labor, and capital in the course of societal change. America's indigenous groups are closely tied to the exchange of land, while its immigrant groups have been more fully implicated in the nation's changing labor needs. Capital is also important in ethnic history, and the role of capital and the ethnic subeconomy is analyzed in the chapters on Asian Americans, 12 through 14.

The final part, consisting of Chapter 15, is a summary of the perspectives in the social sciences on the minority community, namely, social pathology and ethnic communalism. From the first perspective, the minority group is said to disintegrate under the pressures of prejudice and discrimination, while from the second perspective it is said to be preserved. The chapter is organized around the expression of and evidence for these points of view. Pathology and communalism in our framework represent two perspectives on the exclusion of ethnic groups and their divergence. When excluded, do minority groups lose or conserve their community?

The author welcomes comments from both students and instructors. He can be reached at the Department of Sociology, Iowa State University, Ames, Iowa 50011, or by e-mail at s1.jxh.isumvs.

INTRODUCTION

CHAPTER
1
◎◎

THE SOCIAL SCIENCES AND ETHNIC RELATIONS

T he history of America is inseparable from that of its racial and ethnic groups, and thus interest in American ethnicity is tantamount to interest in America itself. Reflecting the ethnic diversity in this country, we have always had diverse opinions about racial and ethnic relations. This is as true for social scientists as it is for the American public at large. One purpose of this book is to present the variety of perspectives on race and ethnicity provided by the social sciences.

Notable contributions to understanding racial and ethnic relations have come from the social sciences. First was the realization that there are no pure races, which turned the study of race and ethnicity away from biological differences among groups. The sociological study of race and ethnicity began around the end of the nineteenth century, when "social thought was almost completely dominated by biological concepts and points of view" (Reuter, 1945:454). This idea, known as Social Darwinism, was more of an ideology than a science, a point of view that paid almost exclusive attention to biological differences among races. These differences supposedly rendered some groups more fit than others to rule and prosper. Social Darwinism was an outgrowth of the larger Darwinian view on evolution, which saw it as a process of universal competition, lethal selection, and the survival of the fittest. This metaphor of a natural struggle for subsistence and the survival of the fittest was applied directly to the study of race relations in human society.

3

Social science changed, however, as social thinkers moved beyond biological analogies and began to analyze race, ethnicity, and society itself as social phenomena. Human society is part of the natural order, to be sure, but it is also above that order and incapable of being fully explained by analogies to the natural world. This is as true for race and ethnic relations as it is for society at large. Beginning early in the twentieth century, social scientists increasingly turned to the evocative metaphors of nineteenth-century social evolutionism, leaving behind those of Social Darwinism.

Social evolutionism is a tradition of understanding human society as a social entity apart from the natural order, on the assumption that culture distinguishes human society from nature. More specifically, it is a tradition of analyzing the change of human society in this manner. Nearly all social thinkers of the nineteenth century were concerned with changes in Western society, including industrialization, the spread of education and literacy, urbanization, the growth of bureaucracy, and the diversification of the occupational structure. New kinds of work have been added to American society over the last century and a half, first industrial blue-collar and later white-collar occupations, and thus the nation's division of labor has grown more diverse in the course of societal change.

ETHNIC RELATIONS AND SOCIETAL CHANGE

The social evolutionists predicted the demise of the folk community as a result of societal change. Specifically, the homogeneity and harmony of folk society would become virtually impossible with occupational diversification. People work at too many different kinds of jobs and do too many diverse things now to feel the old consciousness of kind and solidarity with one another. Nor could peasant life be truly transplanted to the growing industrial cities, for the social fabric of the village and the peasants' connection with nature were fractured by their migration to the industrial city. Finally, bureaucracy in modern society would more and more serve the functions once entrusted to the family in traditional society. Education, work, and welfare would all be accomplished outside the home, in large-scale bureaucracies. The entire process would bring a growing impersonality to life, a loss of community. This analysis was applied to folk groups caught in the change process—that is, ethnic and racial groups who were migrating to industrial cities; this was the beginning of the sociology of race and ethnicity in modern society.

Since the sociology of race and ethnicity has its roots in nineteenth-century social evolutionism, its thematic concern has been the

4

history of racial and ethnic groups in the course of societal change. A notable lore has accumulated in sociology and psychology about ethnic and race relations in the larger change process. This lore will be surveyed in the chapters to follow and used to interpret the histories of ethnic groups in America.

The insight of nineteenth-century social evolutionism is that the structure of society was changing. There were the diversification of the occupational structure and the spread of education, for example. When this insight is applied to ethnic groups in American society, the issue becomes the impact of societal change on these groups and their relations. The modern academic lore on race and ethnicity is organized around this issue, and this is the focus of this book.

Societal change and the histories of ethnic groups are both implicated in and inseparable from the changing labor needs of American society. The originally agrarian American society has undergone two major changes in its labor needs, first the growth of industrial, blue-collar jobs, and then the rise of white-collar work. Thus the change process has three phases: agrarian, industrial and post-industrial. These phases are the context for our analysis of ethnic groups in this country (see Figure 1.1).

Following European colonization, America was first an agricultural society, with most people farming and living in rural areas. This era coincided with the initial contact between indigenous people and immigrant groups, and the expansion of the Western frontier by the immigrants. Later, following the Civil War and frontier settlement, the United States also became an industrial nation, and the stream of immigration from other lands began to flow into American cities. These immigrants helped build the industrial base of the nation during the late nineteenth and early twentieth centuries. After World War II, there was a second change in the nation's labor needs, as the need for white-collar workers grew. This is the post-industrial phase of American society. Ethnic and racial groups have changed in this process, ei-

FIGURE 1.1 THE CHANGE OF AMERICAN SOCIETY AND ITS ETHNIC GROUPS

Agrarian Society c. 1600–1865	Industrial Society c. 1865–1945	Post-Industrial Society c. 1945–Present

$\longrightarrow$ Ethnic change $\longrightarrow$

Note: Dates are approximations only.

ther keeping pace with or falling behind the changes in the larger society. Our task is to understand the different courses ethnic groups have taken in this history, and we begin by turning to the sociological lore on race and ethnic relations in American society.

THE SCHOOLS OF THOUGHT ON AMERICAN ETHNICITY

Assimilationism, ethnic pluralism, and ethnic conflict theory are the three principal schools of sociological thought on race and ethnic relations. As perspectives, they look at the impact of societal change on America's ethnic and racial groups.

Assimilationists contend that racial and ethnic groups assimilate into a changing society (Chapter 2). Ethnic and racial groups move off the land and into large, ethnically diverse cities, send their children to a unitary school system, and eventually disperse throughout the broad range of occupations characteristic of the present era. The theory sees ethnicity today as a survival of folk society with no lasting role in contemporary society, for societal change results in the eventual absorption of ethnic groups into a mass society. This position is closely connected with the early Chicago School of sociology, particularly with the works of Robert Park and Louis Wirth. Gunnar Myrdal, another proponent of assimilationism, took this point of view in his epochal work *An American Dilemma* (1944). The contact hypothesis is yet another expression of this perspective. All these works share the postulation that ethnicity is eclipsed by the force of societal change, and current research continues to chart the assimilation of ethnic groups into the larger American society.

The pluralists, on the other hand, argue that ethnic groups survive in the change process (Chapter 3). Ethnic and racial groups change, to be sure, but they also remain constant as a source of social identity, a sense of community, and the basis for resource competition. Pluralists point to ethnic groups in societies the world over and say that ethnicity is as much a part of modern as traditional society. Pluralism arose originally as a counterpoint to assimilationism, a position taken by Will Herberg (1955), and then by Milton Gordon (1964), and Nathan Glazer and Daniel Moynihan (1970, 1975). In the 1970s an addition to sociological pluralism came from anthropology, in a set of works known collectively as the New Ethnicity School, and pluralism continues in current work by social scientists.

Conflict theory expands on the theme of ethnic competition for resources in a changing society (Chapter 4). According to assimilationists, change brings increased opportunity for the absorption of all ethnic groups into society. The process works principally through the occupational diversification of society and a corresponding expansion of public education. The conflict alternative to assimilationism has its origins in a countervailing view of the change process, one that is also prefigured in nineteenth-century social evolutionism. According to conflict theorists, societal change exacerbates competition and conflict among ethnic groups vying for new opportunities that come with societal change. Groups compete for wealth, power, and status, and competing groups do not assimilate with one another. Chapter 4 examines the exact nature of this competition and conflict, the parties involved, and the resources in American society for which they vie.

The level of analysis shifts in Chapter 5 from ethnic relations in a changing American society to the prejudice of individual Americans— that is, from sociology to psychology. Traditions in the psychology of prejudice and discrimination are examined in this chapter, with the understanding that analysis of ethnic relations at the societal level must be complemented by that of prejudice and discrimination at the individual level. Societal change and the psychology of the people who live through it are in reality inseparable. The social forces of societal change and ethnic exchange are interwoven into the thoughts, feelings, and actions of the individuals involved. This chapter underscores this fundamental fact.

The three social theories of race and ethnic relations, plus the psychology of prejudice and discrimination, are commonly regarded as competing perspectives on American ethnicity. To the exclusion of the others, one theory or another is seen as an essentially correct depiction and explanation of societal and ethnic change. In Chapter 6, however, it is argued that these theories are actually complementary. Each theory is only a partial explanation of societal and ethnic change, but each makes up for what the other theories lack, and together they offer a fuller understanding of ethnic change in the larger change process. Societal change did bring more opportunity for assimilation in America through the mechanisms of white-collar work and mass education, but it also resulted in increased ethnic competition and conflict over these mobility routes. Considerations of race and ethnicity in school admissions, hiring, and promotions today attest to the endurance of ethnicity. The history of ethnic groups is indeed implicated in societal change, a process which has meant, paradoxically, both the assimilation of these groups and their endurance.

This broader view recognizes the possibility that some groups have been included into American society, while others have been excluded from it. Some ethnic groups kept pace with societal change, while others lagged behind it. The products of this dual phenomenon of inclusion and exclusion are both change in and persistence of racial and ethnic groups in American society. The reasons for the inclusion and exclusion of ethnic groups in American society are examined in Chapter 6.

Ethnic groups exchange land, labor, and capital in the course of societal change and their own history. The process began in this country with conflict over land between immigrant and indigenous groups. The more powerful immigrants took land from the indigenous groups, who were subsequently excluded from American society, and the history of indigenous people then diverged from that of the larger society.

The growing need for labor brought more immigrants to the country, and the fate of these groups has since been implicated in the country's changing labor needs. As these needs have changed from agrarian to industrial blue-collar and finally to white-collar work, some groups have kept abreast of these changes while others have not. Some groups, while themselves converging with societal change, have excluded others from the modern mechanisms of assimilation, creating the dual phenomenon of inclusion and exclusion of ethnic groups in American society. Ethnic stereotypes and prejudice have reflected and reinforced these historical facts.

IMMIGRATION

Ethnic history in America began with the immigration of diverse groups into North America and their contact with one another and with indigenous peoples. Since 1820 the federal government has kept records of this immigration, which show that from 1820 to 1989 more than 65 million people immigrated into the country. Immigration into America began before 1820, of course, with the arrival of Africans and northern and western Europeans. At its peak, late in the nineteenth and early in the twentieth centuries, immigration into the United States represented 60 percent of the world's total immigration (Bennett, 1963). Figure 1.2 shows the volume of this human movement into the United States from 1820 to 1986.

The numbers in Figure 1.2 include immigrants from Africa, Asia, Europe, and the Americas, who together comprise most of the immigration into the United States. Immigration into the United States from Africa and northern and western Europe peaked before the twentieth century. In the late nineteenth and early twentieth centuries, immigra-

FIGURE 1.2 IMMIGRATION TO THE UNITED STATES, 1820–1989

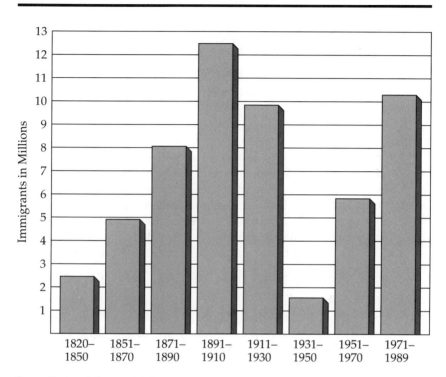

Source: *Statistical Abstract of the United States, 1991.* Washington, DC: Bureau of the Census, 1991.

tion from southern and eastern Europe grew. In the last half of the twentieth century, immigration into the country has been increasingly from the Americas and Asia. In the process, the ethnic composition of America has become ever more diverse.

AFRICANS

From 1502 to 1860, 9.5 to 11.3 million Africans were, without their consent, transported to the New World, and roughly 6 to 7 percent of this total slave trade came to the United States. The majority of slaves were brought to the Americas in the eighteenth century, and between 1780 and 1810 about as many slaves came as in the preceding 160 years. Some slaves still came to the Americas in the early nineteenth century, even after Great Britain (in 1807) and the United States (in

1808) had abolished slave trade. By the time of emancipation, however, almost sixty years later, only 1 percent of the black population in this country was foreign-born. In 1961–1989, there were more than 287,000 African immigrants into the country. (That figure, however, includes North Africa, and roughly one-fourth of that number came from Egypt alone.) Between 1981 and 1989, there were 414,000 immigrants from Haiti, Jamaica, Trinidad, and other islands in the Caribbean with large African-origin populations.

EUROPEANS

Between 1820 and 1986, almost 37 million Europeans immigrated into the United States. Europeans represented 82 percent of the total immigration between 1820 and 1960, making them the largest immigrant group in America. Immigrants came first from northern and western Europe and then increasingly from eastern and southern Europe. Table 1.1 shows this immigration by decade in its peak years and the percentages coming from northern and western Europe and southern and eastern Europe.

Immigrants from northern and western Europe are the so-called old immigrants, having come in greater numbers to the United States before those from southern and eastern Europe. There was a large influx of Irish immigrants into the country from 1830 to 1860, due to the dire poverty of Irish peasants and, more specifically, the potato famine. The percentage of immigrants from Ireland peaked in these years, although Irish immigration has continued. Largely because of political turmoil in Germany at mid-century, many Germans joined the Irish in the United States. The German percentage of total immigration peaked between 1840 and 1860. Later, after the Civil War, many Scandinavians immigrated into the country, settling primarily in the Midwest. Immigration from northern and western Europe continues to this day. For example, between 1961 and 1989 there were more than 328,000 immigrants from Germany and more than 480,000 from Great Britain.

In the 1890s there were for the first time more immigrants into the United States from southern and eastern Europe than from northern and western Europe. Between 1890 and 1920 this new European immigration exceeded that from northern and western Europe. Most of the immigrants from southern Europe were from Italy. More than 3.8 million Italians came to the United States between 1891 and 1920. Immigrants from eastern Europe were principally from Russia and the old Austro-Hungarian Empire, including a large number of Poles. Among these immigrants were Jews, especially those from Russia, who were

TABLE 1.1 EUROPEAN SOURCES OF IMMIGRATION TO THE UNITED STATES,
1820–1920

Decade	Total European Immigration	Northern and Western European	Southern and Eastern European
1821–1830	98,817	68%	2.0%
1831–1840	495,688	82	1.0
1841–1850	1,597,501	93	0.3
1851–1860	2,452,660	94	0.8
1861–1870	2,065,270	88	2.0
1871–1880	2,272,262	74	0.7
1881–1890	4,737,046	72	18.0
1891–1900	3,558,978	45	52.0
1901–1910	8,136,016	22	71.0
1911–1920	4,376,564	17	59.0

Note: Percentages may not total to 100 because of rounding and European immigration from other countries.

Source: Based on data in Marian T. Bennett, 1963. *American Immigration Policies*. Washington, DC: Public Affairs Press.

fleeing from religious persecution there. Immigration from southern and eastern Europe continues to this day. Between 1961 and 1989, for example, more than 366,000 immigrants into the United States came from Italy, nearly 194,000 from Poland, and more than 117,000 from the former Soviet Union.

ASIANS

From 1820 to 1960, over 1 million Asians immigrated into the United States, most from China (409,439) and Japan (329,886). Immigrants from China came to the United States before those from Japan, in connection with the Gold Rush in California in the 1850s, the building of the first transcontinental railroad in the 1860s, and the development of California agriculture in the 1870s and 1880s. After 1880 Chinese immigration fell off due to the Chinese Exclusion Acts. Japanese immigration picked up where Chinese immigration left off, the mass of it occurring between 1890 and 1920. Many of these Japanese immigrants had earlier immigrated to Hawaii, and from Hawaii they came to the continental United States, replacing at first the Chinese in the fields of California. Substantial Japanese immigration stopped with the Quota Act of 1924 and picked up again only after World War II.

Between 1960 and 1989, more than 4.5 million Asians immigrated into the United States. These include over 640,000 Chinese from the mainland and Taiwan, and 123,900 Japanese. However, Asian immigration is now more diverse, and people are coming to the United States from virtually all parts of Asia. More than 600,000 Koreans, about 537,000 Vietnamese, over 893,000 Filipinos, and nearly 440,000 Indians immigrated into the United States during the period 1960–1989. Asian immigration began to increase significantly after 1970, and between 1960 and 1986 it was the second largest immigration to the United States during that period, following only that from the Americas. Since 1981, Asian immigration into the country has exceeded that from any other region of the world.

AMERICANS

Mexicans are the largest immigrant group into the United States from the Americas. Mexican Americans are considered in Chapter 8 as both an indigenous people and an immigrant group. At least 200,000 Hispanos were living in the Southwest in the middle of the nineteenth century, when the United States took control of that region with the Treaty of Guadalupe Hidalgo and the Gadsden Purchase. Thus, Hispanos as well as Indians are indigenous people in the Southwest, at least relative to the rest of us. After the turn of the century there was an influx of Mexican immigrants into the country as a result of the Mexican Revolution and the growing agricultural economy of the Southwest. Mexican immigration rose after the Mexican Revolution began in 1910, declined with the Great Depression and repatriation programs, but increased again in recent decades. The peak decades of Mexican immigration are shown in Table 1.2.

Current controversy over Mexican immigration is on the number of undocumented migrants to the United States from Mexico. Table 1.2 shows only documented immigration, but some speculate that there are as many as 12 million undocumented aliens in the country, and the majority are Mexican. Not all undocumented Mexican immigrants come to settle in the United States permanently, however, which is also true for other immigrants. Some are settlers, but many are sojourners or commuters, who stay only temporarily in the United States. With this in mind, Passel (1986) estimated that in 1980 there were between 1.5 and 2 million undocumented Mexican settlers in the United States. Estimates of Mexican sojourners temporarily in the United States run around 400,000. These figures are substantially smaller than speculative accounts of undocumented immigration from

TABLE 1.2 MEXICAN IMMIGRATION TO THE UNITED STATES, 1911–1989

Decade	Number of Mexican Immigrants
1911–1920	244,705
1921–1930	448,648
1931–1940	17,936
1941–1950	59,217
1951–1960	299,811
1961–1970	443,300
1971–1980	637,200
1981–1989	974,200

Source: Joan W. Moore, 1970. *Mexican Americans*. Englewood Cliffs, NJ: Prentice-Hall, Inc., p. 41, and *Statistical Abstract of the United States, 1991*, p. 10.

Mexico, but should be added to those in Table 1.2 to complete the picture of Mexican immigration.

More than 6 million immigrants from the Americas came to the United States between 1961 and 1989. Well over 3 million were Mexican, but these immigrants came from many countries. There was significant immigration from Canada, Cuba and other Caribbean islands, and Central and South America as well as Mexico during this period.

THE ETHNIC COMPOSITION OF THE NATION

In 1980, the three largest ethnic groups in the United States were English, Germans, and Irish (Lieberson and Waters, 1988). There were 49,598,000 English, or 21.9 percent of the total population; 49,224,000 Germans, 21.7 percent of the population; and 40,166,000 Irish, or 17.7 percent of the population. More Germans than English have been counted in other surveys, but many English might have indicated their ethnic identity as American in 1980 (Lieberson and Waters, 1988). It is difficult to truly estimate which of these two groups was the larger and thus the largest ethnic group in the country.

Other European groups included the French, 12,892,000 (5.7%); Italian, 12,184,000 (5.4%); Scottish, 10,049,000 (4.4%); Polish, 8,228,000 (3.6%); Dutch, 6,304,000 (2.8%); Swedish, 4,345,000 (1.9%); Norwegian, 3,454,000 (1.5%); and Russian, 3,489,000 (1.5%). Except for the Italians, Poles, and Russians, most of these groups are old immigrants from northwestern Europe. Obviously, the longer the residence of immigrant groups in the United States, the greater is their natural increase and percentage of the total population. Other European groups were Czech, 1,892,000; Hungarian, 1,665,000; Danish, 1,518,000; and Portuguese, 1,024,000; each of these groups accounted for less than 1 percent of the total population. Additional ethnic labels used by American people suggest that the numbers of Europeans in the U.S. population was even greater in 1980.

African Americans were the largest non-European group, 26,858,000 (11.9%), and thus they were the fourth largest ethnic group in the country. Mexicans followed, 7,693,000 (3.4%), and there were 1,444,000 Puerto Ricans and 4,251,000 other Spanish. Three percent of the population, 6,716,000, gave American Indian as an ancestry group. The total Asian population was 3,624,000. Over 38 million Americans gave "American" or did not respond to the question about ancestry, suggesting that these figures are only estimates.

IMMIGRATION AS A RESPONSE TO LABOR NEEDS

Immigrants came to America for numerous reasons. Many fled from religious persecution or political turmoil or to evade military draft, and many came for family reunification. Most immigrants came here, however, for land on the frontier, for jobs in the nation's emerging industrial order, or for other economic reasons. That is, the labor needs of the nation have brought the immigrants here. The close connection between the business cycle and cyclical fluctuations in immigration after the Civil War reflects the larger economic reasons for which people came to this country (Jerome, 1926/1973). The volume of immigration was highest at the time of the building of the industrial base of America, after the Civil War and before the First World War. There has always been more immigration into the United States than emigration, or people leaving the country, except during the Great Depression (Simon, 1986). Immigrants are typically young adults with their entire working lives ahead of them, and immigrants have higher labor force participation rates than natives, suggesting that immigrants are job seekers. The immigrant—the free one, at least—is a seller of labor and migrates towards its demand. Thus, the history of immigrant groups in America is tied to the nation's labor needs.

Immigrants were not only pulled to America, they were also pushed out of their native lands. Changes in agriculture and early industrialization in Europe displaced peasants and artisans. For example, "high rents, lack of available industrial opportunities, and evictions, as well as population pressures" pushed the Irish to America (Bodnar, 1985:18). After the end of serfdom in Poland, peasants needed money and thus emigrated in search of work. They moved to different parts of Europe and then to the United States (Morawska, 1985). Industrialization in Bohemia pushed artisans out of their traditional jobs and toward emigration. In short, commercialization of farming pushed people off the land and industrialization undercut the economic niche of skilled artisans throughout Europe, pushing them into international migration.

Current conditions in Mexico provide another example. The population of Mexico was 51 million in 1970, but is expected to be 109 million by 2000, a 113 percent increase (Simcox, 1988a). For more than three decades, the Mexican economy has not been able to provide full employment for its citizens. The Mexican gross national product (GNP) shrunk in dollar terms in the 1980s, with no net increase in employment. Projections to the year 2000 anticipate that 27 million of the 40.5 million Mexican labor force will be either under-employed or unemployed. Thus the incentive for migration to the United States continues, and we see people pushed northward by conditions back home. As its younger population (15–34 years of age, those most prone to emigrate) grows, the Mexican economy is expected to provide jobs for only one-half, or at best three-quarters, of those entering its labor force (Simcox, 1988a). This will likely mean continued Mexican immigration into the United States unless this is reversed due to the North American Free Trade Agreement (NAFTA). Immigration flows to the United States depend on economic and social conditions in home countries as well as labor needs in the United States (Bodnar, 1985).

Immigrants were not necessarily pushed and pulled as single individuals into international migration. They were more likely to flow through social networks (Boyd, 1989). First, the decision to emigrate was typically a family one. Family members migrated to relieve economic pressure at different stages of the family life cycle. For example, married men with a few young children emigrate from Mexico to the United States to help meet the financial needs of a young family. Where family land was passed only to the eldest son, as was the case in late nineteenth-century Ireland and Japan, younger sons and daughters were forced to find opportunity elsewhere, in immigration to America, for example. By the same token, older people who are grandparents are not likely to emigrate.

Second, relatives and friends who had emigrated earlier wrote home about opportunities in America and sent remittances that were used to pay the cost of transportation for later migrants to the United States. Unmarried Irish women in the United States often helped female relatives still in Ireland to emigrate with both information about employment in this country and money for passage to America (Diner, 1983). Finally, many people immigrated to the United States simply to be reunited with family members already in the country. That is, some family members will emigrate for economic reasons and then other family members will follow to be reunited. However, there were still family separations due to immigration (Byington, 1910:181):

> As I waited one day in one of the little railroad stations of Homestead, a Slav came in and sat down by a woman with a two-year-old child. He made shy advances to the baby, coaxing her in a voice of heart-breaking loneliness. She would not come and finally her mother took her away. The Slav turned to the rest of the company, and taking us all into his confidence said very simply, "me wife, me babe, Hungar."

In the past, immigrant laborers as a class usually found nothing better than unskilled work. This does not mean that the immigrants lacked skills and were capable of only crude physical work. On the contrary, many were skilled artisans or small farmers who became members of a class of blue-collar workers or domestic servants in the United States. The bulk of the immigration into this country occurred in its industrial phase, and industry provided the jobs available at the time. There were exceptions, of course; many Scandinavian and German immigrants settled as farmers, and some of America's present minority groups spent many years as farm laborers. This is true of Asians, African Americans, and Mexican Americans, for example. Today, immigrants are concentrated in two occupational groupings, farm laborers and professional and technical workers. The latter is a result of changes in the nation's labor needs—the growing demand for skilled white-collar workers—and it reflects the "brain drain" from other countries into the United States. Although the shift to white-collar work has been a force for assimilation in America, it also means that recent immigrants enter a different economy than did earlier ones. With the shift to mental work, the cultural skills that immigrants bring to the United States is now far more significant than it was in the past, when most jobs were manual.

As the nation's labor needs have changed, so have its immigrant groups. The expansion of white-collar work and public education has meant better inclusion of many immigrants but especially for their native-born offspring into the larger American society (see Chapter 6). At this time, America is losing good-paying blue-collar jobs due to foreign competition and the export of jobs overseas to take advantage of cheaper labor. Thus, the demand for immigrant labor is shifting to white-collar as well as manual work.

Immigrants have helped meet the nation's labor needs at the national level. In particular locales, however, another issue is often at the forefront: That is, do immigrants take the jobs of American citizens? Today, this complaint is heard in California, Texas, Florida, and New York City in particular, and other places where many recent immigrants tend to concentrate. Borjas and Tienda (1987) concluded that such labor displacement is negligible overall at the national level. However, in places where immigrants first settle, and for particular subgroups already in those places, immigrants may have a negative impact. For example, every 10 percent increase in immigrants reduces the average wages of resident alien workers by 2 to 9 percent.

There were 1.8 million immigrants into California during the 1970s, and one million were Mexican. This stimulated the state's economy, and of the 645,000 new jobs in Los Angeles County in the 1970s, two-thirds went to immigrants (Muller and Espenshade, 1985). Although immigrants did not directly displace native-born workers, such as African Americans, the net out-migration of white Americans and resident Hispanics and the declining net in-migration of African Americans suggest that new immigrants might have indirectly displaced workers in California.

There are three theories about the impact of immigrants on American workers. In the first, immigrants are seen to displace American workers on a one-to-one basis, but the evidence for this theory is limited (see above). According to the second, the American labor market is segmented so that immigrants and residents take different jobs and do not directly compete with one another for work. In the triage theory, displacement occurs in some jobs, not in others, and still other jobs are created by immigrants and would not have otherwise existed. Immigrants with few skills might displace unskilled labor already in the nation, but they would not compete with skilled white-collar workers, for example. Their sheer numbers mean additional jobs for others, of course. Some of the jobs toward which many, but not all, immigrants gravitate, are the high turnover jobs with low pay and few fringe benefits, such as hotel cleaning, landscape services, some light manufacturing, and farm labor. Immigrant crews can come to monopolize these jobs by bringing family and friends from back home to the United States, for example from villages and towns in Mexico.

IMMIGRATION AND GENDER

Female immigrants have outnumbered male immigrants into the United States since 1930 (Donato and Tyree, 1986; Houstoun, et al., 1984; Pedraza, 1991; Seller, 1975). Except for 1922, men were the majority of immigrants into the country from 1857 to 1929 (Houstoun, et al., 1984). This was not true for all immigrant groups. For example, more

Irish and Czech women than men were immigrating to the United States in 1920 (Weatherford, 1986). Since 1930, however, females account each year for 53 to 61 percent of the immigrants.

Immigration laws now give preference to family reunification, and this best explains why women now outnumber men among immigrants (Donato and Tyree, 1986). Men in the United States have been sending for their wives and children in other countries, and families have brought orphans into the country, most of whom are female. More American men than women have been marrying foreign-born spouses and bringing them home. Men are more likely to be in the military stationed overseas, and thus more likely to marry the foreign-born. Moreover, foreign-born women have been immigrating to jobs in the health professions, especially nursing, and this helps explain the higher number of women in some cases (Donato and Tyree, 1986). Immigrant women have always been more likely to work outside the home than the native-born, and today employed foreign-born women find jobs in nursing, housekeeping, secretarial service, dressmaking, and household service (Houstoun, et al., 1984). In the past, immigrant women concentrated as domestic servants and industrial workers.

IMMIGRATION RESTRICTIONS

The change of American society has meant the inclusion of some ethnic groups into the larger American society, but it has at the same time resulted in the exclusion of others. The process of inclusion for immigrant groups began with their immigration, while exclusion began with restrictions on their immigration. Immigration and its restriction symbolize a larger truth about ethnic history and societal change in America; they reflect the dual and paradoxical phenomena of ethnic inclusion and exclusion.

Initially, the United States had no policy restricting immigration. This was the *free period of immigration*, which ran parallel to the agrarian phase of American society and the expansion of the western frontier. While some states had immigration restrictions at this time, there were no federal laws other than those to assist immigration (Bennett, 1963). These acts were meant to improve conditions for immigrants during trans-Atlantic crossings and otherwise to prevent their exploitation.

Immigration policy changed, however, and the federal government passed and implemented several acts meant to selectively restrict immigration. This was the *selective period of immigration*, from 1875 to 1965. Racism was very much a part of these efforts to limit immigration, and it replaced, in part, economic needs in governmental policy on immigration. In the middle of the nineteenth century there was great agitation on the West Coast against Chinese labor; in 1879, the electorate of California voted, 154,638 to 833, to end further Chinese immigration into that state. Even before this vote in California, Congress on March 3, 1875, had passed an act providing "for inquiry by our consular officers into contracts of immigrants from both China and Japan for services to be rendered in the United States which were lewd or immoral in purpose" (Bennett, 1963:16). Note the mixture of racial and moral criteria expressed in this act, a mixture that runs throughout the history of immigration restrictions.

Between 1879 and 1882, Congress passed two bills suspending Chinese immigration, both of which were vetoed for being in violation of international treaties with China. In May 1882, however, Congress passed without presidential veto the first Chinese Exclusion Act, suspending the immigration of Chinese labor into the United States for ten years and barring Chinese aliens from United States citizenship. This act was renewed in 1892 and made "permanent" in 1904. The original act did not exclude all Chinese; tourists and students, among others, were exempt, although the later acts closed many of these loopholes. The intent was specifically to exclude Chinese laborers from the country ("coolie" labor, the Chinese were called), and it obviously served the interests of other laboring groups on the West Coast. With the passage of the First Chinese Exclusion Act, Chinese immigration dropped by half from that of the preceding decade, from 123,201 in 1871–1880 to 67,711 in 1881–1890. Thus began a policy of racial exclusion in the United States, one that continued for the Chinese until 1943, when, in the midst of World War II, Congress repealed the Chinese Exclusion Acts and made Chinese eligible for both immigration and naturalization.

Immigration restrictions did not proceed solely on the basis of race in the past century. Congress and the American public were also concerned with other classes of "undesirables." The Immigration Act of 1891 was an expression of this sentiment, in which Congress moved to exclude the following from immigrating into the United States: "all idiots, insane persons, paupers or persons likely to become a public charge, persons suffering from a loathsome or a dangerous contagious disease, persons who have been convicted of a felony or other infamous crime or misdemeanor involving moral turpitude, polygamists, and also any person whose ticket or passage is paid for with the money of another" (Bennett, 1963:21). Early in the twentieth century, with the passage of immigration acts in 1903 and 1904, more classes of aliens, such as anarchists and children unaccompanied by their parents, were excluded.

The immigration restrictions on racial grounds began late in the 1800s with the Chinese Exclusion Acts. Early in the 1900s, there were widespread public sentiment and political pressures for excluding Japanese immigrants as well. The United States negotiated with Japan a Gentleman's Agreement in 1907–08, which limited immigration from Japan to former resident aliens or relatives of resident aliens. However, due in part to the practice of Japanese residents' taking Japanese "picture brides" the intent of this act was circumvented. Japanese residents married brides in Japan by proxy, knowing them only by their photographs and family background. These brides were then eligible to immigrate into the United States. The Japanese population on the West Coast continued to grow as a consequence, creating even more pressure for restriction of the Japanese. In 1920 picture brides were made illegal, and in 1922 Japanese aliens in the United States were declared ineligible for citizenship. Finally, in 1924, Japanese immigration was almost completely stopped, since Japan was given no quota in the Quota Act of that year. Japanese immigration from 1931 to 1950 amounted to only 3,503 people.

The Quota Act of 1924 was meant to stop immigration from southern and eastern Europe as much as from Asia. Along with Asians, southern and eastern European immigrants were excluded from the United States on ethnic grounds. Two important pieces of immigration legislation were passed just prior to 1924 expressing the sentiments against immigrants from southern and eastern Europe. In 1917 Congress passed, over the veto of President Woodrow Wilson, an immigration act that included a literacy test: "Thereafter every newcomer would have to earn admission into the New World by demonstrating his ability to read" (Handlin, 1973:259). The purpose of this test was to restrict immigration from Italy and the Slavic East, where education and literacy were not widespread, without also restricting immigration from northern and western Europe. The peasants from southern and eastern Europe still came, however, after learning to read and write. All prior immigration legislation inconsistent with the principles of the Immigration Act of 1917 was repealed by this act, and classes of excluded aliens on grounds other than nationality and race were extended.

The Johnson Act of 1921 was actually the first quota act passed by Congress: "Its solution also was to limit the number of a nationality entering the United States to 3 percent of foreign-born persons of that nationality who lived here in 1910, as determined by the census" (Bennett, 1963:41). Since there were fewer immigrants from southern and eastern Europe in 1910 than in 1920, the census of 1910 was used to determine national quotas. This act did reduce immigration from southern and eastern Europe, the intent of Congress all along. Countries in the Western Hemisphere were not assigned quotas, and about this time large-scale Mexican immigration began.

Racism was very much a factor in the literacy test of 1917 and the Johnson Act of 1921, and it had been officially expressed in the earlier reports of the Immigration Commission in 1911. The administration of the immigration service had been reorganized with the Immigration Act of 1907, thus creating the Immigration Commission. In 1911 this Commission issued its 42-volume report on the new immigrants, "proving" that the immigrants from southern and eastern Europe were incapable of assimilation and were even biologically inferior to the Nordic stock out of western and northern Europe. The search for a scientific rationale in the exclusion of southern and eastern Europeans continued in the following years.

Dr. Harry Laughlin, a geneticist in the Eugenics Records Office, was asked by the House Immigration Committee to prepare a report on the new immigrants. In November of 1922 he reported to the committee these "scientific" views:

> We in this country have been so imbued with the idea of democracy, or the equality of all men, that we have left out of consideration the matter of blood or natural inborn hereditary mental and moral differences. No man who breeds pedigreed plants and animals can afford to neglect this thing (Handlin, 1957:132).

To "prove" the genetic inferiority of the new immigrants, Laughlin used the record of committals of old and new immigrants to public institutions, ignoring that because of their poverty the new immigrants were forced to seek help only in such facilities, whereas the older and better-off immigrants could afford the alternative of private care. Besides, there was no consistent pattern differentiating new from old immigrants across such mental-health states as feeble-mindedness, insanity, crime, or epilepsy (Handlin, 1957). The supposed difference between old and new immigrants was little more than a fiction that existed in some people's minds. These views were also expressions of social Darwinism, which gave way to social evolution in the social sciences.

Another proponent of immigration restrictions was Arthur Sweeney, a psychologist, who reported in 1923 to the House Committee on Immigration and Naturalization that:

> We cannot be seriously opposed to immigrants from Great Britain, Holland, Canada, Germany, Denmark, and Scandinavia....We can, however, strenuously object to immigration from Italy,...Russia,... Poland,...Greece,...[and] Turkey....The Slavic and Latin countries show a marked contrast in intelligence with the Western and north-

ern European group....They think with the spinal cord rather than the brain....We shall be degenerated to the level of the Slav and Latin races...pauperism, crime, sex offenses, and dependency...*guided by a mind scarcely superior to the ox* (Pavalko, 1977:19; italics added).

Bennett (1963:32–33) summarized much of the sentiment against the new immigrant in this era:

Immigrants from southern and eastern Europe generally are not only ignorant, but their low standards of living tend to depress the American wage standard and to create slums, unemployment and crime.

By reason of their adherence to cultures of their origin, the new immigration is hostile to the Protestant religion and other free institutions of America and foments views which will undermine the American way of life. This immigration has the effect of replacing native with foreign stock by depressing the birthrate of natives. This is because the native is reluctant to bring children into the world to compete with the low kind of labor competition afforded by the new immigrant.

If a lower race mixes with a higher race in sufficient numbers, history teaches us that the lower race will prevail. The lower race will absorb the higher when the two strains approach equality in numbers. The lowering of a great race means not only its own decline, but that of human civilization.

These preposterous pronouncements on the new immigrant culminated in the Quota Act of 1924, the most restrictive of all immigration legislation. The principle features of this act included the following:

1. Quota restrictions were based on national origin.
2. The quota base was changed from the census of 1910 to that of 1890, to further restrict immigration from southern and eastern Europe.
3. The quota admissible in any one year was reduced from 3 to 2 percent of the foreign-born of a nationality living in the United States based on the 1890 census, thus lowering the total quota.
4. The classes of aliens exempted from exclusion were reduced.

The 1890 census was used as a base for national quotas up to 1929, after which the 1920 census was adopted. This provision represented a compromise struck in Congress between the friends of southern and eastern Europeans and their restrictionist foes. With the passage of this act and the Great Depression that soon followed, immigration into the United States was greatly reduced. There were nearly 2.5 million European immigrants into the United States in 1921–1930, while in the following decade, 1931–1940, there were fewer than 350,000 immigrants from Europe, and for much of the 1930s emigration from this country exceeded immigration into it.

After the Quota Act of 1924, Mexican immigration into the United States continued up to the Great Depression. With the Great Depression, however, Mexican immigration fell off as did European immigration. In 1928, Mexican immigration was over 57,000 people, but it fell to less than 3,000 by 1931 (Mirande, 1985). At this time, Mexican immigrants were actually deported and repatriated to Mexico, and between 300,000 and 500,000 Mexican immigrants were sent back to Mexico (Mirande, 1985). There was a reduced need for Mexican labor, especially in Southwestern agriculture, due to the depression and their displacement by "Okies," who were migrating to California because of the dust bowl in the Midwest. This trend was subsequently reversed with the Second World War, when Mexican immigrants were brought again into Southwestern agriculture under the Bracero program (Public Law 78) of 1942–1964, and otherwise immigrated because of an improving U.S. economy during and after the war. "Before this program ended in 1964, it brought in over 100,000 workers per year..." (Bean, Vernez and Keely, 1989:7).

In 1952 the Walter-McCarran Immigration and Naturalization Act was passed by Congress. With this act the quota system of 1924 was continued, although Asian countries were granted token quotas. While the elimination of race as a barrier to immigration and naturalization was a professed aim of this act, the racial quota system with respect to immigration from southern and eastern Europe was only slightly altered. Other classes of aliens—the insane, the diseased, criminals, and paupers—continued to be excluded.

The immigration laws of the United States were more thoroughly revised in 1965. National quotas were replaced by international ones, and thus began the *international period of immigration*. The Eastern Hemisphere was given a quota of 170,000 per year, with a maximum of 20,000 from any one country. The Western Hemisphere was granted a quota of 120,000 per year, without any specific national limitation until 1976, when a 20,000 ceiling from any one country was imposed. Preferences were extended to relatives of U.S. citizens and resident aliens, and persons with desirable occupational skills. This act was in full operation by 1969, when 359,000 immigrants came to the United States, compared to a yearly average between 1951 and 1960 of just over 250,000.

In this present era of immigration policy, the numerical ceiling for immigration has been 290,000 per year. There are many exemptions, particularly to reunite immediate family members, making the total immigration each year exceed the ceiling. Preferences are given to (1) unmarried sons and daughters of U.S. citizens, (2) spouses and unmarried children of U.S. resident aliens, (3) professionals or persons of exceptional ability in sciences and arts, (4) married sons and daughters of U.S. citizens, (5) brothers and sisters of U.S. citizens, and (6) skilled and unskilled workers in short supply. Preferences for reuniting immediate family members favor the most recent immigrants, those from Asia and the Americas. In 1986, nearly two-thirds of those outside the ceiling were admitted to reunite family members, and another 31 percent were refugees and those seeking asylum in the United States. Immigration by seeking political asylum and because of refugee status now falls under the 1980 Refugee Act. Thousands of Cubans, Indo-Chinese, Haitians, Central Americans and Eastern Europeans have immigrated into the United States in the last 20 years as refugees. Moreover, the number of foreign students in the United States increased fourfold between 1965 and 1985, and petitions for naturalization nearly tripled in the same period (Simcox, 1988b). The new immigrants are concentrating in the cities of California, in metropolitan New York and New Jersey, and in cities such as Chicago, Miami, and Washington, D.C.

In November 1986 Congress enacted the Immigration Reform and Control Act after many years of deliberations. The intent of this act was to better control illegal or undocumented immigration into the country, but left intact was the scheme in the 1965 legislation for legal immigration. The 1986 act granted amnesty to illegal aliens who had resided continuously in the United States since January 1, 1982, and could prove their residency. Employers can now be fined for hiring illegal aliens under this law, although agricultural employers won some exemptions to this provision. The idea was to control illegal immigration by drying up its employment opportunities.

The major provisions of the 1986 Immigration Reform and Control Act were:

1. Employer sanctions for recruiting and hiring aliens not authorized to work in the United States. Employers must attest that they have examined the documents of prospective employees regarding U.S. citizenship for authorization to work in the United States. Sanctions for employer violations range from $250 to $2,000 for the first offense and up to six months imprisonment for a pattern of violations. Employers in seasonal agriculture were exempt from sanctions for two years following enactment of the legislation.

2. Prohibition against employment discrimination based on national origin or citizenship status if the person is a U.S. citizen or a permanent resident alien, refugee, or newly legalized

alien who has filed a notice of intent to become a citizen. Employers in violation of this anti-discrimination provision can be ordered to award back pay.

3. The granting of temporary resident status to aliens who entered the United States illegally prior to January 1, 1982, and who have since resided continuously in the country. In regard to agricultural workers, however, temporary resident status can be granted to a maximum of 350,000 illegal aliens who can prove that they have worked in perishable agriculture for at least 90 days in each of the last three years. Aliens who worked in agriculture for at least 90 days during the year preceding May 1, 1986, also were eligible to apply for temporary resident status.

4. Additional agriculture workers may be brought in as temporary residents for three years after the enactment of the law.

Since illegal immigration became such a public issue in recent years, the U.S. government was straining to preserve the appearance that it was in control of its own borders. The credibility of the state was in jeopardy. Thus, in 1986 the government enacted employer sanctions for hiring illegal aliens. Enforcement since 1987 has been focused on informing employers about the provisions of the 1986 Act (Bean, Vernez and Keely, 1989). The class of employers who are granted the greatest concessions are, however, the very ones who have historically relied on immigrant labor, big agriculture.

Employment may be an increasingly important factor in future immigration legislation. Proposals in Congress in the early 1990s include extending preferences for immigrants with high employment prospects in the United States, including skilled workers, those in jobs that residents cannot fill, and scientists and artists. A Senate bill would create two separate preference systems, the first for reuniting family members and the second for independent immigrants with needed occupational skills (Bean, Vernez and Keely, 1989). It would almost triple the number of visas available on the basis of such skills, from 54,000 to 150,000. Family reunification preferences might also be extended to more distant relatives, but there would be a 7 percent country limit for each of the two avenues of immigration. The Congressional debate also includes an annual ceiling of 630,000 on the number of immigrants, 480,000 for family reunification and 150,000 to independent immigrants with occupational skills.

It is now obvious that immigration to the United States has responded not only to the country's labor needs, but also to governmental policy and conditions in countries of origin. Pushed by the lack of employment and other conditions at home, immigrants became an industrial army in the United States, typically filling labor needs unmet by natives. Often immigrants were seen as competitors by native labor, however, and this feeling was reinforced by the cultural and ethnic differences between the two. Thus, there has been public policy in the form of immigration restrictions. Employer needs for immigrant labor continued, however, and governmental concessions to their interests were often granted (Cornelius and Montoya, 1983). For example, growers in the Southwest had access to Mexican immigrants, evident in the Bracero program, even after the immigration door was supposedly closed by the Quota Act of 1924. The larger story about immigration into the country and its restriction includes a cast of characters: employers, labor unions, the government, anti-immigration leagues, and the immigrants themselves against the backdrop of labor needs, racism, political pressure, and family reunification.

This short history of immigration and its restriction is only part of a larger history of ethnic groups in American society. American society has changed, and this has brought both the inclusion and exclusion of racial and ethnic groups, symbolized here by immigration and immigration restrictions. Both inclusion and exclusion will be analyzed in this book. This analysis reflects not only our ethnic roots but also the roots of contemporary sociology in nineteenth-century social evolutionism.

PERSPECTIVES ON
AMERICAN ETHNICITY

C H A P T E R

2

@/@

ASSIMILATIONISM

A ccording to the assimilationists, ethnic and racial groups assimilate into the mainstream of American society. This theory in twentieth-century sociology was prefigured in nineteenth-century thought about societal evolution. The social evolutionists equated societal change with the eclipse of the folk community, and the assimilationists subsequently applied the same idea to ethnic groups in America (Bash, 1979). The chapter begins with the key terms and basic assumptions of this school. After a discussion of nineteenth-century social evolutionism, early and current expressions of assimilationism are surveyed, and the chapter ends with an assessment of this perspective on American ethnicity.

DEFINITIONS AND ASSUMPTIONS

KEY TERMS

ETHNIC GROUP: *Ethnic groups are self-conscious groups of people who, on the basis of a common origin or a separate subculture, maintain a distinction between themselves and outsiders.* Ethnic boundaries may show up in the territorial segregation of a group, in the circumscribed social interaction of its members, in ethnically distinct patterns of behavior, or simply in a consciousness of ethnic kind and historical continuity. That is, ethnic groups can live apart from others, or, when living among others, maintain themselves by keeping to themselves. Members of an ethnic group can also maintain ethnic boundaries by behaving in distinct ways, for example, by using a different language or preferring distinct styles of dress and food, or they can simply maintain that they have a common descent and/or separate subculture. An ethnic group may be either cultural or racial as long as the above criteria are met.

There has been disagreement in the social sciences over the usage of the term *ethnic group*. The convention in early assimilationism was to define an ethnic group as both a cultural group and an ecological entity. An ethnic group was cultural but also concentrated in a territorial locale, an urban ghetto, for example. The implication was that ethnic groups exist only in cultural and physical isolation. This confusion of ethnicity in general with its more specific manifestation in isolation and segregation is certainly a characteristic of assimilationism, at least its earlier works, and some say it is an important limitation of the school.

One convention among sociologists today is to distill ethnic group diversity into the dichotomy of majority and minority groups. Minority groups in this country include Native Americans, Asian Americans, African Americans, and Mexican Americans, among others, who share the common experience of being objects of majority group prejudice and discrimination. Because of prejudice and discrimination, minority groups are excluded from American society. The majority group is usually considered to be all white Americans, regardless of their ethnic and religious origins. While this convention has merit, it will not be followed in this book for the reasons that it oversimplifies ethnic diversity and tends to be ahistorical. That is, ethnicity has always meant more than a simple dichotomy—majority and minority—and most ethnic groups, even today's majority groups, have been minorities at one time or another in American history. We define an ethnic group more inclusively as a self-conscious group of people who move through time, and we will consider how these groups and their relationships change over time.

Another convention is to make a distinction between racial and ethnic groups. Racial groups today are considered the nation's non-white groups, indigenous and immigrant alike, while the term *ethnic group* is reserved for whites. The term *race* has come to have such ambiguous and often contradictory meanings that it is no longer useful in the study of ethnic groups in American history. For instance, while only non-white groups are now seen as races distinct from white Americans, earlier in the century Jews, Italians, and Slavs were considered distinct races. Racial labels shift from one historical period to another. Furthermore, the distinction between racial and ethnic groups implies that racial groups are not also ethnic groups, which is obviously false. Thus we will define groups regardless of race as ethnic groups, so long as they meet the criteria set forth above.

ASSIMILATION: According to common usage in the social sciences, *assimilation is the process by which diverse ethnic groups come to share a common culture and have equal access to the opportunity structure of society.* There are two components of assimilation: acculturation and integration. *Acculturation* refers to the fusion of groups into a common culture. Different ethnic groups acculturate by becoming similar in their thinking, feeling, and behavior. They share the same basic values and patterns of behavior. To illustrate, members of different groups converge to speak the same language, wear similar clothing, and eat the same foods; this is acculturation. *Integration* refers to the fusion of ethnic groups into society so that what they do and with whom is no longer predicated on ethnic identity. Integration means the inclusion of groups into society rather than their exclusion from it. Because of integration, members of different ethnic groups are not segregated with respect to their residence and social participation, and they experience equal access to education, jobs, and other opportunities in the wider society. Obviously, assimilation comes in degrees. Some groups can be more or less assimilated than other groups, rather than some groups being assimilated and others not.

ETHNIC CHANGE: *Ethnicity is an evolving or emergent phenomenon, because groups as well as their relations with one another and with the larger society continually change.* Assimilation is one aspect of this history—the one emphasized in this chapter.

THE ASSUMPTIONS OF ASSIMILATIONISM

1. The historical course of American society results in the assimilation of the nation's ethnic groups.
2. Assimilation is a result of societal change, that is, an outcome of industrialization, occupational diversification, urbanization, and the spread of mass education.

SOCIAL EVOLUTIONISM

Evolution was the great theme of nineteenth-century science. After Darwin published his theory of organic evolution in 1859, interest in evolution grew in all sciences, including the social sciences. In the emerging science of society—sociology—the concern was with social evolution, or the process of societal change. Initially, the Darwinian principles of organic evolution were applied directly to the study of societal change, but sociological principles replaced those borrowed earlier from biology, and the study of societal change eventually became a social science.

Assimilationists hold that the ethnic group is eclipsed by the change process, an idea that was clearly on the horizon in nineteenth-century social evolutionism. The social evolutionists had predicted the collapse of the folk village and its customs in the course of change. Folkways would disappear with the rise of new occupations and economic classes, in the evolution toward an industrial, urbanized, and politically centralized society. With the migration of rural villagers to industrial cities, their eventual occupational diversification there, their resulting economic class stratification, and dispersion into the suburbs, the very basis of folk life—sameness and isolation—was said to disappear.

This message from nineteenth-century Europe was later translated by American sociologists to mean the eventual end of ethnic groups in America. At the turn of the century, the very beginning of American sociology, pioneer American sociologists adopted nineteenth-century intellectual traditions from Europe in their analysis of the then contemporary American society. Assimilationism was simply part of this larger trend.

Profound changes had been taking place in nineteenth-century Europe. Many countries there were being transformed from rural societies, with simple divisions of labor and largely rural populations, into industrial societies, with complex divisions of labor and growing urban populations. Social evolutionists tried to forecast the future of society on the basis of these nineteenth-century trends. While several aspects of this change were obvious, such as migration of rural people into urban industrial centers, the social evolutionists detected some not-so-obvious changes in the human condition, changes associated with the shift from agrarian to industrial society. A fundamental alteration in human relations was discerned. Social evolutionists envisioned in modern society a transformation of the medieval bonds of blood and place, the basis of peasant life, into individualism and rationally calculated human exchange. Modern people would relate to one another as commodities in marketplaces, each trying to maximize individual profit. The mass-produced consumer goods would be consumed en masse, and once-distinct groups would become indistinguishable by what they wore, ate, and did. Impersonal bureaucracy, one symbol of this change, would replace the communal organization of life. Assimilationists read this legacy as reason for the eventual demise of ethnic groups in American society.

Assimilationists were indebted to both basic variants of social evolutionism, the one that predicted conflict in the course of societal change, and the other that forecast cooperation and harmony in the change process. The first tradition is the conflict branch of social evolutionism, represented by Karl Marx, and the second tradition is the functional branch of social evolutionism, represented by Emile Durkheim.

CONFLICT BRANCH

Karl Marx characterized all history as a class struggle. The capitalist class had displaced the feudal nobility as the dominant class in industrial society by the nineteenth century. According to Marx, social evolution would continue, and industrial capitalism would inevitably evolve toward class conflict between capital and labor, the bourgeoisie and the proletariat. The proletariat would eventually reverse the domination of the bourgeoisie and create a classless utopia. With the realization of this utopian state, the evolutionary process would end.

In Marxist thought, assimilationists found a precedent for their prediction that societal change would bring ethnic assimilation in twentieth-century America. Marx had argued that capitalism would elevate the class consciousness of industrial workers. By becoming class conscious, workers would become correspondingly less concerned with family, land, locality, and nationality, which might otherwise divide them. All of these, of course, are particular expressions of ethnicity. Ethnicity would be erased, first as the proletariat mobilized for the class struggle, and finally as the universal fraternity of workers was established in the utopian state. Class consciousness is the modern mentality, Marx argued, and folk sentiments would become obsolete and fade.

FUNCTIONAL BRANCH

Emile Durkheim, in *Division of Labor in Society*, originally published in 1893, attributed societal change to the increasingly complex division of labor in industrial society. Since his time, the division of labor has grown even more complex. Like Marx, Durkheim argued that this change brought the demise of the feudal order, but, unlike Marx, he argued that the interdependence inherent in a complex division of labor, along with other evolutionary forces, would provide for a gradual transition, without class conflict, from folk to modern society.

Durkheim wrote that "social life comes from a double source, the likeness of consciousness and the division of labor. The individual is socialized in the first case, because, not having any real individuality, he becomes, with those he resembles, part of the same collective type..." (1893/1947:226). Likeness of consciousness comes from people doing the same thing, day in and day out, when there is a simple division of labor. This condition, which characterized folk society in the past, was called *mechanical solidarity* by Durkheim.

According to Durkheim, the division of labor becomes more complex in the course of societal change, moving society away from a state of mechanical solidarity. The like-mindedness of the past is no longer possible when workers are divided into the myriad of occupations available in modern society. Mechanical solidarity is impossible across workers in diverse jobs, although it can be maintained within certain occupational groups. The chance for individuality and, by implication, the pursuit of self-interest increase in the industrial city. Does this mean Marxian class war, or worse yet, the Hobbesian war of all against all? Not according to Durkheim, who foresaw a new order arising out of the fact that people in a complex division of labor are interdependent, each requiring the goods and services of others. This product of specialization is the basis for a new moral order in modern society that Durkheim called *organic solidarity*.

Durkheim believed that occupational specialists would realize their interdependence, appreciate the larger whole of which they are part, and cooperate. A complex division of labor from the start represented a cooperative effort to avoid occupational competition. The larger point is that societal change was to bring a new type of solidarity, providing conditions that would integrate diverse specialists into a complex society, which, according to Durkheim, could be buttressed by state regulation and moral education. By the same token, the diversity of modern society spelled the end of mechanical solidarity for folk groups. Folk solidarity could be transplanted to industrial cities only for a time, while migrant groups themselves lived in isolated ghettos and worked the same jobs at the bottom of the new occupational hierarchy. These groups eventually would diffuse into the modern city's complex division of labor, however, and become diversified into what are now called ethclasses, different economic and social classes within ethnic groups. They would disperse in urban space, lose their solidarity, and ultimately disintegrate. Occupational interdependence and other secondary forms of social control would then supplant the lost solidarity of the folk past. This is what many contemporary sociologists would read from Durkheim in their analysis of twentieth-century American society.

While Durkheim argued with Marx over the role of class struggle in societal modernization, he agreed with Marx that ethnicity would be eclipsed by the formation of modern occupational groups. The idea that the interests of occupation and economic class would replace folk consciousness of kind in the mentality of people is shared by both men and is the theme of social evolutionism in general. It is also the theme of twentieth-century assimilationists. The ethnic group will disintegrate with the occupational diversification of its members, and occupational and class interests will replace ethnic sentiments in the process. Early assimilationists even suggested that all this is inevitable. Lyman (1972) observed that this belief in an inevitable and unilinear evolution of the human condition, which is evident in both social evolutionism and assimilationism, ultimately returns to basic notions of Aristotelian natural history. A set course for historical change is posited in a natural history, and any deviation from this course is judged to be accidental. Some assimilationists do assume a set course for ethnic history, toward eventual assimilation, and some dismiss alternatives to assimilation as accidents or as transitional and merely passing phenomena. With motifs such as these, assimilationists looked at the obvious ethnic diversity in early twentieth-century America and saw concealed there the forces for its cessation.

The image of societal change evoked in assimilationism also derives from historic liberalism, "which put its full emphasis on the free individual, finding in man's liberation from political and military bonds, even those of religion and local community,... the essence of progress....Individual autonomy is the transcending goal of historic liberalism" (Nisbet, 1975:47). In this version of history, the primary consequence of societal change is individual freedom and individuality, due to the expansion of opportunity and increasing complexity of society (e.g., Durkheim, 1983/1947). This has been a popular and pervasive image of American society, as once observed by C. Wright Mills (1951:12): "With no feudal tradition and no bureaucratic state, the absolute individualist was exceptionally placed in liberal society....Individual freedom seemed the principle of the social order....A free man, not a man exploited, an independent man, not a man bound by tradition, here confronted a continent...."

Individual freedom is identified with the absence of social constraint on thought and action (e.g., John Stuart Mill, 1859/1956). This conception is commonly called liberty. Adam Smith (1776/1896) argued that for the market economy to function properly, it must be left alone and natural liberty granted to its participants. Individual freedom was deemed necessary for meeting demand with supply. Another sense of freedom found in liberalism is the existence of "opportunities to make important choices among real alternatives" (Moore, 1970:434). Specialization and a complex division of labor increase these choices and alternatives, particularly the choice of work, career, and life-style (Durkheim, 1893/1947). Societal change decreases social constraint and simultaneously increases real choices for individuals.

If modernity means opportunity, freedom, and individuality for people in general, then it does so for members of ethnic groups specifically. Members of ethnic groups find opportunity in a complex society, so the groups become ever more diversified and ultimately decompose sociologically into a mass of individuals. This basic idea begins our analysis of assimilationism.

ASSIMILATIONISM

ROBERT PARK

> In the relations of races there is a cycle of events which tends everywhere to repeat itself....The race relations cycle which takes the form, to state it abstractly, of contact, competition, accommodation and eventual assimilation, is apparently progressive and irreversible. Customs regulations, immigration restrictions and racial barriers may slacken the tempo of the movement; may perhaps halt it altogether for a time; but cannot change its direction; cannot at any rate reverse it... (Park, 1926/1950:150).

This is Robert Park's race relations cycle, which reveals his belief in a unilinear history of race relations. As ethnic groups move off the land and into industrial cities, they come into contact with one another, compete with one another for a time, eventually reach an accommodation, and ultimately assimilate. The industrial city Park had in mind was Chicago, and the ethnic groups were European and Asian immigrants, as well as black migrants from the South. The cycle is inevitable, according to Park, reflecting the determinism of nineteenth-century social evolutionism.

After their contact, ethnic groups challenge one another's prerogatives in the city, resulting in ethnic competition, a phase of the race relations cycle that recapitulates Darwin's struggle for survival and the concept that evolution is propelled by blind, impersonal forces of competition (Theodorson, 1961). This concept was an axiom not only of Darwinian biology but also of historic liberalism—the idea that human exchange is propelled solely by the competitive forces of the laissez-faire marketplace in accord with the laws of demand and supply. Ethnic groups compete for many things in the city, some of which involve subsistence, such as jobs and housing, while others involve symbolic value, such as the competition for status and the conflict between different cultures. At this stage of the race relations cycle, in-group consciousness, solidarity, and prejudice against others are all evident.

Park believed that the physical and social distance between ethnic groups in the city would be reinforced by their initial competition. The city resembled at first an interdependent collection of *natural areas*, each with its distinct ethnic population or economic activity. "Each separate part of the city is inevitably stained with the peculiar sentiments of its population. The effect of this is to convert what was at first a mere geographical expression into a neighborhood, that is to say, a locality with sentiments, traditions, and history of its own" (Park, 1915:579). That is, ethnic ghettos become cultural enclaves, ethnic communities into which distinct subcultures are transplanted and within which future generations are socialized, continuing the pattern of ethnic pluralism in the course of societal change.

According to Park, ethnic relations evolve past competition and toward accommodation and eventual assimilation. The natural tendency for strife and struggle is supplanted by the equally deterministic trend toward human communication and intimacy, resulting in accommodation and assimilation. Competition is settled in the form of some moral order, as ethnic groups reach a mutual understanding about their exchange, enforced by moral authority. This is the stage of accommodation. Natural areas are also subject to change; as ties of ethnicity weaken, successful individuals move out and find new places in business and the professions, and this is registered in change of residence. With accommodation, groups no longer struggle for survival, and, while competition might still occur, groups now compete for status and prestige only, not for subsistence.

Ethnic relations evolve beyond accommodation, too, and the cycle moves toward and ends with assimilation. Park believed that intimacy inevitably ensues from the secondary relations among members of different ethnic groups as these form with the diffusion of groups into a city's complex division of labor:

> In our estimates of race relations we have not reckoned with the effects of personal intercourse and the friendships that inevitably grow up out of them. These friendships, particularly in a democratic society like our own, cut across and eventually undermine all the barriers of racial segregation and caste by which races seek to maintain their integrity (Park, 1926/1950:150).

Park observed elsewhere that employers of one race ultimately realize that their employees of another race are human beings just like themselves. Personal intimacy between members of ethnic groups apparently replaces impersonal competition as a force behind the race relations cycle and moves that cycle inevitably toward assimilation. This point of view is called the *contact hypothesis* in contemporary research.

Park turned to the old German adage that the city makes men and women free, allowing them to pursue their own individual self-interests as they see fit, unencumbered by the customary authority of the folk group. Members of ethnic groups diffuse throughout the complex division of labor in a modern city, break away from the primary controls of the folk past transplanted for a time in urban ghettos, and relocate in other areas of the city. Finally, in the suburbs, members of different ethnic groups, who now share common vocational interests, status, and life-styles, will eventually assimilate. That is, occupational diversification of ethnic groups ultimately leads to their disintegration. Frazier (1947:270) remarked that Park "regarded race relations in the United States as part of a world process in which culture and occupation was coming to play a more important role than inheritance and race." In Park's own words:

> Every device which facilitates trade and industry prepares the way for a further division of labor and so tends further to specialize the tasks in which men find their vocations....The outcome of this process is to break down or modify the older organization of society, which was based on family ties, local association, on culture, caste, and status, and to substitute for it an organization based on vocational interests (1915:586).

The new order of Park is that of Durkheim. As individuals in industrial cities are freed from the bonds of the folk past and move into a complex division of labor, vocational interests and the economic interdependence of diverse vocational groups replace ethnic bonds as the basis for solidarity in society, and secondary forms of social control replace ethnic loyalties and authority in the governance of the modern city. Lyman (1972) found also in Park's writings the expectancy that once ethnic strife is resolved in accommodation and assimilation, the decks would be cleared in America for class struggle. This shows the influence of another nineteenth-century thinker on Park—Karl Marx. Park (1939:45) stated: "Race conflicts in the modern world, which is already or presently will be a single great society, will be more and more in the future confused with, and eventually superseded by, the conflicts of classes."

Park's race relations cycle is an exemplar of the assimilationist view of ethnic change in modern society. The cycle goes through four stages, terminating in the assimilation of ethnic groups. The forces behind the cycle return to the basic ideas of nineteenth-century social evolutionism and historical liberalism. There is an increasingly complex division of labor and expansion of opportunity, growth in individual freedom, impersonal competition of individuals in the laissez-faire marketplace, and the eventual eclipse of bonds of blood and place by vocational or class interests. To this Park added that human cooperation and intergroup intimacy would ultimately succeed competition, even accommodation, and bring assimilation. At a higher level of abstraction, the race relations cycle represents the effort of society to achieve a new equilibrium and social order.

Park dichotomized the dynamics of social life into natural and social forces. While the natural force of impersonal competition organized life at the biotic level, or that of the territorial community, human communication, cooperation, and intimacy organized life by a different principle at the societal level. Hollingshead (1961:109) summarized this habit of Park's by writing: "Man as animal is organized competitively in the scheme of nature, but man as social being is organized cooperatively into groups through communication."

Does the race relations cycle exist at the biotic or societal level, in the scheme of nature or in human society? Park answered that ethnic relations exist on many levels, including the ecological, economic, political, cultural, and personal (Park, 1950). Of course, ethnic relations can span all these spheres of life, but if ethnic relations exist at the biotic level, how do we explain the inevitable movement toward assimilation? We know Park believed that as members of different ethnic groups disperse in space, they come into contact, cooperate, and grow intimate with one another and ultimately assimilate. Cooperation and intimacy are social principles, of course, and if Park meant to locate the race relations cycle solely in the scheme of nature, it is hard to understand how the cycle could evolve beyond the point of blind, impersonal competition. The fact is, the social principles of cooperation and intimacy are explicitly included in the race relations cycle and are given the upper hand. It is these principles, not natural forces, that bring assimilation.

In practice Park alternated between natural and social principles in explaining the dynamics of human life. However, it is clear that with the race relations cycle social principles supersede natural ones, moral forces succeed biotic ones, and human communication, cooperation, and interpersonal intimacy supplant impersonal competition and inevitably bring assimilation. The larger point is that evolutionary forces, both the biotic and social, are deterministic, and they propel the race relations cycle on an inevitable course. This was the case before Park's experiences in Hawaii (Lyman, 1972; Park, 1950). Because of what he saw there, Park changed his mind late in life about the inevitability of assimilation, arguing instead that ethnic relations can terminate in a caste system, or a majority-minority arrangement, not only assimilation. Moreover, he believed the terminus of the cycle would be fully contingent on the culture in which the cycle takes place. In this manner, the concept of natural history was finally replaced in Park's writings on ethnicity by the image of an open-ended and culturally contingent course of ethnic history. There is no question now that the race relations cycle evolves in accord with sociological rather than biological principles.

Park took seriously the idea of Darwin that evolution is driven by impersonal competition. He also agreed with certain social thinkers who argued that human life is organized around a moral order and by symbolic communication. He tried to reconcile these opposing ideas with a dichotomy, assuming that while impersonal competition organizes human life at the biotic level, communication, understanding, and morality organize human life at another level, that of human society. The dichotomy was permeable in practice, however, and his race relations cycle, for instance, includes both the forces of impersonal competition and those of human communication, cooperation, and intimacy.

Park applied certain Darwinian principles in his analysis of race relations, and he persisted for some time in thinking that race relations are as much a natural history as is the idea of organic evolution. Nevertheless, he always superimposed humanity, or human cooperation and intimacy, on the tendency for competition and domination in nature. These are the very reasons that the cycle moves toward assimilation. Furthermore, he never drew from Darwin, as others had, the analogy of fixed racial traits, nor the implication that some ethnic groups are naturally superior to others (Reuter, 1945). This is very much to his credit, for it helped place the study of ethnic relations in the social sciences rather than in biology, an event that has had great implications for national policy with respect to ethnic and race relations.

LOUIS WIRTH

Not only does the ghetto tend to disappear, but the race tends to disappear with it (Wirth, 1928/1956:125).

This short passage from *The Ghetto*, originally published in 1928, suggests a close connection between Louis Wirth and Robert Park. Louis Wirth was first a student of Park's and later a colleague of his at the University of Chicago. In his dissertation, published as *The Ghetto*, Wirth applied Park's race relations cycle to the special case of Jews in Chicago. Park's race relations cycle is a natural history of ethnic assimilation in the abstract, while Wirth's *The Ghetto* represents the more specific natural history of Jewish assimilation in Chicago. The history passes through the stages of contact, competition, and accommodation, ending with assimilation. Wirth shared with Park the conviction that societal change brings the demise of the ethnic group, in this case Jews. Assimilation of Jews is due to their occupational diversification, residential dispersion, and the growing intimacy between Jews and others, all of which is made possible by societal change.

Wirth followed Park in another way. The dualism of natural and social forces is as evident in Wirth's natural history of Jewish assimilation as it is in Park's race relations cycle. The Jewish ghetto on Maxwell Street was originally a product of the economic competition among Chicago's ethnic groups; it was an economic niche for Jews, although the ghetto became a cultural enclave, or natural area, as well. Eventually, the principles of contact and intimacy between Jew and Gentile would supplant ethnic competition, and Jews would ultimately assimilate. This is the same progression of explanatory principles found in Park's more general race relations cycle.

Wirth measured Jewish assimilation with ecological markers; as Jews moved from one neighborhood to another in Chicago, they also moved toward their assimilation. Thus, "not only does the ghetto tend to disappear, but the race tends to disappear with it." The premise is that the ethnic group survives in modern society only with its residential segregation and isolation from others. Once groups disperse and come into contact, however, they grow intimate with each other and eventually assimilate.

FIRST SETTLEMENT: The first settlement in Chicago for Jewish immigrants from Europe was a ghetto in an area not far from the Loop and near the old marketplace on Maxwell Street.

> Maxwell Street, the ghetto's great outdoor market, is full of color, action, shouts, orders, and dirt....Buying is an adventure in which one matches his wits against those of an opponent, a Jew. The Jews are versatile; they speak Yiddish among themselves, and Polish, Russian, Lithuanian, Hungarian, Bohemian, and what not, to their customers. They know their tastes and their prejudices. They have on hand ginghams in loud, gay colors for one group, and for one occasion; and drab and black mourning wear for others.
>
> The noises of crowing roosters and geese, the cooing of pigeons, the barking of dogs, the twittering of canary birds, the smell of garlic and of cheeses, the aroma of onions, apples, and oranges, and the shouts and curses of sellers and buyers fill the air. Anything can be bought and sold on Maxwell Street....Everything has value on Maxwell Street, but the price is not fixed. It is the fixing of the price around which turns the whole plot of the drama enacted daily at the perpetual bazaar of Maxwell Street.

Source: Louis Wirth, *The Ghetto*. Chicago: University of Chicago Press, pp. 232–233.
Copyright © 1956 by The University of Chicago. Reprinted by permission.

It had been the custom for Jews throughout Europe to reside near marketplaces, in Frankfurt and Prague, for example, and Jewish immigrants quickly became the dominant group on Maxwell Street by transplanting their Old World traits. Moreover, "the immigrants drifted to the slum because here rents were lowest—a primary consideration" (Wirth, 1956:198).

The ghetto was a natural area, an economic and ecological niche for Jewish immigrants at first, and later a cultural enclave as well. Life on Maxwell Street quickly elaborated; by 1900 the Jewish community of Chicago contained 50 congregations, 39 charities, 60 lodges, 13 loan associations, 11 social clubs, and 4 Zionist organizations. These organizations were not the full measure of Jewish communal life in the ghetto. Only by adding the theaters, restaurants, cafes, and second-story bookstores, the informal associations among friends and family, the philosophical discussions over chess or pinochle, and the gambling dens and cigar stores on Maxwell Street does the full picture of ghetto life begin to emerge. The hub of ghetto life was the synagogues. There were 50 of them by 1900, indicative of the religious diversity among these immigrants. Wirth (1956:193) found that "In its initial stages the Jewish community is scarcely distinguishable from the rest of the city. As the numbers increase, however, the typical communal organization of the European ghetto gradually emerges."

Old World class distinctions and tribal prejudices were also transplanted in Chicago. As the ghetto elaborated, it simultaneously differentiated into *Landsmannschaft*, religious groups and economic classes. *Landsmannschaft* were more or less autonomous networks that segregated Jew from Jew, based on geographical origins in the Old World:

> A *Landsmannschaft* has its own patriarchal leaders, its lodges and mutual aid associations, and its celebrations and festivities. It has its burial plot in the cemetery....Hand in hand with the ties of sympathy between the members of a *Landsmannschaft* go also the antagonisms and prejudices between these groups which have been brought over from the Old World.

Source: Louis Wirth, *The Ghetto*. Chicago: University of Chicago Press, pp. 223–224. Copyright © 1956 by The University of Chicago. Reprinted by permission.

Religious differences among the Orthodox, Conservative, and Reform Jews crystallized into separate congregations that were often conterminous with nationality differences. The Russian and other eastern European Jews tended to be more Orthodox or Conservative than the German Jews. The economic class hierarchy of the ghetto also separated Jew from Jew; on the average, the Russians were lower on this hierarchy than the Germans. By the turn of the century, Wirth observed, these divisions were rigidly fixed.

The street market was a highly visible part of the
Jewish ghetto on Chicago's Maxwell Street.

SECOND SETTLEMENT: Over time ghetto residents became more diverse, particularly occupationally diverse, and it was the German Jews who first took up higher status occupations. This diversification is identified by Wirth as the start of the disintegration of the ghetto, and thus the disappearance of the Jewish people in America as a group. Once some of the immigrants were able to afford higher housing prices, they looked for more desirable locations elsewhere in the city. Many families moved to the west-side neighborhood of Lawndale, or Deutschland as it was known among the Jews. This was the second settlement. Not only was this a residential movement in Wirth's scheme, it represented the larger process of Jewish assimilation as well.

◎◎

BOX 2.1   MOVING TO DEUTSCHLAND

His whole world collapsed one evening when his oldest son, after the Friday evening meal, said to him that now, since he was going to law school and the family was pretty well fixed, and as he had acquired some friends whom he would like to invite to his house, they ought to move out of the ghetto. "The ghetto!" said the father, "Are you dreaming? What do other people have that we haven't got? Don't you like this flat? Isn't the furniture good enough? Isn't this home swell enough for you?"

That night the old man could not sleep, and the next morning in Shul he was a little bewildered by the services. His mind was wandering. A month later they moved to Central Park Avenue, in Lawndale. The son felt happier, but the father didn't go down to his store on Roosevelt Road and Jefferson Street on the street car with quite the same zest mornings as he used to when they lived upstairs over the business. Nor did he feel the same way when he went to the synagogue. His *Landsleute*, he noticed, looked at him with a rather quizzical air; they didn't shake hands with the warmth of days gone by, and they weren't quite as familiar as they used to be.

Two years later, when the son had opened a law office, the father sold his store and began to dabble in real estate, using his son's office as his headquarters. He had found the synagogue on the near West Side too far away, and had joined a congregation on Douglas Boulevard, three miles further west. He had trimmed his beard a little, too. He still played chess with his son, but instead of discussing the Talmud they discussed the real estate boom on Crawford Avenue. Once in a while he soliloquized, "And I thought I was rich; why, I have made more money in the last year or two than I made during the twenty years before. Yes, I lived in the ghetto and didn't know it."

Residence in Lawndale was identified with the Americanization of Jews, including the secularization of their Judaism and the desire among the residents to fit into the larger society.

Jewish residential mobility and occupational diversification went hand in hand, and both meant the inevitable end of the Jewish group in America, according to Wirth. This notion comes straight from nineteenth-century social evolutionism. The modal occupational type in the ghetto had been the merchant and peddler, but in Deutschland it was the real estate salesman. The life-style of Lawndale residents became conspicuously American as well as plainly conspicuous. Jews no longer competed for subsistence, only for status through displays of consumption, an indication of their accommodation. At the same time, residents of Lawndale became disinterested in the sacred affairs of Judaism, and, accordingly, the prestige of the religious scholar declined, as did rabbinical influence over Jewish communal life. Many Jews now turned toward Christian Science, ethical culture, and rationalism, according to Wirth. Glazer (1957) termed these changes a transition from Judaism to Jewishness, and one in which the secular aspects of Jewish life survive while the sacred dimensions of Judaism wane.

THIRD SETTLEMENT: It takes a second move to a third settlement in the suburbs for Jews to assimilate completely. Lawndale became a Jewish enclave as Gentiles fled the area, and there the residents continued to be Jewish without much effort. In the suburbs, Wirth predicted, contact with Gentile neighbors and friends would become a daily occurrence, intimacy would grow, and Jews would ultimately assimilate, although in the process they would be reminded of the positive aspects of Jewish life. Assimilation would take the forms of religious conversion, intermarriage, and greater Jewish participation in the associations of the larger society. Jewish customs, communal associations, and even identity would be lost, or modified beyond recognition. "In the ghetto the synagogue…is predominately orthodox; in the area of second settlement it becomes 'conservative'; and on the frontier it is 'reformed'" (Wirth, 1956:256). The intimacy between Jew and Gentile on the frontier—the suburbs—would bring an end to

45

this natural history of Jewish assimilation. Only historical accidents, such as an increase in anti-Semitism, would interrupt this race relations cycle.

Wirth's analysis of the specific case of Jewish assimilation mirrors Park's more general race relations cycle. Initial settlement of Jewish immigrants, in the specific case, was a function of impersonal economic factors and was seen as part of the intergroup struggle for subsistence. Human cooperation and intimacy, however, superseded ethnic competition and eventually resulted in Jewish assimilation. Both Wirth and Park made reference to the principles of Darwinian evolution, or the struggle for survival, and those of nineteenth-century social evolutionism, or the eclipse of the folk community in societal change.

GUNNAR MYRDAL

The main trend in history is the gradual realization of the American Creed, which is carried by high institutional structure, particularly education, which puts a constant pressure on race prejudice, counteracting the natural tendency for it to spread and become more intense (Myrdal, 1944:80).

Believing America's destiny to be the realization of the American Creed, Gunnar Myrdal anticipated the eventual assimilation of African Americans in *An American Dilemma: The Negro Problem and Modern Society* (1944). White Americans, he predicted, would finally embrace and put into practice the racial egalitarianism of the American Creed, resolving their long-standing moral dilemma over the historical discrimination against African Americans, and blacks will finally assimilate.

Gunnar Myrdal was brought to the United States by the Carnegie Foundation to collaborate with American social scientists in a study of American race relations. Myrdal, a Swedish social scientist and politician, was chosen by the foundation to head this study on the premise that race relations was such an emotional issue among Americans that a fresh mind was needed. He was also chosen because Sweden had not been an imperial power over people of color. His work began a preoccupation with race relations, black-white relations, that lasted in American social sciences for decades. White ethnic assimilation was so taken for granted at this time that the only remaining issue was the timing of black assimilation.

The publication of *An American Dilemma* represents a significant development in assimilationism. While Myrdal continued with a natural history of race relations, he discontinued the Chicago School custom of making recourse to both natural and social forces to explain the history of race relations. Thus his work represents a turn away from Darwin and toward social evolutionism, or the exclusive reliance on sociological and psychological principles to explain the course of ethnicity. Myrdal was critical of Park's use of a natural explanation of race relations and was particularly critical of its laissez-faire policy implications. If the race relations cycle is inevitable and thus beyond human intervention, what is there to do? Myrdal sought, by contrast, an intervention into the "vicious circle" of race relations in this country, and that intervention was the resolution of the American dilemma. The irony is that commentators would later judge Myrdal's work to be as much a natural history of race relations as was Park's race relations cycle, with no more specific policy directive (Cox, 1948; Ellison, 1964; Lyman, 1972; Metzger, 1971).

Myrdal's explanation of the course of American race relations is a cultural one, making recourse exclusively to social and psychological phenomena, and specifically to American ideals. Myrdal wrote: "Not since Reconstruction has there been more reason to anticipate fundamental changes in American race relations which will involve a development toward American ideals" (1944:xix). This fundamental change is identified as a change in the racial attitudes of whites.

American ideals have always implied racial equality and have historically been supported by high institutional structures in the United States, such as Christianity, English law, and the enlightened doctrine of human rights evident in founding documents such as the Declaration of Independence. These Myrdal called the "general valuations" of the American people. On the other hand, white Americans have been over time prejudicial and discriminatory toward African Americans, due to their "specific valuations." Nevertheless, whites have tried to adhere to American ideals, and as a result they have experienced a moral dilemma between their more general American ideals and their specific valuations with respect to race. However, Myrdal wrote, this dilemma will be resolved ultimately, the American Creed will win out, and African Americans will at last assimilate. Myrdal was as certain as Park and Wirth in his prediction of assimilation. "The main trend in history is the gradual realization of the American Creed" (Myrdal, 1944:80).

Despite the natural tendency for racial prejudice to grow and spread, the racial equality implicit in the American Creed counters it, according to Myrdal. Since Americans are rational, they will eventually believe in either racism or the American Creed, but not in both. Rationality causes a strain toward consistency between general and specific valuations. Because of the moral authority of and institutional support for the American Creed, specific valuations will be brought into line with the general valuations of American ideals. This spells an end to white racism.

The ultimate success of the American Creed lies in the fact that it is carried by high American institutions whose influence will increase with further industrialization, urbanization, and the spread of mass education and literacy. That is, the success of the American Creed comes with societal change. The resolution of the American dilemma is made certain, in the fashion of a natural history, by Myrdal's coupling of the social forces of change with the rationality of individual Americans. Thus whatever racism remains in modern America is merely vestigial and is sure to wane as the nation proceeds along the course on which it is already set—toward modernity. Black assimilation in America is destiny, and its pace is impeded only by unequal modernization of the regions of the country and, by implication, the unequal eradication of a murky, irrational folk mentality with prejudice in it.

While *An American Dilemma* is rich in its description of African American conditions of the era, black desire for assimilation is unquestionably assumed. Modes of African American thought about black pluralism and racial struggle are discounted. It was Myrdal's frank assumption that the future of African Americans would be determined by the attitudes and actions of white Americans toward them. Thus, the race consciousness of blacks, or any attitudes inconsistent with assimilation they might have, hardly mattered in their evolving relationship with the larger society. The vicious circle between white prejudice and black living conditions would be broken with the resolution of the American dilemma, a resolution made inevitable by societal change, and one which would result in the improvement of black living conditions.

Some are critical of Myrdal's depiction of the African American community, seeing in it the unequivocal support for assimilation and life-styles that are exaggerated, pathological distortions of those of whites (Cruse, 1967; Ellison, 1964). They counter with the observation that not all blacks have desired assimilation and not all blacks have distorted themselves in the image of white society. Hair straightening and skin bleaching were confined to only a few, as were other more subtle imitations of white society. Ellison (1964:316) wrote: "It does not occur to Myrdal that many Negro cultural manifestations which he considers merely reflective might also embody a rejection of what he considers 'higher values.'"

Myrdal looked forward to a fundamental change of heart by white Americans toward putting American ideals into practice. Since these ideals are supported in the higher institutions of the larger society and are spread with societal change, Myrdal was certain that the American dilemma would be ultimately resolved in favor of the American Creed. This version of ethnic history sounds every bit as inevitable as do the natural histories of Park and Wirth. Like the other two, Myrdal followed the precepts of social evolutionism in predicting the assimilation of ethnic groups in modern society, in this case of African Americans. Unlike the others, however, he made no reference to the Darwinian principles of the struggle for subsistence, basing his prediction of assimilation solely on the unfolding of certain cultural ideals.

W. LLOYD WARNER AND ASSOCIATES

W. Lloyd Warner was an anthropologist who carried out much of his research on ethnicity while at the University of Chicago. Warner and his associates continued certain Chicago School traditions, such as measuring assimilation as social class mobility, which was implicit in the works of Park and Wirth. The Warner group discontinued reference to a natural history of assimilation, however, making assimilation not only problematical but also expressly contingent on the cultural and biological differences between an ethnic group and the larger society. Warner and his associates have made a voluminous contribution to the study of ethnic relations in American society (Davis, Gardner, and Gardner, 1941; Warner, 1959; Warner and Associates, 1949; Warner and Low, 1947; Warner and Lunt, 1941, 1942; Warner and Srole, 1945).

Warner was interested in small American towns, particularly the class stratification of these towns, and he placed his study of ethnic relations in this context. He thought that the stratification of American towns with from five to ten thousand people typified the social stratification of the country as a whole. Warner and his colleagues selected among townsfolk of the community being studied a panel of judges who would rank their friends and neighbors into socially inferior and superior positions. In their evaluations of another resident, judges considered the person's occupation, source of income, house type, neighborhood of residence, and participation in community organizations. This is called the *reputational approach* to studying the social stratification of a community. From the judges' rankings, Warner and his associates typically found that residents of small towns fall into one of six social classes: upper-upper, lower-upper, upper-middle, lower-middle, upper-lower, and lower-lower. These classes constitute a hierarchy of socially superior and inferior positions within a community.

Ethnic groups as well as individual residents of a community could be ranked on the class hierarchy. The mobility of an ethnic

TABLE 2.1 OCCUPATIONAL STATUS INDICES OF YANKEE CITY ETHNIC GROUPS, 1850–1933

Group	1850	1864	1873	1883	1893	1903	1913	1923	1933
Irish	1.62	1.76	1.74	1.76	1.84	1.94	2.14	2.31	2.52
French Canadian					1.95	2.10	2.14	2.23	2.24
Jews							3.10	3.22	3.32
Italians							2.32	2.29	2.28
Armenians							2.46	2.51	2.56
Greeks								2.53	2.34
Poles								1.88	1.97
Russians									1.95
Total ethnics									2.42
Total natives									2.56

Source: W. Lloyd Warner and Leo Srole, *The Social Systems of American Ethnic Groups* (New Haven, CT: Yale University Press, 1945. Copyright © 1945 by Yale University Press. Reprinted by permission.

group upward in this hierarchy was the measure of its assimilation. In this fashion, blacks and whites in Old City (Natchez, Mississippi), the Norwegians of Jonesville (Morris, Illinois), and a multitude of ethnic groups in Yankee City (Newburyport, Massachusetts) were studied. In Yankee City both the occupational and residential changes of several ethnic groups over many decades were charted. Table 2.1 shows the occupational changes of ethnic groups in Yankee City. The higher the score, the higher is the occupational status of a group.

Note the unilinear trend among these groups toward improving their occupational status over time. It proceeds in only one direction, toward progressive assimilation, except for Italians and Greeks. The occupational status index consists of IA (unskilled), IB (skilled factory), IC (skilled craft), IIA and B (managerial), and III (professional), and these statuses are assigned scores from 1 through 6.

Changes in residence typically follow occupational mobility, and improvement in residential status was another correlated measure of assimilation in Warner and Srole's (1945) study. Like Park and Burgess (1921), they partitioned a city into zones and assigned a number to each zone representative of its residential status. The mobility of ethnic groups as they moved from lower to higher status zones was thereby charted. Table 2.2 shows this mobility for selected groups.

TABLE 2.2 RESIDENTIAL STATUS INDICES OF EIGHT ETHNIC GROUPS, 1850–1933

Group	1850	1864	1873	1883	1893	1903	1913	1923	1933
Irish	1.70	1.95	2.11	2.11	2.12	2.22	2.37	2.57	2.85
French Canadian					1.67	1.78	1.77	2.13	2.43
Jewish							1.93	2.14	2.77
Italian								2.21	2.38
Armenian								2.39	2.57
Greek								2.40	2.54
Polish								1.25	1.40
Russian									1.32

Source: W. Lloyd Warner and Leo Srole, *The Social Systems of American Ethnic Groups* (New Haven, CT: Yale University Press, 1945. Copyright © 1945 by Yale University Press. Reprinted by permission.

Without exception, ethnic groups moved to higher status locations in Yankee City with passing decades. Advancement in residence and occupation was identified with the assimilation of Yankee City's ethnic groups. Assimilation was judged to be reached when a group's residential and occupational status corresponded to that of the community as a whole.

While Warner and Srole (1945) continued the Chicago School custom of equating assimilation with occupational and residential mobility, they discontinued another convention of positing a natural, inevitable, and completely deterministic course—except for accidents—toward assimilation. Instead, they made ethnic history indeterminate, open to any and all influences. No longer was assimilation considered inevitable; rather it was dependent on factors both external and internal to an ethnic group.

Park and Wirth made recourse to both biotic and social principles in explaining the course of ethnic history toward assimilation. Myrdal made no reference to biotic principles, while he maintained the idea of an inevitable evolution toward assimilation in the modern era. Warner and his associates proceeded one step further, making assimilation an empirical question rather than a presumed fact in American society. They felt that the assimilation of racial minorities is especially problematical.

External factors in the assimilation of a group include its subordination by others, largely on the basis of its cultural or biological dissimilarity to the host society. Cultural dissimilarities between an ethnic group and the host society can involve language and religious differences, for instance, while biological differences refer to physical traits such as skin color. Generally, the greater the differences between immigrant and host, the slower the rate of immigrant assimilation. Assimilation is also contingent on the order of succession of immigrant groups, since early-arriving groups assimilate faster than later arrivals, assuming constant cultural and biological differences.

The rate of assimilation also depends on certain conditions internal to an ethnic group, according to Warner and his associates. These refer to the strength of the ethnic subsystem (ethnic community or communalism), and a strong ethnic community was thought to retard assimilation. The strength of an ethnic community was a function of the size of the ethnic group, its intentions in immigrating into the United States, its proximity to the homeland, and its power to control the lives of its members through a communal network of ethnic associations, schools, church and family. A large immigrant group with many members intent on returning to a nearby homeland would have a strong ethnic subsystem in the host society and would assimilate into that society only slowly, if at all.

Considering the external and internal factors simultaneously, Warner and Srole (1945:285–286) made three summary proposals:

1. The greater the difference between the host and the immigrant cultures, the greater will be the subordination, the greater the strength of the ethnic social systems, and the longer the period necessary for the assimilation of the ethnic group.
2. The greater the racial difference between the populations of the immigrant and host societies, the greater the subordination of the immigrant group, the greater the strength of the social subsystem, and the longer the period necessary for assimilation.
3. When the combined *cultural* and *biological* traits are highly divergent from those of the host society, the subordination of the group will be very great, their subsystem strong, the period of assimilation long, and the process slow and painful.

The third proposal applies particularly to African Americans. "There is a system of white and of Negro castes, and also a system of social classes within each caste, further stratifying groups and defining privileges" (Davis and Dollard, 1940:12–13). This is the summary conclusion drawn by Warner's associates upon studying race relations in

Old City (Davis and Dollard, 1940; Davis, et al., 1941). Race relations in Old City were considered typical of those throughout the South.

Ethnic groups in Yankee City, with few exceptions, moved up the social class ladder with each succeeding generation. This pattern was taken to be indicative of white ethnic assimilation in the entire North. In the South, however, blacks were enclosed in a racial caste, and, generation after generation, blacks did not advance beyond the color barrier. Racial castes were endogamous (that is, marriage was restricted to members of the same caste), and social mobility was confined by caste boundaries. Blacks in Old City could rise to the upper classes only within their own caste, and the black upper class was roughly equivalent to the white middle class. This color barrier to marriage and mobility threw into doubt the assimilation of blacks. The racial caste system of Old City is shown in Figure 2.1.

RACIAL ASSIMILATION

Assimilationists were never as certain about racial assimilation as about white ethnic assimilation. Park wrote about racial visibility's reinforcing social distance between groups, how it heightened racial consciousness, and how it impeded the pace of the race relations cycle (cf. Lyman, 1972; Park, 1950). He had in mind both African Americans in the South and Asians on the West Coast. But, "racial barriers may slacken the tempo of the movement [of the race relations cycle]; may perhaps halt it altogether for a time; but cannot change its direction; cannot at any rate reverse it... " (Park, 1950:150). In other words, racial visibility, stereotypes, and prejudice were merely accidents on the inevitable course toward assimilation; at least this was Park's view until his experiences in Hawaii.

No problem was anticipated with the ultimate assimilation of European immigrant groups, but calling Myrdal to this country implied that racial assimilation was not taken for granted. In the end, however, Myrdal predicted eventual racial assimilation with the resolution of the American dilemma. It was Warner and his associates who later voiced serious misgivings about the prospect for racial assimilation, likening race relations in the South to the seemingly everlasting caste system of India. The assimilation of white immigrant groups was simply a matter of time, by contrast, and the results from Yankee City suggested that white ethnic assimilation in terms of upward mobility was virtually assured.

Thus, the debate over assimilation narrowed to one over racial assimilation—would African Americans follow white ethnic groups on

FIGURE 2.1 WARNER'S DIAGRAM OF THE CASTE SYSTEM IN THE DEEP SOUTH

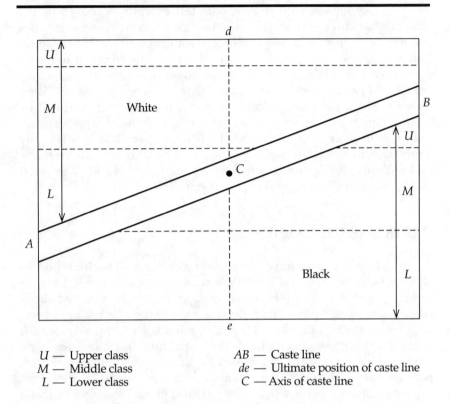

U — Upper class
M — Middle class
L — Lower class

AB — Caste line
de — Ultimate position of caste line
C — Axis of caste line

Source: Allison Davis, Burleigh B. Gardner, and Mary R. Gardner, *Deep South*. Chicago: University of Chicago Press. Copyright © 1941 by The University of Chicago. Reprinted by permission.

the road to assimilation? On one side, some argued that the history of blacks is unique in America, and no analogy can be drawn between whites and blacks in this country. This assumed uniqueness is dramatized by drawing another analogy, one between black history in America and the caste system in India, or by the analogy of African Americans and people who had been colonial subjects in the nineteenth-century. It was assumed that European Americans shared neither experience, although historically white Americans were once colonial subjects of Great Britain, and many European immigrants were, while still in Europe, colonial subjects of old European empires. On the other side, there are those who argue that the experiences of blacks are different only in degree from those of white immigrant groups. The more accurate analogy is with white Americans, not with excluded castes in India and former colonial people around the globe.

AFRICAN AMERICAN HISTORY IS UNIQUE

The caste model draws a comparison between the history of blacks in the South and that of lower castes in India, and the colonial model draws an analogy between blacks in America and colonized people elsewhere in the world. Both suggest that the course of black assimilation might be fundamentally different than that of white Americans.

CASTE MODEL: The caste analogy was proposed in the works of Davis and Dollard (1940), and Davis, et al. (1941), and it continued with Dollard (1957). Berreman (1960) incorporated both the concept and criticisms of it in his description of this analogy. First, the caste system of India and race relations in the southern United States were comparable. In both instances, inequality became a societal institution, it was hereditary and permanent, and it was enforced by the higher castes to better exploit the lower castes. Dollard (1957) wrote that the gains to whites in the South included economic, sexual, and status privileges. The economic gains to whites centered around keeping cheap black labor in its place, and the sexual gains were that white men had access to partners of both races, a privilege others did not share. Deference toward whites was expected from all blacks as a matter of practice, and this had become institutionalized into a racial etiquette. Religion in India and racism in the South justified the respective caste systems.

Berreman (1960) was irritated with critics of the caste model who contended that lower castes in India were content with their lot. They were as much dissatisfied with the caste system as were blacks in the South, he argued. There were several other similarities between the two caste systems. While the advantaged groups were paternalistic toward the disadvantaged groups, members of the lower groups resentfully played their stereotyped subordinate roles for favors. There were rigid rules of avoidance between castes in both instances, and class hierarchies existed within castes in both India and the South. Berreman admitted to one dissimilarity. Abolition of the caste system in India was anticipated with ambivalence, since it meant, for most castes, mingling with inferiors as well as with equals and superiors. Since blacks had no inferiors in the South, they had no ambivalence at all about the end of the caste system.

COLONIAL MODEL: The colonial analogy, too, suggests a gap between European ethnic groups and non-European minority groups. One analogy is between African American history and the experiences of colonized people in the nineteenth century. Blauner (1969) made the distinction between colonialism as a social, economic, and political system and colonization as a process imposed on subordinate peoples. It is the latter that African Americans share with the colonized peoples of the nineteenth century. The values and culture of the colonized groups were destroyed in both instances, according to Blauner. Furthermore, the colonized groups were administered to by representatives of the majority—the police, in the case of African Americans. Finally, racism justified both colonial policies. There is a difference, however. The colonization of African Americans was more complete, Blauner said, for their social structure and culture were less developed, they were less autonomous and a numerical minority, and they were ghettoized more totally (Blauner, 1969).

Moore (1970a) argued that the colonial model describes the history of Mexican Americans without need of analogy. Hispanos in New Mexico were colonized by Anglos in the nineteenth century; theirs is a classic case of colonialism as a system and process. By Blauner's own criteria, the contact between Anglos and Hispanos in New Mexico better fits the colonial model than do the experiences of blacks in this country. On the other hand, Moore wrote that the experiences of Mexican Americans in Texas and California deviate from the classic colonial experience, although these, too, may fall under the colonialism-as-a-process model.

According to Barrera (1979), Hispanics in the Southwest have been caught in a colonial labor system—marked by labor repression, labor-market stratification, and a dual wage system—so that Chicanos have been historically relegated to the bottom of the region's labor market. They served as a reserve labor force in good economic times and buffers for employers during economic downturns. Thus, the representatives of the majority with whom they have had contact are not only the police, but also labor agents, employers, and governmental personnel (Moore, 1978). The colonial model is part of ethnic conflict theory and also discussed in Chapter 4.

The larger significance of these caste and colonial models is the belief that assimilation of non-Europeans is not the same as white ethnic assimilation. While ethnic assimilation appeared inevitable, sociologists began questioning the inevitability of racial assimilation, specifically that of other non-European groups. Thus, new imagery appeared, the likening of African Americans and Mexican Americans to either Indian castes or colonial subjects. Of course, others saw little need for this questioning, assuming that racial assimilation would follow the path of white ethnic groups.

AFRICAN AMERICAN HISTORY IS DIFFERENT
ONLY IN DEGREE

African American history is not unique, although it is different in degree from that of white ethnic groups. This point was made by Nathan Glazer (1971), who argued that Blauner did not truly distinguish between the experiences of African Americans and those of other ethnic groups in America. Glazer summarized what he considers to be Blauner's key points:

> First, the ethnic ghettos arose more from voluntary choice, both in the sense of the choice to immigrate to America and the decision to live among one's fellow ethnics. Second, the immigrant ghettos tended to be a one and two generation phenomenon; they were actually way stations in the process of acculturation and assimilation....The black Ghetto on the other hand has been a permanent phenomenon.... Afro-Americans are distinct in the extent to which their segregated communities have remained controlled economically, politically and administratively from the outside... (Glazer, 1971:450–51).

Glazer observed that while blacks were brought involuntarily to the South as slaves, their later migration to urban ghettos in the North and West was as voluntary as the earlier European immigration into the country. Blauner argued that white ethnics dispersed from their ghettos into the suburbs in a generation or two, while blacks have remained concentrated in racial ghettos far longer because of discrimination. This underestimated the persistence of white ethnic segregation and overestimated black segregation, Glazer argued, observing that Kantrowitz's (1969) index of segregation between Swedes and Russians in New York City is 70.7 and that of blacks is 80. It is a difference of degree rather than kind.

Blauner believed that white immigrant groups quickly took control over their own ghettos, while blacks have not. The rate at which an ethnic group attains control over its own affairs is a measure of self-determination, but is a complex issue. Glazer asked: Is it accurate to compare such rates for blacks with those for all white ethnic groups, since we find that while blacks are behind the Irish they are very much ahead of the Poles in assuming a role in urban politics? Another complexity in making comparisons on rates of assimilation is in the calculation of those rates. Obviously, the numerators must be indicators of assimilation; however, what time span is to be the denominator? If it is the entire history of African Americans in the United States, then their comparative rate of assimilation is so slow as to be virtually unique. However, if the denominator is a shorter historical period, the time African Americans have lived in the nation's cities that have presumably assimilated other immigrant groups, then their rate of assimilation is close enough to those of others that there is only a difference in degree.

> [T]here are almost none [of the elements of continuity] between the experience of the Negro slave in the South and the free immigrant worker in the North. But there are elements of continuity—and important ones—between the experiences of immigrant workers in the North and black migrants in the North (Glazer, 1971:453).

If one sees some comparability between black history and that of white ethnic groups, one can believe that racial and ethnic assimilation, too, are comparable.

O'Kane (1969) observed that white immigrants in the nation's cities took three routes toward assimilation: labor, politics, and crime. Important changes have occurred in the urban labor market, however, since blacks have migrated to urban areas. A decreasing demand for unskilled labor and the more general shift from blue- to white-collar work now limit blacks' chances for mobility up the labor hierarchy, in O'Kane's estimation. On the other hand, blacks can use urban politics and crime as mobility routes, as have other groups, and they will have the same experiences as others have had at dislodging those ahead of them.

THE CONTACT HYPOTHESIS

Intimacy was always considered by assimilationists to be a final reason for assimilation. It moved the race relations cycle from accommodation to assimilation. Beginning with their movement from ghettos, the physical distance between members of different ethnic groups would disappear in the nation's suburbs. There, people from diverse backgrounds would become cordial neighbors, members of the same business and social clubs, and close friends whose children would eventually intermarry. Intimacy brings assimilation.

But could the nation realistically expect interracial intimacy, and thus racial assimilation? The assimilationists were always somewhat uncertain in their answer. Park wrote that racial visibility and stereotypes impeded the pace of the race relations cycle, and Warner and his associates observed that intimacy stopped at the color line in the Deep South. Early interest in the prospect of interracial intimacy has continued and has come to be called the contact hypothesis. "According to this proposition, increased interaction between whites and any minority group, such as Negroes, makes for favorable attitudes on the part of whites, greater acceptance of the blacks, and integration [assimilation] of the racial groups" (Zeul and Humphrey, 1971:464).

Support for the contact hypothesis comes from research on interracial contact in a variety of settings, including the armed forces, neighborhoods, schools, workplaces, and summer camps, as well as from laboratory experiments (cf., Amir, 1976; Cohen and Roper, 1972; Pettigrew, 1969). One historical precedent was the contact between Irish women working as domestic servants and the families for whom they worked. This contact is considered to be a reason for the faster assimilation of Irish women than men (Diner, 1983).

However, other research shows that interracial contact does not always conform to the contact hypothesis (Amir, 1976; Molotch, 1969). Contact can make matters worse, illustrated by clashes between white police and black citizens. The minimal group experiments of Tajfel and his associates (1978, 1981, 1982) clearly demonstrate this possibility. The arbitrary division of subjects into two superficial groups, based on non-existent differences, alone triggered prejudice and discrimination within an hour or so. Subjects favored in-group members in their distribution of rewards and performance and personality evaluations—an in-group bias. They also expressed a preference for being in their own group. The implication is, of course, that such bias is accentuated in the contact between real ethnic groups in everyday life.

Allport (1954) concluded that four conditions must be present in interracial contact for it to produce any measure of intimacy. These are that (1) the black and white participants must be of roughly equal status (2) pursuing common goals (3) in a cooperative manner, and (4) the contact must be sanctioned in law and by political authorities. Pettigrew (1969:56) observed that "all four of his [Allport's] conditions maximize the likelihood of shared values and beliefs." Pettigrew makes an important point. From the perspective of both assimilationism and the contact hypothesis, the point is that blacks and whites must be equally modernized. They must share in the mentality of educational and occupational achievement, middle-class respectability, and racial egalitarianism; they must share in the entire roster of modern traits for there to be any intimacy in their contact.

Zeul and Humphrey (1971) concluded that it is not that interracial contact brings acceptance of blacks, rather it is the degree to which whites were cosmopolitan before contact. It is how modern they are in their tastes, highbrow in their leisure pursuits, educated and non-parochial in their self-identifications that makes whites and blacks, alike, accepting of close contact with one another. Thus we are brought back to the concept that modernity brings the assimilation of ethnic groups into a unitary society.

OTHER RECENT DEVELOPMENTS

While uncertain about racial assimilation, assimilationists have raised few questions about the inevitability of white ethnic assimilation. The latter was assumed to be on its predicted course. Questions about white ethnic assimilation arose later, in the 1970s, with the resurgence of white ethnicity in the larger society. In the current debate over the differences between racial and ethnic assimilation, the idea that the black experience is fundamentally different from the experiences of white ethnic groups has been restated (Pettigrew, 1988). The implication is that white ethnic groups are assimilating while blacks are not, at least not to the same degree. Recent research evidence suggests this is true, with some important qualifications.

Although cultural difference among white ethnic groups still existed in 1980, past ethnic differences in fertility, education, and propensity to marry were converging among European ethnic groups (Lieberson and Waters, 1988). The difference in educational attainment among European groups was slight in 1980 compared to the difference between them and non-European groups. Another indication of acculturation is the shift across generations from a non-English mother tongue to the English language. Stevens (1985:74) found in a 1976 survey that non-English languages "disappear between generations as patterns of social interaction widen to include intimate associations outside of the non-English-language community, and outside of the ethnic descent group." This trend includes the switch from Spanish to English for Mexican Americans (de La Garza, 1985). Assimilation on a number of counts seems to be evident.

European groups are also converging in their occupations, yet another sign of white ethnic assimilation. "[A]mong both men and women in 1980 the major European-origin groups are generally much more similar to one another than to non-Europeans in the broad set of occupations that they hold" (Lieberson and Waters, 1988:135). Russians were the only exception, and Lieberson and Waters believed that most of the Russians are Jewish. Excluding Russians, however, there were still white ethnic differences in specific occupational categories such as farming and services. The old European immigrant groups were still concentrated in farming as compared to the newer groups from southern and eastern Europe, with the exception of Czechs.

Despite such specific differences, European groups in the United States were far more different from non-European groups than they were from one another (Lieberson and Waters, 1988). Women of European groups were even more alike in occupations than were men, and they were more similar to non-European women than were the men. That is, integration of European groups through occupational similarity runs ahead of that for non-European groups with the exception of Asians.

The Census Bureau classified occupations in 1980 into six broad categories:

1. Managerial and professional
2. Technical, sales, and administrative support
3. Service occupations
4. Farming, forestry, and fishing
5. Precision production, craft, and repair
6. Operators, fabricators, and laborers

Whereas 24 percent of the nation's employed whites were managers and professionals, 29 percent of Asian Americans were in these occupations, which are considered the highest-status jobs in the nation. White and Asian participation in technical, sales, and administrative support was relatively the same in percentage terms, 31 percent. A greater percentage of Asians were in service occupations, 16 percent compared to 12 percent for whites. Two percent of the Asian American and 3 percent of the white labor force were in farming, forestry, and fishing. Greater percentages of whites than Asians were in blue-collar work, from the skilled crafts to unskilled labor. Between 1960 and 1976, Asian Americans approached socioeconomic status parity with white Americans (Hirschman and Wong, 1984). Socioeconomic status included earnings as well as occupational status, and the Asian groups included Chinese, Japanese, and Filipinos. By contrast, blacks and Hispanics did not approach parity with whites during this period.

European-origin men were also similar in their conversion of education into occupation and income. The differences among European groups in this conversion were modest, as compared to their differences with both African Americans and Puerto Ricans. The latter groups did not convert education into occupational and income gains as well, and thus had lower incomes. Lieberson (1980) contended that the dissimilarity between blacks and white ethnics on education and occupation has actually increased in recent decades. Mexican Americans were, on the other hand, more similar to Europeans than to African Americans and Puerto Ricans in this regard. European and non-European women were not as dissimilar in income as were the men.

As individual members of ethnic groups climb in socioeconomic status, this change will be registered in their greater residential contact with out-group members. Recall this basic notion from Park and Wirth. In 1970, Massey and Denton (1985, 1988) and Massey and Mullan (1984) found that this model applied also to Hispanics in the United States and somewhat to Puerto Ricans, but African Americans continued to live in racially segregated neighborhoods even after improvement in their socioeconomic status. Thus, distinct racial patterns in occupation, income, and residence continue in the nation.

These black-white comparisons are a bit overgeneralized, however. Since Wilson (1978, 1987) drew attention to class differences among African Americans, researchers have studied the mobility of blacks by social class. Between 1962 and 1973, class differences in intergenerational mobility for blacks were significant. Black men from the most advantaged socioeconomic backgrounds were doing well, those from disadvantaged backgrounds were not, and these class effects were similar to those on upward mobility for whites (Hout, 1984). Moreover, class effects on intergenerational mobility of black men increased between 1962 and 1973. Middle- and lower-class black males were becoming increasingly different from each other. Stolzenberg (1990) found the same pattern in comparisons between Hispanic and non-Hispanic white men. If Hispanic men spoke English very well and had completed at least 12 years of school, then their occupational achievement was close to that of white non-Hispanic men in the same geographic area of the country and with similar English fluency and schooling. However, at lower levels of schooling and English fluency, the occupations of Hispanic men were inferior to the occupations of similar white non-Hispanic men. Thus, racial and Hispanic-European differences in mobility are moderated by class background, for the differences are much less for the advantaged than the disadvantaged.

Ethnic intermarriage has been increasing across the cohorts of all the European groups (Lieberson and Waters, 1988). That is, young women were more likely to intermarry with men of other European groups than were older cohorts of women, who tended to marry within their own nationality group. By the same token, the European groups were not intermarrying at nearly the same rate with non-European groups—including blacks, Mexicans, Puerto Ricans, Native Americans, and Asians—as they were with one another. Intermarriage between blacks and whites in America is tiny compared to that among white ethnic groups. To illustrate, 7 percent of all men married to women who are still in their first marriage are black. However, they are not likely to be married to white ethnic women. Rates of intermarriage for white ethnic women to African American men are well below 1 percent (Lieberson and Waters, 1988).

Intermarriage is the intimacy assumed to be the final step toward assimilation. Intermarriage rates of many white ethnic groups have been rising with succeeding generations, so that an increasing number of white Americans now trace their ancestry to more than one European nation. The rates of intermarriage for the third and fourth generations of white ethnic groups is between 60 and 80 percent, and the rate of mixed ancestry is between 60 and 90 percent. These trends and rates for French and Hispanic Americans are more limited (Alba, 1976 and 1985; and Alba and Chamlin, 1983). Gurak and Fitzpatrick (1982) found in 1975 records that Hispanic groups in New York City were intermarrying with one another at high rates by the second generation, and were marrying white non-Hispanics at a somewhat lower rate. This was true for all groups except Puerto Ricans.

Alba (1985) also found in the specific case of Italians evidence for acculturation. On family issues such as divorce, premarital sex, and abortion, Italians have roughly the same attitudes as other Americans. Nor were they different from other Americans in their attitudes toward child-rearing. Alba took this as evidence that the traditional family-centered Italian subculture is in its twilight, as are presumably the subcultures of other white ethnic groups.

By the same token, white Americans who intermarry and have mixed European ancestry still identify with one or more ethnic groups. Indeed, among the younger generations there is an increasing number of individuals with mixed or ambiguous ancestry who identify with a single ethnic group (Alba and Chamlin, 1983; Lieberson and Waters, 1988). Ethnic identity has risen in saliency, perhaps, but the involvement of white Americans in ethnic communities, their living in ethnic neighborhoods, and their marrying within their own ethnic groups have declined. The current expression of ethnic identity for whites is largely symbolic, according to some, and their participation in ethnic communities and cultures is confined to the occasional festival or rite, and not part of daily routine.

European groups have become more similar to one another than they are to non-European groups, and this is true for education, occupation, income, and intermarriage. This is evidence for both white ethnic assimilation and the relative lack of racial assimilation. On the other hand, Asians have reached parity with whites on socioeconomic status, and the mobility of blacks and Hispanics varies by social class background. The advantaged of both groups are more similar to their white class counterparts than are the disadvantaged to their white counterparts. By the same token, even the black middle class remains residentially segregated and racial intermarriage remains minuscule.

SUMMARY AND ASSESSMENT

Assimilationism has made significant contributions to our understanding of American ethnicity, but there are limitations to this perspective. As long as the assimilationists held to a natural history of ethnic relations, the prediction of assimilation could be neither proven nor disproven. The prediction was not put in a time frame; rather it was stated that assimilation would take place eventually. But exactly what does *eventually* mean? Does it mean that assimilation will occur within a decade, a generation, two or three generations, or in some even more distant future? Moreover, when assimilation did not occur as expected, it was explained that certain accidents or obstacles had interfered with the natural course of race relations, and such cases never were taken as evidence contrary to the tenets of the race relations cycle. Park never found a single case in support of his prediction of inevitable assimilation, but he held to the validity of the cycle into old age (Lyman, 1972).

Ethnic relations in a natural history are likened to a mechanical process. Once set into motion, this process moves like some great machine, inevitably and without purpose toward a final state. This mechanical metaphor of human life was the mainstay imagery of social evolutionism. For example, Gumplowicz wrote in 1899: "The individual simply plays a part of the prism which receives the rays, dissolves them according to fixed laws and lets them pass out again in a predetermined direction and with a predetermined color" (p. 157). The mechanical metaphor was fused with science earlier in Newton's concept of the universe as a great machine (Matson, 1966). The imagery came to be shared in biology, psychology, and the social sciences in the nineteenth century (Polanyi, 1944). Whether the phenomenon under study was physical, biological, psychological, economic, or social, the image was the same: evolution is mindlessly propelled by mechanical forces. Many commentators have noted that this mechanistic metaphor implied a laissez-faire approach about assimilationism, for nothing was to be done since assimilation was inevitable (Cox, 1948; Ellison, 1964; Lyman, 1972; Myrdal, 1944).

In physics, faith in the mechanical motif was seriously shaken early in the twentieth century by the works of Einstein, Heisenberg, and Planck, among others. However, assimilationists were analyzing ethnicity at the same time with the mechanical metaphors of nineteenth-century sciences, apparently unaware of the challenge to mechanism in physics. Moreover, much of the general sociology of the time buttressed the tenets of assimilationism. The theme of American society as a mass society, one consisting of isolated individuals in large cities bereft of social bonds, and the stress on impersonal utility, not personal loyalty or human sympathy, as modern society's flywheel, suggest that assimilationism was but part of general sociology.

Nevertheless, human purpose and sentiment always had an important role in Park's race relations cycle. Human communication, cooperation, and intimacy were all necessary for the completion of the cycle. Neither Park nor Wirth nor any other assimilationist ever expunged humanity from race relations, nor did they reduce ethnic relations to the level of the impersonal struggle for survival. The student can readily imagine what the race relations cycle would have been without reference to communication, mutual understanding, and intimacy. The irony is that, as an explanation of changing ethnic relations, these human variables were every bit as mechanical as was impersonal competition.

With Myrdal's *An American Dilemma*, ethnic relations were put exclusively in the context of human culture, and reference to biotic and impersonal forces was discontinued. Myrdal analyzed American race relations as a moral dilemma—the American dilemma, it was called—and he predicted that it would finally be resolved in favor of racial equality. While the setting of ethnic relations in the context of human culture represents an advance for this school, Myrdal's analysis is still not totally adequate. Cox (1948) observed that race relations are mystified by Myrdal and made part of an American morality play between good (American Creed) and evil (racism), one that takes place in the metaphysical American soul.

Another limitation of assimilationism is its tendency to identify ethnicity in general with ethnic segregation in particular. Ethnicity cannot exist in the scheme outside the ghetto. Not only is this an unnecessarily narrow definition of ethnicity, it has the effect of seriously questioning only the assimilation of Americans of color, especially that of African Americans, who continued to be segregated. Assimilationists began to notice that many African Americans were poor, living in ghettos, and phenotypically distinct. Racial visibility was considered a possible impediment to assimilation even by Park, and Warner and his associates elaborated on this theme in the caste hypothesis. It was felt that when both biological and cultural traits of a group are divergent from those of the larger society, then assimilation of such groups is a slow and painful process. Research in the 1980s on assimilation has generally supported the notion that racial and white-ethnic assimilation have taken somewhat divergent paths.

Questioning only racial assimilation protects the assimilationist thesis to a degree. The implication is that, except for the unique cases of certain racial groups, the assimilation thesis works. Because white immigrant groups no longer live only in ghettos and have risen from the bottom of the nation's social ladder, they have assimilated. With the occupational diversification and residential dispersion of Jewish Americans, for instance, there was assimilation in Wirth's scheme. He did not see the possibility "that members of the third (and later) generations of an ethnic minority may maintain a particular subculture, not lose their identity, although they are neither isolated nor concentrated in specific ecological areas" (Etzioni, 1959:257).

The hypothesis of the uniqueness of color prejudice and the history of people of color possibly errs in two directions. First, the histories of various people of color in America, including those of Native Americans, Asian Americans, and African Americans, are hardly identical. They diverge from one another as much as they diverge from the history of white immigrant groups. For instance, Chinese and Japanese Americans have assimilated to a far greater degree than have African Americans, even more than many white immigrant groups, if we measure assimilation in terms of social class mobility. Is it too obvious to note that these Asians are as physically distinct from whites as are blacks? The emphasis on racial prejudice and discrimination appears unable to make such distinctions among the histories of the different people of color in America.

The proposition that color is virtually the only impediment to assimilation unfortunately never forced sociologists "to abandon the idea that ethnicity is a dysfunctional survival from a prior stage of social development" (Metzger, 1971:644). This is the second error, by implication, of the hypothesis on the uniqueness of racial assimilation (or the lack of it). Ethnicity, even for whites, might be as important in modern society as it was traditionally; at least, we should be open to this possibility. Modernity was equated with expanding individual freedom in historic liberalism, and this idea was applied to ethnic relations in twentieth-century America by assimilationists. As members of ethnic groups experience this freedom, they would disperse into the larger society, and ethnic groups would decompose. This meant assimilation to the assimilationists, but it could also mean the unfolding of ethnicity into new forms and expressions.

C H A P T E R
3
◎◎

ETHNIC PLURALISM

A famous historian of American ethnicity, Oscar Handlin, once confessed that not until he sat down to write a history of America's immigrants did he realize that their history is the history of the country. Assimilationism was the unofficial national doctrine for much of this century, which hardly encouraged widespread appreciation for the nation's ethnic diversity. Ethnicity was a cultural survival that would soon go away, or so the assimilationists thought. However, there have always been those who have maintained that ethnic diversity endures in societal change, and their voices rose in the 1970s and 1980s. Among these are the pluralists, who believe that ethnicity has social, economic, political, and psychological functions in modern American society.

In assimilationism, American society is likened to a melting pot, an image of the absorption of diverse groups into a single culture and society. Only the assimilation of certain racial groups was ever seriously questioned. Pluralists contend, however, that the single melting pot is the wrong metaphor, and suggest that many melting pots better depict ethnic change in American society. Rather than fusing into a single mass society, ethnic groups fuse together in several melting pots, each distinct from the others. Rather than disappearing, ethnicity moves into new forms and expressions in the course of societal change.

This chapter examines ethnic pluralism as a perspective on American ethnicity. The key terms of pluralism are presented and the assumptions of pluralism are identified. Then the works of pluralists are surveyed, and an assessment of pluralism brings the chapter to a close.

DEFINITIONS AND ASSUMPTIONS

KEY TERMS

ETHNIC GROUP: *An ethnic group is a self-conscious collectivity of people who, on the basis of a common origin or a separate subculture, maintain a distinction between themselves and outsiders.* Such boundary maintenance may be manifest in social interaction or simply in patterns of thought and sentiment. This definition allows that ethnicity can take many forms and expressions.

Assimilationists tended to restrict their conception of ethnicity, or, more specifically, of ethnic boundaries, to residential segregation and occupational concentration of ethnic groups. They assumed that ethnic groups exist only in ghettos and when members are concentrated in a narrow range of jobs so that they are isolated from others. Occupational diversification and residential dispersion of an ethnic group were identified with its assimilation, a convention that Warner and Srole (1945) made explicit in their Yankee City study. By implication, ethnic groups disappear with their ghettos.

Pluralists contend that this conception of ethnicity is too exclusive. DeVos (1975:12) commented that "The degree to which some territorial concept is necessary to the maintenance of ethnic identity, symbolically or actually, must be considered in relation to the use of nonterritorial definitions of ethnic uniqueness...." DeVos argued that ethnic "boundaries are basically psychological in nature, not territorial"(p. 6), in line with Barth's (1969) work. Ethnic identity is not necessarily manifest in either territorial isolation or distinctive economic activity; rather, it is more generally the "subjective symbolic or emblematic use of any aspect of culture, in order to differentiate themselves [ethnic group members] from other groups" (DeVos, 1975:16). Ethnicity is a state of mind and always has been, DeVos argued. Ethnicity is a badge phenomenon, which can be voluntarily displayed in the presentation of self and used in both personal and group strategies to achieve certain objectives in society (Bennett, 1975). Therefore, an ethnic group is a self-conscious collectivity of people who maintain a distinction between themselves and outsiders based on origin or a separate subculture, and such boundary maintenance may be manifest in social interaction, including segregation, or simply in patterns of thought and sentiment.

In the pluralist view, ethnicity is constructed in a historical context and, thus, is continually changing (cf., Bean and Tienda, 1987). To illustrate, European immigrants became ethnic groups, not in Europe but in America, by virtue of their immigration. Mexican Americans became an ethnic group when the Southwest was annexed by the United

States in the middle of the nineteenth century. Their group boundaries were constructed in the United States, specifically in the context of their changing relations with other groups in this country. Their sense of "we" always had one boundary, it ended where "they," the out-groups, began, whether this was marked by territory, descent, language, ways of dressing, culinary traditions, or prejudice and discrimination. The construction of ethnicity is interactive, always involving both in-groups and out-groups. At first the boundaries might have been territorial—separate immigrant ghettos—but they later became only symbolic, in food preferences or simply a personal interest in ethnic roots. Thus, European ethnic groups have perhaps evolved toward more open and inclusive boundaries vis-à-vis each other, but this has not necessarily meant their assimilation, according to pluralists.

PLURALISM: There are two dimensions of pluralism: cultural and structural. This corresponds to the two dimensions of assimilation: acculturation and integration. *Cultural pluralism refers to the existence of ethnic subcultures in a society, which affect and make variable the way people think, feel, and act. Structural pluralism means that ethnic identity is evident in social interaction in a society, manifest in either restrictions on social interaction or in the use of ethnic identity in open and free exchange.*

ETHNIC CHANGE: *Ethnicity is an evolving or emergent phenomenon, because groups, as well as their relations with one another and with the larger society, continually change.* The survival of ethnic pluralism is one dimension of this history, and is the one emphasized in this chapter. Ethnic group boundaries may become more inclusive, even start to overlap, in the course of societal change. This can mean the continuation of ethnic pluralism, not assimilation, so long as ethnic boundaries and identity remain meaningful to people. According to pluralists, this is as true today of white ethnics as it is for racial minorities.

ASSUMPTIONS OF ETHNIC PLURALISM

1. While ethnic relations change in the course of societal change, this does not necessarily bring the assimilation of these groups into a single, mass society.
2. As the relations among ethnic groups evolve, the expression of ethnicity can change. In the United States, ethnic boundaries have generally grown more inclusive and less restrictive, and ethnic identity and its expression have become more domestic and less foreign.

3. The persistence of ethnicity in American society is due to the nation's tolerance for pluralism, the psychological functions served by ethnicity, and ethnic group competition for societal resources.

RE-EVALUATION OF PARK AND WIRTH

The discussion of ethnic pluralism begins with critiques of two early works of assimilationism: Park's race relations cycle and Wirth's natural history of Jewish assimilation. This is followed by a survey of several pluralists. The pluralist concept of ethnicity becomes broader and more comprehensive as we go, so that toward the end of the chapter ethnicity is seen as a pervasive and persistent state of consciousness, one that is manifested in a variety of ways.

PARK'S NATURAL HISTORY OF ASSIMILATION

THE RACE RELATIONS CYCLE: In Robert Park's view, the cycle of race relations inevitably ended with assimilation. Emory Bogardus, too, believed that race relations formed a cycle, but he did not believe that it inevitably ends with assimilation. Studying the reception of Asian and Mexican immigrants on the West Coast years ago, Bogardus (1930:621) observed: "There is first curiosity and sympathy followed by economic welcome which brings an increase of numbers. The third stage is industrial and social antagonism as competition develops. Next comes legislative antagonism, succeeded by fair-play tendencies, after which a sixth stage of quiescence is reached. The last phase is found in the second-generation difficulties, the American-born children of immigrants being only partially accepted by natives."

Bogardus's cycle begins with curiosity and sympathy toward Asian and Mexican immigrants. The "strangeness coupled with his original fewness of numbers make him appear helpless" (Bogardus, 1930:613). Apparently, the strangeness of these immigrants invoked curiosity, while their perceived helplessness stimulated the sympathy of natives. Asians and Mexicans also received an economic welcome, especially from employers. The third stage of the cycle is industrial and social antagonism. Bogardus (1930:614) notes that first "sporadic outbursts of prejudice against them [immigrants] have occurred, and the organized movements have gained a tremendous momentum.... Organized labor has usually been the leader in protesting against the...immigrants, on grounds of protecting labor against unfair competition and pulling down of standards built up at great sacrifice by American workers."

Economic threat was not the only issue around which opposition to immigration was mobilized. Fear about the volume of immigration grew—"There has seemed to be uncounted millions on the way"—and this fear was intensified by the perceived high birthrates of Asian and Mexican immigrants. These fears are not unlike those of today. Moreover, as some of the immigrants attempted to move out of their ghettos and into the residential areas of natives, opposition toward them enlarged and grew more heated. Bogardus remarked in a snide manner that at this stage of the cycle, "Natives do not appreciate how they may bring about the assimilation and acculturation of both the first- and second-generation immigrants..." (p. 615). This stage of Bogardus's cycle is similar to Park's stage of competition. Bogardus believed that ethnic antagonism continued into legislative action against the immigrants, the fourth stage of his cycle. An illustration is the immigration restrictions we learned about in Chapter 1.

Invariably a "fair-play" movement developed, and during this fifth stage of the cycle ethnic antagonism was prevented from going to extremes. The fair-play movement, however, did not prevent the expatriation of Mexicans from the United States and the passage of legislation restricting Asian immigration (Chapter 1). After the passage of this legislation, accommodation was achieved. "Assured that the impending danger is safely thwarted, the antagonistic organizations modify their attitudes" (p. 616).

While Park proposed that ethnic change ended with assimilation, due to communication and intimacy, Bogardus's cycle ended on the note of *second-generation difficulties*. He observed that while second-generation immigrants, particularly Asian, were losing contact with the home country, they were being accepted only partially in the United States, the land of their birth and citizenship (p. 617). While Park and Wirth admitted that prejudice and discrimination might impede the pace of assimilation, it was their conviction that such difficulties are passing phenomena and that assimilation is inevitable. Bogardus did not share this conviction, and additional revisions of Park's race relations cycle can be found in Banton (1967), Brown (1934), and Kitano (1969). All these revisions share the idea that a natural history of assimilation should be retired.

THE SOCIAL DISTANCE SCALE: Distance between ethnic groups was an important concept in the works of Park and Wirth. To Park and Wirth, distance between ethnic groups meant primarily their spatial distance, or residential segregation. The residential movement out of the ghetto by an ethnic group was identified with its assimilation.

Along with Park (1924), Bogardus defined the distance between ethnic groups more abstractly, however, as an attitude that may or may not be manifested in physical segregation. This was called social distance, and it can be maintained as an ethnic boundary in the absence of physical distance between groups. The implication is, obviously, that ethnicity can exist without segregation and isolation. Bogardus (1928) constructed a social distance scale by first asking people if they would admit members of 40 different ethnic groups to:

1. Close kinship by marriage
2. My club as personal chums
3. My street as neighbors
4. Employment in my occupation
5. Citizenship in my country
6. My country as visitors
7. Or would exclude from my country

Bogardus proposed that the above items formed a rank order of social distance, with the least amount of distance expressed in item 1 and the greatest amount of distance expressed in item 7. The social distance scale became a popular research instrument, and results from using it over many years show that Americans have consistently wished to maintain social distance between themselves and certain ethnic groups (Bogardus, 1958, 1967, and 1968; Owen, et al., 1981; Smith and Dempsey, 1983). Distance or boundaries between ethnic groups are not only spatial, they are also a more abstract preference to maintain distance in either a spatial or a symbolic way. Ethnic boundaries can persist as social distance in the absence of spatial segregation and, thus, outside ghettos.

WIRTH'S NATURAL HISTORY OF JEWISH ASSIMILATION

On the occasion of the republication of Wirth's *The Ghetto* in 1956, Amitai Etzioni (1959:257) wrote that Wirth viewed Jewish ethnicity as both "a place and a state of mind." These two expressions of ethnicity were so fused in Wirth's scheme that the ecological movement of Jews out of the ghetto was necessarily equated with the extinction of the group. But in Etzioni's words: "Obviously Jews return to Judaism without returning to the physical ghetto.... They return to a group without an ecological base, a phenomenon which Wirth's conceptual scheme does not cover" (p. 258). This habit of seeing in ethnicity nothing so much as its demise follows from the legacy of nineteenth-century social evolutionism. In other words, societal change means the eventual disintegration of the ethnic group.

Ethnicity can exist outside a ghetto, however, and Etzioni found in Wirth's own work evidence of how this might occur:

> There is common identity, tradition, values and consciousness.... common sentiments and interests based on past experience....The common bond is reinforced through ethnic newspapers, organizations, clubs, and synagogues, where members meet, even though they do not live next to each other and are not concentrated in one ecological area (Etzioni, 1959:258).

Another implication of Wirth's own analysis is that settlement outside the ghetto may even activate certain aspects of Jewishness: "contact with others and others' cultures makes the Jew conscious of the positive values of his own tradition" (Etzioni 1959:257).

Herbert Gans (1951) found that the movement of Jews to the suburbs did indeed make them conscious of their own traditions, and, he noted, a Jewish community was soon formed in one suburb of Chicago to conserve these traditions. According to Wirth, Jews would most likely assimilate through religious conversion and intermarriage in the suburbs, but when Gans studied Jewish residents of Park Forest, Illinois, he found there little evidence of such assimilation.

In 1949, 2,000 families resided in Park Forest, of which 141 were Jewish. Jewish families in Park Forest were like their Gentile neighbors in many ways: "The Jews of Park Forest dress as do other Park Foresters, enjoy similar leisure time activities, read the same newspapers, look at the same movies, hear the same radio programs. They observe few traditional Jewish religious practices" (Gans, 1951:333). Nonetheless, Gans found that 100 of the Jewish families had formed a fledgling Jewish community: in just one year a Jewish lodge, a National Council of Jewish Women's chapter, a B'nai B'rith school, and even a board of Jewish education had emerged (p. 333). From the beginning, it was important for these suburbanite Jews to "recognize" whether any of their neighbors were Jewish (p. 333). Gans attributed the emergence of a Jewish community in Park Forest to this sense of Jewish identity or, more specifically, to the desire of parents there for socializing their offspring into Jewish traditions, and to their feeling that they could be more relaxed around their own kind. A Jewish subculture emerged in Park Forest, although it was different from the traditions of the ghetto. In the suburbs, "the Jews are distinguished by a feeling of 'social consciousness,' by concern over political and social problems, by a tendency toward humanistic agnosticism" (p. 337).

Gans noted that the transplantation of ethnicity in this suburb was not confined to that done by Jews: "Both the large Catholic group, and the smaller Lutheran one also consist of a religious body, men's and women's social organizations, and a more or less extensive informal community.... Both communities developed more quickly than the Jewish one...." (p. 337). Years later, Novak (1971) wrote of America's ethnic whites—the Italians, Greeks, Poles, and other Slavs—that they, too, remain unmeltable ethnic groups outside their immigrant ghettos, notwithstanding his own experiences with the Anglo-American establishment:

> I am born of...those Poles, Italians, Greeks, and Slavs, those non-English-speaking immigrants numbered so heavily among the working-men of this nation.... Nowhere in my schooling do I recall any attempt to put me in touch with my own history. The strategy was clearly to make an American of me. English literature, American literature, and even the history books, as I recall them, were peopled by Anglo-Saxons from Boston.... Not even my native Pennsylvania, let alone my Slovak forebears, counted for very many paragraphs.... I don't remember feeling envy or regret: a feeling, perhaps, of unimportance, of remoteness, of not having heft enough to count (pp. 63–65).

Another criticism of Wirth is his underestimation of the durability of the ethnic neighborhood. Not only racial but also ethnic segregation has persisted in American cities. Glazer (1971) cited findings that many ethnic groups in New York City have tended to move en masse to new residential locations, and Rosenthal (1960) documented such movement of Jews in Chicago over three and four generations. Driedger and Church (1974) identified at least two patterns by which ethnic segregation has persisted in Winnipeg, Canada. Jews there tended to move over time to new locations en masse, while the French tended to remain in their old neighborhoods. Guest and Weed (1976) analyzed patterns of ethnic segregation in Cleveland, Boston, and Seattle and concluded:

> The continued existence of ethnic segregation in American cities is clear from these results. There is no evidence that it will disappear in the near future. In particular, its constancy in the 1960s, with slight increases among some groups, supports the idea of continued ethnic ties in American cities. Given the alleged rise of ethnic and racial consciousness in the past few years this finding is hardly a surprise (p. 1109).

More specifically, "for Cleveland the data indicate some clear declines in residential segregation since 1930 for 'new' southern and eastern European ethnic groups; 'old' groups, however, actually increased in segregation" (p. 1088).

This pattern was found not only in central cities but also in suburbs. Thus, the "old" immigrant groups, those from northern and western Europe and Canada, who have been in America for some time and presumably are the most assimilated, have actually become slightly more segregated from one another in all three cities and, in Cleveland, from southern and eastern Europeans as well. Guest and Weed believed that ethnic residential segregation is highly related to differences among these groups in social status, in partial support of Park's and Wirth's thesis. The recent rise in ethnic consciousness, the fact that "ethnic groups may serve as political-interest groups in the metropolis," and the possibility that "residential ties on the basis of ethnicity may counterbalance some of the less agreeable aspects of urban life" (Guest and Weed, 1976: 1109) were given as reasons for the persistence of ethnic residential segregation in America.

The persistence of ethnic segregation in the United States is illustrated above by the movement of groups to new neighborhoods, and in some instances it has grown greater in recent years. Furthermore, even as members of different ethnic groups dispersed into the suburbs and came into contact with one another, ethnic consciousness of kind and nonterritorial forms of ethnicity have endured, as observed by Gans. Ethnicity has also survived in the old neighborhoods, the old immigrant ghettos.

Gerald Suttles (1968) studied such a neighborhood in Chicago. He found that while several ethnic groups lived there together, they maintained a social distance between one another. Since this neighborhood is on the near west side of Chicago, Suttles called it the Addams area, in reference to Jane Addams, whose Hull House had been located nearby. About the residents, Suttles reported that at the time of his study, "approximately one-third are Italian, a quarter are Mexican, 17% are Negro, and 8% or less are Puerto Rican" (p. 22). Earlier, the neighborhood had been an Italian one. In this neighborhood in the inner city, the Italians had not been fully succeeded by other ethnic groups in 1965, and they still comprised one-third of the residents and were the numerically dominant group.

Ethnic boundaries were clearly evident in the daily routines of the area residents. While Italians, Mexicans, blacks, and Puerto Ricans were in constant physical contact and were tolerant of one another, their daily life was still demarcated by ethnic boundaries. Ethnicity circumscribed social interaction in the churches, clubs, business establishments, taverns, and recreational areas of the neighborhood. For example, churches, clubs, and taverns were generally reserved to one ethnic group. People tended to limit their interaction to their own kind, particularly in the case of their primary relationships, such as friendships and family. Ethnicity was a basis for personal trust, and the personal bonds prompted by ethnic consciousness of kind were vital to social intercourse in the area, for otherwise the residents had little reason for trusting one another.

Communication habits and clothing styles also helped maintain ethnic boundaries in the neighborhood. Italian was the daily language of the older Italians, and their English was badly broken. Likewise, Spanish was the daily language among the older Mexicans and Puerto Ricans. The area youth used "jive," a special idiom of English at which the black youths were particularly expert. Young Mexican and Puerto Rican males also engaged in jive talk, but "the Italians seldom use any of this vocabulary, even to the point of not understanding it" (Suttles, 1968:65). Ethnic boundaries were also buttressed by patterns of non-verbal communication. The reluctance of blacks "to look them in the eye" bothered Italians, while blacks complained that Italians "stare you down." Clothing styles also communicated ethnic identity. While wearing leather jackets and black pants was common among young Italian, Mexican, and Puerto Rican males, it was rare among black males. Only blacks wore bandannas around their foreheads, an article of attire locally known as the "rag."

Even in the commercial exchange between store owners and customers, ethnicity was evident. There were establishments that catered to only one ethnic group and sold ethnically specific products. If an outsider entered such a store, she was greeted with "Whatta you want?" and it was assumed that she had lost her way. There were 92 such businesses in the Addams area, and all were quite small. In other stores, outsiders were treated as guests. A guest had to pay deference to his host, the owner, and display an appreciation for the ethnic flavor of the establishment. At businesses open to all ethnic groups, such as the area's short-order cafes, members of different ethnic groups would take turns:

> Thus the typical practice is for one group to enter only when they notice that the cafe is empty. Occasionally, then, one will see a group pass by, look in, and pass on because it is already occupied. However, the group may wait some distance from the cafe and later, after the first group leaves, the second will enter (Suttles, 1968:51).

So it was in this neighborhood that daily life, including commercial transactions, was ordered in time and segmented in space by ethnicity. These studies give evidence of ethnic pluralism in contemporary society. We now turn to the pluralists for their depiction of ethnic pluralism in America and the reasons for its persistence.

Political activism has become a part of the new ethnicity.

THE PLURALISTS

MILTON GORDON

Milton Gordon proposed in *Assimilation in American Life* (1964) that America continued to be a pluralistic society, composed of ethnic subsocieties, as well as those of region, rural/urban residence, and social class. Each of these subsocieties had a distinct subculture which translated more or less the national ethos to the members of the subsociety. An *ethnic subsociety* is "a network of organizations and informal social relationships which permits and encourages the members of an ethnic group to remain in the confines of the group for all of their primary relations and some of their secondary relationships at all stages of the life cycle" (p. 34). The primary relations within any subsociety are the principal sources of self-identification for group members, and they act as crucibles in which the members' interpretations of the larger national ethos are formed. Thus subsocieties have subcultures, or shared styles of thinking, feeling, and acting.

Gordon identified four ethnic subsocieties in this country—blacks, Catholics, Jews, and white Protestants—as well as a residual category for intellectuals. The ethnic mosaic was demarcated by race, religion, and, to a declining extent, by nationality, as people from diverse national origins were assimilating into the larger religious subsocieties. These ethnic subsocieties were, of course, connected to one another, mainly through the secondary relations of their members. None of these subsocieties was a truly homogenous entity, however, for each was stratified by region, rural/urban residence, and the social classes of its members, or by the other subsocieties of America. This matrix of subsocieties formed the basis of the larger American society in the 1960s, according to Gordon.

It was the intersection of ethnic subsocieties and social classes that Gordon stressed. Such an intersection results in *ethclasses*, and there were, within each ethnic subsociety, three ethclasses: higher, middle, and lower. There were three socioeconomic classes of blacks, Catholics, Jews, and white Protestants. Gordon believed that ethclasses were the most fundamental subsocietal units in America. More than any other subsocietal unit, ethclasses confined primary relationships, since friendships, family ties, club memberships, and so on were normally formed within a single ethclass. Thus it is principally within ethclasses that Americans were reared, married, and then reared their own children.

While assimilation has occurred in American history, it has been a complex and uneven process. The components of assimilation according to Gordon are shown in Table 3.1.

TABLE 3.1 VARIABLES IN THE ASSIMILATION PROCESS

Subprocess or Condition	Type or Stage of Assimilation
Change of cultural patterns to those of host society	Cultural or behavioral assimilation (Acculturation)
Large-scale entrance into cliques, clubs, and institutions of host society, on primary group level	Structural assimilation
Large-scale intermarriage	Marital assimilation (Amalgamation)
Development of sense of peoplehood based exclusively on host society	Identificational assimilation
Absence of prejudice	Attitude receptional assimilation
Absence of discrimination	Behavior receptional assimilation
Absence of value and power conflict	Civic assimilation

Source: From *Assimilation in American Life: The Role of Race, Religion, and National Origins* by Milton M. Gordon. Copyright ©1964 by Oxford University Press, Inc.; renewed 1992 by Milton M. Gordon. Reprinted by permission of Oxford University Press, Inc.

According to Gordon, certain aspects of assimilation occurred earlier and more rapidly than others. For instance, acculturation usually began earlier than structural assimilation and proceeded more rapidly. Most ethnic groups in the country conformed to Anglo-American standards of style before they were structurally assimilated, particularly as regards their integration into the primary relations of Anglo-Americans. Barriers to structural assimilation mean that intimacy remained largely confined by ethclasses within the separate ethnic subsocieties of America.

In Gordon's view, assimilation occurred in several melting pots, and race and religion marked the boundaries within the ethnic mosaic. Groups had grown simultaneously larger, from nationality to religious groups, and more diverse, and they were large, stratified subsocieties. Nevertheless, America remained a pluralistic society. This is the essential point of ethnic pluralism. Pluralists reject the notion that assimilation is inevitable in societal change, that occupational diversification and residential dispersion of ethnic groups necessarily mean their disintegration. Ethnic groups changed, however, and nationality groups evolved into larger religious subsocieties stratified into ethclasses, according to Gordon. This thesis was stated earlier by Herberg in his critique of mass society theory.

WILL HERBERG

Herberg's basic point was that people from diverse European origins are assimilating into one or another of the nation's major religious groups: Protestants, Catholics, and Jews. The reasons that this change stopped short of full assimilation include certain individual needs and a societal tolerance for religious, but not national, diversity:

> ... not only was the immigrant expected to retain his old religion, as he was not expected to retain his old language or nationality, but such was the shape of America that it was largely in and through his religion that he—or rather his children and grandchildren—found an identifiable place in American life (Herberg, 1955:40).

According to pluralists, Americans have had an enduring need to have a particular niche in their society, to be a member of a specific group within the larger American society. Since the larger society has tolerated religious diversity but not that of nationality and language, the identity needs of millions of Americans have moved toward religious groups. The United States has not become a mass society, Herberg argued, but instead has changed into one of religious pluralism.

This identity need began for European immigrants with their uprooting in the Old World and transplantation in the New World. Handlin (1973:97) described the feelings of European immigrants this way: "Loneliness, separation from the community of the village, and despair at the insignificance of their own human abilities, these were the elements that, in America, colored the peasants' view of their world." These immigrants felt as if they were cogs in a great machine over which they had little control; they were alienated from American society.

So the immigrants turned to one another for help: "the newcomers took pains early to seek out those whom experience made their brothers; and to organize each others' support, they created a variety of formal and informal institutions" (Handlin, 1973:152). Whenever possible, the immigrants organized with others from the same village or region of the old country. Indeed, many of the immigrants came to America through the social networks of kin and village in the old country (Bodnar, 1985). Vecoli (1970) writes that there once were twenty Little Italys in Chicago alone. Italians from different regions might even live in the same neighborhood but be segregated from one another by residing on opposite sides of the same street or in different houses. Wirth (1928) reported that the Jewish ghetto in Chicago was nothing so much as several European villages and religious communities. These immigrant enclaves represented impersonal adaptation to a new environment, to be sure, but they were also expressions of people's need to relax and celebrate with their own kind.

Language and national culture shaped the immigrant groups' movement into a next stage. Immigrants from different regions of a single country in Europe found in America that they shared a common language and a national identity associated with that language. Other Americans cared little about the regional distinctions among Italians, for instance, and regarded them all simply as Italians. Did they not all speak Italian? At least that is what it seemed to an outsider. Ethnic boundaries were being created in the American context, in the relation between in-groups and out-groups. The general trend was that immigrants from distinct districts, prefectures, or regions of Europe became larger nationality groups in America.

This transformation was more or less completed by the second generation: "The sons of immigrants had no memory of Old Country places, no recollection of the village solidarity" (Handlin, 1973:173). What the second generation remembered were their experiences in America: "By actual membership in the group and by participation in its activities, they knew they were Irish or German or Italian or Polish" (Handlin, 1973:173). They also knew they were Protestant, Catholic, or Jew. Religion had survived the transfer from the Old World, and religion was passed from the first generation to the second, and from the second generation to the third.

Many of the second generation were hyphenated Americans, still a particular kind of American. Some members of the second generation identified with the ethnic nationalism of their immigrant fathers, while others thought of themselves as strictly American. But most were in the middle, both ethnic and American. They had been reared in two worlds, one foreign and one American, and for many this experience resulted in what social commentators of the day called the second-generation phenomenon. At the same time, Herberg (1964) noted, "The various activities of the ethnic group began to shrivel and disappear; the ethnic group itself, in its older form at least, became less and less intelligible and relevant to American reality. It was the end of an era" (p. 100).

Herberg went on to say, "If it was the end, it was also a beginning." By now the third generation had come of age. As to the spirit of this generation, Herberg referred to Hansen's famous dictum, "What the son [second generation] wishes to forget, the grandson [third generation] wishes to remember" (Herberg, 1955:43). Those of the third generation "have no reason to feel any inferiority when they look around them. They are American born. Their speech is the same as those with whom they associate. Their material wealth is the average possession of the typical citizen" (Herberg, 1964:100).

Both the foreignness of their grandparents and the embarrassment it had caused their second-generation parents were largely irrelevant to the third generation. But this brought an identity crisis: What kind of Americans were the third generation to be?

> The old-line ethnic group, with its foreign language and culture, was not for them; they were Americans. But the old family religion, the old ethnic religion, could serve where language and culture could not; the religion of the immigrants was accorded a place in the American scheme of things that made it at once both genuinely American and a familiar principle of group identification (Herberg, 1964:100–101).

Herberg cited Kennedy's studies of intermarriage in support of his thesis that by the third generation ethnic pluralism was transformed into religious pluralism. Kennedy (1952:56) summarized her studies in New Haven, Connecticut, as follows:

> This report…shows that the "triple-melting-pot" type of assimilation is occurring through intermarriage, with Catholicism, Protestantism, and Judaism serving as the three fundamental bulwarks. Protestant British-Americans, Germans, and Scandinavians intermarry; Catholic Irish, Italians, and Poles form a separate intermarrying group; while Jews remain almost completely endogamous.

To the extent that intermarriage reflects structural pluralism in general, this evidence supported Herberg's contention that the pluralism of nationality groups was being transformed into that of religious groups.

Based on data also gathered in New Haven, Hollingshead (1950:627) drew conclusions on intermarriage consistent with those of Kennedy: "[Racial mores] divided the community into two pools of marriage mates. Religion divided the white race into three smaller pools. Persons in the Jewish pool in 97.1 percent of the cases married within their own group; the percentage was 93.8 for Catholics and 74.4 for Protestants…." In New Haven from 1900 to 1950, Catholics with northern and western European origins who did intermarry with Protestants married those with similar national origins, whereas Catholics with eastern and southern European origins did not (Peach, 1980).

Thomas (1951) contended that the findings of Kennedy and Hollingshead on intermarriage in New Haven were not necessarily indicative of marriage trends throughout the country. Examining mate selection among Catholics in various areas across the country, Thomas found that in the decade of 1940–50, one-third of the nuptials sanctioned by the Church were mixed marriages, unions between Catholics and non-Catholics. With respect to marriages that were not sanctioned by the Church but that involved Catholics, Thomas observed that nearly 40 percent of these marriages in the East and Midwest were mixed. On the basis of such evidence, Thomas argued that the triple-melting-pot hypothesis is untenable as it applies to Catholics.

Kennedy (1944:332) had projected that "while strict endogamy is loosening, religious endogamy is persisting and the future cleavages will be along religious lines rather than nationality lines as in the past." Contrary to this prediction, Thomas argued that intermarriages by Catholics would increase in the future. With the halt of European immigration, nationality groups are becoming less of a factor in reinforcing religious endogamy, and as the Church and family lose their control over mate selection, attitudes toward religious exogamy are becoming more tolerant. Indeed, marriage between Catholics and non-Catholics has increased in recent decades (Hirschman, 1983). Moreover, mixed marriages might have a cumulative effect, for offspring of mixed marriages are themselves more likely to intermarry, although Lieberson and Waters (1985) did not find evidence that mixed nationality marriages lead to a rapid decline in ethnic influence on choice of mate for offspring.

The significance of rates of intermarriage for the issue of ethnic and religious pluralism in this country is not clear. Gordon (1964) noted that the conversion of one partner to the religion of the other is extensive in mixed marriages, and after such conversions couples might participate together in one of America's religious subsocieties. He questioned whether "interfaith marriage in American society today serves as an effective bridge between major religious groups or simply as a preliminary step to the entrance of the intermarried couple into the subsociety of one or the other faiths of the spouses. Current research on intermarriage in the United States tells us little or nothing about the answer to this query" (p. 216).

In response to Gordon's query, Greeley (1970) found in two surveys that over 80 percent of the Protestants—including Baptists, Lutherans, Methodists, and Presbyterians—were married to other persons of the same denomination. This religious homogeneity in marriage among Protestants was a product of their practice of marrying within their own denominations as well as a significant amount of conversion after marriage. Similarly, at least 86 percent of the Catholics in the surveys were married to Catholics, and 94 percent of the Jews were married to Jews. On the part of Catholics and Jews, however, this homogeneity was largely the product of people marrying within their own religion, in contrast to the more variable pattern among Protestants.

Other studies report slightly higher rates of intermarriage. For example, Cohen (1988) observed an intermarriage rate for Jews in New York to be between 10 and 15 percent. He also found that marriage partners who convert to Judaism scored high on religious indicators but not on secular indicators of Judaism. Later-generation Jews in the New York area have more non-Jewish neighbors, friends, and even spouses than earlier generations. However, the later generation also maintains social ties with other Jews, participates in the Jewish community, and observes Judaic rituals. There was no clear evidence of the wholesale assimilation of these Jews.

In regard to intermarriage across nationality, Lieberson and Waters (1985, 1988) showed that intermarriage has increased for younger women in virtually all nationality groups. For example, almost 66 percent of the Italian women who were 65 or older in 1980 had an endogamous marriage, married within their own nationality, but this was true for only 23 percent of the Italian women age 25 or younger. This was true of other European groups as well, e.g., Irish, Russian, German, etc., and Gurak and Fitzpatrick (1982) found it to be true for most Hispanic groups in New York City. The exceptions were African Americans, Native Americans, and Puerto Ricans. Endogamy remains stable for African Americans and Native Americans across age cohorts, with about one-fourth of American Indian women and 98 percent of African American women in endogamous marriages.

Herberg believed that religion was replacing nationality as the expression of ethnicity among white Americans. Research shows that religious boundaries are crossed less frequently than nationality ones in marriage. This is not the whole story, however. Even Herberg granted that nationality may continue to be important in politics. Glazer and Moynihan studied ethnic politics in New York City and found the persistence of nationality in the city's political affairs.

NATHAN GLAZER AND DANIEL MOYNIHAN

In the first edition (1963) of *Beyond the Melting Pot*, a classic study of the Italians, Irish, Jews, African Americans, and Puerto Ricans in New York City, Nathan Glazer and Daniel Patrick Moynihan wrote that "Religion and race define the next stage in the evolution of the American Peoples" (p. 315). This prediction is similar to that of Gordon and Herberg, although Glazer and Moynihan did hedge their bet, writing that the American nationality was still changing and no final form was in sight. Nevertheless, from the evidence amassed in the early sixties, they concluded that the nation was moving toward pluralism of race and religion.

In the second edition of the study, however, they wrote: "Thus, religion as a major line of division in the city is for the moment in eclipse. Ethnicity and race dominate the city, more than ever seemed possible in 1963" (1970:ix). They offered three hypotheses for the apparent resurgence of nationality during the 1960s.

First they proposed that occupational identity has lost "status and respect" and was being replaced by ethnicity in the service of self-identification. It was better to be known as Irish, for example, than as an assembly-line worker. To us all, being an ethnic is perhaps preferable to being a proletariat or bourgeoisie, a working stiff or a pencil pusher. Glazer and Moynihan proposed in a second hypothesis that "for the first time a wave of ethnic feeling in this country has been evoked not primarily by foreign affairs but by domestic developments" (1970:xxvi). Many of these "domestic developments" stem from the civil rights movement and have strengthened feelings of nationality while they have weakened religious identity, so that, for example, "the identity of Catholic is no longer self-evident, to those holding it or to those outside the church" (p. xxxvii). While the Catholic Church once helped implement the conservatism of the Italians and Irish in New York City—in its stands on communism, parochial schools, and sex, for instance—many Italians and Irish late in the sixties felt deserted by the Catholic clergy over the issue of race relations. The eclipse of religion in this manner led Glazer and Moynihan to concede that "just as religion in the 1950s covered for ethnicity, ethnicity in the 1960s covers for racism" (1970:xxxviii).

The migration of Puerto Ricans and southern blacks into New York City and the racial strife of the 1960s increased the saliency of race for city politics. Specifically, the liberal elite of Manhattan took political power from working-class Catholics and Jews in New York City and gave expression to Puerto Rican and African American interests at the expense of those of the white ethnics:

> The Protestants and better-off Jews determined that Negroes and Puerto Ricans were deserving and in need and, on those grounds, further determined that these needs would be met by concessions of various kinds from the Italians and the Irish...and the worse-off Jews. The Catholics resisted, and were promptly further judged to be opposed to helping the deserving and needy. On these grounds their traditional rights to govern in New York City *because they were so representative of just such groups* were taken from them and conferred on the two other players, who had commenced the game and had in the course of it demonstrated that those at the top of the social hierarchy are better able to empathize with those at the bottom (Glazer and Moynihan, 1970:xiii).

With each election, politics revived nationality in New York. Of course, appeals to the ethnic vote were at times disguised expressions of the concerns of certain economic classes in the city, and paradoxically, ethnic appeals often allowed politicians to skirt fundamental controversial issues.

It is not only in New York City that ethnicity plays a role in politics, for ethnicity has important political functions in many societies. In a later work, Glazer and Moynihan (1975:9) wrote that at the time:

> The welfare state and the socialist state appear to be especially responsive to ethnic claims. This is everywhere to be encountered: an Indian minister assuring his parliament that "Muslims, Christians and other minorities" will receive their "due and proper share" of railroad jobs; a Czech government choosing a Slovak leader; a Chinese prime minister in Singapore choosing an Indian foreign minister, and so on.

However, the raison d'etre of ethnicity is not to be found merely in political appeals or in the decline of religious and occupational identity, for ethnic identity is far more basic:

> Beyond the accidents of history, one suspects, is the reality that human groups endure, that they provide some satisfaction to their members and that the adoption of a totally new ethnic identity, by dropping whatever one is to become simply American, is inhibited by strong elements in the social structure of the United States. It is inhibited by a subtle system of identifying which ranges from brutal discrimination and prejudice to merely naming. It is inhibited by the unavailability of a simply "American" identity (Glazer and Moynihan, 1970:xxxiii).

This is their third hypothesis: ethnic identity fills a vacuum left by the unavailability of an American identity.

The pluralist version is that due to societal change, ethnic groups have become more diverse—stratified into ethclasses, for example—and simultaneously have grown larger—into ethno-religious groups, for example. Glazer and Moynihan contended that nationality was later revived. The process stops short of full assimilation, as the ethnic group continues to play a role in American society, in politics, and as a source of psychological identity and orientation.

THE NEW ETHNICITY

Ethnicity is considered to be ultimately a psychological phenomenon that can be expressed in any identity display, according to some pluralists; this idea is known as the *new ethnicity*. Ethnic identity is commonly asked for and given in the course of social interaction, for it is helpful and sometimes critical that we know the ethnicity of another person in order to anticipate how that person will respond to us. It would be good to know if someone is a Polish American before starting into a series of Polish jokes, for example. Barth (1969) suggested that when it facilitates interaction, ethnicity of the participants will be made evident, but it will be left latent when it hinders interaction. The implication is that ethnicity is a general state of consciousness, an identity that is not necessarily obvious but that can be voluntarily displayed in overt behavior in a variety of settings.

This conception of ethnicity, the new ethnicity, was popular among several anthropologists. In Bennett's (1975:3) words, this new ethnicity refers to "the proclivity of people to seize on traditional cultural symbols as a definition of their own identity—either to assert the Self over and above the impersonal State, or to obtain the resources one needs to survive and to consume." In the words of DeVos (1975:16), "ethnic identity of a group of people consists of their subjective symbolic or emblematic use of any aspect of culture, in order to differentiate themselves from other groups." Despres (1975:190–191) phrased it this way: "ethnic groups are formed to the extent that actors use ethnic identities to categorize themselves and others for purposes of interaction." The view that all these authors share is that ethnicity is an internal attitude that only predisposes, but does not make necessary, the display of ethnic identity in interaction.

Bennett (1975:4) wrote that the new ethnicity includes both an identity badge in "the search for the self and the definition of group boundaries" and a behavioral strategy "for acquiring the resources one needs to survive and to consume at the desired level." That is, ethnicity is revealed for both expressive and instrumental purposes. On the one hand, it is the assertion of self in an otherwise impersonal world. This usage of ethnicity is akin to its role in resolving the American identity crisis, one referred to both by Herberg and by Glazer and Moynihan. On the other hand, ethnic identity can be utilized in strategies to obtain scarce resources, as Glazer and Moynihan saw ethnicity being used in New York City politics. The ethnic quota system in employment and education is possibly the best contemporary example of ethnicity used in this manner. For whatever purpose it is used, ethnicity and ethnic boundaries in the present world of inter-ethnic communication and contact are emergent in human interaction and can be displayed in a myriad of ways. Thus the expression of ethnicity is by no means limited to isolation and segregation, as the assimilationists implied.

Sociologists today agree that ethnicity is more than segregation and that the latter is as much an ecological adaptation as it is an expression of ethnicity. For example, Yancey, Ericksen, and Juliani (1976) observed that as much as ethnicity itself, it was the concentration of immigrant workers around huge, centralized factories in the absence of rapid local transportation that had formed the ghettos of southern and eastern Europeans in the nation's cities. With the decentralization of work and with the availability of the automobile, such residential concentration is no longer necessary. Of course, ghettos help preserve ethnicity in its traditional forms, but ethnicity can certainly persist outside ghettos and evolve into new forms and expressions.

The ideas about a new ethnicity owe a debt to Barth (1969). Barth observed that in the social sciences definitions of ethnicity made reference to both biological and cultural criteria. Cultural patterns and breeding pools are as much a product of ecological adaptation, however, as they are indications of ethnicity, Barth argued. Moreover, reliance on such measures of ethnicity loses sight of the fact that all over the world today ethnic groups are in sustained and systematic contact. Nevertheless, ethnic boundaries persist, as the dichotomization of outsiders and insiders continues in the course of ethnic contact and communication. Thus the proper study of ethnicity is the study of ethnic boundaries, how they emerge and are maintained and manipulated in daily encounters. This is the methodological focus of the new ethnicity school.

In no manner do these authors imply that ethnic boundaries are evident in all daily encounters. Many types of social intercourse have little, if any, bearing on ethnic identity. A phone call to make a plane reservation is one illustration. In other types of encounters, however, ethnicity is used in either an expressive or an instrumental way. Research on African workers found that they kept their tribal identities latent while at work, but their personal lives were still organized around tribal affiliations (Vander Zanden, 1973). Minard (1952) studied black and white coal miners in America some years ago and found the same pattern of racial cooperation at work and racial separation at home.

As to the reasons for the persistence of ethnicity, those beyond self-expression and resource acquisition, DeVos (1975:17) speculated that ethnic identity is "a feeling of continuity with the past, a feeling that is maintained as an essential part of one's self-definition." In addition, "ethnicity in its deepest psychological level is a sense of survival." It is "a sense of personal survival in the historical continuity of the group." Ethnic identity can give us both a history and a future.

Recent research in sociology finds that most European Americans do have an ethnic identity even after their families have spent several generations in the United States. Lieberson and Waters (1988) identified two trends over the generations. The major trend is for people of mixed ancestry to simplify their ethnic identity by choosing one European nationality over others, and the other minor trend is for succeeding generations to simply call themselves Americans. Like anthropologists, sociologists are struck by the persistence of ethnic identity, and Olzak (1983) proposed some reasons for its persistence. States keep ethnicity alive through policies of ethnic quotas, illustrated by affirmative action in the United States, and, indeed, governmental involvement in education, civil rights, recruitment quotas, etc., can all reinforce ethnic identity. Second, societal change can result in inequality among ethnic groups, which is true in the United States, and this alone can maintain ethnic identity. Finally, as different ethnic groups have come into contact with one another, the resultant prejudice and discrimination have vitalized ethnic identity.

To illustrate, Portes (1984) found that upon leaving the ethnic colony in South Florida, the ethnic awareness of Cuban exiles increased as they entered the mainstream. As their education, knowledge of English, general information about American society, and occupational status increased between 1972 and 1979, their awareness of Anglo social distance toward and discrimination against Cubans increased. Becoming more aware of the boundaries between in-group and out-group presumably raised the saliency of Cuban identity among the exiles. This supports the basic point of pluralism, but rejects the assimilationist hypothesis that ethnic awareness is greatest in isolated ethnic enclaves, diminishing as group members enter the mainstream.

SUMMARY AND ASSESSMENT

The pluralists and assimilationists both analyzed ethnic change in America but came to different conclusions about it. Both assumed that societal change has brought more opportunity, and thus freedom and individuality, for members of ethnic groups. As a result, group members become diverse in education and occupation and disperse out of ghettos. For assimilationists this meant the end of ethnicity through assimilation. Given their tendency to equate ethnicity in general with segregation and occupational concentration of ethnic groups in particular, the assimilationists' predictions seemed to be supported by the residential dispersion and occupational diversification of America's white ethnic groups in the twentieth century. Only Americans of color remained segregated and were denied full access to the opportunity structure of American society, according to the assimilationists, and only racial assimilation was seen by them as still being problematical.

Pluralists conceded that the distinctiveness of ethnic subcultures has diminished with the geographical dispersion and occupational diversification of America's white ethnic groups, and that there has been a gravitation toward Anglo conformity. They insisted, however, that structural pluralism persists to this day, for some white ethnic groups and racial minorities alike. In terms of Park's race relations cycle, pluralists contended that ethnic change has proceeded to accommodation for many groups, but not beyond it.

Ethnic groups have been integrated into such institutions of the larger American society as politics, education, and the economy. However, this structural assimilation is largely confined to people's public lives, or secondary relationships, while their private lives and primary relationships are still infused with ethnicity. In public life, ethnic pluralism has evolved from residential and occupational separation, to be sure. However, in their private affairs, and at the emotional center of life, people still maintain their ethnicity. This is part of the pluralist version of ethnic change in America.

Ethnicity is and always has been ultimately a psychological phenomenon, an attitude and part of a person's subjective consciousness of kind, according to the new ethnicity. It is not necessarily manifest in any restriction on social interaction—what one can do with whom. In the modern world of extensive ethnic contact and communication, ethnic boundaries are often psychological and voluntarily implemented, either as expressions of self or as behavioral strategies. Nevertheless, the pluralists argued, ethnicity is as real today as it ever was in the past. Ethnicity has not been muted in modern America as much as its expressions have become more and more diverse and less and less exclusive. The evolution of ethnicity is not necessarily linear, moreover; in the future, it might evolve backward toward forms that do exclude outsiders. Ethnic change is indeterminate, contingent on human consciousness, dependent on people's needs as they perceive them, and fully subordinate to human purpose.

Ethnicity endures for white Americans, according to pluralists, but it does so in a way consistent with liberal individualism. Historic liberalism is as much accepted in pluralism as it is in assimilationism. New opportunity, complexity, and individual freedom are assumed to result from societal change in both theories, and the debate is restricted to how ethnicity is transformed in a society characterized in those terms.

While social scientists agree that the pluralist position is an improvement on the early assimilationist view that ethnic change is unilinear and inevitable, not all are happy with where the pluralists have brought us. Some object to equating ethnicity with a subjective consciousness of kind (Gans, 1979; Despres, 1975). Even though these critics have no better alternative, as Despres observed, they still have a sound point. The validity of their criticism does not rest, however, on the common observation that ethnic boundaries as psychological phenomena are so fluid as to be meaningless. LeVine and Campbell (1972) observed that ethnic boundaries have been fluid throughout human history and are no more permeable today than they ever were in the past. Nor is the validity found in their objection to ethnicity's being made an internal attitude. The study of attitudes has been common in American social sciences ever since the demise of instinct theory (cf. Allport, 1968). Rather, the validity of their criticism lies in the observation that when pluralists argue that ethnicity persists because of an American identity crisis, a crisis that seems to continue indefinitely with no end in sight, they appear to grant an inevitable, perpetual existence to ethnicity in the same manner that assimilationists have made its demise inevitable.

In their attempts to explain the persistence of ethnicity in America, pluralists have made repeated recourse to an American identity crisis. However, this concept has never been defined and measured with any precision and remains a vague and even mystical notion. Even if we agree with the pluralists and assume that Americans do face an identity crisis, we could argue that the resolution of such a crisis can come in forms other than ethnic identity. There are alternatives to ethnicity in resolving the American quest for a sense of roots. In any case, recourse to notions such as an American identity crisis, sense of continuity with a historical peoplehood, and a sense of history provides only vague and weak explanations for the endurance of ethnicity.

Linking the resilience of ethnic pluralism to ethnic competition in politics and the economy, as did Glazer and Moynihan, Olzak, and Portes, offers a better understanding of why ethnicity endures. As long as ethnicity can be used in the competition for scarce resources, it will endure. Thus, Glazer and Moynihan (1970) believed that ethnicity was revived in the 1960s due to the ethnic realities of New York politics at the time. Subjective ethnic identities were rekindled and evolved in many instances into the objective forms of political interest groups. Here in the United States and elsewhere in the world, ethnicity has become a legitimate and efficacious way to make resource claims in the modern state, as Olzak (1983) observed. So long as it plays a role in resource competition in American society, along with its other functions, ethnicity will endure here.

CHAPTER

4

☙☙

ETHNIC CONFLICT THEORY

Ethnic conflict theory is a third theory on American ethnicity. This theory provides a new and different perspective on ethnic groups in the course of societal change. According to assimilationists, societal change leads to the demise of ethnic groups with their assimilation into a mass society. Only the assimilation of certain racial minorities was ever considered to be an exception to this principle. Pluralists argued that while ethnic groups change with American society, they still endure. One reason given by pluralists for this endurance is competition among ethnic groups for societal resources.

This competition is the turning point to ethnic conflict theory. From the perspective of conflict theory, competition among ethnic groups increases in the process of societal change, thus creating the conditions for ethnic conflict and exploitation rather than assimilation. The result is continued ethnic pluralism in America. With the addition of ethnic conflict theory, the issues of competition, conflict, and inequality are brought into the analysis of American ethnicity.

Ethnic conflict theory follows from a larger conflict analysis of modern society. The larger theory characterizes society as an arena for the struggle among its subgroups. As new opportunity arises with societal change, groups compete with one another in their struggle for wealth, power, and privilege, and inequality is often the result. The struggle and stratification among ethnic and racial groups in America have certainly been documented by conflict theorists. They occurred between indigenous and immigrant people over land, and they continue today among ethnic groups in the labor market and other routes to the good life. According to this view, not all ethnic groups have had equal access to societal opportunity.

93

The implication is that individual freedom cannot be assumed for all in modern society, at least not for members of oppressed groups. Powerful ethnic groups exclude the weak ones from the wealth, power, and privilege that come with societal change. Thus, the degree of freedom that individuals enjoy in American society is a function of the power of the group(s) to which they belong (DeGre, 1964). This means more freedom and individuality for members of powerful ethnic groups but less for members of minority groups.

By the same token, ethnic conflict theory seems to share with assimilationism and pluralism much of the liberal paradigm. Growth in opportunity with societal change and resultant individuality are both assumed; only their distribution is in question. Only members of minority groups face restricted opportunity and limited individual freedom, implying, of course, that members of the majority group enjoy both. Members of powerful ethnic groups fall within the liberal paradigm, and so liberal conceptions of society and ethnicity apply to them. They have either assimilated or evolved toward the new and increasingly voluntary ethnicity, and this is precisely what distinguishes the majority from the minority. The minority stands outside the liberal conceptions of ethnicity in assimilationism and pluralism.

The format of this chapter is similar to that of the others. Key terms and major assumptions of ethnic conflict theory are first presented, followed by a discussion of historical and current expressions of this theory. The chapter concludes with an assessment of this perspective on American ethnicity.

DEFINITIONS AND ASSUMPTIONS

KEY TERMS

ETHNIC COMPETITION: *Ethnic competition is the mutually opposed efforts of ethnic (or racial) groups to secure the same objectives.* Newman (1973:112) stated, "The term 'competition' refers to any situation in which social groups evidence mutually opposed attempts to acquire the same social resources or reach the same goals." Groups can compete for both material and symbolic resources—for jobs, property, and wealth as well as for honor and status. Competition is not necessarily recognized by the parties involved. When groups become aware that they are in competition they are called *rivals*. Ethnic competition and rivalry continue in the course of societal change in the view of ethnic conflict theory.

ETHNIC CONFLICT: *Ethnic conflict is a form of rivalry in which groups try to injure one another in some way.* Such injury can take several forms. For example, ethnic conflict between white settlers and Native Americans took the form of warfare, that between native whites and Asian immigrants resulted in immigration restrictions, and that between blacks and whites took such violent forms as race riots and lynchings. The reason for ethnic conflict is typically to either change or preserve a system of ethnic stratification.

ETHNIC STRATIFICATION: *Ethnic stratification is a form of rivalry in which powerful ethnic groups limit the access of subordinate groups to societal resources, including wealth, power, and privilege.* Powerful groups stratify societal opportunity, such as jobs, education, politics, etc., reserving the best for themselves and relegating weaker rivals to lower positions within the opportunity structure. For example, Native Americans were pushed onto the less desirable lands, African Americans labored under slavery, and various immigrant groups worked at the lowest jobs, went to the worst schools, and were generally placed at the low end of an ethnic hierarchy, at least for a time. This means that members of powerful groups enjoy more individual freedom than members of weaker ethnic groups. Weaker groups are denied full access to the opportunity that comes with societal change.

ETHNIC CHANGE: *Ethnicity is an evolving or emergent phenomenon, since groups as well as their relations with one another and the larger society continually change.* Competition, conflict, and stratification comprise one dimension of this change—the one emphasized in this chapter.

ASSUMPTIONS OF ETHNIC CONFLICT THEORY

1. Ethnic competition and rivalry are basic to societal change. Groups compete for the opportunities that come with change.
2. Competition and rivalry can lead to both ethnic stratification and conflict, and conflict will either change or preserve a system of ethnic stratification.
3. Ethnic competition, rivalry, conflict, and stratification are dynamic, subject to change in the ongoing process of societal change.

The assumptions of ethnic conflict theory follow from those of a larger conflict analysis of modern society (Dahrendorf, 1959; Horton, 1966; Lenski, 1966). Strife and struggle occur in the course of societal change, and, from the perspective of conflict theory, all history is a process of struggle, oppression, and more struggle.

The two days of rioting in Los Angeles following the acquittal of
Los Angeles police officers in the beating of Rodney King in
April 1992 was an example of consensus-projecting conflict.

HISTORICAL CONFLICT THEORY

Was American sociology preoccupied in the past with assimilationist themes? L. Paul Metzger commented that while conflict and pluralist alternatives to the assimilationist perspective were always to be found in the social sciences, assimilationism "continues to hold sway as a kind of official orthodoxy within the sociological establishment" (1971:638). Specifically, Metzger maintained that implicit liberal ideological assumptions involved in the study of American race relations had left social scientists shortsighted and unable to foresee racial conflict and the continuance of ethnicity to this day. The liberal tenet making for this myopia, Metzger says, is the belief that the United States has been undergoing orderly change toward racial assimilation, and the resolution of the racial problem simply followed from the course on which American society was already set. By this reading, all stages of the race relations cycle prior to assimilation are only transitional, and assimilation is sure to come. Thus, whatever racism remained in the modern era was merely vestigial and sure to wane with further modernization.

Metzger (1971:638) believed that this myopia might be corrected by an analysis "in the Marxian tradition" which cites the determinants of racism "in the economic institutions and the struggle for power and privilege in society." Unlike the liberal tradition in sociology, Metzger argued, the Marxian perspective is capable of predicting the continuation of racism, discontent with it, and racial conflict in modern America.

MARXISM

Is it entirely true, however, that an analysis of ethnicity in the Marxian tradition would remedy the myopia Metzger observed in assimilationism? In our view, Marxism suggests assimilationism as much as it does ethnic conflict theory. Did not Marx predict the eclipse of ethnicity in the evolution of capitalism? People would become increasingly class conscious and would assimilate into one of two economic classes in preparation for the ultimate class struggle. Any remnant of ethnic consciousness in modernity was dismissed by Marx as an instance of false consciousness and out of keeping with the realities of scientific socialism.

Other conflict theorists of the nineteenth century shared with Marx the conviction of the inevitable eclipse of ethnicity in the industrial state. For instance, Gumplowicz (1899:119) observed that while industrial classes have their origins in the historical contact between "primitive hordes," and "no state has arisen without original ethnical heterogeneity," ethnic conflict is transformed into economic class conflict in the modern state. Powerful racial and ethnic groups force weaker ones into compulsory labor, thus changing the character of the conflict into a struggle between economic classes. To regulate class conflict in its own favor, the powerful class establishes state sovereignty and thus attempts to perpetuate through political authority the economic inequality it has forced on others. Through their control of the state, the powerful protect their property and enforce their exploitation of others' labor. In the larger sense, property rights and all forms of contractual relationships replace the folk bonds of blood and locale in the evolving nature of group conflict in the industrial West.

On the other hand, the tradition of conflict theory certainly does alert us to the possibility of ethnic conflict in modern society. Does not this tradition locate the dynamics of social change in the struggle for wealth, power, and privilege? If we do not confine our anticipation of conflict to that between economic classes—between the bourgeoisie and the proletariat, in particular—should we not expect that in contemporary society racial and ethnic groups, too, will struggle for wealth, power, and privilege? An expansion of the term *folk* is required in the translation of orthodox Marxism into ethnic conflict theory. This means we must entertain the possibility that ethnic groups, not only economic classes, will struggle for wealth, power, and privilege in the course of societal change.

SOCIAL DARWINISM

Social Darwinism was another precedent for a conflict perspective on American ethnicity. Charles Darwin wrote in 1859 that the natural force behind organic evolution is the lethal struggle among the species for survival, and the naturally fittest survive. This epochal work was entitled *On the Origin of Species by Means of Natural Selection, or the Preservation of Favoured Races in the Struggle for Life*. The Social Darwinists argued by analogy that social evolution is the struggle for survival between racial and nationality groups, and in the course of this struggle the more powerful groups naturally dominate the weaker races (ethnic stratification). Conflict and domination were seen as part of the larger natural order, impervious to human intervention. Racial and ethnic traits were also considered to be naturally determined and fixed, which rendered some races more fit than others to rule. This ideology helped justify racial realities in the United States, including Jim Crow in the South, the conquest of Native Americans, the nation's experiment with imperialism in the late 1800s, and the restriction of immigration from Asia and southern and eastern Europe in the twentieth century (cf. Banton, 1967; Handlin, 1957; Hofstadter, 1944). The representative works of Social Darwinism include Walter Bagehot's *Physics and Politics* (1869/1948), Benjamin Kidd's *Social Evolution* (1894/1921), G. V. de Lapouge's *Les Selections sociales* (1896), H. S. Chamberlain's *Foundations of the Nineteenth Century* (1911), Madison Grant's *The Passing of a Great Race* (1916), and Lothrop Stoddard's *The Revolt Against Civilization* (1922), among others.

However, as Hofstadter (1944) observed, it is easy to exaggerate the significance for race theory of Darwin's work. Arthur de Gobineau published *The Inequality of Human Races* (1915) originally in 1854, five years prior to the publication of Darwin's theory of natural selection. Still, the authority of Darwin's work did stimulate explanations of racial inequality as products of natural selection. In the end, however, Social Darwinism and other variants of this position faded from the American scene. Social Darwinism lost its popularity among the American public after World War I, according to Hofstadter (1944), for in the public mind it had been associated with German militarism. According to Oberschall (1972), public opinion also turned against the business trusts and monopolies, arrangements that the Social Darwinists had supported. In the social sciences, arguments for hereditarily fixed racial traits were supplanted by notions that human nature was environmentally conditioned and always alterable. The emerging social psychology of twentieth-century America preferred to see humankind as a bundle of propensities, triggered by the social environment, rather than a fixed product of biology.

These changes in theory were part of a larger process in the social sciences. From 1890 to 1920 American sociology was undergoing professionalization, searching for its proper role in the American university. Sociologists had to convince others that theirs was an independent academic discipline, with its own content, assumptions, and methods, and not a mere derivation of the more established discipline of biology. This required sociologists to relinquish the naturalism of biology, and it necessitated an end to the organic analogy in the science of society:

> After 1906, as the seventeen sociologists [fathers of sociology] discussed the boundaries of their new discipline, there were the unmistakable signs that some of them were beginning to recognize the contradiction between insisting that sociology was an autonomous science with its own order of phenomena to account for and their continued reliance upon naturalistic analogies…(Cravens, 1971:13).

At the same time sociology allied with the Progressive movement, and particularly with the social reformers of the era (Oberschall, 1972). The naturalism of Social Darwinism and its laissez-faire approach to

social problems were obviously not in the game plan of the social reformers.

By the time Park formulated his race relations cycle, only remnants of Social Darwinism were left in the sociological study of race. In
Park's work, for instance, one finds the concepts of competition and
conflict, reflecting the influence of Darwin on Park. There is also the
undercurrent of naturalism and inevitability in his cycle, by implication a laissez-faire approach, to racial problems. The race relations
cycle proceeds to assimilation due to human sympathy and intimacy,
however, which are strictly non-Darwinian notions. Moreover, scholars who followed Park moved even further away from Darwinism.

Social Darwinism was not to be a vehicle for bringing ethnic conflict theory into twentieth-century American sociology. It was rather
the Marxian tradition that led to ethnic conflict theory, and this chapter is organized around that version of ethnic conflict theory and de-
partures from it.

ETHNIC CONFLICT THEORY

Ethnic relations in a society can be either hierarchical or parallel; ethnic groups are either ranked in a system of ethnic stratification or un-
ranked (Horowitz, 1985b). In the case of parallel groups there is little
ethnic inequality; each group is a separate and full subsociety wherein
members can live their entire lives. With a hierarchy of groups, however, access to wealth, power, and privilege is determined in part by
ethnicity. Most societies are a mix of these two systems. Ethnic relations in the United States are toward the hierarchical side, according to
ethnic conflict theory.

SOCIETAL CHANGE AND ETHNIC CONFLICT

Conflict theorists contend that societal change brings increased
struggle and strife, continually reviving ethnic boundaries and consciousness and making them current. At the very least, industrialization
would adapt to the ethnic and racial status quo; the costs of upsetting it
would be greater than the gains (Blumer, 1965). Ethnic competition and
conflict replace the paternalistic race relations of traditional society in
the course of societal change, according to Van den Berghe (1967). Traditional society was pastoral, had little manufacturing, was based on a
simple division of labor, and was characterized by extreme ethnic stratification and rigid racial caste systems. Social mobility was virtually impossible for subordinate groups in traditional society. With industrial

capitalism, a complex division of labor, and greater opportunity, ethnic relations become competitive. This competition brings increased ethnic prejudice and conflict. As people from different racial and ethnic groups compete openly in modern society, ethnic hostility is exacerbated, while segregation averts constant conflict.

William Newman (1973:115) hypothesized that "the degree to which different social groups view each other as competitive threats, and therefore the frequency of social conflict between them, is directly proportional to the degree to which competition and achievement are prescribed norms in society." To the extent that achievement and competition characterize modern society more than traditional society, Newman's hypothesis is consistent with Van den Berghe's (1967) proposition that societal change brought competitive race relations, not assimilation. Newman amplified the hypothesis with the idea that normative emphasis on success and social mobility predisposes members of different groups to view one another as competitive threats, and this increases the chances for conflict. Ethnic conflict may be expressed through conventional channels for grievances or it may transcend these channels. The former is called *consensus-bound conflict* and the latter is termed *consensus-projecting conflict*. Legal tactics exemplify the former, while attacks on property and people illustrate the latter.

The greater the disparity in wealth between two groups, the more likely is the deprived group to engage in consensus-projecting conflict, according to Newman. A deprived group usually does not have ready access to societal channels for the legitimate expression of grievances, and even if such access were available, because of its historical deprivation it is likely to reject societal norms, including those over the channeling of grievances. By the same token, material parity among a nation's racial and ethnic groups will shape conflict into consensus-bound expressions of it, and conflict will validate the basic norms and institutions of the nation. Moreover, groups are less likely to go to extremes in such cases, for they are unwilling to destroy the society in which they all benefit to some degree.

In summary, Newman's argument is that societies with "a competitive ethos, regardless of the source of that ethos, will exhibit more frequent social conflicts than societies that exhibit a paternalistic ethos" (1973:138). The implication is that ethnic conflict characterizes modern society more than traditional society. Originating in societal values of competition and achievement, conflict in contemporary society is structured by the comparative wealth among groups. The greater the disparity in wealth, the more likely conflict will be an all-or-nothing affair.

According to conflict theory, oppression often results from strife and struggle. Competition for wealth, power, and privilege results in oppression when a powerful group comes to dominate a weaker one. This is ethnic stratification, a form of ethnic rivalry in which powerful groups limit the access of weaker groups to societal resources. However, systems of ethnic stratification can change as wealth, power, and privilege are won and lost.

THE EMERGENCE OF ETHNIC STRATIFICATION

Stratification begins with competition for wealth and privilege, and it results directly from the power of one party to dominate others in the course of their rivalry. Ethnic stratification occurs when an ethnic group dominates its rivals. Along with competition and power, a third element is thought to be important in ethnic stratification: ethnocentrism, or racism (e.g., Barth and Noel, 1972; Blalock, 1967; Kinlock, 1974; Noel, 1968; Vander Zanden, 1972; Wilson, 1973). In the words of Barth and Noel (1972:345), "we suggest that ethnocentrism, competition, and relative power of the groups involved constitute a set of variables which are necessary and sufficient to explain the emergences of ethnic stratification." Let us now analyze each of these elements—competition, comparative power, and finally ethnocentrism.

People share wealth in accordance with human needs at the subsistence level, but, once a surplus of wealth is produced, there is competition for this surplus (Lenski, 1966). To the extent that surplus wealth grows with societal change, Lenski's notion means that ethnic competition increases in the change process. Furthermore, power, rather than human need, will determine the distribution of wealth in modern society. Powerful groups will restrict the access of weaker groups to not only wealth, but also power and privilege. Thus, ethnic stratification also grows in the change process. The powerful and the weak will diverge as a consequence. Powerful groups modernize while the weaker ones do not, at least not to the same extent and at the same rate.

While power originates with and is ultimately based on force, coercive control is so costly to a dominant group that it will try to transform raw force into political authority, or legitimate rule. Gumplowicz (1899:121) found that the transformation of power gained by force into political and legal rights is the foundation of the modern nation-state: "the conditions established by force and accepted in weakness, if continued peacefully, become rightful." When successful at legitimizing its power into political authority, a dominant group not only enjoys power and the privileges associated with power, it also has prestige, or the deference of those deprived of power and privilege.

Authority confirms the status or honor of a powerful ethnic group, and with authority it can avert threats to its collective worth. Authority and power protect not only wealth and privilege, but also the honor of powerful ethnic groups. Nevertheless, authority may be lost for one reason or another, and as its authority wanes a dominant group will typically turn to force again in order to maintain its position. This has been the case with white rule in South Africa. Force can further erode, however, the authority of the dominant group. Thus power evolves and forms political cycles: force, its legitimization and institutionalization into political authority, and the return to force (Lenski, 1966).

The power of a group is based on its size, its control of other power resources, and its capacity to mobilize these resources (Blalock, 1967). The size of a group relative to that of other groups is the best measure of its numerical strength. The larger the comparative size of an ethnic group, the greater is its comparative power, if all other things are equal. The issue of additional power resources is complex (Blalock, 1967). At the risk of oversimplifying, it can be said that a group can exercise power through force or through political authority. It follows that power is based on control of the military, of violence in general, or of legitimate political rule. There is a common denominator to which both force and political authority reduce, however, and that is control over the means of production, or a group's possession of surplus wealth. If all other things are equal, the greater the surplus wealth of a group, the greater is that group's power. This principle has been demonstrated again and again in the course of American history. The conquest of the Native Americans and the subordination of black labor by white landowners in the South are two illustrations that come immediately to mind.

The power resources of a group must be mobilized for it to dominate others effectively in a system of ethnic stratification. Mobilization of power depends on the generality and liquidity of a group's power resources. Wilson (1973:17) argued that "the greater the generality of the resources a group controls, the greater is the scope of the group's power ability; the larger the number of resources a group has at its disposal, the more alternative means it has to reach its goal." In other words, the greater the generality of a group's power, the greater is the range of power application and the stronger is the group's dominance. If an ethnic group controls several societal institutions—the economy, the state, the cultural establishment, for example—then its power is general and its application is wide.

The liquidity of power resources is "the extent to which they can be deployed or mobilized to exert influence. Some resources can be deployed easily and quickly because the mechanisms that facilitate their mobilization or application exist" (Wilson, 1973:17). A good illustration of the principles of the generality and liquidity of a group's power resources is found in frontier contact between settlers and Native Americans. White settlers possessed surplus wealth and a monetary economy that made the surplus a general and liquid power resource. They also controlled the state. Butter was turned into guns, which were used in a coordinated military campaign by the state in the conquest of Native Americans. One claim is that each Indian battle casualty cost nearly a million dollars, a cost that the wealthy side could absorb.

Virtually all conflict theorists share the conviction that ethnic competition and comparative power are elements in the rise of ethnic stratification, but the role of ethnocentrism in ethnic stratification is a matter of some disagreement. *Ethnocentrism* is the tendency of members of a racial or ethnic group to consider their own physical appearance and way of life as superior and most honorable, while their respect for the styles of other groups is a function of how closely those styles approximate their own. In the context of modernization, a group can consider itself modern or advanced and regard other groups as backward and primitive. Ethnocentrism ultimately involves the issue of honor. Some theorists feel that honor is as important in ethnic stratification as are competition and comparative power. Often one group will subordinate another because of its abhorrence for the culture or race of that group, or to avert another group's threat to its honor, and not merely for economic advantage. Those in the Marxian tradition oppose this view, however, and consider ethnocentrism merely incidental to the economic determinants of ethnic stratification. They feel that ethnocentrism or racism is nothing more than a ruse for the more fundamental reality of the exploitation of labor by capital.

THE MARXIST TRADITION: Oliver Cromwell Cox was an exponent of the Marxian tradition. In his classic study of traditional race relations in the South (*Caste, Class and Race*, 1948), he wrote: "The fact of crucial significance is that racial exploitation is merely one aspect of the problem of the proletarianization of labor, regardless of the color of the laborer" (1948:333). Marx had observed that there are those who labor and those who live off the labor of others. Cox saw the essence of southern race relations as white capital living off black labor.

Of course, Cox was critical of the assimilationist school, and particularly the caste hypothesis of Warner and his associates (see Chapter 2). He read in this school the tendency to locate racial exploitation in the folk customs of the South, while, in his mind, racial exploitation was rooted in economic incentives:

Sometimes, probably because of its very obviousness, it is not realized that the slave trade was simply a way of recruiting labor for the
purpose of exploiting the great natural resources of America. This
trade did not develop because Indians and Negroes were red and
black, or because their cranial capacity averaged a certain number of
cubic centimeters; but simply because they were the best workers to
be found for the heavy labor in the mines and plantations (Cox,
1948:332).

Not custom but coercion has historically kept African Americans
in their place in the South, according to Cox. The shootings, whip-
pings, and lynchings of African Americans made evident the extrale-
gal status of black people, who, because they were outside the
protection of the law, had to turn to their white bosses for personal
protection. This further guaranteed for white capital the dependability
and tractability of cheap black labor. White capital used political authority, too, in its domination of black labor, while violence buttressed
this domination.

Cox conceded that there is one slight difference between race relations and class struggle: "Although both race relations and the struggle of the white proletariat with the bourgeoisie are parts of a single
social phenomenon...in race relations the tendency of the bourgeoisie
is to proletarianize a whole people" (1948:344). Nevertheless, he wrote
that racism is merely a "socio-attitudinal facilitation" of the capitalist
exploitation of black labor. In his view, racism was first made possible
when the capitalist class defeated the moral authority of the Roman
Catholic Church and was later reinforced by the rise of Social Darwinism, or scientific racism.

In suggesting correctives for race relations in the South, Cox again
demonstrated his belief that racial exploitation is essentially the capitalist exploitation of labor: "As a matter of fact, the struggle has never
been between all black and all white people—it is a political class
struggle" (1948:573). As to the leadership in this struggle, Cox comments: "These leaders [African American] cannot give Negroes a
'fighting' cause. None can be a Moses, George Washington, or Tous-
saint L'Ouverture; he cannot even be a Mohandas Gandhi—*a Lenin
will have to be a white man*" (p. 572; italics added).

V. O. Key (1949) shared many of the same assumptions about race
relations in his study of southern politics. Key, too, put race relations
into an elite-mass conflict formula, one that specifically included an
elite of white landowners and the mass of black and white labor in the
South. Key set the study of race relations in southern politics, thereby
turning our attention away from raw force toward the control of black
labor through politics. Specifically, the disfranchisement of blacks

105

meant that they were excluded from political power, while their rivals monopolized it.

White capital from the South's black-belt counties had thwarted a two-party system in the South by the 1890s, according to Key. White landowners established a single-party system instead, the Bourbon Democrats, one that they dominated. A two-party system would have been fatal to the interests of white landowners in the black-belt counties, for it might have led to their losing political and economic control of those counties. The Populist alliance between black and white labor near the turn of the century might have assumed political leadership over much of the region, and thus over its black-belt counties. This might have meant the end of the exploitation of cheap black labor by landowners in those counties. But that did not happen, and, as blacks were disfranchised, the yeoman whites of the South were politically manipulated. They were bribed when necessary, but the political instrument of racism often kept this class of propertyless whites in line with the class interests of the elite and disconnected from their own class interests. Thus, capital dominated the proletariat of both races by playing workers of one race off against those of another. Ethnocentrism (racism) was a tool of capital to perpetuate its exploitation of labor. Other writers also attest to the role of racism in uniting different classes of whites in the post-Reconstruction South (Woodward, 1955/1974).

It was not only the planters from the black-belt counties who used this formula. Key observed that once the Populists had gained control of the Democratic party in both Georgia and South Carolina, they too disfranchised the black voters. They needed to prevent any alliance between blacks and their white political opponents. Indeed, "The progressives had special reason for disfranchising Negroes; The Bourbon element usually had the longer purse to meet the cost of the purchasable vote" (Key, 1949:550).

In *Black Awakening in Capitalist America* (1970), Robert Allen wrote that economic incentives have always been at the root of racial colonialism (ethnic stratification) in America. First there was the exploitation of black labor in agriculture and domestic service, and, with the diminishing need for unskilled black labor, exploitation has evolved into abuse of the black consumer. Allen called this more recent instance of black exploitation *neocolonialism*. To appeal to and exploit the black consumer, white corporate power has a need for the cooperation of the black middle class; they need black faces in advertising and in finance offices, for instance. White capital had always needed the cooperation of black intermediaries to exploit black labor fully, but the softer sell required in the milking of the black consumer necessitates more than ever the cooperation of the black middle class.

White corporate power must pension off the black masses through income maintenance programs, in Allen's view, as it simultaneously co-opts the black middle class. The former can be accomplished with little cost to white corporate power, since most of the financial support for such programs comes from the taxpayers. As Allen read it, the ultimate result of this strategy is the enlargement and intensification of the class divisions within the African American community. African American solidarity will disintegrate in the process, and any black challenge to white corporate power will be arrested by dividing blacks in this manner.

The Marxian analysis has been applied also to Mexican Americans in the Southwest. Once Anglos had expropriated Hispanic land in the region, they established a colonial labor system that relegated Mexican Americans to the bottom of the region's labor hierarchy (Barrera, 1979). In agriculture, mining, and railroads, Mexicans were forced into the hardest, lowest-paying jobs; they were cheap and tractable labor for the region's employers. Their numbers would swell in economic good times, when employers needed additional workers, and fall off in bad times, when the labor needs of employers declined. The beneficiaries were Anglo employers, and the losers were Mexican American labor.

Recent Korean immigrants to the United States have gravitated to small business enterprises such as food outlets, service stations, and retail liquor stores. This would appear to be a case of enterprising Asian immigrants pursuing the American dream through businesses of their own. On the contrary, Light and Bonacich (1988) argued, these small businesses are another illustration of the exploitation of ethnic labor, another instance of the Marxian version of ethnic stratification.

୧୧

BOX 4.1 KOREAN GROCERS IN NEW YORK

Mr. Kim, who is 30 years old, is a Korean grocer in the Flatbush section of Brooklyn, a largely black area that has seen an influx of immigrants, mostly from Haiti, Jamaica, and Guyana, but also from Southeast Asia and China. His family has two stores less than a block apart, Sugar Cane Fruit and Grocery and L & P Farm....

Five blocks away, on Church Avenue, two other Korean produce markets have been targets of a boycott and protests by blacks since January, after a dispute between a Haitian customer and one of the stores. The protestors say that the customer was beaten and that both stores treat black customers disrespectfully.

Mr. Kim said the events have not directly affected him. His customers continue giving him the same brisk business that has made him toy with the idea of opening another store in the neighborhood. But the boycott has rocked Mr. Kim's sense of security after five years in the area, and underscored for him the problems that may arise when communication falters in the linguistic and cultural distance between Asia and the Caribbean. He said he now wonders whether a misunderstanding could lead to a boycott against him and threaten his livelihood.

Source: Mireya Navarro, "For a Store Owner, Boycott Raises Fears of Misunderstandings," New York Times, May 17, 1990. Copyright © 1990 by The New York Times Company. Reprinted by permission.

These ethnic business enterprises are actually a way in which cheap labor is exploited by American business corporations. Owners of these small ethnic firms, Marxian theorists argue, are not really owners; they are actually workers in their stores, putting in long hours, making sacrifices, and often using family members as either unpaid or low-paid employees. There is no separation between owners, managers, and workers in these small firms, as one would expect of a business enterprise, for everyone is a worker.

For whom do they work if not for themselves? Many of these Korean immigrants have franchise business outlets, and profits flow from franchises toward a parent corporation in the same way as profits flow from workers to capitalists. Others are subcontractors, doing smaller jobs for larger corporations, and the flow of profits is the same. Many set up shops in high-crime areas and in neighborhoods that parent corporations would not otherwise penetrate. Thus, parent corporations benefit by the increased marketing of their products and services, and these small firms can also pioneer new products into new markets at high risk. If successful, parent corporations can then take them over.

Why have some groups risen from the bottom rungs of the ethnic ladder, as have many European groups, while others have not, at least not to the same degree and at the same rate? Lieberson (1980) answered that since immigrant groups came in successive waves, these groups queued for opportunity in America, and the older groups moved ahead of the newer ones. Landale and Guest (1990) found that newer immigrants actually pushed up older groups, as southern and eastern Europeans pushed up the older immigrants from northern and western Europe around the turn of the century.

If this is so, why have African Americans remained on the bottom for so long? Both Cox and Key (above) provided some of the answer in their analysis of historic southern race relations. But African Americans have since migrated to the urban North and West. Lieberson (1980) was struck by the contrast between Asian and African Americans as they entered the northern labor market. He proposed that because of their greater numbers, African Americans posed a bigger threat to whites, and thus were kept down to a much greater extent than Asian Americans. This obviously departs from a strictly Marxian and economic interpretation of race relations.

In the Marxian position, ethnic stratification is simply another form of economic-class exploitation. Capital exploits labor, and ethnocentrism is no more than a racist defense for ethnic stratification. William Wilson (1978) wrote, however, that racism (ethnocentrism) was an independent force and not an incidental one in the oppression of African Americans in the pre-industrial South. In this regard, he disagrees with Cox's interpretation of southern race relations. Black-white relations have changed, however, and Wilson believes that today economic-class stratification in the Marxian tradition and not racism explains the poverty of low-income African Americans.

To illustrate, talented and educated African Americans "are experiencing unprecedented job opportunities...." On the other hand, "poorly trained and educationally limited blacks of the inner city...see their job prospects increasingly restricted to the low-wage sector, their unemployment rates soaring,...their labor-force participation rates declining,...and their welfare roles increasing" (Wilson, 1978:151). Thus, it is difficult for Wilson to believe that the plight of this black underclass is due to racism. Instead, he concludes that "economic class is clearly more important than race in predetermining job placement and occupational mobility" (p. 152).

In 1987, Wilson focused on the African American poor, especially those in the nation's inner cities. As opportunity expanded for the advantaged black middle class, they moved from the ghettos. Left behind, the circumstances of the black poor, the truly disadvantaged, had grown worse in the nation's ghettos. Gone were the communal institutions once supported by the black middle class in the inner city— e.g., businesses, organizations, and churches—which had represented middle-class values, and middle-class people themselves, who had offered role models to the young. Now, the poor were cut off from the black middle class as well as from the larger society, left with a ghetto of inadequate schools, unemployment, welfare, and crime. The civil rights movement, the War on Poverty and affirmative action have done little for the African American poor. The primary reasons for the deterioration of the African American poor, in Wilson's view, include historical racism as well as the current shift in the occupational structure of the nation away from manual to white-collar work (see Chapter 6).

In a test of Wilson's ideas, Hout (1984) found on the national level significant class differences among blacks in intergenerational mobility between 1962 and 1973, in the favor of the already advantaged. These class differences were the same as those found among whites, and class differences in mobility increased during this period. That is, the advantaged were getting ahead, but the disadvantaged were falling behind, the same picture presented by Wilson.

The Marxian view is that ethnic stratification comes down to capital's exploiting cheap, ethnic labor, be it in cotton fields, factories, or small businesses. The elite exploits the masses, and economic competition and comparative power lie behind ethnic stratification. Once the laboring masses are no longer needed, their circumstances are allowed to further deteriorate, an observation made by Wilson. Ethnocentrism is, however, merely an afterthought of economic exploitation and neglect in the Marxian view.

THE WEBERIAN TRADITION: Other theorists argue that ethnic competition and stratification cannot be reduced to economic exploitation. These writers share the view of Max Weber that social stratification is multidimensional and not reducible to the single dimension of economic-class relations. Weber discerned three separate dimensions of social stratification: class, power, and status. Members of different economic classes have different life chances, including unequal amounts of wealth, and thus there are gaps between their material living conditions and other life experiences. In regard to power, political parties are rationally organized efforts toward the attainment and maintenance of social power. They are implicated in political decision making, whatever the issue. While political parties can advance the interests of an economic class or a status group, they may not necessarily do so, and a political party may operate with the intention of simply expanding or maintaining its power. Status groups are theoretically distinct from both political parties and economic classes and are situated in the distribution of honor. Honor ultimately follows from the monopolization of fashion and rests on the preservation of social distance between the honorable and those who are disreputable, pedestrian, and lacking in proper taste.

Ethnic competition, conflict, and stratification involve all three of these dimensions, these theorists argue. Ethnic groups struggle over the control of surplus wealth, and comparative power determines the outcome of this struggle. But ethnic struggle and stratification also involve the issue of honor. For instance, Noel's (1968) theory of ethnic stratification holds that "competition [for surplus wealth, we have argued] provides the motivation for stratification, ethnocentrism channels the competition along ethnic group lines, and relative power determines whether either group will be able to subordinate the other" (Barth and Noel, 1972:337).

In these expanded formulations, ethnocentrism is seen to play a role in the formation of ethnic stratification equal to those of economic competition and comparative power. For one thing, ethnocentrism facilitates the identification of rivals in ethnic competition for wealth. Those groups who stand in sharp contrast to another in physical appearance and cultural style will be most likely identified as rivals by that group. Skin color and cultural style can become emblematic of ethnic rivalry. Moreover, systems of stratification not only serve in the protection of wealth and power, they also help a wealthy and powerful group in the preservation of its honor. In a system of ethnic stratification, subordinate groups are limited not only in their access to wealth and power but also in their access to the symbols of prestige, privilege, and honor. Is it not fair to say that for much of American history white has been considered more beautiful than black, brown, or yellow? Conflict and stratification involve the issue of honor as much as they do the distribution of wealth and the use of power.

The personal experiences of Malcolm X attest to the saliency of racial honor in America: "The mirror reflected Shorty behind me…. And on top of my head was this thick, smooth sheen of shining red hair—real red—as straight as any white man's" (Malcolm X, 1966:52–54). Later in his life Malcolm looks back at this experience:

> This was my first really big step toward self-degradation: when I endured all of that pain, literally burning my flesh to have it look like a white man's hair. I had joined that multitude of Negro men and women in America who are brainwashed into believing that the black people are "inferior"—and white people are "superior"—that they will violate and mutilate their God-created bodies to try to look "pretty" by white standards (p. 54).

Frantz Fanon wrote, in *The Wretched of the Earth* (1963), that racial violence was necessary for Africans in their revolt against white colonialism. Violence will cleanse their sense of racial inferiority, which was instilled in the minds of African natives by their colonial masters. The revolt against colonialism was a racial struggle between black natives and white settlers, and one that surged in accord with a racial rhythm, conducted by native leaders and not by a "white Lenin."

Racial conflict is not some disguised form of class struggle, in Fanon's view, and was very much attuned to racial honor.

In his book *Who Needs the Negro?* (1971), Sidney Wilhelm observed that racism existed before the rise of capitalism, exists today in non-capitalist society, and historically has brought racial subordination in whatever economic system it has occurred. As capital displaces labor in the American economy, through the mechanization and automation of the production process, it is specifically the black worker who is displaced. White corporate power will promote the dismissal of blacks from any meaningful and secure place in American society, according to Wilhelm, and this process has already begun with the simultaneous mechanization of southern agriculture and northern industry. Much of black labor is obsolescent; now that unskilled black workers are no longer needed, they will be dismissed from both American agriculture and industry. Wilhelm felt that white workers did not share in this plight, for it is racism that shapes the displacement of American workers, and the process might ultimately result in black extermination. In Wilhelm's view, ethnocentrism is much more than a mere afterthought in the neglect of the laboring masses once they are no longer needed.

It is obvious that ethnocentrism has a role in ethnic conflict and stratification, and to argue otherwise is to overlook an important dimension of American ethnic and race relations. This is demonstrated by Tajfel and his associates in their minimal group experiments (Billig, 1985; Brown, 1985; Doise, 1986; Tajfel, 1978, 1981, 1982; Tajfel and Turner, 1986). Experimental subjects were divided into in-groups and out-groups based on arbitrary and artificial criteria. There was no face-to-face interaction between the groups, members of the groups seemingly had little self-interest at stake, the groups had no conflicting interests, and there was no history of hostility between the groups. This is the meaning of a minimal group.

The subjects were asked to distribute rewards and evaluate and indicate a preference for one another. They could maximize the rewards to both groups, maximize rewards to the in-group, or maximize the difference in rewards between in-group and out-group. Subjects consistently chose the third alternative, sacrificing rewards not only to the out-group but also to their own group. What mattered most was the favorable comparison between one's own group and an out-group, not the absolute amount of reward. Subjects also consistently evaluated in-group members higher than out-group members and showed a preference for in-group members.

The conclusion of Tajfel is that subjects were motivated to maintain a positive social identity for their own group. This led to their making invidious comparisons between groups, in rewards, evaluations, and preferences, biased toward the in-group. Why are group members motivated to attribute more worth to their own group and less to out-groups? This is a question of honor, or ethnocentrism. Tajfel felt that people's self-esteem is tied to the social identity of their own groups. The honor of your group has a direct bearing on your self-worth, and this is especially true for real groups. These are groups into which we are born, from which we cannot readily escape, and in which we have a substantial stake. If our group does not possess honor compared to other groups, at least in our eyes, this might be a permanent impediment to our sense of self-worth. What ethnic group members struggle for ultimately is honor and a sense of self-worth, and even in minimal groups people stratify honor to favor their own group. A minority group will likely engage in conflict to raise its social identity and its honor when its disadvantaged position and current social identity is seen by its members as undeserved and unfair.

However, to argue that ethnocentrism will result in the extermination of African Americans, as does Wilhelm, is taking this thesis to its extreme. For instance, Edna Bonacich (1976) took exception with Wilhelm's thesis on the displacement of black workers. She argued in a Marxian way that black unemployment since World War II can be explained without reference to racism. The high unemployment rates of African Americans, especially young males, began around 1940, after the equalization of the wage rates of black and white workers in major industries. Without a reserve of cheap black labor, capital turned to other alternatives, including cheaper labor overseas and the automation of production here at home. Blacks in urban ghettos can still find work in sweatshops, but, because of their political-class sophistication and the welfare alternative to such undesirable jobs, they do not take up such work:

> The "displacement" phase was one in which blacks were desirable employees relative to whites but threatened the gains of the latter. Protective legislation equalized the two groups in terms of labor price but also drove up the price of labor, leading capital to seek cheaper alternatives. As a result, black labor has been bypassed for machines and other cheap labor groups, here and abroad, creating a class of hard-core unemployed in the ghettos. This reality took a while to emerge after the New Deal and only became full-blown in the mid-1950s when black unemployment reached its current two-to-one ratio (Bonacich, 1976:49).

Displaced in this manner from mainline industrial jobs, unskilled blacks are unwilling today to work in marginal sweatshops, and in significant numbers they have turned to the alternative of welfare.

113

New ideas have emerged from this branch of ethnic conflict theory, the one emphasizing that ethnocentrism makes ethnic relations more than a mere variation of the Marxian class struggle. For example, a colonialism model posits that minorities can be seen as colonial subjects in their own country. Blauner (1969) made the distinction between colonialism as an historical event and as a process. It is in the latter sense that African Americans are equated with the colonized people of the nineteenth century, and this is a case of internal colonialism. In both instances, the distinct values and cultures of the colonized groups are assumed to be destroyed. Colonized people are seen as backward and the colonizers as advanced, an issue of honor and ethnocentrism. Furthermore, the colonized groups are administered to by representatives of the colonial power—the police in the case of African Americans. Barrera (1979) and Moore (1970a) argued that the colonial model also describes the experiences of Mexican Americans.

Geschwender (1978) proposed an internal colonial-class model of African Americans that utilizes elements from both the colonial metaphor and the Marxian conflict analysis of industrial society. He argued that African Americans were a submerged nation in the "black belt" up to World War I. A nation is a historically evolved stable community of language, territory, economic life, and psychological make-up, manifested in a community of culture. This nation of African Americans was submerged into that of the larger nation. The economic-class model describes better, however, the subsequent entry of African Americans into the industrial order; they became a proletariat in the twentieth century. The author concluded that the concept of nation-class is a good characterization of the full history of African Americans.

THE LABOR VS. LABOR CONFLICT FORMULA: Even though they disagree on the role of ethnocentrism in the emergence of ethnic stratification, the writers above share the conviction that ethnic stratification arises as the elite of one group exploits or neglects the masses of another. It is specifically the struggle between capital and labor that gives rise to ethnic stratification. Some conflict theorists, however, locate the emergence of ethnic stratification in the struggle between workers from different ethnic groups, thus departing from the elite vs. the masses conflict formula.

In *The Economics of Discrimination* (1957/1971), Gary Becker argued that white capital in America realized no economic gain from racial discrimination in workers' wage rates and was actually disadvantaged by such discrimination. When capital pays higher wage rates to white workers because of discrimination against blacks, it loses twice. First, it experiences artificially high labor costs and, consequently, decreased profits and a reduction in its investment capital. Thus, in theory, white capital has less opportunity to sell to black consumers, a second loss, because of the latter's decreased buying capacity. Black labor is also obviously disadvantaged by discrimination in wage rates. The interests of white labor are, on the other hand, served by this sort of discrimination. They thereby monopolize the better jobs, and the interests of black capital are inadvertently met. Their competition with white capital is decreased in direct proportion to white capital's labor costs and inability to sell and invest in the black community.

White capital might have a taste for ethnic discrimination even though it is to its economic disadvantage. However, Becker believed that it has been the white trade unions, not capital, that have discriminated against black workers, and for economic reasons. This has been particularly so in cases where black workers were direct substitutes for white labor and could displace them.

Bonacich argued that the dynamics of ethnic antagonism lie in the competition between workers of different ethnic groups. Ethnic antagonism "is intended to encompass all levels of intergroup conflict, including ideologies and beliefs,...behaviors,...and institutions..." (Bonacich, 1972:549). One institution of particular interest to Bonacich is the *split labor market*, a special instance of ethnic stratification in the labor market.

Three classes of people are involved in the formation of a split labor market: capital and labor from a powerful ethnic group and labor from weaker ethnic groups. Labor from the dominant group has the incentive to exclude workers of weaker groups from the better jobs in the labor market. This can result in a labor caste system, or split labor market, as was once found in the South (Cox, 1948). It is assumed that the motive of capital is to employ the cheapest and most tractable labor group possible, regardless of race or ethnicity, and, as a rule, minority labor is the cheaper and more tractable alternative. Cheaper labor groups can be used by capital to break strikes organized by higher paid labor, for instance, and can otherwise be used to displace majority group labor if capital is free to implement its interests. If such displacement is not possible, capital can turn to automation as a strategy for replacing high-paid labor. Thus, capital cannot be held directly responsible for the formation of the split labor market, for its class interests lie in the inclusion of the cheaper minority labor in the labor market. "This interpretation of caste contrasts with the Marxist argument that the capitalist class purposefully plays off one segment of the working class against the other..." (Bonacich, 1972:557).

Migrant farm workers, like these strawberry pickers in California, demonstrate one aspect of the split labor market.

It is because of its powerlessness that minority labor is often a cheaper and more docile alternative to labor from the majority group. Because of poverty, the lack of both political and informational resources, and the sojourning motives in some cases, minority labor is frequently willing or forced to work for less. Minority labor also wishes to avoid strikes, other sorts of labor disputes, and efforts at unionization, as was true for many immigrant groups into this country. Under these circumstances labor from majority and minority groups do not ally. Instead, there appears to be an alliance between minority labor and majority capital against labor from the dominant group, and the latter will attempt to meet the perceived threat of minority labor.

If minority labor must be imported, domestic labor will attempt to restrict the entry of immigrant labor into the country, and such immigration restrictions have been common in American history (see Chapter 1). If cheaper labor is indigenous or had immigrated prior to restrictive legislation, dominant labor will attempt to undermine it through a form of stratification called a *split labor market*, whereby "the higher paid group controls certain jobs exclusively and gets paid at one scale of wages, while the cheaper group is restricted to another set of jobs and is paid at a lower scale" (Bonacich, 1972:555). Bonacich continued: "Caste systems tend to become rigid...developing an elaborate battery of laws, customs and beliefs aimed to prevent undercutting." Cheaper labor groups are not only excluded from job apprenticeships, they are denied "access to general education, thereby making their training as quick replacements more difficult" (p. 556), and they are politically weakened as well. Thus, "the solution to the devastating potential of weak, cheap labor is, paradoxically, to weaken them further, until it is no longer in business' immediate interest to use them as replacements."

Racial and ethnic stratification in the labor market has been a recurrent phenomenon in American history, and many immigrant groups have shared in this experience. Blacks were excluded from the textile mills in the post-Reconstruction South and remained sharecroppers under white landowners. In the nineteenth century, Chinese were forced out of mining and all sorts of desirable jobs on the West Coast; in the twentieth century, Japanese immigrants had some of the same experiences there. Mexican farm labor duplicated in the Southwest some of the dimensions of the African American experience in the South. In the Northeast, Poles worked in factories under Irish foremen, who in turn worked under Anglo managers. It was the Irish who had been the common laborers in the nineteenth century, and so concentrated were they in unskilled labor that a joke of the era asked why the wheelbarrow was man's greatest invention, to which Americans answered, because it had taught the Irish to walk on their hind legs. Such has been the character of the ethnic and racial stratification of labor in this nation.

Ethnic conflict theorists disagree over the reasons for ethnic stratification. In the Marxist tradition, the reasons are that majority capital exploits cheap, ethnic labor, and thus ethnic stratification is simply an instance of economic-class exploitation. This applies to minority business owners as well as workers, and it applies to the neglect of the laboring masses when they are no longer needed. In the Weberian tradition, the role of ethnocentrism is elevated, meaning that ethnic stratification is not merely a derivation of economic-class exploitation. Ethnocentrism identifies rivals, and rivals compete for honor as well as for wealth and power. Ethnic minorities are likened to internal colonies in this tradition. Geschwender (1978) synthesized these two perspectives in his nation-class model of African American history. In the labor vs. labor formula, it is the higher paid workers of the majority who relegate ethnic labor to the bottom of the labor market.

CHANGE IN ETHNIC STRATIFICATION

In conflict theory, society is characterized as undergoing continuous change, and systems of ethnic stratification are no exception to this rule. So it is not the case that minority workers have had no recourse but to remain at the bottom of the nation's labor hierarchy, held there in perpetuity by either more powerful labor groups or capital. Other possibilities for minority groups have been the focus of recent sociological research.

Four patterns of minority adjustment have been identified. First, an immigrant group can suffer economic hardship at the bottom of the nation's labor hierarchy for a time, which then gives way to their gradual acceptance and mobility (Landale and Guest, 1990; Lieberson, 1980). As some groups move up the social and economic ladder, others replace them at the bottom. Ethnic stratification changes in the process.

A second pattern is evident for current immigrants into the United States. Some go directly into the nation's better jobs (Portes and Stepick, 1985). "In 1980, 16.1 percent of employed natives were professionals and technical workers; the corresponding figure for immigrants who entered between 1971 and 1979 was 26 percent..." (Simon, 1986). This reflects the international "brain drain" into the country.

Recent immigrants are also overrepresented in the lowest jobs in the country. This represents a third pattern, one that implies the entrapment of immigrant labor at the bottom. They enter a country that now has a segmented labor market (Bonacich, 1972; Portes and Stepick, 1985; Wilson and Portes, 1980). At the core of the American economy, firms exercise control over both supply and demand, translating into a financial advantage for their employees. On the economic periphery, however, small firms are highly competitive, meaning low wages and few benefits to employees. Immigrants who enter this periphery have little opportunity to get ahead. Unable to find work at the economic core, they turn to the peripheral labor market and non-market activity. Uzzell (1980) called such adjustments mixed economic strategies, which range from moonlighting, mixing welfare with wages, and home production, to crime.

A fourth adjustment is found when immigrants erect an ethnic subeconomy, or enclave (Portes and Stepick, 1985; Wilson and Portes, 1980). In an enclave, ethnic firms can limit the open competition prevalent on the economic periphery by developing "ethnically sympathetic" sources of supply and demand, meaning a better deal for their workers. For example, the Cuban enclave in Miami concentrates in cigar-making, restaurants, supermarkets, law firms, funeral parlors, and private schools. The Cuban enclave is characterized by a set of highly interdependent firms that are relatively independent of the majority economy (Wilson and Martin, 1982). Wilson and Portes (1980) found that workers in the Cuban enclave compared favorably to workers in the primary economy in the conversion of human capital into occupational gains.

Chinese and Japanese immigrants were once relegated to the bottom of the labor hierarchy on the West Coast at the same time as further Asian immigration into the country was restricted. In the face of this exclusion, both groups evolved more or less into middleman minorities, that is, they developed ethnic subeconomies.

Bonacich (1973) feels that this evolution of Asian immigrants was as much rooted in their motives for immigrating as it was in the fact that they faced discrimination in America. Asian immigrants were sojourners who were willing to work hard and suffer short-term deprivation in the United States with the hope of accumulating savings here and then returning with these savings to their homelands. This resulted in antagonism toward them. Chinese and Japanese immigrants subsequently took up work in particular industries, retail sales and import-export businesses, for instance, and still put a premium on hard work and thrift. They financed their own businesses through rotating-credit associations, and concentrated in enterprises open to them. Industrial concentration enhances in-group solidarity among the members of a middleman minority, since they are in similar trades and have little incentive for making more than superficial contact with outsiders. In short, they do not assimilate. Their solidarity gives them a competitive edge over others in the host society by providing access to cheap and docile labor from within their own ranks, by facilitating the internal generation of capital, and by vertically integrating an entire industry, as occurred in the case of Japanese growers, wholesalers, and retailers of fruits and vegetables in Southern California before World War II (Bonacich, 1973:587).

On the other side of the coin, minority labor can be exploited by their own kind in ethnic subeconomies. Sanders and Nee (1987) argued that ethnic enclaves benefit ethnic entrepreneurs but not their workers. While enclave entrepreneurs compared favorably to similar non-enclave businesses, workers were not as fortunate as those at the economic core in converting human capital into economic gains. Zhou and Logan (1989) found that male workers in New York's Chinatown, an economic enclave, did far better than female workers.

Moreover, a minority may face hostility from several sectors of the larger society, antagonism that can be aggravated by their becoming a middleman minority. Japanese shopkeepers on the West Coast were in conflict with certain interests of white customers, with white business owners, and with organized labor. Their ability to use cheaper Japanese labor undercut both white business competitors and labor unions. As a consequence all three groups—customers, capital, and labor—could unite against Japanese Americans during World War II on the issues of their clannishness and presumed disloyalty to the country. The result was their internment during the war (Chapter 13).

Individuals from minority groups have always made it into the national elite despite ethnic and racial stratification. Alba and Moore (1982) identified the ethnic background of 545 top people in business, organized labor, political parties, voluntary organizations, mass media, Congress, political appointees, and civil servants. This was the American elite of prominent people. The authors categorized ethnic background into Protestant with ancestry from the British Isles (WASP), Protestants with ancestry from elsewhere in Europe, Jews, Irish Catholics, Catholics from elsewhere in Europe, and minority groups, including all non-whites and Hispanics. WASPs, Irish Catholics, and Jews were overrepresented in the national elite, while other Protestants, Catholics, and minorities were underrepresented. However, members of the underrepresented groups were younger, indicating perhaps that members of these groups were catching up. Individuals from different ethnic groups took different paths to elite positions. It was primarily the WASPs who came from privileged backgrounds of old-stock families and elite educations and concentrated in business and politics (Alba and Moore, 1982). Irish Catholics in the elite were concentrated in organized labor, and Jews in mass media and voluntary associations.

Lieberson and Carter (1979) compared ethnic groups and African Americans listed in *Who's Who* in 1924–25, 1944–45 and 1974–75. The ethnic groups were English, Italian, Jewish, Scandinavian, and Slavic. Only the English exceeded the national average of people in *Who's Who* up to the Second World War. Since 1944–45, Jews exceeded both the English and the national average. Among the ethnic groups, the paths to elite positions have converged on college professors and administrators and business executives. Although the largest group of African Americans in *Who's Who* were college professors and administrators in 1974–75, many blacks took a different path to elite status. "Sports and entertainment are both major sources of national distinction for blacks in a way that is unmatched for any other group. The singer-musician and athlete categories are the second and third most important sources of blacks in *Who's Who* in 1974–75..." (Lieberson and Carter, 1979:354).

The African American athlete illustrates an escape from racial stratification. Only a small number of individuals rise from the bottom of the socioeconomic hierarchy in this manner, and many minority athletes never reach elite status but can be exploited with the promise that they will (Edwards, 1969). Nevertheless, African Americans entered professional sports and found equal opportunity there long before such a situation could even be imagined to exist in the general labor market (Blalock, 1967).

There are several reasons minority members find opportunities first in sports. While racial barriers prevented African Americans from cultivating skills needed in other areas of the economy, the development of athletic skills was virtually unaffected by caste barriers. African American baseball talent had actually been nurtured in the Negro leagues. Moreover, families of aspiring athletes were not required to make large investments—money African American families as a class did not have—in the sports training of their young, for much of these costs was covered in public services like recreational centers and sports programs in the schools, and there were also athletic scholarships. Thus, sports has been a niche in the labor market that has been relatively open to talent from all backgrounds, and one in which ethnic and racial barriers have been more difficult to maintain.

Since the racial integration of professional and collegiate sports, African Americans still gravitate toward basketball, football, baseball, track, and boxing. They are still underrepresented in sports such as swimming, golf, skiing, and tennis (Eitzen and Sage, 1982). It appears that African American access to certain sports is greater than for others, due in part to public funding for some sports but not others. Expensive private training is typical for skiing and tennis, for example, but public finances are the norm for basketball and football. Even in sports with high African American participation, stratification can be still evident. African Americans dominate men's basketball as players, but they are underrepresented as coaches and administrators.

Ethnic enclaves and athletics are just two examples of how ethnic barriers may be circumvented. A system of ethnic stratification itself may change as well. As competition, comparative power, and ethnocentrism change, so can the larger system of ethnic stratification. Social forces in the larger society can alter ethnic competition, comparative power, and ethnocentrism and thereby affect ethnic stratification. Some of these forces are technological innovations, demographic shifts, catastrophes, and value transformations (Shibutani and Kwan, 1965). To illustrate, Native Americans experienced phenomenal rates of natural decrease after their contact with European settlers. This drastic demographic change helped alter the comparative power of Native Americans and white settlers, which finally resulted in white dominance and the exclusion of Native Americans from their own land.

People seek privilege as long as there is a surplus of wealth, and as a rule the powerful find it, while the weaker do not (Lenski, 1966). The struggle for privilege may be endless in the abstract, but a particular case of ethnic competition for surplus wealth can nevertheless terminate as long as two conditions are met. Competition can end with either assimilation or exclusion. Once a dominant group fully absorbs another, formerly subordinate group, stratification between these two groups is no longer possible. The struggle for privilege and stratification might well continue past assimilation, but the process can no longer involve these two as distinctive ethnic groups.

Ethnic competition can also terminate with exclusion. A subordinate group might break off contact with a dominant group by migrating elsewhere, as exemplified in America by the movement of indigenous peoples further into the interior in the hope of escaping European encroachment. Rivalry and conflict were only temporarily halted in this case, for they occurred again and again on the frontier as European settlement expanded. This is an example of voluntary exclusion, but exclusion can also be involuntary or forced. Involuntary exclusion can come in the form of forced migration or extermination. The latter took on horrendous proportions during World War II; the Nazis went so far as to engage in genocide and then plan a museum in Prague, Czech Republic, dedicated to an exterminated people, European Jews.

Furthermore, there have been times when ethnic groups have simply ceased to regard one another as competitors, at least for a time. Because of a catastrophe, for instance, competitive groups may fuse their efforts into a joint, cooperative endeavor for their mutual survival. Such cooperation often accompanies war, when groups forget their differences and unite in a larger national effort against an external enemy. Once the external threat disappears, however, there is often a return to intergroup competition.

Power enables one group to dominate another in a system of ethnic stratification, but power can be lost as well as won. For one thing, rulers of one group can lose their authority to govern other groups; the authority of whites to rule over blacks has been declining throughout southern Africa. This is an instance of what Shibutani and Kwan (1965) called a transformation of values. If a dominant group is to maintain control as it loses its authority, it must resort to the use of force. However, with the resort to force the dominant group further erodes its claim to political authority and the legal right to rule.

Mastery over force comes ultimately from the monopolization of the means of production, or the control over land, labor, and capital in the creation of surplus wealth. A group must have a surplus above the level of subsistence to sustain the use of force since wealth is expended in warfare. Any loss of control over the means of production diminishes military capacity. For instance, as Native Americans lost more and more of their land, a loss that was not offset by gains in other power resources, their comparative power declined.

Power must be mobilized for a group to dominate others in a system of ethnic stratification. This mobilization depends in part on the generality and liquidity of a group's power resources, or the degree to which a group's wealth can be converted into political authority or raw force and focused on the maintenance of inequality. Power resources and their mobilization are not, strictly speaking, the possession of ethnic groups. Control over wealth and power has become concentrated in the corporate economy and/or state (Coleman, 1974; Galbraith, 1971). The use of power resources by ethnic groups has become increasingly difficult without their involvement in the corporate core of modern society. The upper classes of white ethnic groups have dominated the American economy. With the consequent resource advantage, they have excluded other ethnic groups from powerful and wealthy positions at the economic core.

However, minority groups can also turn to the corporate core in their rivalry with the majority. African Americans and other minorities have recently called upon the federal government for help in their rivalry with the dominant group, and the results have been civil rights legislation and affirmative action. The rivalry between ethnic groups can be mirrored in the rivalry between modern megastructures—big government and big business in this case. One result can be a change in ethnic stratification.

When ethnic groups relate to the corporate core, moreover, they tend to take on the organizational forms found in that core. To better deal with bureaucracy in the economy and state, agencies of ethnic groups become bureaucratized, with paid managerial staffs and boards of directors. This happened with civil rights organizations, for example. Thus, with the addition of conflict theory, we see that societal change can make for organizational growth and change in ethnic groups as much as it can reduce ethnicity to an expression of individuality (Dworkin and Dworkin, 1976; Hannan, 1979).

Ethnocentrism has also changed in the course of American history. As prejudice toward a group has waned, that group, more often than not, has found greater opportunity in the wider society. Lyman (1974) observed that as ethnocentrism toward Chinese Americans declined during World War II, they benefited from opportunities never before open to them in this country. The result was a drastic improvement in the position of Chinese Americans in the nation's system of ethnic stratification. Commentary not unlike this could be made about the nation's Irish and several other Roman Catholic nationality groups. So, with changes in ethnocentrism, comparative power, and ethnic competition, the relative positions of particular groups in a system of ethnic or racial stratification will change, although as a phenomenon ethnic stratification may persist in modern society.

THE FUNCTIONAL THEORY OF ETHNIC CONFLICT

Conflict theory often leaves the impression that competition and conflict are necessarily disruptive and divisive in a society. That is, ethnic conflict is something a society should avoid. Is it possible that this is only one side of the coin, and that conflict can and does play a positive role in society? The functional theory of conflict answers in the affirmative and proposes that conflict can unite groups in a society and will not necessarily drive them further apart. Conflict contributes to the maintenance of society, for as George Simmel (1908/1955) put it, "a certain amount of discord...and outer controversy is organically tied up with the very elements that ultimately hold the group together" (pp. 17–18).

Lewis Coser, in *The Functions of Social Conflict* (1956), elaborated on Simmel's functional theme of social conflict. Occasionally groups must search for a new relationship to replace their old one, as when an established system of ethnic stratification becomes dysfunctional. This search often requires a test of the relative strength of the parties, and the outcome of this test helps determine the nature of the new relationship. In the course of conflict, the ultimate values around which groups will forge a new relationship are revitalized.

Alliances are often created in conflict, and new forms of association emerge out of it. Moreover, in-group solidarity can be strengthened, in-group authority can be centralized, and consciousness of kind can be intensified in conflict with outsiders. This means that the internal structures of conflicting parties tend to be vitalized in the course of their conflict. Another positive function of conflict is that it can prevent the buildup of tension to the point where its release would virtually wreck a society. Occasional conflict is a safety valve of sorts, and this can actually maintain rather than change the status quo.

The functional theory of conflict applies primarily to realistic conflict. Realistic conflicts "arise from frustration of specific demands within the relationship and from estimates of gains of the participants, and which are directed at the presumed frustrating object" (Coser, 1956:49). Realistic conflict is rooted in actual rivalries, whereas nonrealistic conflict is occasioned by the need for tension release. Whether the group be Jews, African Americans, or some other group is of secondary importance to the aggressor in nonrealistic conflict.

The importance of this distinction is that realistic conflict can be replaced by other methods for achieving the desired end. "It has functional alternatives as to means while nonrealistic conflict has only functional alternatives as to objects" (Coser, 1956:50). Those who are pathologically hateful will always need someone or some group to hate. By contrast, realistic conflict can bring the reintegration of society without the need for finding another scapegoat and alienating another segment of society.

Himes (1966) found racial strife in this country an instance of realistic conflict, one that has had essentially positive functions for the nation. The pattern of traditional race relations in the United States was anachronistic and needed reform. Through intergroup conflict, race relations were changed in the needed direction, toward racial equity and better interracial understanding. This understanding brought the realization by members of both races that they shared certain basic values, according to Himes. The personal identification of African Americans with American ideals was strengthened, as the sense of African American alienation and cynicism was reduced, and so conflict paradoxically brought the unification of black and white Americans into a single moral community. The larger point is that ethnic conflict does not always result in renewed racial stratification; several outcomes, including assimilation, can follow from conflict. Of course, the condition of a group can actually worsen in the course of inter-group conflict.

SUMMARY AND ASSESSMENT

Ethnic conflict theory accentuates the role of competition, rivalry, strat-ification, and conflict in the change process. There is ethnic competition for surplus wealth, for new kinds of jobs, political power, property, and so on. Systems of ethnic stratification arise out of this struggle and en-dure for a time, but ultimately change. What remains are ethnic groups and their relations, which continue to exist into the modern era. This is the conflict version of ethnic relations in societal change.

Ethnic conflict theory is part of a larger tradition that characterizes societal change as a process of strife and struggle. It is class struggle that the Marxists stressed, and the translation of that legacy into ethnic conflict theory has been an underlying theme of the chapter. In the Marxian tradition, ethnic conflict and stratification are viewed as parts of the larger class struggle, in which ethnocentrism plays no more than a secondary role. Other theorists have contended, however, that eth-nocentrism is as important in the emergence of ethnic stratification as are economic competition and comparative power. That is, honor is considered to be an additional, significant dimension of ethnic stratifi-cation and conflict. Another departure from the Marxian tradition is represented by those writers who believe that the dynamics of ethnic stratification lie in the competition between labor of different groups, not between capital of one group and labor of another. Workers of powerful ethnic groups often become an aristocracy of labor and rele-gate others to the bottom of the labor hierarchy.

Ethnic conflict theorists are critical of both assimilationism and pluralism, by implication. While pluralists see an accommodation among ethnic and racial groups in modern society, the conflict theo-rists see strife, struggle, and the oppression of the weak by the power-ful. Rather than seeing assimilation at work, conflict theorists accentuate its absence, due to ethnic struggle and stratification. How-ever, there is as much evidence for ethnic and racial assimilation in America as there is for ethnic conflict and oppression. In the abstract, conflict and consensus, unity and disunity, are inseparable parts of the larger process of ethnic change in the course of societal change. These three theories—assimilationism, pluralism, and conflict theory—are complementary, each making up for some of what the others lack for a fuller understanding of American ethnicity.

5

⊘⊘

THE PSYCHOLOGY OF PREJUDICE AND DISCRIMINATION

T he sociological study of race and ethnic relations can be complemented with a psychological analysis of prejudice and discrimination. Psychological explanations of prejudice round out the sociology of ethnic relations with reference to the psychology of the individuals involved. American psychologists have produced a voluminous literature over the years on prejudice and discrimination in this country. After World War II, as racial protest gained momentum, prejudice and discrimination became a public issue, and psychologists became increasingly interested in racial attitudes. Their interest was also stimulated by developments within psychology itself. For example, a classic psychological study of racial and ethnic attitudes, *The Authoritarian Personality*, published in 1950, inspired research on the psychology of prejudice and discrimination. Research on ethnic attitudes continues to this day.

Ethnic and race relations are implicated in individual psychology as well as in a changing society, and ethnic attitudes exist in the psychology of the individual as well as in the broader American society and culture. To better depict this fact, social scientists use sociology and psychology together. The implication is that somehow social and psychological theories on ethnicity are complementary and, together, offer a more comprehensive view of ethnicity. Thus, while sociologists are wary of psychological reductionism, they also have been aware of the need to supplement a sociological analysis of ethnic relations with a psychology of prejudice and discrimination.

Psychology complements all three sociological perspectives on American ethnicity. Study of the psychological reasons for prejudice can complement conflict theory's emphasis on ethnic competition and conflict at the societal level. Pluralism is based on the premise that a multitude of ethnic groups can cooperate in a single society. The issue of bigotry is thus a central concern of pluralists, for unchecked ethnic hostility might divide a pluralistic society beyond repair.

It is assimilationism that the psychology of prejudice and discrimination may complement the most, however. According to the assimilationists, social change makes society ready for assimilation. No reason for prejudice and discrimination can be found today in the nature of society, but both might be due to the psychology of individuals. Assimiliationism left a vacuum which psychological explanations could fill.

Key terms and basic assumptions of the psychology of prejudice and discrimination will be presented, followed by a discussion of the major psychological perspectives on prejudice and discrimination. Research on the exact relationship between prejudice and discrimination will be then reviewed, and the chapter ends with an assessment of this approach to American ethnicity.

DEFINITIONS AND ASSUMPTIONS

KEY TERMS

PREJUDICE: According to Allport (1954:9), "ethnic prejudice is an antipathy based upon a faulty and inflexible generalization....It may be directed toward a group as a whole, or toward an individual because he is a member of that group." In the words of Simpson and Yinger (1972:24), prejudice is "an emotional, rigid attitude toward a group of people." In these definitions there is a common understanding about what prejudice is and what it is not. Prejudice is not overt behavior; it is always an *attitude,* an internal state, or a set of beliefs and feelings about some ethnic or racial group. Prejudice may predispose the individual to act in a certain way toward an ethnic group, but prejudice is by definition an attitude, not an act. Prejudice is also a particular kind of attitude, one about social groups such as ethnic and racial groups.

Prejudice is a set of beliefs, involving stereotypes and strong, often negative emotions about a group of people, that predisposes one to act in a certain way toward that group. There are three dimensions to this definition: Prejudice involves cognition, emotion, and a predisposition to act in a certain way.

The *cognitive dimension* is the thinking that goes into prejudice. While this thinking may be simple or complex, it is the simplicity and rigidity of prejudicial beliefs that are stressed. Beliefs about ethnic and racial groups often take the form of *stereotypes,* which are oversimplified and uncritical mental pictures we carry in our heads. Ethnic stereotypes are mental images of racial and ethnic groups. Walter Lippmann (1922:16) wrote that life contains "so much subtlety, so much variety, so many permutations and combinations...we have to reconstruct it on a simpler model before we can manage with it." We reconstruct human variation, for example, into simple, often rigid, and rather homogenous categories, evident in racial and ethnic stereotypes. These stereotypes abound in America; who has not heard jokes about "dumb Pollacks and Bohunks," "emotional Italians," "lazy blacks," and "greedy Jews"? The point is that stereotypes hardly allow for the realistic individual variation that occurs within ethnic and racial groups, and thus prejudice may be considered a faulty and inflexible generalization.

Are stereotypes corruptions of rationality, justice, and human-heartedness? If we are rational, seeking accurate, correct, and complete information about ourselves and others, then the simplicity and slantedness of stereotypes seem to be a failure of rationality (Harding, et al., 1969). This is akin to what Allport meant when he termed prejudice a "faulty and inflexible generalization." The idea that prejudice is a failure of justice and human-heartedness is clearly expressed in Myrdal's *An American Dilemma* (1944). Prejudice was believed to be inconsistent with American ideals for justice and fair play, with the very meaning of modernity.

In the 1970s and 1980s, most research on stereotypes was in the cognitive tradition of psychology (Stephan, 1985). In this view, stereotyping is not necessarily seen as a failure of rationality; rather it is a result of ordinary thinking. According to Tajfel (1969), people simply categorize others into distinct types or categories, and proceed to emphasize the dissimilarity between members of different categories, simultaneously accentuating the similarity among members of the same category. This represents ordinary thinking that can result in stereotypes about groups of people. For example, McArthur (1982) argued that simple and obvious physical differences among people coupled with the above cognitive processes can lead to elaborate racial stereotypes.

Stereotypes also can be implicit personality theories about members of ethnic groups (Ashmore, 1981; Cantor and Mischel, 1977 and 1979; Grant and Holmes, 1981). That is, the traits attributed to group members are arrived at on the base of one's theory about the prototypical personality of the group's members. We type people as having one kind of personality or another (e.g., introvert or extrovert) in a similar way. Group stereotypes can also be decomposed into distinct subtypes (Ashmore, 1981; Deaux and Lewis, 1984; Hamilton, 1981). For example, Ashmore (1981) found that females decomposed their stereotypes of women into subtypes of nervous Nellie, wallflower, etc., while men decomposed their stereotypes into girlfriend, nurturant, submissive, etc.

Furthermore, stereotypes may serve to protect the social identity of one's own in-group and thus one's self-esteem, according to Tajfel (1978, 1981, 1982). A slanted and negative stereotype of an out-group makes one's own group that much more favorable in the comparison, and this has a positive impact on self-esteem. What all these ideas have in common is that stereotypes result from ordinary thinking (Billig, 1985). These cognitive processes and the biased assimilation of new evidence explain the persistence of stereotypes (Hamilton, 1981; Pettigrew, 1989).

The *emotional, or affective, component* of prejudice refers to the fact that prejudice involves feelings or sentiments, usually negative and intense, toward an ethnic or racial group. Prejudice is not normally considered to be a neutral attitude; rather, its meaning is reserved for intensely held and strongly felt sentiments about an out-group. Most often, feelings about the out-group are negative, while those about one's own group are positive. This reflects the debt that current conceptions of prejudice owe to William Graham Sumner's writing on ethnocentrism (cf. LeVine and Campbell, 1972).

Prejudice toward certain racial and ethnic groups is thought to predispose one to discriminate against them. This is known as the *conative component* of prejudice. Like all attitudes, prejudice implies a readiness, based on beliefs and sentiment about some group, to discriminate against that group. However, the exact correspondence between prejudice and discrimination, between all attitudes and overt behavior, is a matter of debate. Some say that there is essentially no relationship between prejudice and discrimination, at least not an obvious one, while others argue that prejudice clearly predisposes one to discriminate. This debate will be surveyed later in the chapter.

DISCRIMINATION: Discrimination is an act—overt behavior—while prejudice is an attitude and only a predisposition to action. Like prejudice, however, discrimination is directed toward a group of people, particularly racial and ethnic groups, although a single individual may be the object of discrimination. The individual is discriminated against because of his/her perceived group membership. Typically, the intent behind discrimination is to keep members of a group in their "place."

Discrimination is action that can limit a target ethnic group's access to opportunities in the larger society. Discrimination can occur with respect to employment, housing, and all sorts of public services, including education. That is, members of the target group can be denied jobs, choice of residential location, and access to better schools. Thus, members of the target group share only exclusively in the larger society and culture and are likely to diverge from the course of change in that society.

Discrimination has been persistent in American history, and it certainly has become an important concern in the study of American ethnic and race relations. Nevertheless, discrimination is hard to discern case by case. Some of the conditions specified in various definitions of discrimination are difficult to ascertain in practice. The point of this chapter, however, is not the difficulty of proving discrimination; rather the purpose is to survey those psychological and social psychological theories that view American ethnicity from the "prejudice-discrimination axis," as Blumer (1958b:420) phrased this outlook: It rests on the belief that the nature of the relations between racial groups results from the feelings and attitudes which these groups have toward each other. It follows that in order to comprehend and solve problems of race relations it is necessary to study and ascertain the nature of prejudice.

ASSUMPTIONS OF THE PSYCHOLOGY OF PREJUDICE

1. Ethnic relations, and especially prejudice and discrimination, can be understood in the terms of the psychology of individuals.

2. The reasons given for prejudice and discrimination vary by psychological theory, but all agree that individual prejudice rather than the nature of contemporary society is the cause of discrimination.

PSYCHOLOGICAL THEORIES OF PREJUDICE

There are three major traditions in American psychology, and each gives its own reasons for prejudice. These are the psychoanalytic, cognitive, and behaviorist theories. The exact nature of the internal psychological processes that underlie prejudice and discrimination is the issue on which these theories differ.

Frank Beard's 1885 cartoon portraying "Columbia's unwelcome guests" demonstrates ethnic stereotyping at its worst.

THE PSYCHOANALYTIC TRADITION

The psychoanalytic tradition began with Sigmund Freud and has continued for many years with his many followers. *The Authoritarian Personality* (Adorno, et al., 1950) is an important contribution from this tradition to the study of ethnic prejudice and discrimination—specifically, anti-Semitism. Although this study applies several theoretical sources to the study of prejudice, as major works often do, its thrust is a psychoanalytic account of anti-Semitism. Actually, this work is an expansion of earlier Freudian hypotheses on the roles of projection, frustration, and aggression in prejudice. The authors proposed that prejudice is a personality type, and while prejudice involves projection and the displacement of aggression, for instance, it is not an isolated trait or some specific defense mechanism. There is a prejudiced personality, which the authors termed the *authoritarian personality*. The authoritarian personality is composed of interrelated characteristics or needs that lie behind the ideological preferences and ethnic prejudices of an individual. These needs originate in early childhood, in the family, and are the consequence of particular child-rearing practices.

While *The Authoritarian Personality* was completed in the United States after World War II, the work began in Germany before the war (Robinson, 1969). It represents a study of the psychology behind the appeal of the Nazi movement that ultimately led to the extermination of millions of people in Central Europe during the war, when approximately 14 million noncombatants were systematically destroyed by the Nazis with grim efficiency, many in extermination camps. Jews, Gypsies, and Slavic groups were the primary targets for the extermination.

Anti-Semitism was found to be an integrated set of attitudes about Jews, including beliefs about their "offensiveness," "threatening character," "seclusiveness," and "intrusiveness," and the desirability of segregating Jews. Aside from some surface contradictions in these beliefs—e.g., Jews are seen as both intrusive and seclusive—these beliefs tended to be highly correlated in the minds of anti-Semitic people. The study expanded into an inquiry about the possibility that anti-Semitism is part of a larger set of beliefs, a general rejection of all outgroups, not just Jews. This resulted in the development of an ethnocentrism scale that included subscales of attitudes about blacks, Filipinos, "Okies," Japanese, and "zoot-suiters," all minorities at that time in California, where the study was carried out in this country. It also included attitudes about people from other countries. These subscales were found to be correlated with one another, and the entire

133

scale of ethnocentrism correlated with the anti-Semitism scale. These findings appeared to justify the theoretical premise that prejudice is part of a broad personality syndrome.

Another facet of the research was people's ideological preferences, specifically their antidemocratic or fascist attitudes. The assessment of sociopolitical attitudes was intended to serve as an indirect measure of prejudice. This led to the development of the F scale (or implicit Antidemocratic Trends or Potentiality of Fascism Scale). People who scored high on the F scale possessed the following characteristics: conventionalism, submission to authority, aggression toward the unconventional, opposition to the imaginative and gentle, superstition and stereotype, emphasis on power and toughness, destructiveness and cynicism, projectivity, and concern with sexual "goings-on." Examples of the items on the F scale include:

1. Obedience and respect for authority are the most important virtues children should learn.

2. Young people sometimes get rebellious ideas, but as they grow up they ought to get over them and settle down.

3. Homosexuals are hardly better than criminals and ought to be severely punished.

To score low on the F scale, one had to disagree with these items. The F scale correlated with the ethnocentrism scale, although the correlation coefficients depended on the groups studied and the forms of the scales used. Clinical interviews of respondents and results from projective techniques supplemented data obtained through the attitudinal scales, and all results were interpreted as supporting the authors' basic contention that there is a prejudiced personality. This personality is characterized by the factors in the following list.

Highly authoritarian persons:
- have an emotional need for unconditional submission to authority which expresses itself in family interaction, other interpersonal relations, political attitudes, and attitudes toward supernatural figures.
- desire the polity to be ruled by a powerful, autocratic leader to whom all would grant total allegiance, unquestioning obedience, and extreme deference.
- believe that obedience and respect for authority are paramount values and the most important virtues children should learn.
- believe in extremely severe punishment of deviants: not only those who defy leaders but also offenders against conventional mores such as sexual restrictions.
- have a preoccupation with power, viewing all relations in terms like strong-weak and dominant-submissive, and admire displays of militancy, strength, and punitiveness ("toughness") by respected leaders.

- think in rigid categories, believe oversimplified explanations of natural and social events, and dogmatically apply these categories and explanations to ambiguous phenomena (that is, cannot tolerate ambiguity).

Source: From Robert A. LeVine and Donald T. Campbell, *Ethnocentrism? Theories of Conflict, Ethnic Attitudes, and Group Behavior.* New York: John Wiley and Sons, Inc., 1972. Reprinted by permission of the authors.

In keeping with the psychoanalytic tradition, the authors of *The Authoritarian Personality* sought the origins of authoritarianism in early childhood, particularly in certain types of parents and family structures. It was found that authoritarian people had parents who were extremely concerned with status distinctions and who despised those below them in the status hierarchy. These parents were seen to be harsh and rigid, and as a rule they made the expression of love for their children conditional on the children's obedience. Relationships among family members tended to be stratified into positions of dominance and submission. Duties, chores, and obligations, rather than exchanges of mutual affection and love, were emphasized in the home. The result was a child forced to submit to stern, aloof authority and rigid, arbitrary discipline, often involving physical punishment or the threat of it. Always there was the demand for obedience.

While children became understandably hostile toward their parents because of these experiences, they also learned that they could not express this hostility toward them. The parents were far too threatening and punitive for that. Besides, any child would feel guilty about hating his or her parents. Instead, the children learned to repress hostility toward their parents and thus began a pattern of submission to authority. Children grew more dependent on and unable to defy authority, first parents and then all authority figures. Eventually, there was identification with authority and the idealization of it, all of which helped the children hold in check their natural hostility toward authority figures like parents and political figures.

Simultaneously, the children learned to displace aggression onto substitute targets or scapegoats. This pattern also began at home, learned from the prejudice of the parents. Not only was some of the hostility for authority ventilated in this way, hostility the children could never express toward authority, but they also gained the approval of parents and other authority figures for being prejudiced in this manner. Nevertheless, authoritarian persons must always defend themselves against their own impulses, avoid looking too closely at themselves, forever condemn the unconventional, and, of course, hate the scapegoat. This is the psychoanalytic portrait of the prejudiced personality: the repression of hostility toward authority figures, the idealization of authority figures, and the displacement of hostility onto scapegoats.

The popularity of *The Authoritarian Personality* did not mean an uncritical acceptance of it. Only six years after the publication of this work, Vander Zanden (1972:148) estimated that "at least 230 publications appeared dealing with authoritarianism." Much of this commentary was critical on a number of counts. First, critics pointed out that the people who had been studied by the authors of this work were in no manner a representative sample of all Americans. Instead, they tended to be the middle class, college students, members of patriotic or civic associations, and so on, and thus they were different in certain social characteristics from other segments of the nation's population.

Another criticism of *The Authoritarian Personality* has to do with the fact that to get a low score on any one item in the original F scale, a respondent had to disagree with the item (e.g., disagree that obedience and respect for authority are the most important virtues children should learn). Some people tend to agree with any and all statements, while others tend to disagree, possibly irrespective of authoritarianism. This tendency is perhaps one type of a response set rather than authoritarianism (Bass, 1955; Chapman and Campbell, 1957; Couch and Keniston, 1960; Messick and Jackson, 1957; Peabody, 1961).

A major theme of *The Authoritarian Personality* is that prejudice is part of a personality syndrome, not an isolated psychological trait. However, there is some question as to whether responses to the F scale do indeed represent a unified, single psychological orientation. Studies have shown through factor analysis that six or seven distinct traits are measured by the F scale, none of them very well. Authoritarianism was also identified solely with right-wing (fascist) political ideology. Critics say that authoritarianism is just as likely to be found on the political left as the political right.

THE COGNITIVE TRADITION

Authoritarianism can be found across the entire political spectrum, not only on the political extremes, according to Milton Rokeach (1956; 1960). It can be associated with any political ideology and is not unique to a right-wing or left-wing political orientation. Not only may communists be as authoritarian as fascists, but also political moderates may be as authoritarian as those on both political extremes. Furthermore, people may be as authoritarian about their religion, philosophy, and scientific viewpoints as they are about their political attitudes. In other words, the authoritarianism analyzed by the authors of *The Au-*

thoritarian Personality was seen by Rokeach as a single instance of a more general phenomenon, that of dogmatism and opinionatedness, or closed-mindedness. Closed-mindedness can be found in all political camps and connected with nearly any viewpoint. This means that one may be dogmatically unprejudiced as well as prejudiced, dogmatically tolerant as well as intolerant.

The term *dogmatism* means "(1) a relatively closed cognitive organization of beliefs and disbeliefs about reality, (2) organized around a central set of beliefs about absolute authority which, in turn, (3) provide a framework for patterns of intolerance and qualified tolerance toward others" (Rokeach, 1956:3). Dogmatic persons have a closed belief system, meaning that they reject a far wider range of beliefs and opinions than they accept, make little effort to keep consistent their central and peripheral beliefs, and are categorical in their opinions, showing little flexibility and awareness of situational nuances. That is, dogmatic and opinionated persons tend to view the world from a single perspective, reject essentially all viewpoints other than their own, and are unconditional in their judgments about people and their actions, whatever the circumstances. By contrast, open-minded individuals view the world from a variety of vantage points, are more flexible in their judgments, attempt to maintain better consistency between central and peripheral beliefs, and are less likely to reject out of hand the opinions of others.

Dogmatic people also tend to see history from a single, fixed point in time. They may be past oriented, as are fascists; present oriented, like psychopaths; or future oriented, as are some religious enthusiasts. Regardless of the time perspective favored, the dogmatic individual tends to see the flow of events through time from only that one perspective, and thus the present is blurred with the past and the future. A fascist, for example, would see the present and the future only in terms of the past, while a religious enthusiast would view the past and the present as only leading up to the future, toward salvation, for example. Open-minded people clearly distinguish among these time frames and appreciate the fact that the human condition can be viewed from all three perspectives.

Rokeach argued that all belief systems, dogmatic or not, have three levels: primitive, intermediate, and peripheral. Primitive beliefs are basic ideas about the nature of the world. The dogmatic person sees the world as threatening, while the open-minded person views the world as basically friendly. With respect to intermediate and peripheral beliefs, the dogmatic individual has the habit of making reference to some authority behind them, implying somehow that authority is absolute, categorical, and correct in all cases. People who are open-minded are less likely to believe in absolute authority and do not appeal to it as often in their more specific beliefs.

Rokeach's formulation represents an extension of historical Gestalt psychology. Gestalt psychology postulates that humans are basically cognitive beings who need to know the world around them. Through perception and cognition we organize our world into coherent and balanced wholes, and our feelings about the world follow from our knowledge of it. Not only are people's beliefs at various levels mutually consistent, but there is also a balance between thought and sentiment. This is the picture of the open-minded person.

The portrait of the closed-minded individual, in contrast, reproduces the essentials of the authoritarian personality in the psychoanalytic tradition. Dogmatic beliefs follow from feelings, specifically from the need to ward off threat, not from the need to know. Inconsistencies between primitive and peripheral beliefs are kept in isolation, as if in defense. That is, there is no attempt to maintain a balance between the various parts of the larger belief system. Moreover, dogmatism and opinionatedness involve identification with absolute authority. Rokeach does not locate the causes of racial prejudice in inner psychic conflict, however. He favors the cognitive perspective that prejudice follows rationally from certain beliefs about other ethnic groups.

Prejudice in this view is a function of perceived *belief similarity-dissimilarity* between races, rather than a result of deep-rooted, internal psychological turmoil. Prejudice follows from the dissimilarity perceived between one's own values and those associated with members of other racial or ethnic groups. The greater the dissimilarity, the greater is the prejudice felt, which is especially true when basic values and important beliefs are involved. Prejudice does not necessarily imply a rejection of another person on the basis of race or ethnicity per se. Rather, the rejection is based on the perceived discrepancy between that person's values and one's own, although this perception may be unreal and based on ethnic stereotypes. Presumably, there will be no prejudice when it is evident that members of different races share the same basic values.

Some writers object to Rokeach's position that all racial prejudice is belief prejudice; their studies show that there is both conventional and belief prejudice (Triandis, 1961; Triandis and Davis, 1965). Conventional prejudice is not necessarily the sort that follows from inner psychic conflict; it simply means that the rejection of another person is indeed based on that person's ethnicity or race per se. In support of Rokeach's position, other studies attest to the existence of belief prejudice.

The findings of Stein, Hardyck, and Smith (1965), like those of many other researchers, illustrate the workings of both belief and conventional prejudice. White teenagers in this study were first asked about their own values, values considered by the authors to be relevant to adolescents. From the same set of values, value profiles of four hypothetical teenagers were constructed by the researchers. Two of the hypothetical teenagers were white and two were black, and their values were fabricated to be either similar or dissimilar to the values of each of the respondents. Thus, for each respondent the hypothetical teenagers formed a four-cell table: black and similar, black and dissimilar, white and similar, and white and dissimilar. In this way the weights given by respondents to race and belief in their acceptance or rejection of the hypothetical teenagers could be ascertained. Respondents' attitudes toward the hypothetical teenagers were measured by a social distance scale, that is, in terms of how friendly they anticipated they would be with the hypothetical teenager in various social settings. Some of these settings were quite formal and implied some of the traditional distance between the races, while others were informal and intimate (e.g., date my sister or brother).

Analysis of the responses showed that these white teenagers weighted belief similarity-dissimilarity more heavily than race in their anticipated friendliness/unfriendliness toward the four hypothetical peers. This was true except for certain "sensitive" items, in settings that implied intimacy. In the intimate settings the respondents weighted the race of the hypothetical teenager more heavily than beliefs; that is, social distance was more a function of the hypothetical teenager's being black than any belief similarity-dissimilarity. We see here the working of both belief and conventional prejudice; belief prejudice stops with intimacy, where conventional prejudice begins. Moreover, when these respondents knew nothing of a hypothetical teenager except for race, they anticipated that a black teenager would have values unlike their own, while the values of a white peer were expected to be similar to their own. This suggests that in the absence of information to the contrary, whites will think blacks are essentially dissimilar to themselves.

More recent research supports these conclusions (Berndt and Heller, 1986; Bodenhausen and Wyer, 1985; Deaux and Lewis, 1984; Grant and Holmes, 1981 and 1982; Locksley, Hepburn and Ortiz, 1982a and b; Rasinski, Crocker and Hastie, 1985). Locksley, et al. (1982a and b) found that when making a judgment about an individual, personal information about that individual is more important than group stereotypes when the two are inconsistent. For example, you would weigh what you know about a particular person as being more important than the stereotypical stupidity of his/her ethnic group in your opinion of the person's intelligence. Rasinski, et al.

(1985) found, however, subjects to be cautious about revising stereo-typical judgments in such cases. If personal information and group stereotypes are consistent, one's judgment of the individual will round out into the full group stereotype.

The notion that prejudice is based on perceived belief dissimilarity is prominent among those who detect recent changes in prejudice. In Europe, for example, there is a new racism based on perceived cultural differences between new immigrants and established in-groups (Bark-er, 1981). The old racism was based on supposed biological differences between groups, but it has been largely replaced by this newer form of prejudice. The cultures of new immigrants, such as Turks, are seen as threats to the basic values of the in-groups, e.g., Germans, French and Dutch. This explains the difficult reception of new minorities in Eu-rope, according to Barker.

Symbolic racism in the United States is essentially the same as the new racism in Europe. Ethnic out-groups are thought to violate, and thus threaten, basic American values such as individualism, hard work, and self-discipline (Kinder, 1986; Kinder and Sears, 1981; McConahay and Hough, 1976; McConahay, et al., 1981). This racism is expressed symbolically in negative attitudes toward affirmative action and school busing, for example, symbols of contemporary race relations. There is the wish to conserve in-group values, even defend them from per-ceived threat, along with the idea that minorities can be too demand-ing. The new racism is rooted in perceived belief dissimilarity and the threat minorities can pose to the in-group's values. We must note, how-ever, that a number of social scientists argue that there is no new or symbolic racism (e.g., Bobo, 1983; Sniderman and Tetlock, 1986).

Kleinpenning and Hagendoorn (1993) found in Holland that dif-ferent types of prejudice lie on a single dimension and are cumulative. There is no old and new prejudice. Prejudice begins with simply wish-ing to avoid contact with out-group members (aversive), proceeds to the belief that one's own group is culturally superior and other groups should conform to the in-group's standards (ethnocentrism), then the notion that out-groups are a cultural threat and have more rights than they deserve (symbolic), and culminates with the attitude that there are innate differences between ethnic groups (biological). One who is biologically prejudiced is also symbolically prejudiced, ethnocentric, and believes in aversive prejudice. That is, the states of prejudice are cumulative from the mildest to the strongest, aversive to biological. The implicaton is that newer have not replaced older forms of preju-dice, at least not in Holland; rather newer and older forms are cumu-lative stages in the unfolding of a single prejudice from aversive to biological.

THE PSYCHOANALYTIC VS. COGNITIVE DEBATE ON PREJUDICE

The debate between psychologists in the psychoanalytic and cognitive traditions is over the relationship between prejudicial beliefs and feelings. Those in the psychoanalytic tradition emphasize that inner feelings, rooted in unconscious psychic conflict, are externalized onto minority groups. The result is prejudice. Beliefs about a minority group are then formed in the service of these ego-defense mechanisms. For instance, anti-Semitism as a set of beliefs about Jews is explained as the repression of hostility toward parents and its displacement onto a scapegoat. Cognitive theorists see the roles of beliefs and feelings in reverse order. Prejudice as a sentiment follows directly and sometimes rationally from one's beliefs about a minority group. For example, Rokeach argued that prejudice for most people is simply a result of their perception that they and minority group members are essentially different, implying that we dislike those unlike us. However, how does this explain the fact that prejudicial beliefs often appear irrational, narrow, and overly stereotypical? Emotion distorts logic, those in the psychoanalytic tradition answer. From the cognitive point of view, Henri Tajfel (1969) explained that prejudice is simply a function of three cognitive processes: categorization, assimilation/contrast, and the search for coherence.

People categorize what is actually continuous in the real world into distinct types or categories. For example, imagine what you would see if the world's people stood shoulder to shoulder in a single line from the lighest to the darkest and you rode past them in a car, as if in a military review. Would you not see a single continuum of color? There would be no clear and distinct racial categories; one race would not abruptly end and another begin. However, in our mind's eye we tend to see people belonging to one distinct racial group or another. Indeed, we categorize virtually everything in this manner, which helps bring some order and definition to our world. This process is called *perceptual grouping* in Gestalt psychology. It is also seen as an essential psychological process in other forms of cognitive theory, such as the works of Piaget (cf. Flavell, 1963).

Once we categorize our world, we proceed to emphasize the differences between members of different categories and simultaneously to accentuate the similarity among members of the same category. The similarity of the members of a single category becomes greater, while the dissimilarity between members of different categories is accentuated. Members of one racial group come to look all the same, and basically different from members of other groups. This is the *assimilation/ contrast principle*.

Values and beliefs are also attributed to members of the different categories in the process of categorization. These attributes, too, undergo the dual phenomenon of assimilation/contrast. People in one category are seen to be essentially similar in their beliefs and values, while people in different categories are seen to be essentially dissimilar. This is the stuff of stereotypes. It also reminds us of the study by Stein et al. (1965). In the absence of information to the contrary, a member of one race will believe that all members of another race have similar values, and that those values are essentially different from his or her own. Stereotypes are learned in childhood, Tajfel noted, when they are often taken as factual, due to the child's developmental inability to question the authority behind the stereotype (Kohlberg, 1968; Piaget, 1932). This alone can result in prejudice.

Prejudice is rooted in categorization, assimilation/contrast, and the search for coherence, to be sure, but there are additional motives behind prejudice. Thus, Tajfel and his associates formulated their *social identity theory* (Tajfel, 1981; Tajfel and Turner, 1979; Turner, 1975). Ethnic groups provide a social identity to their members, and this identity contributes to members' self-esteem. People are motivated to make comparisons between their in-group and out-groups in favor of their own group. This is in-group bias. Validating the social identity of one's own group and thus maintaining one's self-esteem is a prime motive in prejudice toward out-groups, the flip side of in-group bias. This process was demonstrated in the minimal group experiments of Tajfel. Members of artificially formed groups showed a distinct bias in favor of their in-groups, and prejudice emerged toward out-group members.

The theme of cognitive theory is that prejudice is a rational process. We learn to categorize people into different races or ethnic groups and to attribute values and beliefs to them on this basis. In the process members of one group come to appear more like one another and unlike members of another group, the assimilation/contrast effect. Once we know that a member of another race or ethnic group is not different from us, however, we tend to like that person. In other words, prejudice is a rational consequence of assumed belief dissimilarity. Prejudice is also a consequence of in-group bias, which confirms both our social identity and our self-worth.

Research has found that much of the racial prejudice in the United States is just such belief prejudice. In some situations, however, race is more important than is belief similarity-dissimilarity. In situations involving interracial intimacy, whites tend to reject blacks on the basis of race rather than comparative beliefs (Stein et al., 1965).

While Tajfel (1969) is correct that the cognitive component of prejudice had been ignored in the psychoanalytic school, he appears to err in the opposite direction, overlooking the emotional element in prejudice. All cognitive theorists may overstate the role of cognition and rationality in prejudice. All prejudice does not neatly follow from belief similarity-dissimilarity, as we already know. Years ago, Merton (1957) observed that in-group virtues may be out-group vices. For instance, members of one ethnic group may consider their own striving for success as appropriate ambition, a case of honest effort, but they find the same behavior in another group to be pushiness, an indication of greed. In Merton's (1957:428–429) words:

> The very same behavior undergoes a complete change of evaluation in its transition from the in-group Abe Lincoln to the out-group Abe Cohen or Abe Kurokawa...Did Lincoln work far into the night? This testifies that he was industrious, resolute, perseverant, and eager to realize his capacities to the full. Do the out-group Jews or Japanese keep these same hours? This only bears witness to their sweatshop mentality, their ruthless undercutting of American standards, their unfair competitive practices. Is the in-group hero frugal, thrifty, and sparing? Then the out-group villain is stingy, miserly, and penny-pinching.

It is not clear how cognitive theorists can explain such beliefs, which on the surface appear to be irrational and made to conform with prior feelings about one's own kind and others. How can a rational person judge the same traits in his group and in the out-group to be essentially different? Beliefs about other ethnic and racial groups may at times be in the service of one's feelings or emotional needs. Perhaps, Tajfel's social identity theory quiets these criticisms with its emphasis on our need for a positive social identity to maintain a sense of self-worth.

The cognitive and psychoanalytic approaches to prejudice proceed from very different assumptions on the basic psychology of humankind. Cognitive theory simply proposes that prejudice is based on fundamental cognitive processes, perceived belief dissimilarity, and social identity, unlike the more complicated Freudian explanation of instincts, psychic conflict between those instincts and morality, and the externalization of that conflict onto members of minority groups. Prejudice is a rational process from one viewpoint and irrational from the other. Research shows that prejudice is both rational and irrational, the latter based on beliefs in the service of strong emotions. These two theories, when considered together, make it clear that both cognition and emotion play important roles in the psychology of prejudice.

THE BEHAVIORIST TRADITION

Behaviorism is the third great tradition in American psychology, one that began in the nineteenth century in both the United States and Europe. Behaviorists assume that humans are rational and hedonistic, that we can learn from our environment and will select from our behavioral repertoire those actions that will bring us reward. Behaviorists also prefer to depict human psychology solely in terms of observable stimuli and overt responses. Thus behaviorism is often known as S-R (Stimulus-Response) theory.

This S-R aspect of behaviorism presents somewhat of a problem in the study of prejudice. Prejudice is typically defined as an attitude, an internal state of beliefs and feelings that only predisposes people to respond in certain overt ways and is usually not considered the response itself. Discrimination is the response. However, since behaviorists prefer not to deal with internal psychological states like attitudes, they must recast the meaning of prejudice. The ethnic and racial groups toward whom prejudice is directed are seen as stimuli, and prejudice itself is seen as some sort of overt response.

Prejudice is learned, meaning that the bond between the stimulus object and the overt response to that object is acquired, not innate. Behaviorists believe that there are two basic learning methods. Learning may occur through either classical or instrumental conditioning, because of either association or reinforcement.

Ivan Pavlov, the early Russian behaviorist, paired a bell with meat powder and conditioned dogs to respond to the bell in a way they had responded to the meat powder. In this classical-conditioning paradigm, the bell is the conditioned stimulus and the meat powder is the unconditioned stimulus. The response to the bell is the conditioned response, while the original response of salivation to the meat powder is the unconditioned response. The learning of the conditioned response follows from the association between the conditioned and unconditioned stimuli. The second paradigm of learning in behaviorism is instrumental or operant conditioning, which is closely connected with the works of B. F. Skinner. A pigeon in a Skinner box, for instance, learns to respond so as to attain a reward by pecking in the right place for a pellet of food. The response is instrumental, or an operant for obtaining a reward, and learning in this case conforms to the law of reinforcement rather than the law of association.

PREJUDICE AND CLASSICAL CONDITIONING: A study by Staats and Staats (1958) illustrates how prejudice can be learned through classical conditioning. In classical conditioning two stimuli are paired, the condi-

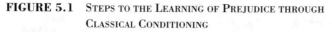

FIGURE 5.1   Steps to the Learning of Prejudice through
Classical Conditioning

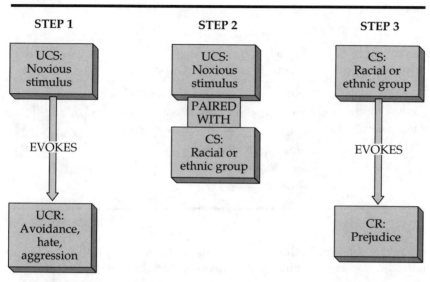

tioned stimulus (CS) and the unconditioned stimulus (UCS). After several of these pairings, even animals learned to respond to the conditioned stimulus (CR) as they had to the unconditioned stimulus (UCR). In the Staats and Staats experiment, college sophomores were told that they were being tested on their ability to learn two lists of words simultaneously. One list of words contained names of nationalities and was presented visually. Immediately after each of the visual words was presented, another word was spoken to the subjects from a second list. Words from this second list had strong evaluative meaning, both positive (e.g., *beautiful*) and negative (e.g., *ugly*). The visual words from the first list were the conditioned stimuli, obviously, and the spoken words were the unconditioned stimuli.

It was predicted that the subjects would eventually learn to respond to names of nationalities from the first list as they had responded to the evaluative words from the second list. The subjects were asked to rate the names of nationalities on pleasant-unpleasant semantic differential scales. It was found that nationalities paired with negative words, such as *bitter, ugly,* and *failure,* were rated as more unpleasant than nationalities paired with positive words, consistent with the prediction. This study suggests that prejudice is a condi-

FIGURE 5.2 STEPS TO THE LEARNING OF PREJUDICE THROUGH
INSTRUMENTAL CONDITIONING

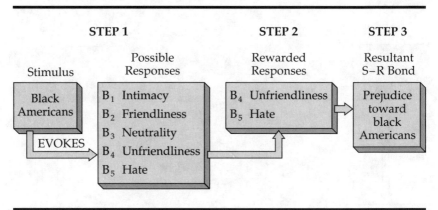

tioned response to a stimulus—a racial or ethnic group—that has been paired in someone's mind with a noxious stimulus (see Figure 5.1).

PREJUDICE AND INSTRUMENTAL CONDITIONING: In instrumental conditioning, the correct response is learned in order to obtain a reward. This response is termed an operant. Prejudice is an operant in instrumental conditioning, a means to obtain reward or avoid punishment. The bond between the stimulus object of black people and the response of prejudice is a function of the reward that prejudice brings. Skinner has shown that reward need not be continuous; the bond between the stimulus and the response is actually stronger when reward is periodic or intermittent. If a child learns that prejudice brings reward from his parents or others significant to him, or if it allows him to avoid punishment, even if this is only occasional, he will become prejudiced, in accord with the principles of instrumental conditioning. Figure 5.2 illustrates this process.

PREJUDICE AND IMITATION: You have probably seen children imitate adults. Children playing "dress up" try to look like mommy or daddy, a practice we often find cute and even charming. We may be embarrassed by our own children, however, when they go so far as to mock the quirks of their mother or father. Imitation is actually a serious part of the social learning process. By imitating adult models, children begin to learn about the adult roles they will be expected to play one day. Children learn many things about society by imitating the grown-ups around them, and prejudice and discrimination are among the things that children learn in this way. A child may learn prejudice by imitating a parent after seeing such feelings expressed in the privacy of the home or in public. That the parent is infrequently, if ever, reprimanded for being prejudiced is also noticed by the child. This serves as a model for the development of the child's own racial and ethnic attitudes, which may ironically come as something of a surprise to the parents.

The role of imitation in learning prejudice might be illustrated by Bandura and Walters' studies of children imitating adult aggression (cf. Bandura, 1962). Young children were exposed to a variety of models, adults in person, adults on film, and cartoon characters on film, who were either aggressive or nonaggressive. It was found that the children who viewed aggressive models responded in an aggressive manner by punching and kicking a plastic Bozo doll when later frustrated. Children who had not been exposed to aggressive models did not respond to frustration with aggression. If children can learn aggression in this way, then they also can learn prejudice thorough imitation. Prejudice is simply a product of imitating prejudiced models. Moreover, parents may be unintentional models, and the children need not be directly rewarded for imitating the prejudice of their parents in order for prejudice to develop.

Once prejudice is learned as a correct response to a certain class of stimulus objects, say African American athletes while watching televised sports, it may then generalize as a response to all African Americans, possibly to all people of color. It might come to include members of other minority groups, whatever their color. This process is called *generalization*. The scope of generalization is a function of how closely related, in either a physical or thematic sense, additional stimulus objects are to the original stimulus object. Of course, prejudice toward a given minority group may be directly learned and not be a function of the generalization of prejudice toward some other group. The opposite side of generalization is *discrimination*, whereby one learns to differentiate responses to different classes of stimuli. A child who learns to be prejudiced toward black athletes may also learn that prejudice is not the proper response to other classes of African Americans, and certainly not to members of other racial groups. The dual phenomena of generalization and discrimination help determine toward whom one learns to be prejudiced, from the perspective of S-R theory.

Like all learning, prejudice can be reversed, or unlearned, a process the behaviorists call *extinction*. Through extinction, response strength diminishes; for instance, the probability that one will respond with prejudice toward African Americans becomes less. Extinction can occur with counterconditioning or through the manipulation of rein-forcement schedules. Through counterconditioning the connection be-tween the conditioned stimulus, some ethnic group, and the noxious unconditioned stimulus is broken, possibly by pairing the ethnic group with other positive stimuli. Prejudice diminishes as a conse-quence. If we assume that prejudice was originally learned as an oper-ant, a means of securing reward, then prejudice should diminish if it is not rewarded.

Not all psychologists are happy with the behavioral model of prej-udice, particularly those who are not behaviorists. A basic criticism of the behavioral formulation is that prejudice is not a response. It is dis-crimination that is the response; prejudice is the attitude behind it. Chein (1948) observed that responses come and go, while attitudes such as prejudice endure. Prejudice toward a certain ethnic group may last a lifetime, and it is hard to imagine how such an attitude is actual-ly a response. Doob (1947) stated that an attitude once learned can also be "drive producing." This might account for the persistence of an atti-tudinal response over time, except that drives are stimuli, not respons-es, for they initiate behavior and are not behavior itself. Doob suggested that attitudes are also habits. Is prejudice all three—a re-sponse, a stimulus, and a habit? It clearly cannot be all three, and it may be none of these. Aside from these criticisms, it is obvious that prejudice can be learned through conditioning and imitation, and be-haviorism adds to understanding of the psychology of prejudice.

THE FUNCTIONAL THEORY OF PREJUDICE: A SYNTHESIS?

Three perspectives on the psychology of prejudice have been re-viewed, the psychoanalytic, cognitive, and behavioral theories. Each of these certainly has something to say about the psychological roots of prejudice, but each also has its shortcomings. Here again we are faced with a plurality of perspectives on a single phenomenon, none of which seems to be a complete explanation. A fuller view of the psy-chology of prejudice may emerge, however, when these theories are used together in a complementary manner.

This is what Daniel Katz (1960) suggested in his call for a function-al approach to the study of attitudes, including prejudice. Writers have taken one of two basic approaches to the study of attitudes, Katz ob-served, one based on the irrational model of people and another based on the rational model of humans. The first approach posits that preju-dice is an outcome of irrational and emotional forces, unconscious in their origins. In our review, it has been represented by the psychoanalytic theory of prejudice, including the version found in *The Authoritarian Personality*.

The second approach to attitudes is based on the rational model of humans, which explains prejudice as an essentially rational process, a product of conscious and even logical thought. Attitudes are part of the larger process by which humans adjust to their surroundings. This approach is seen in both behaviorism and the cognitive theory of prejudice. Prejudice is either a rationally conditioned response or an operant for reward, from the perspective of the behaviorists, and it brings a semblance of order to an otherwise chaotic world and serves to bolster our social identity, according to cognitive theorists.

The complementarity of these three theories—psychoanalytic, cognitive, and behaviorist—becomes clear when we consider the many psychological needs that attitudes like prejudice can serve. Katz argued that attitudes serve four classes of psychological needs; that is, they perform four major functions for an individual.

"First, attitudes have an *instrumental, adjustive, or utilitarian function,* facilitating the attainment of rewards from the external environment..." (Katz, 1960:171). Hyman and Sheatsley (1954) have shown that prejudice can bring acceptance from one's own kind, for instance, when prejudice is a norm of that group. The utilitarian function of attitudes is stressed by the behaviorists.

Second, the *ego-defensive function* of attitudes is to protect individuals from basic but threatening truths themselves. Prejudice of the authoritarian personality is a means to displace hatred and hostility away from parents and onto a scapegoat. The authority personified by the parents is idealized in the process, protecting individuals even further from facing any guilt over hating their own parents. It is the psychoanalytic tradition that stresses this ego-defensive function of prejudice. From this perspective, prejudices:

> ...proceed from within the person, and the objects and situation to which they are attached are merely convenient outlets for their expression. The point is that the attitude is not created by the target but by the individual's emotional conflicts. And when no convenient target exists the individual will create one (Katz, 1960:172–173).

The *value-expressive function* of attitudes refers to the fact that one's attitudes can express to others one's basic beliefs and central values. Prejudice can serve as an assertion of self, a statement on one's world view and self-identity. This perspective on prejudice is evident in the cognitive approach, particularly in the social identity theory of Tajfel and the view that prejudice follows from assumed belief dissimilarity. The very process of rejecting the dissimilar out-group confirms the values of one's own group, and thus one's social identity and self-worth. This function of attitudes would also be accented in ego psychology and in any psychology on self-concept and self-realization.

Finally, Katz said, attitudes have a *knowledge function*. Prejudice, like any attitude, can provide some order and clarity in a chaotic and complex world. Tajfel (1969) stressed this very function of ethnic and racial stereotypes, illustrated by the assimilation/contrast effect. If Katz is correct and attitudes do serve a variety of needs, a variety that has been merely suggested by reference to these four personality needs that prejudice can serve, then the different theories on the psychology of prejudice seem to be complementary. While each theory stresses only one or two major needs met by prejudice, each one, in its narrow emphasis, makes up for some of what the others lack in their equally narrow points of view. Together they give a fuller understanding of the psychology underlying prejudice. Oversimplification in the psychological study of prejudice can be avoided to some extent by using these theories in a complementary manner.

SOCIAL REPRESENTATIONS

Up to this point, we have been talking about prejudice solely as an attitude of an individual (Allport, 1935). Due to an authoritarian personality, cognitive processes, or conditioning, an individual is prejudiced. The initial conception of attitudes in sociology was, however, that attitudes were group-held and shared widely by members of an in-group (Thomas and Znaniecki, 1918–1920). This group-held conception of attitudes has been revived in social representation theory, and now we shift to a discussion of recent research on group-held ethnic attitudes.

Members of an ethnic in-group can represent a nation's ethnic groups into a hierarchy, a representation which they share. This representation would include first the categorization of the population into ethnic groups, e.g., Asians, blacks, whites, etc. Invidious comparisons among these groups could follow, and thus embedded in the representation would be a hierarchy of groups. If a social representation, this hierarchy would be widely shared across members of an in-group. A social representation has also been termed a *folk* or *cultural model*, "a cognitive schema that is intersubjectively shared by a social group" (D'Andrade, 1987:112).

Hraba and Mok (1990) found a shared ethnic hierarchy among white students at a large, midwestern university in the United States.

The hierarchy from bottom to top was Asian, Hispanic, African American, Native American, Jewish, and white Americans. Most social distance was toward Asians and the least toward the in-group. There were minor changes in the adjacent positions of groups from one contact domain to another. In the domain of marriage, for example, the group sequence was African American, Asian, Hispanic, Native American, Jewish, and white Americans on top. The position of African Americans dropped below those of Asians and Hispanics, but the rest of the group sequence was the same. These students shared this hierarchy of ethnic groups in social distance whatever the level of their individual prejudice, and thus it was their group-held social representation.

In Holland the Dutch in-group shared a hierarchy of that nation's ethnic groups (Hagendoorn and Hraba, 1987 and 1989; Hraba, et al., 1989). The Dutch were asked about their social distance toward eight groups in the Netherlands. They discriminated among these groups in social distance; some groups were kept at a greater distance than others. On top of the hierarchy were the Dutch themselves, followed by English, Jews, Spanish, Surinamers, South Moluccans, and Turks, all ethnic groups in Holland. Social distance was greatest toward the groups on the bottom of the hierarchy. The same group sequence was shared by virtually all members of the Dutch in-group, and thus the hierarchy was a social representation.

People can unfold and collapse an ethnic hierarchy across contexts of use (Hraba, et al., 1989). More discriminations in social distance are made among ethnic groups in an unfolded hierarchy and fewer are made in a collapsed hierarchy. To illustrate, one might make only a black-white distinction in social distance at a party, congregating with one's own kind, for example, but discriminate much finer among whites by nationality or religion as potential marriage partners. The cognitive image contained in a social representation serves pragmatic purposes. According to the situation, it is able to bring out the number of ethnic distinctions that are more relevant when ethnicity is particularly salient, consequences of contact are lasting and significantly affect life chances, and when norms do not inhibit ethnic preferences. Discriminations are not so refined in domains where consequences of contact are not so great and norms run counter to the display of ethnic preference.

Ethnic stereotypes may be one of the reasons for the specific group sequence in an ethnic hierarchy. Recall that the Dutch hierarchy had the Dutch on top, followed by English, Jews, Spanish, Surinamers, and Moluccans, with Turks at the bottom. The Dutch respondents were also asked about their stereotypes toward these same groups, and the association between stereotypes and group rank in the ethnic hierarchy was studied (Hagendoorn and Hraba, 1989). The Dutch first distinguished between themselves and all out-groups primarily on the foreign appearance of the others. This included dress, food habits, language spoken, etc. Next, they distinguished the English and Jews from others lower on the hierarchy by stereotypes of deviancy and working class. Compared to the others, English and Jews were seen as less deviant and less working class. Deviancy included stereotypes of uncivil and criminal behavior, such as selling drugs, and working class referred to being unskilled, dirty, irrational, etc. The Spanish were then differentiated from the others yet lower on the hierarchy on the basis of seclusiveness. Compared to Surinamers, Moluccans, and Turks, the Spanish were seen as less seclusive, that is, more open and attractive. This process proceeded until Moluccans and Turks were distinguished at the low end of the hierarchy (Hagendoorn and Hraba, 1989).

The stereotypes anchored the Dutch ethnic hierarchy to familiar points of reference, namely, Dutch institutions and values. To illustrate, foreign appearance refers to Dutch dress codes, food preferences, and language use. Deviance relates ethnic groups to Dutch legal codes and cultural norms. Even the seclusiveness of groups is a comparative judgment, for being closed and unattractive must be judged against familiar Dutch standards. It appears that increasing perceived deviation from Dutch norms or combinations of perceived deviations lead to a disproportionate increase in social distance towards out-groups, unfolding an ethnic hierarchy.

Ethnic attitudes can be the possession of an ethnic in-group or a single individual. Members of an in-group might share the same ethnic hierarchy, for instance, but vary in other attitudes toward the target out-groups—for example, in how negative their stereotypes are about the out-groups and the degree to which they want to exclude out-groups from their lives. Psychological theory can help explain why some individuals become more extreme than others in their prejudice. Social representation theory reminds us that some of the prejudice in society is, however, shared by people and part of our culture.

THE RELATIONSHIP BETWEEN PREJUDICE AND DISCRIMINATION

The debate over the relationship between prejudice and discrimination revolves around a larger issue, the relationship between all attitudes and any kind of behavior. Some believe that there is a basic consistency between attitudes and behavior, a belief that is based on what is called the *latent process* conception of attitudes. In this view, attitudes function within the individual, intervene between stimulus and response, and give direction and consistency to the response (De-Fleur and Westie, 1963). But is there a basic consistency between prejudice and discrimination? Do prejudiced people always discriminate, and do nonprejudiced people always act in accord with their attitudes by not discriminating?

There is evidence that no such consistency between prejudice and discrimination exists. LaPiere (1934) and a Chinese couple took long motor tours of the United States in the early 1930s, during a period of intense and widespread prejudice toward the Chinese in this country. From notes he took on these trips, LaPiere concluded:

> In something like ten thousand miles of motor travel, twice across the United States, up and down the Pacific Coast, we met definite rejection from those asked to serve us *just once*. We were received at 66 hotels, auto camps, and "Tourist Homes," refused at one. We were served in 184 restaurants and cafes scattered throughout the country and treated with what I judged to be more than ordinary consideration in 72 of them (p. 231; italics added).

That is, there was only one instance of discrimination during these motor trips. Later, LaPiere wrote to the 250 hotels and restaurants where he and the Chinese couple had been served, asking "Will you accept members of the Chinese race as guests of your establishment? One hundred twenty-eight of the 250 proprietors replied. Ninety-two percent of the restaurants and cafes and 91 percent of the hotels, auto camps, and tourist homes replied that they would not. The remainder replied "Uncertain; depends on circumstance" (p. 234). Only one proprietor, a woman who had remembered the Chinese couple and had liked them, answered yes.

LaPiere identified the proprietors' responses to the questionnaire as prejudice, of which there was a considerable amount, and their actual receptions of the Chinese couple and LaPiere with discrimination, of which there was almost none. He concluded that there is no inherent consistency between attitudes and action, at least when the former is measured by responses to a questionnaire, as it usually is, while the latter is measured by observed behavior in real settings. Other researchers have drawn similar conclusions.

After reviewing these studies, Wicker (1969) argued that on the average only about 10 percent of people's behavior can be attributed to their attitudes. This would mean that there is essentially no relationship between prejudice and discrimination. But this may be an oversimplification of the issue.

Robert Merton (1949) devised a typology of four kinds of persons who combine prejudice and discrimination in different ways. This typology is useful in showing how the connection between prejudice and discrimination can vary from person to person and from one situation to the next. Unprejudiced nondiscriminators, or all-weather liberals, adhere to the American Creed in both belief and action. Such persons will act in accord with their beliefs in nearly all situations, by not discriminating, save for those instances where there is strong cultural support for discrimination. Unprejudiced discriminators, or fair-weather liberals, are persons of expediency who will act in accordance with their own beliefs only insofar as nondiscrimination is the easier and more profitable course of action. Thus, they will act inconsistently, depending on whether there is weak or strong cultural support for discrimination. Merton added that such persons often suffer from guilt and shame for having deviated in action from their beliefs in the American Creed.

Prejudiced nondiscriminators, or fair-weather illiberals, are reluctant conformists to the American Creed. They do not discriminate because they fear that such an action would be costly and painful. For instance, a merchant would lose minority group customers. Like the fair-weather liberal, this is a person of expediency. The basic difference between these two types of people, however, is that the fair-weather illiberal is under a strain when conforming with the American Creed, while the liberal is under strain when deviating from it. The prejudiced discriminator, or all-weather illiberal, is consistent in beliefs and actions in nearly all situations, by discriminating consistently except in those instances where there is strong cultural support for nondiscrimination. This typology of persons and situations is illustrated in Figure 5.3, where inconsistency between belief and action is shown in the area of poor prediction.

Of course, it is too simple to think that prejudice alone determines people's behavior. Prejudice alone does not determine whether people discriminate or not. Even common sense tells us that we consider many things in deciding how to act in a given situation. For one thing, we reflect on the possible consequences of our actions before acting. Even a highly prejudiced person is likely to demur from discriminating when that action is against the law and he or she is aware of the likelihood of getting caught at it. A second consideration people often make in decisions about interracial contact is just how intimate the contact between them and members of another group will be. It is much easier for nonprejudiced persons to act in accord with their professed feelings and lack of prejudice and discrimination when the contact with members of another group is impersonal rather than

FIGURE 5.3   THE RELATIONSHIP BETWEEN PREJUDICE AND CONDITIONING

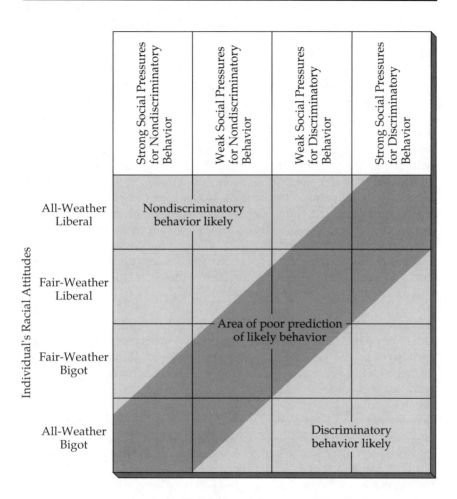

Source: Lyle G. Warner and Melvin L. DeFleur, "Attitude as an Interactional Concept: Social Constraint and Social Distance as Intervening Variables between Attitudes and Action," *American Sociological Review* 34: 1532–169 (April 1969), Figure 3, p. 168. Adapted by permission.

intimate. People also bring competing attitudes and motives into any action situation, which was described as part of Myrdal's (1944) American dilemma in Chapter 2. All of these possibilities have been researched, and it has been found that the correspondence between prejudice and discrimination does indeed vary in accord with these additional considerations.

Some observers of the attitude-behavior controversy feel that attitude-behavior inconsistency is a "straw man" issue, an issue of little substance based on the false premise that while there is only an imperfect correspondence between people's attitude and behavior, there is somehow a perfect correlation between people's behavior in one situation and that in another. But "the problem of correlating attitudes and behavior is no different from the problem of correlating behavior in one situation with behavior in another situation" (Kiesler, Collins, and Miller, 1969:27). While it is true that people sometimes act inconsistently with their true beliefs and feelings, is it not equally true that people behave inconsistently from one situation to the next, quite apart from their attitudes? Actually, when trying to determine the correspondence between measures of prejudice and discrimination, for instance, are we not simply asking about the correlation between two types of behavior in different situations?

To illustrate, let us reexamine the LaPiere (1934) study. LaPiere took proprietors' responses to a questionnaire as an indication of their racial attitudes. Is not the answering of a questionnaire about serving Chinese a type of behavior, rather than an attitude, to be considered just as much a behavior as checking a Chinese couple into a hotel or waiting on them in a restaurant? The issue in LaPiere's study is not so much an inconsistency between attitudes and action as it is an inconsistency between actions in different situations. The problem is that it is clearly easier to discriminate against Chinese when answering a questionnaire than it is when a well-dressed Chinese couple show up with a European at the front desk of a hotel, seeking accommodations for the night. In the parlance of psychology, these responses have different thresholds, holding constant the underlying attitude. A psychologist, D. T. Campbell (1963:160), explained: "But this is no evidence of inconsistency. Inconsistency would be represented if those who refused face to face accepted by questionnaire, or if those who accepted by questionnaire refused face to face. There is no report that such cases occurred."

Moreover, note that the stimulus objects, those to which the managers and clerks responded, change in LaPiere's study. On the questionnaire, they were asked, "Will you accept members of the Chinese race as guests in your establishment?" But, on the "behavioral" measure, the managers and clerks responded to more than a cultural stereotype; they responded to all sorts of things about a particular Chinese couple and their European companion. LaPiere (1934:232) admits as much: "My Chinese friends were skillful smilers...Finally, I was impressed with the fact that even where some tensions developed due to the strangeness of the Chinese it would evaporate immediately when they spoke in unaccented English." But only race was salient on the questionnaire.

The controversy over the consistency between attitudes and behavior, and thus that between prejudice and discrimination, belongs primarily to a theoretical tradition in American psychology called *cognitive consistency theory*. Actually, cognitive consistency theory is a collection of theories, all of which share in the conviction that people attempt to keep in balance the ways in which they perceive, think, evaluate, and then act in their environment (cf. Fishbein, 1967; Insko, 1967). When people experience an inconsistency or imbalance in their perceptions, cognitions, feelings, and actions, they will take steps to restore the balance, making the world as they see it into a coherent whole again. We touched on this tradition earlier in the chapter, in regard to the cognitive approach to prejudice.

Leon Festinger (1957; 1964) formulated a theory of cognitive dissonance which is part of the larger cognitive tradition. He made an important distinction in this theory, one that is surely worth noting here. There are two types of dissonance, he wrote: predecision dissonance and postdecision dissonance. The former precedes any given action, while the latter follows and is, in a sense, a consequence of prior action. It is his focus on postdecision dissonance that made Festinger's theory new and different. Festinger observed that dissonance often follows from making a decision, any decision, although not all decisions arouse dissonance. "On the whole, the evidence is clear that simply making a decision does not guarantee the onset of dissonance-reduction processes" (Festinger, 1964:156). One must voluntarily commit oneself to a course of action, having freely chosen among alternatives, and this course of action must have real and lasting consequences, as long as one sticks to the decision, before dissonance over a decision is experienced. Buying a car is often given as an example of such a decision.

To validate a choice and simultaneously reduce any dissonance aroused by thinking about passed-over alternatives, people will often accentuate the attractiveness or worth of the chosen course of action after they have already set out on it. That is, they will try to bring their attitudes into line with their actions after, not before, they have acted. They may do this in a number of ways, for instance, by systematically avoiding exposure to any information critical of the choice. A new owner of a car might refrain from reading anything complimentary about other cars she might have bought but that are now passed-over alternatives.

Festinger's point is that once action is taken and a decision is made, that choice may sometimes set into motion pressures for a person to rationalize the course of action as attractive, valuable, or at least the best alternative possible. Might not this be the relationship between prejudice and discrimination, or more correctly, between discrimination and prejudice? Because of the felt need to discriminate, or because the person or those dear to her or him have done it in the past, a person might become prejudiced to vindicate the discrimination. Because a person has discriminated in the past, and seemingly has made the decision to do so, he or she may feel the need for prejudice so as to validate the course of action on which he or she is already set. The person elevates the value of discrimination by being prejudiced, and simultaneously depresses the value of the rejected alternative. This is consistent with the view of sociological conflict theory on the psychology of prejudice. It also appears to be consistent with the stand of the Supreme Court and other branches of the federal government with respect to racial integration and affirmative action programs. Discrimination is being dealt with, and it is assumed that attitudes will subsequently fall in line.

SOCIOLOGICAL THEORY AND PREJUDICE

Conflict theory contends that groups struggle for wealth, power, and privilege in modern society, and this often brings discrimination and ethnic stratification. From this perspective, members of ethnic groups become prejudiced toward one another by simply pursuing their respective self-interests. That is, "prejudice appears to be one of the results rather than a cause of intergroup conflict" (Bernard, 1951:248). Prejudice on the part of the majority can justify its subordination of the minority by making it seem that the minority got what it deserved, or by making it appear that the condition is the fault of the minority. Prejudice vindicates a course of action on which people are already set, one of blatant self-interest in dealing with a rival, and it serves to reduce dissonance over having taken this course of action.

Perhaps it is Herbert Blumer (1958a) who has most forcibly formulated this sociological view of prejudice. From the sociological perspective, prejudice is a set of beliefs and feelings about racial and ethnic groups. It can include feelings of superiority, beliefs about innate racial traits, claims to certain privileges and prestige, and fear and mistrust of the minority group. Moreover, prejudice is a predisposition to action, for it can motivate behavior: "It guides, incites, cows, and coerces" (Blumer, 1958a:5).

In this perspective prejudice is also a sense of group position and "fundamentally a matter of relationship between racial groups" (Blumer, 1958a:3). Its origins belong to the historical relationship between groups, not to the personality composition of a single, contemporary individual. Prejudice is a social phenomenon. It waxes and wanes with public sentiment and through the transmission of information. As race relations become a public issue, at least in a pejorative sense, as political leaders focus on the ethnic struggle for wealth and power, as racial stereotypes are invigorated and sharpened, prejudice intensifies and becomes more widespread. "It is this *sense of societal position* emerging from this collective process of characterization," Blumer concludes, "which provides the basis of race prejudice. The dominant group is not concerned with the subordinate group as such but it is deeply concerned with its position vis-à-vis the subordinate group" (p. 4). Recall that the ethnic hierarchy as a social representation taps this form of prejudice. It refers to group positions on an ethnic hierarchy.

The contrast between the sociological and psychological perspectives on prejudice is illustrated in their respective explanations of anti-Semitism in Nazi Germany. It is explained in *The Authoritarian Personality* that anti-Semitism is a product of internal psychic conflict. This conflict begins with harsh and rigid discipline in the home, representing authority that the child comes to hate. Over the years, however, the individual learns to displace this hostility away from parents and toward out-groups.

Historically, Jews have been such scapegoats in the minds of their oppressors. Note that in this version of prejudice, Jews have only a shadowy existence, like inkblots, being merely passive objects in the tormented minds of others. This seems to reduce ethnic relations not only to psychodynamics, but also to the relation between members of only one group and their distorted imaginations.

From the sociological perspective, German prejudice toward Jews was a sense of group position activated by leaders of the Nazi movement. Jews were a middleman minority in Central Europe, playing a social and economic role that can bring a group into conflict with many powerful sectors of the surrounding society. Their ethnic solidarity enables the middleman minority to undercut their competitors, and "the result is a tremendous degree of concentration in, and domination of, certain lines of endeavor" (Bonacich, 1973:587). This can antagonize business interests, organized labor, and the general public in the larger society.

Prejudice, from this perspective, is a tactic in trying to dislodge the middleman minority from its economic position. Blumer (1958a:5) wrote that the source of prejudice is a felt challenge to a sense of group position, and "it may be in the form of encroachment at countless points of proprietary claim; it may be a challenge to power and privilege; it may take the form of economic competition." Bonacich (1973:592) took an extreme view when she wrote:

> The difficulty of breaking entrenched middleman monopolies, the difficulty of controlling the growth and extension of their economic power, pushes host countries to ever more extreme reactions. One finds increasingly harsh measures, piled on one another, until, when all else fails, "final solutions" are enacted.

The point is that psychology is hardly a full explanation of ethnic relations, even anti-Semitism, and the student must keep this in mind. Ideally the psychological and sociological perspectives complement one another, each making up for some of what the other lacks.

Some writers in sociology go so far as to say that discrimination has essentially nothing to do with prejudice. Knowles and Prewitt (1969) wrote that much of the racism in American society exists in societal institutions, not in the psychology of individuals. Indeed, such institutional arrangements as racial discrimination in hiring and school admissions and racially biased I.Q. tests require neither prejudice nor commitment to discrimination. They require only people's conformity to such practices.

The position taken in this book, however, stops short of such sociological determinism. Our own view on ethnic change is complemented best by social representation and cognitive dissonance as theory, although we feel that virtually all schools in sociology and psychology can be used together in a fuller understanding of the dynamics behind ethnic change. Discrimination is rooted in ethnic competition in modern society, from our own sociological perspective, and not in the psychological traits of individuals.

Discrimination does produce prejudice, however, as it simultaneously results in the exclusion of a minority out-group and its divergence from the majority in-group. Prejudice can be shared by in-group members in the form of an ethnic hierarchy, for example, and it is a way an in-group reduces for its members any postdecision dissonance over their discrimination against out-groups, along the lines of cognitive dissonance theory. Discrimination sets into motion two types of drift. One is at the societal level, the divergence between the life chances of the minority and majority groups, and the other is psychological, the perceived belief dissimilarity between members of the diverging groups.

The latter process follows the principles of postdecision dissonance reduction and assimilation/contrast effect, but it is also grounded in the social reality of the diverging groups. That reality often includes increasing social distance, even physical distance, between members of the diverging groups, so that stereotypes and prejudicial feelings are not checked by close and continuous human contact. The result is sharply contrasting stereotypes of in-group and out-group members. These stereotypes are easily learned by each succeeding generation, through deliberate conditioning or unintentional modeling and imitation, and fulfill several psychological functions for in-group members. For example, prejudice against others maintains a positive social identity, and thus self-esteem for in-group members, and the out-group can serve for some as an inkblot for their own internal turmoil. Prejudice formed in this manner can lead to more discrimination, perpetuating the discrimination and its results, which appear more and more to support the original discrimination and subsequent prejudice. Cause and effect blur, and a vicious circle forms.

SUMMARY AND ASSESSMENT

Prejudice serves certain psychological needs, arising as it does out of the need to know, the need to have an orderly view of the world, the need for affiliation and a positive social identity, and even the need to displace certain psychic conflicts onto out-groups. It is learned in many ways, through conditioning and modeling, for example. These are among the reasons for prejudice in modern American society, none of which have much to do with ethnic relations and societal change. Once prejudice is formed, however, it helps shape the character of ethnic relations in society. Prejudiced people are predisposed to discriminate, an action which, if it is on a large enough scale, can lead to the exclusion of minority out-groups and their divergence from the majority in-group. This can and does occur, even though modern society is supposedly ready for ethnic and racial assimilation. The role for the psychology of prejudice and discrimination in the academic study of American ethnicity in recent years has been to explain prejudice and discrimination in a society in which it should not occur.

Psychological perspectives complement the broader sociological theories on ethnic and race relations. By their reference to subjective states of mind, such as prejudice, the psychological perspectives round out the sociological emphasis on objective conditions of society as the true forces behind ethnic change.

Assimilationism is complemented the most in the psychological approach, although it can certainly complement other sociological theories on ethnicity as well. The assimilationists have argued that societal change would mean an end to ethnicity, including prejudice and discrimination. That has not happened, of course, but the idea that prejudice and discrimination are due to the psychology of individual Americans, who unfortunately lag behind the evolving nature of society, helped explain the stubborn persistence of ethnocentrism.

Psychology can be used with conflict theory, too. For instance, the psychological thesis that prejudice causes discrimination complements the reverse contention of sociological conflict theory that discrimination causes prejudice. This contradiction suggests that objective competition and subjective feelings can reinforce one another; both are merely parts of a large whole. Thus the psychology of prejudice and sociological conflict theory are complementary, together providing a more comprehensive view of ethnic and race relations.

We must always be mindful that the psychology of prejudice is only a partial explanation of ethnic relations. Its emphasis on subjective, internal, and psychological states as the dynamic but often hidden forces behind ethnic relations must always be counterbalanced by the sociological perspective, with its emphasis on the societal conditions of ethnic relations. We must understand how the social reality of ethnic relations shapes the internal psychological states of the people involved, not only how psychology can affect social reality. Writers in both psychology and sociology have tried from time to time to reduce the study of ethnic relations to their own perspective. The dynamic exchange between proponents of these perspectives can be a positive stimulant to the study of ethnic and race relations, in our view, and psychology will always have a role in the larger study of ethnicity. In this chapter on the psychology of prejudice and discrimination, we should allow a psychologist (Gordon Allport, 1962) to have the last word:

> In order to improve relationships within the human family it is imperative to study causes. One valuable and valid approach lies in an analysis of social settings, situational forces, demographic and ecological variables, legal and economic trends.... At the same time, none of these social forces accounts for all that happens—in technical terms, for all the variance in group relations. Deviant personalities, if they gain influence, can hasten, alter, or retard social forces. What is more, these forces in and of themselves are of no avail unless they are channelized through the medium of conforming personalities. Hence to understand the full causal chain, we require a close study of habits, attitudes, perceptions and motivation (pp. 129–130).

CHAPTER

6

୭/୭

SOCIETAL AND ETHNIC CHANGE: TOWARD THEORETICAL COMPLEMENTARITY

T he possibility that there are two trends in societal change—one that brings the inclusion of some ethnic groups into American society and another that results in the exclusion of other groups—was presented in the preceding chapters as a correct depiction of ethnic and societal change. The assimilationists argued that change brings the fusion of ethnic groups into a unitary society. Groups integrate, acculturate, and finally fuse into a single structure and a common culture. By contrast, conflict theorists said that groups compete for societal resources, a competition that they say actually grows more intense in the change process. Powerful groups oppress weaker ones, excluding them from wealth, power, and privilege. Thus there is no final fusion between the powerful and the weak; rather they diverge, sharing unequally in society. The continuation of ethnic differences in the course of societal change was also seen in pluralism, and psychologists added that ethnic prejudice and discrimination also continue into our time.

The position taken in this chapter is that societal change has brought the inclusion of some ethnic groups into American society and the exclusion of others from it. The task is to identify the historical forces behind the dual phenomena of inclusion and exclusion. The variable impacts of these historical forces on Native Americans, Mexican Americans, European Americans, African Americans, and Asian Americans will be examined in Part III.

KEY TERMS

ETHNIC CHANGE: *Ethnicity is an evolving or emergent phenomenon, because groups as well as their relations with one another and with the larger society continuously change.* In the change process, groups can be included into the larger society or they can be excluded from it. Thus some ethnic groups can converge with the change process, while others can diverge from it.

INCLUSION AND EXCLUSION: *Inclusion of an ethnic group into the larger society is evident when that group shares with others a common culture, similar socioeconomic characteristics, and societal resources by virtue of its nonexclusive participation in the larger society. Exclusion is evident when an ethnic group does not share with others a common culture, similar socioeconomic characteristics, and societal resources because of its exclusive participation in the larger society.* It is by degree that any ethnic group has been either included into or excluded from American society. At one extreme of this continuum is the full assimilation or fusion of an ethnic group with others into the wider society, and at the other extreme is the complete and permanent exclusion of a group from society, possible only through its extermination or forced emigration. The instances of inclusion and exclusion of ethnic groups in American history, however, fall somewhere between the two extremes.

ETHNIC CHANGE IN AMERICAN SOCIETY

Both inclusion and exclusion have occurred in American society. Reasons for the dual phenomena of inclusion and exclusion in the nation's history will be discussed in a series of seven propositions.

PROPOSITION 1

Ethnic groups and their relations in America have changed with a changing society. Ethnic change has revolved around the intergroup exchange of land, labor, and capital.

Theories should place ethnic relations in the context of the larger society in which they occur. This advice is often given by social scientists (Bernard, 1951; Lieberson, 1961; Newman, 1973; Van den Berghe, 1967). Moreover, society is frequently considered a process in sociology, or a social and economic network that is continuously changing (e.g., Buckley, 1967; Olsen, 1968). Indeed, the United States has changed from an agrarian to an industrial and now a post-industrial society (Chapter 1). The plan of this chapter is to analyze ethnic change in the context of these changes in American society.

Ethnic relations have been implicated in the intergroup exchange of land, labor, and capital, as well as the three phases of societal change. There was first the exchange of land on the frontier between Native Americans, Hispanos in the Southwest, and white settlers during the agrarian phase of American history. The settlers eventually expropriated all but small parcels of Indian land, transplanted a European market economy and made capital improvements on it, and otherwise brought the land into the production of surplus wealth. Hispanic land in the Southwest was also expropriated in the process. From this point, the histories of Native Americans, Hispanos, and the larger American society began to diverge.

Expropriation of Indian land was followed by the need for immigrant labor in America. Immigrant groups first settled on the land and took up work in American agriculture. Later, in the nation's evolution toward an industrial society, the stream of immigrants began to flow into its industrial centers. Children and grandchildren of immigrants would later become college-educated white-collar workers in the post-industrial phase of American history. That is, immigrant groups have changed as America's labor needs evolved from an agrarian to an industrial and then post-industrial society. It is in the context of the country's changing labor needs that the history of its immigrant groups must be set.

To meet the labor needs on an expanding southern frontier, up to 678,000 Africans were brought to what became the United States from the seventeenth century to the outbreak of the Civil War, and most became slaves in the southern plantation economy. European immigrants worked throughout America, and nearly 37 million came to the United States between 1820 and 1986. First came immigrants from northern and western Europe, followed by those from southern and eastern Europe. Early Asian immigrants were primarily from China and Japan, and they concentrated in the work force on the West Coast. Current Asian immigration comes from virtually all parts of Asia. Immigrants have also come from the Americas, particularly from Mexico. Hispanos were actually living in the Southwest prior to the coming of Anglos, and Mexican immigration into the United States picked up in the twentieth century. The largest ethnic groups in 1980 were English and German Americans, followed by Irish, African, French, Italian, Scottish, Polish, and Mexican Americans (Lieberson and Waters, 1988).

While the history of ethnic groups is situated in the economic history of the nation, ethnic and racial groups are not equivalent to economic classes. Economic classes result from humans' relation to production, while ethnic groups are products of commonalities in race, culture, and nationality, all of which are theoretically independent of the economic order. Ethnic groups can exist prior to their entry into any given economic order, while economic classes cannot. Nevertheless, once ethnic groups enter into production or otherwise become part of an economic order, their histories are shaped by economic change. Ethnic change in the course of societal change—agrarian, industrial, and post-industrial—is shown in Figure 6.1.

Ethnic and racial diversity, or pluralism, is the beginning state of ethnic change, and in the United States it appears that pluralism is also the end state, at least up to this point in time. In American history there have been the dual forces of inclusion and exclusion, immigration and its restriction, and the results have been both assimilation and the continuation of ethnic and racial diversity in American society. To depict and explain this process, assimilationism and conflict theory must be viewed in a complementary manner. Assimilationism and conflict theory are each only partial explanations of ethnic change in America, but each theory makes up for some of what the other lacks. Thus a more complete explanation of ethnic change can emerge by using the two theories together.

PROPOSITION 2

Ethnic relations in America have evolved from two types of ethnic contact.

Ethnic relations obviously begin with intergroup contact, and there have been two kinds of ethnic contact in American history. First, contact occurred between immigrant settlers and indigenous Americans on the frontier, namely, Native Americans across the continent and Hispanos in the Southwest. This was contact between indigenous and immigrant groups. Following their fight for control of the land, as the more powerful settlers gained control and subordinated the indigenous peoples, Native Americans were largely excluded from the revised social and economic system of the settlers and were restricted to reservations. Hispanos and later Mexican immigrants were subordinated in a system of ethnic stratification, or colonial labor system (Barrera, 1979).

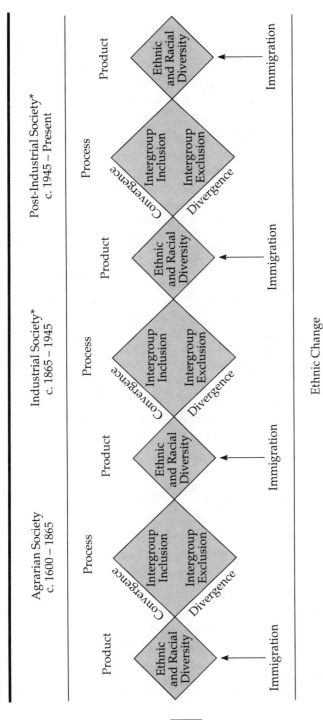

FIGURE 6.1 SOCIETAL AND ETHNIC CHANGE

Agrarian Society
c. 1600 – 1865

Industrial Society*
c. 1865 – 1945

Post-Industrial Society*
c. 1945 – Present

Process

Product

Ethnic and Racial Diversity

Immigration

Convergence

Divergence

Intergroup Inclusion

Intergroup Exclusion

Ethnic Change

*Industrial society is identified with the building of urban, industrial centers and the growth in industrial, blue-collar work, while post-industrial society is identified with the expansion of white-collar work.

The second type of contact was the immigration of labor into the country from virtually every corner of the world. Africans, Asians, Europeans, Mexicans, and others came here to work. This was contact between immigrant groups. In most cases this contact was voluntary; immigrants willingly came to the United States. In the case of African Americans, however, the contact was involuntary, for it was imposed on them. Although the experiences of immigrant groups in this country vary, and these variations are significant, all immigrant groups share the experience of meeting the country's labor needs. The difference in immigrant and indigenous contact is significant, as noted by Lieberson (1961:906):

> ...where the migrant group is dominant, frequently the indigenous population suffers sharp numerical declines.... Conflict often accompanies the establishment of migrant superordination. Subordinate indigenous populations generally have no alternative location and do not control the numbers of new ethnic populations admitted into their area. By contrast, when the indigenous population dominates the political and economic conditions [which is true of the contact between early and late immigrant groups], the migrant group is introduced into the economy of the indigenous population.... [T]he migrants may fare better than if they remained in their homeland. Hence their subordination occurs without great conflict. In addition, the migrants usually have the option of returning to their homeland and the indigenous population controls the number of new immigrants in the area.

The contact between white settlers and Native Americans did result in conflict, and the conflict frequently involved the use of raw force. Settlers took land from Native Americans by force, gradually assumed control of the frontier, and ultimately transformed that force into legitimate political rule (cf. Glazer, 1954). Force was also used in the expropriation of Hispanic land. Later immigrants were comparatively willing to accept Anglo-Saxon cultural, political, and economic hegemony when they entered the country on the other side of Lenski's (1966) political cycle—force, legitimate rule, force (see Chapter 4).

PROPOSITION 3

Relations between America's immigrant and indigenous people evolved out of their conflict over land proprietorship and use on the frontier. As the more powerful immigrants transplanted their market economy and a European legal system onto American soil, the indigenous peoples were either excluded from the revised economic and social order or found some measure of accommodation to it at the bottom of the labor hierarchy. Both involved exclusiveness between the immigrants and indigenous people,

and this exclusiveness has meant a divergence between America's indige-
nous groups and the larger society.

There was conflict between Native Americans and white settlers on the frontier over land use and proprietorship. The settlers expropriated Indian land, established a market economy and a European political system, and brought the land into the production of a surplus. To European settlers, land represented a tool of production and a means to create wealth. Surplus wealth was extracted from the land, distributed through a system of markets, and consumed at points distant from its production. Picture farmers growing grain that is then shipped by rail or barge to distant cities. Investments of capital and labor were required to bring the land into production and build a distribution system, and European notions of private property were established on the frontier with settler political hegemony to protect these investments. That is, immigrant farmers owned their land in the sense that it was their private property, and this secured for them the benefits of their work. It was a case of capitalist penetration into a frontier.

As their wealth and numbers grew, the settlers became the superior power in North America. From a position of power, settlers expropriated more and more Indian land and became more powerful and wealthy in the process. Thus, land in America was converted to new uses and ownership, consistent with the principles of a market economy and a European system of law and land proprietorship. This same Anglo-European economic system reached Hispanos in the Southwest during the 1800s, and the result was the same—land expropriation.

Although great labor needs were created, Native Americans were largely bypassed as a potential source of labor. Instead, the country turned almost solely to immigrant labor, and Native Americans were excluded for generations from the wider social and economic order. Some might wish to put it more strongly by saying that the American Indian was nearly exterminated. Native Americans were certainly isolated on reservations, out of the way, where they stayed on a course divergent from that of the larger society. Even today, evidence for this divergence can be found in the relatively low rates of Native American participation in the labor force, as well as their low levels of education and high rates of mortality and morbidity.

Once Hispanic land was expropriated in the Southwest, the indigenous Hispanos and later Mexican immigrants were relegated to the lower jobs in the region's labor hierarchy. They faced both a split and segmented labor market, for they concentrated in segregated work gangs and were paid at lower wages even when they worked alongside Anglos. It was a colonial labor system (Chapter 8). Hispanos and Mexican immigrants worked at first in agriculture, as well as mining and railroads, and then in the region's industry. Immigration from Mexico fluctuated with the region's labor needs, reinforced by state immigration policies, such as the repatriation program in the 1930s and the later Bracero program for farm labor.

PROPOSITION 4

Immigrants came to this country as labor, and as the nation's labor needs have changed so have the immigrant groups.

Immense numbers of immigrants came to the United States in the eighteenth, nineteenth, and twentieth centuries—more than 60 million, either as free individuals, contract laborers, or slaves—to meet the labor needs of a growing country. It was the largest migration of people in the history of the world. During this period, the southern plantation economy expanded from the Atlantic Coast to the Mississippi Delta, and the larger national boundaries expanded from the Atlantic coast to the Pacific. This huge expanse of land absorbed thousands of immigrants and native-born settlers alike; one need only recall the Louisiana Purchase of 1803, the Treaty of Guadalupe Hidalgo in 1848, and the Homestead Act of 1862 to sense the scale of the national policy for populating a frontier that would stretch to the Pacific with immigrant settlers. The expansion of the frontier for immigrant settlement and the expropriation of Indian land were simply different sides of the same coin.

After the Civil War, the United States became an industrial nation. The opposition of southern planters to measures required for industrial growth had been nullified, and hundreds of factories, foundries, mills, and packinghouses were built. This industrial growth pulled literally millions of immigrants into the country and put them to work. Immigrants by the thousands worked on building the railroads, one of the great construction endeavors of the era, and labored in industries in the nation's cities. While many people stayed on the land and in agriculture beyond the second half of the nineteenth century, the percentage of farmers and farm workers to the total labor force declined from this point forward, going down to less than 2 percent today.

American agriculture played a critical role in the nation's industrial development. Agriculture and extraction (e.g., mining and logging) provided industry with the raw materials for production, with food for an urban labor force, and with a domestic market for industrial goods. Agriculture and extraction also furnished much of the investment capital for the construction of the country's industrial base. The construction of industrial plants and transportation systems required large sums of capital, and since prosperous American farmers had accumulated savings by early in the nineteenth century, they, along with wealthy merchants, helped finance American industry. While the savings of individual farmers and merchants were modest, corporations later concentrated these individual holdings into larger pools of venture capital, achieving a scale of investment necessary to build an industrial nation. Money still had to be borrowed from foreign nations, however, and American agriculture played an important role in these international dealings as well. Agricultural and mineral surpluses, even the land itself, were used as collateral in these foreign loans, and the sale of the surpluses to foreign countries helped Americans retire these debts. The expropriation of the Indian land, the conversion of this land into the production of a surplus, the sale of this surplus in a market economy, and the demand for industrial goods created by this transformation were all important in the growth of American industry in the nineteenth century.

From 1870 to 1950 the nation's labor force grew fivefold, from 13 million to 65 million workers (Hauser, 1964). Many of these workers were immigrants who, with their children, met the nation's growing and changing labor needs. As the country's labor needs expanded, they also changed from farming to industrial work, and the stream of immigrants shifted away from settlement on the frontier to the nation's industrial cities. While only 17 percent of the nation's labor force was engaged in manufacturing by 1820, nonfarm blue-collar workers represented over 40 percent of the labor force in 1920, and the number of workers in agriculture to the total labor force declined from 80 percent to 35 percent in this same period (Hauser, 1964). The transformation of the United States into an industrial society is the second phase of societal change.

During the industrialization of America, many laboring jobs were deskilled from the crafts to the more simple routines of factory workers (Bodnar, 1985). Mechanization of the production of goods such as textiles and machinery resulted in the specialization of jobs into routine tasks, symbolized by the simple and repetitive work on an assembly line. Thus, the nation's labor needs gravitated toward the unskilled, the niche that many immigrants filled.

The experiences of many immigrant groups, people from all over the world, converged in this country to meet its labor needs in agriculture and extraction, and then in industry. There were German and Scandinavian farmers in the Midwest, African slaves (and, after the Civil War, black sharecroppers) in the plantation South, Irish construc-

171

tion workers and industrial laborers in the Northeast, and Chinese miners and construction workers in the West. All of these groups and others shared experiences at work in America; all provided manual labor, more or less.

There was also divergence, however, as some groups were to enter the urban, industrial labor market sooner than others. For example, African Americans became industrial workers in the twentieth century, later than many European immigrants. It was the European immigrants who first entered the industrial order of the North, in the nineteenth century. The significance of this divergence became clear in the twentieth century, when the modern institutions for the greater inclusion of immigrants and their children first appeared in the northern cities.

The structure of nineteenth-century American society permitted only a limited measure of ethnic inclusion. The process of inclusion is facilitated greatly by secondary institutions that enable immigrants to enculturate quickly, disperse throughout a variety of jobs and geographical settings, and come into frequent contact with members of other ethnic groups and with the cultural symbols of the society at large. Secondary institutions for such integration and acculturation of the masses simply did not exist in the nineteenth century.

The occupational structure of a society is one institution that can facilitate ethnic inclusion. The more diverse is a nation's occupational structure, the greater is the chance for the occupational diversification of any of its ethnic and racial groups, and this is an important step toward inclusion. There is also a greater potential for the occupational mobility of all when a goodly portion of a nation's total jobs are at the middle and upper levels. If, in addition, much of the work requires schooling, as white-collar jobs do, then the chance is greater for the enculturation of immigrant groups. None of this was true, however, for nineteenth-century America.

The occupational structure in the nineteenth century was neither broad nor diverse. Rather it was narrowly confined to manual labor, the bulk of which was in unskilled work. The chances for occupational mobility, and thus the occupational diversification of ethnic groups, was limited to some members moving up to skilled trades and not much further, although sons and daughters of farmers could and did move out of agriculture and into the urban labor market. Missing from the nineteenth-century labor market was the multitude of white-collar jobs now found in the nation's occupational structure. Furthermore, manual workers, skilled and unskilled, rural and urban, were not put in touch with a national culture and the larger society in the course of their work. Thus they could exist easily in ethnic subsocieties and subcultures, without reaching into the larger society. Their work required neither schooling nor enculturation in the general sense. By way of illustration, children typically attended school for only five or six years and then took on a job apprenticeship.

All of this would change in the twentieth century with the expansion of white-collar jobs. Because white-collar workers require prolonged education (often through college) and must constantly manipulate cultural symbols, they are put in touch with the national culture. Combined with the spread of education, literacy, mass communication, and patterns of mass consumption, the growth of white-collar jobs has resulted in a greater capacity to assimilate diverse ethnic groups, in potential if not in practice. This observation is obviously consistent with the theme of assimilationism.

Moreover, it was typical in the past century for unskilled manual laborers to work in ethnically homogenous gangs, and the labor market was ethnically stratified. For example,

> In the ready-made clothing industry, Jews predominated in small firms with minimal mechanization...while Italians concentrated in large factories.... Serbs and Croats in New York City were heavily involved in freight handling. Italians dominated construction gangs and barber shops in Buffalo, Philadelphia, and Pittsburgh. By 1918, Italians represented 75 percent of the women in the men's and boy's clothing industry and 93 percent of the females doing hand embroidery in New York City. Nearly all of the 3,000 employees in the Peninsular Car Company in Detroit by 1900 were Polish. Polish women dominated restaurant and kitchen jobs in Chicago by 1909.... By 1920, one study found an incredible 69 percent of Slovak males in coal mining and about one-half of all Mexicans working as blast furnace laborers (Bodnar, 1985:64).

This ethnic concentration occurred within and across industries, and it isolated immigrant groups from one another as well as from the larger society. This tendency was also the case in the construction of railroads in the West and with farm labor in the South and Southwest. In the construction of the transcontinental railroad, for instance, Chinese gangs laid track from the west, the Irish and Italians laid it from the east, and they met only in Utah. In the South, around the turn of the century, blacks were cultivating the land for white planters, while white labor was working at the mills in the towns. About this same time in New England, Anglo-Americans were the managers, the Irish were the foremen, and the Polish were the common laborers in the textile mills (Collins, 1946). Work done in this manner kept the contact of immigrant groups with one another on the job at a minimum, and this slowed the rate of their assimilation as it maintained their ethnic diversity. Labor needs and the organization of work fostered segrega-

tion on and off the job, in other words, and this segregation was reinforced in the patterns of social participation of the era.

The isolation of immigrant farmers in rural areas and the urban
concentration of immigrant workers in ethnic enclaves near factories
circumscribed people's patterns of social participation to doing things
with their own kind. This also had the effect of maintaining ethnic pluralism through the early twentieth century. For instance, industrialization fostered ethnic segregation in the nation's industrial cities from
late in the 1800s to World War II (Yancey, Erickson, and Juliani, 1976).
Factories needed enormous pools of labor, and in the absence of rapid
transportation or the widespread use of the automobile, immigrant
workers concentrated in large numbers in neighborhoods near their
work. Neighborhoods near packinghouses were for years ethnic enclaves; my own roots are in just such a neighborhood. Many of these
neighborhoods achieved institutional completeness, so that nearly all
of the needs of immigrant residents were met within these segregated
areas (Breton, 1964). The residential isolation of ethnic groups in rural
and urban areas reinforced ethnic exclusiveness in the past century.

The lack of mass public education played a role equal to that of the
occupational structure in maintaining ethnic diversity in America. It is
primarily through mass education that ethnic groups are enculturated
into the larger national culture. Of course, the occupational structure
and educational system of a society are thematically related. So long as
labor needs in America were confined to manual and unskilled work,
employers and society at large took little interest in the education and
enculturation of immigrant labor. What need had an immigrant for a
formal education when virtually all the nation's jobs required nothing
more than motor skills? Only bodies were needed, not minds. Moreover, children exited from education and became part of the labor
force at an early age. In the absence of the white-collar work that characterizes the current labor market in America, the government, private
capital, and organized labor had little interest in mass public education—that is, in the enculturation of immigrant labor—and the minimal investments made at the time in public education attest to this indifference. There was no large-scale mechanism for ethnic groups,
either in industry or on the land, to adopt a common culture rapidly.
This mechanism would come in the twentieth century, however, with
white-collar work.

The causes for ethnic exclusiveness and diversity in the past century were limited neither to the nation's occupational structure nor to
the lack of mass public education. In this era, many members of ethnic
groups were first-generation immigrants in this country who had
strong and relatively fresh memories of their homelands and the old

ways. This alone made for ethnic pluralism. Nevertheless, ethnic diversity persists in a society when its institutions for the absorption of immigrants are limited in scope, and this was the case in nineteenth-century America. Although Anglo-Saxons controlled the cultural, economic, and political apparatus of the larger society, including that on the frontier, their control was significantly circumscribed by the nature of the nation's labor needs. The nation needed field hands and factory workers; there was no need for the systematic and thorough enculturation of immigrant labor, nor for their occupational mobility. This allowed for the continuation of immigrant subsocieties and subcultures. The national character of America did not begin to take shape until the twentieth century (Handlin, 1973), the result, we contend, of changes in the country's labor needs.

Some mobility was certainly possible in the past for immigrant labor through rural-to-urban migration, politics, and the labor movement. For example, old European immigrants, those from northern and western Europe, were being pushed up in occupational status during the last two decades of the 1800s by the influx of new immigrants from southern and eastern Europe, and for many the route was from the farm to some form of white-collar work in town and city (Landale and Guest, 1990). Research in the latter half of the twentieth century has found almost 40 percent of the nation's prominent Irish in organized labor, with another 17 percent in politics, the two big routes for Irish mobility (Alba and Moore, 1982). Immigrants could also become entrepreneurs, a route taken by Asian Americans, among others, at the time. But careers in crime, business, politics, and organized labor brought people back into contact with their ethnic roots as much as with the larger society. This is illustrated by the Irish labor boss and by the lack of assimilation on the part of Chinese businessmen in the past century. Nevertheless, these mobility routes were important in the preparation of a group for later changes that permitted greater ethnic inclusion. Groups that were able to establish "turfs" successfully in business, crime, politics, and the trade unions could take better advantage of the growth of white-collar work and the expansion of education in the present century.

The limits to ethnic inclusion in the past century are only comparative and a matter of degree. Relative to the mechanisms for the absorption of ethnic groups that exist in the present century, there were few secondary institutions for inclusion in nineteenth-century America. If the experiences of the immigrant groups in the nineteenth century are compared with the exclusion of the Native Americans in the same period, however, it would seem that there was ample opportunity for the inclusion of immigrants. Our point is that the opportunity for the inclusion of immigrant labor expanded as America became a post-industrial society.

More than the native-born, immigrant women in the nineteenth century worked outside the home. For many immigrant families, it was necessary to put as many family members to work as possible, not only wives but also children (Bodnar, 1985). The women worked as domestics, in the garment industry and packinghouses, and elsewhere in industrial America. Many immigrant women who did not work outside the home took in boarders, often providing them with food and laundry service as well as lodging, or served other families from their own homes by taking in washing, for example. Other immigrant women worked at piece work from the home in the putting-out system of the garment industry.

The norm for better-off native-born women was to be a housewife, a role that crystallized by 1850 as a counterpoint to capitalism at the foundry and factory (Matthews, 1987). The housewife was the mainstay and protectress of a national culture, which was so rapidly changing with industrialization and immigration. Immigrant as well as black women were often servants in such homes, since neither could afford the luxury of not being employed. The role of housewife would change early in the twentieth century into that of a consumer of the mass production put out by industry, as other duties of the housewife began to decline with modern home appliances. By late in the twentieth century, however, most married women, native-born or immigrant, were working outside the home.

PROPOSITION 5

Because of the rise of white-collar work and the corresponding expansion of public education, strong forces for ethnic inclusion were set into motion in twentieth-century America. The histories of many immigrant groups in this period have converged with that of the larger society and culture.

There have been two great changes in the labor needs of this country; the first was the growth of industrial, blue-collar work in the past century, and the second was the rise of white-collar work in this century. These changes represent the second and third phases of societal change, the transformation of the United States into an industrial and then a post-industrial society. White-collar workers represented less than 18 percent of the nation's labor force in 1900, but by 1990 such workers represented over 65 percent of the country's labor force. Employment in agriculture has continued to decline, from nearly 38 percent of the labor force in 1900 to only 2.5 percent in 1990. The proportion of nonfarm blue-collar workers in the total labor force rose to over 40 percent by mid-century, but it has declined to less than 25 percent today. There has been a trend toward mental and service work in this century (Tables 6.1 and 6.2).

The growth in white-collar work has meant a growing number of clerks, teachers, medical specialists, engineers, and salaried managers in large public and private organizations. Trow (1966:438) pictured these changes:

> Since the Civil War...an economy based on thousands of small firms and businesses has been transformed into one based on large bureaucratized organizations.... When small organizations grow large, papers replace verbal orders; papers replace rule-of-thumb calculations of price and profit; papers carry records of work flow and inventory that in a small operation can be seen at a glance on the shop floor and materials shed. And as organizations grew, people had to be trained to handle those papers—to prepare them, to type them, to file them, to process them, to assess and use them. The growth of the secondary-school system after 1870 was in large part a response to the pull of the economy for a mass of white-collar employees with more than an elementary school education.

Since the 1960s, paper work has been increasingly replaced by computers.

With the two transformations of the American occupational structure, from an agrarian to an industrial and then to a post-industrial society, there have been accompanying changes in American public education. Thus the history of American education also consists of three distinct phases, as shown in Figure 6.2.

When the American economy was agrarian, only a small fraction of the American labor force needed a high school or college education, and only a small fraction were so educated (around 2 percent). Later, as the United States became an industrial and urban nation, still only a minority of eligible Americans were enrolled in the nation's high schools and colleges. About 12 percent of the eligible youth were attending high school in 1900, and only 2 or 3 percent were enrolled in college. As long as the nation's labor needs were manual and its occupational structure was confined in large measure to physical and blue-collar work, and as long as the nation needed bodies rather than minds, America had little in the way of mass public education.

The number of white-collar workers has grown phenomenally in this century, from under 18 percent of the labor force in 1900 to 66 percent in 1989. First, the number of clerks expanded at an extraordinary rate: a 28-fold increase in clerks occurred from 1900 to 1960. Later, after World War II, there was a great growth in the number of profes-

TABLE 6.1 AMERICAN OCCUPATIONAL DISTRIBUTION, 1900–1970

Occupation	1900	1920	1950	1970
White collar	17.6%	24.9%	36.6%	48.1%
Professional and technical	4.3	5.4	8.6	14.8
Managerial, official, professional	5.8	6.6	8.7	8.3
Clerical	3.0	8.0	12.3	17.9
Sales	4.5	4.9	7.0	7.1
Blue collar	35.8	40.2	41.1	36.0
Craftsmen	10.5	13.0	14.1	13.9
Operatives	12.8	15.6	20.4	17.6
Laborers (except farm)	12.5	11.6	6.6	4.5
Services	9.0	7.8	10.5	12.8
Private households	5.4	3.3	2.6	1.5
Farm workers	37.5	27.0	11.8	3.1

Source: Sar A. Levitan and William B. Johnston, *Work Is Here To Stay, Alas* (Salt Lake City, Utah: Olympus Publishing Company, 1973).

TABLE 6.2 AMERICAN OCCUPATIONAL DISTRIBUTION, 1970–1990

Occupation	1970	1980	1990
Managerial and professional	19.0%	22.7%	25.5%
Technical, sales, and administrative support	29.2	30.3	31.5
Service occupations	12.7	12.9	13.5
Precision production, craft, and repair	4.1	12.9	11.5
Operators, fabricators, and laborers	21.2	18.3	15.5
Farming, forestry, and fishing	3.8	2.9	2.5

Source: U.S. Bureau of the Census, 1983: 1-45; 1990: Equal Employment Opportunity File.

sional, technical, and kindred workers: "between 1950 and 1960 the total labor force increased by only 8 percent; but the number of professional, technical, and kindred workers grew by 68 percent, and these, of course, are the occupations that call for at least some part of a college education" (Trow, 1966:442–443). Not surprisingly, college enrollments have increased tremendously since 1950. Correlated with the increasing educational needs of American labor have been two transformations of American education in the twentieth century, one

FIGURE 6.2 CHANGE IN AMERICAN EDUCATION, 1870–1986

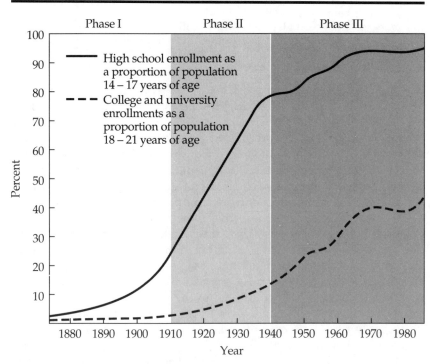

Source: Adapted from Martin Trow, "The Second Transformation of American Secondary Education," in Reinhard Bendix and Seymour Martin Lipset (eds.), *Class, Status, and Power*, 2nd ed., New York: Free Press, 1966. For 1960–1980: *Current Population Reports, School Enrollment—Social and Economic Characteristics of Students, October 1986.* Tables 1–3, p. 80. Washington, DC, Bureau of the Census.

associated with the training of clerks and another with the education of professionals and technicians.

First, the private academies, where a small number of elite students had been given a classical liberal education in the nineteenth century, were replaced by public high schools, where a mass of students were vocationally trained for clerical work. Until 1950, the high school diploma was for most students a terminal degree. After 1950 college enrollments climbed, as the nation's technical and professional workers were educated in colleges and universities (see Figure 6.2). This was the second transformation of American education. Trow (1966:441) summarized these two changes in American education:

The period 1870–1980 with which we are dealing falls naturally then into three phases. In Phase 1 secondary and higher education were by and large offering an academic education to an elite minority. Phase II, between roughly 1910 and 1940, saw the rapid growth of mass terminal secondary education, with higher education still offered to a small but slowly growing minority. Since 1940, or more precisely since World War II, we are (in Phase III) seeing the rapid growth of mass higher education.

The rise of white-collar work and the expansion of education have provided a greater potential for the inclusion of ethnic groups into American society. The occupational structure of the United States has become relatively broad and presently permits more occupational mobility for the nation's ethnic and racial groups. Children and grandchildren of immigrants can now move into a greatly expanded stratum of work, namely, the white-collar jobs. Moreover, children from diverse ethnic backgrounds have gone to public schools together for the first time on a mass scale, and they now stay together in school for longer and longer periods. They initially learned skills suitable for clerical work—reading, writing, and arithmetic—and later in the century they learned the more advanced skills for carrying out the complex functions of engineers, professionals, and technical workers.

Students were also enculturated in the process. They were Americanized at the very time they were learning job-related skills. As they were taught the Anglo core of American culture, the process of acculturation necessarily ran ahead of the structural assimilation of immigrant groups (Gordon, 1964). This enculturation continues for many young Americans through late adolescence and into early adulthood in the nation's colleges, especially the large state universities, which have increasingly replaced private and parochial institutions of higher learning in the education of most students.

Enculturation is not merely incidental to technical learning, for cultural facility is indispensable in the discharge of many white-collar duties. The middle-class style of life, its "respectability," and those verbal skills and sense of taste and discretion involved in the selling of oneself in the great salesroom—as Mills (1951) called the role of white-collar functionaries in twentieth-century America—all of these enculturated traits became vital in ethnic labor's search for a livelihood in the nation's economy. Immigrants' habits, their foreign ways, the apparent backwardness of the immigrants themselves—none of these would do in the white-collar salesroom, as American conformity and other-directedness became characteristic of the era (Mills, 1951; Riesman, 1950).

White-collar workers manipulate the symbols of a national culture, putting them in touch, day in and day out, with that culture, and

the enterprise requires prolonged enculturation and a working famil-
iarity with the national ethos. This is not to say that these workers are
all fully assimilated, or that they are far more assimilated than blue-
collar workers in all aspects of that process. Because of compulsory education, the spread of literacy, and the diffusion of mass media—all
products of the change process—blue-collar workers are also in touch
with a national society and culture. Often they show signs of greater
Americanization, in their patriotism, for instance. The basic contention
remains that societal change brings a greater potential for assimilation
through occupational diversification, educational expansion, and a
virtual explosion in the variety of experiences that put one in touch
with the larger nation.

One of the additional experiences that increased the potential for
ethnic inclusion is the contemporary mass consumption of goods and
American popular culture. Casual observation seems to corroborate
with Galbraith's (1971) conclusion that corporations produce standardized products and services, and through the consumption of these
goods levels the diversity of Americans. Clothing fashions are standardized, as shopping at the local mall attests; cars look the same, as
do many of our homes; and much of our food preferences converge
under McDonald's golden arches and at the local pizza franchise. We
seem to share a standardized version of the good life by consuming
the same products in unison. Some time ago, Georg Simmel saw this
coming with societal change (Frisby, 1986). He said that this external
culture would dominate our inner lives, but ironically there would be
always a distance between us and these externally made products.
Today, this means a throwaway society, for we have little attachment
to what we buy and consume, each unit being cheapened by its widespread diffusion as fashions come and go. More to the point, mass
consumption can level ethnic diversity, although slight ethnic variations in styles can persist.

First with their high-school diplomas and then with their college
sheepskins, many Americans from immigrant and working-class backgrounds took up white-collar work and became middle class: "moving
into the middle class was 41.1 percent of the sons of skilled workers,
33 percent of the sons of semi-skilled workers, and 23.8 percent of the
sons of unskilled workers" (Schneider, 1969:439). It was the offspring
of the more skilled blue-collar workers who on the average moved
into white-collar work, but of course middle-class children had the
best chance for finding such positions. While the children of working-
class origin generally found work at lower-level white-collar jobs,
there has been a significant movement of these children into the upper
levels of the middle class as well. For instance, Blau (1965) found that

40 percent of the salaried professionals in the early 1960s came from the working class and another 11 percent came from rural origins. Studies have found that, without exception, members of the nation's ethnic and racial groups have moved in large numbers into white-collar work and have attained higher levels of education in this century (Abramson, 1973; Greeley, 1974). Indeed, there is a pattern of European ethnic groups converging in education, occupation, culture, even intermarriage, and Asian Americans are reaching parity with European Americans (Alba, 1976 and 1985; Hirschman and Wong, 1984; Lieberson, 1980; Lieberson and Waters, 1988).

Comparing his study of occupational and income mobility in nineteenth-century Newburyport, Massachusetts, with similar studies of other cities in the twentieth century, Thernstrom (1966:614) came to a similar conclusion:

> ...but it is surely significant that the six studies covering the 1933–1956 period show two to three times as many laborers' sons in nonmanual positions as the figures for Newburyport in the latter half of the nineteenth century and for Indianapolis in 1910. In recent decades white-collar and professional occupations have made up an ever-increasing segment of the American occupational structure, and during the same period the American educational system has become markedly more democratic. The fruits of these two developments are graphically displayed here, in the rising proportion of laborers' sons who no longer face the necessity of making a living with their hands.

The expansion of public education and the growth of white-collar work have become major mechanisms for ethnic inclusion in American society. These mechanisms brought by societal change have expanded the opportunity for the integration and enculturation of the nation's ethnic and racial groups. Additional changes have occurred in twentieth-century America, and they, too, permit a greater degree of inclusion. Now there are mass media, mass consumption, and the spread of a mass culture. Due to the decentralization of the workplace, the growth of the suburbs, and the increasing convenience of transportation, there has also been a dispersion of ethnic groups out of the ghettos and into the metropolitan areas (Massey and Denton, 1985 and 1988; Massey and Mullan, 1984). That is, many immigrant groups have recently become more dispersed in residence and diversified in educational and occupational status. In the process, members of these groups have converged with the national trends in work, education, consumption, and media, becoming less distinct in the process.

The present century has also brought more opportunity for intergroup contact and the rise of more ethnically inclusive patterns of social participation. This process began with immigrant groups adopting American forms of social participation, particularly the voluntary association, as they turned away from Old World ascriptive patterns of participation based on blood and place (cf. Light, 1972; Treudley, 1949). As certain immigrant groups became more diversified, their middle classes in particular began to participate in voluntary associations that brought them into contact with people from a variety of ethnic and social backgrounds. As a consequence, the middle classes, those with higher levels of education and white-collar jobs, became exposed to a wider and more cosmopolitan range of interests and concerns (Axelrod, 1956; Babchuk and Booth, 1969; Curtis, 1971; Foskett, 1955; Wilensky, 1961). By contrast, the social participation of blue-collar workers and those with lower levels of formal education has been largely confined to family and friends in local settings, that is, to informal relations with people from essentially similar backgrounds. The participation of blue-collar workers in formal associations outside of unions and churches has been minimal (Dotson, 1951; Suttles, 1968). That is, it is the middle classes of various immigrant groups, those with white-collar jobs and higher levels of education, that have become most included into the larger society.

As societal change occurred and ethnic inclusion proceeded, the internal differentiation of immigrant groups grew. The immigrant brotherhoods and sisterhoods in America became more heterogeneous, due to the increasing diversity of experiences among the members of these groups. Gordon (1964) noted that the most important divisions of immigrant groups to emerge out of the process were the ethclasses. Immigrant groups became stratified into distinct economic classes—ethclasses—due to the different experiences among members in the changing larger society. The middle classes of ethnic groups were the first to participate in the wider American society, to adopt the homemaking methods and take up the child-rearing practices and so on, advised by the cultural bearers of that larger society. Convergence came sequentially to different classes of immigrant groups, first to the middle classes and later to the working and lower classes. Thus, convergence also meant divergence within a single ethnic group, as the experiences among its members became diversified and the brotherhood itself became differentiated into ethclasses.

A good example is the recent differentiation of African Americans due to affirmative action programs as well as the larger change process. While blacks were excluded by other immigrant groups earlier in the century, many of them are now moving into white-collar work, while poor blacks are not (Wilson, 1978 and 1987). The result is the differentiation of African Americans into ethclasses:

On the one hand, poorly trained and educationally limited blacks of the inner city...see their job prospects increasingly restricted to the low-wage sector, their unemployment rates soaring to record levels, ...their labor force participation rates declining, their movement out of poverty slowing, and their welfare rolls increasing. On the other hand, talented and educated blacks are experiencing unprecedented job opportunities in the growing government and corporate sectors, opportunities that are at least comparable to those of whites with equivalent qualifications (Wilson, 1978:151).

The same class differences in mobility into the good life among African Americans and Hispanic Americans have also been found by others (Hout, 1984; Stolzenberg, 1990).

The immigrant groups have changed in the process. They have changed from foreign and homogeneous groups, distinct from one another and the wider community in their subcultures, to domestic and heterogeneous groups that have become differentiated into ethclasses, and each ethclass has become less and less distinct from its class counterparts in other ethnic groups. Ethclasses have also become less segregated from each other in residence and social participation. This is especially true for the growing middle classes within the nation's ethnic groups. Not only have these middle ethclasses become more dispersed in the larger community, they now reflect that larger community, including its norms and values with respect to thinking, feeling, and acting. They are the most thoroughly enculturated of the ethclasses. The larger process is that these groups, swept up in societal change through educational attainment, occupational diversification, mass media, and mass consumption, have converged with one another and with the wider society.

The process of ethnic inclusion has not meant the full assimilation of immigrant groups into a unitary society. First, the middle classes of ethnic groups were more included than others in the post-industrial American society. Moreover, acculturation, or the adoption of the Anglo core of American culture, proceeded ahead of the structural assimilation of all ethclasses. Labor had to be culturally standardized for white-collar work before taking it up, and this brought acculturation before structural assimilation. Furthermore, while members of various ethnic groups have been significantly enculturated and do participate more freely in the secondary institutions of the larger society, their private lives and primary relations are still infused with some measure of their own distinct ethnicity. Ethnic identity has not been eclipsed by modernity.

Ethnic boundaries have, however, become more inclusive and permeable, less restrictive and definitive, and the expression of ethnic identity is now more voluntary, done selectively and purposefully in domestic idioms. It is a new ethnicity (see Chapter 3). Nevertheless ethnic boundaries do persist, though often only as psychological phenomena. It is evident that the existence of ethnicity is not limited to its manifestation in the residential segregation and occupational concentration of groups. Indeed, there appears to be a current resurgence of ethnicity as an egocentric expression, an assertion of self in the seemingly impersonal modern world.

Furthermore, some ethnic groups continue to be excluded from American society to some degree. Obviously, the nation's indigenous people—the Native Americans—have not been absorbed as others have into the larger American society. Some immigrant groups have also been bypassed to varying degrees in the modernization of American society. The nation's ethnic and racial groups, immigrant and indigenous alike, have not been equally included into American society, and they do not all participate openly and freely with one another in the nation's secondary institutions. Racial and ethnic stratification persists, and racial and ethnic diversity are still evident in American society. There have been two trends in societal change: one that has brought the greater inclusion and convergence of some ethnic groups and a second that has resulted in the exclusion and divergence of other groups. This has meant both change in and continuance of ethnic pluralism in America.

PROPOSITION 6

Some groups have diverged from societal change, due mainly to ethnic competition, conflict, and exclusion.

The error of assimilationism is that, while it pointed to the forces of change that provide for ethnic inclusion, it neglected other forces that are no less a part of the change process and that make for ethnic exclusion. These forces are rooted in the struggle among ethnic groups for societal resources. This competition has meant at least the partial exclusion of some ethnic and racial groups from society by more powerful rivals. The expansion of opportunities that can free individuals from the folk past has been counterbalanced in the change process by powerful groups erecting barriers to those opportunities, in effect denying to others that freedom. The products of the dual forces of inclusion and exclusion, convergence and divergence, are both assimilation and the persistence of ethnic and racial pluralism into the modern era. Whereas ethnic exclusion was neglected by assimilationism, it was clearly shown in conflict theory, which hypothesized the exclusion of the weak by the powerful. Thus, by combining both theories in a complementary way, we can see that societal change creates the conditions for both inclusion and exclusion, as well as a divergence between those groups included into and those excluded from modern society.

Ethnic competition and conflict have been evident in every phase of American history. These historical forces have often resulted in some form of ethnic exclusiveness, either the stratification or the geographical separation of the rivals. The latter took place on the frontier when, after conflict over land, the powerful settlers isolated the weaker Indians on reservations, an isolation that continues to this day. After Anglos expropriated land on the Southwest frontier, both Hispanos and then Mexican immigrants were forced to the bottom of the region's labor market, entrapped in a system of ethnic stratification, another form of ethnic exclusion.

Immigrant groups came to the country as labor, and it has been in the labor market that they have competed with one another for the nation's better jobs. In the course of this competition some groups have erected for their benefit systems of stratification that split or segmented the labor market so that one group "controls certain jobs exclusively and gets paid at one scale of wages, while the cheaper group is restricted to another set of jobs and is paid at a lower scale" (Bonacich, 1972:555). A split labor market is evident when ethnic groups work at the same jobs, but the dominant group is paid at higher wages than subordinate groups. For example, while both blacks and whites worked on the railroads, whites monopolized the better jobs, relegating blacks to the lower ones, such as porters and cooks. Differential pay for black and white teachers in segregated schools is another historical example of a split labor market. A segmented labor market is evident when dominant and subordinate ethnic groups work at different jobs; minority groups concentrate in types of work that are different from those of the majority (Olzak, 1983). For example, southern whites concentrated in textile mills and blacks in field work late in the nineteenth century. Subordinate groups not only have been excluded from job apprenticeships, they have been denied "access to general education, thereby making their training as quick replacements more difficult" (p. 556), and they are politically weakened, according to Bonacich.

The exclusion of minority labor from better jobs has happened to Asians on the West Coast, to Chicanos in the Southwest, and to African Americans in the South and North. The histories of these groups are developed in the following chapters, but the list of instances and groups involved in the ethnic and racial stratification of labor in America could go on and on. The condition of ethnic exclusiveness and official inattention to the enculturation of labor has lasted longer in some parts of the country than in others, as the historical apathy toward the education of African American labor in the South and of Chicanos in the Southwest suggests.

Other ethnic groups, however, have been swept into society through the mechanisms of public education, white-collar work, and politics. European immigrants were entering American politics at the same time blacks were disfranchised, and public schools were enculturating white immigrants at the time that blacks were relegated to inferior schools because of segregation (Lieberson, 1980). Ethnic stratification has been an enduring social phenomenon, one that results in the continuance into the modern era of ethnic and racial subcultures. Members of white immigrant groups became professionals, managers, and proprietors, at the top of white-collar work, while blacks became clerks and salespeople, at the bottom. In blue-collar work, whites monopolized the skilled trades and became foremen, while blacks were relegated to the level of operatives and laborers (Broom and Glenn, 1965; Schmid and Nobbe, 1965). "Keeping Negroes down in the occupational structure keeps whites up" (Glenn, 1965:110). The white-black gap in education, occupation, and income has widened since World War II, and the conversion of education into occupational gains is still greater for whites than for blacks as well as Puerto Ricans (Kaufman, 1983; Lieberson, 1980:Lieberson and Waters, 1988). By the same token, the black middle class has been doing reasonably well compared to its white counterparts, and Asian Americans are reaching parity with whites (Hirschman and Wong, 1984; Hout, 1984; Wilson, 1978 and 1987).

Both capital and labor have played roles in the stratification of the nation's labor market. Ethnic competition in the labor market is part of the larger class struggle between capital and labor. Capital has historically sought the cheapest labor possible, and the newer immigrant was typically the cheapest and most docile laborer. In many cases, capital turned to new immigrants as a displacement for the more expensive and better organized labor of older immigrant groups. This process took the form of strikebreaking on occasion, but often new immigrants were not completely aware of their role in the class struggle. In response the older immigrant groups erected barriers, often through their unions, to the full and rapid inclusion of the new immigrant into the labor market. Labor stratification is not the only result of labor competition, for immigration restrictions, the full inclusion of the new immigrant, and a radical alliance of workers from different ethnic groups are all possible outcomes of labor competition.

Ethnic and racial stratification has been as common in business circles as it has among laboring groups. Big business corporations have assumed increasing control of the country's economy, a course of events that Collins (1975:440) described:

> The history of business enterprise in America shows that the most successful industries are those that amalgamate relatively early with the largest banking interests.... A related tactic...is for organizations to generate internally as much capital as possible, through such devices as employee stockholding, management of insurance and pension plans, and so forth. The point here is that the control of ready sources of cash at any one point in time is crucial for maintaining the political position of the organization in the system of credit, and thus for keeping it solvent; this is a precondition for continual control in the hands of a particular group.

The White Anglo-Saxon Protestant (WASP) upper class took control of big business, becoming in disproportionate numbers the executives of the national and international business corporations.

Newcomer (1955) found that Jews and eastern and southern Europeans, among others, have been absent from the ranks of the nation's big business executives. Many of these executives are of European origins, but their ancestry is from the west and north. When Jews and eastern and southern Europeans have broken into this circle, they have been concentrated in entertainment, merchandising, and mass communication, enterprises in which ethnic barriers have been harder to maintain. Other studies in the same era supported Newcomer's findings (Mills, 1963; Taussig and Joslyn, 1932; Warner and Abegglen, 1955). The elite of American business are still predominately WASPs and Protestants with ancestry elsewhere in northern and western Europe (Alba and Moore, 1982). Racial minorities have been almost completely absent from the ranks of big business executives. With respect to minority businessmen, Collins (1971:1013) stated: "Those organizations more likely to be dominated by members of minority ethnic cultures are the smaller and local businesses in manufacturing, construction, and retail trade; in legal practice, solo rather than firm employment." "[A]lthough blacks are 12 percent of the U.S. population, their businesses in the late 1980s still accounted for only one-third of 1 percent of the nation's total sales receipts" (Jaynes and Williams, 1989:181).

The picture is somewhat different in government employment. Sowell (1975:183–184) concluded that minority employment in government service fluctuates with politics, and the civil rights movement has had positive effects on the employment of blacks in the federal government:

> In the military, Negroes were slightly overrepresented. In the civilian federal agencies, Negroes gained 20 percent of all new employment in a five-year period following the establishment of the equal-

employment program, with almost a doubling of blacks in the top six grades during this period, and blacks often received fancier perquisites than their white counterparts as well.

Hout (1984) also found that much of the recent occupational gains of the black middle class was in the public sector of the American economy. Still, blacks and other racial minorities are underrepresented in certain areas of government, such as the State and Treasury departments.

The upper classes of white ethnic groups have dominated the private economy throughout American history (Alba and Moore, 1982; Lieberson and Carter, 1979). Minority groups turned to the state in their rivalry with the white majority in the last half of the twentieth century. Civil rights and affirmative action can be seen in this light. To better deal with bureaucracy in the economy and state, agencies of ethnic groups become bureaucratized, with paid managerial and legal staffs and boards of directors, exemplified by black organizations during the civil rights era. Such an observation is consistent with the theory that societal change can mobilize ethnic groups (Chapter 4).

It is also consistent with the notion that the modern state mediates between various interest groups, not only ethnic groups but also economic classes (Quadagno, 1984). Reacting to the racial turmoil of the 1960s and 1970s, the federal government passed and implemented civil rights legislation, an example of the state's mediating role. During the Reagan era, however, there was an attempt to dismantle the state's civil rights policy. Whatever interests it serves, the state acknowledges ethnic inequality when addressing issues of income redistribution and civil rights, and ethnic boundaries are reinforced when state policies flow along ethnic lines (Olzak, 1983).

The picture that emerges with conflict theory is one of ethnic stratification in twentieth-century America. In the private sector of the economy, both white- and blue-collar jobs have been stratified, as whites have taken the better and blacks the less desirable positions in both job markets. While racial stratification is not as prevalent in the public sector, as it is in the private sector, it is still evident in government service. This is the other side of the coin to the assimilationist version of modern society.

The assimilationists argued that mobility for all groups increased in societal change. The great expansion of educational and occupational opportunity absorbs all groups alike. From the larger perspective of sociological functionalism, to which assimilationism belongs, modern society reduces ethnic inequality by preparing all competent individuals, regardless of ethnic-group membership, to take positions vital to society. Because of the highly specialized division of labor and the growing interdependence among specialists, each specialist is increasingly vital to society and must be the most qualified and best prepared for the job. There is no room for racism in the modern order. Of course, the jobs that are most functional or most vital to society must be rewarded best. This creates stratification, obviously, but it is one based on individual achievement, not on race, creed, or color. All of this can be found in Davis and Moore's (1945) classical statement on the functional theory of stratification.

Conflict theorists argued, on the other hand, that while opportunities do expand with societal change, they are not equitably shared by all groups. Powerful groups erect barriers against weaker rivals to the better positions in the labor market and to various other privileges. The results are split and segmented labor markets, an ethnic division of labor. All sorts of case studies show "the operation of ethnic and class standards in employment based not merely on skin color but on name, accent, style of dress, manners, and conversational styles" (Collins, 1971:1008). Conflict theorists see the recent inflation of educational requirements for work, blue- and white-collar alike, and the emphasis on Anglo-American cultural styles in the selection and promotion of employees as evidence of group barriers in the labor market. Employers interpret Anglo-American cultural styles not as barriers but as signs of employee motivation, maturity, and even good character. Squires (1977:445) gave the reasons college graduates were sought by job recruiters at a large Midwestern state university for sales, managerial, and junior executive positions: "A person develops a sense of *maturity* in college; we like our engineers to have a college degree not because of the specific knowledge learned in school, but for the *social skills* developed in school" (italics added). Thus, in recent years we see mobility chances for the advantaged exceeding those for the disadvantaged in all ethnic groups.

Many conflict theorists argue that racial stratification has replaced ethnic stratification since World War II. This is true to some extent, but it is also true that some racial minorities have been included into the larger society through education and white-collar work. Opportunity for acculturation and structural assimilation did grow, even for racial minorities in America. For instance, Wilson (1978:19) observed that "with the passage of equal employment legislation and the authorization of affirmative action programs the government has helped clear the path for more privileged blacks, who have the requisite education and training to enter the main stream of American occupations." Recent research shows that this has been the case for blacks, and it is true for other minority groups as well.

For example, Asian Americans are reaching parity with whites (Hirschman and Wong, 1984). Among others, they and Cubans erected ethnic enclaves that research shows to be comparatively successful (Chapter 4). We also know that recent immigrants to the United States are taking up professional and technical work. Ethnic and racial barriers are not insurmountable, and this was stressed in Chapter 4. The point is that assimilationism and conflict theory must be used together for a fuller understanding of ethnic change in American society. Societal change does indeed increase the potential for ethnic inclusion, but ethnic competition and stratification with respect to land, labor, and capital are also a part of the change process. This has meant the inclusion of some groups into modern society and the exclusion of others, at least in a relative sense, and thus it has meant divergence as well as convergence of ethnic groups.

The historical divergence between ethnic groups sets the context for prejudice. Discrimination sets divergence into motion, but it is easy to believe that group differences make for the divergence, forgetting that the differences are mainly due to historical discrimination. Divergence can translate into restricted interaction among members of the groups involved. Thus the optimistic dictum of W. I. Thomas does not always apply: "race prejudice could be dissipated through human association" (Frazier, 1947:268).

Several of the psychological theories on prejudice can help explain the perpetuation of prejudice in such a social setting. Diverging groups can become each other's living inkblots, stereotypes can solidify in accord with the principles of the assimilation/contrast effect, and these ideas and feelings can be easily passed on through conditioning, modeling, and imitation to succeeding generations. Indeed, ethnic stratification can be psychologically represented in an ethnic hierarchy. Historical divergence can be rooted in people's minds as a sense of ethnic group position, and that representation, when implemented into action, can perpetuate exclusion and divergence. The psychoanalytic, cognitive, and behavioristic traditions, as well as social representation theory, all have something to say about the relationship between ethnic exclusion, divergence, and prejudice.

Prejudice can also be generated between converging groups as they compete for the expanded opportunities that societal change brings. The content of the stereotypes and prejudice in the cases of converging and diverging groups will likely be different. Converging groups who are in competition will typically see each other as threats, holding stereotypes about each other's pushiness; while diverging groups will likely view each other in superordinate-subordinate terms, infused with stereotypes of the boss and shiftless workers. The larger point is, however, that societal change perpetuates prejudice as much as it eradicates it, and psychology can help us understand the process.

191

PROPOSITION 7

Due to changes in the American occupational structure late in the twen-tieth century, forces for ethnic inclusion in the economy have moderated. A likely result will be increasing inequality among and within the na-tion's ethnic groups.

One type of American worker today is the "yuppie." This man or woman has a high-paying job—possibly a broker, a junior executive in a large firm, or a professional. Employment was preceded by a college, graduate, or professional education, perhaps at an elite school. Yup-pies are best known for their life-styles, made possible by their well-paying jobs. This includes driving an expensive imported car, living in a fashionable neighborhood, providing posh private schooling for an only child, and sipping white wine and dining at upscale restaurants. Did the rise of white-collar work and the growth of national wealth el-evate children and grandchildren from ethnic backgrounds into such a life-style?

There are actually very few yuppies in America. Only about one-fourth of the nation's workers have a job with high income and status. These are the managers and professionals, who had 1985 weekly in-comes that averaged $488, equal to about 150 percent of the salary of the typical American worker. These and other white-collar workers continue to grow as a percentage of the total labor force.

However, something else is happening as well, because the aver-age income of working men and women in America is declining. For example, a typical 30-year-old man in 1973 earned $23,580 annually in constant dollars, but in 1984 his income decreased to $17,520. The real weekly earning for working women in 1969 was $266, but in 1984 it was $230. The real median hourly pay for 93 million workers fluctuat-ed from $8.52 in 1973 to $7.66 in 1982, then up to $7.83 in 1988 and down to $7.46 at the end of the decade. In the 15 years through 1988, the poorest two-fifths of American families saw their percentage of na-tional income drop from 17 to 15. The percentage for the richest fifth over the same period rose from 41 to 44 percent.

Once young Americans could expect to live better than had their parents, an expectation underlying ethnic inclusion earlier in the cen-tury, but for many this is no longer true. Median household income in America declined by 4.8 percent from 1979 to 1984. For young house-holds with heads under 25 years of age, the decrease was even greater, 17.7 percent, from $17,048 to $14,028. Even with both partners working and with fewer children, young American families face a deterioration in living standards. To illustrate, the proportion of a typical young

192

man's income required to pay for a medium-priced house rose from 21 to 44 percent between 1973 and 1983. Young couples are now less likely to buy their own homes, but if they do, their houses are smaller than those of their parents. This is hardly a sketch of yuppies, but it does picture what most young Americans now face.

The decline in real wages for American workers is due to the nation's losing unionized, secure, well-paying, manufacturing jobs, according to some observers. Indeed, between 1970 and 1985, precision, production, craft, and repair workers, as well as operators, fabricators, and laborers declined as a percentage of the total labor force. The jobs the nation has been gaining are the non-union, high-turnover, ill-paying, no-future jobs in the service industries. Not only do service jobs pay poorly, they do not give youth a ladder with which to move up; they are dead-end jobs. With jobs such as these, the young will not experience the lifetime income growth that the older generations did.

Not all agree that the American middle class is shrinking because of a decline in manufacturing jobs. For example, Lawrence (1985) believed that middle-class jobs have been declining in all sectors of the economy, not only in manufacturing. He showed that the proportion of jobs providing a middle-class salary was no greater in manufacturing than in other sectors of the nation's economy. Middle-class jobs were those with $250–400 weekly earnings, lower-class jobs paid less than $250 per week, and upper-class jobs paid more than $500 per week. The percentage of middle-class earners was about the same in manufacturing as in other sectors, such as construction, government, and services, but these jobs are shrinking in all the sectors.

Furthermore, part-time workers are increasing faster than full-time workers in the labor force. The labor force expanded by 26.5 percent from 1970 to 1982, but the number of part-time workers rose by almost 60 percent. The number of involuntary part-time workers was increasing faster than that of the voluntary ones, the former being workers who prefer to have full-time jobs. Perhaps this trend is symbolized by the laid-off union worker reduced to flipping burgers part-time at a fraction of his former pay. Part-time workers not only make less money than full-time workers, but also receive fewer benefits.

Before 1970 plenty of blue- and white-collar jobs provided a middle-class income. The wage distribution in the nation resembled a bell-shaped curve, with a few well-paying jobs at one end, a few poor-paying jobs at the other end, and most jobs in the middle. That middle is shrinking, however, and the result could be a two-tier hierarchy of workers, some on the top in well-paying jobs, but most on the bottom in dead-end jobs with poor pay and few benefits. It is a segmented labor market, and the ethnic poor are increasingly trapped at the bottom. In Table 6.2, you can see a modest growth in managerial and professional occupations but a decline in the better paying blue-collar jobs. The good jobs that are growing are in computers, electronics and engineering, and the skilled or professional service occupations. These jobs require educated workers, particularly those with college educations. Most of the declining jobs are semi-skilled manual jobs, and thus the less-skilled face more joblessness in the future.

Not only is the nation's job market changing, but so is its labor force. Currently, white males are about 47 percent (1987) of the new entrants into the American labor force, but over the next 13 years they will be only 15 percent of these new entrants. In other words, older white males who have dominated the job market will be retiring in such great numbers that groups other than white males will be replacing them. Non-whites will make up 29 percent of the new entrants in the near future. Will this mean a structural lift for young and poor blacks? Most research and forecasts say not, because of the mismatch between their skills and the educational requirements of America's growing and better-paying jobs. The advantaged will take these jobs, not the disadvantaged, and the gap between the two will grow.

This forecast of the nation's future is already evident in research on America's ethnic groups. Wilson (1978 and 1987) saw the class division in the black community between the poor and the middle class, a division that clearly reflects a two-tier society. Other research confirmed his observation, not only for blacks but for other ethnic groups as well (e.g., Hout, 1984; Stolzenberg, 1990). Recent immigrants concentrate at both the bottom and top of the labor market, also reflecting a two-tier occupational structure. For example, immigrant women in 1980 were concentrated at the top in professional jobs (13.3%), many in the medical industry, but also toward the bottom in clerical jobs (26.3%), as operatives (21.7%), and in service work (19.7%) (Tienda, et al., 1984). It is simple, really, for there are good jobs and there are bad jobs, and in the future there will be fewer in between. The key to better jobs is increasingly educational credentials (Hout, 1988).

The impact of occupational change is felt *within* ethnic groups as well as across them. The significance of race in underemployment has been increasing, but so has the significance of educational and age differences within races (Lichter, 1988). Advantaged classes within minority groups compare more favorably with their white class counterparts than do the minority disadvantaged with their white counterparts (Hout, 1988; Stolzenberg, 1990; Wilson, 1987). But college-entry rates for minority youth are falling, and high-school dropouts have already experienced a decline in real earnings. Black male dropouts earned $334 weekly in 1969, but only $268 in 1986.

White male dropouts earned $447 weekly in 1969 and $381 in 1986 (Jaynes and Williams, 1989). In 1986 the poverty rate for households headed by a person younger than 25 years was more than double the rate of 1967. The gap between workers on the top and those on the bottom will grow with a shrinking middle class, and the result will be increasing inequality across and within ethnic groups. Changes in the nation's occupational structure can slow the convergence of ethnic groups with one another.

The four historical patterns of minority-group adjustment to the American labor market will likely continue. The first is working on the bottom of the labor market and gradually moving up. If forecasts are correct, however, this pattern will be less possible in the future, as the middle class shrinks. The second pattern is seen in the many new immigrants now going directly into the nation's professional and technical jobs due to the educational credentials that they bring to the country. This pattern will become even more prominent if job and income qualifications become important criteria for legal immigration into the country.

The third pattern, in which minority groups stay permanently at the bottom of the occupational structure, is already evident in the black underclass as well as among the poor of other ethnic groups. As mentioned above, prospects for the poor are declining with a shrinking middle class. Finally, ethnic groups can erect their own subeconomies, their own enclaves, and this pattern continues especially for Asian immigrants as well as others, such as Cubans in the Miami area. This adjustment will be discussed in following chapters.

SUMMARY AND ASSESSMENT

The experiences of ethnic and racial groups in America have alternated between the poles of inclusion and exclusion. Inclusion became more possible in the post-industrial phase of American society due to the rise of white-collar work and the expansion of public education. Opportunity for inclusion grew with the greater need for enculturated labor. This transformation of American society began early in the twentieth century, during the time Park and Wirth wrote their natural histories of assimilation.

Because of ethnic and racial stratification, groups have converged at unequal rates, however, with the larger trend toward a modern American society. This has occasionally resulted in collective protest. In the 1960s African Americans, among others, protested their exclusion from modern America. This protest was particularly directed at racial discrimination in education and in the work force, at the very barriers that have excluded blacks from American society. During this period of protest, the bulk of ethnic conflict theory was written, and more recent research shows a racial gap in inclusion to this day.

The pluralists wrote that societal change would not result in the full assimilation of the nation's ethnic groups. According to pluralists, ethnicity survives even among groups who have been comparatively included in the larger American society. It survives in people's private lives and primary relationships. Rather than having been eclipsed by social change, the ethnic group has evolved into more inclusive forms, toward the psychological and more voluntary expression of ethnicity. A constant in the entire process, according to some pluralists, is the fact that ethnicity at its root is and always had been a psychological phenomenon that can be expressed in a variety of ways. Societal change has brought to people the freedom to express their ethnicity voluntarily and variously.

Ethnicity also survives because of ethnic competition, a point shared by both pluralists and conflict theorists. Moreover, as the nation evolves, the political state might become the direct arbitrator of ethnic competition and the distributor of societal resources, and this distribution might be accomplished in accord with ethnic quotas. If this does occur, then the political state will replace the labor needs of the nation's private economy as the main force behind ethnic change in the future. If it does not, the future occupational structure of the nation portends a two-tier society, one of "haves" and another of "have-nots," and this inequality will cut into and across ethnic groups.

It should be apparent that each component of the sociological lore on American ethnicity is only a partial explanation of ethnic change. Assimilationists are correct that change brings assimilation—at least it brings a greater potential for integration and acculturation. Modern, more than traditional, society needs enculturated labor in a wide variety of work, and this means more opportunity for the inclusion of ethnic labor into the larger society. This has certainly been true for much of the twentieth century, although recent changes in the labor market might mean that the societal forces for ethnic inclusion have slowed. In no manner is assimilation inevitable in modern society, however, and the fact is that some groups have been excluded and not assimilated. This fact was overlooked by the assimilationists, and this is the reason they have given us only a partial explanation of ethnic change.

Both pluralists and ethnic conflict theorists point to the connection between ethnic competition and the lack of assimilation in American society. Conflict theory is the stronger statement, contending that ethnic rivalry for societal resources intensifies as society changes, and this provides more reason for the oppression of the weak by the powerful. The histories of oppressed groups diverge from those of their oppressors and that of the larger society; there is no necessary assimilation between the powerful and the oppressed. However, because of its preoccupation with competition and oppression, conflict theory is unable to give proper focus to the increased potential for ethnic inclusion and convergence in modern society. For much of the twentieth century the need for enculturated labor set into motion significant forces for the assimilation of labor. Thus, conflict theory and pluralism are also only partial explanations of ethnic change.

These three theories are complementary, however, and while each is no more than a partial explanation of ethnic change in American society, each makes up for some of what the others lack. This is essentially what Hechter (1974) concluded about the impact of industrialization on ethnicity in England from 1885 to 1966. He found both ethnic inclusion and exclusion in Great Britain. A complete description and explanation of ethnic change in America, too, must start with consideration of these theories in a complementary manner. Since the process of convergence and divergence can become rooted in the psychology of individual Americans, and that psychology when manifest in discrimination can perpetuate any historical drift, the psychology of prejudice and discrimination must be used to round out the sociological analysis of ethnic change and societal change. Theoretical complementarity cannot be achieved, however, by merely adding these social theories together and then adding the psychology of prejudice and discrimination. The result would be some summation that would in effect say that all theories apply with equal adequacy to all phases of American history, that all are equally true under all historical conditions, and that each explains with equal validity the history of every single ethnic group in America. Rather, these theories must be used alternately, as the ethnic groups in America themselves have alternated between inclusion and exclusion, and as the historical forces behind inclusion and exclusion have alternated from one era to another.

Niels Bohr faced the same issue in physics: the presence of two theories of matter, the wave and particle theories, each of which was only a partial explanation of matter. According to Matson (1966:132), "both formulations persisted in remaining valid for some observations, but invalid for others; each failed where the other was successful." But comprehensive knowledge of matter was possible, Bohr argued, if only "we accept both theories as valid—not simultaneously but in alternation" (Matson, 1966:132). At times and under certain conditions, matter is a particle, while, under other conditions and at other times, matter is a wave. Likewise, for some groups and under certain historical conditions, ethnic change is a process of inclusion and convergence, while, for other groups and under different conditions, ethnic change is a process of exclusion and divergence.

∾

ETHNIC EVOLUTION
IN AMERICA

CHAPTER

7

☙☙

NATIVE AMERICANS AND AMERICAN SOCIETY

T
wo kinds of ethnic contact have occurred in America: the contact between America's indigenous peoples and immigrant settlers on the frontier and the contact between older and newer immigrant groups. Frontier contact is the topic of this chapter; the study of immigrant groups follows in subsequent chapters. As Europeans dispersed throughout the world in past centuries, they came to North America, dominated the indigenous peoples, and settled what had been (to them) a frontier. This type of ethnic contact, between a powerful immigrant group and a weaker indigenous people, typically results in conflict and the subordination of the native population (Lieberson, 1961). Both conflict and subordination certainly characterize the history of Native Americans following their contact with Europeans, as indicated in Figure 7.1.

BEFORE CONTACT

Estimates of the Native American population in North America above the Rio Grande prior to European contact range from a low of 900,000 to a high of 18 million (Snipp, 1989). The consensus on these estimates ranges from 2 to 5 million at the time of contact. Map 7.1 gives an idea of the diversity of America's indigenous groups prior to European contact. We will examine the indigenous peoples in several regions of the country—Northeast, Southeast, Great Plains, Southwest, and Northwest—to get some idea of their lives before their contact with immigrant groups. In what follows we will describe a representative

FIGURE 7.1   NATIVE AMERICANS AND CHANGE IN AMERICAN SOCIETY

Agrarian Society c. 1600–1865		Industrial Society c. 1865–1945		Post-Industrial Society c. 1945–Present	
Frontier contact and early accommodation	→ Conflict over land	→ Land expropriation	→ Exclusion of Native Americans	→ Present situation

group of Native Americans within each geographical region. Keep in mind that there was great diversity as well as commonalities among the many groups within each region.

THE NORTHEAST

The eastern woodlands stretch roughly from the Atlantic Ocean to the Mississippi River, a region that surrounds the five Great Lakes and includes part of Canada as well as the United States. Individual groups included, among others, the Penobscot and Passamaquoddy on the Atlantic slope; the Potawatomi and the League of the Iroquois along the lower Great Lakes; the Illinois and Miami in the Ohio Valley; and the Ojibwa (Chippewa) and Menomini at the western edge of the region. Other tribes are shown on Map 7.1. Native Americans in this region were farmers as well as hunters and gatherers. It is in this region that early contact with Europeans occurred, of course, the Europeans being predominantly French, English, Dutch, and, increasingly, native-born Euro-Americans of immigrant stock.

The League of the Iroquois consisted of the Seneca, Cayuga, Onondaga, Oneida, and Mohawk. If the protectorates of the League are also counted, the League ranged from the Atlantic Coast to the Mississippi River. (The "Five Nations" of the Iroquois became the "Six Nations" after the Tuscarora were admitted to the confederation in 1722 after migrating northward following their defeat by white settlers in North Carolina.) The population of the Five Nations was estimated at 5,500 in 1600 (Spencer and Jennings, et al., 1977). The exact origin date of the League is not known; accounts vary from 1459 to the early 1600s (Tooker, 1978). Intertribal affairs were managed by a council of fifty *sachems*, with representatives from each of the Five Nations. Rights to sachem titles were restricted to extended families who were hereditary holders of these titles, with clan matrons having the only voice in the selection. Thus family membership and political participation in intertribal governance were interwoven.

Iroquois villages were located near bodies of water, both streams and lakes. A steep bank and palisades of logs protected villages, and within them extended families lived in separate longhouses. Each nuclear family had separate apartments inside a longhouse but shared fireplaces along the central aisle of the house. Sleeping platforms were arranged along the walls, with storage areas below the platforms. Longhouses were constructed from log poles with bark thatch shingles for the walls and roof, and on average were 25 feet wide and 80 feet long (Fenton, 1978). Outside the villages were woodlands and cleared areas for cultivation. Once the soil had been exhausted and firewood became scarce, about twice in a generation, whole villages were moved to new sites.

The extended family comprised the basic social and economic unit of the Iroquois. It was matrilineal, and household authorities were elder females. Women were cultivators, and the men engaged in hunting and fishing. The yearly cycle included the planting, cultivation, and harvesting of the "three sisters," corn, beans, and squash, and, while men did the heavy labor of field clearing, women were the primary cultivators. Women were organized in work parties under the direction of a senior matron.

After the fall harvest, men and a few women took to the woods to hunt for meat, principally deer and bear. Hunting parties then returned to their villages at the winter solstice with smoked and dried meat. In the early spring, work parties returned again to the woods to gather maple sap and boil it down to syrup and sugar. Passenger pigeons were netted during their spring flights, and there were also forays to fishing stations. Berries, nuts, roots, greens, and other edibles were also gathered at different times of the year.

Autumn was also the time that Iroquois men were free to go to war. War raids were undertaken because of council decisions and for personal vendettas. Enemies were either killed or returned to Iroquois villages as prisoners for adoption. Warfare became almost a preoccupation of young Iroquois men during the contact period with whites, and war chiefs ultimately took over the power of hereditary chiefs by the time of the American Revolution (Fenton, 1978). Contact with Europeans began as early as 1534 and evolved into warfare over the beaver trade in the seventeenth century (Trigger, 1978). The Iroquois suffered high mortality because of both warfare and disease epidemics in the contact period, offset somewhat by the taking of prisoners. Nevertheless, the populations of the tribes were drastically reduced (Tooker, 1978). Men were increasingly away from their villages, and local

MAP 7.1 LOCATIONS OF NATIVE AMERICANS BEFORE EUROPEAN SETTLEMENT

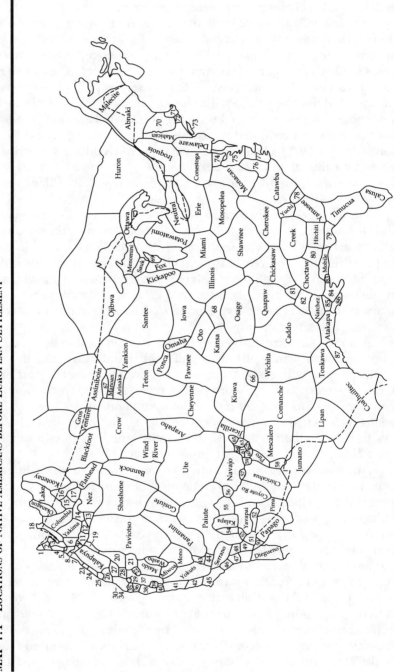

1 Quileute
2 Quinault
3 Twana
4 Chehalis
5 Kwalhioqua
6 Klikitat
7 Tillamook
8 Chinook
9 Wishram
10 Tlatskanai
11 Tenino
12 Umatilla
13 Cayone
14 Wallawalla
15 Spokan
16 Kalispel
17 Coeur D' Alene
18 Snoqualmi
19 Molala
20 Klamath
21 Achomawi
22 Yana

23 Alsea
24 Suislaw
25 Coos
26 Chastacosta
27 Takelma
28 Shasta
29 Chimariko
30 Hupa
31 Karok
32 Tolowa
33 Yurok
34 Wiyot
35 Wailaki
36 Yuki
37 Wintun
38 Pomo
39 Wappo
40 Olamentke
41 Costano
42 Salina
43 Tubatulabal
44 Kawausu

45 Chumash
46 Gabrielino
47 Luiseno
48 Cahuilla
49 Kamia
50 Cocopa
51 Yuma
52 Maricopa
53 Halchidhoma
54 Mohave
55 Havasupai
56 Hopi
57 Zuni
58 Manso
59 Acoma
60 Isleta
61 Queres
62 Tano
63 Tewa
64 Jemez
65 Taos
66 Kiowa Apache

67 Hidatsa (Gros Ventre)
68 Missouri
69 Winnebago
70 Pennacook
71 Massachuset
72 Mohegan
73 Metoac
74 Nanticoke
75 Powhatan
76 Tuscarora
77 Pamlico
78 Cusabo
79 Apalachee
80 Alabama
81 Chakchiuma
82 Tunica
83 Biloxi
84 Acolapissa
85 Huma
86 Chitimacha
87 Karankawa

Source: From *Native American Tribalism: Indian Survivals and Renewals* by D'Arcy McNickle. Copyright © 1973 by Oxford University Press, Inc. Reprinted by permission.

power shifted to Iroquois women at home. The Iroquois still exist as a people, in New York and Ontario, but their society and way of life have been greatly altered by past warfare, loss of land, and the intrusion of immigrant settlers.

THE SOUTHEAST

This region slopes from the Appalachian Plateau toward the Atlantic Ocean and Gulf of Mexico, stretching from Virginia into eastern Texas. Some of the tribes in the region before European contact were the Creek, Cherokee, Chickasaw, Choctaw, Natachez, Seminole, and Yuchi. The people were cultivators, hunters, fishers, and gatherers, and these activities, along with trade, provided their economic base.

The Creek, along with other tribes, were members of the Muscogean language group of Native Americans. The Creek territory was centered in Alabama and Georgia, and their population around 1800 is estimated at nearly 22,000. Creek towns had 100 to 1,000 inhabitants and were often arranged as hamlets strung together along a river, with fields and forests interspersed between the hamlets.

Each town had 30 to 100 houses, and early Creek towns were protected by stockades. At the center of town was a rotunda, outside of which was a square ground, and across the square was a chunk yard for recreational games. Village men and officials occasionally assembled in the rotunda or square ground to discuss civic affairs. Civic authority was divided between civil and war officials, with the former presiding over meetings in the rotunda. The confederacy could organize war parties of up to 1,000 warriors, who raided other tribes and brought captives back home as slaves.

Each family, depending on its wealth, occupied one to four houses in a village. Multiple houses were arranged around a yard, with one dwelling as a kitchen and winter lodge, the second a summer and guest house, the third a granary and storehouse, and the fourth a warehouse. The houses were owned by a woman and shared with her husband and their children. Marriages were typically arranged between the clans, and the prospective husband paid a bride price. Children were lifelong members of the mother's clan. Although sexual license was common prior to marriage, fidelity was expected after marriage, and adultery was a punishable offense.

During the fall and winter, the Creek hunted away from their villages for up to six or seven months. In March, cultivation began near the villages. It centered on corn, although the Creek also grew beans, squash, sunflowers, melons, and pumpkins and gathered wild plants such as wild rice, berries, and nuts. Garden plots were next to each house, and the whole village shared a common field for cultivation marked into plots for each household. During the growing season, people worked in the mornings, and there were ball games in the afternoons and dances in the evenings. The Creek also fished, and thus their food was varied, a mixture of game meats, fish, cultivated vegetables and fruits, and wild plants. By the middle of the eighteenth century, in the course of contact with immigrant groups, the Creek adopted livestock husbandry.

The highlight of the yearly cycle was the *busk,* or Green Corn Ceremony, held in August. This ceremony, signifying the ritual renewal of a village, lasted for days and included feasting and fasting, ritual washing, and the extinction of old fires and the rekindling of new ones. Marriages since the last busk became binding at this time, amnesty was granted for past crimes, and honorific titles were awarded. This ceremonial period confirmed and renewed the social order of the Creek.

During their contact with European immigrant groups in the eighteenth century, the Creek adopted black slavery (Littlefield, 1979). Black slaves performed about the same role in the Creek economy as did Creek women, as cultivators. Between 1833 and 1840, the Creek and their slaves were removed to Indian Territory, present-day Oklahoma, residing there with the other relocated tribes, including the Choctaw, Chickasaw, Cherokee, and Seminole. Up to one-half the Creek perished during and after their removal.

THE GREAT PLAINS

The Great Plains region stretches from southern Alberta, Saskatchewan, and Manitoba to the Rio Grande border between the United States and Mexico, with its western edge at the foothills of the Rocky Mountains. The center of the region includes the Missouri and Mississippi river valleys and the grassland plains that surround these drainage basins. Two types of indigenous peoples occupied the Great Plains before and during European contact. On the grassland plains were nomadic bison-hunting tribes, and in the timbered river valleys were sedentary cultivators. The sedentary tribes included the Pawnee, Wichita, Mandan, Ponca, Omaha, Iowa, Missouri, and Kansas; the nomadic groups included the Cree, Blackfoot, Cheyenne, Arapaho, Kiowa, Shoshone, Comanche, Crow, and Dakota tribes. Tribes could shift from one way of life to the other, as illustrated by the Cheyenne and Crow, who evolved from sedentary farmers into nomadic hunters after the introduction of the horse by Europeans.

The Lakota, also known as the Teton Dakota, were one of the Dakota tribes (Spencer and Jennings, et al., 1977). Their territory was the northern plains, the present-day Dakotas and parts of Nebraska, Montana, and Wyoming. The Lakota were comprised of seven bands, the Brulé, Hunkpapa, Miniconjou, Oglala, Oohenonpa, Sans Arc, and Sihapsa, or Blackfoot.

The Oglala groups came together for a communal bison hunt and the Sun Dance ceremony in the summer. As the time of the Sun Dance drew near, the different Oglala groups moved toward a designated location and joined the encampment. Several days of preparation followed, and the Sun Dance itself lasted four days. The festival was marked by processions, feasting, and group dancing. Candidates for the sacred dances personified the virtues of bravery, generosity, fortitude, and integrity. In one dance the skin of participants was pierced with wooden skewers, a ritual of self-torture symbolizing capture, torture, and escape. After dancing to twenty-four songs, lasting many hours, participants would remove the wooden skewers signifying escape. This ceremonial time reaffirmed the bonds between the Oglala groups, validating them through religious ritual and shared experience. At this time, kinship ties were also renewed, marriages arranged, property exchanged, and stories and exploits told. During the spring and fall, the Oglala disbanded. Smaller groups migrated to their own separate territories, and even smaller groups of families survived the winters in sheltered bottom lands.

Since Lakota life was nomadic, their possessions, including dwellings, had to be portable. The tepee epitomized this portability. It consisted of a tripod base of wooden poles around which bison hides were attached. In the center, directly below the smoke hole at the top, was a fire hearth. The tepee, a home for one nuclear family, was moved by tying the poles together and placing them over a horse's back in an inverted V-shape to be dragged as a travois. Tepees in an encampment were typically arranged in a semicircle.

Most Lakota marriages were voluntary, the choice of the young men and women who met in the course of their daily chores and at dances. Young women also sat with a female relative outside their tepees in the evenings as young men queued to talk to them, each talking about the events of the day and his own exploits (Powers, 1986). In most cases, parents of the young couple would consent to the marriage, with the families exchanging gifts. After marriage, the woman left her family to reside with her husband's hunting band. Plural marriages were also possible, particularly for wealthy men. If a man's brother died, he was expected to marry his sister-in-law and be responsible for her children. The same was true for women, who were expected to marry the husbands of deceased sisters.

The Lakota had a simple division of labor, although men and women shared many of the same tasks. Adult women collected, cultivated and prepared food; for example, women skinned and butchered bison, dried the meat, and prepared hides. The Lakota diet consisted of buffalo, elk, and deer meat, along with wild fruits and vegetables, although other small animals and shelled corn were also eaten (Powers, 1986). Women also put up and took down the tepees. Men hunted bison from horseback with bows and lances. Bows were made from hardwoods and strengthened with a strip of green sinew glued to the back of the bow. Bows were short, a necessity for a hunter on horseback. Bison-hunting was done in groups, and hunting techniques included encircling a herd with grass fires or driving them into a corral or over a cliff, a technique that had been used before the introduction of the horse. Young men were also members of war parties, which raided other tribes for horses, food, and sometimes captives. In this way, the Lakota maintained control over nearby sedentary tribes, such as the Arikara.

Other specializations among the Lakota included shamans, who served as an intermediary between the people and the supernatural world. Shamans cured illness, forecasted the location of bison herds, and were leaders of the Sun Dance. Authority was diffuse, but there was a division between council chiefs and war leaders. Chiefs were older men whose lives exemplified Lakota virtues and who validated their status in public opinion through acts of generosity. Law and order was maintained mainly through interpersonal control—for example, the control by a family over its members. Warrior societies and the *Akacita* also maintained order, particularly during the Sun Dance and communal bison hunts. War leaders were young men who organized war parties, and their status was raised during the conflict with whites. Although successful at the Battle of Little Big Horn, the Lakota were finally forced onto reservations located primarily in South Dakota.

THE SOUTHWEST

Native Americans have lived in the Southwest for at least 12,000 years; the ancient groups of the region include the Mogollon, Anasazi, and Pueblos. The Southwest includes New Mexico, Arizona, southern California, Nevada, Utah, and the northern half of Mexico. The region is arid, and the indigenous people were concentrated in its river valleys before contact with Europeans. They were horticulturists, pastoralists, and hunter-gatherers. The tribes included different bands of Apache, Pueblos, Zuni, Navajo, Hopi, Paiute, Havasupai, Yavapai,

Maricopa, Pima, Papago, Yuma, and Mohave on the American side. On the Mexican side were the Concho, Opata, Tarahumare, Yaqui, and many others (Josephy, 1982).

The Navajo were relatively recent migrants to the Southwest prior to European contact. They came to the Southwest from the north as nomadic hunters and gatherers, settling first in north-central New Mexico. The Navajo soon adopted farming practices from other indigenous people in the region, growing corn, beans, and squash. As the Spanish moved into the region with their livestock in the sixteenth century, the Navajo also became herders of sheep and goats. Thus, their principal foods included mutton along with corn.

The Navajo lived in matrilineal and matrilocal family units, meaning that lineage was on the maternal side and the nuclear family typically resided near the maternal relatives. Each family lived in a hogan, a low house made of logs and mud with a doorway opened to the east for the sunrise. The interior was a single circular room with a fire in the middle below a smoke hole at the roof. The roof itself was earthen. Family members slept on the floor near the fire, radiating out from it as the spokes in a wheel. Outside the hogan were a corral and various outhouses for storage, work, and shade. If an occupant died in a hogan, the body was taken out through an opening on the north side and the hogan was forever abandoned.

Marriages were arranged through the respective families, ritually marked by an exchange of gifts. The Navajo marriage ceremony was held at the home of the bride. About nine in the evening the wedding party assembled. On the west side of the hogan the couple took seats, male spectators to their right and women to their left. A basket of corn-meal mush and two wicker containers of water were brought before the couple. The bride's father then sifted pinches of sacred pollen on the basket of mush. The bride poured water upon the groom's hands, then he upon hers, and both then ate from the basket of mush, dipping from all four sides of the basket. The basket was then passed to the assemblage, who finished its contents. A supper followed the ceremony, and the party ended at dawn.

Divorce was relatively simple. A woman could divorce her husband, for example, by placing his saddle outside the hogan. He would then return to the home of his mother, living among her relatives. While kinship was the primary social organization of Navajo life, the Navajo were also organized into different bands, each with a distinct territory and headman. Over time, bands migrated northwest from north-central New Mexico so that the Navajo range reached ultimately into Arizona and parts of Utah.

Sitting Bull, a Hunkpapa Sioux chief (seen here with his family), was forced to surrender to federal troops in 1881.

The sacred belief system of the Navajo distinguished between supernatural "Holy People" and mundane "Earth Surface People." One of the Holy People is the Turquoise Woman, whose Hero Twins journeyed to the sun to see their father. Along the way, they had several adventures and overcame numerous monsters, except Old Age, Dirt, Poverty, and Hunger, who continued to haunt the Navajo. These beliefs seem to reflect certain realities of life that occur everywhere, but are exaggerated by the harsh, arid climate in which the Navajo lived.

Between 1862 and 1865, the Navajo were transferred to Bosque Redondo in New Mexico. This ended the hostility between them and whites. Conditions at Bosque Redondo were deplorable, however, and the maintenance of the Navajo there was costly to the United States government. A treaty was made with the Navajo in 1868, and in July of that year the Navajo migrated back to their tribal homeland.

THE NORTHWEST COAST

This region runs along the Pacific Ocean from southeast Alaska to northwest California. The indigenous people lived along the coast and were concentrated at the mouths of rivers, along beaches and fjords, and on off-shore islands. If dearth and need fairly characterized living conditions in the Southwest, surplus and even abundance characterized life of the indigenous people of the Northwest. Fish were not merely caught, they were harvested, and on the land there were plentiful game and waterfowl. From Alaska to California, the tribes in this region included the Tlingit, Haida, Bella Bella, Bella Coola, Kwakiutl, Nootka, Quinault, Chinook, Tillamook, Alsea, Kalapuya, Coos, Hupa, and Wiyot, among others.

The Tlingit, in southeast Alaska, were comprised of fourteen tribal groupings with northern and southern branches. They lived in villages along the coast, each composed of up to twelve houses in permanent settlements. The Tlingit also built houses inland during the fur trade. Their houses, which faced the water along the coast, were elaborate wooden structures with average dimensions of 40 feet long and 30 feet wide. Bigger houses were known; the size and elaborateness of a house signified the status of the house group. Each house was home for up to ten to twelve nuclear families.

The house group was the most important economic unit of the Tlingit. It was an extended family, composed of males, their wives and minor children, sons of their sisters, and sons of the daughters of their sisters (Oberg, 1973). That is, boys at the age of 10 went to live with their maternal uncles and great uncles, while daughters left the parental household for another upon marriage. The eldest male was household head. Large and rich households also had slaves. All food gathering and consumption were done in common by household members, and the members also shared ceremonial objects. Most wealth was held in common, although members of a household did have individual possessions, and wealth passed from maternal uncle to nephew, not from father to son. Households or larger matrilineal clans held other property rights in common, such as fishing and hunting grounds, sealing rocks, berry patches, and totemic crests.

The annual economic cycle of the Tlingit began in March with fishing and hunting, followed by deep-sea fishing and waterfowl hunting in April. In May green plants and roots were collected, and June was spent in many economic and social activities. The salmon catch was in July, and the storage of food began in August and proceeded through the fall. The winter months were spent on ceremonies and preparation for the next year's harvest. The division of labor in this cycle was by household group, organized by gender, age, and status of the members. To illustrate, while adult men fished, women cleaned, split, and dried the catch. Additionally, there were a few specialized professions, such as shamans and wood carvers.

It was the *potlatch* for which the Northwest Coast people are best known, and the Tlingit were no exception. Potlatches were ceremonies that drew many people, and during these ceremonies food and gifts were given to the guests. The host group could start with a household but also extend to a clan and even an entire village, and several years could be spent in preparation of a single potlatch. Guests ranged from members of other households to other clans and villages. Huge quantities of food were served during these four-day affairs, and guests often took even more food back home. In grandiose displays, food was even burned or dumped into the sea, as if the giver had so much that food could be wasted. Other gifts included blankets, slaves, and ceremonial objects.

Guests were expected to reciprocate with a potlatch of their own. Not only gift giving, but also dancing, speeches, theatricals, and contests entertained guests and hosts alike at potlatches. The scale of the potlatch was commensurate with the status of the giver and as an equitable payment of a previous debt. Potlatches were given in connection with house building and rites of passage, including mortuary rites. Up to the time of the potlatch, a dead body was considered to be unfinished, but with a potlatch the spirit of the deceased was finally released and even reincarnated in a close matrilineal descendant (Kan, 1989).

The potlatch was a mechanism for the people to distribute their surplus wealth, and it validated the status of the hosts. Boastful re-

213

marks about one's status often accompanied a host's seeming indifference to property at a potlatch. These were the social events of the year, and truly great potlatches would be recounted in stories across the generations.

FRONTIER CONTACT AND EARLY ACCOMMODATION

Upon reaching Haiti, Christopher Columbus remarked about Native Americans:

> They are artless and generous of anything they have. If it be asked for, they never say no, but do rather invite the person to accept it, and show as much lovingness as though they would give their hearts. They are men of very subtle wit, who navigate all those seas, and who give a marvelous good account of everything…(Columbus, 1906).

The characterization of Native Americans by incoming Europeans would later change, as history moved from early accommodation to conflict and the eventual conquest of Native Americans. To put it abstractly, prejudice toward Native Americans would follow the taking of their land, and all sorts of stereotypical beliefs would somehow justify that they did not deserve their own land.

European colonization of North America began with the marches of Coronado in the west and DeSoto in the east. This colonization involved the British, Dutch, French, Spanish, and native-born Americans of immigrant stock. Accommodation between Native Americans and whites was at least possible in the early years, when neither side was the military superior and when Indians were vital economic suppliers to Europeans, as illustrated by the beaver trade. The contact evolved, however, into conflict over land and, ultimately, the conquest of America's indigenous people.

For 300 years following the first European penetration into the region that became the United States, no one people was politically dominant in it (Spicer, 1969:11). Neither the British, Dutch, French, nor Spanish, nor even, later, the emerging American government nor the many Indian nations could truly claim suzerainty in North America until late in the eighteenth century. In 1794, in what became the state of Ohio, Spicer (1969:12) noted, the triumph of the "Americans" in the Battle of Fallen Timbers gave a clear indication that they were destined for military dominance. Even after the turn of the century, British negotiators, for motives of their own, including an attempt to continue British control of the fur trade in America, asked for an Indian buffer state from the Great Lakes to the Ohio River. As Vogel

(1972:79) noted, however, "the stubborn resistance of the American negotiators...stalled the negotiations for months, and the British finally yielded the point." The American negotiators did concede to the British that there would be no more land cessions, a promise that was often made but seldom kept.

In the course of the first 300 years of their contact, immigrant and indigenous nations were rivals in North America. The Americans, British, Dutch, French, and Spanish all fought one another and the indigenous peoples. The conflict of the era cannot be denied. Josephy (1982) described the early assaults on Indians in Florida and New England—for example, the Puritan assault on the Pequots of Connecticut in 1637. Up to 700 died in one assault on a single Pequot village by Puritans aided by Mohicans and Narragansetts. Moreover, diseases introduced by whites reduced native populations drastically in this period; in the winter of 1616–17 a smallpox epidemic killed 50 to 70 percent of New England's coastal Indians (Josephy, 1982).

The consensus is that there were 2 to 5 million Native Americans in North America in 1600, but their numbers were reduced to under one-quarter of a million by 1850 (McNickle, 1962; Snipp, 1989). The Indian population decline was sharpest in the early years of contact. Military campaigns, famine, and slavery took their toll, but it was especially the spread of European diseases that decimated Indian numbers. Smallpox, diphtheria, bubonic plague, influenza, typhoid, measles, and scarlet fever resulted in the deaths of up to 4.75 million in North America between 1500 and 1890 (Snipp, 1989). Only remnants of tribes had to be overcome by the immigrants as settlement expanded to the west.

> One cannot begin to fathom the trauma that must have been experienced by those few Native people who, by genetic chance, survived the onslaught of previously unknown diseases, only to watch their families and friends perish. Yet they not only had to attempt to hold the fabric of their kin-based political systems together, but at the same time try to make a proper response to a growing and increasingly aggressive invading force of foreigners (Dorris, 1981:47).

This mortality in such gigantic proportions resulted in the migration of tribes further beyond the frontier, spreading European diseases and thus mortality, and reduced Native Americans to survival economies.

The early Indian policies of the European powers and the American government were intended to be benevolent by protecting Native American lands from undue settler encroachment. This intent was expressed in the Indian policy of the Spanish from the very beginning and by the British in the Royal Proclamation of 1763; in both instances Native Americans were recognized as the rightful owners of land in the Americas. Land was not be taken from them except in fair exchange. The British Proclamation of 1763 established a boundary at the Appalachian Mountains between European settlers and Native Americans. McNickle (1962:15) wrote "it is reassuring to note that the Dutch were scrupulous in paying for the land and making a record of it. The first important purchase appears to be Manhattan Island in 1626 for sixty guilders, or about thirty-nine dollars at today's silver prices. This would be about 360 acres per dollar, but since the Canarsie Indians had ample acres besides, they probably considered sixty guilders in European trade goods a fair exchange." Indians were needed not only as military allies, but also as producers and suppliers, for example, in the fur trade. Early Indian policy reflected these hard facts.

The early Indian policy of the United States, a policy largely inherited from the British, was also meant to protect Native American lands from settler encroachment. McNickle (1972:84) looked to the Northwest Ordinance of 1787 as an expression of the benevolent intent to these policies:

> Article III...The utmost good faith shall always be observed towards the Indians; their land property shall never be taken from them without their consent; and in their property, rights, and liberty, they never shall be invaded or disturbed, unless in just and lawful wars authorized by Congress; but laws founded in justice and humanity shall from time to time be made, for preventing wrongs being done to them and for preserving peace and friendship with them.

CONFLICT OVER LAND

Early intentions gave way to later realities, however. The expanding appetite of a growing number of settlers for land across the continent in the nineteenth century made competition and conflict between Native Americans and settlers nearly inevitable. European settlers brought a market economy to North America, which gave them the capacity to generate surplus wealth—or, if you like, which produced capital. To transplant this economy on American soil, settlers obviously had to first acquire Indian land and then make investments to bring it into production. Necessary improvements required capital, labor, and technology, for the tasks included clearing the land, cultivating it, and building a system of transportation. Transportation was necessary so that agricultural and mineral surplus extracted from the land could be shipped to distant markets and sold there for a profit. To protect their investments, settlers, from a position of increasing military superiority, established on the frontier European traditions of private property and exclusive ownership of land. Because the economic activities of white settlers and Native Americans were largely incompatible and because the more powerful settlers believed in the private ownership of land, settlers and Indians could not symbiotically share the land, and this meant conflict. About this phase of Indian-white relations, Prucha (1962:139) has stated that "the conflict between the whites and Indians that marked American Indian relations was basically a conflict over land."

The irony of this saga is that many of these settlers had been pushed off their own land in Europe in the transition there from feudalism to modern capitalism. Peasants were pulled into the growing industrial cities of Europe to work in factories and mills. Urban workers had to be fed, creating the need for European farmers to produce a surplus. The creation of an agricultural surplus in Europe included making land a commodity, one that could be bought and sold in the impersonal market. In this way, men and women with capital could first circumvent feudal notions about personal and non-economic ties between people and the land. They could buy land, consolidate their holdings into large estates, invest in labor-saving innovations for cultivation, and construct a system of transportation. Agricultural surpluses were produced and distributed to urban industry and workers through a system of markets, and peasants were displaced in the process.

For example, Scottish peasants by the thousands were forced off their land as it was turned into pasture for sheep by big land owners who sold wool to the growing textile industry in the Midlands of Great Britain. It was a time when sheep ate men. Displaced peasants were pushed into European industrial cities or were forced to migrate to the New World, where there was still room for farmers on the frontier. In America these transplanted peasants pushed the Indians off their land, as they had been forced off their land in Europe in the transition to a market economy.

Hansen (1940) observed that a succession of immigrants moved onto Indian lands. The trader and trapper came first, followed by the frontiersman, who engaged in hunting, gathering, and some subsistence farming. These types were not permanent settlers, however, and they moved on after a short stay in one place. The effect of their encroachment onto Indian lands was to push back the frontier, allowing other settlers to locate permanently where once the trapper and frontiersman had been.

It was a permanent settler who transplanted the European market economy and brought the legacy of private property to the land. Sizable investments of labor and capital were made by settlers, for land had to be cleared, homes and whole towns built, and a system of transportation constructed on the frontier. Hansen (1940) estimated that each homestead site required an initial investment of $1,000 to bring it into production. Private ownership of the land gave a settler some sense of security that he would realize a return on his investments, for he had legal title to the land, and the land and the improvements he made on it could not be capriciously taken from him. Public land was also converted into private holdings of big capital—the railroads, for instance—so that corporations could secure foreign loans with land as collateral. Thus land on the frontier became the private property of individual settlers and land speculators, real and corporate persons, and each parcel of land was under the exclusive ownership and sole control of the party who held legal title to it. There was no longer room for Native Americans on the land; they were now trespassers.

Another fact about the contact between Native Americans and settlers was that their ecological uses of the land were sometimes incompatible. The modifications of the habitat required for cultivation of the land and the construction of roads and railroads seriously interrupted the ecological base of Indian life. A specific case, the near depletion of the buffalo herds during the building of the transcontinental railroad, suggests the broader scale of this disruption. The building of a market economy on the frontier had the consequence of generally undermining the Native Americans' ecological life-style. The transformation in land use from Native American to white purposes also meant conflict between settlers and indigenous people.

Native Americans resisted settler encroachment, engaging occasionally in open conflicts, which were commonly called Indian wars. East of the Mississippi River, the greatest resistance was by the Creek Confederacy in the Southeast and by the Iroquois in the Northeast (Spicer, 1969). Fierce fighting occurred on the Great Plains and in the Southwest, where the Apaches held out until the 1880s. This resistance was tragic and largely ineffective, for settler encroachment eventually extended from coast to coast, at a great cost in Native American lives.

To accomplish military control over the Dakota and other Great Plains tribes, for example, the U.S. government established a series of forts throughout the upper Missouri River region. While treaties between the Dakota and the federal government were signed, these agreements were seldom honored. Gold prospectors rushed into the Black Hills (Dakota Territory) around 1876, and later the Custer massacre took place in Montana. Ultimately all of the Dakota bands succumbed to the superior military force of the United States and were placed on reservations. Fighting flared again later in 1890, when the U.S. Cavalry, on the advice of an Indian agent, mistook the Ghost Dance for an Indian uprising and massacred 300 Sioux at Wounded Knee Creek. Black Elk spoke to John Neihardt (1961:258) about this massacre:

> Men and women and children were heaped and scattered all over the flat at the bottom of the little hill where the soldiers had their wagonguns, and westward up the dry gulch all the way to the high-ridge, the dead women and children and babies were scattered.... It was a good winter day when all this happened. The sun was shining. But after the soldiers marched away from their dirty work, a heavy snow began to fall.... There was a big blizzard, and it grew very cold. The snow drifted deep in the crooked gulch, and it was one long grave of butchered women and children and babies, who had never done any harm and were only trying to run away.

This incident was repeated in its essentials across the frontier, as Native American land throughout North America was expropriated and Indian people were either killed or excluded to isolated reservations.

EXPROPRIATION OF LAND

Map 7.2 illustrates the scale and timing of the expropriation of Native American land across the continent. The European powers, and then the U.S. government, "found it prudent to devise procedures by which title to the land could pass in an orderly manner from Indian to European [and American]" (McNickle, 1962:10). Initially, the procedure was the purchase of Indian land in fair trade; at least this was the stated purpose of European and early American Indian policy. George Washington (Vogel, 1972:75) wrote on the practicality of purchasing, instead of expropriating, Indian land: "I am clear in my opinion, that policy and economy point very strongly to the expediency of being upon good terms with the Indians, and the propriety of purchasing their lands in preference to attempting to drive them by force of arms out of their Country."

However, the exchange of land in this manner proved to be a failure, for neither side truly understood the implications these sales had for the other. As an indication of this mutual ignorance, members of a tribe would return to land which had been previously sold to white settlers by other tribal members and expect to share with the settlers in the use of the land. Of course, the white homesteaders considered the land their private property after such sales, although these sentiments never made much sense to the Native Americans, for among them land had never been merchantable in the European sense. Hostilities between Native Americans and white settlers often resulted from this

MAP 7.2   NATIVE AMERICAN LAND CESSIONS IN THE UNITED STATES

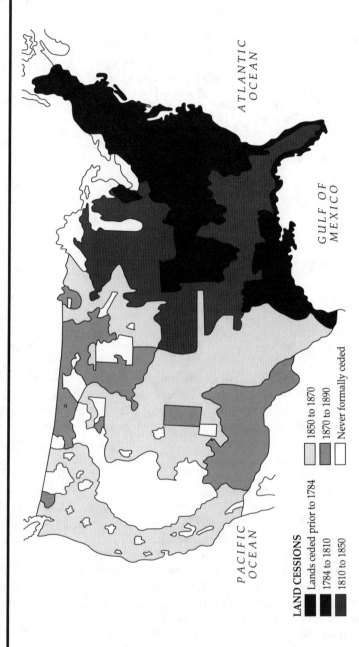

ATLANTIC
OCEAN

GULF OF
MEXICO

PACIFIC
OCEAN

LAND CESSIONS

Lands ceded prior to 1784

1784 to 1810

1810 to 1850

1850 to 1870

1870 to 1890

Never formally ceded

Source: "Land Cessions" map by Jean Paul Tremblay, reprinted from *The Indian Heritage of America.* Copyright © 1968 by Alvin M. Josephy, Jr. By permission of Mr. Josephy.

confusion over land ownership and use. It also made for ethnocentrism such as the following:

> Our savage Indians had no idea of the ownership of land.... The idea propagated by some modern sentimentalists that in resisting the march of civilization the wild Indians were fighting for their homes and firesides belongs to fiction rather than to fact.... They had no home and no fireside, in the civilized sense of these terms (quoted in Humfreville, 1964).

Neither group knew what to make of the other, illustrated in the Native American case by the "...idea of the Southern Cheyenne that mountain men—the early European trappers in the Rockies—represented the return to the world of a class of long-departed excrement-eating clowns" (Dorris, 1981:46).

Early in the contact period, European nations implemented the Right of Discovery, meaning that "...legal jurisdiction fell to the European nation first landing on, and laying claim to territory not formerly held by other Europeans" (Dorris, 1981:48). As the number of settlers increased, the need for land and the desire to pacify the frontier for further white settlement grew. Native American land rights were increasingly ignored by the U.S. government, and thus the precedents of earlier Indian policies, such as the Royal Proclamation of 1763 and the Northwest Ordinance of 1787, were discontinued in the 1800s. First, the Trade and Intercourse Act of 1790 stated that Native American land could "...pass out of Indian hands only when the federal government...is involved in the transaction" (Dorris, 1981:50). Later, there was the Louisiana Purchase from France in 1803 and then, under the discretionary powers granted to President Andrew Jackson by the Indian Removal Act of 1830, the eastern tribes were removed to lands west of the Mississippi River:

> In the succeeding ten years the Atlantic and Gulf States were cleared of the Cherokees, Choctaws, Chickasaws, Creeks, and Seminoles.... The Ohio River and Great Lakes tribes were also rounded up and removed, with the Sauk and Fox Indians making a last desperate stand in Illinois against overwhelming numbers. All were moved—Ottawas, Potawatomies, Wyandots, Shawnees, Kickapoos, Winnebagoes, Delawares, Peorias, Miamis, and finally the Sauk and Fox—all were sent out of their homes to strange lands beyond the Mississippi (McNickle, 1962:40).

The stage was set for the removal of the Cherokee from the Carolinas and Georgia by the Indian Removal Act of 1830 and the earlier Louisiana Purchase in 1803. The forcible relocation of the Cherokee began in 1838; they were marched to Indian Territory (Oklahoma), a march known as the Trail of Tears. The Cherokee were first rounded up and brought to detention camps, and then the bands began the trek to Oklahoma in the fall of 1838. They took a route through Tennessee and Kentucky, after which some went through Missouri and others through Arkansas to Oklahoma. Some detachments of Cherokee were on the trail for up to 139 days. Many walked that winter, while the infirm rode in wagons. In the end, four thousand Cherokee died on the Trail of Tears, nearly one-fifth of the entire Cherokee population.

Some tribes were forced to move again in a few years out of Iowa, Kansas, and Nebraska because of the mounting pressure for further white settlement. The Kansas-Nebraska Act of 1854 and the Homestead Act of 1862 paved the way for the white settlement of Iowa, Kansas, and Nebraska. Mineral deposits were discovered even further into the frontier, in the Dakotas and Colorado, for instance. Between 1869 and 1893, five transcontinental railroads were built to link the east and west coasts of the country. This meant the expropriation of more and more Native American land and the removal of Native Americans to even more remote corners of the frontier, out of the way of white settlement.

According to Spicer (1969:66–67), "the dominance of the settlers led steadily to the elimination of any conception of Indian political rights. A major step in the legal codification of this view came in 1871 when the United States Congress acted to put an end to the making of treaties with any Indian group." So ended the era of treaties; this action reversed the earlier concept of Native Americans as domestic nations and as the rightful owners of American land on the basis of their historical occupancy. In theory if not always in practice, Native Americans had been considered as self-governing political entities, capable of deciding for themselves the manner in which they would exchange land with others. Even the Indian Removal Act of 1830 had "authorized such removal only on the condition that the Indians gave consent" (Spicer, 1969:46). Actual practice had always been somewhat ahead of legal principle, but now with this legislation in 1871 and later Congressional actions, even the principle of Indian self-determination was abandoned:

> So long as the Indian tribes could hold the policy makers at arm's length, as they managed to do through the treaty process, they could determine for themselves what internal controls they chose to exercise over land or any other sphere of interest. With that barrier breached in 1871, only the judicial process remained to inhibit. A countervailing legislative process was needed, and would soon be proposed (McNickle, 1962:45).

This legislation came in 1887 with the passage of the General Allotment Act, or the Dawes Act. Under this legislation Indian families were each allotted 160 acres, with titles to these allotments held in trust for 25 years by the government. "Surplus" Indian land was to be sold. "Each Indian allottee was granted a share or a portion of a share, usually not exceeding 160 acres...there was considerably more remaining Indian land than there were Indians to distribute it to individually,...[and] almost one-half of all the lands controlled by Indians in 1885 were declared 'surplus' and passed out of Native control" (Dorris, 1981:51). Vogel (1972:175) noted: "No lands were to be kept in reserve for future generations of Indians, because of the assumption that their population would continue to decline."

The net effect of the Allotment Act was to separate Native Americans from much of their remaining land: "In 1887, approximately 140,000,000 acres were owned in joint tenure by the Indians of the United States. The allotment law, as amended in succeeding years, set up procedures which resulted in the transfer of some 90,000,000 acres from Indian to white owners in the next forty-five years" (McNickle, 1962:49). Thus the procedures for acquiring Indian land evolved from the concept that land was to be acquired only with Indian consent and in a fair exchange to the concept that tribal lands were to be held in trust by the federal government and could be sold without Indian permission. This change in legal notion facilitated land expropriation, although the practice of the unilateral grabbing of Indian land generally preceded changes in legal theory.

Whatever means settlers might have chosen to secure Indian land, they were certainly powerful enough to do it, even in the face of Indian resistance. The superior power resources of white settlers included numerical superiority, social organization, and, most importantly, surplus wealth. Settlers reached numerical superiority soon after their initial contact with America's indigenous groups, and Native Americans quickly became a numerical minority on their own land. This prompted a Pawnee scout, Little Warrior, to say in 1879 that "it is of no use for you to try to fight the white people. I have been among them, and I know how many they are. They are like grass....If you try to fight them they will hunt you like a ghost" (Forbes, 1964:66). Not only were Native Americans unable to restrict the immigration of white settlers so that the numbers of settlers grew ever greater, but their own numbers were simultaneously on the decline, due mainly to the diseases brought to America by the immigrants.

The settler economy generated surplus wealth, a surplus that grew as the frontier enlarged and the economy expanded. Thus, settlers possessed an increasing margin of wealth above the subsistence level, which they could and did direct in military and political efforts to expropriate more Native American land. The capacity of settlers to generate wealth was rooted in their market economy and followed from their takeover of a bountiful land. Technology helped make possible the production of an agricultural and mineral surplus and its shipment through a system of markets to various consumption centers, and thus it, too, was important in the creation of surplus wealth. The steam engine aided the transportation of crops to market, for instance, as the steel plow allowed settlers to break for the first time the rich sod of the Midwest. These technological innovations facilitated cultivation and extraction at a profit, stimulated settlers' desire for more land, and resulted in relatively dense white settlement. From numbers and wealth came power, and the power of settlers was extremely liquid, since in a monetary economy surplus wealth can be easily turned into military force. Butter was indeed turned into guns, and $1,000,000 for each Indian casualty was not too high a price.

Native American resources for conflict were simply no match. Not only were Native Americans short of the wealth and numbers necessary for successful resistance to settler encroachment, but also they never effectively mobilized the resources they did share in a united stand against invasion. Across the frontier and with few exceptions, the indigenous peoples were organized into small groups lacking linguistic unification and other ingredients essential for the effective pooling and easy mobilization of their power resources. This was on top of the fact that Native American numbers had been decimated by European diseases and their economies reduced to subsistence ones. Thus Native American attempts to repel encroachment were reduced to ineffective retaliation which had the net result of strengthening settlers' resolve to take more Native American land. The whites were not only more powerful, they were also better organized, having a centralized political authority and military force in the U.S. government, which itself was the legacy of centuries of political evolution in Europe.

The result of this mismatch in power resources is sadly evident in the surrender speech of Chief Joseph of the Nez Perces:

> I am tired of fighting. Our chiefs are killed. Looking Glass is dead. Too-hul-hul-sote is dead. The old men are all dead…. It is cold and we have no blankets. The little children are freezing to death…. I want to have time to look for my children and see how many of them I can find. Maybe I shall find them among the dead. Hear me, my chiefs. I am tired; my heart is sick and sad. From where the sun now stands I will fight no more forever (Vogel, 1972:171).

Prejudice, reinforced by violence but rooted in the dissimilarity between European and Native American cultures, was generated in the course of the conflict over the land and helped settlers justify their expropriation of it. One suspects that as settlers agitated for Indian removal, they argued that Indians wasted the potential of the land by not extracting surplus quantities from it. To settlers this was a sign of innate laziness and a convenient rationalization for Indian removal. Even when settlers met Native Americans who were accomplished agriculturalists, as they did in the Southwest, the stereotype of the ever-lazy and sometimes violent Indian prevailed (Spicer, 1962). That several Native American cultures had been virtually destroyed and many Indians were wandering aimlessly about the frontier were undoubtedly construed as final proof in the minds of many settlers that the Indians had gotten what they deserved.

Underlying the conflict over land was a deep ethnocentrism, and thus this era can be also characterized as a clash of cultures. The immigrants valued progress, technology, materialism and individualism. With these values, they saw native life, rooted in stability, subsistence, ecological harmony, and communalism, as hopelessly stagnant and inefficient. Native Americans, for their part, saw the immigrants obsessed with change, the here-and-now, not the spiritual, and creating chaos rather than peace and harmony (Olson and Wilson, 1984).

BOX 7.1   THE STORY OF ISHI

On August 29, 1911, in the California gold country, a prospector found a middle-aged Indian crouched against a corral fence, and he called the sheriff. The sheriff took the "wild man" into custody. Near starvation, Ishi (as he came to be called) suffered from exhaustion and fear. He was unresponsive, and the sheriff put him in jail to protect him from curiosity seekers. It could be assumed that Ishi expected to be killed, for after all he was captured by his enemy, the white man.

An anthropologist at the University of California, T. T. Waterman, went to the jail to see Ishi. He established a rudimentary communication with Ishi, and later the University of California received permission to make room for Ishi at the University Museum of Anthropology in San Francisco. The museum became Ishi's home until he died four and a half years later.

During his years at the Museum, Ishi never revealed his own, private Yahi name. He remained a man apart from the surroundings in other ways as well. Although he learned to shake hands in the way of the white man, he never initiated a handshake, and he discouraged others from coming too close or touching him. The crowds of white people in the city and on the beaches overwhelmed Ishi. He did adapt a new dining etiquette (a knife and fork), and he appreciated having a job and income of his own. Ishi even accumulated a modest savings, which he willed upon his death to the medical school in San Francisco.

◉◉

EXCLUSION OF NATIVE AMERICANS

The fate of the Native Americans eventually fell into the hands of the more powerful settlers. In their position of dominance, white settlers could have either included America's indigenous peoples into the revised society or excluded them. The latter course was chosen, and the Indian policy of the U.S. government became one of exclusion whereby Native Americans were isolated on reservations and removed from white society. This was a policy of peace through isolation. Along with their physical isolation on reservations, Native Americans were excluded from any meaningful participation in the American economy and state. This allowed the history of Native Americans to diverge from that of American society (see Fig. 7.1).

The full-scale implementation of this exclusionary policy began with the actions of President Andrew Jackson, who apparently had the interests of Georgian settlers in mind when he ignored the opinion of the Supreme Court and executed the Indian Removal Act of 1830. Under this act, the Federal government removed Indians living east of the Mississippi River—supposedly with their consent—to reservations west of the river. It was in the course of this move that the Cherokee were forcibly marched out of the South to Indian Territory in present-day Oklahoma. As Vogel (1972:70) noted: "Oklahoma, already the home of the Five Civilized Tribes of the Southeast, was soon to become a vast concentration camp into which Indians from tribes as far apart as the New York Senecas and the West Coast Modacs were to be squeezed."

Thus America's indigenous peoples were trapped in an historical cul de sac on reservations, where, without capital and technology, they had no chance of competing as farmers and ranchers with white settlers in the new market economy. Moreover, on reservations they had virtually no access to industrial work or access of any kind into the larger society. Native Americans were unprepared for the later changes in American society, that toward industrial and then white-collar work. The geographical distribution of reservations and major Native American groups is shown in Map 7.3. By population size in 1980, the five largest reservations were the Navajo, Pine Ridge in South Dakota, and Gila River, Papago, and Fort Apache in Arizona (Snipp, 1989).

MAP 7.3 MAJOR NATIVE AMERICAN GROUPS AND RESERVATIONS

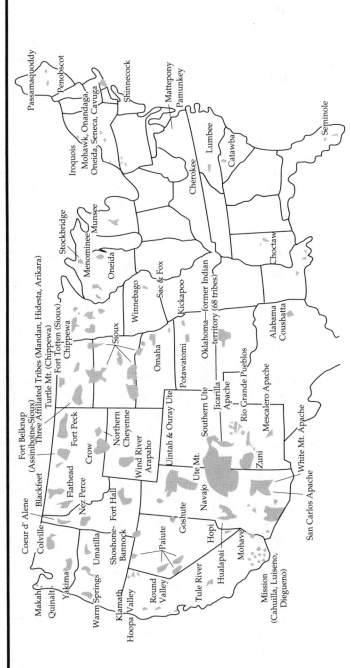

Source: From *To Live on This Earth* by Estelle Fuchs & Robert J. Havighurst. Copyright © 1972 by Estelle Fuchs and Robert J. Havighurst. Used by permission of Doubleday, a division of Bantam Doubleday Dell Publishing Group, Inc.

227

The effects of geographical isolation on Native Americans were compounded by those of the General Allotment Act of 1887, which had a tenure of over forty years. Under the Allotment Act and its auxiliary programs, reservation Indians were expected to emulate white settlers, or at least some fancied version of settlers, by becoming farmers and tilling allotments of privately owned land. Two ideas about farming were evident among the European immigrants: plantation and yeoman farming. After the Civil War, yeoman farming predominated the ideology of agriculture, and this was the idea transplanted on reservations. European conceptions of property rights and proper land management were forced on reservation Indians, at least on many of them, and the broader expectation was that Native Americans, through their experiences as a class of property owners, would eventually assimilate into American society. This assimilationist notion was buttressed by other efforts, such as the bringing of immigrant religion and education to the reservations. Indeed, for a time the United States gave responsibility to churches for reservation management before turning over this responsibility to the federal government (Josephy, 1982). Tribes in Indian Territory were exempt from the allotments, as were the Senecas in New York and the Sioux in Nebraska (Olson and Wilson, 1984).

The provisions of the General Allotment Act were generally contrary to Native American cultural norms, particularly those concerning the communal ownership and management of land. Equally important, the act was inconsistent with the actual course of economic development—toward the consolidation of land holdings—in the regions where the reservations were located. While Native Americans were scratching at small plots of arid and unproductive earth in the West, settlers of the same region were systematically consolidating their land holdings and evolving toward an economy of scale. Some of the land in this consolidation was Indian land, as Indians lost nearly two-thirds of their reservation land (90 million acres) during the tenure of the General Allotment Act. During the years of the General Allotment Act, Native Americans were unable to compete with the larger and better equipped settler operations and were forced to either sell or lease much of their land to whites.

Along with its provisions for land allotments, the General Allotment Act of 1887 attempted to suppress native traditions in religion and education. One instance of this repression was the establishment of Indian boarding schools. Children were taken from their homes and sent to distant boarding schools, where they were taught to relinquish their heritage and conform to white ways. The intent of the Allotment Act had been to assimilate Native Americans or to accomplish their inclusion into and convergence with the larger society. The net consequence, however, was the economic and political exclusion of Native Americans from the larger society, so that Indians as a people diverged from the national history. The discrepancy between intention and fact in this instance was acknowledged in later Indian policy. In 1898, the Curtis Act repudiated Indian self-determination and dissolved the governments of the so-called Five Civilized Tribes.

The problems engendered by conquest and loss of tradition were recognized later in the course of the Indigenismo movement, specifically in the Meriam Survey of 1928. The Meriam Report (Institute for Government Research, 1928:5) stated:

> In some instances the land originally set apart for the Indians was of little value for agricultural operations other than grazing. In other instances part of the land was excellent but the Indian did not appreciate its value. Often when individual allotments were made, they chose for themselves the poorer parts because those parts were near a domestic water supply or a source of firewood, or because they furnished some native product important to the Indians in their primitive life. Frequently the better sections of the land set apart for the Indians have fallen into the hands of the whites, and the Indians have retreated to the poorer lands remote from markets.

This recognition helped bring about the Indian Reorganization Act of 1934 discussed below.

The ostensible reason for isolating Native Americans on reservations was to pacify the frontier, making it safe for further white settlement, while the apparent intent of the General Allotment Act was to somehow assimilate the Native Americans isolated on these reservations. But behind these reasons are more basic ones, or so say conflict theorists.

In the course of ethnic relations, groups exchange certain resources, including their land, labor, and capital, which act as assets and affect how they treat one another. Typically, according to conflict theory, the group with the larger share of such resources dominates the others. Domination can come in several forms, however, and the match between a powerful group's needs and a subordinate group's resources can greatly affect how the subordinate group is treated. If a conquered group possesses resources needed and desired by its conqueror, especially if these resources are not easily gotten elsewhere or not easily substituted for, then its domination is likely to be relatively benevolent. For instance, if Native Americans had been good wage workers in sufficient numbers, and if there had been no immigrant labor in the country, American capital might have incorporated Native Americans into the society as labor and treated them in accord with labor supply and demand. Such assets as labor can be termed *competitive resources*, following Blalock's (1967) usage. A conquered group's possession of competitive resources usually brings its inclusion into the society of the conqueror.

Once their land had been expropriated, however, Native Americans possessed few competitive resources. They had little in the way of labor and capital with which to influence the Indian policy of the United States. Land is potentially a competitive resource, but Native American land was obviously detachable from the Native American people, and thus was not, in practice, a competitive resource. Nor did Native Americans comprise an attractive labor pool. Their numbers had declined to 250,000 people by 1850, and their physical health in the late nineteenth century was dreadful, with widespread malnutrition and morbidity. So there is some question as to whether Native Americans were healthy enough to have been brought into the revised frontier economy as workers.

Furthermore, the fragmentation of the Native American population into diverse groups precluded the easy mobilization of what healthy Native American labor there was into labor pools large enough to have been useful in the labor-intense operations of the emerging economic empire in the West. Moreover, few Native Americans had any experience as contractual wage workers, and potential employers were aware that earlier attempts at using Indian labor had been largely futile. Native American slaves in the South had a history of running away, and their presence "raised the danger of conspiracies with enemy Indians" (Forbes, 1964:90). Into this setting came large numbers of immigrant laborers who were cheap and relatively docile and who would work in large labor pools, as did Africans in the South, the Chinese in the construction of the transcontinental railroad in the West, and Mexicans in the farming operations of the Southwest. These immigrants met the nation's labor needs.

The exclusion of Native Americans also followed from certain precedents set in the era of treaties, when they had been treated in almost all instances as political collectivities, as independent and then dependent domestic nations, and not as free, autonomous individuals. When these precedents are combined with a Native American inclination toward self-exclusion, with the fact that other people were pulled into the country's labor force as free labor, and with the Native Americans' low level of health, the exclusion of Native Americans from the larger society seems in hindsight nearly inevitable.

Native Americans stood between a powerful group and its goal, to put it abstractly, without having either competitive resources or the protection of a third party to temper the powerful group's inclination to take the most direct and least costly route toward its goal. Thus, the U.S. government legitimated the unilateral expropriation of Native American land, catching up with actual practice as it did so. Following this expropriation, neither American capital nor labor had any interest in assimilating Native Americans into the revised American economy. So Native Americans were excluded to reservations, and it was hoped that there the "red people" would vanish.

THE PRESENT SITUATION

Steps toward reversing the exclusion of Native Americans began early in the twentieth century. By 1920, observed Spicer (1972), it was obvious that the Allotment Act had failed in its intent to assimilate Native Americans. Realizing this, certain influential whites, including John Collier, who later became Commissioner of Indian Affairs, proposed changes in Indian policy. These suggestions were ultimately incorporated into the Indian Reorganization Act of 1934. Edward Spicer (1972) expressed the opinion that such efforts toward improving Indian welfare, which he called Indigenismo movements, represent a later phase in a cycle of conquest that comes when the conquered people are no longer a military threat.

The initial stage of the Indigenismo movement in the United States was the years 1870–1920, which were associated with the General Allotment Act, while the second stage, begun in 1920, consisted of a reappraisal of that act. The Indian Reorganization Act of 1934 repealed the allotment laws, restored a small portion of lost reservation land, and permitted the voluntary exchange of allotments for interests in tribal corporations (Olson and Wilson, 1984). Many Native Americans were excluded, however, from the Reorganization Act because they were not recognized as tribes by the Bureau of Indian Affairs, as were Native Americans in Oklahoma. In a referendum, 181 tribes accepted the act and 77 rejected it (Olson and Wilson, 1984).

The belief behind the Indian Reorganization Act was that Native Americans would find their own accommodation to American society if left to themselves. This policy rationale was a reversal of the common practices under the earlier General Allotment Act. The Indian Reorganization Act included a return to tribal management of reservation land, the replacement of distant boarding schools with day schools near home, and the encouragement of tribal practices, including native religions. All these measures were directed toward the reestablishment of traditional ways, the authority of which had been so badly undermined during the tenure of the Allotment Act. Many tribes became economic corporations and political entities under the new act. The intent was to have Indians move into the future in their own way, and it was hoped that the process would be facilitated by the return to traditional authority patterns.

Since the Indian Reorganization Act, Indian policies have moved steadily toward greater self-determination. In 1946 the federal government waived its immunity from legal suits for having inadequately compensated Native Americans for their land, as well as for having mismanaged tribal lands under the General Allotment Act. In the 1950s the federal government even attempted to terminate its special relationship with Native Americans and to dissolve essentially all of its historical obligations toward them. Between 1953 and 1962, Congress terminated federal services to more than sixty separate Native American groups (Olson and Wilson, 1984). The passage of this legislation was resisted by Native Americans on the premise that they were neither prepared nor willing to abandon their ties to the federal government and their land. Termination had nearly disastrous consequences for some tribes that undertook it—for example, the Klamath and Menomini. Between 1952 and 1972, the Bureau of Indian Affairs also relocated about 100,000 Indians from reservations to American cities (Snipp, 1989).

Passage of the Indian Self-Determination and Educational Assistance Act of 1975 now allows tribes to provide services to their members in their own way with federal funds. It also recognizes the right of Native Americans to "'control their relationships both among themselves and with non-Indian governments, organizations and persons,' and goes on to observe that 'the prolonged Federal domination of Indian service programs has served to retard rather than enhance the progress of Indian people and their communities'" (Dorris, 1981:55). At the present time several tribes are also seeking the return of their lands, and some tribes have been successful (Box 7.2). This signals the intention of Native Americans to find their own accommodation to the larger society.

☙❧

BOX 7.2 TRIBAL INVESTMENT BANK LIFTS INDIANS IN MAINE

Mr. Zilkha is president of Tribal Assets Management, an investment bank set up to help oversee the $81.5 million settlement the federal government gave the Penobscot and Passamaquoddy Indians in 1980 in compensation for land taken from them over the past two centuries....Indeed Mr. Zilkha and state officials agree that Tribal Assets Management now has the largest pool of private capital in Maine, which ranks 39th in the nation in per capita income and badly needs investment funds.

"The Indians are becoming major players in the state economy along with the banks and timber companies," said Thomas N. Tureen, a public-interest lawyer who masterminded the tribe's ten-year lawsuit to win the settlement and then founded Tribal Assets Management....They're like a venture capital firm specializing in Maine.

Of the $81.5 million settlement given to the Penobscots and Passamaquoddys, who together number only 4,200 and live mainly on three isolated reservations, one-third has gone toward purchasing 300,000 acres of timberland they considered their patrimony. Another third has been put into liquid government securities whose earnings are distributed annually on a per capita basis. The remaining third is being used to acquire a portfolio of commercial and industrial investments in Maine....

The Indians have sought an investment program that combines financial gain with social benefits. "They want to make money but do something for Maine, too," Mr. Zilkha said.

Thus, the Passamaquoddys acquired two profitable radio stations in Rockland and the state's third-largest blueberry farm, another lucrative venture. But they have also bought a cement plant in Thomaston, Me., the largest such plant in New England, to keep it from closing and thus save 200 jobs of non-Indians.

...The Penobscots are also building a $2.5 million factory to make audio cassettes on their reservation in collaboration with an electronics company in southern Maine....In addition, the tribe has created the Penobscot guarantee fund to lend money to small, rapidly growing companies in Maine that cannot get financing from regular banks.

...Mr. Tureen's success on behalf of the Penobscots and the Passamaquoddys has recently begun to attract business from other Indian tribes, from the Navajo in Arizona to the Cherokee in North Carolina. "The Indians are well positioned as potential investors," he said, because "they own 55 million acres of land in the lower 38 states, which they can use as assets."

The Indian Reorganization Act and the legislation following it represented the cessation of the forced enculturation of Native Americans. The current policies of the federal government appear to be on a course of cultural pluralism for Native Americans. This policy may also bring a change in the Indian subeconomy, which since the past century has been running in a direction opposite that of the larger American economy. This real possibility is symbolized by the tribal investment bank in Maine (Box 7.2) and by the Alaskan Native Claims Settlement Act (1971) on our last land frontier: "Here, for the first time, very large economic resources are placed in the hands of native people with very few external controls over the way they use those resources" (Havighurst, 1977:13). Forty million acres of land were restored to Alaskan natives, and $962.5 million was promised them for land taken over by the state and federal governments. The way Alaskan natives will receive this money is also important:

> The valuable thing they receive is 100 shares in one of 12 Native Regional Corporations which take title to the land and which keep for investment purposes 90 percent of the money paid under the Act. ...The Regional Corporations were formed as quickly as possible after the passage of the Act, and have been using approximately $200 million they received from the government in the first five years to invest in productive enterprises-such as hotels, supermarkets, mineral exploration, reindeer herds, and fish canneries (Havighurst, 1977: 13–14).

By 1980 there were over 1.3 million Native Americans living in the United States, indicating considerable growth in numbers since the nineteenth century. This population growth is due to better health care, sanitation, and housing, as well as the more inclusive counting of the Native American population (Snipp, 1989). Native American life expectancy for both males and females increased dramatically between 1940 and 1980, and now it exceeds that for African Americans, although it is still behind that for white Americans: 51 years vs. 64.9 years for whites in 1940, but 71.1 years vs. 74.4 years for whites in 1980 (Stuart, 1987).

Nearly one-half of the adult Native Americans lived in urban areas in 1980. Like the American population at large, Native Americans have been moving to urban areas in the West and South. The most important of these flows is from the Mountain to the Pacific states. "Overall, American Indian migrants tend to be younger than nonmigrants and single. Their motives for migration include seeking employment, attending college, or serving in the armed forces. They also tend to be better educated" (Snipp, 1989:303).

Tables 7.1 and 7.2 show how Native Americans are currently following the labor history of immigrant groups, moving from agriculture to urban residence and industrial work. Note the decrease in Native Americans employed as farm workers since 1940, and the increasing percentage in blue- and white-collar work. Native Ameri-

TABLE 7.1 PERCENTAGE DISTRIBUTION OF NATIVE AMERICANS AND ALL
EMPLOYED PEOPLE BY OCCUPATIONAL GROUPS, 1940–1970

Occupational Group	Native Americans				All People			
	1940	1950	1960	1970	1940	1950	1960	1970
White-collar workers								
Professional and technical	2.6	3.2	6.2	9.8	7.5	8.7	11.1	14.9
Managers, officials, and proprietors (except farmers)	1.3	1.9	2.6	4.1	8.4	8.7	8.4	8.3
Clerical and sales	2.6	4.5	8.7	16.6	16.8	19.2	21.6	25.0
Blue-collar workers								
Craftsmen and foremen	4.6	9.1	11.2	14.1	11.3	14.3	13.5	13.9
Operators	13.7	16.1	19.9	18.1	18.4	20.3	18.4	13.7
Laborers except farm and mine	19.8	14.4	14.7	8.6	6.8	6.5	4.8	4.5
Service workers								
Private household	3.7	3.3	5.2	2.6	6.2	2.5	2.7	1.5
Other service	4.0	7.0	11.9	16.4	6.2	7.8	8.4	11.3
Farm workers								
Farmers and managers	37.9	20.5	7.4	1.6	11.5	7.6	3.9	1.9
Laborers and foremen	9.2	20.1	12.2	4.2	6.9	4.4	2.2	1.3

Note: Percentages may not total 100 because of rounding.

Sources: 1940 Census, *The Labor Force*, Table 62, p. 90; 1940 Census, *Characteristics of the Non-White Population by Race*, Table 3, pp. 29–36; 1950 Census, *Characteristics of the Nonwhite Population by Race*, Table 10, p. 32; 1960 Census, *Occupational Characteristics*, Table 2, pp. 11–20; *Characteristics of the Nonwhite Population by Race*, Table 33, p. 104; 1970 Census, *Occupational Characteristics*, Table 39, pp. 593–600.

cans have remained behind other groups in this transition, however, indicative of their continued divergence.

For example, Native Americans are overrepresented in administrative support, service occupations, and as operators, fabricators, and laborers, but they are underrepresented in managerial and professional jobs as compared to all people in the labor force (Table 7.2). Nevertheless, Native Americans' occupational history since 1940 has been consistent with, not contrary to, trends in the larger society.

Across the nation, in cities as well as on reservations, labor force participation rates for Native American males have been declining; 70 percent of the Native American adult males in this nation were in the labor force in 1940, but this rate dropped to 59.5 percent in 1960 and

TABLE 7.2 PERCENTAGE DISTRIBUTION OF NATIVE AMERICANS AND ALL
EMPLOYED PEOPLE BY OCCUPATIONAL GROUPS, 1990

Occupational Group	Native Americans 1990	All People 1990
Managerial and professional	17.2%	25.5%
Technical, sales, and administrative support	25.8	31.5
Service occupations	19.0	13.5
Precision production, craft, and repair	14.0	11.5
Operators, fabricators, and laborers	20.4	15.5
Farming, forestry, and fishing	3.6	2.5

Note: Percentages may not total 100 because of rounding.

Source: 1990 Census, *Characteristics of the Population*, Chapter C, General Social and Economic
Characteristics, Table 125, pp. 1–102; U.S. 1990 Census of Population, Equal Opportunity File.

was 58.5 percent in 1980. Forty-eight percent of the adult females were
in the labor force in 1980. Moreover, "The median level of schooling of
the Indian male in 1960 was about the same as the 1940 level of all
males..." (Sorkin, 1971:16). In 1980, 8.4 percent of Native Americans 25
years old or over had less than five years of schooling, 55.5 percent
had graduated from high school, and 7.7 percent had four or more
years of college. Among non-Indians, over 67 percent of this age cohort have graduated from high school. Such evidence testifies to the
continued exclusion of Native Americans from major institutions of
the larger society, such as education and the labor force. Commentary
on Native American adjustment to urban life has been pessimistic
about the rapid transition of significant numbers of Native Americans
into the ranks of urban wage earners. Moreover, federal Indian policy
became less responsive to the pro-Indian lobby in the 1980s (Gross,
1989). These observations portend an uncertain forecast for the future
of Native Americans.

   Whatever the future brings, the present situation shows the signs
of historical divergence over the past 100 years or so. Native Americans are still one of the least educated groups in the country and still
reside more than others in rural areas. "American Indians still bear the
markings of a population outside the economic mainstream. By the
standards of white Americans, American Indians are not well educated; they are marginally attached to the labor force; they do work that
is not highly valued; and the consequences of these liabilities are

poverty and economic hardship....The fate of American Indians in the next century may depend on their success in passing along their culture at the same time that they learn to cope with the demands of post-industrial American society" (Snipp, 1989:264–265).

The point is that indicators of the current health, wealth, education, and welfare of Native Americans still attest to their historical divergence as a people. The current cultural idioms of Native Americans and the general pattern for them to restrict social participation to their own kind are also evidence of their continued exclusion and divergence. Some assimilation has occurred, of course, but, when compared with other ethnic groups, the inclusion and historical convergence of Native Americans have been minimal.

This is not meant to dismiss the obvious signs of Native American assimilation. Field research finds significant degrees of acculturation, even among reservation Indians. McFee (1972) observed that the acculturation of the Blackfeet began immediately after their conquest, and a conscious decision was made by some families to adopt white ways. Today, the different degrees of enculturation among the Blackfeet divide the tribe into two camps: Indian-oriented and white-oriented. Not only do these two groups have different value systems and status hierarchies, but they are also partially segregated from each other in their patterns of social participation. Social occasions for Indian-oriented Blackfeet and those for white-oriented Blackfeet are mutually exclusive. When the two groups do participate together in public, it is on a neutral site at a large, impersonal event. Moreover, social distance between members of the two groups is maintained in town and on shopping and business trips. Thus, the assimilation of Blackfeet varies by ethclass.

> ...what appears to be taking place is the creation of two somewhat distinct populations of persons with American Indian background. One is a core population of individuals strongly connected to their American Indian heritage. In terms of their residence, lifestyle, socioeconomic characteristics, and even appearance, this group constitutes a population easily identifiable as American Indian.... A second population consists of persons who can recall, legitimately, some amount of Indian ancestry but have little knowledge of Indian culture and in most respects do not resemble the core population of American Indians (Snipp, 1989:310).

Once the Oglala lived in a social world distinct and separate from the dominant American society, one that was described at the beginning of this chapter. That continued even after their defeat, but, once Oglala children began to attend boarding schools away from home, they had to live in two worlds, one Indian and the other white. Today, the two cultures still coexist but are as opposed as ever (Powers, 1986). The traditionalists fear the demise of Indian culture, however, and point to the loss of the Oglala language among the young and to how the young forget kinship terms and how to act properly toward their kin. The old ways of courtship are gone, and traditional rites of passage into adulthood are no longer observed. Practices from the dominant society have been adopted by the Oglala, ranging from having high-school cheerleaders to organizations for dealing with domestic violence against women and children, such as the Sacred Shawl Society. Although a cleavage exists between the traditional and the modern, most Oglala organize their lives flexibly along three dimensions: traditional versus modern; white versus Indian; and male versus female (Powers, 1986).

Native Americans are converging too fast in one way for some interest groups. They have gone into the gambling industry in a big way, operating more than 100 legal gambling operations across the country, mostly on reservations, that bring in $500 million a year. Indian bingo casinos are the big winners. Gambling was widespread among Native Americans prior to contact, with games of chance including dice, sticks, and other objects as part of guessing exercises as well as betting on sports events (Oxendine, 1988). Now tribes are locating gambling operations off reservations, near big population centers, made possible by the Indian Gaming Regulatory Act of 1988 (see Box 7.3). However, some of the nation's state governors are opposed to this expansion, citing unfair competition with charities and their own state-run gambling operations. Native Americans counter that gambling proceeds provide a needed stimulus to their tribal economies, as profits go toward other businesses, and health and social services. The governors' pressure has resulted in the Interior Department's forming an Indian Gaming Commission to oversee Native American gambling operations across the country.

℗℗

BOX 7.3   THE PEQUOT TAKE ON ATLANTIC CITY

Each week, busloads of bingo players from New England and the New York metropolitan area arrive at the tiny Mashantucket Pequot reservation near the Rhode Island border for the high-stakes games that were legalized in 1986. By next fall, these gamblers and thousands more may find something else: a new casino, the first on the eastern seaboard outside of Atlantic City....

The Pequot, a tiny 200-member tribe, were the first Indian tribe east of the Mississippi to secure a gambling compact with a state under the Indian Gaming Regulatory Act....

The Pequot casino in Ledyard, a small, rural town of 14,500 residents about 15 miles north of New London, would greatly enhance the economy in New London County, which has been hit hard by job losses at major defense-related companies....It would create about 1,500 jobs and provide tribal members with funds for a museum, a research center, and additional housing....The operation will gross about $80 million annually.

The casino itself will be modest, about half the size of the smallest casino in Atlantic City, with a capacity of about 1,000 customers....

...A casino in Ledyard is minutes away from the coastal towns of Mystic and Stonington, and it would be a serious competitor with Atlantic City because southeastern Connecticut is a far more attractive region....

Source: Nick Ravo, "How a Tribe in Connecticut Is Taking On Atlantic City," *The New York Times*, April 14, 1991. Copyright © 1991 by The New York Times Company. Reprinted by permission.

෧෧

Throughout their history, Native Americans have resisted immigrant encroachment. In the past, there was warfare, but it led to a total war against the indigenous people, and we know the results. There were also native revitalization movements as military conquest became inevitable. There was the Ghost Dance in 1869 and again in 1889, but it ended with the slaughter at Wounded Knee. Other expressions of revitalization in the past were the Dream Dance, Sun Dance, and Peyote cults in the Southwest. These movements acknowledged defeat and interpreted it in terms of supernatural punishments for wrongdoing. But there would be repentance, atonement, and thus the return of the Indian way of life and repulsion of the invaders. Today, Native American resistance takes the form of religious revival and a return to tradition, but it also includes the political mobilization of Native American groups.

☯

BOX 7.4 THE NEW INDIAN WARS

The Lake Superior Chippewa...ceded land under treaties of 1836, 1837, 1842, and 1854, but retained the right to harvest resources on that land. Indian rights to hunt, fish, and gather in the ceded territory were not "granted" by the U.S. Government; they were *retained* by the tribes. And the validity of those rights has recently been affirmed by Federal court decisions.

But when the Indians attempt to exercise their rights by spear fishing on northern Wisconsin lakes, they are likely to be met—as they have been in recent years—by vocal and sometimes violent anti-treaty protesters. SAVE A WALLEYE. SPEAR A PREGNANT SQUAW was a common slogan in northern Wisconsin last spring....

Wisconsin's state government has responded to the conflict, which is widely perceived as a threat to the peace and to Wisconsin's tourist industry, by insisting that the solution lies in buying out or leasing the Indians' treaty rights in exchange for cash or government services....

Last year, the state of Wisconsin offered an economic and developmental aid package worth more than $50 million to the northern tribes in exchange for suspension of their treaty rights. Some tribes rejected the offer, and others announced they had no intention of selling their rights at any price....

In Wisconsin, while Indians spear fish, protesters hurl rocks and racial slurs. Two men were charged with criminal conspiracy to interfere with Chippewa civil rights by building and exploding a pipe bomb near spear fishers last spring. And the tension is mounting rather than subsiding. The bulletin board at a bowling alley in the northern Wisconsin town of Eagle River cautions against shooting Indians: "That will only get more sympathy for them, but if you put holes in their boats they can't spear and holes in their tires they can't get to the lakes. Stop being wimps. Yelling or simply watching will not intimidate anyone....Force confrontation and overreactions, escalate....Nothing will change until you escalate."

Source: Scott Kerr, "The New Indian Wars," *The Progressive*, April 1990. Reprinted by permission from *The Progressive*, 409 East Main Street, Madison, Wisconsin 53703.

☯

Pan-Indian interest groups were formed early in the twentieth century, exemplified by the Society of American Indians. The National Congress of American Indians was founded in 1944, the National Indian Youth Council in 1961, the American Indian Civil Rights Council in the mid-1960s, the National Tribal Chairman's Association in 1965, the United Native Americans in 1968, and the American Indian Movement (AIM) in the late 1960s. Since the 1960s, Native American protests have become public events, illustrated by the occupation of Alcatraz in 1969, the Trail of Broken Treaties Caravan and occupation of the Bureau of Indian Affairs (BIA) offices in 1972, the standoff between AIM and federal marshals at Wounded Knee in 1973, as well as recurrent protests over water rights in the Southwest and fish-ins in various parts of the country. The trail of Broken Treaties Caravan was organized by several tribes and AIM, and each contingent converged on Washington, D.C., from separate starting points. For example, the caravan from Oklahoma followed the Cherokee's Trail of Tears part of the way to Washington, and the Lakota started from Wounded Knee. "This had a special symbolic meaning for us Sioux, making us feel as if the ghosts of all the women and children murdered there by the Seventh Cavalry were rising out of their mass grave to go with us" (Crow Dog and Erodes, 1990:84). The issues have remained much the same over the years: sovereignty, self-determination, and self-governance, seen today in conflicts over fishing rights, gambling, and land claims (Box 7.4).

"In the area of water rights, some fifty Indian suits have recently been filed in the West and Southwest. These assert...that treaties guarantee the tribes as much water as it takes 'to make their reservations flourish,' and that they have prior claim on the use of any waters that lay under or flow by or through their territory" (Dorris, 1981:61). Indian land contains valuable minerals as well. Nearly two-thirds of the nation's low-sulfur coal and virtually all the uranium reserves are on Indian land. "Other tracts of tribal lands contain, or are adjacent to, large copper reserves, have significant geothermal production, or have the potential for lucrative oil and gas production" (Dorris, 1981:63). To assist members in developing and managing these resources for their own benefit and in accordance with their own values, twenty-five Indian tribes formed the Council of Energy Resources Tribes (CERT) in 1975.

Indian women are part of this overall effort, and note the mixture of comparisons with other ethnic groups and the women's movement in this regard (Box 7.5). Women have become tribal leaders in increasing numbers since the 1960s and are now council members and tribal chairs in at least one-fourth of the federally recognized tribes (Allen, 1986).

Today's Native Americans have learned the usefulness
of protest marches and other militant actions.

◎◎

BOX 7.5 CHARTING NEW DIRECTIONS

I submit to you three pathways—pathways which can lead us once again through hardships ahead. First, let us examine the roads other minority groups have traveled. Second, let us learn how to impact political power, Third, let us re-examine the scope, the total scope of the women's movement....

Let us learn from the Hispanics. Let us learn how to maintain our tribal distinctiveness but keep it internal, and how to present an external coalition to the common good of us all....

We will remain powerless until leadership of our nation's Indian organizations enter into real dialogue with each other. It isn't that we don't have national organizations but it's too infrequently we hear of them coming up with common priorities... with a unified voice...with a solid position....

We will remain powerless until we learn to seize power. Seizing power begins at your own ballot box. Far too many Indians don't vote. Too many of us don't participate—participate in the process of choosing our Congressman or our tribal council....

So, let us now turn to the much maligned topic of the women's movement. I ask that we re-assess its scope. Let us look at it to determine what is—and what is not—applicable to Indian women....

I say to you the heart and soul of the women's movement is sheer economics. It will continue to be an economic issue for so long as there remain those awful inequities in the paycheck.... And, what happens at the payroll office is an Indian woman's issue. More than one-third of our women are in the work force and ours remains the lowest median annual income of all the nation's ethnic women. For those working outside the home, $1,695 is a yearly average, according to the latest available statistics. Employer of the greatest number of Indian women is Uncle Sam himself—but our grade levels are way below the national average....

There's an ever-increasing number of Indian women who work because we have to. We're the head of the family.

Source: Owanah Anderson, "Keynote: Charting New Directions." Pp. 5–10 in Sedelta Verble (ed.), *Words of Today's American Indian Women: Ohoyo Makachi.* Wichita Falls, TX: Ohoyo Resource Center.

☐

SUMMARY

Frontier contact between America's indigenous peoples and immigrant settlers led to their conflict over land, the expropriation of Native American land, and then the exclusion of Native American people from the economic and social order of the settlers. Ethnic conflict theory and pluralism provide good interpretations of this history. Ethnic conflict theory helps explain land expropriation and the exclusion of Native Americans and their divergence, and thus the pluralism of Native Americans and the larger society. Historically, these two groups competed for land, and because the immigrant settlers were more powerful they were able to expropriate Native American land. The power resources of settlers included their numbers, centralized political authority, and capacity to generate surplus and fluid wealth within the framework of a market and monetary economy. The settlers' desire for Native American land followed from their intention to make permanent settlements on the North American frontier. From a position of power, the settlers transplanted a European economic, political, and social order on the frontier. Because of white ethnocentrism and the fact that Native Americans had few competitive resources, Native Americans were largely excluded from this revised society.

As a consequence of their exclusion, Native Americans proceeded along an historical course divergent from that of the larger society. Native Americans grew more and more dependent on the federal government as first the ecological base to their way of life disappeared and then little was accomplished to bring their inclusion into the larger society. Today the pluralism of white and Native American societies is still evident.

The prospects for Native Americans are far from clear, but current trends, if they persist, should bring the greater inclusion and enculturation of Indians. The nadir of the material conditions of Indian life is in all probability behind us. Their levels of health, wealth, education, and welfare should continue to improve, it is hoped, to a point of parity with those of other groups in the country. We should also expect more convergence of Native American culture with the trends in the total society. This convergence of material conditions and cultural content of Indian life will come with increased Indian participation in the secondary institutions of the larger society, in the labor force and in the nation's schools, for instance, and it will be first in evidence among the young, well-to-do Native Americans.

By the same token, conflict continues between Native Americans and others. The historic conflict between Native Americans and the larger society involved military force, and it resulted in something close to the extermination of Native Americans. The cycle of conflict has swung away from the use of force, however, and toward the legal litigation of Indian-white grievances. This is an instance of Lenski's political cycle (see Chapter 4). The channeling of Indian-white conflict through the institutions of the larger society, such as the courts, law offices, and universities, necessitates the enculturation of many Native Americans into practices and skills of the larger society. This means the acquisition of language skills, the reading of law, practical experience with bureaucracy, and so on. The likely result is that more Native Americans will come to share with others cultural idioms, common experiences, and the same material conditions of life. The more successful Native American leadership is, the more it will reflect the characteristics of its adversaries. Thus Native American leaders will become modern men and women with modern skills.

Moreover, to press their demands on the larger society, Native Americans will increasingly organize themselves into voluntary organizations, as they have already done in the National Congress of American Indians, the National Indian Youth Council, and CERT. It is significant that these associations are tribally inclusive and follow organizational principles adopted from the larger society, being established by Native Americans who have had previous extensive experience in the secondary institutions of the larger society, such as schools and the military. These trends can be taken as indicators of the convergence of Native Americans, at least of certain leaders. If this is so, then the first level of convergence is the inclusion of several tribes in common organizational endeavors and the corresponding growth of a pan-Indian consciousness. It may also mean a growing divergence between Native American ethclasses, however. In any case, as Native Americans prepare themselves to negotiate with the larger society, and as they acquire competitive resources through education and business to do so, their future should converge more with that of the total society. Now that the nature of Indian-white conflict has changed, and now that Native Americans must become an organized political interest group and players on the business stage, the future of Native Americans should be more convergent, at least to the extent that they are successful at realizing their claims on American society.

Undoubtedly, traditional idioms will be rediscovered and circulated in the future. This must be done to mobilize Native Americans for collective action against the larger society. While this will revitalize certain traditional themes in Indian cultures, as the Ghost Dance did in the past century, ideology for collective action must now be of a pan-Indian nature to appeal to people from diverse tribes. The risk of the entire endeavor is that Indian ethnicity will be stripped of its tribal traditions, even its authenticity, and become contentless. That is, Native Americans might become just another organized political group in the modern state.

The future could also truly revitalize Native American identity, even tribal identity, and shore up ethnic boundaries. This could happen in those cases where single tribes pursue their land claims and return the land to its former uses, thus committing themselves and the land to the preservation of the old ways. Even tribal members living elsewhere, off tribal lands, could return home for personal succor and ethnic rejuvenation.

But, more than anything else, it is the mismatch between Native American labor skills, as these exist today, and the current need for socially skilled (Anglo skills) and highly technical labor that points toward the continued divergence between Native Americans and the larger society. Unless this discrepancy is significantly diminished, Indian participation in the mechanisms for ethnic inclusion of postindustrial society will be limited, and we should expect the continued divergence of Native Americans.

C H A P T E R
8
❦❧

HISPANIC AMERICANS AND AMERICAN SOCIETY

T he Hispanic population in the nation stood at 22.4 million in 1990, a 53 percent increase since 1980. There are several ethnic groups within this population, including people with origins in Mexico, Puerto Rico, Cuba, the Dominican Republic, Colombia, El Salvador, Guatemala, and other countries in Central and South America. Mexican Americans comprise about 60 percent, Puerto Ricans about 14 percent, and Cuban Americans about 5 percent of the Hispanic population in the United States. These three groups are discussed in this chapter.

❦❧

BOX 8.1 AN INVISIBLE PRESENCE GROWS

The only decoration on the wall in Sergio Munoz's new office as executive news director of KMEX television is a color-coded map showing the density of the Hispanic population of Los Angeles....

"This is the real story, as shown on this map," he said the other day...."You can see it very clearly. The growth of the Latin population is a fact of life. But if you look at the power structure, look at the government, it's not there. From the outside, it's some sort of ghost, and it frightens people...."

As an administrator and executive editor of *La Opinion*, the city's largest Spanish-language daily, for 12 years until last January, and as executive news director of the largest Spanish-language television station for the last four months, Mr. Munoz has observed the fast and silent expansion of the city's Hispanic pop-

ulation. Over the decade beginning in 1980, it swelled by 70 percent, from 816,00 to 1.4 million, and now comprises approximately 40 percent of the city's population of 3.7 million....

In addition to the massive influx from neighboring Mexico,
which has mushroomed in the last decade and a half, the growth
since the 1970s has included a continuing wave of refugees from
war and economic dislocation throughout Central America.

"I was once asked how it was to be the editor of a newspaper that is trying to cater to so many groups, to Nicaraguans,
Salvadorans, Mexicans," Mr. Munoz said. "My answer was
'that's not the worst part. The worst part is trying to please a
community that is fragmented even within these groups.' On the
newspaper itself there were Sandinistas and Contras, and all the
Argentineans that were for the Sandinistas and all the Chileans
on the other side."

Drawn first to the traditional Mexican-American neighborhoods of East Los Angeles, the various national groups have
radiated through the center of the city, their progress traced in
red, purple, and green that show their density on Mr. Munoz's
map....

Source: Seth Mydans, "An Invisible Presence Grows in the Barrios of Los Angeles," *The New York Times*, May 24, 1992. Copyright © 1992 by The New York Times
Company. Reprinted by permission.

@@

MEXICAN AMERICANS

The Mexican-origin population in the United States grew from 4.5 million in 1970 to 8.7 million in 1980, an increase of 93 percent (Bean, et
al., 1985). By 1990 there were nearly 13.5 million Mexican-origin people in the country. This increase is due to both a more accurate counting of Mexican Americans by the U.S. Census and an actual increase in
the number of Mexican Americans because of immigration and natural increase. What makes the news is the growing number of Mexicans
in the country, particularly stories about undocumented immigrants,
and related issues concerning the rise of Chicano culture (Box 8.1). But
the story of Hispanos and Anglos goes back to the nineteenth century.

As white settlement expanded across the western frontier in the
1800s, Anglo settlers came into contact with Hispanos in the Southwest. The Hispanic community of the Southwest numbered about
200,000 people at the time of contact early in the nineteenth century,
although estimates of the Hispanic population in 1848 run as high as

350,000 people. This community was composed of three economic classes: elite landlords who possessed large tracts of land and could trace their property rights back to early Spanish land grants in the New World, a large class of poor Mexican-Indian laborers, and a small number of middle-class merchants, small ranchers, and farmers.

Hispanos had migrated from Mexico into the Southwest as had Anglo farmers, pastoralists, and prospectors in the search of gold and silver. For example, a band of Spanish colonists under Juan de Oñate left Mexico in January 1598 and established a colony along the upper Rio Grande (Samora and Simon, 1977). Indians rebelled against the colonists in 1599, but the rebellion was put down and friars were then sent among the Pueblos to Christianize them. Another Indian rebellion in 1680 pushed the Spanish out of New Mexico, but the colonists moved again into the province following a military campaign against the Pueblos in 1692. The Spanish crown granted land to a small number of individuals, who became *hacendados*, or landowners. They possessed huge tracts of land, haciendas, used for grazing in an arid climate, and these landowners ultimately replaced the *conquistadors* and silver barons as the elite class in much of the Southwest. For example, the elite de Baca family in New Mexico had 1 million sheep on the Llano Estacado, and under this *patron* family were *mayordomos* (managers), *caporales* (overseers), and herders.

The Hispanic community in California was originally a string of missions that stretched from San Diego to San Francisco. The Jesuits had founded missions in Baja California by 1697, and later the Franciscans built twenty-one missions along the California coast (Samora and Simon, 1977). Each mission was a self-sufficient economic and social system, with the friars on top and Indian labor on the bottom. Indian population declined between 1769 and 1835, the mission period, from about 70,000 to 15,000 people (Samora and Simon, 1977). Although the missions became quite wealthy, the mission system was replaced in the nineteenth century with a secular pastoral economy. Under this pastoral economic system, the labor hierarchy was the *rancheros* at the top, followed by *mestizo* small ranchers and laborers, and the colonized Indians on the bottom.

Because of encroachment threats by other European powers, the Spanish also built a string of *presidios*, or forts, from Texas to California. The French were a threat from the east (Louisiana), the British from the north, and the Russians in northern California. Of course, the presidios also protected the colonists from the indigenous Indians throughout the Southwest.

Then, in the nineteenth century, Anglos from the United States migrated into the region, replacing Hispanos as the dominant population

FIGURE 8.1   MEXICAN AMERICANS AND CHANGE IN AMERICAN SOCIETY

Agrarian Society c. 1600–1865		Industrial Society c. 1865–1945		Post-Industrial Society c. 1945–Present
Frontier contact and early accommodation	→ Conflict over land →	Land expropriation →	Ethnic stratification →	Present situation

in the Southwest by century's end. Anglos outnumbered Hispanos in Texas by five to one as early as 1835 (Samora and Simon, 1977). Anglos were 90 percent of the population in southern California by 1890, although Hispanos had been a numerical majority there as late as 1870 (Mirande, 1985). Although the pattern of Anglo replacement varied across the Southwest, especially in its timing, the United States had annexed the entire region by 1853 with the Treaty of Guadalupe Hildago and Gadsden Purchase (see below). Anglos with their capitalism and culture eventually displaced the Hispano gentry-peasant economy and way of life, dominating the whole region, and people of Mexican descent became an ethnic minority in the Southwest. It was a clash between two cultures and two economies, as well as two ethnic groups. The history of Mexican Americans is outlined in Figure 8.1.

FRONTIER CONTACT AND EARLY ACCOMMODATION

Frontier contact between Anglos and Hispanos took place across the borderlands, from Texas in the east to California in the west (see Map 8.1). The initial contact between Anglos and Hispanos varied across the region, so writers typically depict it state by state (e.g., McWilliams, 1968; Moore, 1970b; Rosenbaum, 1981; Stoddard, 1973). This variation in contact will be noted below.

There was such a rapid influx of Anglos into Texas and northern California in the nineteenth century that Hispanos quickly became a minority in these areas. In 1848, there were 10,000 *Californios,* and only four years later there were 250,000 Anglo newcomers in California. Anglo settlers quadrupled in number in Texas between 1820 and 1830, and by 1850 *Mexicanos* were only 5 percent of the Texas population (Rosenbaum, 1981). Ironically, part of this influx of Anglos into Texas was made possible by Mexico. Fearing that its unpopulated northern borderlands would be annexed by the United States, Mexico had initially welcomed Anglo colonists to Texas. Stephen F. Austin had the

MAP 8.1 MEXICAN LAND CESSIONS TO THE UNITED STATES

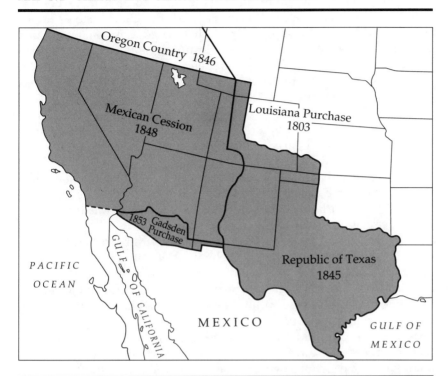

permission of the Mexican government to establish a settlement in Texas in 1823, but he later became one of the leaders of the Texas revolution against Mexico.

Anglo immigrants faced few natural barriers between Texas and the rest of the United States. Although there are such barriers in northern California, the lure of quick riches in the gold fields brought large-scale migration from the East. Anglos first settled in northern California, in and around the gold fields, where they became the dominant group, and only later in southern California, where they became the majority group by late in the nineteenth century.

There was an early alliance in Texas between Anglos and the 5,000 or so Hispanos. Actually, the Hispano population in Texas contained a significant number of Indians assimilated into the Spanish settlements, up to 38 percent of the Hispano population (Valdez and Steiner, 1972). The Hispanos had been dissatisfied for some time with Spanish and Mexican rule, since neither government had been able to provide them

251

with effective protection against the Indians of the region, especially the Comanches. Furthermore, most of the Hispano trade in the borderlands was, by the nineteenth century, with the United States rather than with Mexico. Unhappy with a distant government in Mexico City, Texas Hispanos turned to Anglo immigrants as allies, and together they fought for Texas's independence from Mexico in 1836. Texas was annexed by the United States in 1845, and this precipitated the Mexican-American War (1846–1848).

Unlike Texas, New Mexico was protected from Anglo invasion by natural barriers, and a numerical imbalance between Hispanos and Anglos did not occur early in their contact. The Hispanic population did not drop below 50 percent of the total population of the state until after 1940 (Rosenbaum, 1981). More than in any other state, there has been an equitable accommodation between the two groups in New Mexico, particularly in state politics. But even in New Mexico, Anglo-Hispanic relations evolved into conflict over land.

Original land grants to Hispanos in New Mexico had come in three forms. Grants were given to communities of at least ten households, to patrons for settling a town site with at least thirty families, and to a hacienda, or ranch (Rosenbaum, 1981). Along with the gentry, Hispanic peasants in the Southwest were engaged in subsistence grazing and farming for over two centuries before the coming of Anglos. Peasants lived in *jaccales*, huts made of posts plastered with mud, thatched roofs, and dirt floors. These were typically single rooms, and often kitchens were attached as open shelters. The *casa grande* of a *rico* (rich) family was much more elaborate, of course.

In Arizona, Anglos and Hispanos also allied, not against Mexico but against Indians in the region. Unable to pacify the Apaches, Hispanos had been forced to concentrate in a few towns of Arizona, particularly Tobac and Tucson. Tucson—along with San Antonio in Texas, Santa Fe in New Mexico, and Los Angeles in California—was one of the most populous Hispanic towns in the Southwest prior to 1848. By the late nineteenth century, largely due to the campaigns of the U.S. Cavalry, the Indians of Arizona were conquered and sent to reservations.

CONFLICT OVER LAND

The Spanish borderlands became Mexican possessions after Mexico won its independence in 1821. Thus, in their efforts to gain control of the Southwest, Anglos came into conflict with both the Mexican government and their Hispanic neighbors as well as with the Indians of the region. Conflict occurred between the Republic of Texas and Mexico (1835–1836) and between the United States and Mexico in the Mexican-

American War of 1846–1848. The United States government had approved statehood for Texas in 1845, and then sent General Zachary Taylor with a largely volunteer force to the Rio Grande in 1846. Fighting broke out in April between Taylor's forces and the Mexican army, and, in a related action that July, Commodore John D. Sloat captured Monterey and declared California to be an American possession (Samora and Simon, 1977). The American army under Taylor eventually pushed further into Mexico, and an armistice was announced in August of 1847. The war was particularly brutal, with American troops committing numerous atrocities on the civilian Mexican population.

Mexico ceded most of the Southwest to the United States after the war, first in 1848 with the Treaty of Guadalupe Hidalgo, and then in 1853 with the Gadsden Purchase (see Map 8.1). Under the Treaty of Guadalupe Hildago, Hispanos in the Southwest could elect to be either Mexican or American citizens, and their property was to be protected (see Box 8.2).

ॐ

BOX 8.2   GUADALUPE HIDALGO TREATY OF PEACE, 1848,
               ARTICLE VIII

Mexicans now established in territories previously belonging to Mexico, and which remain for the future within the limits of the United States, as defined by the present treaty, shall be free to continue where they now reside, or to remove at any time to the Mexican republic *retaining the property which they possess in the said territories, or disposing thereof, and removing the proceeds wherever they please, without their being subjected, on this account, to any contribution, tax, or charge whatever.*

Those who shall prefer to remain in the said territories, may either retain the title and rights of Mexican citizens, or acquire those of citizens of the United States. But they shall be under obligation to make their election within one year from the date of the exchange of ratifications of this treaty; and those who shall remain in the said territories after the expiration of that year, without having declared their intention to retain the character of Mexicans, shall be considered to have elected to become citizens of the United States.

In the said territories, property of every kind, now belonging to Mexicans not established there, shall be inviolably respected. The present owner, the heirs of these, and all Mexicans who may hereafter acquire said property by contract, shall enjoy with respect to it guarantees equally ample as if the same belonged to citizens of the United States. [Italics added.]

253

This failed attempt to enter the U.S. illegally from
Mexico was photographed by agents of the U.S.
Immigration and Naturalization Service.

☙❧

After the Treaty of Guadalupe Hildago, Anglo settlers turned their attention to the private land holdings of their Hispanic neighbors. Both groups resorted to open violence on occasion, as occurred in the Lincoln County Wars of New Mexico, the Cortina War in Texas, in the burning of courthouses across the region to destroy documentation of land rights, and during the periodic range wars between cattlemen (Anglos) and sheepmen (Hispanos). There were also lynchings of Mexican miners in California during the gold rush. Violence between Anglos and Hispanos continued even into the present century. In 1915, for example, the Plan of San Diego was found on Basilio Ramos at McAllen, Texas, a plan that called for an insurrection against Anglos in the Southwest, including kidnapping and ransoms and political assassinations. News of this event sparked Anglo riots against Hispanos in South Texas, and it was later charged in an official investigation that the Texas Rangers had executed 200 to 300 suspects without trial (Maril, 1989).

While such incidents cannot be denied, the true character of this conflict is found more in legal and political battles over property rights, during elections, and in courtrooms than in gunfights, arson, riots, and range wars. The issue was political hegemony in the region, and thus control of the courts in the settling of rival land claims. One Anglo-Texan admitted to some of the difficulties in gaining political control over land ceded by Mexico:

> Mexico! What the hell do we want of it. It isn't worth a cuss. The people are as bigoted and ignorant as the devil's grandchildren. They haven't even the capacities of my black boy [Negro slave]. Why, they're most as black as niggers anyway, and ten times as treacherous.... You go any further into Mexico...and you'll get Mexicans along with your territory; and a dam'd lot of 'em too. *It'll be fifty year before you can out vote 'em* (Olmsted, 1857: 126; italics added).

But Anglos did get political control of the Southwest.

Anglo settlers had the advantage, for they brought their law and political machinery to the Southwest once the United States had annexed it. Anglos controlled the courts, and thus the jurisdiction of property rights in the region. The land conflict between Anglos and Hispanos hinged on legal proceedings and financial dealings within the larger framework of a Western political economy, which both sides shared as relocated Europeans. The conflict between whites and Native Americans was characterized by more violence and military action, since Indians shared neither a Western political economy nor a legal framework with the white settlers. Nevertheless, the outcome was the same:

In the end, the Hispanos were caught up in the meshes of Anglo-American banking, finance, and legal intrigue. Prior to the conquest, there had been no land tax in New Mexico; but, with Anglo rule, came taxes, litigation over land titles, mortgages, and the other incidents of a monetary economy (McWilliams, 1968:76).

Hispano-Anglo conflict was not merely over land; it was also a clash between two cultures (Rosenbaum, 1981). Anglo prejudice against Hispanos centered on differences in language, religion, food, work habits, even race, and the contrast was sharply drawn in the image of the Mexicano as a bandido (Mirande, 1985; 1987). This prejudice was used to justify the expropriation of even more Hispano land, while the Hispano saw the bandido image in terms of resistance to this expropriation and takeover. The Anglo self-image was one of the rugged individual from a superior culture and race, a group that was vindicated in what it did. To Hispanos, however, Anglos were rude, arrogant, and overbearing.

EXPROPRIATION OF LAND

With the Treaty of Guadalupe Hidalgo, most of the borderlands, including California, became the possession of the United States—nine days after gold was discovered in California. The Gadsden Purchase in 1853 brought even more of the Southwest under American political control (see Map 8.1). Once the borderlands were under their political control, Anglo settlers got the upper hand in their conflict with Hispanic landowners. Dominating the political machinery of the region, from county courthouses to territorial and state capitols and on to Congress, Anglo-American settlers typically found their legal challenges to Spanish land grants were successful in the courts of the region. McWilliams (1968:77) described the situation in New Mexico:

> Many of the villagers neglected to bring their papers into court and often had lost evidences of title. Most of them lacked funds to defend titles; or, if they retained an Anglo-American lawyer, a large part of the land went in payment of court costs and fees. The confusion became so great that in 1891 a Court of Private Land Claims was established to pass upon the land grants in New Mexico. Needless to say, the members of this court were all Anglo-Americans; and, as nearly as I can determine, there was not a single Spanish-American lawyer in the territory. Litigation over land titles was highly technical and involved; cases dragged on in the courts for years; and, in the general process of settling titles, control of resources shifted to the Anglo-Americans.

In parts of Texas and California, great numbers of land squatters among the Anglo immigrants simply ignored legal niceties. By legal and illegal means, land ownership passed from Hispanos to Anglos. For example, between 1840 and 1859, all Hispano land in Nueces County, Texas, except for one ranch, was transferred to Anglos. Even in New Mexico, only 30 percent of the pre-Anglo landowners held their original lands in 1910 (Moore and Pachon, 1985).

Taxation was one of the mechanisms by which Hispanic land was expropriated. American politicians levied property tax rates at levels that only the largest of Spanish landholders could afford, thereby forcing small Hispanic farmers off their land and into wage labor. Such maneuvers were particularly effective during economic hard times, when first the ranchero system and then dry farming faltered because of droughts and low prices (Moore, 1970b).

By 1900 American capital, particularly the railroads and agribusiness, as well as the federal government owned the Southwest. As the Hispanic economy slumped, American capital flowed into transportation, irrigation, and all the improvements needed to make the region an Anglo economic empire. King Cotton moved into Texas (1890–1930) and eventually into Arizona and California. Hispanic forms of extraction in mining were improved and made more profitable with American capital and technology. The extraction industry grew in the Southwest and came to include the powerful petroleum industry. Equally important, rail lines were built so that the region's surplus of foodstuffs, fiber, and minerals could be shipped to consumption centers in the East and North by the early 1900s.

To illustrate the flow of capital into the Southwest, Griswold Del Castillo (1984) reported that the cash value of farms and ranches in Los Angeles County between 1850 and 1880 increased by over 264 percent, and for Bexar county in Texas (San Antonio) it was over 291 percent. During the same period, the capital invested in farm machinery in Los Angeles County grew by 275 percent, and that of Bexar County increased by 183 percent. Capital invested in manufacturing grew by 175 percent in Los Angeles County and by 259 percent in Bexar County. Of course, people came with the capital. In 1850, 75 percent of the 1,610 people of Los Angeles were Hispano, but only 19 percent of the 11,183 residents in 1880 were Hispano.

The scarcity of water had always been a limiting factor in agricultural development in the Southwest. Steps taken at the turn of the century to offset this limitation included the National Reclamation Act of 1902. Public funds were expended to ensure an adequate supply of water for the growers in the San Joaquin, Imperial, Salt River, Mesilla, and Lower Rio Grande valleys. Cities in the region would later do the same, capture water, usually from distant sources, financed by public utility companies. While the intent of the Reclamation Act was to extend the Homestead Act into the Southwest, its consequence was to provide water to large growers at public expense. Public lands were also given to the railroads, among others, with the intent of furnishing them with collateral for borrowing investment capital. Tariffs were also passed at the national level to foster the economic development of the region, as was the case with the Dingley Tariff of 1897, which helped the sugar beet industry by taxing imported sugar at 75 percent of its market value (McWilliams, 1968).

An alliance of big capital and the U.S. government came to dominate the economy of the Southwest. Anglos eventually owned most of the land in the borderlands, in both private and public holdings, and the private holdings became increasingly concentrated under the ownership of railroads and big ranchers and growers. These business interests, with governmental assistance, made capital improvements in farming, ranching, mining and transportation (e.g., irrigation, canning operations, refrigerated cars). By the early twentieth century the economy of the region was positioned to take off, but labor was needed. That labor would come from Mexico, and the Southwest became an economic empire with the convergence of land, labor, and capital.

ETHNIC STRATIFICATION

Irrigated truck farming, cotton cultivation, and the construction and maintenance of railroads were at this time all labor-intensive endeavors. The population of the Southwest was not sufficient to fully satisfy these growing labor demands. The small Hispano farmers who had been forced into wage labor, Indians, immigrants from Asia and Europe, and migrants from other parts of America could not adequately meet the region's labor needs in the early 1900s.

The economic boom of the Southwest occurred at roughly the same time as the Mexican Revolution in 1910. Before the Revolution, under the Diaz regime, Mexican peasants had lost their rights to communal lands due to enclosures, and 97 percent of the rural families were landless by 1910 (Massey, et al., 1987; Moore and Pachon, 1985). In addition, farm wages were falling. Food prices were increasing, however, with the shift in Mexican agriculture to cash crops; the price of corn rose by 60 percent between 1890 and 1910 (Massey, et al., 1987). Mexican peasants were being pushed into migration northward.

Jobs created by capital investments in farming and transportation in the Southwest pulled Mexican labor into the region's economy by the second decade of the twentieth century. Furthermore, the restriction of European immigration in the 1920s stimulated Mexican immigration, as employers looked elsewhere to replace immigrant labor from Europe. Simultaneously, the turmoil of the Mexican Revolution pushed Mexican labor out of Mexico and into the borderlands. By this time, rail lines could bring Mexican workers to the Southwest by the thousands, while labor recruiters from the borderlands had been in Mexico since late in the nineteenth century (Massey, et al., 1987). McWilliams (1968) estimated that 10 percent of the Mexican population came to work in the Southwest. Mexican immigration into the United States was 18,000 per year before 1910, but over 51,000 in 1920, almost 39,000 in 1929, and then dropped off with the Great Depression to 2,627 in 1931 (Massey, et al., 1987; Mirande, 1985). Immigration increased again in the 1940s with World War II, the Bracero program, and the rise of in the number of landless peasants in Mexico (Massey, et al., 1987). Labor came together with land and capital investment in the Southwest.

The migrant stream from Mexico to the United States was at first peasants and their sons who sought extra earnings in the United States to return and buy land in Mexico (Bodnar, 1985). Over the years, however, this migrant stream grew and widened to include people from a variety of backgrounds, until the migration touched all sectors of Mexican society (Massey, et al., 1987). More women migrated with male relatives over time, due partly to family reunification in the United States. The migrants flowed to the United States through networks composed of family, friends, and members of the same villages, connecting people on both sides of the border.

The labor demand was greatest in truck and cotton farming, railroad construction and maintenance, and mining. Into these industries Mexican workers came, comprising two-thirds of the laborers in cotton farming and 70 percent of the section crews and 90 percent of the extra gangs on the railroads (McWilliams, 1968). Mexicans became an agrarian laboring class or otherwise filled the bottom positions of the regional labor hierarchy formed during the preceding decades, when Anglos had taken control of the Southwest. The labor market of the region became split and segmented along ethnic lines, Anglos on top and Hispanos on the bottom. For example, prior to Anglo dominance in 1860, over 30 percent of the Hispanos in San Diego had been ranchers and farmers, another 39 percent skilled workers, and almost 16 percent unskilled labor. After Anglo control, over 80 percent in 1880 were unskilled labor (Mirande, 1985).

Barrera (1979) characterized the ethnic stratification in the Southwest in the following terms. Most Hispanos and later Mexican immigrants were incorporated into Anglo capitalism as labor subordinates, becoming a colonized population:

1. There was *labor repression*, meaning that Chicano labor was under the total control of employers.

2. There was *occupational stratification*, or a segmented labor market along ethnic lines. Chicanos were relegated to the least desirable jobs in the labor hierarchy, such as field labor in agriculture.

3. There was a *dual wage system*, whereby Anglos were paid higher wages than Chicanos even for the same jobs.

4. Chicanos acted as a *reserve labor force*, their presence and immigration translated into an ample labor supply that kept wages depressed even in a time of rapid economic expansion.

5. Chicanos were also *labor buffers*, who were laid off during economic downturns and rehired as the economy improved.

In addition, a peripheral sector of largely rural Hispanos was unaffected by Anglo dominance, a marginal sector was completely displaced by the Anglo economy, and a fourth sector was incorporated into Anglo capitalism as equals, as illustrated by the alliance of Anglo and Hispano elites known as the Santa Fe Ring in New Mexico.

Mexican immigration now flowed into this colonial labor system. The immigrants came to the company towns of the mining areas, the agricultural camps, and the urban barrios of the region. It was certainly different from the earlier Anglo migration to the Southwest. Anglos had come from a more advanced economy and a more powerful state to a less developed region, and they developed it in the image of their origin with themselves in control. One group came to dominate and the other to be labor subordinates (see Box 8.3).

☺☺

BOX 8.3   I'M TALKING FOR JUSTICE

I am Maria Moreno, forty years old, mother of twelve children. Born in Karnes City, Texas. Raised in Corpus Christi. Since 1928 I start working in agricultural work. I been a worker all my life. I know how to handle a man's job and I'm not ashamed to say it. I'm American citizen, and I'm talking for justice....

1940, we came to California. Waiting and hoping to find a better living condition for ourselves and for our family. The braceros came in. We had to move on from the Imperial Valley. We hit Salinas. Here come the braceros. Well, we're tickled anyway when we work a little. We can earn a little money. We can feed our children. Half eat....

I've got a twenty-three-year-old son. When he was nineteen years old he was blind because he was without eat. 1958 it start raining so hard we can't earn very much money....All our money was gone...

People been forgotten. They don't care about us. Our home is under the tree. That's the way that we have been treated. We never screamed. We never had a word until now. Like I said, I'm mother of twelve children and I'm working for discovering the things that been hiding for so long—that people must know what we been suffering, what we been through....

Source: Maria Moreno, "I'm Talking For Justice." Pp. 181–182 in Magdalena Mora and Adelaida R. Del Castillo (eds.), *Mexican Women In The United States: Struggles Past and Present*. Los Angeles: Chicano Studies Research Center Publications, Occasional Paper No. 2.

This was also the point at which the history of Mexican Americans and Native Americans began to differ. While the treatment of Mexicans was exclusive, most were a labor caste in the revised economy of the Southwest; Indians were more completely excluded from the larger society and isolated on reservations, even in the same region. There are several reasons for this difference.

Hispanos and Mexicans had a history of labor in farming, ranching, and mining in both Mexico and the borderlands. For example, in rural Mexico before the Revolution most labor on the *haciendas* was landless peasants, either permanent labor or seasonal workers, restricted to toil through debt peonage. They were a labor caste even before American capital came into the Southwest. Their niche was then undermined by changes in Mexican agriculture, pushing them north. Indians in the Southwest did not comprise a comparable labor pool, having had virtually no history as wage labor in agriculture, ranching, or mining except for those in the earlier missions. Furthermore, Indians who had earlier made the transition into wage labor had been assimilated into the Hispanic culture and community, so that by the twentieth century their progeny were more often considered Mexican than Indian.

Hispanos had lived in the areas of the Southwest where the greatest labor needs arose, that is, in the fertile river valleys of the region. Before the coming of Anglos, Hispano settlement in the Southwest had resembled a fan, with the people concentrated along the ribs of the fan, the river valleys of the Southwest as well as along the Pacific Coast. Thus, Hispano labor was right at hand, and the human ties between these areas and Mexico acted as conduits for labor emigration from Mexico. In the same region, Native Americans were, by the turn of the century, located in isolated corners, on marginal land where a comparable labor demand never developed.

Mexican labor was also more easily organized by employers in the Southwest. Employment of Mexican labor typically took the form of the traditional patron-peon system, in which a single labor boss brought a gang of laborers to a grower to meet most of the grower's labor needs. In South Texas, border guards also acted as labor agents (Foley, 1988). For employers this was an efficient hiring method, since they needed nothing so much as gang labor. In its efficiency, it would not have been matched by the employment of Indians. Compared to the linguistic and cultural diversification of the region's Indians, Mexicans were integrated by a common language and culture and thus were more easily mobilized into large but manageable labor gangs. Behind the labor bosses and their crews were, of course, the family and village networks in Mexico and the United States through which new immigrants came.

Mexicans faced virtually no competition from other ethnic groups for their position as a labor caste in the Southwest. African Americans did not move in great numbers into the Southwest with King Cotton, due to their earlier emancipation. If that labor migration had occurred, it would have most certainly meant fewer positions for Mexican labor, at least in the fields and orchards of the Southwest. Because most Anglo labor could secure other opportunities, few of them were willing to work for long in the fields at low wages, until the Great Depression, when labor migrants headed west from the Dust Bowl and Mexican labor was repatriated. The same may be said about European immigrant laborers, who, like the Volga Germans in the sugar beet industry, would exit after a few short years in seasonal work for better opportunities elsewhere in the economy. Further European immigration had also been restricted by the 1920s, as had Asian immigration. Thus there was no adequate supply of European, Chinese, or Japanese field workers for southwestern agriculture. Almost by default, then, Mexicans became the farm workers of the Southwest.

Mexicans were incorporated into the economy in an exclusive manner, and this has had implications for their history:

> The basic factor retarding the assimilation of the Mexican immigrant, at all levels, has been the pattern of his employment. With few excep-

> tions, only a *particular class* of employers employed Mexican labor in
> the Southwest: large-scale industrial enterprises; railroads; smelters;
> copper mines; sugar-beet refineries; farm-factories; large fruit and
> vegetable exchanges. These concerns have employed *many* Mexicans,
> in gangs, crews, and by families, as in the sugar-beet industry. It is
> not the individual who has been employed but the group
> (McWilliams, 1968:215).

Because they have been employed as a group and worked together in
gangs and at migratory jobs, Mexican American workers have been
isolated from workers of different ethnic backgrounds and from other
potentially assimilative mechanisms in the Southwest. Thus, Mexican
workers were not totally unlike Indians; they, too, took a course somewhat divergent from that of the larger society.

If the generation of Hispanos who witnessed the Anglo transformation of the Southwest was the creation generation, then the Mexican immigrants were the migrant generation (Alvarez, 1985). Both
shared the experience of a split and segmented labor market and ethnic prejudice, and both were labor buffers, in the words of Barrera
(1979). The latter became particularly evident during the Great Depression, when up to 500,000 Chicanos were repatriated to Mexico as
labor demand fell off and its supply in the Southwest went up with
migrants from the Dust Bowl. In the 1950s, Mexicans were deported
again in Operation Wetback.

The concentration of Mexican Americans at the bottom of the
labor hierarchy and apart from mechanisms for their assimilation into
American society lasted until the 1940s. With the increasing mechanization of agriculture in the Southwest and the growing urban man-
power needs during and after the 1940s, Mexican Americans migrated
to the cities of the Southwest. In the rural Southwest, growers needed
less stoop labor and fewer ranch hands, although new jobs in packing
sheds, canning plants, and feedlots did emerge. Thus the Mexican
American entered America's urban economy a generation later than
even the most recent of European immigrants, those from southern
and eastern Europe. As they did, labor needs in Southwest agriculture
went unmet, and growers turned again to Mexican immigrants under
the Bracero program that ran from World War II up to the 1960s.

In the intervening years, other ethnic groups had established their
occupational turfs in the nation's cities, had organized themselves in
unions, had taken advantage of cheap but good urban educational services, and had in numerous other ways prepared themselves for societal change toward white-collar work. When Mexican Americans arrived in the cities, they faced prejudice and discrimination from these
other ethnic groups. There were instances of violence against urban

Chicanos in the 1940s; the best known is the zoot-suit riots in Los Angeles (see Box 8.4). There were barriers against the entry of Mexican Americans into the institutions for ethnic inclusion—education and the white-collar labor force. This was the beginning of the Mexican American generation (Alvarez, 1985).

With this generation, new organizations emerged in the Mexican American community, including the Order of Sons of America, the League of United Latin American Citizens, The Mexican American Movement, and the American G.I. Forum (Barrera, 1988). Furthermore, immigrants from the same villages in Mexico organized their own soccer clubs in American cities, playing and socializing on Sundays (Massey, et al., 1987). Although varied in their membership and some priorities, the civil rights groups were assimilationist and focused on the elimination of prejudice against Mexican Americans, their equality before the law, and the improvement of their political representation at different levels of government.

The difficulties urban Mexican Americans faced in preparing themselves for the post-industrial society reached into their history, their agrarian past. While laboring in the fields in the Southwest at low wages, Mexican Americans could accumulate neither the savings nor the skills necessary to prepare themselves for white-collar occupations. Migratory work, a necessity for many Mexican agriculture workers, precluded the adequate education of Mexican American children in the cultural skills required in the urban labor market. Schools for children of migratory workers have been notoriously inadequate, and inadequacy in school facilities, curriculum, and faculty has been compounded by the fact that the children of migratory workers attend school less than other children do. Children in classrooms for only a portion of the year, year after year, cannot learn as much as those who attend on a regular basis. Due to the prevailing low wage rates for field workers, many children of migratory workers quit school and entered the farm labor force at an early age to help with the family income. What parents could not do the schools did not do, that is, prepare a generation of Mexican Americans for a new type of work in this country which required a large degree of enculturation.

@@

BOX 8.4   THE PACHUCOS AND THE ZOOT-SUIT RIOTS

Many Mexican American youths in the east side barrio of Los Angeles...spent much of their time in one another's company—in what the newspapers referred to as "gangs." These Pachucos flaunted their distinctiveness by dressing in a manner that most Anglos considered "outlandish." They wore tight-cuffed trousers that bloused at the knee and were belted high on the body. Their costumes also included wide-brimmed hats, long-tailed coats, high boots, ducktail haircuts, and ankle-length watch chains. Anglos called these costumes "zoot suits" and tended to identify those who wore them as "hoodlums." The newspapers exacerbated this tendency by referring to pachucos as "gangsters" and by giving their activities sensational coverage.

The summers of 1942 and 1943 produced two widely noted events involving the pachucos. The first event concerned the death of a young Mexican American named Jose Diaz near an East Los Angeles swimming hole. Twenty-four pachucos were arrested,...but an autopsy showed that he might have died in an automobile accident. After a trial that lasted several months, nine of the defendants were convicted of second-degree murder, and eight others were convicted of lesser offenses. Throughout the trial the press coverage was highly sensationalized. The swimming hole was referred to as "The Sleepy Lagoon," and the fact that the defendants were of Mexican heritage and wore "zoot suits" was emphasized. The convictions were appealed on the grounds that the trial had been conducted in a biased and improper way, and, after the defendants had suffered nearly two years of imprisonment, the convictions were overturned....

The publicity surrounding the Sleepy Lagoon Trial strengthened a widely held impression among Anglos that there was some sort of innate connection between Mexicanness and criminality....

The U.S. Navy had located a training facility in the east side barrio of Los Angeles. In time, various misunderstandings arose between some of the sailors and some of the Mexican American residents of the area, and on 3 June 1943 the accumulated tensions erupted into a number of disorders that became known as the "Zoot-Suit Riots." The "riots" may be more accurately described as a series of mob attacks by U.S. servicemen and off-duty policemen directed at Mexican Americans who wore zoot suits.

After a group of sailors allegedly were beaten by a gang of pachucos, a large group of servicemen "invaded" the east side barrio and severely beat at least four Mexican American youths wearing zoot suits. By 7 June the number of people engaged in the disorders had swelled into the thousands. The Los Angeles police department took few steps during this period to protect the Mexican Americans or restrain the servicemen. In some cases, the police merely followed the servicemen and arrested the Mexican Americans who were the victims of an attack! Miraculously, no one was killed in these disorders.

The "Zoot Suit Race Riots" in Los Angeles ended in about ten days....

☯☯

Better attention to the education of children of farm workers by educators and public officials in the rural Southwest did not materialize largely because the tax base was the owners of large tracts of land—the big growers and the railroads, or the very interests who opposed property taxes and needed cheap Mexican labor. What interest did big growers, absentee landlords, and corporation comptrollers have in the education of Mexican Americans, a service which would cost them money? As a class of employers, they needed only bodies, not minds. Moreover, until recently, the Southwest never had a large middle class, due to land consolidation and the historical marginality of urban industry in the region. Thus there was only a small middle class in the history of the region to invest in good schools, which would have prepared Chicano children better for the realities of post-industrial society.

Such were the circumstances behind the historical divergence of Mexican Americans. Barnes (1971:23) summarized the impact of such conditions in the Southwest on the historical exclusion of Mexican Americans from the larger society:

> Schools, shops and civic institutions never blossomed in those parts of the South and West dominated by giant land holdings. Enormous disparity of wealth and power is rarely conducive to widespread involvement in public affairs, and is even less so when large portions of the population are emigrants, or are barred by one means or another from voting. Why after all, should an absentee landlord spend his taxes on good public schools, when his own children go to private school and an educated work force is the last thing he wants?

One suspects that for much of the Anglo working class of the Southwest, which was composed of Americans from a variety of ethnic backgrounds, the indifference of Anglo capital toward improving the conditions of Mexican American laborers was equally strong. Through their unions Anglo workers formed, in significant respects, an aristocracy of labor, particularly in construction and on the railroads. On the railroads the Mexicans, along with some Indians, laid and maintained the tracks, hard and dirty work, while whites ran the trains as engineers, firemen, and brakemen—a neat instance of ethnic stratification. Even at the same jobs on the railroads, Mexicans got lower pay than Anglos (Reisler, 1976). Opening their craft unions to Mexican Americans and educating Chicano children would have been obviously inconsistent with the interest of the Anglo aristocracy of labor (Bonacich, 1972).

To compound the exclusion brought about by their work concentration and their limited participation in public schools, Mexican Americans have lived apart from other Americans, segregated in the barrios. At work and at home, Mexicans have avoided contact with outsiders and outside social institutions, preferring instead their own kind and relying on their own ethnic services. While nearly all of America's ethnic groups have lived in ethnic neighborhoods, segregated for a time from others, Mexicans in the borderlands have lived in barrios for centuries, and into these barrios came new arrivals from Mexico. Segregation of this sort and the proximity of Mexico have also played roles in the historical exclusion of Mexican Americans from the larger American society.

Land consolidation in the Southwest meant that Mexican American families faced nearly insurmountable barriers to buying their own farms. This mobility route ordinarily requires few cultural skills and allows for the direct application of job-related experiences; it was used by the Japanese on the West Coast at the turn of the century (see Chapter 13). However, in much of the Southwest, land holdings and agricultural production had become so concentrated in the hands of big growers that small farms were not competitive, and it was only the small farms that Mexican American workers could afford to buy. For Mexican Americans this mobility route has been used only by the few families who have come to own small-to-modest truck farms and produce stands outside the cities of the Southwest and Midwest. Only a minuscule proportion of the table fruits and vegetables eaten by American families is purchased from such operations.

By the same token, there were mobility routes for the Mexican American generation. For example, families in the rural Southwest could purchase a truck, nurture political and economic contacts, and thereby become labor agents. Some evolved into informal bankers, merchants, and landowners. Then, there was the chance to migrate North. Three or four families, or perhaps a group of friends, might migrate together, working in the North for better wages, saving money, and eventually settling in the Midwest, for example, or returning home to the Southwest better off. During the Second World War, with young males out of the labor force and in uniform, Chicana women found new opportunity in the war industry, especially in Los Angeles,

(Romo, 1983). This was happening even as the zoot-suit riots were taking place.

The Chicano community also contained mutual aid societies at this time, originally burial-insurance societies (Barrera, 1988). These societies evolved over time into multi-purpose insurance and welfare societies, as well as elaborating into social clubs that held dances, barbecues, and celebrations on Mexican patriotic holidays. The largest of these *mutualistas* was the Alianza Hispano-Americana, founded in Tucson in 1894 (Barrera, 1988).

Some writers contend that unlike many other immigrant groups, Mexicans did not and still do not come to America with a commitment to establish themselves and work toward their assimilation (e.g., Grebler, et al., 1970). Many Mexican migrants are sojourners, who work for a time in the United States and then return to Mexico with their savings. Because they are willing to work at low wage rates—dollars go further in Mexico than in the United States—these sojourners have had the effect of depressing wage rates for other Mexican families who have wanted to establish themselves in this country. While this argument has some merit, many ethnic groups who have established themselves in America were also sojourners (see Chapter 12). Moreover, millions of Mexicans have settled permanently in the United States, and to characterize even those who return occasionally to Mexico as sojourners overlooks the history of the Southwest. It was once Hispanic and the possession of Mexico.

Mexican Americans were particularly hard hit in the Great Depression. Many field workers lost their jobs, due to increased competition with migrating Anglos from the Midwest and South and the increasing mechanization of agriculture in the Southwest. Displaced workers either returned or were repatriated to Mexico, but many more migrated to the cities of the Southwest, and they have done so since in increasing numbers. The Bracero program begun in the 1940s and lasting into the 1960s meant renewed migration from Mexico into the United States, although Operation Wetback in the 1950s meant more repatriation.

The trend since World War II is clear, however; Mexican Americans are evolving into an urban people. Grebler, et al. (1970:71) noted the significance of this internal migration of Mexican Americans and the continued immigration of Mexican nationals in the context of the country's changing labor needs:

> In the late decades of the nineteenth and the early years of this century, the American economy could easily absorb millions of unskilled Irish, Polish, Italian, and Scandinavian immigrants. But since the 1920s (when the mass immigration from Mexico began) and particu-

268

larly since World War II the absorption of people with low-grade job qualifications had become increasingly difficult. The mechanization of industry, the more recent automation of manufacturing and other processes, and the growing importance of consumer and business services have placed a high premium on skills.

According to ethnic conflict theory, systems of ethnic stratification are used by dominant groups to relegate their rivals to the bottom of the opportunity structure. Ethnic stratification is enforced in a number of ways, including job discrimination, poor schooling, and the threat of violence for those who step beyond the boundaries of the stratification lines. Violence against Chicanos is evident, to be sure, illustrated in the raids of the Texas Rangers and the zoot-suit riots. Prejudice also enforces and justifies ethnic stratification and has been directed toward Mexican Americans, represented in images of *bandidos, pachucos,* and the association of Mexican Americans with urban gangs and criminality in general.

The fuller story of ethnic stratification in the Southwest includes the cooperation between Anglo interests there and the U. S. government. First, Anglos had the government, through military conflict, expropriate land from Mexico, culminating in the Treaty of Guadalupe Hidalgo and the Gadsden Purchase. Next, it manipulated the state legal apparatus in the expropriation of Hispanic land in the Southwest. Thirdly, it had the government invest in the region, exemplified by the National Reclamation Act. Anglos also enlisted state support in labor recruitment of Mexican immigrants. When labor was needed, the border was open, illustrated in the Bracero program. When labor needs fell off, the state expatriated Mexican immigrants to Mexico. In a sense, Mexican labor was criminalized, making it more vulnerable, cheaper, and tractable (Portes and Walton, 1981).

According to ethnic conflict theory, the oppressed resist, and Chicano resistance is also evident. With the coming of the Chicano generation later in the twentieth century, for example, several protest leaders emerged. Reiss Tijerina launched a campaign in New Mexico during the 1960s to use land grants to recover lost Hispanic land there. In 1963 he established the *Alianza Federal de los Mercedes*, and its members were engaged in a shoot-out at the court house in Tierra Amarilla, New Mexico. José Angel Gutierrez organized Hispanic students while in college in the 1960s and then returned home to Crystal City, Texas, and politically organized Chicanos in that city. He helped found La Raza Unida in 1970. Rodolfo "Corky" Gonzales organized Chicanos in Denver during the 1960s and 1970s, founding the Colorado La Raza Unida Party in 1970. Gonzales was a writer as well as a political personality, and his poem "Yo Soy Joaquim" expressed his frustration with Chicano oppression:

I am Joaquin
      lost in a world of confusion
      caught up in the whirl of a
      gringo society,
      confused by the rules,
      scorned by attitudes,
      suppressed by manipulation
      and destroyed by modern society.
My fathers
      have lost the economic battle
      and won
      the struggle of cultural survival.

Source: J. C. Hammerback, et al., *A War of Words: Chicano Protest in the 1960s and 1970s*, Greenwood Press. 1985, p. 59. Copyright © 1985 by Greenwood Press, an imprint of Greenwood Publishing Group, Inc., Westport, CT. Reprinted by permission.

Cesar Chavez began organizing farm labor around Delano, California, in the 1960s, and the United Farm Workers was established in 1965 with 2,000 members under his leadership. By 1972 the United Farm Workers had 30,000 members and was affiliated with the larger AFL-CIO (Hammerback, et al., 1985). Obviously, these protest leaders vary in their demands for change and level of militancy, but they have in common the goal of reversing the economic, political, and cultural repression of Chicanos and a corresponding resurrection of Chicano heritage.

THE PRESENT

Immigrants come from Mexico through social networks composed of family members and *paisanaje,* or members of the same village (Browning and Rodriquez, 1985; Massey, et al., 1987). Single men and women or entire families cross the border to towns and cities in the United States, where family and neighbors from Mexico already live. The most common destinations in the 1980s were Los Angeles, Chicago, El Paso, and San Diego (Portes and Rumbaut, 1990). A young man may search out his father, an uncle, cousins, or simply friends from back home. These people help him find a job, often at the same place where they work. Over time immigrants acquire new friends, job skills, and even savings, part of which is returned home to Mexico. At first, they may share housing with many others to save on rent, although each may have their own phone because no one wants to get stuck with someone else's expensive calls to Mexico. Later, some can afford cars, household goods, and even homes, thus taking on some symbols of success as well as making life more comfortable.

The immigration stream creates a counter stream, the occasional return of immigrants to Mexico:

> Now imagine that it is December, just before Christmas, and you are driving along a highway in the Mexican state of Jalisco.... Judging by the traffic, you wonder whether you haven't taken a wrong turn out of Guadalajara and driven into California. Every other vehicle that passes has license plates from that state, and now and again one from Texas or Illinois goes past. Turning off the main highway onto a cobbled road, you see a small farm town in the valley below.... As you pull into town, late-model cars, trucks, and vans with American license plates line the narrow streets where not long ago donkey and cattle were the only traffic.... Many [migrants] will pass the next few weeks relaxing in homes newly outfitted with color televisions, tape decks, video recorders, stereos, refrigerators, and washing machines brought from the United States. Others will get right to work build- ing a new home,...still others will pursue some local investment op- portunity,...and by February they will begin to disappear again, heading to el Norte (Massey, et al., 1987:1–3).

Such trips home to Mexico will encourage even more to migrate to el Norte.

Mexican Americans are not only increasing in numbers; they, along with other Hispanic groups, also are evolving toward blue-collar and even white-collar work (see Tables 8.1 and 8.2). They are converging with the country's changing labor needs as they shift from the rural Southwest to the cities of California and even the Midwest (Moore and Pachon, 1985). They are still behind other groups, howev-er, as Tables 8.1 and 8.2 also show. The discrepancy between the occu-pational composition of Mexican Americans and all people in 1990 was greatest in white-collar work, especially managerial and profes-sional, the type of work that indicates a good degree of integration into the larger society and requires a good measure of acculturation. If the future of Chicanos is to truly converge with that of other groups and the larger society, this discrepancy must be diminished.

In 1980, 45.4 percent of the Spanish-origin males 25 years old and over in the United States had completed high school, compared to 68.5 percent for all other males of the same age group. For females 25 years old and over, the figures were 42.7 and 67 percent, respectively. Clear-ly, there is an educational gap between Hispanics and the larger popu-lation. This gap is also evident in rates of higher education. In 1980, 5.2 percent of the same Spanish-origin males had four or more years of college, but 10.5 percent of the males from all other groups had four or

TABLE 8.1 PERCENTAGE DISTRIBUTION OF SPANISH SURNAME AND ALL EMPLOYED PEOPLE BY OCCUPATIONAL GROUPS, 1950–1970

Occupational Group	Spanish Surname			All People		
	1950	1960	1970	1950	1960	1970
White-collar workers						
Professional and technical	2.7	4.6	7.7	8.7	11.1	14.9
Managers, officials, and						
proprietors except						
farmers	7.4	4.1	4.2	8.7	8.4	8.3
Clerical and sales	10.4	14.1	19.4	19.2	21.6	20.0
Blue-collar workers						
Craftsmen and foremen	10.6	12.6	14.0	14.3	13.5	13.9
Operators	21.1	24.8	22.6	20.3	18.4	13.7
Laborers except farm						
and mine	15.0	11.5	7.2	6.5	4.8	4.5
Service workers						
Private household	3.0	3.1	1.7	2.5	2.7	1.5
Other service	8.1	9.9	14.1	7.8	8.4	11.3
Farm workers						
Farmers and managers	4.9	1.8	0.5	7.6	3.9	1.9
Laborers and foremen	20.7	13.5	4.1	4.4	2.2	1.3

Note: Percentages may not total 100 because of rounding.

Sources: 1950 Census, *Occupational Characteristics*, Table 3, pp. 29–36; 1950 Census, *Persons of Spanish Surname (except Puerto Rican)*, Table 6, pp. 23–39; 1960 Census, *Occupational Characteristics*, Table 2, pp. 11–20; 1960 Census, *Persons of Spanish Surname (except Puerto Rican)*, Table 6, p. 38; 1970 Census, *Occupational Characteristics*, Table 39, pp. 593–608.

TABLE 8.2 PERCENTAGE DISTRIBUTION OF MEXICAN AMERICANS AND ALL EMPLOYED PEOPLE BY OCCUPATIONAL GROUPS, 1990

Occupational Group	Mexican Origin 1990	All People 1990
Managerial and professional	11.5%	25.5%
Technical, sales, and administrative support	26.0	31.5
Service occupations	21.0	13.5
Precision production, craft, and repair	11.0	11.5
Operators, fabricators, and laborers	23.5	15.5
Farming, forestry, and fishing	7.1	2.5

Sources: U.S. Department of Commerce, 1983, *1980 Census of Population, Volume 1: Characteristics of the Population*, Chapter C: General Social and Economic Characteristics, Table 169. U.S. Bureau of the Census, Current Population Reports, Series P-20, No. 455, *The Hispanic Population in the United States, March 1991*, U.S. Government Printing Office, Washington, DC, 1991.

more years of college. For females, the comparative figures were 2.9 for Spanish-origin and 5.4 percent for all others. There will have to be a convergence in education before Chicanos also converge in occupation and income with the larger population. In 1979, however, working Chicano males made about 68 percent of the median annual income of white males, and Chicano females made about 85 percent of the annual income of white females.

By the same token, Hispanic men who have completed at least 12 years of school and are fluent in English have similar occupational attainments as non-Hispanic men with the same characteristics and living in the same geographic area (Stolzenberg, 1990). It is at the lower level of schooling and English proficiency that occupational attainments of Hispanic men are lower than that of others. The Hispanic advantaged compare more favorably with their non-Hispanic class counterparts than does the Hispanic disadvantaged with its non-Hispanic class counterpart. Integration into the larger society is coming first to the higher ethclass of Hispanics.

This same point is demonstrated in other research. Labor force participation rates, occupations, and income of Chicanos are associated with language capacity. Those who speak only Spanish are lower on these dimensions than those who are bilingual or speak only English. However, the attrition of Spanish across generations of Mexican Americans is about the same as was loss of home language for earlier European immigrants (Connor, 1985; Stevens, 1985). For example, in a 1976 sample of Hispanics 14 years old and over who reported that Spanish was the usual language spoken at home when they were children, one-half said that English was now the usual language spoken in the home (Grenier, 1985). "Of those born and raised in Mexico, 84 percent speak mostly Spanish at home. By the third generation, 84 percent use mostly English" (Horowitz, 1985a:78). De La Garza (1985) summarized other research that shows the same trend; Spanish monolingualism does not outlast the immigrant generation. Thus, Chicano mobility should proceed with successive generations. By implication, Chicano support for bilingualism and retention of the Spanish language is not support for Spanish monolingualism (see Box 8.5).

Keefe and Padilla (1987) showed that occupational mobility, as well as generation, of Chicanos was associated with declines in Chicano cultural awareness, social orientation, and ethnic loyalty. Cultural awareness refers primarily to Spanish language use, social orientation to associating with Chicanos and eating Mexican food, and ethnic loyalty means a preference for Spanish and high regard for Mexican culture.

☙❧

BOX 8.5   ENGLISH AS OFFICIAL LANGUAGE SPLITS
CALIFORNIA CITY

Filmore, Calif.—A battle is being waged in this citrus-growing community between Hispanic and non-Hispanic residents over a new ordinance that declares English the city's official language.

Passage of the measure...started the dispute between Hispanic people...and City Council members allied with a group that opposes bilingual teaching....

Filmore's economy depends on the orange and lemon groves around the city. People of Hispanic heritage have lived here and worked in the groves for generations. Their children have found professions and founded businesses here. About half of the city's 10,000 residents are Hispanic....

Today more than 60% of the children here are Hispanic. Before the ordinance was passed, in some classes non-Hispanic children had been getting about 20 minutes of bilingual education daily along with children not yet fluent in English. A community group, the ABC Committee, called the practice a waste of time.

Then a Deputy Sheriff married to an ABC Committee activist urged the Council to adopt a resolution that would say, "The English language is the official language of the city of Filmore." ...The Council adopted it as an ordinance....

Backers say an official language can unify different cultures; parents say Hispanic children now sit on one side of the classroom and non-Hispanic children on the other....

The Hispanic people are also boycotting a market whose management supported the move for an official language. Hispanic people from out of town are refusing to buy anything in Filmore.

Mayor Cloyd, a principal defender of the language plan... said a second language should be taught only at home on a voluntary basis.

"Are the signs on the road going to be in Japanese, Chinese, Oriental, or Spanish or Anglo?" he asked.

"There could be another Quebec in the United States of America," he went on...."Who would want that?"

Mr. Morales said the ordinance's backers did not recognize the culture of the region or the contributions of Mexican heritage. "It's an insult to the Spanish community," he said.

To succeed, he said, his people must become fluent in English, but he added, "By saying English is the official language, they're saying we're second-class citizens. As far as we're concerned, we're equal in all respects."

◎◎

Moreover, with a rise in socioeconomic status, Hispanics move to suburbs and have contact with Anglos (Massey and Denton, 1985 and 1988; Massey and Mullan, 1984). The rate of intermarriage between Chicanos and others has also been increasing over recent decades (Horowitz, 1985). Early in the 1960s, 40 percent of the Chicano marriages in Los Angeles were exogamous, and in the 1970s they hit the 50 percent mark in all of California. The same trend is seen in other areas of the country, only the percentage of intermarriages varies from place to place. In some locales, outmarriage by Chicanos is now over 90 percent. The trend toward intermarriage is clearly seen across the generations as well. By the second and third generations, Chicano men and women are more likely to marry Anglos. "In the third generation, the probability of marriage between a Mexican-American and an Anglo was higher than between a Mexican-American and either a first- or second-generation Mexican-American" (Horowitz, 1985a:81). English fluency, educational and occupational attainments, residential mobility and intermarriage are all signs of inclusion, but they are coming first to the Chicano middle class.

This does not mean the assimilation of the Chicano community, however. The poor and recent immigrants continue to be traditional in culture and occupational niche. Moreover, institutions in the Hispanic community are growing. Between 1970 and 1980, Spanish-language radio stations in the United States increased from 60 to 200, newspapers from 40 to 65, magazines from 25 to 65, and the markets served by Spanish television grew from 12 to 167 (Moore and Pachon, 1985). This is hardly a picture of a dying ethnic community.

Indeed, the growing Chicano community is having an impact on how business is done in this country. Companies no longer serve a homogenous mass market in many parts of the United States. Thus, telephone companies now have customer service representatives who speak Spanish as well as English. One supermarket chain in California has recently opened a separate chain of stores designed for Spanish-speaking customers. All employees and signs are bilingual, and 50 percent of the markets are given over to fresh produce and meat, since

Mexican customers favor fresh foods. (In traditional stores only 25 percent of the floor space is for fresh produce.) The meat department stocks beef lips, pigs heads, and snouts, and the butchers work out in the open. Money orders and Western Union services are available in the markets, the latter service to wire money to relatives in Mexico. The stores are designed to duplicate the feel of a Mexican open-air market.

Inclusion and enculturation is a good bet for the Chicano middle class, but immigration from Mexico continues. What will be the impact of this immigration on the Chicano community in the United States? On the one hand, Lieberson (1981) showed that increasing numbers of recent arrivals helped the new European immigrant groups, those from eastern and southern Europe, earlier in the century. On the other hand, the increasing size of the African American population in northern cities, once European immigration had fallen off, meant greater discrimination against blacks.

Sullivan (1986) argued that both can happen to the Chicano community; continued immigration can help, but it also can hurt. For example, in communities where Chicanos are landlords, store owners, employers, etc., and in a position to make rents, profits, and interest, then a stream of new arrivals, and thus customers, can be an economic benefit. In communities where Chicanos are only wage labor, however, new arrivals can undercut Chicano workers' economic security by their sheer numbers, by being a cheaper alternative for employers. Local employers can drive down wages and benefits when the supply of cheaper workers is great. Thus, tension should be greatest between new arrivals and the Chicano working class.

Research shows that Chicanos and *indocumentados*, undocumented immigrants, have negative stereotypes of each other. In one Texas study, Chicanos saw indocumentados as rate busters at work, taking harder, dirtier, and more dangerous jobs without standing up to employers for their rights (Rodriguez and Nunez, 1986). Chicanos also saw new arrivals as backward and themselves as more urbane and sophisticated. For their part, indocumentados saw working-class Chicanos as lazy, relatively incompetent workers who spoil their children. In addition, language use and musical tastes separated Chicano from indocumentado. Even when both speak Spanish, their dialects, idioms, and vocabularies differ so much that language is not a common bond.

The impact of Mexican immigrants on the nation's job market for all groups is a national concern. One theory is that new immigrants displace American workers on a one-to-one basis, but the evidence does not support this theory. According to a second theory, the labor market is segmented so that immigrants and residents take up different jobs and do not directly compete with each other. Evidence supports this theory at the national level, but in places where immigrants first settle, immigrants can displace American workers, especially those on the bottom of the labor hierarchy (Borjas and Tienda, 1987). Actually, immigrants can displace resident workers in some jobs but not in others, and immigrants can create new jobs. Two-thirds of the new jobs in Los Angeles County during the 1970s went to immigrants (Muller and Espenshade, 1985).

The division between resident Mexican Americans and new Mexican immigrants is only one dimension to the diversity of Mexican Americans today. Mexican Americans are separated by ethclass, with the middle class living outside barrios and otherwise including themselves in American life. Many are college educated, career oriented, and have the same general values and life-styles of the Anglo middle class. It is a long way from their homes to the 300 or so Mexican youth gangs in Los Angeles. These ethclass differences intersect with the generational differences among Chicanos, that is, the length of a family's residence in the United States. The longer that residence, the more likely we see signs of inclusion in terms of education, occupation, residence, and intermarriage.

It might be overly optimistic to forecast that the immigrants, poor and working-class Chicanos, will experience the same upward mobility possible in the past, due to recent changes in the occupational structure of the country (Chapter 6). Box 8.6 contains an account of one neighborhood in Houston, Texas, that suggests a pessimistic forecast.

☙

BOX 8.6 MAGNOLIA PARK

Bordered by factories and docks, the Magnolia Park neighborhood has long been a beacon for generations of Mexican immigrants seeking sturdy homes and steady wages. Over time, most found jobs, assimilated, and moved on to a better life.

But that is much less the case nowadays. The neighborhood is as much a place to stay poor as it is to start poor. Upward mobility among the 14 million people of Mexican descent in the United States...is faltering, and on Magnolia Park's shady streets the signs of trouble are everywhere: high-school dropouts and teen-age mothers, families doubled and tripled up in bungalows, day-laborers who gather at street corners hoping to sell their services....

The neighborhood's troubles started with the oil bust of the early 1980s and continued as the nation's labor market underwent vast changes, shifting more and more from a blue-collar, manufacturing base to high-technology and service industries. With the loss of those jobs went the traditional stepping stones that Mexican immigrants had long used to get ahead....

Immigrants still get lots of help from relatives and friends in finding work, but they usually end up in dead-end, low-paying service jobs—cleaning offices, mowing lawns, babysitting or sewing....

The story is much the same in other big cities where people of Mexican descent are concentrated, in neighborhoods like East Los Angeles and the Pilsen area of Chicago. While the upheaval in the labor market hurt urban working-class neighborhoods of all ethnic or racial groups in the 1980s, Mexican-American neighborhoods particularly suffered because it occurred just as their populations were exploding....

...Income for workers of Mexican origin across the nation rose from the 1950s through the 1970s. They were concentrated in areas experiencing robust growth, especially Texas, the Southwest, and California. Meanwhile, blacks and Puerto Ricans increasingly suffered from the decline of manufacturing in the Midwest and the Northeast. In the 1970s family income for people of Mexican origin rose by 7 percent, compared with about 3 percent for whites and blacks.

But in the 1980s a national recession, the restructuring of the labor market, and competition from new immigrants all took their toll.... Real family income for people of Mexican origin fell by more than 13 percent between 1979 and 1987. During that time, the earnings of whites remained comparatively flat and those of blacks fell by almost 7 percent.

Source: *The New York Times*, January 19, 1992. Copyright © 1992 by The New York Times Company. Reprinted by permission.

Another division in the Mexican American population is between Chicanas and Chicanos, women and men. Lieberson and Waters (1988) showed that the dissimilarity between European and non-European women, including Chicanas, in occupations is much less than it is for males. Occupations for women are more compressed, and thus there is less dissimilarity between women of different ethnic groups. Perhaps, this reflects in part the gender barriers imposed on Chicanas, in addition to the ethnic barriers they face. Chicanas share with other women a segmented labor market, whereby males concentrate in certain jobs and females in others, and even a split labor market, whereby women in the same jobs as men get less pay. These Chicana experiences are not necessarily shared by their men, although ethnicity is.

Other issues can separate Chicana from Chicano, such as reproductive rights, child care, and the sexual division of labor in the home. Chicanas talk and write about how they are expected to serve men in the home, although they, too, are working full-time outside the home. Another issue is that Chicanos exercise too much social control over Chicanas. One writer traced this to the legacy of Malintzin Tenepal, who is seen to have betrayed her own kind in the service of Hernan Cortez during the Spanish conquest of Mexico (Moraga, 1986). Chicanas can be labeled, even today, with the stigma of betraying La Raza, the threat of which allows their men to exercise control over their lives.

Mexican Americans are perhaps a unique ethnic group in America. Only they, and to a lesser extent French-Canadian immigrants, are a border people, living in a part of the United States adjacent to their country of origin. The national loyalty of border people is often suspect around the world (Weiner, 1985). Border ethnic groups can make irredentist demands, a call for regaining lost territory for a mother country. In the case of Chicanos, this would be the return to Mexico of the entire Southwest of the United States. Evidence does not support any such expectation on the part of Mexican Americans, however. For example, Chicano ethnic loyalty toward Mexico, Mexican culture, and the Spanish language declines significantly across the generations, as do cultural awareness and ethnic social orientation (Keefe and Padilla, 1987). Even in the 1960s, fewer than 2 percent of Chicanos in Los Angeles and San Antonio expressed a desire for retaining a sense of Mexican patriotism (De La Garza, 1985). Moreover, Chicano voting on social and political issues is indistinct from that of the larger electorate.

PUERTO RICAN AMERICANS

Puerto Ricans are the second largest Hispanic group in the United States. There were nearly three million (2,727,754) Puerto Ricans living in the country in 1990, and most resided in the Northeast, especially in New York City. Over 40 percent of the world's Puerto Ricans now reside outside Puerto Rico. The historical connection between the United States and Puerto Rico goes back to the past century, a connection that became a conduit for Puerto Rican immigration into the United States.

IMMIGRATION AND CONTACT

Puerto Rico was a Spanish colony from 1593 to 1898. At the conclusion of the Spanish-American War, Puerto Rico became a U.S. pos-

FIGURE 8.2 Puerto Rican Americans and Change in American Society

Industrial Society c. 1865–1945		Post-Industrial Society c. 1945–Present	
Immigration	→ Puerto Rican community →		Present situation

session in 1898. Under the Foraker Act of 1900, the U.S. president appointed the governor of Puerto Rico and members of the island's executive council, but members of a lower house were elected by the Puerto Rican electorate (Fitzpatrick, 1971).

Puerto Ricans became U.S. citizens with the Jones Act of 1917, which also provided for popular elections to both house of the legislative branch of the island's government. A resident commissioner was also elected to represent Puerto Rico in the U.S. Congress, but without voting rights (Fitzpatrick, 1971). With the Elective Governor Act of 1947, the governor of Puerto Rico was elected by popular vote, and the governor appointed most governmental officials in Puerto Rico once appointed by the U.S. president. Luis Muñoz Marin took office as the first elected governor in 1949. Puerto Rico became a Free Associated State by referendum vote in 1952.

Since that time, the island's politics have centered on a debate over the political status of Puerto Rico: was it to be an independent nation, a state of the United States, or continue with commonwealth status as an Free Associate State? It has remained as the Free Associate State of Puerto Rico. Although Puerto Ricans are U.S. citizens and serve in the U.S. armed forces, they have no voting representation in Congress and are not subject to U.S. income tax.

Since the United States annexed Puerto Rico, there have been significant economic ties between the island and the mainland. Puerto Rico was integrated into the United States economy with the Foraker Act by free trade between the island and the mainland, protection under the U.S. tariff system and cabotage laws, and inclusion into the U.S. monetary system (Sanchez-Ayendez, 1988). Thus, American capital reached into the island's economy, and as a consequence there began a subsequent flow of Puerto Rican labor to the mainland (Portes and Walton, 1981). This flow was facilitated by the fact that Puerto Ricans were U.S. citizens and thus faced no immigration barriers.

Before its annexation by the United States, Puerto Rico had a diversified subsistence economy. That is, most people lived in rural areas, growing crops for themselves and their families. This changed with U.S possession of the island. Puerto Rican agriculture was brought into the world economy, and it concentrated on commercial agriculture, specifically the growing of cash crops for export (Fitzpatrick, 1971; Rodriguez, 1989; Sanchez-Ayendez, 1988). These crops included sugarcane, tobacco, and coffee. Sugarcane was the principal export crop, and 60 percent of the island's sugar production was controlled by absentee U.S. firms. Concentrating on export crops, Puerto Rico had to import staples to feed its population.

In the process, rural Puerto Ricans became farm labor for large landowner's. Because of a downturn in coffee production, farm labor began to migrate from the highlands to the coastal areas of the island, where sugarcane was grown and where the tobacco-processing plants were located (Sanchez-Ayendez, 1988). In the sugarcane fields, labor was needed for about six months each year, with the slack seasons coinciding with the growing seasons in mainland agriculture (Fitzpatrick, 1971). Even during good times, it was possible for farm labor in Puerto Rico to work in the sugarcane fields for half the year and become migratory farm labor on the mainland for the other half.

The Great Depression resulted in a declining demand, and thus prices, for Puerto Rican agricultural exports. After 1935, not only sugar production but also the smaller manufacturing sector of the island's economy declined (Sanchez-Ayendez, 1988). Since the population of Puerto Rico doubled between 1899 and 1940, there was surplus labor, and thus unemployment, particularly during economic hard times.

Soon after World War II, Puerto Rico undertook industrialization in an effort to deal with unemployment on the island. At first, this was a state-sponsored effort under the Puerto Rican Development Corporation (Rodriguez, 1989). This was followed by Operation Bootstrap, an attempt to bring branch plants of U.S. firms to Puerto Rico. Tax holidays were given to plants relocating to the island, and an additional lure for firms was the skilled but cheaper labor in Puerto Rico. Products from Puerto Rico could be shipped to the mainland duty free because of the free trade between the island and the mainland.

During the 1960s, manufacturing in Puerto Rico shifted toward petrochemicals, chemicals, and pharmaceuticals. This did not eliminate unemployment, however, because many of the new industries were capital-intensive, with only modest labor needs, and the island's agriculture was being mechanized at the same time. Today, the government is the biggest employer in Puerto Rico, followed by commerce and manufacturing (Sanchez-Ayendez, 1988). Unemployment in 1983 was still relative high, around 20 percent. Economic conditions in Puerto Rico and its ties to the United States led to the migration of

Puerto Ricans to the mainland. This migration came in two waves, before and after the Second World War (Falcon, 1984; Fitzpatrick, 1971; Sanchez-Ayendez, 1988).

In the nineteenth century, political exiles caught up in the struggle with Spain over Puerto Rican independence emigrated, and a small number came to New York City (Falcon, 1984). Between 1898 and World War l, Puerto Ricans continued to migrate to the mainland, particularly to New York. In 1918, there were 4,500 Puerto Ricans in the cigar-maker unions in New York City, and there were more than 44,000 Puerto Ricans in New York by 1930 (Falcon, 1984). Puerto Ricans in New York were employed as cigar makers, factory operatives, domestics, laundry workers, and in hotel services and the needle trades. The men concentrated as laborers, construction workers, hotel porters, stevedores, etc., while the women were domestics, machine operators, laundry workers, and in the needle trades (Falcon, 1984). Puerto Rican neighborhoods also included lawyers, dentists, doctors, and pharmacists, as well as small businesses such as grocery stores and restaurants.

Puerto Ricans also found work as farm labor in the United States, particularly along the East Coast but also in the Midwest and Southwest. Farm laborers amounted to about 5 percent of the Puerto Rican population on the mainland. Some settled out of migratory farm work and into towns and cities, especially in the Northeast, and these were the initial Puerto Rican settlements outside New York City.

The earliest Puerto Rican immigrants were merchants, skilled workers in the tobacco industry, and political exiles. Over time, the class composition of the Puerto Rican community on the mainland changed toward a concentration in blue-collar work, in services as well as industry. Another pocket of Puerto Rican workers was found in mainland agriculture. Labor needs in the country dropped with the Great Depression, however, and it is estimated that nearly 20 percent of the Puerto Ricans on the mainland returned home to the island during the 1930s (Falcon, 1984; Sanchez-Ayendez, 1988).

A mass migration of Puerto Ricans to the mainland followed World War II. Fewer than 70,000 Puerto Ricans were living in the United States in 1940, and the total emigration from Puerto Rico to the mainland from 1898 to 1944 was 90,000 (Falcon, 1984; Fitzpatrick, 1971; Sanchez-Ayendez, 1988). By contrast, 18,700 Puerto Ricans emigrated on average each year to the mainland during the 1940s, over 41,000 each year during the 1950s, and 14,500 each year during the 1960s (Sanchez-Ayendez, 1988). By 1990, there were nearly 3 million Puerto Ricans in the United States.

Much of this second wave of Puerto Rican migration consisted of unskilled farm workers displaced by the mechanization of Puerto Rican agriculture since World War II. Despite the industrialization efforts on the island with Operation Bootstrap, surplus farm labor could not be absorbed by the industrial sector. The pull of labor needs in the United States, especially during the 1940s through the 1960s, was another reason for this great migration, as was the availability of cheap air fares between San Juan and New York.

The migration slowed during the 1970s and 1980s, and thousands of Puerto Ricans returned to the island in those two decades. Economic growth in the United States declined in the 1970s and 1980s, and there has been a loss in manufacturing jobs in particular (see Chapter 6). This helps account for the decline in Puerto Rican migration and the return of many to Puerto Rico. Nevertheless, Puerto Rican migration has always been circular, first to the mainland and then back to the island (Mills, 1957). Past declines in labor needs on the mainland, during the Great Depression, for example, resulted in the return of Puerto Ricans to the island. Indeed, the Puerto Rican immigrant has been characterized as a sojourner or a migrant laborer, who got a job in the United States with the intent of returning home as soon as possible.

PUERTO RICAN COMMUNITY

Puerto Ricans settled near the Brooklyn Naval Yard and in Harlem around the time of World War I (Fitzpatrick, 1971). After the 1924 Quota Act greatly restricted further European immigration, the demand for Puerto Rican labor rose. Their migration continued throughout the 1920s, and from Harlem the Puerto Rican community spread to East Harlem and the South Bronx, and from the Brooklyn Naval Yard to the Williamsburg section. The early Puerto Rican community in New York City became a cultural and political enclave, with many political and social organizations flourishing in the 1920s (Falcon, 1984:26).

Violence against Puerto Ricans in New York was common at this time, according to Falcon (1984). The community reacted by organizing self-defense groups and protesting to authorities about the lack of police protection. Police brutality against Puerto Ricans was also an issue. There were additional protests about the mistreatment of Puerto Rican contract farm laborers in Arizona and New Mexico.

During the 1960s, at the height of Puerto Rican immigration to the mainland, Sexton (1965) described Spanish Harlem (Box 8.7).

Puerto Rican Americans seeking greater influence in the
New York City school system march across the Brooklyn Bridge.

BOX 8.7 SPANISH HARLEM

At 6:30 A.M., while silk-stocking Manhattan is asleep, East Harlem is starting to bustle. The poor are early risers. They have the jobs others don't want: the early-hour jobs, the late-hour jobs. Many rise because it is a rural habit.

Along about 7:30 the streets are filled with fast-moving people: men, women, and swarms of children of all sizes....

Some will stand at the bus stops, but most will crowd into the downtown subways that speed them to jobs in commercial or silk-stocking areas: to serve the affluent, or work in their stores or small industrial shops.... The Puerto Rican women, to their sewing machines in the garment shops.

Later in the day, if it is warm, the men who have no jobs will come out and stand on the sidewalks and talk together.... Later, when the children return from school, the sidewalks and streets will jump with activity. Clusters of men, sitting on orange crates on the sidewalks, will play checkers or cards. The women will sit on the stoop, arms folded, and watch the young at play.... Vendors, ringing their bells, will hawk hot dogs, orange drinks, ice cream....often jarring noise of honking horns, music, children's games, and casual quarrels, whistles, singing, will go on late into the night....

The most striking contrast between the rich and the poor areas of Manhattan is in the visible wealth of the one and the visible children of the other. Also, there is the obvious restraint of the one and the expressiveness of the other. In East Harlem, music is everywhere, and visible gaiety, anger, fear, love, hatred....

The spirited Latin music of East Harlem, pouring out from open tenement windows in every block, is Puerto Rican. Many signs, directions, conversations are in Spanish. The culture, the dark and tight style of dress, and the way of life, the store front Pentecostal churches, the pleasantness and gentleness are among Puerto Rico's contributions to East Harlem....

East Harlem is special because, except for a number of small Puerto Rican *bodegas,* it has few of Manhattan's accessories.... It is rather like a barracks, a place of residence for some 180,000 people—who populate a community big enough to call itself a city.

Source: Patricia Cayo Sexton, *Spanish Harlem,* pp. 1–4. Copyright © 1965 by Harper & Row, Publishers. Reprinted by permission of HarperCollins Publishers.

Sexton (1965) went on to describe community political organizations in East Harlem and their leaders, who used the antipoverty programs of the 1960s to developed a political presence in New York (Rivera, 1984). Other Puerto Rican organizations in New York City were the Puerto Rican Forum and the Puerto Rican Family Institute (Fitzpatrick, 1971), both of which addressed issues concerning the family and education of Puerto Rican youth.

Puerto Rican politics on the mainland also involved issues at home, in Puerto Rico. The debate was over the status of the island, whether it would continue as a commonwealth, or become a state or an independent nation. The *Fuerzas Armadas de Liberacion* (FALN) was one organization that advocated Puerto Rican independence and used terrorism as a means. It was linked to several bombings of businesses and public places in the United States.

In the past decade or so, Puerto Ricans have become more politically active. Sanchez-Ayendez (1988:192) reported that "national organizations, such as the Puerto Rican National Coalition, and community-based agencies, such as Inquilinos Boricuas en Accion in Boston and La Casa de Puerto Rico in Hartford, have been...promoting grass-roots movements among Puerto Rican communities...to improve the socioeconomic condition of their people." This note brings us to consider the present condition of Puerto Ricans in the United States.

THE PRESENT

Puerto Ricans are the largest Hispanic group in the Northeast, and over 70 percent of Puerto Ricans in the United States live in the Northeast (Sanchez-Ayendez, 1988). The largest concentration of Puerto Ricans in the country is still in New York City, but large numbers are living in Newark, New Jersey; Hartford, Connecticut; Chicago, Illinois; Boston, Massachusetts; Philadelphia, Pennsylvania; and Miami, Florida. Ninety percent of the nation's Puerto Ricans lived in New York City during the 1950s, but under 50 percent lived there by 1980. Puerto Ricans have migrated from New York City to other locations, although they are still concentrated in the Northeast.

Economic changes in New York City since 1960 help explain this shift in the Puerto Rican population (Moore and Pachon, 1985; Rodriguez, 1989; Sanchez-Ayendez, 1988; Sassen-Koob, 1985). Puerto Ricans were once concentrated in the manufacturing sector of New York City, but the city lost 173,000 manufacturing jobs in the 1960s and another 268,000 jobs in the 1970s due to firms' relocating out of the city and changes in the production process, such as automation and computerization, that displaced labor. This declining sector of the city's

TABLE 8.3 PERCENTAGE DISTRIBUTION OF PUERTO RICAN AMERICANS AND ALL
EMPLOYED PEOPLE BY OCCUPATIONAL GROUPS, 1990

Occupational Group	Puerto Rican Origin 1990	All People 1990
Managerial and professional	16.7%	25.5%
Technical, sales, and administrative support	34.2	31.5
Service occupations	18.6	13.5
Precision production, craft, and repair	9.8	11.5
Operators, fabricators, and laborers	19.3	15.5
Farming, forestry, and fishing	1.3	2.5

Source: U.S. Department of Commerce, 1983, *1980 Census of Population, Volume 1: Characteristics of the Population*, Chapter C: General Social and Economic Characteristics, Table 169. U.S. Bureau of the Census, Cuurent Population Reports, Series P–20, No. 455, *The Hispanic Population in the United States*, March 1991, U.S. Government Printing Office, Washington, DC, 1991.

economy affected Puerto Ricans, who were not finding jobs in the growing sectors of the New York economy, namely, in the professions, finance and insurance, and real estate (Rodriguez, 1989). These changes in the occupational structure of New York City resulted in blue-collar unemployment, and this forced Puerto Ricans to move or find lesser jobs in the city's peripheral economy.

These changes in New York City were a national trend as well (see Chapter 6). They have impacted Puerto Ricans and other Hispanic groups in particular. To illustrate, median family income of Puerto Ricans was 70 percent of non-Hispanic family income in 1970, but it fell to 46 percent in 1980 (Moore and Pachon, 1985). Median family income for Cuban and Mexican Americans also fell relative to non-Hispanic family income. According to Fitzpatrick (1987), the median family income of Puerto Ricans in 1980 was $9,900, compared to $15,100 for all Hispanics in the United States and $19,500 for all U.S. families. Part of this story is that Puerto Rican women left the New York City labor force in the 1970s and 1980s in significant numbers due, in part, to structural unemployment, although this was not a national trend.

By the same token, Puerto Ricans living outside of New York City were doing better economically than those in the city (Rodriguez, 1989). This suggests that the population shift of Puerto Ricans from New York to other locations was a search for economic opportunity. In particular, Puerto Rican women outside of New York are more likely to work outside the home.

In Table 8.3, it is evident that Puerto Rican workers are overrepresented as operators, fabricators, and laborers, their historical niche in the United States. This is more true of Puerto Rican men than women. Puerto Rican workers in 1990 were also overrepresented in the service occupations. It is in the managerial and professional occupations that Puerto Rican workers are significantly underrepresented, and this is especially the case for Puerto Rican men. It has been found that education and English-language proficiency do not translate into comparable occupational attainments for Puerto Ricans as for non-Hispanics and other Hispanic groups (Rodriguez, 1989). Moreover, Puerto Ricans are more likely to have jobs toward the lower end of the occupational groups in Table 8.3, and are making less money than their non-Hispanic counterparts.

On the other hand, there was intergenerational mobility (occupation and education) of Puerto Ricans in the United States during the 1950s and 1960s, although the pace of that mobility has since slowed (Massey, 1981). Puerto Ricans born in the United States are still better off than those born in Puerto Rico. In contrast to other Hispanic groups, rising class standing of Puerto Ricans does not result in their becoming less residentially segregated (Massey, 1981). Rather Puerto Ricans are comparable to African Americans; they remain segregated whatever their economic class, although Puerto Ricans are not as segregated as African Americans.

There has been competition between Puerto Ricans and African Americans in the cities. It is a struggle for jobs and political influence, and it has occurred in both New York and Chicago, for example. The symbolic issue is often education, specifically the decentralization of city schools and the introduction of bilingual education. Puerto Ricans and other Hispanics pushed for community control of local schools in Chicago, while African Americans opposed it. In other instances, there have been alliances between Puerto Ricans and African Americans over school issues.

Puerto Ricans vary in racial characteristics, from African to European with many shades in between. In Puerto Rico, race was a continuum, or color gradient, not a dichotomy of black and white (Rodriguez, 1989). Puerto Ricans in the United States experienced another ideology, race as a black or white dichotomy. It was expected that black Puerto Ricans would eventually assimilate into the African American community, identifying themselves as black in the process; white Puerto Ricans would assimilate into white America. While there has been some of this, most Puerto Ricans, as well as other Hispanics, continue to define themselves as Hispanic (e.g., Cuban, Mexican, or Puerto Rican), not black or white American (Rodriguez, 1989).

The traditional Puerto Rican family emphasized a strict sexual division of labor, with the wife in the home as a mother and the husband concerned with breadwinning. Families were once extended and other support systems surrounded the family, including godparents (*compadrazgo*) and the informal adoption of children during a crisis (*hijos de crianza*). Family forms and dynamics began to change with immigration to the mainland. Most significantly, Puerto Rican women went to work outside the home, sometimes finding work more easily than did their men. Consequently, sex roles began to shift toward egalitarianism. Although the family and extended kin continued to be the primary support system for immigrant Puerto Ricans, they report a loss of family unity and closeness with residence in the United States (Sanchez-Ayendez, 1988). Four family types are evident among Puerto Ricans (Sanchez-Ayendez, 1988; Fitzpatrick, 1971): (1) an extended family living under one roof, (2) nuclear family, (3) blended families with children from previous marriages or unions, and (4) female-headed households. In recent years, there has been an increase in female-headed households in particular.

Intermarriage rates of Puerto Ricans increases with the generations born in the United States (Sanchez-Ayendez, 1988). Rates of Puerto Rican exogamy in New York City at mid-century were comparable to the rates of intermarriage for European immigrants earlier in the century. However, Puerto Rican outmarriage rates in New York City in 1975 were below those for all other Hispanic groups, not over 30 percent (Gurak and Fitzpatrick, 1982). Moreover, Puerto Ricans who do intermarry are more like to marry other Hispanics than Anglos.

Puerto Ricans report that they are more likely to stay permanently in the United States over the generations of residence in the country. Immigrants may want to return to Puerto Rico, and many do, but succeeding generations appear to be rooted in the United States. Those who return to Puerto Rico are seen as *Nuiyoricans* there, not Puerto Rican but New York Puerto Ricans. Nevertheless, Puerto Ricans do not identify themselves as exclusively American, nor black or white American, but rather as Puerto Rican and Hispanic.

CUBAN AMERICANS

Cuban Americans share with Mexican and Puerto Rican Americans the Spanish heritage and language. Like Mexico and Puerto Rico, Cuba was once a Spanish colony in the New World. Cuba, like Puerto Rico and the Philippines, became a U.S. possession in 1898, after the Spanish-American War. Cuba became an independent nation in 1902,

FIGURE 8.3 CUBAN AMERICANS AND CHANGE IN AMERICAN SOCIETY

Industrial Society c. 1865–1945	Post-Industrial Society c. 1945–Present

Early and recent immigration → Cuban community → Present situation

following a brief period of U.S. military government from 1898 to 1902. There were significant economic ties between Cuba and the United States up to the Cuban Revolution in 1959, and these were the lines along which Cuban immigration flowed to the United States before and after 1959.

IMMIGRATION AND CONTACT

There were over 1 million (1,043,932) Cuban Americans in the United States in 1990, making Cuban Americans the third largest Hispanic group in the country. Cuban immigration into the United States was comparatively small before the 1959 Cuban Revolution. There were about 124,000 Cuban Americans (79,000 Cuban-born) in the United States in 1960, concentrated in Key West, Tampa, and Miami, Florida, and the New York metropolitan area (Boswell and Curtis, 1983). This early immigration included Cuban political exiles, escaping from political conditions at home and plotting for their return to Cuba. It also included cigar manufacturers, who relocated their operations to the United States, principally Key West and Tampa, Florida, and their workers (Boswell and Curtis, 1983; Moore and Pachon, 1985). This early immigration continued to fluctuate with political and economic conditions in Cuba, and in the 1930s Miami emerged as the center of the Cuban community in the United States.

The present immigration of Cubans began in 1959. By the 1950s, American interests had sizable investments in Cuba, owning much of the island's utilities, railroads, and tobacco and sugar industries. The United States bought about 75 percent of Cuba's exports and provided 65 percent of the island's imports (Boswell and Curtis, 1983). Fulgencio Batista dominated Cuban politics from 1933 to 1959. Fidel Castro led a revolutionary movement against the Batista regime during the 1950s, and on New Year's Day of 1959 Batista fled the country. Castro and his army entered Havana a few days later,

One of the more modest of the hundreds of restaurants
serving Miami's large Cuban American population.

on January 8, and thus began a new era for both Cuba and Cuban Americans.

The Castro regime soon implemented land reforms, established state farms, and nationalized industry and businesses in Cuba. In 1961 Castro announced that the revolution would follow Marxist-Leninist ideals. By that time, trade and diplomatic relations between Cuba and the United States had been severed, and the island turned toward the Soviet Union. Cuban-American political and diplomatic relations deteriorated again with the unsuccessful Bay of Pigs invasion of Cuba by exile forces trained in and supported by the United States. The Cuban missile crisis in 1962 strained relations further. Russians had installed offensive nuclear missiles on Cuba, and the American diplomatic and military response resulted in the removal of the missiles from Cuba and a United States promise not to invade Cuba. Cuban international policies in both the Americas and Africa continued to run counter to American political interests, and the international relations between the two countries continued to deteriorate, punctuated by conflicts in South and Central America, and Angola in Africa, and by the inception of Radio Marti to beam American broadcasts into Cuba.

Over time, changes brought by the Castro regime touched all sectors of Cuban society, and Cuban immigration into the United States came ultimately from all classes and regions of Cuba. Cuban immigration since 1959 formed six stages (Boswell and Curtis, 1983; Larzelere, 1988; Llanes, 1982; Moore and Pachon, 1985; Szapocznik and Hernandez, 1988). In the first stage after Castro's takeover, departees came to the United States by commercial flights from Havana between 1959 and October of 1962. Between 153,000 and 248,000 Cubans came to the United States during this first wave (Szapocznik and Hernandez, 1988).

Immigration slowed in the second stage, 1962–1965. The 1962 Cuban missile crisis strained relations between the two countries, and emigration policy in Cuba became more restrictive. Most of the 30,000 to 55,000 Cuban immigrants in this wave were escapees who came to the United States by boats and rafts (Szapocznik and Hernandez, 1988). The third stage brought close to 300,000 Cubans to the United States by a U.S. airlift, the freedom flights, between 1964 and 1973 (Boswell and Curtis, 1983; Szapocznik and Hernandez, 1988). The flow of immigration slowed again in the fourth stage, 1973–1978, restricted by Cuban emigration policy to largely third-country arrivals.

In the fifth stage, small numbers of ex-political prisoners and family members of Cubans already in the United States arrived by air and sea directly from Cuba. The immigration flow swelled again in 1980 to over 100,000 Cubans with the Mariel boatlift, from Mariel Harbor in Cuba to Key West, Florida. People in this sixth wave of Cuban immigration are known as the *Marielitos,* and the wave contained a goodly portion of people Castro deemed undesirable. Many were criminals, disabled, mental patients, and street people, for example. It is estimated that up to nearly 1 million Cubans came to the United States between 1959 and 1980. This represents 85–90 percent of the total Cuban emigration during the period.

The Cuban immigration was initially a response to political events in Cuba rather than labor needs in the United States. The immigrants reported that their primary motives for leaving Cuba were pending imprisonment or the fear of it, political harassment and disruption of daily life, loss of livelihood for failing to go along with the revolution, and their stance against Castro and communism (Fagen, et al., 1968). In those cases where later arrivals joined family already in the United States, family reunification was a prime motive as well. "By the 1970s, however, it...became apparent that economic motives were beginning to replace those of political and religious persecution" (Boswell and Curtis, 1983:57). Thus, economic incentives began to play a role in Cuban immigration in its later stages. Moreover, the Mariel boatlift turned into a political embarrassment for the American government. Almost 4,000 Marielitos were still in American jails by 1987, and the Cuban community in America was decidedly cool toward the Marielitos (Boswell and Curtis, 1983; Schaefer, 1990). This prompted restrictions on further Cuban immigration with the 1980 Refugee Act, and Cuban immigration significantly slowed in the 1980s.

The Cubans in the early immigration waves after the revolution in 1959 were well educated, had both job skills and significant capital, and most (up to 94 percent) were white. In a word, they were the elite of pre-revolutionary Cuba: professionals, government officials, and business people. During the middle waves, the immigrants became more modest in background and were younger and less likely to be white. Toward the end, the immigrants were even poorer, more likely to be young and single, and less likely to be white (only 80 percent were white). The flow of emigration from Cuba sloped down the Cuban hierarchy over time in regard to education, class, and race, although white Cubans were overrepresented in the total immigration compared to the racial composition of Cuba (Massey, 1981).

CUBAN COMMUNITY

By early in the 1980s, the Cuban American population was concentrated in Florida, New York, and New Jersey. Nearly 60 percent lived in Florida, with nearly 600,000 in the Miami area alone (Boswell and Curtis, 1983; Moore and Pachon, 1985). Just over 10 percent lived in New Jersey and almost another 10 percent resided in New York. Other pockets of Cuban population were in California and Illinois. The metropolitan areas with the largest Cuban American populations were Miami, New York and northern New Jersey, Los Angeles, and Chicago. Cubans lived in other cities, of course, and indeed were dispersed throughout the nation. Their concentration in south Florida, however, stands out.

Many Cuban immigrants who were originally settled in other parts of the country through the Cuban Refugee Program returned to Miami. In 1978, 40 percent of the Cuban Americans in Miami had previously lived in other parts of the United States (Boswell and Curtis, 1983). They moved to Miami to be reunited with family and for the climate. The Cuban community in Miami began as a Little Havana, a 800-block neighborhood just west of Miami's central business district. Over time, Cubans have expanded beyond Little Havana toward the west and south, and into Hialeah, Florida (Boswell and Curtis, 1983). It is Little Havana that has been most thoroughly Latinized.

BOX 8.8   Little Havana

Although the shops are generally small, the range of commercial activities in Little Havana is impressive; virtually all essential (and some exotic) consumer goods and services are available. It is easy to appreciate how the enclave could function as a self-contained area for non-English speaking Cubans. In addition to the large American chain supermarkets in the enclave, which all have Spanish-speaking employees, there are numerous small, mostly family-run grocery stores (called *bodegas*) that carry a full line of Cuban food products.... Little Havana is also noted for its many Cuban bakeries. These formal establishments are supplemented by Cuban peddlers who sell...out of the back of their pick-up trucks or off the hood of their cars.... Virtually all of the pharmacies have signs on the window that announce, "*Envios de Medicinas a Cuba.*"... Concentrated along *Calle Ocho* and Flagler Street...are a score of Cuban cooperative health clinics, staffed by Cuban physicians. Cuban-owned furniture stores are also clustered along *Calle Ocho*. Chairs are usually lined up along the front of these stores in keeping with an old Spanish custom.... For followers of *Santeria*, an Afro-Cuban cult religion ...there are over a dozen *botanicas* that stock an utterly baffling array of items.... Beyond these stores and shops, there are in addition banks, bars, barbershops, beauty salons, book stores, car dealerships, flower shops, gift shops, jewelry stores, hardware stores, insurance offices, nightclubs, theaters, travel agencies....

Perhaps more so than any other activity, Little Havana is most noted for its multitude of Cuban restaurants and *cafeterias*. ... A majority of the many *cafeterias* in the enclave are small, inexpensive, and usually crowded. They also typically have counters that open to the sidewalk for pedestrians to stop by for a quick cup of *cafe cubano* and perhaps some fresh *pasteles* (pastry).

Compared to the bustling street life of the commercial strips, the residential areas of Little Havana are relatively quiet and subdued.... Wrought iron grill work over windows and decorative Spanish tiles also embellish many homes. Certainly one of the more distinctive features of the residential district is the large number of yard shrines, literally hundreds, that grace the area.... The vast majority of the shrines are erected in honor of Catholic saints, especially Santa Barbara, Our Lady of Charity, and Saint Lazarus....

Source: Thomas D. Boswell and James R. Curtis, *The Cuban-American Experience: Culture, Images, and Perspectives.* 1983. Rowman and Allanheld, Publishers. Pp. 94–96.

⊘⊘

There are about 25,000 Cuban-owned businesses in the Miami area. Many of the immigrants who arrived shortly after the Castro takeover brought both capital and business skills to the country (Moore and Pachon, 1985; Portes and Truelove, 1987). A Cuban American subeconomy has resulted, and Cuban Americans are something of a middleman minority (see Chapters 12–14). In an ethnic subeconomy or enclave, such as Little Havana, ethnic firms nurture ethnic sources of supply and demand (Portes and Stepick, 1984; Wilson and Portes, 1980). In other words, Cubans employ their own ethnic kind, often family members, and are otherwise supplied within the ethnic group by yet other Cuban-owned firms with Cuban employees. Cuban businesses also cater to ethnic needs or demand, concentrating in the selling of goods and services to other Cuban Americans.

New arrivals into Little Havana were typically assisted by their family members in finding a place to live and getting a job, often in a Cuban-owned firm. *Municipios en el exilio* (municipalities in exile) also assisted new immigrants. These sociopolitical organizations are rooted in the municipalities of Cuba itself, and each municipality sprung up in Little Havana as an organization. For example, the *Municipio de Santiago de Cuba en el Exilio* represented immigrants from Santiago de Cuba, a city in the east of Cuba. This *municipio* assisted immigrants from that city in finding work, if necessary, and with information on

U.S. citizenship and voter registration. It provided news of friends from home through newspapers and held cultural events. The purpose was to help immigrants adjust to a new life, on the one hand, and help them to keep in touch with old ways, on the other.

Cuban Americans in Miami have experienced competition and conflict with other ethnic groups in the area. There has been job competition between Cuban and African Americans and black resentment about Cubans' getting ahead. Riots have resulted, and there is a high level of segregation between Cuban and African Americans in the Miami area (Boswell and Curtis, 1983; Moore and Pachon, 1985). The conflict with Anglos has centered on the symbol of Spanish language use. In 1973, Miami and Dade County became officially bilingual, with Spanish as well as English as official languages, but the county's electorate, by a two to one majority, repealed the earlier ordinance in 1980, at the time of the Mariel boatlift (Boswell and Curtis, 1983). A new ordinance of 1980 stipulated that no public funds were to be used to teach languages other than English.

As the Cuban community has expanded out from Little Havana, Cuban Americans have become less segregated from Anglos in the suburbs of Miami. On average, residential segregation of Cuban families declines with their continued residence in the country and as their class standing rises, along with their move to the suburbs (Massey, 1981). Whereas the model of Little Havana is one of an ethnic subeconomy and cultural enclave, the one of the suburbs is more assimilationist. At the very least, this is evidence for ethclasses within the Cuban community.

THE PRESENT

Many Cuban immigrants experienced downward mobility with their arrival in the United States. Their initial jobs and class standings in the United States were below those they had in Cuba. Some professionals had a more difficult time than others in the United States. Downward mobility was particularly true for lawyers, who could not transplant their professional acumen to the United States, but this was less so for physicians, scientists, and engineers, for example (Boswell and Curtis, 1983). Nevertheless, Cubans have experienced upward mobility and earnings parity with white Americans with their continued residence in the United States (Boswell and Curtis, 1983; Massey, 1981).

The occupational composition of Cuban Americans in 1990 is shown in Table 8.4. Note that Cuban Americans are somewhat underrepresented in managerial and professional occupations when com-

TABLE 8.4 PERCENTAGE DISTRIBUTION OF CUBAN AMERICANS AND ALL EMPLOYED
PEOPLE BY OCCUPATIONAL GROUPS, 1990

Occupational Group	Cuban Origin 1990	All People 1990
Managerial and professional	20.8%	25.5%
Technical, sales, and administrative support	36.0	31.5
Service occupations	14.2	13.5
Precision production, craft, and repair	12.6	11.5
Operators, fabricators, and laborers	16.2	15.5
Farming, forestry, and fishing	0.7	3.5

Source: U.S. Department of Commerce, 1983, *1980 Census of Population, Volume 1: Characteristics
of the Population*, Chapter C: General Social and Economic Characteristics, Table 169. U.S. Bureau of
the Census, Current Population Reports, Series P–20, No. 455, *The Hispanic Population in the United
States*, March 1991, U.S. Government Printing Office, Washington, DC, 1991.

pared to all people in 1990 and overrepresented in laboring jobs, but
otherwise they are comparable to the total work force. In 1988, nearly
one-quarter of the Cuban-American population 25 to 34 years of age
had completed college, comparing favorably to their Anglo counterparts.

Other trends seem to point toward the better inclusion of Cuban
Americans into American society. One of these is the political participation of Cuban Americans (Boswell and Curtis, 1983; Moore and Pachon, 1985). At first, they engaged in exile politics focused on Cuba.
Several nationalist Cuban organizations emerged in this country, such
as the Anti-Castro Liberation Alliance, Revolutionary Movement of
the People, and the Democratic Revolutionary Front. The last two organizations merged in 1961, forming the National Revolutionary
Council, which had as its aims the overthrow of Castro, the return of
property confiscated by the Castro regime, and free elections for a new
Cuban government. Nationalist politics have continued in the Cuban
community, evident in the sending of arms to Cuba and the presence
of paramilitary groups such as Alpha 66 and Omega 7; but interest in
nationalist politics has declined since 1963.

Interest in American politics has replaced nationalist politics in the
Cuban community. This is surely an indication of inclusion into American society. Cuban Americans are noted for the rate of naturalization
and their voter turnout in American elections. They vote heavily Republican, an anomaly for a new immigrant group, in part reflecting

their staunch anti-communism, particularly in regard to the Castro regime. Cubans also contribute to political action committees (PACs) such as the National Coalition for a Free Cuba. In American elections, Cubans elect their own when possible, and Cuban American elected officials have been prominent in the Miami area, for example.

Exclusive use of the Spanish language among Cubans declines with length of residence in the United States. The immigrant generation spoke Spanish, of course, and a considerable number were also fluent in English. By the second generation, two-thirds speak mostly English, and the generation is fluent only in a limited Spanish called "Spanglish," a patois that mixes Spanish and English words, sometimes in a single phrase (Boswell and Curtis, 1983). Surveys among Cuban Americans in Miami indicate that the desire to stay permanently in the United States increases over time. In a 1966 survey, about 83 percent said they wanted to return to Cuba if it were freed. In 1977, however, 93 percent intended to stay in the United States (Boswell and Curtis, 1983).

Changes in the Cuban American family also reflect a trend toward inclusion. Cuban immigrants brought with them to the United States the traditional Cuban family. One's place in life was centered on the family, both maternal and paternal surnames were used, there was the tradition of godparents or *compadrazgo,* and there was a double standard for males and females. Females were protected and dependent within the family circle, illustrated by low rates of women's working outside the home and the chaperoning of females on dates.

Many of these traditions have eroded with time. Wives entered the labor force in the United States, and gender relationships within the family shifted toward the egalitarian. Most second-generation Cubans no longer use maternal surnames, the days of chaperoning are largely past, the significance of *compadres* has declined, and outmarriage has become common. Rates of intermarriage for Cuban males climbed from 16 to 74 percent over the first two generations in a national sample (Massey, 1981). Forty-six percent of the second-generation females intermarried by 1970 (Boswell and Curtis, 1983). Exogamy rises steadily with Cuban American inclusion into the larger society, evident at higher levels of education, occupational status, and residential dispersion, as well as across generations.

SUMMARY

Mexican, Puerto Rican, and Cuban Americans share a Spanish past and the experience of Spanish-speaking ethnic groups in the United

States. The history of Chicanos goes back several centuries in the Southwest. This history was characterized by the takeover of Hispanic lands by Anglos, the relegation of Hispanos and then Mexican immigrants to the lower rungs of the region's labor hierarchy, and Chicano resistance and protest. Now, there are signs of the inclusion of a Mexican American middle class into the nation.

To make the transition from manual to mental work in this country, Mexican Americans must quickly acquire cultural and technical skills through formal education, but this is where a gap still exists between Anglo and Chicano children. If this gap does not close, we should expect more of the same exclusion and divergence of Mexican Americans:

> Americans have thought of their country as one of the few in the world without an identifiable proletariat as a *social class*, that is, a group of people who are and feel permanently relegated to poverty and whose expectations for their children are conditioned by this hopeless outlook. Regardless of the historical validity of this view, the problems posed by a continued existence of an *ethnic* proletariat will be particularly acute in the Southwest with its two disadvantaged minorities (Grebler, et al., 1970).

Even as some Mexican Americans rise with the occupational structure of American society and the Chicano middle class grows larger, there are important limits on the full assimilation of Mexican Americans into the larger American society. One limitation Mexican Americans share with many other groups in the country is the use of ethnicity, and particularly minority status, as a strategy for the acquisition of certain resources in the welfare state. It is particularly the middle class of a minority group that benefits from quota systems, which are meaningless at the bottom. This will tend to keep alive ethnic identity among the Chicano middle class. The risk in this has been mentioned before, in regard to Native Americans: the use of this tactic may mean that eventually the group becomes nothing more than a contentless interest group. But will Hispanic culture grow shallow with the rise of the Chicano middle class? There is reason to believe it will not. The exchange, including migration between this country and Mexico, especially along the borderlands, should continuously invigorate the Hispanic subculture in this county. The prospects are for the cultural pluralism of Mexican Americans coupled with a decreasing measure of exclusion and divergence with respect to material life chances and social participation.

Puerto Ricans share with Mexican Americans a Spanish heritage and a colonial past. Due to subsequent economic conditions on the island and labor needs on the mainland, there have been two waves of

Puerto Rican immigration into the United States. Most immigrants have come to the United States since World War II, although this immigration has slowed in recent decades. Puerto Ricans concentrated initially in New York City, but there has been a more recent shift out of that city to other locations. Puerto Ricans are still concentrated in the Northeast.

Intergenerational mobility, and thus ethnic inclusion of Puerto Ricans in the United States, is evident. By the same token, there is still exclusion in regard to education, occupation, and segregation. Moreover, there has been a decline in the relative family income of Puerto Ricans with a corresponding rise in female-headed households. This portends for a continued pluralism between Puerto Ricans and the larger society as well as significant ethclass differences within the Puerto Rican community.

Significant Cuban immigration into the United States occurred only after the Cuban Revolution in 1959, although small Cuban enclaves existed in Florida as early as the nineteenth century. Over the waves of the recent immigration, the Cuban population in the United States has looked more like that back home in Cuba. Initial settlement concentrated in Florida and New Jersey and New York, but Cubans were also dispersed throughout the country through refugee resettlement programs. Many then concentrated in south Florida.

In Miami, the first settlement was Little Havana, which developed into a Cuban subeconomy and cultural enclave. Cuban Americans have since expanded into the suburbs, and by most indications they are moving toward a better inclusion into American society. This is evident in their occupational and educational attainments, changing politics, language use, and family patterns.

CHAPTER

9

@/@

EUROPEAN AMERICANS AND AMERICAN SOCIETY

N early 37 million Europeans immigrated into the United States between 1820 and 1986, making them as a single entity the largest ethnic group in the country. European immigration came in two stages. There was first the immigration of northern and western Europeans, most of whom came before 1890. They are generally called the "old" European immigrants. The next stage was the immigration of southern and eastern Europeans, most of whom came after 1890—the "new" European immigrants. In this chapter we analyze Irish Americans, part of the older European immigration, and Italian and Polish Americans, part of the newer immigration.

IRISH AMERICANS

There were three waves of Irish immigration to the United States: Irish Protestants in the eighteenth and early nineteenth centuries, the famine and increasingly Catholic immigrants in the middle of the nineteenth century, and then dwindling numbers of Irish immigrants up to the present (Fallows, 1979). Over 5 million Irish immigrated into the United States in the nineteenth and twentieth centuries.

BACKGROUND TO IRISH IMMIGRATION

The Irish Republic and Northern Ireland occupy the island of Ireland in the North Atlantic Ocean, separated from Great Britain on the

FIGURE 9.1 IRISH AMERICANS AND CHANGE IN AMERICAN SOCIETY

Agrarian Society c. 1600–1865	Industrial Society c. 1865–1945	Post-Industrial Society c. 1945–Present
Early immigration and contact →	Famine immigration and contact →	Accommodation, competition, and conflict → Present situation

east by the Irish Sea. The land alternates between uplands and lowlands and is generally rocky with persistent rainfall. Several rivers drain the island into the surrounding sea. Temperature extremes are rare. Much of Irish history is a story of British domination and its consequence for the Irish, including their immigration to the United States.

The Irish are a Celtic people, originally from northwestern Europe, who are believed to have settled Ireland around 350 B.C. (Shannon, 1963). Later, they were converted to Christianity under the leadership of St. Patrick, who came to Ireland in A.D. 432 (Shannon, 1963). The story of Ireland then became a tale of foreign invasion and domination. The first invaders were the Danes, who raided coastal areas in the east along the Irish Sea around 800. It is the invasion and domination by the British, however, that has shaped Irish history the most. The Normans under Henry II crossed the Irish Sea in 1169 and conquered the eastern portions of Ireland by 1171 (McCaffrey, 1971; Shannon, 1963). This began the manorial system in Ireland consisting largely of British landlords and Irish tenant farmers. With the Statutes of Kildenny (1366) the British in Ireland were forbidden to associate with native Irish, marry Irish, wear their costumes, adopt Irish children, or use the services of their priests (McCaffrey, 1971). Despite these efforts to prevent assimilation, the Normans became fully absorbed into Irish society by the sixteenth century (Shannon, 1963).

All of Ireland came under British rule by the seventeenth century (Fallows, 1979). Elizabeth I of England colonized more of Ireland between 1560 and 1580 by establishing more English landlords on manors (Griffin, 1973). In response to an insurrection in Ulster in 1641, Cromwell of Great Britain invaded Ireland, and during the years of this fighting about one-third to one-half of the Irish population perished (Greeley, 1981; Shannon, 1963). In one battle at Drogheda, Cromwell executed 2,800 people. In the end, Irish Catholic landlords were driven west of the Shannon River into Connacht, their former lands were confiscated, and Protestant landlords controlled 75 percent of the land in Ireland (Fallows, 1979; McCaffrey, 1976). The collapse of the old Irish leadership came later with their surrender to William of Orange at the Siege of Limerick in 1691 (Brown, 1966). About this same time, Irish peasants began to rely increasingly on the potato as their main food crop, for the potato was hard to confiscate by invading armies (Beckett, 1966).

☯☯

BOX 9.1 A MODEST PROPOSAL

In 1729, Jonathan Swift wrote "A Modest Proposal," brilliantly using irony to shock his readers into an awareness of the conditions of the Irish poor.

...a young healthy child well nursed is at a year old a most delicious, nourishing, and wholesome food, whether stewed, roasted, baked, or boiled; and I make no doubt that it will equally serve in a fricassee or ragout....

I grant this food will be somewhat dear, and therefore very *proper for landlords*, who, as they have already devoured most of the parents, seem to have the best title to the children....

It would greatly lessen the number of Papists, with whom we are yearly overrun, being the principal breeders of the nation....
The poorer tenants will have something valuable of their own...and help to pay their landlord's rent, their corn and cattle being already seized, and *money a thing unknown....*

This food would likewise bring great custom to taverns, where the vintners will certainly be so prudent as to procure the best receipts for dressing it to perfection, and consequently have their houses frequented by all the fine gentlemen, who justly value themselves upon their knowledge in good eating....

☯☯

Persecution of Irish Catholics intensified, illustrated by the Penal Laws of 1695. Under these measures, Catholic estates in Ireland were broken up; the Catholic clergy was banned and Catholic schools were forbidden; Catholics were denied the right to vote, hold public office, bear arms, serve on juries, serve in the army and navy, marry a Protestant, or inherit or purchase land; they were barred from the universities, teaching, the trades and professions; and they were forced to tithe to the Protestant Church of Ireland (Beckett, 1966; Brown, 1966; Connery, 1970; Fallows, 1979; Greeley, 1981; Kennedy, 1973; Shannon,

1963; Wittke, 1970). The Celtic clan society was breaking down under British pressure. The Penal Laws divided further the religious subsocieties of Ireland, relegated the Catholic Irish to the bottom of society, and bonded Irish nationalism and Catholicism. Although the British Parliament briefly surrendered its claim to legislate for Ireland (1782–1800), there was no repeal of the Penal Laws, and thus Protestants still monopolized the government and the economy. This period is called the Protestant Ascendancy (McCaffrey, 1976). Home rule for Ireland was subsequently abolished in 1801 with the Act of Union, when Ireland became part of the United Kingdom of Great Britain and Ireland, dominated by the British Parliament in London.

The worst abuses of the Penal Laws were abolished by the Catholic Relief Act of 1829 (Fallows, 1979). Thereafter, upper-class Catholics could sit in the British Parliament, hold all but the highest civil and military offices, and were allowed more social and professional opportunity (Brown, 1966; McCaffrey, 1976). The rural masses, however, were no better off, as would become clear during the Great Famine. The social hierarchy of the country consisted of upper-class Anglicans on top, then middle-class Presbyterians, with lower-class Irish Catholics at the bottom (Fallows, 1979).

British rule in Ireland served the interests of Great Britain, not those of Ireland. The policy objective was to maintain Ireland as an agricultural colony to industrial England. For example, the export of Irish woolens was stopped in 1699, the importation of hops for Irish breweries was forbidden in 1710, the exportation of Irish glass ceased in 1756, and imported British goods generally undersold Irish ones in the home market (Beckett, 1966). Irish trade and industry stagnated in the 1800s, and the number of non-agricultural laborers actually declined from 1821 to 1841 (Brown, 1966; Kennedy, 1973). Thus, Irish industry did not expand to provide an alternative for peasants in time of need. Ireland was reduced to exporting grain and livestock products.

Rents from Irish tenant farmers flowed to absentee landlords in Great Britain, their tithes and taxes went to British officials, and the Irish were obligated to pay almost 12 percent of the British government's budget. Capital critical to both agricultural and industrial development in Ireland was leaving the country. Irish tenants had no incentive to make agricultural improvements because of the insecurity of their leases, and more land was being taken out of tillage and put into pasture for livestock. But there were more people than ever before on the land. The population of Ireland increased from 5 to 8 million between 1780 and 1840; Irish peasants married early and had large families (Brown, 1966). Land was divided equally among the family heirs, with the result that with each generation it was further subdivided into smaller and smaller plots. The only feasible food crop under the circumstances was the potato. As long as the potato kept up with the population increase, Irish tenants could live off the land.

BOX 9.2   THE IRISH PEASANT

In the middle of the eighteenth century, Irish peasants were the most miserable representatives of their class in Western Europe. Their standard of living was probably lower than that of black slaves in North America. Peasants fortunate enough to have rented farms usually occupied less than fifteen acres—five was the average—and many residents of rural Ireland were agricultural laborers or bog squatters attempting to feed large families with the produce of an acre or less. Irish peasants lived in mud huts, usually windowless, with dirt floors and a hole in the thatched roof to serve as a chimney. Cabin interiors were dirty and smoky from turf fires, constant rains turned dirt floors into mud holes, and thatched roofs, although attractive from a distance, hosted a variety of vermin. Since animals were precious— their sale paid the rent—large families shared their wretched hovels with pigs and chickens.

Source: Lawrence J. McCaffrey, 1976. *The Irish Diaspora in America*. Bloomington: Indiana University Press. P. 52.

Irish Catholics were limited to tenant farming for Protestant landlords, and, because of population increases, rural families had subdivided their meager holdings into small plots on which they grew potatoes for subsistence. As more land was converted from tillage into pastures, the standard of living in rural Ireland steadily declined early in the 1800s (Beckett, 1966). There were periodic crop failures even before the Great Famine of the mid-1800s. Bad seasons between 1727 and 1730 and the resulting famine caused up to 400,000 deaths (Beckett, 1966). Even in good years it was hard to store potatoes for a full year, and thus the summer months were often hungry times for Irish peasants. Still the potato was the food crop, for wheat and corn required three times the land for cultivation (Fallows, 1979). Eighty percent of the 8 million Irish people prior to the Great Famine lived on the land, and 50 percent depended on the potato for subsistence (Beckett, 1966). It was a disaster waiting to happen, and happen it did.

305

IRISH IMMIGRATION

During the 1830s, before the potato famine in Ireland, 200,000 Irish immigrated into the United States (Fallows, 1979). With the Famine, 1844–1849, Irish immigration increased to nearly 1.5 million between 1845 and 1854, more than a million between 1855 and 1870, and more than another 1.5 million between 1870 and 1900 (McCaffrey, 1971). Most of these immigrants were Catholic and from rural Ireland. Irish immigration then declined in the twentieth century, and emigration from Ireland did not return to the levels of the late 1800s until the 1950s, when labor-saving technology was displacing Irish farmers (Kennedy, 1973). Most Irish emigrants came to the United States, followed by Canada, Great Britain, and Australia.

EARLY IMMIGRATION: The reasons for Irish emigration reach back for centuries, although the famine years of 1845–1847 were a nadir of Irish history. Early Protestant Irish immigrants came mainly from Ulster, or Northern Ireland, and were descendants of people who had even earlier migrated to Ireland from the British Isles (Wittke, 1970). There were 3,000 immigrants from Ulster between 1721 and 1742, and by the mid-1700s Ulster immigration to North America had reached 12,000 per year (Beckett, 1966; Griffin, 1973). The maritime trade in timber, tobacco, and cotton from North America to the British Isles provided passage for these immigrants on the return voyages to Canada and the United States. Some of those who landed in Canada walked south into New England, but most disembarked at American ports from Boston to New Orleans. In the first U.S. Census in 1790, there were 44,000 Irish-born in the country and another 150,000 of Irish ancestry in a total population of 4 million. Over one-half were living south of Pennsylvania (Fallows, 1979; Griffin, 1973; McCaffrey, 1976). These early Irish immigrants, who became small farmers, artisans, frontiersmen, and indentured servants in America, had assimilated by the time of the Catholic immigration following the Great Famine.

FAMINE IMMIGRATION: The Great Famine began in 1845 when the potato crop failed, but farmers still had a reserve of food and were hopeful for a better crop the following year. The blight occurred again, however, in 1846, and the despair became absolute. Potatoes were black, pulpy, oily, and foul-smelling, and famine set in. Although the blight did not return in 1847, the area sown with potatoes was very small, and the hunger continued. Farmers planted potatoes extensively the following year, but the blight returned in 1848. People begged at farmhouses for scraps of food, and each day many having no strength

306

to go on simply died in the farm yards. Country lanes were strewn with bodies, and people resorted to mass burials in open pits. One million died between 1845 and 1850, and another 3 million emigrated between 1845 and 1870 (Beckett, 1966; McCaffrey, 1976). There were over 8 million people living in Ireland in 1841, but only half that number in 1900 (Beckett, 1966).

Tenant farmers with less than five acres suffered the most during the famine. In order to pay their rents, tenant families sold rather than ate their cash crops and livestock (Kennedy, 1973). There was food in Ireland, but it was being exported. Landlords also evicted tenant families, adding to the problem, and people had to move or die. The decision to emigrate was usually made by an entire family, selecting the members who were to go to America. After 1830, remittances from the United States flowed into Ireland, and letters and pamphlets told of a better life there, thus providing families with both the motive and the money for the trans-Atlantic passage (Wittke, 1970).

Not only famines pushed the Irish toward emigration (Bodnar, 1985). Population pressure, high land rents, evictions, and the lack of industrial jobs must be added to the list. Indeed, the famine was in part the result of these other conditions, most of which were rooted in the economic and political domination of Ireland by Great Britain. Furthermore, Irish immigrants were pulled into the United States by the growing need for industrial labor and domestic servants, the latter especially in the case of young women. The human ties between earlier Irish immigrants and family and friends still in Ireland were the networks through which continued Irish immigration flowed.

The Catholic Irish emigrants came mainly from rural Ireland, and women were more motivated to leave than were men (Kennedy, 1973; Shannon, 1963). Women were subordinate to men in rural Ireland, symbolized by their eating only after males had finished their meals. Mortality rates were higher for females, also indicative of their lower status. Moreover, girls married by birth order in Ireland, and many younger sisters preferred to emigrate rather than wait their turn. Thus, in most decades after the Great Famine up to the 1950s, more Irish females emigrated than males (Kennedy, 1973). For example, women were almost 54 percent of the total Irish immigration in 1900, whereas they were only 35 percent in 1830 (Diner, 1983).

> The Ireland of the last half of the nineteenth century, birthplace of the hundreds of thousands of women who flooded into the United States, held out very little for women. Few of its resources or honors went to women. It had evolved a family system that...produced surplus sons and daughters.... Such women left Ireland because they could not find a meaningful role for themselves in its social order and

because American opportunities for young women beckoned.... *Ireland became a place that women left* (Diner, 1983:28–29; italics added).

There were only three European immigrant groups in which women outnumbered men in 1920 (Weatherford, 1986). The Irish led by having only 74 men per 100 women. By contrast, there were 148 Danish men per 100 women. Irish women in America sent remittances back home, providing passage money to the United States for their unmarried siblings (Diner, 1983). These women also helped their relatives find work here. Female-headed households were common among the Irish in America, a reflection of the sex composition of Irish immigration and the fact that Irish women delayed marriage or never married in significant numbers.

The passage from Ireland was horrible in the early years of the immigration, and 17,000 of the 100,000 who left Ireland for Canada in 1847 died en route (Greeley, 1981). The passengers in steerage often caught ship fever, a kind of typhus, and were covered with body lice. At times, the ships' provisions of food and water ran out before the voyage's end (Wittke, 1970). Wearing green clothing, runners for Irish boardinghouses often met the ships at dockside to gather up newcomers for their establishments. The exploitation was so bad that both the federal government and Irish charitable societies eventually stepped in to improve passage conditions and better manage the disembarkation of immigrants (Wittke, 1970).

After the famine Irish farmers changed. First, the families began to practice primogeniture, leaving the land to only the first-born male. This stopped the endless subdivision of family land into smaller and smaller plots, and it forced other siblings to find alternatives to farming, in emigration for example. Marriage was delayed for the first son until he inherited the farm, typically in his mid-thirties (Greeley, 1981). If they stayed in Ireland, other sons and daughters often remained unmarried, with daughters increasingly going into religious orders as nuns. The Irish birth rate fell as a consequence (McCaffrey, 1976).

In the late 1800s, Irish farmers acquired more rights over their land, and the pattern of landlordism by which Protestant landlords ruled over Irish Catholic tenants ended by early in the twentieth century (Beckett, 1966). The Irish Church Act of 1869 severed the connection between the state and the Protestant Church of Ireland, and pressure for Irish home rule escalated. The Easter Rebellion in 1916 led to a guerrilla war between Irish nationalist organizations and the British constabulary, and in 1920 Ireland was divided into two states, the Irish Free State (later the Republic of Ireland) to the south and Northern Ireland in Ulster. A civil war followed over the issue of dominion status of the Irish Republic with Britain, but it was settled in 1923. Guerrilla warfare and civil rights agitation in Northern Ireland began in 1968 and continues to this day.

ACCOMMODATION, COMPETITION, AND CONFLICT

By 1890 there were nearly 5 million Irish-born or Irish-origin people in the United States, 200,000 more Irish than in Ireland at the time (Brown, 1966). Irish Catholic immigrants concentrated in the nation's cities, particularly those in the Northeast and Midwest. In 1870, three-quarters of the Irish lived in Massachusetts, Connecticut, New York, New Jersey, Pennsylvania, Ohio, and Illinois (Fallows, 1979). They were one-third of New York City's population in 1890, when New York was the largest Irish city in the world (Glazer and Moynihan, 1970). The Irish stayed in urban America, not far from where they disembarked, due largely to their poverty upon arrival, their having little intention of returning to farming, and their ability to find work, family, and friends from Ireland in the cities rather than the countryside (Shannon, 1963). The Irish immigration was a rural-to-urban one which happened to cross international boundaries (Kennedy, 1973).

Between 1860 and the first decade of the twentieth century, two-thirds to over three-quarters of Irish immigrants were either common laborers or servants (Fallows, 1979; Kennedy, 1973). Laborers made 75 cents per day in the 1850s, and women as domestic servants made a dollar per week plus room and board. Irish women also gravitated into the garment trades, while Irish men worked in manufacturing, trade and transport, mining, and construction. "As early as 1818, there were three thousand Irishmen working on the Erie Canal" (Wittke, 1970:35).

Canal digging was tireless and dangerous work:

> When it rained, workers lost their pay, but the charge for board and lodging in the bunks of their crude shanties continued. The diggers often stood knee-deep in water, and cholera epidemics and dysentery killed many of them. They had to cut out trees through the width of the canal area, and they toiled through hot summer days infested with swarms of mosquitoes carrying malaria.... Deaths from "canal fever" were numerous. In 1826, digging was stopped on the canal out of Cleveland for several months in the summer when health conditions became too bad.... Accidents, injuries, tuberculosis, cave-ins, and deaths were numerous along the canals. Many an unmarked grave along the route was the last resting place of an Irish pick-and-

shovel worker killed in the line of duty and unceremoniously buried to make room for the next hand (Wittke, 1970:34).

After the era of canal building, many Irish workers built the nation's railroads.

Irish women gravitated toward domestic service, working in the homes of the native-born. Prior to modern appliances, domestic servants were common in middle- to upper-class American homes, and these servants were predominately foreign-born or African Americans (Matthews, 1987; Weatherford, 1986). Among the immigrant groups, the Irish had a high number of young, unmarried women, and thus they fit this niche.

Irish women faced prejudice in American homes, suspected of being Roman Catholic agents bent on turning their juvenile charges over to popery. Nevertheless, they made comparably good wages as domestics and saved much of their income, and exposure to American family life meant the earlier enculturation of Irish women than men (Diner, 1983). Irish women gained more economic independence from Irish men with their own incomes, and their earlier enculturation resulted in their easier transition over a generation to white-collar work as teachers, stenographers, nurses, and clerks.

The Irish formed an ethnic community in the process of their accommodation to American society. The community began in neighborhoods with parish churches, parochial schools, political clubs, and saloons. There were also militia and volunteer-fire companies, Irish newspapers, and, of course, St. Patrick's Day celebrations, which began in Boston in 1737 and New York in 1762. The Irish community contained several charitable organizations, nationalistic groups, and secret societies in some cases. Some of the elements of the community would be mobility channels for the Irish to middle-class status and even prominence in the United States, while others were focused on fighting for the independence of Ireland.

The Irish soon dominated the Roman Catholic clergy in the country, displacing the French and other native-born Americans, as well as successfully competing with German Catholics. For example, of the 69 Catholic bishops in the United States in 1886, 35 were Irish, with Germans a distant second at 15 bishops (Wittke, 1970). Although they had little experience with labor unions in Ireland and were often used as strikebreakers in the United States, the Irish became leaders in organized labor as well. They were instrumental in founding the Nobel Order of the Knights of Labor and the American Federation of Labor, and Peter J. McGuire is the father of Labor Day (Shannon, 1963; Wittke, 1970). The Irish also used urban politics as a mobility route from the neighborhood to city hall, and ultimately to state and national levels.

They controlled political machines in the nation's largest cities by the end of the nineteenth century. One was Tammany Hall in New York City. The Irish literally broke into Tammany Hall one night in 1817 and were in complete control of this political machine later in the 1800s (see Box 9.3). The first Irish Catholic mayor of New York was elected in 1880, and the Irish made Tammany the most effective political organization in America. The Irish dominated political machines in Brooklyn by the 1870s, and those in Boston, Buffalo, Chicago, Philadelphia, San Francisco, and St. Louis by 1890 (Fallows, 1979). Not all of these machines were as effective as Tammany Hall in New York, however (McCaffrey, 1976). In the twentieth century, Irish politicians reached prominence even at the national level. They were moving up from block captains, precinct leaders, and aldermen to state and national leaders. Alfred E. Smith was governor of New York and ran for president in 1928, losing to Herbert Hoover. Joseph Kennedy of Boston was appointed American ambassador to Great Britain in 1938, and his son John was elected president in 1960.

☯

BOX 9.3 THE IRISH CONFRONT TAMMANY HALL

On the night of April 24, 1817, there was a gathering in Dooley's Long Room in New York City. The subject under discussion was the discrimination practiced against the Irish by the Tammany Society, the city's dominant political organization. The men in the room, mostly laborers and small tradesmen, raised their voices in anger as they expounded their long-standing grievances. It was time, they concluded, that Tammany was compelled to nominate some Irish leader such as Thomas Emmet for Congress.

Two hundred strong, the men stamped out of Dooley's and headed for Tammany Hall. They broke in upon the caucus of party leaders that was then underway and demanded Emmet's nomination. When their request was not politely received, the Irish began to overturn the tables and break the furniture, the better to use pieces of it to inculcate learning on Tammany minds. The Tammany men fought back. Windows were smashed, eyes blackened, and noses broken. The Tammany men obtained reinforcements from neighboring taverns and finally drove the Irish away. Emmet was not nominated, but it was undoubtedly a highly educational evening.

311

@@

Politics had always been important in Ireland, and it is one of many reasons that the Irish took up politics in America. They included sizable voting blocs in many cities, they had past experience with Anglo-Saxon politics, and they spoke English. The political machines dispensed patronage, privileges, and welfare, and the Irish became the middleman between the larger WASP society and the new immigrants from southern and eastern Europe, including Italians and Poles. Irish control in urban machine politics faded in the twentieth century, due in part to federal welfare programs that provided many of the services once rendered by local political machines.

Secret societies had been important in the expression of political grievances in Ireland. There were the Whiteboys and Ribbonmen, for example, who fought against the Protestant landlords. In America, too, the Irish formed secret societies on the same model. The Molly Maguires and Hibernians were violent participants during labor troubles in Pennsylvania, for example. "They terrorized the area for years, committing outrages, mayhem, arson, and murder and intimidating voters at the polls" (Wittke, 1970:221).

Irish immigrants participated not only in American politics, but also in the politics of Ireland. Irish nationalism came of age in America, and the immigrants established a number of nationalistic groups. For example, the Fenian Brotherhood began in New York in 1858, and the *Clan na Gael*, founded in the same city in 1869, joined with the Irish Republican Army in 1877 (Glazer and Moynihan, 1970; Griffin, 1973; McCaffrey, 1976). The Irish came to America as members of clans, towns, parishes, and counties, but in the United States they became a nationality, the Irish (McCaffrey, 1976). They went to the same church in this country, voted as a bloc, worked together, and were seen by others as Irish. Irish nationalism held the Irish together by transcending the regional differences of their origins in Ireland (Glazer and Moynihan, 1970).

The aims of Irish nationalistic organizations were a combination of agrarian reform and home rule for Ireland. According to Greeley (1981), there were three types of Irish nationalist organizations: one type sought constitutional home rule for Ireland, another worked for land reform, and the third included the secret revolutionary societies, such as the Fenians and Irish Republican Brotherhood. Their activities ranged from fund raising to putting pressure on the United States government for military invasions in the cause of Irish nationalism. Irish nationalists in America "... decided to use the United States as an arsenal for Irish freedom by providing money and guns for liberation movements in Ireland and by using Irish political power to shape American foreign policy in an anti-British context. During the 1844–1846 dispute between America and Britain over the Oregon boundary, the American Irish were in the front ranks of the war hawks" (McCaffrey, 1976:117). Irish veterans of the Civil War returned to Ireland to fight for its independence, and the American Fenians invaded Canada three times to agitate against the British, twice in 1866 and once in 1870 (Brown, 1966; Wittke, 1970). Irish nationalists cooperated with German American organizations in the United States prior to World War I to keep the country from allying with Great Britain in that war, an effort that ultimately failed (Glazer and Moynihan, 1970). Irish nationalists competed with the clergy and Irish American politicians for influence over the Irish in the United States. With the independence of Ireland in 1921, however, nationalism among the Irish in America waned.

Contributions to Ireland from the American Irish took additional forms. The immigrants sent remittances to family and friends in Ireland for passage to America, as well as to help with rents and other expenses in Ireland. Remittances were especially heavy at Easter and Christmas (Wittke, 1970). Between 1848 and 1900, about $260 million was sent to Ireland (Fallows, 1979). The Irish also organized charitable groups for assisting the immigrants in America, such as the Irish Immigrant Society of New York, and they contributed to the building of Catholic churches and schools.

Their accommodation to American society brought the Irish into competition and conflict with other ethnic groups in American. The Irish soon dominated the Catholic Church, became prominent in politics and labor, and played a middleman role between the WASPs and the newer immigrants. Their competition and conflict with others ran along these very lines. The Irish competed with other Catholic groups for prominence in the Church, and with yet others in the political arena and the labor market. This competition resulted in occasional conflict. A Protestant mob invaded the Irish ghetto of Philadelphia in 1844 and burned homes and dynamited Catholic churches. Anti-Irish violence occurred in Boston, New York, Louisville, and New Orleans at about this same time. "In the early 1850s, a Protestant mob attacked and burned the Irish section of Lawrence, Massachusetts, and in 1855, Boston's older families...dismissed their Irish servants after hearing a rumor that the women were Vatican agents in a plot to poison the Protestant leadership of Massachusetts" (McCaffrey, 1976:94). The stereotype of Irish immigrants centered on not only their Catholicism, but also on the attributions of their being violent, common laborers, drunks, and a drain on the American welfare system. An example of this anti-Catholicism is described in Box 9.4.

☉☉

BOX 9.4   MARIA MONK

Maria Monk was the heroine of the Protestant, anti-Catholic crusade. Her *Awful Disclosures of the Hotel Dieu in Montreal* (1836) was anti-Catholic nativism's equivalent of the anti-Semitic *Protocols of the Elders of Zion*. Maria Monk was a mentally-retarded and deranged Protestant girl who ended her days as a prostitute. Her only contact with Catholicism was as a patient in a Catholic hospital, but she claimed to be an escaped nun, and anti-Catholics decided to exploit her story. In her account of convent life in Montreal, Maria Monk told of seductions by priests in the confessional and of frequent sexual encounters between priests and nuns. She described tunnels connecting the rectory and convent which were used as passages to lust and as burial grounds for babies resulting from the illicit unions between priests and nuns. According to Monk, the unfortunate infants were baptized and then murdered so that the secrets of the convent would never leak to the outside world. Maria Monk's revelations became an immediate best-seller and led to a number of convent inspections, all disproving her allegations... Protestants wanted to believe the most gruesome stories of Catholic depravity, so Maria Monk's tale of horror and lechery continued to anger and stimulate American nativists. It was even unearthed in 1960 as an argument against the election of John F. Kennedy to the presidency.

Source: Lawrence J. McCaffrey, 1976. *The Irish Diaspora in America*. Bloomington: Indiana University Press. P. 93.

☉☉

Anti-Irish nativism was mobilized by political parties. One example was the Know-Nothing Party, which had many successes in 1854 and 1855 in local, state, and national elections on a platform of restricting immigration, tightening citizenship qualifications, and disqualifying naturalized citizens from holding public office (McCaffrey, 1976). There had been legislative attempts as early as 1704 to restrict Irish immigration, and the Naturalization, Alien, and Sedition Acts of 1798 extended the waiting period for naturalization from five to fourteen years in an attempt to make application for citizenship harder for both Irish and French revolutionaries (Griffin, 1973; Shannon, 1963). Nativism receded with the Civil War but returned in the 1880s, when the American Protective Association had 1 million members. The Ku Klux Klan revived anti-Catholicism in the twentieth century, combining it with anti-Semitism and racism.

The Irish, for their part, also engaged in political violence and racism. A famous example is the 1863 draft riots in New York. Men could escape from being drafted into the Union Army by paying $300 or providing a substitute draftee. Added to the inequity of the conscription law was a fear on the part of the Irish poor that blacks recently freed by the Emancipation Proclamation would compete with them for jobs. "Conscription merely added insult to injury, since it compelled Irishmen to fight for the freedom of the very class which threatened to deprive them of work" (Jones, 1960:174). The Irish protested and protests escalated into riots in a number of cities.

> In New York, violence lasted for five days in July with mobs of . . . Irish people fighting the police, killing eleven blacks and an Indian mistaken for a black, burning a black orphanage, and destroying three million dollars worth of property. Finally, city officials had to call in the army to restore order. During the long disturbance, police and the military killed twelve hundred rioters and wounded many more while members of the mob killed three policemen and injured others. Interestingly, almost all of the police and a large number of soldiers on riot duty were as Irish as their opponents (McCaffrey, 1976:69).

The Irish immigrant Dennis Kearney was a leader of agitation against the Chinese on the West Coast in the 1870s, shouting "America for Americans" at demonstrations in San Francisco (Wittke, 1970). In the labor market and politics, and with respect to religion, the Irish competed with groups above them, the WASPs; groups at the same level, e.g., Germans; the newer European immigrants, such as the Italians and Poles; and black Americans. The results were open conflict, the mobilization of anti-Irish and anti-Catholic sentiment by interest groups and political parties, and attempts to restrict Irish immigration and application for citizenship.

THE PRESENT

One-quarter of the Irish in America are descendants of families who migrated before 1870, two-fifths are descendants of those who came between 1877 and 1900, one-quarter are descendants of those who migrated between 1900 and 1921, and 7 percent are either immigrants or descendants of immigrants who arrived after 1925 (Greeley, 1981). Over 70 percent of the Irish Catholics in America are either third or fourth generation, and over the generations the Irish have changed. According to Greeley (1981), Irish Catholics took a leap in status between 1895 and 1905, and the First World War generation was more white-collar, managerial, and professional than the general population. Irish women were becoming teachers and nurses, and the men were rising through the ranks of politics and civil service (McCaffrey, 1971). In Newburyport, Massachusetts, the social class distribution of the Irish in the 1930s was:

> 13 percent in the lower-lower class, 54 percent in the working class,...28 percent in the lower-middle, and 6 percent in the upper-middle. When the third generation of native-born Irish was considered separately, however, only 2 percent remained in the lower-lower class, 39 percent were in the working class, 42 percent were now lower-middle, and 17 percent were in the upper-middle. Clearly, each successive generation, even in this conservative New England community, included a larger proportion in the upper reaches of the stratification order (Fallows, 1979:60).

The Irish reached educational parity with the general population by the 1930s, and in the 1970s the attainment of Irish Catholics in years of education compared favorably with British Protestants in the United States (Fallows, 1979; Greeley, 1981). Immediately following the Second World War, Irish Catholics went to college in higher numbers than others except for American Jews. In 1971 the Irish equaled or exceeded national averages on education, occupation, and income (Fallows, 1979). Irish males over 16 were more likely to be in high-level white-collar jobs (29.6%) than the national average (28.2%), and Irish women were more likely to be in those same jobs (20.7%) than the national average for women (18.7%). In 1969 Irish median family income was slightly higher than the national average. Consistent with their improving status, the Irish, by the second and third generations, were moving out of the immigrant neighborhoods and into the suburbs (Fallows, 1979; Ware, 1935).

A few Irish families became wealthy in the United States. They built an elite Catholic subsociety consisting of boarding schools, debutante balls, Catholic universities, charities, and elite Catholic clubs (Fallows, 1979). These families include familiar names, such as McDonnell, Cudahy, Cuddihy, Grace, and Kennedy. These families ". . . strove earnestly to achieve an aura of respectability to accompany their wealth.... They also wanted to be honest and churchgoing and devout.... Because they were aware of the Irishman's reputation for drunkenness, they were teetotalers or, at the most, cautious drinkers.... Even such families as the Joseph P. Kennedys cared enough about being accepted socially to move out of Boston, where they knew they could never make the grade, and follow the example of the Murrays and McDonnells and come to New York..." (Birmingham, 1973:103).

Between 1964 and 1974, however, the children attending Catholic schools declined by a third, as parents found good public schools in the nation's suburbs (Fallows, 1979). Catholic Church attendance also fell off in this period. There are even more indicators that the Irish Catholic subsociety is in decline. Across the generations, intermarriage between the Irish and other ethnic groups has significantly increased, so that while only 28 percent of the first generation are of mixed ancestry, 68 percent of the fourth and later generations are (Fallows, 1979). Intermarriage for the Irish is now higher than that for any other group. Studies of the social characteristics of Catholic Irish males show acculturation, for the Irish are essentially no different than British Protestant males in the United States, except that they are more likely to vote and participate in politics (Fallows, 1979). Comparisons of Irish women with their Anglo-American counterparts showed the same trend toward acculturation. There are no differences between the Irish and others on "...drinking behavior, the likelihood of having drinking problems, degree of sexual restrictiveness for males, and degree of sexual restrictiveness for females" (Fallows, 1979:108).

Not only have the Irish converged with the larger nation, but also the country has absorbed Irish culture into the mainstream (Glazer and Moynihan, 1970). Through cartoon characters, songs, and movies, the Irish came to symbolize the larger nation:

> ...when Hollywood undertook to synthesize the Christian religion, they found it most easy to do in the person of an Irish priest: Pat O'Brien as Father Duffy in the trenches. When it came to portraying the tough American, up from the streets, the image was repeatedly that of an Irishman. James Cagney...was the quintessential figure: fists cocked, chin out, back straight, bouncing along on his heels (Glazer and Moynihan, 1970:256–257).

Even the most Irish of all celebrations, St. Patrick's Day, is now an American one.

FIGURE 9.2   ITALIAN AMERICANS AND CHANGE IN AMERICAN SOCIETY

Agrarian Society c. 1600–1865		Industrial Society c. 1865–1945		Post-Industrial Society c. 1945–Present
Early immigration, contact	→	Mass immigration, contact	→	Accommodation, competition, and conflict	→	Present situation

ITALIAN AMERICANS

CONTACT

Over 25 million people emigrated from Italy between 1876 and 1976, but not all came to the United States, and many returned to Italy after a temporary stay abroad (Cordasco, 1980). Over 5 million Italians immigrated into the United States between 1820 and 1967, making Italian second only to German immigration during this period (Lopreato, 1970; Moquin and Van Doren, 1974). Only a few thousand Italians immigrated into the United States before 1881, but then Italian immigration began to increase significantly up to the 1920s. The peak years of Italian immigration were 1880 to 1924 (Rolle, 1980). Over 300,000 Italians came in the decade 1881–1890; 651,893 came between 1891 and 1900; over 2 million immigrated between 1901 and 1910; 1,109,524 came in the following decade; and 455,315 came to the United States between 1921 and 1930 (Alba, 1985). After 1930 Italian immigration declined to a few thousand each decade until 1950, due in large measure to the Quota Act of 1924, which granted Italy a yearly quota of 3,845 immigrants, reduced from over 42,000 in the Quota Act of 1921 (Lopreato, 1970; Nelli, 1983). After 1951 Italian immigration increased again to well over 100,000 each decade because of changes in immigration laws (see Chapter 1).

BACKGROUND TO ITALIAN IMMIGRATION

Italy is a peninsula in southern Europe shaped like a boot sticking into the Mediterranean Sea. To the north is continental Europe, to the east is the Adriatic Sea, and the islands of Sardinia and Sicily lie to the west in the Mediterranean Sea. Mountains run the length of Italy, with coastal planes on each side. The country is divided into several provinces, but the division between northern and southern Italy is most important with respect to Italian immigration.

Reasons for Italian immigration reach back into Italian history. The peninsula was dominated by Spain from roughly 1500 to 1700, during which time the former Italian city-states, such as Venice, went into decline (Beales, 1971). In the 1700s, Italian industry and commerce were also in decline. The economy was largely agricultural, with the nobility and the Church owning much of the land (Woolf, 1979). Agricultural production was controlled by these powerful and often absentee landlords, and prices of agricultural goods were set low in the interests of urban customers. Although agricultural exports increased in the second half of the eighteenth century, Italian peasants were trapped in a state of indebtedness, and many lost their small holdings and became day laborers in order to survive (Woolf, 1979). Economic stagnation characterized the entire peninsula. Trade was confined to local regions, and the rural population was fragmented into villages. Italy was not unified into a single state, and the masses of people were poor.

During the nineteenth century, the movement to unify Italy known as the *Risorgimento* gained momentum. A series of revolts against foreign domination, which then included the French and Austrians, occurred in the first half of the century (Gooch, 1986). Not until 1860 was the *Risorgimento* accomplished, when much of Italy was unified under King Emmanuel II. Later, Venice and Rome joined in Italian unification. The movement for independence and unification was a movement led by the rich, and economic and social conditions for workers and peasants remained much the same. They were still poor and isolated, and the country was still characterized by illiteracy, economic stagnation, and poverty. This was the context for Italian emigration in the nineteenth century, although industrialization was picking up late in the century, primarily in the north.

ITALIAN IMMIGRATION

In the past two centuries, Italians have immigrated to North and South America, to other countries in Europe, and to Africa, Asia, and Oceania (Davie, 1936). Northern Italians were the first to emigrate, going to continental Europe, South America, and the United States from the provinces of Piedmont, Liguria, Venice, Marches, and Latium (Lopreato, 1970). Most of the immigrants from northern Italy went to elsewhere in Europe and to South America. Italians are the largest immigrant groups in both Brazil and Argentina, and 90 percent of the Italian immigration to South America came from northern Italy (Nelli,

1983). Ninety percent of the Italian immigration into the United States came from southern Italy, however, and the total Italian immigration into the United States is greater than that to the two South American countries (Davie, 1936; Nelli, 1983).

Northern Italian immigrants were the first to arrive in the United States, settling in significant numbers in California, Louisiana, and New York (Nelli, 1983). Northern Italians in California became prominent in truck gardening, wine-making, commercial fishing, and banking. Amadeo Giannini, an American-born son of northern-Italian immigrants, founded the Bank of America in 1904, then called the Bank of Italy, and created the TransAmerica Holding Company in the 1920s (Nelli, 1983).

Southern Italians followed northern Italians to the United States, most coming to the country after 1890 (Nelli, 1983). The reasons for this emigration from southern Italy, the *Mezzogiorno,* were many. The *contadino,* or peasants, of southern Italy lived in villages and small cities built on hillsides and cultivated land in the valleys below the villages, walking to and from work each day, sometimes for great distances. Housing in southern Italy was described in the following terms:

> For many their homes were one-room hovels with no windows or chimneys. The floor was earth or stone. Furniture was limited to a bed, and maybe a chair, bench, or wooden chest. Food, mostly potatoes and corn, was stored under the bed or, in the case of drying peppers, hung down from the walls. Often the inhabitants shared their accommodations with domestic animals (Iorizzo and Mondello, 1971:39).

Agricultural conditions were harsh and poverty widespread in the Mezzogiorno. The region is dry, and what little rainfall there is comes in the winter months, contributing to soil erosion rather than crop yields. The land was worked with hand tools, for innovations in agriculture had not reached the Mezzogiorno by the 1800s. The region was also overpopulated, its soil poor, and land rents high. Several events in the late 1800s had particularly harmful effects on agriculture in the Mezzogiorno (Alba, 1985; Iorizzo and Mondello, 1971; Lopreato, 1970; Lord, et al., 1970; Moquin and Van Doren, 1974; Rolle, 1980). The importation of wheat from Russia and the United States resulted in the collapse of the Mezzogiorno wheat market, and a declining demand for Sicilian textiles meant unemployment for weavers, spinners, and sheepherders. Overseas markets for wine and citrus fruits from the region also collapsed for a variety of reasons, including the destruction of wine grapes by phylloxera in the 1890s (Nelli, 1983). From 1870 to 1900 per capita income in southern Italy declined (Iorizzo and Mondello, 1971). In addition, the peasants were severely taxed by the government. The result was desperation in the countryside, evident in malnutrition and the spread of diseases, including malaria and cholera. As late as 1953, 25 percent of the farmers of the Mezzogiorno were classified as wretched and another 24 percent as needy (Lopreato, 1970).

Moreover, there was little mobility within the region out of these circumstances for the peasants. Industry had developed in northern Italy but not in the south. The class structure on the land in the Mezzogiorno precluded any mobility for peasants within agriculture. Landed aristocrats held much of the prime land (65 percent of the acreage in Italy was in big estates), and they, with a few professionals and priests, made up the gentry, which was no more than 2 percent of the population. Aristocrats were often absentee landlords who kept private police armed with shotguns in their fields to prevent the looting of crops, indicative of the conditions at the time. Craftsmen, shopkeepers, and minor officials constituted a small middle class of perhaps 10 percent of the population. The remainder of the population were the peasants, who owned small plots or were sharecroppers, and the day laborers. A peasant from Abruzzi captured this class structure and consequent confinement for the poor in a poem:

> At the head of everything is God, Lord of Heaven.
> After Him comes Prince Torlonia, lord of the earth.
> Then come Prince Torlonia's armed guards.
> Then come Prince Torlonia's armed guards' dogs.
> Then, nothing at all. Then nothing at all. Then nothing
> at all. Then come the peasants. And that's all.
> (Quoted in Lopreato, 1970)

When laborers in the United States were making between $1.50 and $2.00 per day, those in southern Italy were making 25 cents for a 12-hour day in the fields. After 1870, agents representing steamship companies and labor bosses in the United States roamed the Mezzogiorno looking for recruits to this country (Iorizzo and Mondello, 1971). Moreover, in 1888 the Italian government declared emigration to be free except for some minor restrictions on military personnel, and it assisted emigration. Perhaps the Italian government began to understand the value of the remittances immigrants were sending back to Italy from America, which totaled three-quarters of a billion dollars by World War I (Iorizzo and Mondello, 1971). Thus, small farmers and artisans as well as landless peasants were pushed out of the Mezzogiorno and pulled into the United States, a process facilitated by both labor agents and the Italian government (Bodnar, 1985). Most of these immigrants were men at first, and then early in the twentieth century they were joined by women and children. It was a chain migration during which initial Italian immigrants to American later sent for their families.

ACCOMMODATION, COMPETITION, AND CONFLICT

Immigrants from northern Italy concentrated in western states, as well as New York and Louisiana, and those from southern Italy settled primarily in the Northeast of the United States. In 1920, there were 139,000 foreign-born Italians in California, but the concentration of foreign-born Italians was far greater in the Northeast. There were 862,000 in New York, 351,000 in Pennsylvania, 248,000 in New Jersey, 174,000 in Massachusetts, 127,000 in Connecticut, and 51,000 in Rhode Island (Rose, 1922). In addition, there were 149,000 in Illinois, 96,000 in Ohio, 48,000 in Michigan, and 23,000 in Missouri, all industrial states in the Midwest. In 1970, 70 percent of the Italians in America still lived in the Northeast (Nelli, 1983).

Italians also concentrated in the nation's cities; 93 percent of them initially settled in urban America (Lopreato, 1970). The Italian population of San Francisco grew from 1,622 in 1870 to 16,918 in 1910, that of New York City from 2,794 in 1870 to 340,765 in 1910, that of Philadelphia from 516 to 45,308, and Chicago's Italian population grew from 552 to 45,169 in the same period (Nelli, 1983). Even medium-sized cities throughout the country had large numbers of Italians. For example, Omaha, Nebraska, had an Italian population of 12,000 in 1940 (Rolle, 1968).

A number of reasons have been given for the Italian concentration in urban America. Many immigrants from the Mezzogiorno were sponsored by labor recruiters in Italy representing labor bosses in this country who placed the immigrants in urban industry. Moreover, the jobs most plentiful and paying the best wages when they arrived here were in industry and urban construction, not in agriculture. Having little money upon arrival, most immigrants simply could not travel to the nation's hinterland; thus they stayed in the cities at which they disembarked, particularly those on the East Coast. It was in these same cities that the immigrants found family and friends from back home.

In the cities, Italians tended to settle within walking distance of work in neighborhoods that came to be predominately Italian (up to 60%). There was not typically a single "Little Italy" but many Little Italys in a single area, seventeen of them in Chicago alone (Vecoli, 1970). Immigrants from the same town or region of Italy often lived on the same block, even the same tenement, while those from other regions lived on adjacent blocks, each living closest to his or her own *paesani*. Ware (1935) observed this pattern in Greenwich Village in

New York City, for example. Italian immigrants went to work in America but returned home in the evenings to Old-World ways.

The communal associations of Italian immigrants were also organized along provincial origins. There were over 400 such associations in Chicago alone, according to Vecoli (1970). Immigrants from the same town or province also organized their own *festa*, a celebration of their local patron saint (Whyte, 1955). This pattern of settling next to and associating with paesani reflects the localism of the immigrants and their isolation from one another in the old country. It is called *campanilismo*, meaning that one's world was confined by being within earshot of the local *campanile* (bell tower), a notion symbolized today in America by campaniles on college campuses. Among northern Italians, a person from a nearby town, perhaps no more than a few miles away, was known as *forestiero*, that is, like a forest, unknown and impenetrable (Lopreato, 1970). Another reason for associating with paesani was that they spoke the same dialect, which was often incomprehensible to immigrants from other regions of Italy. Indeed, to communicate, Italians from different regions had to make recourse to an Americanized Italian, whereby *street* was called *stritto, car* was *carro*, and *store* was *storo* (Moquin and Van Doren, 1974). Provincial ties and affiliations fell off, however, not long after the immigrants settled into American cities. For the second generation in particular these ties had little relevance (Ware, 1935). Newer organizations replaced the older ones as second-generation Italian American boys formed youth gangs or social clubs irrespective of the provincial origins of their parents (Whyte, 1955).

Italian neighborhoods in the immigrant generation became ethnic enclaves with churches, businesses, and fraternal lodges. Box 9.5 gives an impression of what it was like. Immigrant Italians lived in tenements, in which a 8 × 10 room often held ten people, and single men lived in boardinghouses where they sometimes slept in shifts, sharing the same beds.

☙☙

BOX 9.5 THE NEIGHBORHOOD

Along the principal street of an Italian colony are to be seen, besides the banks, numerous grocery shops and markets, great and small, displaying fruits and vegetables, and wares peculiar to the race, the Italian pharmacy, undertaking establishment, cobbler shop, barber shop, macaroni manufactory, ... a printer's shop, perhaps the home of a local paper, the public school, the

Italian Roman Catholic Church, and frequently the Protestant mission. There may be a cooperative store, a form of business which often has had marked success among Italian Americans. There has been the saloon, as much a place of resort as of drinking; there are many bottled soda shops and pool-rooms patronized by or maintained by clubs, sometimes gangs, for amusement, or for political or less legitimate purposes. The shingle of the doctor and mid-wife are to be seen, these persons, especially the latter, enjoying great repute among their people because of the high standing of their professions in Italy.... Upstairs along the street are to be found cheap lodging houses, the headquarters for Italian bands, and the large number of lodges, both of Italian name and of American name with Italian constituency. Besides these, the large colonies will have their own theater and moving picture halls, charities, hospital, consulate, chamber of commerce, and luxurious club. In and around these institutions, social and business life flows....

Source: Philip M. Rose, 1922. *The Italians in America*. New York: George H. Doran and Company. P. 71.

☯☯

In addition, one could attend musicals and operas and watch marionette shows in Italian neighborhoods. There were also Italian communal organizations that spread across specific locales to include virtually all Italians in America. For example, there were 110 Italian newspapers in the country in 1918, and many had circulations far beyond a local area (Alba, 1985). The first was *L'Eco d'Italia* established in New York in 1849 (Nelli, 1983). *Il Progresso* had a daily circulation of 110,000 in 1921, with its subscribers located in all parts of the country. The Missionary Sisters of the Sacred Heart established hospitals, schools, and orphanages for Italians throughout the country. Fraternal societies became national organizations; for example, the Order of the Sons of Italy once had 3,000 lodges across the country. The purposes of this organization, described in Box 9.6, are a combination of assimilationist and ethnic preservation themes.

☯☯

BOX 9.6   THE PURPOSES OF THE SONS OF ITALY

1. to enroll in its membership all persons of Italian birth or descent...who believe in the fundamental concept that society is based upon principles of law and order, and who

adhere to a form of government founded upon the belief in God and based upon the Constitution of the United States of America....

2. to promote civic education among its members.
3. to uphold the concept of Americanism.
4. to encourage the dissemination of Italian culture in the United States.
5. to keep alive the spiritual attachment to the traditions of the land of our ancestors.
6. to promote the moral, intellectual, and material well-being of our membership.
7. to defend and uphold the prestige of the people of Italian birth or descent in America.
8. to encourage the active participation of our membership in the political, social, and civic life of our communities.
9. to organize and establish benevolent and social welfare institutions for the protection and assistance of our members, their dependents, and the needy in general, with such material aid as we are able to give.
10. to initiate and organize movements for patriotic and humanitarian purposes, and to join meritorious movements for such purposes which have been initiated by other organizations or groups.

Not all Italian immigrants settled in the nation's cities; over 6 percent worked in agriculture in 1900 (Nelli, 1983). There were Italian truck farmers throughout the United States, and Italian immigrants also established agricultural colonies in some locales. There were Italian truck farmers outside several cities in the Northeast, in North Carolina, Alabama, Mississippi, near Memphis, Tennessee, and near San Francisco in California. There were Italian colonies in Vineland, New Jersey; Tontitown, Arkansas; Bryan, Texas; and the Italian-Swiss Colony in Asti, California, among others (Lord, Trenor, and Barrows, 1970; Moquin and Van Doren, 1974; Nelli, 1983). Over one-half of the 60,000 Italians in California in 1900 were engaged in agriculture (Iorizzo and Mondello, 1971). Some Italians became prominent in agriculture and food processing, evident in the number of Italian wine makers in California, such as Gallo, Martini, Mondavi, and Petri; and the list includes Marco Fontana behind the Del Monte label and Amedeo

Obici, the founder of Planters Nut and Chocolate Company. Large numbers of Italian immigrants also worked on the railroads in western states in the late 1800s and early 1900s. "From 1908 to 1909 over nine thousand Italians secured jobs on railroad lines to the West" (Rolle, 1968:153). Moreover, Italians were miners from West Virginia and Alabama to California.

In large cities, Italian women gravitated to the needle trades. "By 1918, Italians represented 75 percent of the women in the men's and boy's clothing industry and 93 percent of the females doing hand embroidery in New York City" (Bodnar, 1985:64). Near Buffalo, New York, they concentrated in food-processing and the canneries (Lamphere, 1987). In cities and mining towns, Italian wives also took in boarders and did other work at home. A few Italian immigrant women became prominent in America (Box 9.7).

☯

BOX 9.7   THE STORY OF ANTONIETTA ALESSANDRO

Antonietta Pisanelli Alessandro came from Naples to New York as a child. As a young woman, she made her living singing, dancing, and acting in the major eastern cities. She made her New York debut at an Italian benefit in Giambelli Hall.... Personal tragedy marred her career, however; first her mother died, then her husband, then one of her two children.

With her remaining young son and few other resources... she arrived in San Francisco in 1904. She assembled a group of amateur performers, rented a ramshackled hall, and opened an Italian theater. According to an early patron, the settings were so crude they were liable to fall apart at any moment.... But the performance earned $150. By the time the fire department closed the building, Pisanelli was able to open the more substantial Cafe Pisanelli Family Circle, a combination theater, club, opera house, and cafe.

Featuring the finest actors and singers imported from Italy, the Circle was soon known as the liveliest theater in San Francisco. Through road tours as well as home performances, Antonietta Pisanelli Alessandro and her company brought Italian drama and Italian music, from folk songs to opera, to Italian Americans and others throughout the country.

Source: Maxine S. Seller, 1975. "Beyond the Stereotype: A New Look at the Immigrant Woman." *Journal of Ethnic Studies* 3:59–68, p. 60. Reprinted by permission.

☯

Italian men found work first as common laborers in industry and construction. In 1905, 80 percent of the Italians in New York were manual laborers, and, in 1916, one-half of all employed Italians were laborers (Alba, 1985; Lopreato, 1970). Italian immigrants were also tailors, barbers, merchants, contractors, quarrymen, longshoremen, shoemakers, and restaurant owners (Lord, et al., 1970; Moquin and Van Doren, 1974). In short, Italians worked in a variety of jobs, although they concentrated at first at the bottom of the labor hierarchy. In the early 1930s, the Italian labor hierarchy in Greenwich Village, New York City, included janitors, watchmen, and scrubwomen on the bottom; longshoremen and teamsters at the next level; office workers, telephone operators, firemen, and policemen at the next rung of the ladder; and doctors, lawyers, politicians, and real estate salespeople at the top (Ware, 1935).

Many Italian immigrants were initially placed in jobs by Italian *padroni*, or labor bosses (Iorizzo and Mondello, 1971; Lopreato, 1970; Moquin and Van Doren, 1974; Nelli, 1983; Rolle, 1968). Laborers would pay padroni commissions for finding them work, and at times the padroni would provide housing and food as well. In some cases, ties to padroni were formed in Italy prior to emigration, as labor recruiters would contract prospective recruits and even pay for their passage to the United States. A padrone often provided other services, such as letters to home, remittances to Italy, and help in securing home mortgages. According to Rolle (1980), Italian immigrants worked under a padrone for an average of eleven weeks and four days after reaching the United States.

The benefits of the padrone system for the immigrants included getting them to the United States and placing them in jobs, especially those outside cities that required transportation to the work site, as well as the additional services. There were abuses, however, and padroni often overcharged for passage to the United States and collected commissions, rents, and reimbursements for food that were exorbitant. The padrone system declined as more Italian immigrants came and new immigrants were able to turn to paesani for help in finding work and as more and more Italians joined labor unions. Moreover, the importation of immigrant laborers under contract was forbidden under the Foran Act of 1885.

As Italian immigrants sought their accommodation to American society, they began to compete with other groups, and both prejudice and conflict resulted. For example, Italians often moved into formerly Irish neighborhoods, such as Greenwich Village and the North End in Boston, and the Irish resisted at first. This resulted in street fights between the Irish and Italian newcomers (Ware, 1935; Whyte, 1955). Italian workers also began to replace the Irish in the mines, packing houses, steel mills, and on the railroads. This, too, resulted in conflict at times. In 1874, 150 Italians were brought into Armstrong, Pennsylvania, to break a strike organized by Irish workers and were met by gunfire (Iorizzo and Mondello, 1971).

Conflict occurred with other groups and in other places as well. Eleven Italians were lynched in New Orleans in 1891 on the suspicion that they were Mafia members who had killed the chief of police a year earlier, although nine of the eleven had been acquitted of that crime in trials (Moquin and Van Doren, 1974). Around the turn of the century, Italians were lynched and murdered throughout the country, for example, in Colorado, Illinois, North Carolina, and Florida. Two hundred Italians were driven out of Altoona, Pennsylvania, in 1894, and the Buffalo, New York, police detained 325 Italians in 1888 (Iorizzo and Mondello, 1971). The Palmer Red Scare raids of 1920 incarcerated 6,000 Italian and other aliens (Rolle, 1980). Prejudice associated Italians with lawlessness, radicalism, primitiveness, and violence:

> This "dago" it seems, not only herds, but fights. The knife with which he cuts his bread he also uses to lop off another "dago's" finger or ear, or to slash another's cheek.... More even than this, he sleeps in herds; and if a "dago" in his sleep rolls up against another "dago" the two whip out their knives and settle it there and then.... When infuriated with liquor, he will upon any fancied occasion use the only argument he possesses—his knife (quoted in Moquin and Van Doren, 1974:261).

In this atmosphere, the Italian immigrants Sacco and Vanzetti were convicted of the 1920 murder of a paymaster and guard at a shoe factory in South Braintree, Massachusetts. In the end, there was the exclusion of further Italian immigration into the country. Italy was granted a token annual quota of 3,845 with the Quota Act of 1924.

Since the arrival of Italians in America, the connection between this ethnic group and organized crime has received much attention. Italian organized crime was once known as the Black Hand, but now is known as the *Mafia* or *La Cosa Nostra*. The national organization of the Mafia is composed of twenty-four crime groups, or families (Herbert and Tritt, 1984). A commission oversees this confederation composed of members from the different families. The five crime families of New York are always represented on this commission, and its chair is *capo di tutti capi*, or boss of bosses.

The origins of the Mafia are in southern Italy, the Mezzogiorno. The Mafia was one of several secret societies in Sicily and throughout southern Italy. The organization began as the armed guards of absentee landlords in the Mezzogiorno, but later became a power in its own right (Nelli, 1983). The Mafia was a state of mind as well as an organization (Ianni, 1972). Family was the first loyalty, and the Mafia organization was infused with kinship terms and expectations. Within the family, relations were personal, protective, hierarchical, and made for a strict social order. Outside the family, there was distrust, and every man was expected to protect himself and his family in his own way.

Organized crime is hardly an Italian monopoly. "Since 1984, convictions obtained under the Racketeering Influenced and Corrupt Organizations—or RICO—Act have dismantled most of the nation's 24 organized crime families" (Raab, 1989:30–92). Law-enforcement officials view the current leadership as a sign of decay within the Italian Mafia. By the same token, there are signs of new ethnic groups in organized crime, many profiting from the drug trade. The illegal business empire might look something like this in the near future. The Italian American control of organized crime might be gradually relinquished to black, Puerto Rican, Chicano, and Cuban Americans, and other minorities (Herbert and Tritt, 1984). Organized crime has been historically a mobility route for minorities on the bottom; Italians once used it and now newer minorities will do so. Italian Mafia interest will increasingly turn to legitimate businesses.

THE PRESENT

With the second generation, there were important changes in the Italian American community. The old provincial ties were irrelevant to the American-born generation. The group became Italian Americans, and the new generation faced a serious choice. To be and identify oneself as Italian meant fewer chances for social mobility, for making it in the larger society. On the other hand, identification with Americans could lead to rejection by both groups, Italians and Americans. There were three responses to this conflict by the second generation (Child, 1943). The in-group response was to be Italian, the rebel response was to identify oneself as American, but most took the apathetic response of trying to ignore the conflict.

A rift between the generations occurred in Italian families. The American experience had individualized family members, wives as well as children, and this showed up in different values concerning arranged marriages, size of families, dating, husband's authority at home, divorce, and the children's role in the family (Ware, 1935). Children had been taught American ways in the nation's public schools, and the family no longer worked together as a single unit in America as it had in the Mezzogiorno. The Italian community changed in other ways as well. Ethnic newspapers and radio stations declined in sub-

TABLE 9.1 EDUCATIONAL AND OCCUPATIONAL ACHIEVEMENT OF ITALIAN
AMERICAN AND WASP FEMALES BY BIRTH COHORT

	1931–1935 Birth Cohort	1951–1956 Birth Cohort
Four or more years of college		
Italian females	6.5%	26.3%
WASP females	16.4	26.3
Professional, technical, and managerial positions		
Italian females	17.6	36.7
WASP females	36.7	36.5

Source: Figures from R. D. Alba, 1985. *Italian American: Into the Twilight of Ethnicity*. Englewood Cliffs, NJ: Prentice-Hall, Inc.

scribers and listeners, fraternal lodges declined in membership, and the second generation began to move to the suburbs (Alba, 1985).

As the nation's occupational structure turned toward more white-collar jobs in the post-industrial period, Italians caught up with other groups in both education and occupation. Alba (1985:128) reported:

In the aggregate, then, Italian Americans lag notably behind Protestants of British ancestry, but this is because of the wide gap that exists for the first two generations and older cohorts of Italians and...for those whose ancestry is derived entirely from the group. Parity with WASPs has very nearly been obtained by the third and later generations, those born after World War II, and individuals of part Italian ancestry.

Table 9.1 illustrates how rapidly Italian women moved toward parity with WASP women in educational achievement and in the job market. For men, the same convergence is evident in education and high white-collar jobs (Alba, 1985).

Nelli (1983) also observed that Italians were catching up occupationally with other ethnic groups and moving into the middle class. In average family income in 1974, Italians were behind only Jews and Irish Catholics among European ethnic groups. Lieberson and Waters (1988) concluded that European ethnic groups, including Italians, were fast converging in occupational composition by 1980. According to Alba (1985), Italian Americans are also acculturating. On family issues, such as premarital sex, abortion, and divorce, attitudes of Italians were essentially no different than those of other Americans. Nor were Italians different than others in their attitudes about child rearing.

While Italians were a bit more distrustful of others and less likely to value the intrinsic rewards of work, these differences could be explained by demographic factors other than ethnicity. Only 2.8 percent of the Italians still belonged to Italian organizations. Intermarriage rates among Italian Americans are steadily rising, and, for those under 30 years of age in 1979, 67 to 80 percent married outside the Italian group. Alba (1985) concluded that the Italian culture in America is in its twilight.

POLISH AMERICANS

Poland is located in the geographical center of Europe, with the Baltic Sea to the North and the Carpathian Mountains to the South. The country is slightly smaller than the state of New Mexico. Poland is now bordered on the West by Germany; on the East by Russia, Lithuania, Belarus, and the Ukraine; and on the South by the Czech Republic and Slovakia. The Poles are a Slavic people; their name means dwellers in the fields, or on the plains (Wytrwal, 1961). The Poles are the largest immigrant group from eastern Europe in the United States, part of the "new" European immigration to America. Over 8 million people in the United States identified themselves as Polish Americans in 1980.

BACKGROUND TO POLISH IMMIGRATION

The reasons for Polish immigration to America reach back into Polish history. Poles were not only pulled to America, but they were also pushed out of Poland. A review of Polish history will add to our understanding of these forces. The first period of Polish history was the Piast dynasty from the tenth to the fourteenth century (Fox, 1970; Lopata, 1976; Reddaway, et al., 1950; Szczepanski, 1970). The first Piast king, Mieszko I, consolidated the Slavic tribes on the Polish plain into a national kingdom. With his marriage in 966 to the Bohemian princess, Dubrovka, Mieszko also brought Christianity into Poland, namely Roman Catholicism, although Catholicism had already made its way onto the Polish frontier. Thus, the Poles are one of the easternmost Catholic groups in Europe.

Several wars were fought during the Piast dynasty, with Germans, Czechs, Hungarians, Danes, Lithuanians, and Tatars. Polish territory expanded during the Piast dynasty, although there were occasional reversals. Under Boleslaus Chrobry, for example, the Poles, Czechs, and Slovaks were united into one state, and the Polish frontier extended to

331

FIGURE 9.3 POLISH AMERICANS AND CHANGE IN AMERICAN SOCIETY

Agrarian Society c. 1600–1865	Industrial Society c. 1865–1945	Post-Industrial Society c. 1945–Present	
Early immigration and contact →	Mass immigration and contact →	Accommodation, competition, and conflict →	Present situation

---

the Elbe and Elster rivers in the west, the Danube River in the south, the Baltic Sea in the north, and the Lwow area and Kiev to the east. The last Piast king was Casimir the Great (1333–1370), who established uniform legal codes in the kingdom, contributed to town development, and founded the University of Cracow, the third oldest in Europe.

The second period of Polish history is the Jagiellonian dynasty (1386–1572). The Jagiellonian dynasty began with the marriage of the Polish queen, Jadwiga, to the grand duke of Lithuania, Jagiello. The Polish kingdom was now a union between Poland, Lithuania, and Ruthenian lands, and it stretched from the Baltic to the Black Sea. Not only did the Polish kingdom expand to the East during the Jagiellonian dynasty, it also expanded to the West with the defeat of the Germanic Teutonic Knights and the acquisitions of the port city of Danzig, Pomerania, and part of East Prussia. The Poles also fought the Russians and Turks during this period. The University of Cracow was reorganized under the Jagiellonians, flourished, and was renamed Jagiellonian University, the name it carries to this day. The last of the Jagellons was Sigismund Augustus, who died in 1572.

The Polish nobility, the *Szlachta*, gained ascendancy during the last phase of the Jagiellonian dynasty. By the sixteenth century the nobility established a parliament, the *Sejm*, which gave them control over the state. The Szlachta was a landed gentry with large estates engaged in export agriculture. From these estates, wheat, rye, hemp, honey, wax, fats, lumber, skins, and furs were exported. To better secure agricultural labor, the nobility instituted serfdom on their manors in the fifteenth and sixteenth centuries, tying peasants to the soil. By 1496, no more than one peasant son could leave the soil without the master's consent (Reddaway, et al., 1950). In addition to peasants, there were a paid staff for care of the livestock, gardeners, and seasonal laborers on the large estates. In the towns, there were merchants, craftsmen, small shopkeepers, and administrators. The mining of iron ore, other metals, and salt were also fixtures in the Polish economy of the era.

332

The Chicago Stockyards furnished employment for
many Polish immigrants in the 1890s and later.

The third period of Polish history is that of the elected kings (1587–1772). The Szlachta gained nearly complete control of the Polish state in this period, symbolized by the *Liberum Veto* in the eighteenth century, whereby all laws had to be passed unanimously, without a single dissent, by the Sejm. Poland was now a republic, and the nobles elected the kings, often foreigners whom they could better control. Gentry at the regional and county levels elected the deputies to the Sejm.

Poland was a granary for western Europe in the sixteenth and seventeenth centuries, exporting agricultural goods from large estates owned by the crown, nobles, and the Church. During this period, Poland fought wars with the Tatars, Cossacks, Swedes, Russians, and Turks. A Polish army under Sobieski liberated Vienna from the Turks in 1683, but the intrusion of Prussia, Russia, and Austria into Polish affairs grew toward the end of this period of history and would later result in the partition of the country. Poland was in decline, isolating itself from the West, neglecting education and learning, and pauperizing the towns. And the peasants were sinking to the status of slaves.

The fourth stage of Polish history was the partition of Poland by Austria, Prussia, and Russia from 1772 until its independence in 1918, following World War I. There were three stages to the partitions, the last coming in 1795, whereby Austria ruled Galicia, Prussia most of western Poland and Russia eastern Poland. In the middle of the country, around Warsaw, there was a Warsaw Duchy from 1806 to 1813, and a Congress Kingdom of Poland from 1815 to 1830. Poland at this time literally disappeared from the map of Europe. Uprisings among the Poles against foreign rule occurred in 1830, 1846, 1848, and 1863, all of which failed to liberate the country and resulted in the emigration of Polish exiles.

In each partition, the occupying power undertook a policy to eradicate Polish culture, and Polish property and wealth were confiscated as well. In Prussian Poland, for example, Polish landholdings were lost to the Germans, and Prussia took control of the Catholic schools, forbidding the use of the Polish language under Bismarck's *Kulturkampf* policy of Germanizing Polish society (Reddaway, et al., 1941; Wytrwal, 1961). Emigration started in Prussian Poland, peaking between 1880 and 1893, and the population in Poznania and West Prussia fell by 41,000 between 1882 and 1895 (Bukowczyk, 1987; Fox, 1970). Most came to the United States, but after 1891 Polish emigration from Prussian Poland turned toward industrial Germany.

In Russian Poland, there was a similar policy to eradicate Polish culture, punctuated by executions and imprisonment in Siberia. Poles were forbidden to speak Polish in public, and Polish land was taken by Russians. Due to this Russification policy, emigration from Russian

Poland to the United States began, and 740,438 emigrants from this region came to America between 1899 and 1914 (Wytrwal, 1961). In Austrian Poland it was the same story; emigration from this region peaked in 1910. Between 1870 and 1914, a total of 1.2 million emigrated from Prussian Poland, 1.3 million from Russian Poland, and 1.1 million from Austrian Poland (Bukowczyk, 1987).

The reasons for the mass emigration of Poles were primarily economic. Serfdom was abolished in the different partitions of Poland during the 1800s, and the financial state of the Polish nobility declined. The old manorial system collapsed, the number of impoverished and landless peasants increased, and 80 percent of the rural population was in a state of economic distress (Bukowczyk, 1987). Peasants farmed smaller landholdings, faced higher taxes but lower wages, and had little economic alternative in Poland, due to the slow pace of its industrialization. People migrated to find work, needing wages with the end of serfdom, and the migration distances grew to include immigration to the United States (Morawska, 1985). Polish society changed with the release of peasants from servitude and the impoverishment of rural Poland, and opportunity beckoned in America, transmitted through letters from previous emigrants (Thomas and Znaniecki, 1984).

> As with all movements of history, a multiplicity of factors was responsible for Polish emigration. Foreign oppression, an overflowing population, primitive methods of agriculture, meager productivity of the soil; all were instrumental in producing the Polish exodus. In addition to land hunger, the Poles suffered from low wages, excessive taxation, and insufficient industrial development.... This exodus was the result of the unrestrained agitations of transatlantic ship agents, Russian crop failures of 1876, Bismarck's cruel policy of extermination directed against the Poles, and the German, Austrian and Russian practices of assisting the exportation of "undesirable Poles" to America (Wytrwal, 1961:148).

Many young men also sought to escape from being drafted into the armies of the occupying powers. Young men and women from the same family or village often left Poland together, destined for an American city where they knew someone. The village they left behind is described in Box 9.8.

The social hierarchy in rural Poland began with a few families of great nobility on top; followed by numerous middle nobility; lower nobility; peasant farmers, including crown peasants, peasants under the control of the church, and private serfs of landowners; and finally landless peasants on the bottom (Lopata, 1976). The peasants' lives were contained within a local area, often a single village, something like the *campanilismo* of Italian peasants. This was known as the *okolica*, "...the area within which a person's reputation is contained, the social area in which the person lives and interacts, the social life space which contains his identities. The *okolica* of the peasant includes the family, home, lands, the village of families, and sometimes other villages" (Lopata, 1976:19). Of the Polish immigrants to the United States in 1900–1911, 43 percent were agricultural laborers, 33 percent were independent farmers, 17 percent were servants, and 7 percent were in the skilled trades (Bukowczyk, 1987).

၍

BOX 9.8 THE POLISH VILLAGE

The main business of the community is farming. The farms are small, averaging about twelve acres. From sunrise to sunset the men and women work in the fields, the younger children tending the cattle and doing the chores. One reason for the small size of the farms is that they have been subdivided for the dowries of children....

The general condition of the peasantry is one of poverty. ...Moreover, the land holdings are too small for the support of large families; the church exacts heavy payments for mass offerings; the one miller in town charges exorbitantly for grinding the grain....

The poorer class live in three-room huts, consisting of a store room, a bed room, and a living room with fire place that also serves as a kitchen....

Among the peasants large families are the rule....

Parental authority is also manifest in the marital selection of children. Since all values are subordinated to the ownership of land, parents have a sharp eye to the acres which a proposed marriage will bring and they may interfere with the match. Otherwise, romance is a factor in selection, and a man will send a proposer, as an intermediary, to the girl of his choice. If she accepts from the latter a drink of vodka, the engagement is concluded....

Education in the village is of a more or less primitive pattern. That is, the children learn their necessary functions and duties through imitation of their elders. The Russian government attempted to introduce schools in which the Polish language was prohibited, and to tax the people for them. Such efforts were vigorously opposed by the peasants. The result was that the people were generally illiterate....

The life of the folk is enveloped in religion. Rarely does anyone question the authority of the Roman Catholic Church, which gives color to the life of the people through its festivals and holidays. The onerous exactions of the church are met submissively; ...as the people pay to safeguard their fortunes in this and the next world....

Equally important to religion and the priest for keeping people in line is the role of gossip. The closeness of contact between the families of the village make it a primary group, where everyone knows what everybody else is doing. Thus, there are no secrets, and woe betide anyone guilty of a too flagrant violation of the mores.

Source: Arthur Evans Wood, 1955. *Hamtramck: Then and Now.* New York: Bookman Associates. Pp. 31–2.

☺☺

Poland was restored as an independent state after the First World War. Polish independence had been the thirteenth of President Wilson's Fourteen Points at the Versailles Peace Conference. After short wars with Germans, Czechs, and Russians, the Polish frontiers were established by 1922 (Szczepanski, 1970). When Nazi Germany invaded Poland in 1939, Poland again lost its independence, and 6 million of the 35 million Poles were killed in the course of World War II (Szczepanski, 1970). After the war, Polish independence was restored again under a communist government, and its boundaries were moved toward the West, gaining territory from Germany and losing it to the Soviet Union. In recent years Poland has become a democratic state.

POLISH IMMIGRATION

There were three waves of Polish immigration into the United States The first two waves constitute early Polish immigration and the last mass Polish immigration into America (Sandberg, 1974; Wytrwal, 1961).

EARLY IMMIGRATION: The colonial immigration of Poles from 1608 to 1776, the first wave, consisted of individual Poles intermixed with other settlers from a variety of European nations coming to America. There were Poles at the founding of Jamestown, Virginia, in 1608, for example, and Poles were among the citizens of New Amsterdam, now

337

New York City. Doctor Kurczewski was headmaster at a school in New Amsterdam in 1659, and other Poles were residents of the city at that time (Fox, 1970; Grzelonski, 1976; Wytrwal, 1961). Early Polish immigrants settled throughout the eastern seaboard of the United States, from New England through Pennsylvania and into the South.

The colonial immigration of Poles was followed by their political immigration from 1776 to 1865, the second wave (Sandberg, 1974; Wytrwal, 1961). Political troubles pushed these political exiles out of Poland, and some of the exiles became prominent in American history. For example, Kosciuszko and Pulaski served as officers and commanders on the American side in the Revolutionary War. Kosciuszko was known for his construction of defensive fortifications, and Pulaski became a Brigadier General, leader of the Pulaski Legion, and is known as the father of the American cavalry. Additional Polish refugees immigrated to America following political turmoil in Poland in the 1830s, 1848, and 1863 (Grzelonski, 1976; Wytrwal, 1961). These men and women either returned to Poland or eventually assimilated into American society.

During the 1800s, small groups of Polish immigrants also settled on the American frontier and took up farming. Poles from Silesia arrived in Texas in 1854 and founded the agricultural colony of Panna Maria (see Box 9.9). Polish immigrants also established agricultural settlements in Wisconsin (Grzelonski, 1976; Wytrwal, 1961). In 1856, immigrants from the Poznan area and Pomerania founded Poland Corner in Wisconsin, and "... in the years that followed such settlements as Pulaski, Kazimierz, Poniatowski, Cracow, Sobieski and others sprang up nearby" (Grzelonski, 1976:133). By 1860, Polish settlements were located in Michigan, Illinois, Ohio, Louisiana, Indiana, Texas, and Wisconsin. There were about 50,000 Poles in America by 1870 (Wytrwal, 1961).

☯☯

BOX 9.9 PANNA MARIA

In 1854, a sailing vessel arrived at Galveston, Texas, and a weary group of eight hundred men, women, and children disembarked. Father Leopold Moczygemba, a Franciscan monk, was their leader. Carrying their ploughs and other implements, their bedding, kitchen utensils, and a large cross from their old parish church, these peasants began their long trek inland until they finally reached the site for the future colony, which they hopefully and nostalgically named Panna Maria in honor of the Virgin Mary. The established small agricultural community was the location of the first Polish church in America. ... Polish settlements in San Antonio, Bandera, Yorktown, and St. Hedwig followed soon after. Still later came Czestochowa, Kosciuszko, Falls City, and Polonia, all in Texas. By 1906 the Polish population of Texas was estimated at between 16,000 and 17,000.

Source: Joseph A. Wytrwal, 1961. *America's Polish Heritage: A Social History of Poles in America*. Detroit: Endurance Press. P. 62.

@@

MASS IMMIGRATION: The mass immigration of Poles into the United States began after 1870 and continued into the twentieth century. Two million Poles immigrated to America between 1880 and 1910, and there were over 3 million Poles in the country in 1910 (Fox, 1970; Thomas and Znaniecki, 1984). Another 174,365 arrived in 1912–1913, 122,657 in 1914, and by 1950 there were over 5 million first- and second-generation Poles in the United States (Fox, 1970; Wytrwal, 1961). Many Polish immigrants eventually returned to Poland from the United States; 30 percent of those who came between 1906–1914, for example, returned to Poland (Bukowczyk, 1987).

Whereas the earlier waves of Polish immigration were from the Polish elite, this third wave was representative of all strata in Poland and thus contained high numbers of Polish peasants (Lopata, 1976). This emigration began in Prussian Poland and then spread to Russian and Austrian Poland. In the United States, the Polish immigrants began to concentrate in the industrial cities. To illustrate, in 1920 there were 400,000 first- and second-generation Poles in Chicago; 200,000 each in New York and Pittsburgh; 100,000 each in Buffalo, Detroit and Milwaukee; and 50,000 in Cleveland (Bukowczyk, 1987).

ACCOMMODATION, COMPETITION, AND CONFLICT

When the Polish peasants reached America around the turn of the century, the earlier Polish emigrants, the political exiles, had already assimilated into American society (Wytrwal, 1961). Most of the new immigrants settled in the nation's industrial cities, reaching from New England to Chicago. In 1910, the states with the largest Polish populations were, in descending order, Pennsylvania, New York, Illinois, Wisconsin, Michigan, Massachusetts, Ohio, New Jersey, Minnesota, and Connecticut (Fox, 1970). The Polish immigrants found jobs as unskilled laborers; "according to the findings of the Immigration commission, 6.4% are in the trades, 3.8% in domestic and personal service, and the rest in unskilled labor" (Fox, 1970:69).

339

Early in the twentieth century, the occupations of Poles in America were non-farm labor (29%); mine, mill, and factory workers (23%); skilled trades (5%); business, professional, and clerical (9%); and farmers (6%) (Fox, 1970). Up to 80 percent of the Poles worked in industry, including iron and steel mills, machine shops, naval piers, packing houses, textile mills, and coal mines (Thomas and Znaniecki, 1984).

The Poles entered the American market at the bottom in industries that were rapidly expanding at the time.

> ...employers established the pecking order of their workers on the basis of race, ranking white native-born Americans on top; Irish, Scots, English, Welsh, and Germans below but near them; Poles, Magyars, Italians, Slovaks, and Russians next, in various orders; and black Americans in the bottom category (Bukowczyk, 1987:21).

In one specific locale, the Cambria mills in Johnstown, Pennsylvania, there were two occupational circuits. "The first, with higher wages and better working conditions in more prestigious finishing departments, employed predominately native-born American and western European workers. The second, largely unskilled, with unhealthy and dangerous jobs in open-hearth, blast furnace, and railroad departments, and in the foundries and coal mines, employed the immigrants" (Morawska, 1985:101). Poles also went into farming, and Polish farming communities were concentrated in Massachusetts, New York, Ohio, Indiana, Illinois, Wisconsin, and Texas. "In 1901 the number of Polish farming settlements was estimated at seven hundred" (Fox, 1970:73).

Polish women found work in textile mills, the apparel industry, cigar-making, packing houses, and canneries (Fox, 1970). In only 30 percent of the Polish households was the husband the sole breadwinner. When the women did not work outside the home, they managed large families and some took in boarders, often to help buy a home (Box 9.10). "Wives could expand their reproductive work to support other wage earners who paid for room and board. Young women could remain employed after marriage if the couple continued boarding..." (Lamphere, 1987:35).

The traditional Polish peasant family was patriarchal, under the authoritarian control of the father. "The prestige of the family was in accordance with its land holdings. The conjugal bond was less that of romantic love than that of mutual respect for the contributions made by each spouse...and little freedom was permitted children in choice of occupation.... In short, the peasant family was a close, confining system which held its member in the iron bonds of custom and necessity" (Wood, 1955:206). In the United States, Polish women took over more family functions, since their husbands were out of the house and at work most days (Lopata, 1976). The mothers exercised control over the children, expecting them to financially contribute to the household. Mothers also took in boarders, as previously mentioned, and their status rose. Over time, second- and third-generation children gravitated toward a more American model of family life.

⊚⊚

BOX 9.10 MARIA KOWALSKA

"Maria Kowalska" is John J. Bukowczyk's composite of a typical Polish immigrant wife of the early 1900s.

...Maria Kowalska's toil would literally never have been done. For a woman, the workday began well before dawn. She would have lighted a fire in the wood stove, after emptying out the ashes from the previous day, and cooked breakfast before she roused her husband and male lodgers....After the men left for work, Maria would have turned her attention to the daily and weekly round of household chores. If her house or apartment did not have indoor plumbing yet, hauling water for cooking and washing was by far her most arduous task....Once a week, this immigrant wife scrubbed laundry by hand in a steaming tub set on a chair in the kitchen and ironed next to the crackling stove. She might make a weekly trip to the farmers' market and the corner store—where she had to negotiate credit—for goods she could neither make or grow. More regularly, she would have tended the family's vegetable garden—canning produce in the summer—and looked after the ducks and chickens the family probably kept in a shed behind the house. As the afternoon wore on, she might have had time to mend or sew....By then it would have been time for her to serve the evening's pot of soup, which had simmered all afternoon, and wait on the men as they returned at dusk, dirty and tired from a day in the mines or mills.

Source: John J. Bukowczyk, 1987. *And My Children Did Not Know Me: A History of the Polish-Americans*. Bloomington: Indiana University Press. P. 24.

⊚⊚

Polish immigrants settled near their work. At first, immigrants from the same village located in a neighborhood, often boarding with either friends or relatives. "Eventually, the community became so large as to attract new immigrants from other parts of Poland or Poles from other parts of America. These local ethnic settlements were located near large industrial work sources and in the poorer section of the city. . ." (Lopata, 1976:43). For example, thousands of Polish immigrants settled in Hamtramck in the Detroit area near a Dodge automobile plant that opened in the second decade of the twentieth century (Wood, 1955).

As the size of Polish communities grew, they became more complex. Some Poles opened businesses to serve the Polish clientele; there were butchers, bakers, dressmakers, shoemakers, and undertakers, for example; and Polish professionals, such as attorneys and physicians, established offices in the community. There were, in 1916, seventy-four Polish savings and loan associations in Chicago alone (Bodnar, 1985). The immigrants also built Polish parishes and established Polish mutual aid societies (Lopata, 1976; Wytrwal, 1961). The St. Stanislaus Kostka was founded in Chicago in 1864, and the first Kosciuszko Club was established in 1871 in Philadelphia (Wytrwal, 1961). Both the churches and the clubs became community centers (see Box 9.11). By 1960, there were some 10,000 Polish organizations and 830 parishes in the United States (Wytrwal, 1961). Some of these parishes were very large; for example, St. Stanislaus Kostka parish in Chicago had 50,000 parishioners around the turn of the century (Wytrwal, 1961).

Examples of Polish organizations include the Polish National Alliance (PNA) founded in 1880, the Polish Roman Catholic Union (PRCU) in 1880, Polish Falcons in 1888, Polish Women's Alliance of America in 1898, and Polish American Congress in 1944 (Sandberg, 1974). The PNA had 220,000 members in 1924–1925; and it had served earlier, before Polish independence in 1918, as a shadow Polish government in America, a fourth partition (Bukowczyk, 1985). Although there was tension between the aims of these different organizations, as a group they promoted independence for Poland prior to the First World War; provided insurance, education, and aid for Polish immigrants; advocated for separate Polish parishes; and developed civic and cultural pride in things both Polish and American. The objectives of the PRCU specifically were (1) "to uphold and spread the Catholic Faith, (2) to maintain and spread the Polish language, Polish traditions, and the Polish spirit, (3) to aid Poland, (4) to help members attain higher positions in the civil and religious fields, and (5) to raise children in the Polish and Catholic spirit" (Wytrwal, 1961:212). The PNA was decidedly more secular, composed of middle-class nationalists rather than clergy. Such organizations were started at a local level but later became national associations with local chapters and a press.

☺☺

BOX 9.11 POLISH COMMUNITY CENTERS

The center was usually a large hall filled with tables and chairs. Here Polish songs, rhythmic folk dances, lively music and stirring dramas were developed and perpetuated...and many episodes of Polish history were related. The walls of the center were adorned with framed lithograph pictures of Polish revolutionary heroes, of a battle in which the Poles emerged the victor and the Turk or Prussian the loser, or of a Polish castle, manor, or church. The rooms were also supplied with newspapers.... In these newspapers, the immigrants might read shipping news, stories of crime and accidents, poems, moral advice, essays.... More important, the newspapers carried political articles on current issues in the United States and in partitioned Poland....

The atmosphere of the center, clouded with foul cigarette or cigar smoke, was hardly inviting to the eye or nose. But this was the place to hear local gossip, who had died or was getting married, who was leaving for partitioned Poland, or returning to America; to exchange information or misinformation on the latest trend in employment or on the competence or incompetence of the officers of the club.

Source: Joseph A. Wytrwal, 1961. *America's Polish History: A Social History of Poles in America*. Detroit: Endurance Press. P. 157.

☺☺

Polish parochial schools were often connected to parish churches, and there were over 500 Polish elementary schools in the country teaching at one time about two-thirds of the Polish-American youth (Bukowczyk, 1987; Sandberg, 1974). Marian devotion, prayer, humility, respect, and loyalty to family and community were among the values taught by Polish nuns. In addition to elementary schools, the Poles founded high schools and colleges; there were 71 high schools and 6 colleges in the 1960s (Sandberg, 1974). Furthermore, a Polish press emerged in America, and there were 1,356 separate Polish serial publications between 1842 and 1966 (Lopata, 1976). Individual Poles and Polish families kept their ties to relatives and friends in Poland through both letters and remittances (Lopata, 1976; Thomas and Znaniecki, 1984). Remittances to relatives in Poland ran as high as $15 million each year (Lopata, 1976).

Most Poles came to this country as members of local villages, not as a single nationality. This was the *okolica* of the peasants, and it was local and confined. The national consciousness of Polish immigrants was formed in the United States through their daily contact with other Polish immigrants from other parts of Poland and the activities of Polish nationalist organizations already mentioned (Wytrwal, 1961). These same organizations also encouraged Americanization, reflecting the accommodation of Poles to American society.

There were also competition and conflict along the way. Polish immigrants were at times used as strikebreakers, resulting in competition with others on the job. The hierarchy Americans had in mind put the Polish on the bottom in the unskilled, heavy, and poor-paying jobs, and Poles were not expected to take the better jobs. The stereotype of the Pole in America was one of an uneducated, stupid, and crude manual laborer, pictured in the Polish jokes as late as the 1970s and 1980s. The Poles also competed with Germans and particularly the Irish over control of the Roman Catholic Church, especially over their local parishes. This led to the formation not only of the Polish Roman Catholic Union, but also the Polish National Independent Catholic Church with fifty parishes at one time (Fox, 1970). Prejudice against Poles and other southern and eastern Europeans resulted in the Quota Act of 1924, which granted no more than a token quota to the Poles. In 1929, Polish immigration to the United States had an annual quota of 6,488 (Lopata, 1976).

THE PRESENT

After World War I, Polish immigrants began to acculturate (Wytrwal, 1961). There was a shift in orientation from returning to Poland to building a good life in this country, having a home, nice furnishings, good clothes, and some savings (Morawska, 1985). In a sample of second-generation Poles living in Buffalo in 1927, only 7 percent identified themselves as Poles, whereas 57 percent identified themselves as American and another 39 percent as Polish American (Wytrwal, 1961). Polish nationalism in the United States faded with the independence of Poland after the First World War. English was replacing the Polish language in Polish parishes and in the Polish press, and instruction in Polish in parochial schools fell off. Third-generation families were becoming less dominated by the father and more egalitarian, and there was an increasing adoption of the American style of life (Wrobel, 1979). After the Second World War some 160,000 Polish refugees and displaced persons immigrated into the United States, and Polish immigration continues to this day, but not at the level it was early in the century.

By 1970, 35.6 percent of employed Polish American women were clerks, 19.2 percent were operatives, 15.5 percent had service jobs, and

13.1 percent were in professional and technical work (Bukowczyk, 1985). Of employed Polish American men, 24.4 percent were in the crafts and foremen, 19.6 percent were operatives, 15.2 percent were managers, officers, and proprietors, and 14.5 percent were in professional and technical work (Bukowczyk, 1985). In short, Poles were reaching occupational parity with other ethnic groups, and this trend continues (Lieberson and Water, 1988).

Some Polish Americans reached prominence in their professions. In some cases, this has meant playing down Polish roots by name changes. "Many 'Polish-American' television and motion-picture celebrities changed their names—Charles Bronson (Buchinski), Stephanie Powers (Stefania Federkiewicz), partly-Polish Jack Palance (Walter Palaniuk), and Michael Landon (Orowicz)... " (Bukowczyk, 1987:113). Others, such as baseball stars Carl Yastrzemski, Stan Musial, and Joe and Phil Niekro, kept their Polish names.

Past ethnic differences in fertility, education and propensity to marry were converging among European ethnic groups, and these include the Poles (Lieberson and Waters, 1988). European groups are also converging in their occupations, although the older immigrant groups are still more likely to be in farming than those from eastern and southern Europe (Lieberson and Waters, 1988). "...[M]ost studies show that older Polish Americans of the old emigration are at the top rungs of the blue collar world, and recent generations are at the lower rungs of the white collar world. An increasing number are entering the professions, shortcutting the traditional rung-by-rung movement of prior generations" (Lopata, 1976:95).

More recent studies have found a decline in Polish ethnicity with succeeding generations and social class (Lopata, 1976; Sandberg, 1974). For example, Sandberg (1974) studied Poles in Los Angeles on three measures of ethnicity. The first was cultural ethnicity, meaning opinions about the importance of Polish schools, centers, organizations and press, as well as the perpetuation of the Polish language, music, dance, traditions, and history. Religious ethnicity was the second, and it referred to feelings about participating in a Polish church and the importance of the church for both the individual and the group. Finally, national ethnicity meant feelings of kinship, mutual responsibility and a sense of belonging with others of Polish background, as well as sensitivity about Polish jokes and the propriety of Anglicizing Polish names. He found that all three measures of Polish ethnicity declined with succeeding generations, and the upper and middle classes were less ethnic than the working class. Other studies find that later generation Poles show more approval of ethnic intermarriage, are less likely to support a political candidate on the basis of Polish identity, and have a decreasing preference for use of the Polish language in the Roman Catholic service (Lopata, 1976). Rates of marital endogamy have fallen significantly for Polish women in the younger generation (Lieberson and Waters, 1985). By the same token, Polish Americans still attend Polish parishes and live in Polish neighborhoods in some cities.

SUMMARY

European Americans are the largest immigrant group in the United States. European immigration came in two phases, the old immigrants from northern and western Europe, illustrated by the Irish in this chapter, and the new immigrants from southern and eastern Europe, represented by the Italians and Poles. The history of all European groups has been tied to the changing labor needs of the nation, and all three of these groups have more or less kept pace with these changes. In all three cases, there is evidence for convergence and inclusion after each became a nationality in America, although the timing of convergence and inclusion varies across these groups. Along the way, however, these three groups have faced barriers to their inclusion, seen in ethnic competition, conflict, and even immigration restrictions, especially in the cases of Italians and Poles.

CHAPTER

10

☯

AFRICAN AMERICANS AND AMERICAN SOCIETY: THROUGH THE NINETEENTH CENTURY

T he history of African Americans is part of the larger, ethnic legacy of America. As land was expropriated from America's indigenous peoples, the need grew for immigrant labor on the frontier. African Americans are one ethnic group who met this need. Immigrants from Africa share with others a long, hard history of labor, and this history, like that of other immigrant groups, has been implicated in the changing labor needs of the nation. The history of African Americans is unique, however. Only immigrants from Africa were once slaves and the property of southern planters. The history of African Americans is outlined in Figure 10.1. In this chapter the slave trade, slavery, and emancipation are analyzed. The period of northern migration through the present accommodation of African Americans will be discussed in the following chapter.

CONTACT

It is true, of course, that the New World was richly endowed by nature with fertile soils, a great spectrum of climates, and enormous reserves of precious metals. These resources, however, were in themselves worthless. In order to farm the soil, there must be farmers, and in order to mine the earth, there must be miners (Harris, 1964/1974:11).

347

FIGURE 10.1 AFRICAN AMERICANS AND CHANGE IN AMERICAN SOCIETY

Agrarian Society c. 1600–1865		Industrial Society c. 1865–1945		Post-Industrial Society c. 1945–Present	
Contact, slave trade, southern slavery	→	Emancipation, conflict, and caste	→	Northern migration, racial conflict, and caste	→ Civil rights → Present movement situation

This quotation makes a fundamental point; human power was needed on the frontier to exploit fully the land expropriated from Native Americans. Europeans found it difficult, however, to harness native labor to their extraction endeavors on the expropriated land. When Europeans did press natives into forced labor on southern plantations, the Indians ran away, disappearing beyond the frontier, or they died in great numbers (Blassingame, 1972). Indian slaves also constituted a security threat since they could ally with free natives in retaliatory raids against planters. This was true not only in the South of this country but also throughout the Americas. The same story may be said for whites, who could easily escape from plantations into the surroundings. Both the French and British had turned initially to indentured labor from Europe for labor in the New World, and this lasted until the 1670s (Braudel, 1984). Then, planters and mine owners throughout the Western Hemisphere increasingly relied on slave labor from Africa.

African slaves could do none of these things, and their blackness became a visible sign of their bondage, eliminating for planters many of the security problems associated with pressing other groups into forced labor. There are several reasons African slaves were an attractive alternative to native labor, in spite of the fact that they had to be imported across a great distance and at a considerable cost.

First, "it is well known that slavery, serfdom and corvée were ongoing institutions in many sub-Saharan African societies before European contact" (Harris, 1974:14). Moreover, Africans "probably had acquired immunities to certain common European disease organisms which were lethal to the American Indians." In particular, Africans had a higher immunity to malaria and yellow fever than both Europeans and Indians. For these reasons and others, West Africans were a good and dependable labor pool in the absolute and comprised a superior labor supply compared to American Indians, and this was true throughout the New World.

While the practice of indentured servants from Europe was widespread in colonial America, European servants were never enslaved for life or for future generations. Moreover, European labor immigration in the volume needed for the American frontier was not available until after the abolition of slavery. For one thing, serfdom in Eastern Europe lasted until the nineteenth century, and thus labor from the Elbe River east was not free from bondage in the seventeenth, eighteenth, and early nineteenth centuries and able to migrate to the New World (Blum, 1957). For another thing, those willing to emigrate from western Europe were too few in number and would have made less than ideal workers in the New World (Rawley, 1981). To put it simply, there was a shortage of indentured European labor (Braudel, 1984).

Africans were brought to the New World over a span of more than three centuries, from 1502 to 1860. It is estimated that between 9.5 and 11.3 million Africans were brought as slaves to the Americas, and 6 to 7 percent of this total came to the United States (Fogel and Engerman, 1974; Rawley, 1981). The entire slave trade between Africa and the New World totaled about 10,000 human beings per year by 1650, 40,000 per year by 1713, and 60,000 per year between 1741 and 1810 (Rawley, 1981). Most of the slaves brought to the New World, 60 to 70 percent, were laborers in sugar production; another goodly number were miners, particularly in Brazil; and the rest cultivated a diverse number of crops, including tobacco and cotton in the United States. Sugar plantations began in northern Brazil and later expanded into the entire Caribbean. About 38 percent of the African slaves went to Brazil, and over 50 percent went to the Caribbean (Johnson and Campbell, 1981). Slave traders preferred males and people between the ages of 15 and 25.

In the United States, the plantation economy expanded from tobacco growing in the Upper South to cotton production in the Lower South. The peak period of African immigration into the United States was between the years of 1741–1760 and 1781–1810, coinciding with the expansion of cotton production in this country and the rise of the British textile industry (Rawley, 1981). Once the slave trade ended, and as slaves became increasingly valuable in the expanding plantation system due to innovations in cotton farming and the textile industry, the living and working conditions of slaves improved.

Slaves were principally from West African agricultural tribes, and thus had skills useful for cultivation and extraction in the New World. The West African tribes were never in a position to stop the great European powers in their slave trade, although they, too, participated in this trade. Europeans entered West Africa from below the Sahara in the north to Angola in the south. From coastal ports, they took out slaves by the thousands, and groups from the Yoruba, Dahomey, Ashanti, Ife, Oyo, and Congo tribes came to the New World as slave labor. They came in ships sailing under the flags of the then maritime powers of Europe: Britain, France, the Netherlands, Portugal, and Spain. So long as African labor remained in Africa it was of little use to Europeans. African labor had to be exported to be of use to Europeans elsewhere in the world. At least this was the case until the middle of the nineteenth century, when the European powers eventually colonized much of Africa and could use African labor at home. At this time the slave trade finally stopped.

The slave trade was a triangular operation, according to Williams (1966). The triangle began in Europe, ran South to West Africa, crossed over the Atlantic to the Americas, and ran across the Atlantic again to continental Europe. In this triangle, the British, for example, shipped finished products such as cooking pots, iron bars, textiles, guns, and spirits to Africa in trade for slaves; transported the slaves to the New World in trade for raw materials; and then took the raw materials from the Americas home to England, where the raw materials were either consumed or turned into finished products in English factories. Then the cycle was started again. Think of textiles to Africa, slaves to the Americas, and cotton to Europe as an illustration of the triangular trade. A profit was made at each point on this triangle. Thus, the slave trade was part of a world economy, with industry at the core in Europe, particularly in Britain, and on the periphery of Africa and the Americas were slave labor and the production of raw material for the industrial core, illustrated by African slaves working in southern cotton for export to the British textile industry.

The route from Africa bringing slaves to the Americas is called the Middle Passage. One child when placed on a slave ship looked around and saw "a multitude of black people of every description chained together, every one of the countenances expressing dejection and sorroe, I no longer doubted my fate.... I fell motionless on the deck and fainted" (quoted in Rawley, 1981:290–291). The mortality rate for slaves ranged from 10 to 25 percent during the Middle Passage, although on average mortality of crews was higher (Fogel, 1989). Killing diseases included dysentery, measles, smallpox, and scurvy. Death rates were higher for longer voyages, and especially when ships ran low on water and provisions.

Ironically, the rise of the industrial order in Britain, itself made possible in part by profits from the slave trade, resulted in the subsequent British attack on the trade. It was in the interest of Britain as an industrial nation to buy raw materials from the colonies in the New World at the lowest possible price, but the sugar monopoly of West Indian planters stood in the way of this scheme. Thus, the British, early in the nineteenth century, undermined that monopoly by prohibiting the slave trade, thereby eliminating the planters' labor supply.

SLAVERY

Not only the slave trade, but also slavery itself was part of a world economy. The southern plantations were on the American frontier, obviously, as were the mines in Brazil and the sugar plantations in the Caribbean. For example, cotton from the South was exported to Europe or shipped to the textile industry in New England. Imported into the South were foodstuffs from the North and, later, the Midwest; work animals such as mules from the border South; manufactured goods from both the North and Europe; and slaves from Africa and the Caribbean. Planters in the South were linked to this national and international trade through middlemen, e.g., merchants, bankers, and wholesalers, who were collectively called the "cotton factors" (Ransom and Sutch, 1977). Plantations were profit-maximizing, large-scale farms producing staples for an external market within this larger economic context (Mandle, 1978).

Slavery is a period of American history about which much has been said and written, but it is still surrounded by debate and controversy. More often than not, accounts of slavery are a weave of hard, historical evidence, political ideology, and academic or popular fashion. Accounts of slavery fall on a continuum of being either critical or apologetic of this "peculiar institution."

Those critical of slavery present it as most inhumane and cruel, a version that has its roots in the Abolitionist movement. By this account, African American slaves were regularly brutalized and reduced to beasts of burden. In the fields of the South there were grindingly hard field labor and routine physical punishment. With the whip, sadistic white masters and their overseers coerced slaves into labor and often forced sexual attention on black women. African American bodies and souls alike were abused in the process. These critics of slavery disagree, however, over the degree to which black people were degraded by enslavement. Some believe that the African American character and community were broken during slavery and that this condition is still evident (Frazier, 1949). Other critics argue that, on the contrary, the black family and community remained intact during slavery (Gutman, 1976).

The apologists of slavery portray it as an institution in which African slaves were humanely treated. Since slaves were innately lazy and incompetent, in this view, compulsory labor in the form of slavery was necessary. However, slaves were neither regularly brutalized nor sexually molested in any systematic way. White masters were genuinely concerned for the welfare of their slaves, and the relationship between master and slave was nothing more than one between a watchful white parent and an innocent black child. Physical brutality was no more common in slavery than it is when a father occasionally corrects his own children. It is not surprising that many of the apologists of slavery were slaveholders who tended to fashion their cultural image—what would now be called a media image—after that of a moralistic Christian father.

Both of these versions are caricatures of southern slavery and are faulty depictions of it. Both views blend together hard evidence, political ideology, and blatant self-interest. Of course, any history of slavery is necessarily an interpretative one. Our hope is to interpret slavery sensibly from the perspective of ethnic and societal change, during which groups exchange land, labor, and capital. Slavery was a labor regimen on the southern frontier, a way to extract wealth profitably from the land, and it began for African people a long history of menial agrarian work for others, even as the labor needs of the larger nation changed. It is beyond the scope of this chapter, however, to try to settle once and for all the controversy surrounding slavery.

PROFIT AS A GOAL OF SLAVERY

In our view, the bottom line in plantation life was profit. Slavery was neither instituted nor maintained on the whim of planters' racial prejudice, although many of them were certainly prejudiced. It was instead an economic arrangement, as Cox (1948:332) observed:

> Sometimes, probably because of its very obviousness, it is not realized that the slave trade was simply a way of recruiting labor for the purpose of exploiting the great natural resources of America. This trade did not develop because Indians and Negroes were red and black or because their cranial capacity averaged a certain number of cubic centimeters; but simply because they were the best workers to be found for the heavy labor in the mines and plantations.

Southern planters were agrarian capitalists, and by most accounts they were as a class successful entrepreneurs, first in tobacco in Virginia and Maryland and then in cotton in the Lower South. Planters were engaged in commercial agriculture, raising cash crops that were shipped elsewhere in the world. Slavery was a way to organize labor in this enterprise, and slave labor certainly played a part in making the endeavor profitable. The slave represented a good investment and an important tool of production, and this was the basis of the relation between white master and African slave.

Slavery was also a perverse extension of the concept of private property. With the rise of capitalism, the feudal obligations between lord, land, and labor were replaced with the concept that land and labor were mere commodities in an impersonal marketplace. Land once purchased became the private property of the owner, and its use was restricted only by the law of supply and demand. At least this was the theory of laissez-faire capitalism. Land was considered a commodity by nearly all European settlers in America, something that never made sense to Native Americans. Southern planters took the additional step of viewing the slave, a human being, as a piece of private property. Themselves the property of others, slaves were forbidden to accumulate any property of their own, and this also greatly affected the history of African Americans (Gutman, 1975).

This is an essential truth about slavery, even though planters liked to fashion themselves as having a feudal sense of noblesse oblige toward slaves. Slavery was the only feature that distinguished planters from other capitalists who relied on free and contractual labor. As capitalism evolved toward industrialization, pressures arose to free labor from the land, out of serfdom in Europe, for example, so that rural workers could migrate to industrial cities. Enclosure Acts in England even pushed rural peasants off the land. Displaced peasants either found work in Europe's industrial cities or migrated to the New World. African Americans did not, however, become part of this trend until the twentieth century.

Current estimates of the profitability of the plantation system give every indication that southern plantations and slave labor were good economic investments. It has been estimated that the rate of return on investment in slave labor of both sexes and all ages was 10 percent (Fogel and Engerman, 1974). Investment in northern textiles in the same period yielded about the same rate of return, while investment in southern railroads brought a smaller return of 8.5 percent. Comparisons within agriculture itself tell the same story. Southern agriculture was 35 percent more efficient in 1860 than was northern agriculture, due in large measure to the economies of scale made possible by cheap slave labor (Fogel and Engerman, 1974). Plantations with slave labor were 28 percent more efficient than were farms in the South using free labor. Slaveholders were in a position to force small, independent farmers off the best land and control the market for staples by price cutting (Bonacich, 1975:608). The economic advantage in southern agriculture enjoyed by slaveholding planters was rooted in their monopolization of cheap slave labor and their economy of scale.

353

The slave-auction posters of the pre–Civil War period demonstrate the "commodity" status of the African American slave.

Another indication of the relative economic value of slave labor is the fact that while one-third of the free population at the time of slavery were active participants in the nation's labor force, at least two-thirds of the slaves were in the labor force. Virtually all the slaves worked, women and children as well as men, working 16 hours per day during harvest, and they worked for less than did free labor. It was not the number of hours slaves worked that distinguished them from free labor in agriculture: it was their working harder per hour (Fogel, 1989). Slaves labored under two basic systems, the task and gang systems (Stampp, 1968).

Under the task system, each slave was given a daily work assignment that could be done at his or her own pace, and a slave driver inspected the completed work to insure that it was satisfactory. This system was best suited for rice cultivation.

Under the gang system, slaves were divided into gangs supervised by slave drivers. By 1800, most slave drivers were blacks, not whites, and throughout slavery most of the field hands were women, not men (Fogel, 1989). Thus, the pace of work was forced on slaves. Gangs were in the fields " 'fore daylight" and back home after sunset. In his travels in the South, Olmsted (1970:432) reported: "We found in the field thirty ploughs ... turning the earth from the cotton plants, and from thirty to forty hoers, the latter mainly women, with a black driver walking among them with a whip, which he often cracked at them, sometimes allowing the lash to fall lightly upon their shoulders. He was constantly urging them also with his voice. All worked very steadily. ... " Breakfast was eaten at slave cabins before daylight, and the noon meal was brought to slaves in the field; they stopped work only long enough to eat. "All worked as late as they could see to work well, and had no more food nor rest until they returned to their cabins. At half-past nine o'clock the drivers... blew a horn, and at ten visited every cabin to see that its occupants were at rest, and not lurking about and spending their strength in fooleries..." (Olmsted, 1970:433).

Spero and Harris (1931) wrote that while free labor cost capital at least $106 per year, slave labor cost as little as $75 per annum. Bonacich (1975:603) cited another example of the slave's labor value for capital from Linden (1940): a mill in DeKalb, Georgia, reported that a slave cost $75 a year, while a white operative cost $116. In short, the surplus value of slave labor for planters exceeded that of free labor for their employers.

Slave labor was also flexible. Planters frequently rented slaves to enterprises off the plantations, particularly during the slack seasons, to serve as construction workers and skilled workmen such as carpenters, masons, and tailors. This obviously added economic value to slave labor. As for certain extra costs in the surveillance of slave labor, the southern states often picked up most of these costs by providing police, militia, and court services with public money (Sowell, 1975).

SLAVES AS TOOLS OF PRODUCTION

To planters, slaves represented nothing so much as capital investments and tools of production in a labor-intensive, agrarian economy. "Massa, he look after us slaves when us sick, 'cause us worth too much money to let die like you do a mule" (Yetman, 1970:91). The price of a slave was a function of his or her laboring potential and, thus, age, skills, lack of physical handicaps, and absence of habits that would undermine his or her working (Fogel, 1989). Next to land, the purchase of slaves was the planter's largest investment. Moreover, in labor-intensive endeavors, profits are won or lost by the cost of labor. Thus the price and productivity of slaves was a prominent concern of planters as a class of entrepreneurs, and this concern set parameters to the planters' treatment of their slaves. If this is so, then we should expect that slaves were physically well maintained, like any significant capital investment or tool of production. Brutality and abuse of slaves were necessarily checked by the degree to which such excesses interfered with the health and productivity of slave labor. Nevertheless, brutality and abuses of all sorts did occur on southern plantations; enslavement alone is abusive, and some slaveholders and their overseers were particularly barbarous.

> Slaves have been stripped naked and lashed, often to death. Dey would be left strapped after from twenty-five to fifty lashes every two or three hours to stand dere all night. De next day, de overseer would be back with a heavy paddle full of holes dat had been dipped in boiling water and beat until de whole body was full of blisters. Den he'd take a cat-and-nine-tails dipped in hot salt water to draw out de bruised blood and would open every one of dem blisters with dat (Yetman, 1970:182).

However, some planters were benevolent masters. "I ain't goin' to talk against my white folks like some cullud folks do, 'cause Massa Lewis was mighty fine man and so was Miss Mary.... There was mighty little whippin' goin' on at our place, 'cause Massa Lewis and Miss Mary treated us good" (Yetman, 1970:25–26). Abuse and kindness were both meted out. We should expect, therefore, that slaves were treated as capital investments and a class of labor for whom there was no better substitute. The sadism, sexual mistreatment, or kindliness of white masters were all secondary to their utilization of

356

slave labor in the southern plantation economy. Slaves were a major capital investment, and certainly the most important tool of production. It was these hard economic facts that affected the use and treatment of slaves on southern plantations.

Evidence indicates that the physical welfare of slaves was at least equal to, and in some instances exceeded, that of free labor in the nineteenth century. From records kept by planters on their daily operations, Fogel and Engerman (1974) found that the diet of some slaves exceeded modern recommendations on the daily intake of chief nutrients, and it surpassed by a wide margin the dietary levels of the entire population of the United States of the time. By even a wider margin, the slave diet exceeded that of the average white southerner in the past century. Slaves consumed up to 4,000 calories per day, as much an indication of how hard they worked as the adequacy of their diet (Ransom and Sutch, 1977). This varied from plantation to plantation, however: "Old Massa always see that we get plenty to eat. O' course it was no fancy rations. Just corn bread, milk, fat meat, and 'lasses, but the Lord knows that was lots more than other poor niggers got. Some of them had such bad masters" (Yetman, 1970:36). On plantations a slave's diet was determined by his/her labor productivity, rated as a full-hand, three-quarters of a hand, etc., and thus children and some women were fed less than able-bodied men. The nutritional gap between slaves and whites was only for children 5 years old or younger (Fogel, 1989). Of course, family members shared food, and slaves reported supplementing their diets by hunting, gardening, and stealing food if necessary.

Slaves experienced less crowded housing than some classes of free men and women did, especially the urban, industrial workers of the early nineteenth century:

> Mostly the slave houses had just one big room with a stick-and-mud chimney, just like the poor people among the Creeks had. Then they had a brush shelter built out of four poles with a room made out of brush, set out to one side of the house where they do the cooking and eating, and sometimes the sleeping too. They set there when they is done working, and lay around on corn shuck beds, because they never did use the log house much, only in cold and rainy weather. Old Chief just treat all the Negroes like they was just hired hands, and I was a big girl before I knowed very much about belonging to him (Yetman, 1970:186).

In this case, the master was a Creek Indian in Oklahoma. On large plantations, slave quarters "... consisted of a single or double row of cabins or multiple-unit tenements for families and dormitories for unmarried men and women" (Stampp, 1968:292). Slaves got also a clothing allowance, one of which was:

Each man gets in the fall 2 shirts of cotton drilling, a pair of woolen pants and a woolen jacket. In the spring 2 shirts of cotton shirting and 2 pr. of cotton pants.... Each woman gets in the fall 6 yds. of woolen cloth, 6 yds. of cotton drilling and a needle, skein of thread and 1/2 dozen buttons. In the spring 6 yds. of cotton shirting and 6 yds. of cotton cloth similar to that for men's pants, needle, thread and buttons. Each worker gets a stout pr. of shoes every fall, and a heavy blanket every third year (Stampp, 1968:291).

It is not surprising that southern slaves had longer life expectancies in the nineteenth century than did free industrial labor in America and Europe. However, Fogel and Engerman (1974) compared the material conditions of slave life with some of the worst conditions faced by free industrial workers of the era, and records kept by planters could be self-serving.

Another indication of the quality of physical maintenance of African slaves in the United States is found in their rate of natural increase. Their birth rates were the highest of any slave population in the New World. While only 6 to 7 percent of the African slaves imported to the New World ever arrived in the United States, by 1825, 36 percent of the slave population living in the Western world was in this country (Fogel and Engerman, 1974). This comparison is strengthened by the fact that slaves were continuously imported into the Caribbean and South America to offset the high mortality rates of slaves there. According to Van den Berghe (1976:535), "The mines of Brazil, especially in the eighteenth century, were undoubtedly the greatest consumers of black flesh in the New World, with mortality rates up to 40 percent a year." In this country slaves increased their numbers, an indication that they were maintained as valuable property and tools of production. W. E. B. Du Bois (1935:9), a black leader and scholar, seemed to agree with the essentials of this interpretation of slavery:

The slavery of Negroes in the South was not usually a deliberately cruel and oppressive system.... The victims of southern slavery were often happy; had usually adequate food... and shelter sufficient for a mild climate.... When the mass of their field hands were compared with the worst class of laborers in the slums of New York and Philadelphia... the black slaves were as well off and in some particulars better off.... Their [slaves'] hours were about the current hours for peasants throughout Europe. They received no formal education, and neither did the Irish peasant, the English factory laborer nor the German *Bauer*, and in contrast with these free white laborers, the Negroes were protected by a certain primitive sort of old-age pension, job insurance, and sickness insurance.

However, Du Bois noted, "no matter how degraded the factory hand, he is not real estate" (p. 10). Du Bois helps us express our feelings about southern slavery, reminding us also that slavery must be judged in the context of the treatment of all labor in the era, including industrial workers and the serfs of eastern Europe.

Recent historical research on slave fertility and mortality in the South reveals the following pattern: Mortality rates were actually worse than abolitionists charged. These high rates were often caused not by the malice of masters but by the backfiring of well-intentioned practices, as when masters fed raw milk to weaned infants or rewarded field hands with liberal allotments of rum. Masters were not generally guilty of working field hands to death but they were guilty of so overworking pregnant women that infant death rates were pushed to extraordinary levels. Fertility rates were high not because masters manipulated the sexual behavior of slaves as they did their cattle, but because they housed slaves in family cabins rather than barracks. When economic motives led masters to interfere with the sexual lives of slaves, such interference did not usually raise fertility but reduced it, as when husbands were sold from wives or when young adults were prohibited from seeking marital partners beyond the boundaries of their plantations (Fogel, 1989:153).

While there were definite economic limits to the physical mistreatment of slave labor, some slaves were certainly overworked. "De rule on de place was: 'Wake up de slaves at daylight, begin work when they can see, and quit work when they can't see'" (Yetman, 1970:58). Slave women worked from early in the morning to late at night, laboring in the fields and managing their own households. They also spun, wove and dyed cloth, sewed clothing, made soap and candles, and grew, preserved, and prepared food (Jones, 1985). Overwork was especially true in cases of absentee landowners, when the management of a plantation was turned over to an overseer. This "enabled the planter to place between himself and the black slave a series of intermediaries through whom better pressure and exploitation could be exercised and large crops raised" (Du Bois, 1935:36). An overseer tended to drive slaves in their work. He was paid in proportion to the current year's crop, rather than the average crop over several years, and his wages and attractiveness to other planters, and thus his career, were all tied to short-term production (Sowell, 1975). These labor bosses seldom cared about the eventual costs of practices that included the exhaustion of both land and labor, since they did not share in these costs. The economic interests of overseers rested solely in the maximization of short-term production, which often led to the exploitation of slave labor.

Both rewards and punishments were used as inducements to ensure the productivity of slave labor. On most plantations there was a system of rewards for hard work, which included incentives such as bonuses, prizes, and opportunity for occupational mobility. Bonuses for hard-working slaves ranged up to $1,000 in 1974 dollars, according to Fogel and Engerman (1974). Opportunity existed for ambitious slaves to move into skilled trades and even into managerial and professional work on many plantations. At the end of the Civil War, 83 percent of the mechanics and artisans in the South were black. Throughout slavery, slave society was hierarchical, with family connections being important for mobility into the better jobs (Fogel, 1989).

Slaves in the cities, particularly, were engaged in a variety of work: "Our butchers are Negroes; our fishmongers Negroes; our vendors of fruit, vegetables, and flowers are all Negroes; and generally slaves" (Wade, 1964:29). In Richmond, Virginia, slave labor was used extensively in the tobacco and iron industries, and much of this work was highly skilled. Slaves were also used in the building of railroads in the South, as well as in the construction of other means of transportation. They were also dockworkers in many southern seaports, as well as naval carpenters, tailors, bakers, and tanners. Positive inducements such as bonuses and the promise of occupational mobility insured labor productivity and maintained slave discipline in the South. Fogel and Engerman (1974) went so far as to conclude that the occupational structure of slavery was not unlike that of free labor of the period.

Gutman (1975) objected to much of the detail in this portrait of slavery. He specifically questioned the proposition that the occupational structure of slavery was comparable to that of free labor and the corollary suggestion that slaves were nothing so much as black Horatio Algers. Fogel and Engerman make slavery sound like a Skinner box, Gutman complained; that is, through the use of stimuli, cues, and reinforcement schedules, Africans were made over into black Anglo-Saxons, complete with the Protestant ethic for hard work. Gutman argued that this is an overly mechanistic and simplified depiction of slavery. In his view, slavery was as much rooted in the realities of property ownership in the South and in the informal system of slaves as it was in any formal inducements for labor productivity.

The strictly economic view also overlooks other realities about southern slavery. First, planters were not only wealthy, they also had political control over the South. Thus, they had power over both blacks and whites, and they used the state in support of their own class interests, for example by having states finance patrols to catch runaway slaves. Moreover, the planter class had high status; they enjoyed deference from others. Because of planter wealth, power, and status, the culture of the South justified the plantation economy with racism.

Despite all this, there were over 200 recorded slave revolts in the United States between 1526 and 1860 (Aptheker, 1939). These insurrections were only a small but extreme part of slave protest. Slave discontent was more commonly expressed in work slowdowns, strikes, sabotage, destruction of tools, feigning illness, flight, and even suicide. Slaves were known to set fire to a master's house and barns in protest, and the cooks at the big house poisoned the food and drink of their owners on occasion. Flight was so common that southern states had armed militias and patrols moving throughout the countryside to control slave movement and prevent possible rebellions. "Then the patterrollers they keep close watch on the poor niggers so they have no chance to do anything or go anywhere. ... If you wasn't in your proper place when the patterrollers come they lash you til you was black and blue. The women got fifteen lashes and the men thirty" (Yetmen, 1970:36). On the plantations, planters and overseers were typically armed, and we already know of the physical punishment meted out there for insubordination and running away. This is hardly a happy picture of contented slaves, irrespective of adequate diets, housing, and other material conditions of life.

THE SLAVE SUBCULTURE

When men and women work together, their work and the meaning it has for them are elaborations on what is strictly required by their bosses. Out of the formal organization of labor evolves an informal system of workers, one that may or may not conform to the formal rules and regulations. Thus neither slavery nor any other organization of labor is like a Skinner box. Even in total institutions like concentration camps (and slavery has been likened to a total institution), where it might appear that life is totally governed by routine and official orders, unique, self-initiated adjustments are often made by inmates. On occasion these adjustments can seriously subvert the operation, meaning, and purpose of the formal institution (Goffman, 1961). Goffman called the informal system of a total institution its *underlife*.

There was an underlife to slavery everywhere it was found. It was organized into family bonds and friendships, crystallized into values and roles unique to slaves, and manifested in the habits and personal styles of slaves. It was the African subsociety and subculture of the South. The subculture of slaves was primarily an oral tradition that was passed from one generation to the next by word of mouth. The perpetuation of this black subculture, rooted in West Africa, was partly the result of the exclusion of slaves from the dominant white society. Slaves did not share with planters in certain privileges, nor were

361

they welcomed in the subsociety of white workers and farmers in the South. We will trace the evolution of this subculture through the stages of the larger history of African Americans.

The foundation of the slave community was the family (Gutman, 1976). Throughout the South during slavery, the slave family was primarily a two-parent nuclear family, surrounded by extended kin. Seventy-five percent of the slave families were two-parent families, and their marriages were typically long-lasting (Gutman, 1976). Courtships were based on romantic love, although planters did interfere with marital choices (Jones, 1985). Wedding ceremonies were described by one ex-slave in these terms: "...I seen cullud folks marry before de war and Massa marry dem dis way: Dey goes in de parlor and each carry de broom. Dey lays de broom on de floor and de woman put her broom front de man and he put he broom front de woman. Dey face one another and step across de brooms at de same time to each other and takes hold of hands and dat marry dem. Dat's de way dey done, sure 'cause I seed my own sister marry dat way" (Yetman, 1970:90). The average age of slave women at the birth of their first child was 21 years (Jones, 1985).

Slave families reinforced labor discipline in the interest of the planter class. Slaves remained on plantations, worked hard, and stayed out of trouble largely because of their families. Slave runaways often occurred after the separation of family members by sales or decisions to move slaves a great distance (Gutman, 1976). But slave families were much more; they represented human bonding, and families socialized each new generation. Slaves had family names, sometimes unknown to their owners, and practiced sexual exogamy outside of these blood ties. Kinship ties could extend beyond a single plantation, and this was true even for marriages. Slaves from different but nearby plantations married; these were called broad marriages (Gutman, 1976). Partners would travel to see each other once or twice per week in these cases.

The migration of slaves to the Lower South, particularly from 1815 to 1860, meant family separations. Approximately three-quarters of a million slaves moved from the Upper to the Lower South, from tobacco to cotton, going by ship, railroads, and overland marches (Johnson and Campbell, 1981). Gutman (1976) found that about 40 percent of the slaves in the Lower South reported an earlier marriage with another spouse, and one-sixth of these earlier marriages were involuntarily broken by the forced migration. However, slaves soon formed family ties in new locations, many doing so through remarriage. Slave families could also be broken because of estate sales, following an owner's death for example, and thus slave marriages were insecure. However, 75 percent of the families were intact with two parents.

The church was another institution in the slave community. Slaves regularly attended religious services, and sermons were given by both black and white preachers. "We were allowed to have prayer meetings in our homes and we also went to the white folk's church" (Yetman, 1970:16). The slave family and church fortified one another; the church held up family life as an ideal and censured adultery, for example. Slave men worked, as did free farmers of the era, but slave women worked in the fields as well as being wives and mothers (Jones, 1985). An indication of their strong family values is seen in their exit from field work and into the home after emancipation.

The slave subculture was in part due to the labor needs of the planters. It has been observed that slavery is suited only for the organization of labor for crude physical work. Forced labor is less practical and efficient for work that is more complex, skilled, and mental in nature. Thus slaves were necessarily concentrated in manual labor. If capital's labor needs are largely confined to manual work, as were those of the planters, little investment is made in the enculturation of labor. The subculture of slaves was a direct outcome of planters' labor needs. Planters had no need for enculturated slaves, and it was also in the interest of white labor to keep slaves largely uneducated, save for instruction in the manual arts. "Us poor niggers never allowed to learn anything. All the readin' they ever hear was when they carried through the big Bible. The massa say that keep the slaves in they places" (Yetman, 1970:36). Furthermore, the vast majority of slaves worked and lived in isolated rural areas, and three out of every four slaves toiled in all-black work gangs, often under black supervision. Most slaves had only occasional and asymmetrical contact with whites, and as a result black-white cultural pluralism prevailed in the antebellum South. Of course, in this era of American history there were few mechanisms for the enculturation of any laboring group, slave or free.

The planters in every practical sense controlled the Old South, both its economic and political systems, although they comprised only 7 percent of the population of the region. Plantations were the central economic institution of the southern economy, and planters exercised virtual mastery over the land, labor, and commodity markets in the South. Property qualifications for the voting franchise and the outright restriction of public office to members of the planter class also gave planters political domination over the Old South (Spero and Harris, 1931). Du Bois (1935:33) noted:

Into the hands of the slaveholders the political power of the South was concentrated, by their social prestige, by property ownership and also by their extraordinary rule of the counting of all or at least three-fifths of the Negroes as part of the basis of representation in the legislature. It is singular how this "three-fifths" compromise was used, not only to degrade Negroes in theory, but in practice to disfranchise the white South.

There was a class of free blacks who before the Civil War constituted approximately 11 percent of the black population of the country. In fact, Sowell (1975) considered this figure to be an underestimation, and Meier and Rudwick (1970:99) found that "Free blacks monopolized barbering, practically controlled the building trades, and were prominent among the shoemakers and butchers." There was also a small class of free black professionals. As older immigrants have been generations ahead of more recent arrivals from the Old World, free blacks have been ahead of slaves with respect to education and economic position. Sowell observed that the free black business class in northern cities had been, by most indicators, rather comfortable, at least until the twentieth century, when the black migration to the North inflamed the racial prejudice of white clients and business fell off. The descendants of this class, along with the children of black families in the South who were fortunate enough to have acquired land or a profession after emancipation, made up the bulk of black college students well into the present century. The "talented tenth," as they have been called, has been moving closer than the black masses to inclusion in and convergence with the larger society.

The exclusion and divergence of African Americans during slavery can be overemphasized. There are many indications that there was some racial assimilation in the South. First, the material welfare of slave labor was at least equal to that of southern white labor, which suggests some measure of convergence in material living conditions. There was also cultural blending. On their part, black slaves in this country converted in great numbers from pagan beliefs and Islam to Christianity, although in parts of Brazil blacks remained essentially Islamic (Harris, 1974). Slaves also adopted Anglo names, both voluntarily and as a result of force, and mother tongues from West Africa were lost. The perpetuation of Africanisms was more difficult in this country than elsewhere in the New World. Here the plantations were smaller, and thus there was seldom a critical mass of slaves from a single tribe on one plantation, which is necessary for the survival of tribalisms. Slavery saw the beginnings of the assimilation of tribal identities into a single social entity, African Americans, which was American as well as African.

By the same token, white southerners adopted many aspects of African culture. The ingredients and preparation of southern cooking are more West African than English. Rice, grits, yams, okra, greens, and hot spices are not staples of the British diet but are common in the dishes of West Africa. The British preferred rather blandly prepared meats, particularly roast beef and mutton stews. Southern cooking consists of highly seasoned casseroles and meat dishes that are fried, baked, or barbecued—anything but bland. I know of a white woman, formerly of Georgia, who bought her first standing rib roast and promptly boiled it—so much for her British ancestry. She was much taken with a party dish that included black-eyed peas, several meats, and spices and that had been literally envisioned in a dream of a Yoruba woman. The woman from Georgia exclaimed that she had not enjoyed such cooking since leaving the South.

In the preparation of food and other domestic practices, and in music, African idioms have been diffused throughout the South and the entire nation. These were the corners of the larger labor market in which black creativity was allowed to flourish. As musicians and cooks, blacks were expected to entertain and serve whites, and along these lines African styles crossed over into the white community.

We are not suggesting that blacks and whites imitated each other in the antebellum South, however. Their assimilation of each other's ways was interpretative and selective, and the adoptions each made were translated into their own respective idioms. African American Christianity is no mere copy of the worship of whites; the rite of baptism, for example, was filtered through memories of Dahomey river-cult ceremonies. African American dialect is no mere regional patois; English was translated through West African semantics and phonetics as slaves adopted it. Full-scale racial assimilation was severely limited in the South because of the social distance between planter and slave and the competition between black slaves and free white workers. This made for a good measure of racial exclusion during slavery and permitted a black subculture in the South.

While white planters and black slaves were allied in a sense against white labor during slavery, the social distance between planter and slave prohibited the full inclusion of blacks into the society of planters. Racial assimilation in this manner was not on the agenda of the powerful planters. Moreover, the antagonism between slaves and poor white workers and small farmers prevented assimilation at the level of labor. Slaves were an ever-present threat to the economic position of white labor, for capital always had the option of displacing white workers with cheaper black labor. White workers in the cities of the South were aware that their employers could always turn to

365

cheaper slave labor, perhaps renting slaves as hirelings to avoid the purchase price of a slave. White yeomen on the land also knew that they were subordinate to the planters, since only large planters could afford the best land and control the staples market (Bonacich, 1975). This made for a great deal of resentment on the part of poor whites, not only toward planters but toward slaves as well. Thus the assimilation of slaves, both vertically into the society of planters and horizontally into the society of white workers, was restricted.

In the course of slavery, poor whites made little headway in competition with white planters and slave labor (Spero and Harris, 1931). Capital had the ultimate weapon, of course; it could flood the labor market by setting free approximately 4 million slaves (Harris, 1974). Thus there were mutual exclusion and enmity between black and white labor during slavery. If significant assimilation occurs between groups, it typically comes when class counterparts in different ethnic groups converge, but this did not happen between black and white labor in the antebellum South. Moreover, if the day ever came (and come it did) that planters could no longer protect African Americans from hostile poor whites, then the spirit of whites such as the one Cash (1960:52) described could be turned loose in full-blown racial conflict:

> ...to stand on his head in a bar, to toss down a pint of raw whisky at a gulp, to fiddle and dance all night, to bite off the nose or gouge out the eye of a favorite enemy, to fight harder and love harder than the next man, to be known eventually far and wide as a hell of a fellow— such would be his focus. To lie on his back for days and weeks, storing power as the air he breathed stores power under the sun of August, and then explode, as that air explodes in a thunderstorm, in a violent outburst of emotion—in such fashion would he make life not only tolerable but infinitely sweet.

EMANCIPATION, CONFLICT, AND CASTE

It surely seemed at the time that emancipation would hasten the inclusion of African Americans into the larger American society. Slaves were free at last. Although emancipation might not have been the fundamental reason for the Civil War, slavery was always an issue in the conflict. President Lincoln issued the Emancipation Proclamation while the war was still being fought, and the eventual Union victory led to the implementation of the decree in the South. Moreover, the shortage of labor created by the war meant that the South had to rely more and more on black labor behind the battle lines. African Americans by the thousands took up positions in industry and transportation that had been vacated by whites serving the Confederacy. More than 200,000 African Americans also served in the Union armed forces, 93,000 from the Confederate states (Jones, 1985). This signaled some progress for black labor, but the trend collapsed at the end of the war.

After the Civil War, the potential existed for bringing ex-slaves into the larger society. African American workers could have migrated north and taken up positions in the emerging industrial order of that region, or they could have gone west, becoming homesteaders on the frontier. There was also a plan for land redistribution in the South, so that ex-slaves could become independent farmers and property owners with "forty acres and a mule." This was the plan initially of the Freedmen's Bureau and then of Thaddeus Stevens, an antislavery leader of the Radical Republicans in Congress. Its theory was similar to that of the General Allotment Act for Native Americans (see Chapter 7)—assimilation through property ownership. This was a fundamental theme of the era, the thought that capital acquisition was the route to civilization, if not salvation. This plan for ex-slaves was blocked, however, by President Johnson. Still, there was at least the potential for black people to become a class of either industrial workers or independent farmers after the Civil War, thereby converging with nineteenth-century American society.

The potential for African Americans following emancipation is illustrated in the Reconstruction Era. After the Civil War, the Union Army occupied the South until 1880. During this short period, freed slaves experienced some significant improvements in their standard of living. First, black men could vote in southern states after 1867, and they became the majority of the registered voters in several former-Confederate states by the next year (McPherson, 1990). Three years later, black men were 15 percent of the officeholders in the South, including U.S. Senators.

This change in political power was reflected in economic changes for African Americans in the South. For example, slaves in the seven cotton states of the Lower South had received in the form of food, clothing, and shelter only 22 percent of the income produced by the plantations on which they worked. This figure jumped to 56 percent after freedom. Between 1857 and 1879, average per capita income for African Americans in southern agriculture increased by 46 percent, from 23 percent to 52 percent of white income by 1880 (McPherson, 1990). These changes, among others, have led some historians to call the Civil War the second American Revolution. With regard to African Americans, however, the revolution was short-lived. By the 1880s, a counter-revolution in the South reversed many of these gains, putting into place a racial caste system based on tenancy, the crop-lien system, debt peonage, and legal restrictions on the civil and political rights of African Americans, all of which were meant to keep black workers "in their place."

THE RACIAL CASTE SYSTEM

After Reconstruction, race relations took a turn for the worse, entering into a period of prolonged conflict that is remembered as one of the ugliest periods of American history. The outcome of emancipation was racial strife and stratification, with black people in the South on the bottom in agrarian tenancy and domestic service. A racial caste system, the product of racial competition, conflict, the superior power of anti-black forces, and a growing racial ethnocentrism, replaced slavery in the South in the latter half of the nineteenth century. Some freed slaves did migrate, many to southern cities, others to better lands on the Mississippi delta, and there was even a Kansas Exodus in 1877. However, over 90 percent of the ex-slaves stayed in the South.

The racial caste system established after emancipation had essentially the same effect on African Americans as had slavery. It continued the exclusion of blacks from American society and perpetuated their divergence. Bonacich (1972:555) saw caste as the exclusion of an ethnic group from certain types of work. Furthermore, "caste systems tend to become rigid and vigilant, developing an elaborate battery of laws, customs and beliefs aimed to prevent undercutting." According to Bonacich, the success of a caste system is the denying of the target group's access to general education and political power: "the solution to the devastating potential of weak, cheap labor is, paradoxically, to weaken them further, until it is no longer in business's immediate interest to use them as replacements" (Bonacich, 1972:556). The racial caste system that followed emancipation meant the exclusion of black labor from nearly all trades save agrarian labor and domestic service, the segregation and exclusion of blacks from decent education, and the almost complete exclusion of blacks from the political process in the South. This caste system was an extreme form of ethnic stratification.

After the war, and with emancipation, southern planters could no longer rely on slave labor, of course. They turned first to work gangs on the plantations, giving ex-slaves fixed wages as well as provisions in food and housing (Jones, 1985; Mandle, 1978; Ransom and Sutch, 1977). This labor regimen did not work well, however, for at least two reasons. First, currency was in such a short supply in the South following the war that planters did not have the wherewithal to pay wages to field hands. Second, ex-slaves understandably objected to this arrangement, for it was so similar to slavery. Nothing had really changed with emancipation, or so it appeared, for ex-slaves were working again just like slaves in large work gangs under the direct and constant supervision of bosses. African American labor voted with its feet by exiting from field labor in the South. The hours worked per capita by black labor fell between 28 and 37 percent below slavery levels (Ransom and Sutch, 1977). On the one hand, black women and children drastically curtailed their working hours; women were using their freedom to become mothers and housewives (Jones, 1985). On the other hand, even adult black men worked fewer hours per week, approximating the work norms for free labor rather than slave labor.

Planters also turned to recruiting immigrant labor for the field work in the South. Agents were sent to Europe, but with little success. Immigrant Chinese were brought onto the plantations, but this also failed, as the Chinese soon found better jobs on the railroads or as independent truck farmers (Mandle, 1978). Something new had to be tried, and any new arrangement would have the purpose of keeping ex-slaves in southern agriculture as labor and preventing their mobility to new jobs and opportunities, either in the South or elsewhere in the nation. This new arrangement would be *farm tenancy*, especially *sharecropping*.

With tenancy, a plantation was divided into two major sections: one owned and farmed by the owner and the remainder farmed by tenants. Tenant lands were subdivided into smaller farms, each worked by tenant families. There were no more slave quarters, for each family lived on its own section away from others. Also gone was the direct and constant supervision by bosses, for each family farmed its own fields without overseers and drivers of the slave years. The arrangement gave black families more independence, and families could work together in their own fields. Each tenant got 30 to 50 acres at either a fixed rent or in a share of the crop. Sharecropping was far more popular; about 72 percent of the black tenants were sharecroppers and the rest renters (Ransom and Sutch, 1977). The tenant and owner typically split the crop in half, and thus tenants received their yearly earnings in December after the harvest. During the year, tenants bought their provisions and supplies from either the plantation store or a rural merchant, paying off these debts plus interest from 30 to 70 percent at the end of the year (Ransom and Sutch, 1977).

Moreover, planters and other employers used work fines to supplement the labor supply. "A black man found guilty of vagrancy or any trivial offense... would be fined instead of jailed, and any planter who paid his fine would have the right to the black man's labor until he had worked out the amount advanced" (Henri, 1975:28). This "working-out" often took months, even years, and the system was so popular for employers that they showed up at courts regularly on Monday mornings to pay fines of black men rounded up over the weekend.

Up to 1900, nearly 90 percent of the nation's black population was locked into tenancy or domestic service at the bottom of the southern labor hierarchy. African American tenants did move from plantation to plantation at the end of the year; it is estimated that one-third moved each year either voluntarily or because of eviction (Mandle, 1978). They moved from one tenancy to another, from one plantation to another, rather than moving out of tenancy and into other opportunities. Very few blacks became independent farmers, owning and farming their own land, because they did not have the money to buy or rent land and other property. Very few became skilled workers in southern industry and urban trades. Very few migrated to the North and the industrial jobs there, which were being filled by European immigrants. Fewer still went west as homesteaders. Nor were black children being educated. Jim Crow laws buttressed these barriers.

With the passage of Jim Crow legislation in the 1880s and 1890s blacks were disfranchised in southern states, segregated in public accommodations and on common carriers, and curtailed in their access to due process of law. With the Plessy v. Ferguson decision of the U.S. Supreme Court in 1896, they were also segregated in public education (Miller, 1967). Disfranchisement was accomplished in a number of ways. There were poll taxes, excluding poor blacks from voting; grandfather clauses as a voting requirement, limiting the vote to only those whose grandfathers had the vote prior to the 14th and 15th Amendments, which gave voting rights to blacks; and literacy and understanding requirements, meaning that voters had to interpret passages of the Constitution to the satisfaction of white southern election officials before being allowed to vote. Black Codes in southern states restricted the entry of blacks into jobs other than tenancy and domestic service. For example, black artisans were prohibited by vagrancy laws from traveling town to town. Labor recruiters from the North were restricted in recruiting southern blacks by false-pretense and anti-enticement laws (Mandle, 1978). African Americans were made powerless, in a word, and set up as targets for white hostility, which also helped keep in check any black challenge to the racial caste system.

The effect of this racial caste system showed up in the divergence of blacks from the trends in the larger American society (cf. Bonacich, 1975; Fogel and Engerman, 1974; Johnson, 1939; Sowell, 1975; Spero and Harris, 1931). After the Civil War, black life expectancy actually declined by 10 percent, black morbidity increased by 20 percent, and the gap between the wages of blacks and whites in comparable occupations grew. In 1880 for the first time a decline was noted in the absolute number of black artisans, although at this time the black population was growing. African Americans were becoming more concentrated than ever in agrarian labor and domestic service. By 1900, 58.3 percent of the gainfully employed black males in the country were engaged in agriculture and another 23.7 percent were employed in domestic and personal service (Schmid and Nobbe, 1965). Spero and Harris (1931:33) summarized the effects of this period on the black worker: "The emancipation of the slaves in the perspective of the labor movement produced the following results. The major portion of the Negro labor supply was shunted away from the labor movement and industrial employment into agriculture and domestic service." Thus, after emancipation blacks diverged from the trend in the larger society toward industrial work and settlement on the frontier, and blacks lost ground to other immigrant groups.

Moreover, the southern economy stagnated after the Civil War, and thus black tenants were trapped in poverty. Per capita income in the South was 50 percent of that in the North in 1900 (Ransom and Sutch, 1977). Between 1880 and 1900 per capita income in the Cotton South grew at less than 1 percent per year. Up to 1920 labor productivity in cotton was less than half that in wheat and 60 percent that in corn. All these figures mean that the South was poor, and black tenants in particular were the poorest. Sharecropping meant little incentive to make productive improvements in farming, for the landowners had to make such investments but share one-half of the profits with their tenants. Moreover, the South did not diversify its economy into rapid industrialization, as did the North in this era.

> In 1865 emancipation from chattel slavery permitted black Americans one kind of freedom…. They gained a degree of independence that was significantly greater than they were allowed in bondage. Yet this freedom was incomplete…. blacks received no freedom dues; land distribution was aborted and the blacks were forced to begin their lives as free men and women without money, without tools, without work animals, without assets of any kind. Their…freedom was under constant attack by the dominant white society determined to preserve racial inequalities. The economic institutions established in the post-emancipation era effectively operated to keep the black population a landless agricultural labor force, operating tenant farms with a backward…technology. What little income was generated in excess of the bare essentials was exploited by monopolistic credit merchants (Ransom and Sutch, 1977:198).

The triangle of capital, white labor, and black labor was the shape of the forces behind the formation of the racial caste system in the

South. Before the Civil War, planters had been in the position to undercut both white and free black workers with cheaper slave labor. However, the situation changed after the war. The planters lost much of their power, for they had suffered a military defeat, the South was occupied by Yankees, and the franchise had been extended to labor, black and white. Du Bois (1935) likened the Reconstruction era to a dictatorship of the proletariat. Of course, the war had been a disaster for the entire South, not just for the planters, and southern conservatives were aware of the widespread desperation. According to Cash (1960:176), the planter class read the times in these terms:

> . . . that the South was hurrying fatally, was indeed already distinctly coming into a time when there wouldn't be room enough on the plantation to take care of both the main body of the blacks and this always multiplying army of white candidates—when these whites would be hurled, not only into competition with these blacks, but into the most naked and brutal competition—into a struggle to the death for the means of subsistence.

"Who could not see, in a word, that here was chaos?" Cash asked.

Chaos was certainly evident in race relations: the lynching, burning, beating, and shooting of blacks were commonplace during the era. The Ku Klux Klan and other organizational versions on the same racist theme were on the rise. "De Ku Klux, dey was a-ridin' de country continually, and de niggers dey scared plumb sick by dem tall white lookin' haunts with dey hosses all white with de sheets. And some say dey just come outen dey graves and a-lookin' for niggers to take back with 'em de daylight come" (Yetman, 1970:80). There were 1,449 lynchings in the South between 1882 and 1903, and over 83 percent of the victims were black (Mandle, 1978).

The conviction grew in the minds of the southern leadership that the resolution lay in progress, in the Yankee formula of industrialization: "Let us introduce the factory in force. Let us, in particular, build cotton mills, here in the midst of the cotton fields. Let us build a thousand mills—and more than a thousand mills, and erect the South into a great industrial and commercial empire" (Cash, 1960:177). With industry came the compromise between southern capital and white labor, and the relegation of blacks to a class of agrarian laborers and domestic servants. For both white capital and labor, some class interests were served by this compromise, while it was black labor that lost the most in the process. Both parties in the compromise had ideal outcomes in mind.

The white landowners sought the cheapest possible agrarian labor, and in those days that meant black labor. However, the landowners could not forge anew their historical alliance with black labor against white workers. African Americans were no longer the private property of planters and were free to enter into alliances of their own making. A Populist alliance of free slaves and poor whites was particularly feared by the white landowners. Such an alliance was a serious threat to their political control of the South in the late nineteenth century, when labor, black and white, might have gotten the upper hand in the southern class struggle. Black and white labor had to be divided if capital was to stay in control. In other words, capital was as concerned with the Populist alliance as with racial antagonism and possible chaos, and the powerful landowners eventually turned to the white poor with a deal.

White labor sought at least some protection against its displacement by cheaper black labor, and in some quarters it hoped for nothing less than a class revolution in the South. In addition to the release of 4 million slaves, the ranks of white labor had been swelled as the yeomanry were forced into wage labor by the economic catastrophe that followed the war. Cash (1960) located the quandary of the small farmers in the lack of capital in the South, which resulted in the crop-lien system, credit arrangements with "supply merchants" that all too often brought bankruptcy and the dispossession of their land. According to Ransom and Sutch (1977), these supply merchants had territorial monopolies on goods and credit throughout the cotton South, and they locked farmers into a dependency on cotton as a cash crop to service their debts: "... farmers had no alternative but to accede to the merchants' demand that they grow cotton to repay their debts. Farmers soon found that this practice locked them into the continued need for credit to begin each new season. The merchant had been quick to seize an opportunity to prevent a shift to greater grain production" (p. 165). White workers and small farmers were in a desperate condition and in an ugly mood, and capital had to compromise with these poor whites.

Outside of agriculture, whites took up positions in the mills and in unionized trades or otherwise came to monopolize the better jobs in the labor hierarchy of the South. Most of the labor for the southern cotton mills was obtained from "two classes, the tenant farmers and the mountaineers, as well as from the lowest class, known as *poor whites*" (Hawk, 1934:479). At the close of the Civil War five out of every six artisans in the South (83 percent) were black, but by 1900 their numbers had been reduced to approximately 5 percent (Landry, 1977). Some whites became an aristocracy of labor in the new industrial order of the South, while others located on the land, either as peasant proprietors or, like blacks, agrarian tenants (Vance, 1939). It is easy to exaggerate the movement of whites into southern industry. While industry did expand in the South after the war, manufacturing employed only 6.5 percent of the region's labor force in 1900 (Ransom and Sutch, 1977). African Americans remained bereft of land and largely excluded from industrial work. "In 1890, when the Census Bureau first gathered data on Negro occupations, almost 90 percent of Negro workers were engaged in agriculture or domestic and personal service" (Broom and Glenn, 1965:107).

This was the deal southern capital gave poor whites. African Americans were forced to the bottom of the region's labor hierarchy, disfranchised and pushed out of the southern political arena, and segregated in public services, including education. Du Bois (1935:611) saw the meaning of the end of Reconstruction for black people in their relationship to the land: "The German and English and French serf, the Italian and Russian serf, were, on emancipation, given definite rights in the land. Only the American Negro slave was emancipated without such rights and in the end this spelled for him the continuation of slavery." The entrapment of blacks in agricultural and domestic service continued into the twentieth century in a racial caste system that served the interests of both capital and white labor. As white labor evolved into industrial work and land proprietorship it realized some security against the economic threat of cheaper black labor, although poor whites did not get the upper hand in the class struggle with southern capital. It was the landowners and rural merchants who benefited the most; the former kept their cheap black labor and gave the southern industrialists (many of whom were Yankees) the higher priced white labor, and the latter profited from exorbitant interest rates and inflated prices on goods. Moreover, they broke the Populist alliance between black and white labor, and the "Bourbon Democrats," as Key (1940) called the political party of the landowners, thereby maintained their political and economic control over the South.

There were several reasons external to the South for the failure of Reconstruction. One is that the United States began a venture in international colonialism late in the nineteenth century, using racism as it did. For example, the United States took control of the Philippines after the Spanish-American War (Chapter 14). This use of racism represented a moral corruption of northern liberals, the political force behind Reconstruction, a hypocrisy that southern conservatives turned to their advantage. Most importantly, however, immigrant labor in the North was opposed to the migration of black labor out of the South, fearing that black labor would undermine their economic position, as slave labor had been detrimental to white workers in the South. Thus landowners in the South were left free to virtually reinstate slavery; there was no effective intervention by a more powerful outside party.

Sharecroppers in the post–Civil War South often did the same
kind of work in the same fields they worked on as slaves.

FIGURE 10.2 PERCENTAGE OF AMERICANS 14 YEARS OLD AND OLDER CLASSIFIED AS ILLITERATE, BY RACE, 1870–1969

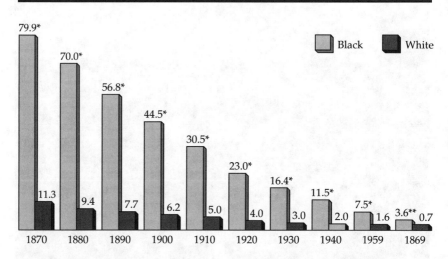

Source: *Historical Statistics of the United States: Colonial Times to 1970.* Washington, DC: Bureau of the Census, 1976.

Scientific racism (Social Darwinism) became a popular ideology regarding racial inferiority during this era (Chapter 4). This conveniently justified the racial caste system as it added to the irrational frenzy of southern racism. Nevertheless, violence and cruelty toward blacks occurred in the South because it was allowed, and it was allowed because it served the rational ends of the compromise between the planters and poor whites. All along the line, according to Woodward (1966:81), "signals were going up to indicate that the Negro was an approved object of aggression. These 'permissions-to-hate' came from sources that had formerly denied such permission." This reinforced the caste status of blacks and thus satisfied the rational interests of the planters and white workers. Sowell (1975:48) commented on the effect of the caste system on black history:

> The economic realities of white land ownership, near-monopoly of technical and business skills, and control of financial institutions meant that blacks had to work for whites on whatever terms were available. A form of sharecropping came into being in which the sharecropper was kept perpetually in debt to the local merchants. . . and so tied to the soil in de facto peonage. Severe vagrancy laws and harsh enforcement by local police and courts made it very difficult

376

for many Negroes to get free even momentarily and to change their occupations.

The caste system meant also educational deprivation for blacks, most of whom lived in the South. The majority of African Americans were illiterate in the nineteenth century, and the rates of illiteracy among blacks far exceeded those of whites (see Figure 10.2). Only 31 percent of blacks 5 through 20 years of age were enrolled in school in 1900, compared to 54 percent of the country's white population. About 15 percent of the education budget in southern states went to black schools (Henri, 1975). The significance of the inequality of educational services offered to blacks in the past century would become manifest later, as the nation's labor needs moved toward mental, white-collar work and blacks had to make up the tremendous gap between their educational level and that of other groups.

Between 1880 and 1915, 1 million blacks migrated to the urban South and were 30 percent of the region's urban population (Jones, 1985). "Unlike their sharecropping counterparts, urban black women had to rely almost exclusively on wage-labor.... Most of these women— girls and married, separated, or widowed mothers—toiled either as domestic servants or laundresses" (Jones, 1985:113).

> A woman would usually collect clothes on Monday from two or three families. She set up a large pot in the yard of her house and instructed the children to help her draw water. The clothes had to be boiled in the pot, scrubbed on a washboard, rinsed, starched, wrung out, hung up, and ironed.... On Saturday she would deliver the clothes and, she hoped, collect her money (Jones, 1985:125–126).

Black women rose at 5 A.M. to get to work as domestic servants in white homes. These women also took in boarders and did seasonal farm work in order to get by. Black men in the urban South were confined to low-paying and occasional work, excluded from labor unions, and targets of white prejudice. Middle-class black men were in skilled trades or were entrepreneurs, and the women worked as teachers and dressmakers.

This is not to say that black people at this time had no resources of their own and that there was neither integrity nor sweetness in their lives. There were a viable black community, a subsociety, and a subculture. African American subculture continued to evolve as an essentially oral, folk tradition, along the lines it had followed during slavery. It celebrated and soothed the soul, giving a melancholy meaning to the economic reality of black life in the South, and it continued to cross the race line into the larger world as entertainment and an art form. The black subsociety included a wide network of interlocking institutions—benevolent societies, fraternal associations, burial societies, cultural groups, and, most importantly, churches and schools. After emancipation, and with financial help from white philanthropists, black people established a network of colleges, including Fisk, Howard, and Tuskegee, which have trained the bulk of the black middle class well into the present century (Sowell, 1975). African American scholars in this era made important technical and cultural contributions to American life, achievements often personified by George Washington Carver. The black church helped its parishioners, mostly common people, face a harsh reality:

> A primary function of the church was to nourish and maintain the souls of black folk by equating them with the essence of humanness. Religion was molded into an adaptive mode of resistance to the dehumanizing oppression, degradation, and suffering of slavery. The black church developed as the institution which counteracted such forces by promoting self-worth and dignity, viable identity, and by providing help in overcoming fear (Holt, 1972:189).

There was also the black family, of course, and all these institutions—family, fraternal organizations, mutual aid societies, schools, and churches—constituted a community in which people came to understand the meaning of their life.

African American couples became legally married after the Civil War, registering for marriage in the same proportion as whites (Gutman, 1976). Freed slaves also moved throughout the South searching for previously separated family members. Multiple marriages in cases of separation during slavery were settled at this time. Blacks began to marry at younger ages, with the intention of establishing their own households (Tolnay, 1984). The average black family remained intact, with both a husband and wife, but in cities nuclear families increasingly lived with other relatives and unrelated boarders, which was obviously an economic adjustment.

An exodus of blacks out of the South after the Civil War might have been expected, but such a migration did not materialize until the twentieth century. Cheap and plentiful land was available in the West as a result of the Homestead Act, and the North was just entering a period of rapid industrial growth (Chapter 6). There were attempts to resettle slaves by the Bureau of Refugees, Freedmen, and Abandoned Lands, for instance, but these efforts failed for lack of necessary support. Indeed, there was active resistance in many northern and western states against any migration of freed slaves into those areas (Bonacich, 1975). Instead, the opportunities elsewhere in the country were taken up by immigrants from Europe and Asia, and it was not until European and Asian immigration had virtually stopped in the twentieth century that blacks moved out of the South.

The failure of the resettlement of freed slaves is possibly the most significant nonevent in African American history. In the South, where they stayed, blacks were essentially trapped in an historical cul de sac as a result of the compromise between southern capital and white labor. Unlike other immigrant groups, blacks did not benefit from the union movement for industrial labor until much later in the twentieth century. While blacks remained on the land in the South, they never came to own much of it, and many of them were caught in debt peonage. Thus in the early thirties Charles Johnson heard this tale from a black tenant in Macon County, Alabama:

> Last year I drawed $10 to the plow [meaning $10 a month for four to six months for each 20 acres cultivated] but I ain't getting but $7 this year. I rents the whole place [400 acres] and then subrents it, and pays 4 bales of cotton for rent. But I don't never make nothing offen it. Didn't clear nothing last year. I paid out $200 last year. Interest steps on me time I pay my rent [for money borrowed from the bank] and interest cost 15 cents on the dollar. I haven't made nothing since 1927. I clears $210 then and ain't cleared nothing since. I got 21 cents for cotton that year (Johnson, 1934:110).

Through the nineteenth century blacks were the majority of the labor force in the rural South, from 71 percent in 1860 to approximately 50 percent in 1900, but they never owned more than a small fraction of the region's farms, no more than 6 percent (Vance, 1939), and these were typically small operations on marginal land. Furthermore, there was little in the way of a class of black businessmen in southern cities, although there were prosperous black entrepreneurs in several northern cities (Sowell, 1975). Thus black labor was almost without exception at the mercy of more powerful parties in the economic and political arena, and these parties had agreed to establish a racial caste system.

Du Bois (1935:626) summarized the larger meaning of the failure of Reconstruction:

> The white capitalist of the South saw a chance of getting rid of the necessity of treating with and yielding to the voting power of fully half the laboring class. It seized this opportunity, knowing...that the United States, instead of marching forward through the preliminary revolution by which the petty bourgeois and the laboring class armed with the vote were fighting the power of capital, was disfranchising a part of labor and on the other hand allowing great capital a chance for enormous expansion in the country. And this enormous expansion got its main chance through the thirty-three electoral votes which the counting of the full black population in the South gave to

that section. It was only necessary now that this political power of the South should be used in behalf of capital and not for the strengthening of labor and universal suffrage. This was the bargain of 1876.

In the nineteenth century, great changes occurred in American society. Indian land was expropriated, the frontier was settled by immigrant groups, and the industrial base of the nation was built. All of these were important elements in the larger process of societal change. These changes largely bypassed African Americans, however, resulting in their divergence. Most blacks did not resettle on the frontier, nor did they migrate north and into industrial work. Instead, they stayed in the South, where, in the context of a larger class struggle they were forced into a caste of propertyless agrarian workers and domestic servants. Black people were excluded from the modernization of American society, in other words, and this is the essential meaning of the failure of Reconstruction from our perspective.

Were black people locked into a racial caste everywhere in the country at this time? This is an interesting question, for it makes us wonder about exceptions to the national history described above. Let us look at one local history of black people around the turn of the century, for we see in it an exception to racial caste.

This local history took place in south-central Iowa between 1880 and 1915 (Schwieder, Hraba, and Schwieder, 1987). This part of Iowa was rich in coal deposits and thus dotted with coal mining communities. Two of these communities, Muchakinock and Buxton, were managed and operated by the Consolidation Coal Company, a subsidiary of the Chicago and Northwestern Railroad. In 1881 the Consolidation Coal Company brought black people from Virginia, primarily from Charlottesville and Staunton, to break a strike by white miners in Muchakinock. The company continued to recruit blacks as miners, and blacks were between 37 and 66 percent of Muchakinock's population between 1881 and 1900.

In 1900 the company moved its mining operation further south and west to Buxton, and Muchakinock's black population moved as well. In the South, black people were a caste at the bottom of the class structure, working as sharecroppers or domestic servants. The class structure of Buxton had the company manager on top, followed by business and professional people, skilled workers and mine foremen, and miners. Except for company managers, who were always white, blacks were proportionately represented in all these economic classes. The black population of Buxton ranged from 55 percent in 1905 to 40.4 percent in 1915. About one-half of the town's doctors and lawyers, one-half of its school teachers, and one-half of the miners were black. The richest man in Buxton was black; he owned meat stores and farms and was a mule buyer for the company. In the mines, blacks and whites worked side by side and were paid equal wages. In short, there was no segmented or split labor market by race, and this distinguished Buxton not only from the South but also from northern industrial towns in this era. For example, Bodnar (1977) found ethnic stratification in the steel mills, with both blacks and Slavs on the bottom.

Furthermore, the company assigned housing to blacks and whites on a first-come first-served basis, and thus there was no residential segregation by race within Buxton. Outside of Buxton, however, there was racial segregation, for the Swedes tended to live apart from others. There was no segregation in Buxton's schools; in public services, such as stores, hotels, and restaurants; or on common carriers. A miner's train took miners each morning from Buxton to the mines, and white and black miners were evenly dispersed on the cars of this train. That is, there was no Jim Crow. African Americans developed an elaborate community composed of eight churches, and forty lodges, clubs, musical groups, political associations, and sports teams. Moreover, the company built in Buxton the country's largest black YMCA, complete with tennis courts and a swimming pool. By 1910 blacks were moving out of Buxton, and the town was completely abandoned by 1920 because mining operations had moved again. Buxton illustrates that African Americans did well in the era when a racial caste system was not imposed on them.

SUMMARY

Before the twentieth century, the history of African Americans passed through the stages of slave trade, slavery, and emancipation. An economic history of slavery and the slave trade was emphasized, one that put slavery in the context of the world economy and capitalism on the American frontier. Profits were made in the slave trade, which was only a part of a larger trans-Atlantic trade pattern. Profits were also made in the plantation economy based on slave labor. Our contention was that the profit goal set parameters around the treatment of African slaves by white planters. The political power and social status of the planter class in the Old South reinforced the economic tie between white capital and black labor. In this setting, a slave subculture developed, crystallizing into kinship networks and the African American church.

With emancipation, there were great possibilities for African Americans. These prospects collapsed, however, with the end of Reconstruction, and African American history continued in southern agriculture with tenancy. The economic niche of ex-slaves in tenancy and domestic service was buttressed by the politics of Jim Crow and the Black Codes as well as maintained by violence. The twentieth century started with the migration of African Americans from the rural South to the urban North.

CHAPTER

11

⊘⊘

AFRICAN AMERICANS AND AMERICAN SOCIETY: THE TWENTIETH CENTURY

T he history of African Americans began with the slave trade and slavery. The Civil War ended slavery, but emancipation brought little improvement in the economic and political conditions of African Americans. Jim Crow laws and farm tenancy simply replaced slavery in the South, and they helped solidify a racial caste system. In this chapter, we come to a new era of African American history, one that begins with the migration of black people to the North early in the twentieth century. In the North, too, African Americans faced racial barriers, if not the obvious signs of Jim Crow. The chapter continues through the civil rights movement to the present accommodation of African Americans in the larger society.

THE GREAT MIGRATION

Between 1910 and 1970 there was a great migration of African Americans from the South to the urban North and West. In 1910, almost 90 percent of the African Americans in the nation lived in the South. By 1970 the percentage had fallen to only 52 percent, and today the majority live in the nation's cities. This represents a significant migration during which African Americans moved not only regionally, but also moved off the land and into cities. In the process, African Americans have evolved from agrarian and domestic work toward industrial blue-collar and white-collar work.

383

Two million African Americans migrated north from the South between 1900 and 1930 (Jones, 1985). This migration slowed during the Great Depression, but then picked up again in the 1940s. "Black migration from the six plantation states [North Carolina, South Carolina, Georgia, Alabama, Mississippi, and Louisiana] during the 1940s totaled in excess of one million, a level almost three times that of the 1930s decade..." (Mandle, 1978:85). Another 1.5 million African Americans migrated from the South in the next two decades. The percentage of African Americans living in the South declined from 89 percent in 1910 to 77 percent in 1940 to only 52 percent in 1970. Broom and Glenn (1965:159–160) described this migration in some detail:

> During the decade following 1910, the great migration of Negroes from the rural South began with the push of a depression in Southern agriculture and the pull of new opportunities for industrial employment in the North.... World War I reduced immigration [of Europeans] and increased the demand for new workers, thus creating a labor vacuum into which thousands of Southern workers could move. The northward migration subsided during the depression of 1920–1921, resumed by 1924 when the heavy flow of European immigrants was permanently stopped, and subsided again during the Great Depression of 1929–1939. The Negro exodus from the South reached a new high during World War II and the period of postwar prosperity, but in this later migration large numbers of Negroes joined the movement to the West.

Prior to 1910, African American migration was from farm to city within the South, with secondary streams of black migrants to Kansas and Oklahoma, for example. After 1910, and especially after 1916, black migration turned to the North, particularly to northern cities. The states with the biggest increases in black population were New York, Illinois, New Jersey, and Pennsylvania, and the cities were New York City, Chicago, Detroit, and Philadelphia (Johnson and Campbell, 1981). The migrants tended to move due north from their southern origins, that is, one stream up the Atlantic Coast to the Northeast, another from the mid-South to the North-Central region, and a third along the Mississippi River from the South to the Midwest (Johnson and Campbell, 1981). A typical pattern was for an individual or family to move off a farm into a nearby town, then, later, to a larger southern city, and finally move out of the region into a northern city (Bodnar, et al., 1982).

African Americans were first pulled into the industrial North in connection with World War I and the cessation of European immigration, and only after World War II did they move in significant numbers to the West. Most African American migrants to the West were from the trans-Mississippi South, particularly Louisiana and Texas.

This migration north has been likened to the crossing of the river Jordan sung about in Negro spirituals, or the passing over to the Promised Land. Detroit was a rather gray Jordan, and the entire North was a somewhat cheerless and certainly cold Promised Land. But it was economics that brought African Americans to the North; there were jobs in Mr. Ford's place in Detroit, for example. Henry Ford announced in 1914 that none of his workers would earn less than $5 per day. The same year he began to hire African Americans, and word of this spread among poor African Americans throughout the South (Jones, 1963). African American migrants experienced increases in income between 50 and 100 percent with their move north. They entered many of the old heavy industries in the North: steel in Pittsburgh and Gary, metal trades in Detroit, brick making in Newark, and meat packing in Chicago and East St. Louis. African Americans also entered coal mining in Pennsylvania, food processing in Chicago, longshore work on the eastern seaboard, and numerous other trades in the nation's industrial order. In this way, African American history began to converge with the trend toward an industrial nation

African Americans in the South were contacted by labor recruiters representing northern employers, they received letters from friends and relatives who had already gone north, and black newspapers in the North also spread the word. Robert Abbott, editor of the *Chicago Defender*, had a network of Pullman porters on the railroads, and African American entertainers spread the newspaper, with its job advertisements and editorials about work in the North, throughout the South. The newspaper's circulation grew from 10,000 in 1916 to 283,571 in 1920 (Henri, 1975). Between 1910 and 1920, the African American population in Detroit grew by over 600 percent, that of Cleveland by over 300 percent, Chicago by almost 150 percent, and New York by over 66 percent (Henri, 1975).

African American labor was not only pulled into the North, and later into the West, it was also pushed out of the South. The southern compromise that followed emancipation had meant severe social and economic hardship for blacks. African Americans were bypassed in the process of bringing industry to the South; they were disfranchised, segregated in public services, and, in a word, weakened. The racial caste system served the interest of capital and white labor and was maintained as much in lawlessness and violence as it was by the law. There were approximately 100 lynchings in the South each year in the 1880s and 1890s (National Advisory Commission on Civil Disorders, 1968). The North symbolized to southern African Americans personal safety for themselves and their families, schools for their children, and some semblance of dignity, as well as economic opportunity (Palmer, 1967).

Economic factors were nonetheless the primary forces for pushing African Americans out of the South. Around World War I, a combination of inflated farm prices and damage done to cotton by the boll weevil freed African American tenant farmers from debt peonage in one sense and forced them off the land in another. Many fled North. However, it was not until after World War II that the push of African American labor out of the South took on truly mass proportions. According to Wilhelm (1971:182), the full impact of industrial technology was not felt by the African American farm worker until the postwar era, when "'factories in the fields' took over the production of farm produce and displaced the Negro farm hand in the process." More specifically:

> A virtual revolution took hold in Southern agriculture because there was a dramatic shift from pre-industrial to industrial technology. For the 20-year period from 1940 to 1960, the farm labor dropped from 4.2 million to 1.7 million; crop acreage declined from 111 million to 81 million for the same time. Average farm size increased by 1960 to twice the acreage of the 1930s, but in spite of the expansion, owners employed less than half the amount of labor required twenty years earlier (Wilhelm, 1971:183).

After the Civil War cotton production meant sharecropping with mule-power for planting and cultivation, and then hand-picking the crop. The second stage, in the twentieth century, was the mechanization of the pre-harvest process, particularly on a planter's section, and the introduction of the tractor in land preparation. In the third stage, mechanization was completed except for cotton picking. The last stage was the mechanization of cotton picking (Mandle, 1978). In 1958, only 27 percent of the Mississippi Delta cotton crop was harvested by machine, but 81 percent was harvested by machine in 1964 (Johnson and Campbell, 1981). African American labor in southern agriculture was becoming obsolete in the twentieth century, due to the mechanization of agriculture, which pushed African American farm workers to the North and the West.

The old southern formula was behind the entry of African American labor into the industrial North around World War I. Industrial capital in the North sought in the African American worker a more tractable and cheaper alternative to white labor, which was becoming increasingly militant and organized into labor unions. That is, capital sought to counter the growing labor movement by bringing African American workers north. Moreover, with the end to mass European immigration later in the 1920s, migrating southern African Americans became northern capital's last alternative to high-priced union labor. African Americans were specifically used as strikebreakers in many

TABLE 11.1 STRIKES IN WHICH AFRICAN AMERICANS WERE USED AS STRIKEBREAKERS, 1916–1934

Industry	Year	Locality
Aluminum	1917	East St. Louis
Brick making	1923	Newark
Building	1919	New York
Coal mining	1922	Pennsylvania
	1925	Northern West Va.
	1927	Western Pa.
	1928	Ohio
	1934	Birmingham
Corn refining	1919	Chicago
Fig and date packing	1926	Chicago
Garment industry	1917	Chicago
	1920	Chicago
Hotel industry	1918	Chicago
Longshore work	1916	Baltimore
	1923	New Orleans
	1929	Boston
Meat packing	1916	East St. Louis
	1919	Chicago
	1921	Chicago
	1921	Widespread
Metal trades	1921	Detroit
Railroads	1916	Chicago
	1922	Unspecified
Restaurants	1920	Chicago
Steel	1919	Widespread

Source: Edna Bonacich, "Advanced Capitalism and Black/White Relations," *American Sociological Review*, Vol. 41, February 1976, p. 41. Reprinted by permission.

industries and at several locations in the North and Midwest (see Table 11.1), and generally the intention was for African Americans to displace unionized white workers (Bonacich, 1976; Spero and Harris, 1931). Early in the century, for example, employers brought black workers north in cattle cars to break a strike in the meat-packing industry in East St. Louis, Illinois (Jones, 1963). Such a scene was not uncommon in industrial centers throughout the North and Midwest (Table 11.1).

To many white workers, southern blacks appeared to be the lackeys of capital, scabs used to destroy the white worker. Southern blacks were equally suspicious of white workers and tended to avoid involvement in labor unions. Instead, there was a paternalistic and protective relationship between white capital and black labor, which was reminiscent of arrangements in the Old South between planter and field hand. Employers often formed company unions for black workers, and black preachers were known to take the occasion of a Sunday sermon to advocate the alliance of black labor with capital against white labor. Competition between white and black workers in this era can, however, be overstated. Many black workers did join with whites in labor unions or took only jobs that had been vacated by whites. Moreover, many of the strikebreakers were white, themselves migrants from the rural South. African Americans were not the only migrants serving as replacements for unionized workers; it just seemed that way.

In the 1920s, the Union Stock Yards in Chicago had 101 packers employing over 33,000 workers (Herbst, 1932). The old immigrants from northern and western Europe had been the initial workers in the yards, and they were later replaced by immigrants from southern and eastern Europe. Blacks were brought into the Union Stock Yards as strikebreakers in 1894, 1904, and 1921, and during the 1920s up to 12,000 African Americans were working at the yards. The pattern was for black men and women to take jobs on the bottom of the labor hierarchy in the packing industry. For example, 68 percent of the black men were common laborers, but only 38 percent of the white workers were at the bottom. Black women at one packer were excluded from the pharmaceutical and gut-string departments, all clean, light, and comfortable work (Herbst, 1932). "In the casing room, where working conditions are poor and wages low, Negro women predominate..." (Herbst, 1932:76). This segmented labor market occurred in other industries as well (Bodnar, 1977).

RACIAL CONFLICT AND CASTE

The competition between white and black labor in the North, some of it real and some of it fancied, brought racial conflict in the North just as it had in the South. Race riots were evident as early as the 1860s in Cincinnati and New York City, for instance. But it was after the turn of the century, with the acceleration of black migration North, that race riots took place with some regularity in the region. Around World War I, there were race riots in Chicago, Philadelphia, Washington, D.C., Omaha, and East St. Louis, Illinois (see Box 11.1). The 1919 riot in Chicago left almost a thousand people homeless and 38 dead. Riots occurred again in connection with black migration during World War II, in Harlem, Detroit, and throughout the country.

BOX 11.1   1917 RACE RIOT IN EAST ST. LOUIS

East St. Louis, a city of about 75,000 situated across the Missis-sippi River from St. Louis, was noted for huge industrial plants, including chemicals, aluminum, slaughtering and meat-packing. The whole city in 1917 was an industrial slum....

...the Negro population about doubled from 1910 to 1917, when it numbered 10,600, and whites whose neighborhoods were being encroached on feared further migration of southern blacks.

...although black migrants were not snatching jobs away from whites, labor organizers encourage white workers to be-lieve they were, in order to induce the white workers to join unions for protection.... Further complicating the situation, it seems pretty clear that employers sometimes gave job prefer-ences to blacks, because they were not nor were they likely to become union men. Worst of all for any sort of racial harmony, employers in some cases did bring in blacks as strikebreakers, and union men instigated by union leaders came to think of all blacks as strikebreakers who weakened the unions.

Tensions kept building up as more and more blacks arrived. In 1916–17, about 2,400 blacks migrated to East St. Louis. In July of 1917 the riot broke out. Both whites and blacks had guns. Days and nights of violence ended with eight whites and at least thirty-nine blacks dead, over a hundred blacks shot or mangled into helplessness, and perhaps six thousand blacks left homeless by the burning of the black neighborhood.

Source: From *Black Migration: Movement North, 1900–1920*, pp. 264–266, by Flo-rette Henri. Copyright © 1975 by Florette Henri. Used by permission of Doubleday, a division of Bantam Doubleday Dell Publishing Group, Inc.

The competition between black and white labor was not settled by street violence in northern cities, however. There was an accom-modation between black and white workers in the North that was not unlike the old southern caste system. The labor market was seg-mented along racial lines. Whites took the better white-collar and blue-collar jobs, leaving vacant for blacks jobs at the bottom of the labor hierarchy:

During and since the war [World War II], hundreds of thousands of new jobs have been created at intermediate and upper levels, and many Negroes have been able to move up without displacing whites. Between 1940 and 1960, the total number of employed white-collar workers increased by nearly 12 million, or 81 percent, while the total employed labor force increased by only 37 percent. Hundreds of thousands of white workers have moved into new higher-level jobs leaving vacancies at intermediate levels that could be filled by Negroes (Broom and Glenn, 1965:108).

In white-collar work, whites were the proprietors, professionals, and managers, while most blacks in white-collar work were employed in sales and as clerks. Blue-collar work was also stratified; whites monopolized the skilled trades and positions of foremen, while blacks became operatives and laborers (Schmid and Nobbe, 1965). This was the trend until recently. In the twentieth century, African American workers also began to lose positions in domestic service because of labor-saving appliances in homes (Bodnar, et al., 1982; Jones, 1985; Lieberson, 1980). More African American families turned to welfare, and men left their families so that their wives and children could qualify for it. Twenty percent of the African American households in northern cities were female-headed in 1930, but, by 1940, 25 percent were (Jones, 1985). As a consequence, African Americans fell behind European immigrants from eastern and southern Europe.

The segmented labor market in the industrial cities of the North was accompanied by racial residential segregation. The black ghetto in Chicago, for example, took time to emerge, but as neighborhoods became black they also deteriorated because of landlord neglect. During peak periods of black migration, 1916–1918 in Chicago, "landlords no longer had to lower rents or make any repairs or improvements to fill their by now dilapidated apartments" (Henri, 1975:85). White opposition to the spread of black residence prevented blacks from moving to more desirable housing. Thrown together in the ghetto were respectable families along with gamblers, pimps, and prostitutes. In virtually all urban ghettos, African America families brought lodgers into their homes, and families were increasingly crowded into apartments of one and two rooms (Bodnar, et al., 1982; Gutman, 1976; Henri, 1975).

Although the labor market was racially segmented, African Americas from the South found better jobs in Chicago, and they were relieved by the lack of Jim Crow in Chicago's stores, public transportation, and public facilities. They worked side by side with whites, shopped in the same stores as whites, and jostled with whites on the elevated trains and buses. The color line was much less distinct and degrading than it was in the South. But there was a color line, and it showed in the residential segregation of blacks from whites. While it expanded with new migrants, the "black belt" on Chicago's South

Side was always contained by white resistance to further black encroachment (Drake and Cayton, 1945). The South Side was known as Bronzeville, and it had vitality:

> Stand in the center of the black belt—at Chicago's 47th St. and South Parkway. Around you swirls a continuous eddy of faces—black, brown, olive, yellow, and white.... In the nearby drugstore colored clerks are bustling about.... In most of the other stores, too, there are colored salespeople.... In offices around you, colored doctors, dentists, and lawyers go about their duties.... Two large theaters will catch your eye with their billboards featuring Negro orchestras and vaudeville troops, and the Negro great and near-great of Hollywood. ... If you wander about a bit... you will note that one of the most striking features of the area is the prevalence of churches, numbering 500 (Drake and Cayton, 1945:379–381).

In Bronzeville lived the black upper, middle, and lower classes. The upper class was the social and economic world of doctors, lawyers, school teachers, and business people. Both the upper and middle classes stressed orderly and disciplined family life and church attendance. The upper class had a network of exclusive social clubs and a routine of entertaining with dinner parties, teas, debuts, etc. The middle class was composed of some professional people, but was primarily clerks and service workers. Their core values were having a nice home, raising a family, making something out of their children, and striving to get ahead (Drake and Cayton, 1945).

There was also racial segregation in public education for much of the twentieth century. Despite the decision of the U.S. Supreme Court in 1954 that "rigid and arbitrary separation of the races in the public schools solely on the basis of race is no longer legal" (Simpson and Yinger, 1972:549), the equal opportunity report by Coleman, et al. (1966) found that even in 1965, 80 percent of white children in the nation attended schools that were from 90 to 100 percent white, while around 65 percent of the nation's black children attended schools where 90 percent of the students were black. Furthermore, the research showed that, as a class, black students across the nation scored below whites on academic achievement tests that included standardized measures of verbal and math ability and reading comprehension. As indicators of racial differences in preparation for the skills necessary in white-collar occupations, these tests are related to the racially stratified labor market.

While the factors involved in academic achievement are many and complex, the Coleman Report gave special attention to the impact of racial integration in the schools on the academic achievement of black students:

...the general pattern is an increase in average test performance [for black students] as the proportion of white classmates increases, although in many cases the average for Negro students in totally segregated classes is higher than the average for those in classes where half or less of the students were white (Coleman, et al., 1966:331).

It was also found that black students who attended integrated schools in the early grades showed slightly higher achievement scores than those who attended integrated schools only in the later grades. This relationship, while not strong, held when controlling for the family backgrounds of the students.

With respect to the relationship between the racial composition of classrooms and the academic achievement of black students, Pettigrew (1967:287) proposed that "many of the consequences of interracial classrooms for both Negroes and whites are a direct function of the opportunities such classrooms provide for cross-racial self-evaluation." When black students are accepted by their classmates, are expected to do well academically, and can publicly express their competence before whites, they overcome their sense of futility, raise their academic self-concept, and perform well. Coleman, et al. (1966) concluded that childhood and family experiences primarily accounted for black students' attitudes toward academic achievement. Pettigrew suggested that interracial interaction in classrooms intervenes between family background and black students' attitudes toward education, and the sooner black children are introduced into interracial classrooms the stronger and more positive effect this has on their academic achievement. If this is so, racial segregation in the nation's schools helped perpetuate the racially stratified labor market.

THE BEGINNING OF CONVERGENCE

Nevertheless, the twentieth-century migration of African Americans to the urban North and West was a significant step toward their inclusion into the larger American society. It was the first time that African Americans in significant numbers were included in industrial blue-collar trades and white-collar work. The inclusion was not complete, however; African Americans were still at the lower levels of the labor hierarchy in blue- and white-collar work. But until this migration, and before the middle of the twentieth century, the vast majority of African Americans were far more extensively excluded from the larger American society. Not only were they concentrated in one region of the country, a region which itself lagged behind the rest of the nation, but also they had been restricted to farm labor and domestic service and completely segregated in public education. In the rural

South, African American culture had continued as an oral folk tradition, and the material living conditions of the African American masses remained divergent from those of many citizens of the nation.

However, as African American workers swung into industrial jobs and the lower levels of white-collar work, their material living conditions began to converge with those of other industrial and white-collar workers. Indicators of health, wealth, education, and welfare showed tremendous improvement in the material base of black life in twentieth-century America (Broom and Glenn, 1965; Levitan, et al., 1975; Schmid and Nobbe, 1965; Sowell, 1975). Although these gains were somewhat overshadowed by the even larger gains made by other ethnic groups, such as Asians and Jews, there was improvement nonetheless. African American cultural traditions also changed in the process, and they too converged with those of the larger society.

African American folk traditions were intellectualized, their circulation was increasingly through the printed media rather than by word-of-mouth, and their expression was professionalized in the twentieth century. A Negro press emerged in northern cities that exists to this day; dozens of newspapers and several magazines give testimony to the modernization of African American folk culture. African American art, theater, literature, and music have all become professional pursuits in the cities, where they have been made into consumable products that can be bought by all. For instance, the folk tradition of blues music, which began in slave work songs, became the "race record" in the North. Because of its consumer appeal, the Columbia Record Company roamed the South in a mobile unit to record "people like Barbecue Bob, Peg Leg Howell, Blind Willie Johnson, … Aaron T-Bone Walker, and many other singers who sang what was essentially folk material" (Jones, 1963:116–117). The works of contemporary African American musicians are now available to virtually everyone in American society.

African American protest too was rationalized along the lines of organizations in the larger society and became structured into voluntary associations like the NAACP, founded in 1909, with full-time directors and professional staffs. NAACP membership grew from 6,000 in 1915 to over 88,000 in 1919 (Henri, 1975). Even the cultural image of African Americans changed. The African American male, for instance, was transformed from the stereotypical field hand to the equally stereotypical street-corner hipster or militant about whom so many books have been written. It was a categorical imperative for these cultural types to have nothing but contempt for the old "Toms" down South. Jones (1963:118) saw the convergence of blacks even in the Great Depression and observed that this convergence brought costs as well as benefits:

A 1933 political cartoon demonstrates the plight of the educated African American during the Great Depression.

The Depression was the first real economic crisis—an economic crisis experienced by the Negro, based on the general fortunes of the entire society. Before the Depression, it is quite easy to see how in the paternalized stratum of American society inhabited by Negroes an economic crisis would be of no great importance. The movement by Negroes into the mainstream of American society had also placed them in the path of an economic uncertainty that they had never known before.

Two important movements emerged from the nation's urban African American community in the 1920s. The first was the Universal Negro Improvement Association (UNIA) led by Marcus Garvey. Marcus Garvey was born in 1887 at St. Ann's Bay in Jamaica and emigrated to New York in 1916. He traveled and spoke throughout the United States that next year, and he established UNIA in New York in 1918. Over the next few years UNIA established branches throughout the country and the world. The membership in Harlem alone was 35,000, and it was over 1 million worldwide (Martin, 1983). Only people of African descent were eligible for membership. UNIA had its own businesses, cooperatives, the Black Star Line Steamship Corporation, Universal African Legions, Black Star Nurses, and its own press. *Negro World*, its weekly newspaper from 1918 to 1933, had a circulation of 200,000 readers in 1920, making it the largest African American newspaper in the country. Garvey spoke on Sunday evenings in Harlem, and his message was essentially one of black nationalism. He told audiences to stop imitating whites and guide their lives by self-reliance and by putting race first. The objectives of UNIA included a universal confraternity among the race, the promotion of race pride, and assistance for the needy of the race. Garvey was convicted of mail fraud in 1923, imprisoned for a time, and deported from the country in 1927. The movement subsequently splintered and declined, and Garvey died in London in 1940.

While Garveyism appealed to the masses, the Harlem Renaissance, the second movement, was intellectual. At the core of this movement were African American writers writing about black America, both urban black America and its roots in Africa, the South, and the West Indies. This movement spread into the visual arts, theater, and music. The writers included Claude McKay, Jean Toomer, Countee Cullen, Langston Hughes, Nella Larsen, George Schuyler, Arna Bontemps, and Zora Neale Hurston (Whitlow, 1973). African American literary organizations were established in several cities, exemplified by the Writers' Guild in New York. On stage, Josephine Baker was the brightest entertainment star in Paris, Paul Robeson began his acting career, and African American musicians by the score were hits the world over. The lyrics of Langston Hughes (1958) in "The Negro Speaks of Rivers," first published in 1921, are an example of the Harlem Renaissance:

I've known rivers:
I've known rivers ancient as the world and older than the flow of
    human blood in human veins.

My soul has grown deep like the rivers.

I bathed in the Euphrates when dawns were young.
I built my hut near the Congo and it lulled me to sleep.
I looked upon the Nile and raised the pyramids above it.
I heard the singing of the Mississippi when Abe Lincoln went down
    to New Orleans, and I've seen its muddy bosom turn all golden
    in the sunset.

I've known rivers:
Ancient, dusky rivers.

My soul has grown deep like the rivers.

Source: From *Selected Poems* by Langston Hughes. Copyright 1926 by Alfred A. Knopf, Inc. and renewed 1954 by Langston Hughes. Reprinted by permission of the publisher.

While African Americans early in the twentieth century were moving toward convergence with the larger society, their divergence was still evident. Fein (1965) found that the median education of non-white adults 25 years and older was 8.2 years in 1960, while that of white adults had reached 8.7 years in 1940, a gap of 20 years. In 1964, the median income of black families was $3,839, but the median income of white families had reached $3,800 in 1951. Black males had a life expectancy of 61.5 years at birth in 1959–61, a level that had been reached by white males in 1931–33. The rate at which black children were born in a hospital in 1962 was reached for whites in 1946, a sixteen-year gap. While black-white occupational gaps were closing, they were still evident. If discrimination against blacks was to end, it would still take several years for these gaps to close (Lieberson and Fuguitt, 1967).

With the migration north, the African American middle class changed. The roots to the African American middle class go back to slaves who were freed before the Civil War and who had established themselves in urban trades and ownership of real estate in both the North and the South. Frazier (1957) identified many of these families as mulattoes, who maintained a rigid social distance between themselves and the African American masses. Segregated from whites and voluntarily separated from the black masses, this class was proud of its culture, refined manners, and genteel ways. A new African American middle class resulted from the migration north, one that virtually replaced this older, mulatto middle class.

The new African American middle class were white-collar workers in occupations ranging from the professions, clerks, and salespeople to craftsmen and foremen. Some were business proprietors with businesses in the African American community, such as beauty parlors, barber shops, and funeral parlors. Most were employees, however. Whereas the status of the old middle class revolved around culture and refinement, status in this new middle class was based on money, or at least the appearance of having money, displayed in conspicuous consumption. Not having any secure place in the larger society, according to Frazier (1957), this class bought expensive homes, furnishings, cars, and clothing and participated in a segregated world of make-believe:

> The homes of many middle-class Negroes have the appearance of museums for the exhibition of American manufacturers and spurious art objects. The objects which they are constantly buying are always on display. Negro school teachers who devote their lives to "society" like to display twenty to thirty pairs of shoes, the majority of which they never wear. Negro professional men proudly speak of two automobiles which they have acquired when they need only one. The acquisition of objects which are not used or needed seems to be an attempt to fill some void in their lives (Frazier, 1957:230–231).

Frazier locates this striving for status through showy consumption in feelings of inferiority and insecurity. "The frustrations that haunt their inner lives" stem from the fact that they cannot escape from being black in America no matter how hard they try. Thus, "their escape into a world of make-believe...leaves them with a feeling of emptiness and futility..." (Frazier, 1957:213). Aside from Frazier's obvious moral indictment, the African American middle class was changing in America, a change that was consistent with the larger change in the nation toward white-collar work.

Racial stratification in the North did not last nearly as long as the old racial caste system had in the South. Beginning with legislation under Roosevelt's New Deal, the alliance of capital and cheaper black labor was assailed by "making it illegal for employers to use blacks as strike-breakers or 'strike insurance,' denying the legitimacy of the company union and taking away the advantage to be had in paying blacks lower wages for longer hours" (Bonacich, 1976:45). Although

397

the intent of this legislation was not immediately realized, it still signaled the start of a new era in northern race relations (see Box 11.2).

☙☙

BOX 11.2 MABEL K. STAUPERS

One black leader, Mabel Keaton Staupers,...executive secretary of the National Association of Colored Graduate Nurses (NACGN), successfully challenged the highly racist top echelons of the U.S. Army and Navy and forced them to accept black women nurses into the military nurses corps during World War II....

Between 1934 and 1940 Stauper's efforts to win for black women nurses unfettered membership in the major professional associations ... had been unsuccessful. Staupers resolved therefore to seize the opportunity created by the war emergency and the increased demand for nurses to project the plight of the black nurse into the national limelight.... Staupers viewed the acceptance of black nurses into the Army and Navy Nurse Corps as critical to the achievement of her major objective, that is, the full integration of black women into American nursing....

Plans to effect the complete integration of black women into the U.S. armed forces unfolded gradually as the war progressed. During the first year of peace time mobilization, 1940–41, Staupers concentrated on preventing the exclusion of black women from the Army and Navy Nurse Corps; once the war began she fought to have abolished the quotas that had been established by the Army. Throughout 1943 and 1944 she challenged the Army's practice of assigning black nurses only to care for German prisoners of war and not to white American soldiers. In addition Staupers cooperated with other groups to ensure that legislative measures proposed in Congress concerning nurses and hospitals contained anti-discrimination clauses....

Frustrated by her inability to persuade the Navy and War Department to abolish quotas completely and to institute plans for the ... integration of black nurses, Staupers resolved to present the case of black nurses to America's First Lady. Shortly after she made contact with Eleanor Roosevelt, the First Lady sent discreet inquiries to Secretary of War Stimson.... She wrote, "I have received several protests lately that, due to the shortage of nurses, the colored nurses be allowed to serve where there is not serious objection to it...."

On January 20, 1945 ... nurses would be accepted into the Army Nurse Corps without regard to race. On January 25, 1945, Admiral Agnew announced that the Navy Nurse Corps was now open to black women....

In 1948 the ANA [American Nurses Association] House of Delegates opened the gates to black membership, appointed a black women nurse as assistant executive secretary in its national headquarters....

Source: Darlene Clark Hine, 1982. "Mabel K. Staupers and the Integration of Black Nurses into the Armed Forces." Pp. 242–255 in John Hope Franklin and August Meier, eds., *Black Leaders of the Twentieth Century.* Urbana: University of Illinois Press.

The immediate effect of the New Deal legislation was to strengthen the hand of labor in its struggle with capital. Bonacich (1976) noted that union membership expanded in the 1930s and up to World War II, and this expansion included a goodly increase in black union membership. But the long-term effect of equalizing the wage rates and general treatment of black and white labor in major industries has been something else again. American capital faced for the first time an alliance between black and white labor, one backed by the federal and some state governments. After World War II capital sought an alternative to expensive union labor, black and white.

One option capital pursued was the relocation of some of its labor tasks overseas, to take advantage of cheap labor outside the United States in the so-called Third World (Bonacich, 1976). This process reversed the historical practice of importing cheap labor into the country and has been referred to as the "runaway shop." The ability of American capital to relocate labor needs overseas was undoubtedly aided by the international position of the United States after World War II, when American political influence made American investments there secure.

Capital also relocated its labor force within the country, generally away from the expensive union labor in the North to cheaper nonunion labor in the South. As the meat-packing industry took up this practice in the 1950s and 1960s, black men in the North lost their jobs, while black women in the South, among others, found employment in the relocated packing operations. Expensive union labor was also displaced by mechanization and automation, and blacks were disproportionately hurt in the process. They were concentrated in jobs with low technological content, in industries that were economically inert, had declining labor needs, and were easily automated (Baron, 1971). At the same time, African Americans by the thousands were being displaced by the mechanization of southern agriculture (Wilhelm, 1971). All of this has meant African American unemployment, according to Edna Bonacich

(1976). Sometime in the 1930s, in connection with the passage of the National Recovery Act in 1933, the unemployment rates of blacks and whites underwent a reversal. Contrary to what is commonly understood, until 1940 white unemployment rates in this nation had always exceeded those of blacks. After 1940, black unemployment began to exceed white jobless rates, and it climbed rapidly to the current two-to-one ratio (Bonacich, 1976:35). As this trend continues, it is black youth who are hurt the most. Inner-city black youth have little access to industries in the suburbs and so are unable to undercut labor costs there and as a consequence they find no work at all.

Little reference is made in Bonacich's argument to active discrimination against black workers, much of it in the skilled trades and white-collar work in the private sector of the economy. This discrimination persisted in northern cities long past the New Deal and World War II. Nevertheless, her argument is insightful; it ties black history to changes in the larger American society, which she sees as on a course of advanced capitalism. The essentials of her argument are illustrated in the life cycle of East St. Louis, Illinois, since World War II.

This city was a meat-packing center and a heavy industrial complex up to the early 1960s. In East St. Louis and throughout the nation, a stockpile of investment capital and personal savings had been accumulated during World War II. These savings created a great postwar demand for consumer goods by the American public, who had been starved for such possessions during the war. People bought cars, homes in the suburbs, appliances, clothing, and meat; the per capita consumption of meat in this country tripled after World War II. All of this created jobs, and there was an economic boom.

Because of this boom, the old plants in East St. Louis, even with their outdated production processes and expensive union labor, were in full production after World War II. East St. Louis was a vibrant place, if a bit corrupt and rough and tumble. It was a good place for a working man and woman to be, and southern African Americans by the hundreds moved into the city. The good times did not last long, however, as plants began moving out of town in the 1950s to avoid antiquated production processes, expensive labor, and "union troubles." Nevertheless, southern African Americans continued to move into East St. Louis. The town "died" as an industrial center in the 1960s, and these people were trapped. Unlike the earlier European immigrants to this city, the African American migrants on the average did not benefit as much from the better days and had less of a chance to prepare their children for technical and professional employment. Today many of them live in East St. Louis, essentially jobless, amid the rubble left from the riots of the 1960s.

Fortunately, unemployment is only part of the current picture of black America. There has been considerable occupational mobility for many African Americans in recent years:

> Blacks moved into better paying and higher status jobs. The proportion employed as managers and administrators, professional and technical workers, and craftsmen and kindred workers—the three highest paying occupations—almost doubled between 1958 and 1973, while the proportion employed in service work, nonfarm, and farm labor—the three lowest paying occupations—fell by one-third. Occupational patterns of whites did not change as much, so that non-whites caught up somewhat (Levitan, et al., 1975:44).

THE CIVIL RIGHTS MOVEMENT

The modern era of the civil rights movement in the United States began in the late 1950s, and the Reverend Martin Luther King, Jr., of the Southern Christian Leadership Conference (SCLC) was its leader in the South and perhaps the entire nation. Martin Luther King, Jr., was a graduate of Morehouse College in Atlanta, Crozer Theological Seminary in Pennsylvania, and Boston University, and was first called to the ministry at Dexter Baptist Church in Montgomery, Alabama. In 1955, he helped organize a boycott of Montgomery's buses after Rosa Parks had refused to go to the back of a bus. The SCLC was founded in 1957 in Atlanta, and Dr. King was chosen as its president. During the Pilgrimage Day in Washington, D.C., May 17, 1957, Dr. King emerged as the nation's premier civil rights leader (Patterson, 1989). His philosophy combined the non-violence of Gandhi, the civil disobedience of Henry David Thoreau, and the social gospel of Christianity. His goals were to end segregation in the South, improve the economic conditions of African Americans and poor people, and guarantee the vote for black people in the South. The last goal was established in the Crusade for Citizenship, begun in 1958, and the objective was to double the black vote within two years. Dr. King's tactics were non-violent protest, relying on peaceful marches, sit-ins, mass rallies, and moral and political persuasion.

A wave of sit-ins at segregated lunch counters swept the South once they had started in Greensboro, North Carolina, in 1960. The SCLC assisted these student protesters in forming their own organization, the Student Nonviolent Coordinating Committee (SNCC). The Congress of Racial Equality (CORE) initiated the freedom rides in 1961–62 throughout the South. Volunteers rode interstate buses and used bus terminals to protest segregation in the buses and bus stations. SNCC later took the lead in the freedom rides, and in November of 1961 the federal government banned segregation in interstate travel.

Dr. King and the SCLC moved their attention to Birmingham, Alabama, in 1963. Birmingham was known as the most segregated town in the South. The issues were segregated public facilities in downtown businesses and facilities such as restaurants, restrooms, and drinking fountains and improved hiring of blacks by local businesses. Dr. King led the first march in Birmingham on Palm Sunday, and then a second on the following Good Friday. He was arrested by the Birmingham police, and spent the weekend in jail. From his cell he responded to complaints from Birmingham's white ministers about his civil disobedience. His reply in "Letter from Birmingham Jail" was that the demonstrations were moral, but their causes in racial segregation and bigotry were not: "It is unfortunate that demonstrations are taking place in Birmingham, but it is even more unfortunate that the city's white power structure left the Negro community with no alternative." "...I am in Birmingham because injustice is here. Just as the prophets ...left their villages and carried their 'thus saith the Lord' far beyond the boundaries of their home towns, and just as the Apostle Paul left his village... and carried the gospel of Jesus Christ to the far corners of the Greco-Roman world, so am I compelled to carry the gospel of freedom beyond my own home town." Children then joined the marches to downtown Birmingham, and the police chief, "Bull" Connor, ordered the fire hoses and police dogs even on them. The news pictures horrified the nation. Finally, in May a truce was established with Birmingham leaders. Segregation in public facilities was to end in ninety days and improved hiring practices and promotions of black employees were to begin in sixty days.

Dr. King and the SCLC then organized the March on Washington in August of 1963. About one-quarter of a million people attended the rally at which Martin Luther King, Jr., gave his "I Have a Dream" address. The federal government subsequently passed the Civil Rights Act of 1964. This act forbade racial discrimination in public places of business; any inequality in public accommodations; and discrimination in state programs receiving federal aid, in labor unions, in employment, and in voting (Scott, 1976). In September of that same year, the 16th Street Baptist Church in Birmingham was bombed on a Sunday leaving four girls dead. Violence was still being used to keep blacks "in their place," a method of intimidation going back to slavery days. Late in 1964, Dr. King accepted the Nobel Peace Prize in Oslo, Norway.

The focus of the civil rights movement in 1965 was on Selma, Alabama. A march from Selma to Montgomery, Alabama, was undertaken on March 7, but once past the Edmund Pettus Bridge at Selma, it was stopped by Alabama law-enforcement officials, and marchers were beaten by the police. A second march led by Dr. King began on March 21 and reached Montgomery on March 25.

Responding to the civil rights movement, Congress passed the Voting Rights Act of 1965, which eliminated all qualifying tests that were discriminatory and gave the Attorney General the power to protect federal registrars in the South. A review of civil rights actions during this period is presented in Box 11.3.

◎◎

BOX 11.3 FEDERAL CIVIL RIGHTS ACTIONS, 1948–1968

1948   President Truman, in Executive Order 9981, directs the Armed Forces to institute equal opportunity and treatment among the races.

1954   The Supreme Court, in *Brown v. Board of Education of Topeka*, rules against segregation of blacks and whites in public schools.

1955   President Eisenhower, in Executive Order 1059, establishes the President's Committee on Government Employment Policy to fight discrimination in employment (replacing the Fair Employment Practices Committee established by President Truman in 1948).

1955   The 1955 Interstate Commerce Commission issues an order banning segregation of passengers on trains and buses used in interstate travel.

1957   The 1957 Civil Rights Act creates a six-member presidential commission to investigate allegations of the denial of citizen's voting rights.

1960   The 1960 Civil Rights Act strengthens the investigatory powers of the 1957 civil rights commission.

1961   President Kennedy establishes the Committee on Equal Employment Opportunity aimed against discrimination in employment.

1961   The Justice Department moves against discrimination in airport facilities under the provisions of the Federal Airport Act and against discrimination in bus terminals under the Interstate Commerce Commission Act.

1962   President Kennedy, in Executive Order 11063, bars discrimination in federally assisted housing.

1964   The Civil Rights Act prohibits discrimination in public accommodations and employment.

1965   The Voting Rights Act suspends literacy tests and sends federal examiners into many localities to protect rights of black voters.

1968   Fair housing legislation outlaws discrimination in the sale
or rental of housing.

❧❧

In 1967, Martin Luther King, Jr., became increasingly critical of the Vietnam War, breaking with President Johnson over this issue. This threatened the alliance between the civil rights movement and the federal government. Early in 1968 he was again involved in domestic civil rights issues, as the SCLC was busy organizing a poor people's march on Washington. King also joined in the protest of garbage collectors in Memphis, Tennessee, over their wages and working conditions. It was during this campaign that he was shot and killed on April 4, 1968, at the Lorraine Hotel in Memphis.

Riots in 100 cities followed Dr. King's assassination. During the 1960s race riots occurred in many American cities, and in 1967 alone there were 164 such disorders. Although not confined to northern cities, most of the riots took place in the cities of the North. According to the Report of the National Advisory Commission on Civil Disorders (1968:117), the background to the riots was a reservoir of grievances over employment, housing, severely disadvantaged living conditions, prejudice and discrimination, and "a general sense of frustration about their [African Americans'] ability to change those conditions." The incidents that precipitated the riots were often police actions against African Americans witnessed by others, actions that were seen as discriminatory and even brutal, occasionally resulting in a death. A cycle of street violence then unfolded, peaking at night and falling off during the daylight hours. Once store windows were smashed by bottle and rock throwing, looting followed. Arson followed as well. Efforts to control the riots relied on not only the police but also the National Guard.

At about this time, there was a change in the civil rights movement. More militant leaders emerged who advocated violent means and separatist goals in contrast to King's non-violent tactics and integrationist goals. These were black nationalist leaders, reflecting the precedent of Marcus Garvey earlier in the twentieth century. The geographical focus of the movement shifted as well, from the South to the North and West.

For example, the Black Panther Party was formed in Oakland, California. It was organized originally as the Black Panther Party for Self-Defense in 1966 by Huey P. Newton and Bobby Seale. It drew its philosophy from Malcolm X and Franz Fanon as well as from Marxism and socialism, and it projected racial pride and rejected capitalism. In the early years, the Black Panther Party was a neighborhood patrol in Oakland, checking on police abuse in the African American community. The party became a national movement, adding well-known personalities such as Eldridge Cleaver and chapters around the country. It allied with SNCC and other groups in 1968. Ultimately, the Black Panthers went into decline, due in part to harassment and infiltration by the police. Perhaps, the Panthers are remembered most for their penchant for calling the police "pigs" and their free food and breakfast programs for children in Oakland.

Malcolm X, another African American leader to emerge at this time, appealed particularly to poor and working-class blacks in the nation's cities. Malcolm, born in Omaha as Malcolm Little, spent his youth in the North as a street hustler and petty criminal. In prison he converted to the Nation of Islam, known also as the Black Muslims, led by Elijah Muhammad. Muhammad began this movement in Detroit early in the 1930s, but moved in 1934 to Chicago and organized there the Allah Temple of Islam (Essien-Udom, 1962). Malcolm X began proselytizing for the Nation of Islam on street corners in northern cities, and by 1963 he became a national spokesperson for the Black Muslims. His message was that black Americans still carried the chains of slavery in their minds, and, to break these chains, violence and conversion to Islam were both necessary. This message stood in sharp contrast to that of Martin Luther King, Jr., although Malcolm X's advocacy of violence moderated over the years.

The Nation of Islam had temples in several northern cities and established businesses such as grocery stores, restaurants, and farms. It was an ethnic self-help organization, meant to lift blacks up with self-discipline, religion, and their own hard work and sacrifice. The relation of Malcolm and Elijah Muhammed deteriorated, especially after Malcolm publicly commented on President Kennedy's assassination that the chickens had come home to roost. Malcolm finally broke with the Nation Of Islam and formed his own organization, the Organization of Afro-American Unity. In 1965, Malcolm X was assassinated at the Audubon Ballroom in Harlem.

The more militant groups, exemplified by the Black Panthers and Black Muslims, stood opposed to the state. By contrast, other civil rights groups, such as the SCLC and the NAACP, worked through the state to meet their goals. For example, the NAACP pursued litigation in the court system that resulted in over twenty Supreme Court decisions from 1915 to 1967 in the favor of African Americans (Scott, 1976). The SCLC as well as the NAACP were powerful lobbying forces for the passage of civil rights legislation in the 1960s. That is, the moderate civil rights groups allied with the federal government in their rivalry with other ethnic groups. Getting out the black vote, Dr. King's primary goal, was obviously critical in persuading the state to support the civil rights of African Americans.

Citizenship rights in America and Europe began with civil and legal rights in the eighteenth century, evolved into political rights, especially voting, in the nineteenth century, and expanded into social rights in the twentieth century (Marshall, 1950). Social rights of citizenship in the United States include social security, medicare, and unemployment insurance. The history of citizenship rights shows us how far African Americans were behind. In the civil rights movement of the late twentieth century, southern African Americans had to fight for civil and legal rights, for their right to vote, and for the elimination of racial barriers in their social rights. All of these rights had been extended to other citizens much earlier in American history. The civil rights movement reversed the historical alliance of white landowners with the state, evident during slavery and later with the passing of Jim Crow laws. The alliance forged by civil rights organizations with the state subsequently brought affirmative action.

Affirmative action is an active effort toward redressing any racial, sexual, or other minority imbalances in an employee work force. The federal and state governments have become sponsors and enforcers of affirmative action. Government-sponsored affirmative action began with Roosevelt's Executive Order 8802, obligating defense contractors not to discriminate against any worker because of race, creed, color, or national origin (Ringer and Lawless, 1989). There was no provision for affirmative action in the Civil Rights Act of 1964, but both Presidents Kennedy and Johnson issued executive orders about affirmative action on the part of firms and agencies doing business with the federal government. The codification of affirmative action plans was in place by 1971.

Employers were directed to take affirmative steps toward correcting any imbalances in their work forces. University officials were requested to do the same in their admissions policies. Written affirmative action plans include a policy statement, the assignment of executive responsibility within an agency or firm for affirmative action, analysis of the work force, goals and timetables for minority employment, and internal auditing and reporting systems. Goals and timetables translate into ethnic quotas in the minds of many Americans, and the American public in opinion polls appears to reject quotas. Moreover, there have been several legal challenges to affirmative action, for example, *Defunis v. Odegaard, Bakke v. Regents of the University of California,* and *Weber v. Kaiser Aluminum and Chemical Corporation.* Affirmative action continues as law, although the rigor of its enforcement waxes and wanes with political administrations. In Box 11.4, we see that informal affirmative action has been the historical rule rather than the exception in America.

☺☺

BOX 11.4 ETHNIC BONDS IN THE WORKPLACE

We misread history if we believe that white immigrants participated as individuals in an open, merit-based competition for employment. Rather, the early record shows that most white immigrants secured employment directly or indirectly through compatriots. This process was cloaked in favoritism and operated quite independently of qualifications. The result can be called "ethnic mobility, collective style."...

This situation evolved because employers had quite definite ethnic preferences in hiring.... Over time, these ethnic employment patterns solidified still further and social networks provided the new foundation for recruitment. Personal contacts proved cheaper than formal middlemen.... Not surprisingly, these networks rarely crossed ethnic boundaries....

By a process that today might be called "ethnic affirmative action," workers with no relevant experience were indiscriminately hired by the clothing trades, the construction industry, or the steel mills. They got their jobs simply on the basis of their ethnic heritage....

Today, a new government-mandated ethnic niche called "affirmative action" has affected black welfare. While the directive ostensibly embraces all industries, state employment has become the arena most open to black penetration. By 1980, 25.5 percent of the employed black males in New York were government employees, while the percentage of all New York men in government was 15.9 percent....

Formal qualifications had little to do with the very early distribution of white immigrants among selected industries. Government does not operate in this fashion. While ethnicity and perhaps even social networks play a part in job attainment, proper credentials are a prerequisite for consideration.

If the blacks who profit most from the implementation of affirmative action are the more educated and talented of the race, what happens to the "unqualified"? The decline in low-skill opportunities across the economic structure and the growing "credentialism" in the job market suggests an increasing gap between the Afro-American haves and have-nots.

Even as some blacks have moved ahead, they can do little in the job market for those they leave behind. Today, few interpersonal channels of influence can obtain a decent job for a school dropout or an unskilled laborer.... How different is this scenario from the ability of the turn-of-the-century Italian or Jew to assist his or her less fortunate cousins....

Source: *Reporting for the Russell Sage Foundation*, No. 6, May 1985, pp. 6–7. Reprinted by permission.

๑๏

THE PRESENT SITUATION

There were over 30 million African Americans in 1991, just over 12 percent of the nation's population (O'Hare, et al., 1991). The five cities with the largest African American populations are, in descending order, New York, Chicago, Detroit, Philadelphia, and Los Angeles. African American suburban population has increased by 70 percent since 1970, but the number of African Americans in high-poverty areas also increased by 19 percent between 1980 and 1990 (O'Hare, et al., 1991). The median net worth of the nation's African American households was $4,169 in 1988, compared to $43,279 for whites. Almost one-third of the African American households had a zero or negative net worth.

Tables 11.2 and 11.3 show the occupational changes of African Americans over the past five decades. Note the decline in African American household servants and farm workers, reflections of the old racial caste system, and the increase in black white-collar workers. These trends have continued up to 1990, although parity with others has not been reached. In 1990, black workers were concentrated in the low- and semi-skilled blue-collar jobs—operators, fabricators, and laborers—and in the service occupations and technical, sales, and administrative support. The historical absence of black proprietors and entrepreneurs, as well as business managers, public officials, and elected politicians, should also be noted. With a rising number of black public officials and politicians in recent years, this picture is changing somewhat, but not by an increase in the number of black capitalists. The history of African Americans is not only one of people laboring for others, it is also comparatively devoid of entrepreneurs and property holders. The effect is that black labor has had no economic alter-

TABLE 11.2   PERCENTAGE DISTRIBUTION OF AFRICAN AMERICANS AND ALL
EMPLOYED PEOPLE BY OCCUPATIONAL GROUPS, 1940–1970

Occupational Group	African Americans				All People			
	1940	1950	1960	1970	1940	1950	1960	1970
White-collar workers								
Professional and technical	2.7	3.2	5.2	8.3	7.5	8.7	11.1	14.9
Managers, officials, and								
proprietors except farmers	1.1	1.7	1.6	2.2	8.4	8.7	8.4	8.3
Clerical and sales	1.8	4.6	8.1	16.0	16.8	19.2	21.6	25.0
Blue-collar workers								
Craftsmen and foremen	3.0	5.6	6.7	9.1	11.3	14.3	13.5	13.9
Operators	10.4	19.2	21.5	18.0	18.4	20.3	18.4	13.7
Laborers except								
farm and mine	14.3	16.8	13.7	9.3	6.8	6.5	4.8	4.5
Service workers								
Private household	22.9	14.8	16.1	8.3	6.2	2.5	2.7	1.5
Other service	11.4	15.4	18.4	20.0	6.2	7.8	8.4	11.3
Farm workers								
Farmers and managers	15.0	9.1	3.0	1.0	11.5	7.6	3.9	1.9
Laborers and foremen	17.5	18.9	5.8	2.5	6.9	4.4	2.2	1.3

Note: Percentages may not total 100 because of rounding.

Sources: 1940 Census, *The Labor Force*, Table 62, p. 90; 1950 Census, *Occupational Characteristics*, Table 3, pp. 29–36; 1960 Census, *Occupational Characteristics*, Table 2, pp. 11–20; 1960 Census, *Occupational Characteristics*, Table 3, pp. 21–30; 1970 Census, *Occupational Characteristics*, Table 39, pp. 593–608.

native to working for whites, and thus no option to facing the prejudice and discrimination of others at work:

> In 1982, 339,239 black businesses in the nation had $12.4 billion in sales receipts, which represented about one-third of 1 percent of the total U.S. sales receipts of $4.12 trillion. Five years later, the share of black sales revenue was unchanged…. Thus, although blacks are 12 percent of the U.S. population, their businesses in the late 1980s still accounted for only one-third of 1 percent of the nation's total sales receipts (Jaynes and Williams, 1989:181).

Their recent occupational gains point toward a gradual convergence of some African Americans with the larger society. Current mobility among blacks is most striking for the young and for black women. Working black women now make 90 percent of the income of their white counterparts, up from 62 percent in 1959 (Levitan, et al.,

TABLE 11.3   PERCENT DISTRIBUTION OF AFRICAN AMERICANS AND ALL
EMPLOYED PEOPLE BY OCCUPATIONAL GROUPS, 1990

Occupational Group	African Americans 1990	All People 1990
Managerial and professional	16.9%	25.5%
Technical, sales, and administrative support	21.2	31.5
Service occupations	22.6	13.5
Precision production, craft, and repair	8.2	11.5
Operators, fabricators, and laborers	21.5	15.5
Farming, forestry, and fishing	1.6	2.5

Note: Percentages may not total 100 because of rounding.

Sources: 1980 Census, *Characteristics of the Population, Chapter C, General Social and Economic Characteristics*, Table 89, pp.1–45. U.S. Bureau of the Census, 1983:1–45; 1986:402–403; 1990 Equal Opportunity File.

1975). More than ever, black women are playing an important and even dominant economic role in the African American community. When both partners of a young black family work, they now make 90 percent of the income of their white counterparts.

In all of these comparisons it has been the better educated African Americans who have made the greatest gains. There was a 370 percent increase in the number of African American college students between 1960 and 1973. More recently, from 1986 to 1988, African American college enrollment rose from 1.08 million students to 1.13 million. Among young African American women, enrollment rose from 646,000 to 687,000, and African American male enrollment rose from 436,000 to 443,000. Educated African Americans now find opportunities in white-collar work, particularly in the public sector of the economy, that is, in governmental bureaucracy and publicly regulated industries (Sowell, 1975).

Whereas 17 percent of the total work force is in government employment, 27 percent of the African American work force is employed by the government. The impact of racial quotas in hiring and promotion is most evident in the sectors of the nation's economy under direct or indirect governmental control. Of course, political reaction to the civil rights movement would first show up in these parts of the economy. African American families in which both partners have good educations and both partners work now converge with others in material well-being and cultural values.

A Confederate flag waves behind a banner celebrating
the achievements of Martin Luther King, Jr.

This has brought changes in the African American elite and middle class (Jaynes and Williams, 1989). In 1940, 26 percent of the African American elite (*Who's Who among Black Americans*) were physicians, 14 percent were clergy, 14 percent were educators, and none were business executives and government officials. In 1980, 12 percent of the African American elite were business executives, 11 percent were government officials, 32 percent educators, and only 5 percent were clergy (Jaynes and Williams, 1989). In 1940, most of the African American middle class were teachers, self-employed, or clergy. In 1980, most of the African American middle class was salaried managers in both private firms and public agencies, as well as teachers. In short, the African American elite and middle class have converged with the trend toward a post-industrial society.

The convergence of African Americans began before the civil rights movement of the 1950s and 1960s and was to some extent a cause of that protest. The acculturation of African Americans into the broad, consumptive American society preceded their inclusion into its opportunity structure. African Americans developed the taste for the "good life," or middle-class status and life-styles, before they acquired the resources to support those life-styles. Having migrated out of the rural South, African Americans found themselves surrounded in northern cities by postwar prosperity, but it was the whites who prospered the most. The whites lived in the best suburbs, possessed modern appliances, sent their children to good schools, and experienced economic security and personal safety. African American migrants acquired a taste for these elements of the good life as black children were becoming better prepared for white-collar jobs, the route to this life.

Inclusion ran behind enculturation, due in large measure to racial discrimination. Through discrimination, other groups were protecting their own positions in the skilled trades and white-collar work, trying to perpetuate the black-white segmented labor market. The organized nonviolent protest of the 1950s and 1960s was directed at the barriers faced by aspiring middle-class blacks. It was an ethclass movement aimed at realizing the good life. It was also a southern movement aimed at eliminating Jim Crow. The subsequent militancy and street riots appear to have been cries of frustration from working class and underprivileged black youth, unprotected from unemployment due to mechanization and automation. The skills of these youths were obsolete in a technological society, and they were not only discontented with American society, they were also alienated from middle-class blacks. Their protest was unstructured, violent, and expressive rather than goal-oriented, and it was void of black middle-class leadership.

Farley (1977) found that current trends for African Americans, those begun in the 1960s, continued largely uninterrupted in the 1970s. On the one hand, labor force participation rates for black males continued to decline, while, on the other hand, blacks were still making gains into the middle class through educational and occupational mobility. Farley (1977:206) concluded:

> During the prosperous 1960s, racial differences in education, occupation, and income generally declined. We investigated whether this trend continued into the 1970s and concluded that the gains of the 1960s apparently were not solely attributable to the prosperity of that decade, since racial differences in status narrowed in the 1970s as they did in the previous decade. Blacks and whites, especially the young, are more alike in years of school completed than ever before. Racial differences in the occupations of employed workers continue to decline. The income gap separating black and white families has remained constant, but this is largely a consequence of the sharp rise of female-headed families among blacks. Indexes describing the income of specific types of families or the earnings of individuals generally reveal that racial differences moderated during the early years of the 1970s.

The black middle class doubled to one of every four black workers between 1960 and 1970 (Landry, 1987). There was a growing inclusion of a black middle class into the larger American society, while a black proletariat remained economically stagnant. Class differences in the intergenerational mobility of black men increased between 1962 and 1973, with men from advantaged backgrounds doing much better than those from disadvantaged backgrounds (Hout, 1984). By the same token, Lieberson and Waters (1988) found in 1980 that members of European ethnic groups were far more similar to one another in their occupations than they were to African Americans, indicative of the continued divergence of blacks.

African American workers in nearly every occupational category are still underrepresented at the top of the category. While the proportion of employed African American workers who are professionals, managers, administrators, and technical workers rose from almost 7 percent in 1960 to 14 percent in 1973, African Americans in 1973 were at the lower levels of this occupational category (Levitan, et al., 1975). African American professionals in 1973 were concentrated in precollege teaching, nursing, medical technology, social work, personnel, and labor relations. This is only one illustration of the general trend for African Americans to be concentrated at the lower rungs of certain labor hierarchies, while at the same time they have made considerable progress in recent years. Blacks are more concentrated in the lower middle class than whites (Landry, 1987). The picture is complete only when we add that labor force participation rates for blacks are declining, especially for poor, young black males.

Furthermore, the social participation of African Americans tends to be ethnically restrictive. Research has shown that blacks tend to participate almost exclusively with other blacks in voluntary associations such as churches, fraternal organizations, and neighborhood improvement associations (Williams, Babchuk, and Johnson, 1973). Even middle-class blacks still live in racially segregated neighborhoods, and black-white intermarriage is well below that expected by chance (Lieberson and Waters, 1988; Massey and Denton, 1985, 1988; Massey and Mullan, 1984). The inclusion of even middle-class African Americans falls far short of their full assimilation. Of course, many blacks do join with others in some organizations—labor unions, for instance—and this is a function of the degree that they are included in the secondary institutions of the larger society.

The breakdown in the nation's racial stratification has brought greater inclusion of a growing black middle class into the larger society, to be sure, but this does not translate into an economically secure position for the black middle class. "Not only is the struggle to reach the middle class more difficult for blacks ... but, once there, middle-class blacks have a more difficult time than whites in maintaining a middle-class standard" (Landry, 1987:231). It is by having both spouses work that the black middle class can reach a comfortable lifestyle. That level of comfort is also below that of whites in terms of savings and value of homes. If there is a job loss, black middle-class families could survive financially, on average, for only two months (Landry, 1987).

Nevertheless, there is a widening stratification within the black community. By the late 1960s, income distribution was more unequal between wealthy and poor black families than it was between wealthy and poor white families (Wilson, 1973). By the 1980s, black men aged 25–34 years with at least some college earned 80 to 85 percent as much as their white counterparts. On the other hand, the real weekly earnings of black, male high-school dropouts was $286 in 1986, down from $334 in 1969 (Jaynes and Williams, 1989). More than ever, black America is now stratified into ethclasses, although class divisions among blacks go as far back as that between freedman and slave.

From 1970 to 1986, the proportion of black families with incomes less than $10,000 grew from 26.8 to 30.2 percent of all black families. During the same period, black families with incomes over $35,000 also grew, from 15.7 to 21.2 percent, and those with incomes over $50,000 grew as well, from 4.7 to 8.8 percent of all black families (Jaynes and Williams, 1989). Wilson (1978:151) summarized these trends:

> On the one hand, talented and educated blacks are experiencing un-precedented job opportunities.... On the other hand, poorly trained and educationally limited blacks of the inner city ... see their job prospects increasingly restricted to the low-wage sector, their unem-ployment rates soaring,... their labor-force participation rates declin-ing,... and their welfare roles increasing.

There is now a black middle class converging with the national trend toward white-collar work, but it remains excluded at least in terms of segregated housing and lack of intermarriage. There is also a rather permanent African American proletariat in this country, com-posed of people whose skills are obsolete or who have been pensioned off. This class has been displaced by the loss of jobs in southern agri-culture, on the one hand, and the more recent loss of industrial jobs in the northern cities, on the other. These changes in the occupational structure of the nation have contributed to the current condition of the poor African American family.

THE POOR AFRICAN AMERICAN FAMILY

About one out of every eight families in the United States is below the poverty line. However, 56 percent of the African American female-headed families live in poverty. In 1990, over 50 percent (51.2%) of the nation's black children under 18 years old lived with their mother only, compared to about 16 percent for white children (O'Hare, et al., 1991). The poor African American family is today a social issue in the country.

> ... the most critical danger facing female-headed households is pover-ty. Seventy percent of black children under the age of 18 who live in female-headed families are being brought up in poverty. In 1983, the median income for such households was $7,999, compared to almost $32,107 for two-parent families of all races, in which both spouses worked. Without the large increase in female-headed households, black family income would have *increased* by 11 percent in 1970s. In-stead, it fell by 5 percent (Norton, 1985:79).

Other researchers agree that racial differences in family structure ac-count for much of the black-white difference in childhood poverty (Eggebeen and Lichter, 1991).

The issue of the poor African American family was brought to the nation's attention some years ago. Daniel Patrick Moynihan (1965) wrote about the growing number of female-headed households among poor blacks. Similar conclusions were drawn at the time by other social scientists as well, e.g., Rainwater (1966 and 1970), and the point was made by E. Franklin Frazier as early as 1939.

415

The reaction by some African American intellectuals was swift. Moynihan's report was claimed to be racist, for it seemed to imply that the problems of poor African Americans was their own doing rather than the result of prejudice and discrimination. Moreover, books and articles followed that emphasized the strengths of the black family and its ability to survive, and insisting that not all black families were female-headed (e.g., Billingsley, 1968). Meanwhile, the number of female-headed families among poor blacks has continued to increase. The majority of black children in the United States are now born to single women. Births to single black women rose from 38 percent of the total black births in 1970 to 57 percent in 1982, and some believe the figure to be even higher today.

One explanation is that slavery had torn apart the African American family. Slave husbands and wives were sold apart, for example, and this prevented stable family life during slavery. Today's black female-headed family is a result of this history, or so this theory goes. But the historical evidence does not support this theory. "As recently as the early 1960s, 75 percent of black households were husband-and-wife families.... Indeed, the evidence suggests that most slaves grew up in two-parent families reinforced by ties to large extended families" (Norton, 1985:93). The rise of the black female-headed household is a recent phenomenon, not an historical one, as we learned in the preceding chapter.

Another explanation is the high unemployment rates for young black males in the post-industrial economy following the Second World War. Since 1950, black males have lost their niche in agriculture due to its mechanization, and more recently in blue-collar jobs due to the de-industrialization of America (Wilhelm, 1971). White-collar jobs have expanded since World War II, but have been filled by white women. Rising unemployment for young and unskilled black males is the result, and these men cannot support a family.

"The [family] breakdown begins with working-class black men, whose loss of function in the post–World War II economy has led directly to their loss of function in the family" (Norton, 1985:93). These black men can no longer maintain a stable family life because of their under-employment and unemployment. For example, Bane (1986) found that most black women do not become poor because they are household heads and thus without the economic support of a man. Rather, they are poor when married and simply reshuffled their poverty to a new household after a divorce, separation, or death of the husband. Moreover, Guttentag and Secord (1983:201) reported that "it appears that in 1970, for the age cohorts most eligible for marriage, there were almost two black women for every man." The reasons were the relatively high

death rates of young black males, their imprisonment, and their disproportionate presence in the U.S. armed forces stationed in foreign countries. The odds are stacked against marriage and stable family life.

A final explanation begins with the migration of rural southern
blacks to northern ghettos in recent decades. Middle-class blacks simultaneously moved out of these same ghettos, as better housing became available to them (Wilson, 1987). In the 1940s, Drake and Cayton
(1945) found both the upper and middle classes in Bronzeville. The
middle class had personified and promoted middle-class values in
ghettos, and stable, two-parent family life was part of the value system. But the middle class is now gone from the ghetto. The African
American poor have become separated from both the black middle
class and the larger society and have transplanted their southern roots
in the nation's ghettos. Underclass culture today in ghettos is traceable
to southern roots—the South of a generation ago, not slavery. "The
similarities between sharecropping and welfare are eerie: dependency
on 'the man'; more money for having more children; little value placed
on education; no home ownership; an informal attitude toward marriage and childbearing" (Lemann, 1986:47). Whatever the reasons,
poor blacks continue to be excluded from the larger society.

SUMMARY

The mechanisms for inclusion and convergence of ethnic groups have
increased with societal change. The nation changed from an agrarian
to an industrial society beginning in the middle of the nineteenth century, and then evolved into a post-industrial society in the twentieth
century. This brought changes in the nation's labor needs, first from
agricultural to industrial blue-collar work and later, in the twentieth
century, to white-collar work. White-collar work requires an enculturated labor force, and there has been an expansion of public education
along with the rise of white-collar occupations. These two changes
have meant increased opportunity for inclusion and the convergence
of ethnic groups with one another and with the larger society.

But these opportunities have not been shared equally by the nation's ethnic groups, due in large measure to ethnic competition and
the persistence of ethnic stratification. While some groups have been
included into the larger society, others have been excluded. While
some groups have converged with one another and the larger nation,
other groups have diverged from the course of societal change. Much
of the history of African Americans illustrates this ethnic exclusion
and divergence.

417

Far longer than nearly any other ethnic group, African Americans were largely agricultural laborers and domestic servants, well into the twentieth century. They were slaves during the agrarian phase of American history. Slavery is an extreme form of ethnic stratification, and it was never meant to be a mechanism for assimilation. Nevertheless, some black-white assimilation did occur during slavery with respect to language, religion, cooking, music, and so on, and it followed along the lines where blacks came into contact with whites in the course of their work. The assimilation of blacks was severely limited during slavery, however, by the nature of the planters' labor needs as well as the antagonism between slaves and white workers.

As the nation entered its industrial phase after the emancipation of the slaves, black labor was excluded once again, this time from the emerging industrial order of the nation and from resettlement on the frontier. The historical antagonism between white workers and freed slaves surfaced in widespread acts of violence in the post-Reconstruction South. There was at the same time, however, the possibility of an alliance between black and white labor in the Populist movement. Southern capital feared both chaos and the Populists, and it struck a compromise with white labor that resulted in a racial caste system. Blacks were largely excluded from industrial work, remained propertyless, and stayed for another two or three generations on the land under the domination of the southern landowners. This they did as the rest of the nation followed a course of industrialization. Thus African Americans continued to diverge from other immigrant groups through the nineteenth and into the twentieth century.

In the twentieth century, however, there began a mass migration of African Americans out of the rural South and into the industrial North and West. Black workers again faced racial stratification, this time in the industrial North, although the northern version did not last nearly as long as had the southern caste system. So in many ways, the migration of African Americans out of the rural South has been a significant step toward their greater inclusion in the larger society. Black labor has been transformed in the twentieth century from a class of uneducated, agrarian workers and domestic servants into a better educated class of blue- and white-collar workers. In the process, the African American subculture changed from an oral folk tradition into an urban expression that has made significant intellectual contributions to the larger national culture. The Harlem Renaissance in the 1920s symbolized this change and these contributions.

The inclusion of African Americans in white-collar work has been particularly significant in recent years, since the civil rights movement. But this tells only half the story. There is also a growing African American proletariat in this country, as indicated by the increasing number of black women on welfare and the declining labor force participation rates of black males. The labor skills of these people have been made obsolescent by the simultaneous mechanization of southern agriculture and the automation of northern industry. There is little reason to predict the inclusion of the African American poor into the larger society in the near future, given the current discrepancy between their skills and the evolving technology in the nation. Their future rests on political decisions, particularly those that bear on welfare and income redistribution, rather than the economics of labor needs and property ownership. The African American middle class will probably converge with its white counterpart, limited by barriers to interracial intimacy and the use of race as an identity badge and strategy in resource competition.

C H A P T E R
12
☯

CHINESE AMERICANS AND AMERICAN SOCIETY

One-half of the immigrants to the United States in the 1980s were Asians, and by 1990 there were almost 7 million Asians living in the country (Takaki, 1989). By the year 2000, there will be almost 10 million Asians in the United States (Kitano and Daniels, 1988). In this and the two following chapters, we will examine the immigrant experiences of Asian Americans—first the Chinese, next the Japanese, and finally Koreans, Filipinos, and Vietnamese.

Asian and African Americans share a legacy: both were immigrant laborers and both have experienced color prejudice and discrimination as racial minorities in this country. There are important differences, however, between the experiences of these ethnic groups. For example, Chinese Americans became entrepreneurs and proprietors, middleman minorities, who through their own subeconomies circumvented to some extent the economic discrimination and color prejudice of others. Furthermore, in the second half of the twentieth century Chinese Americans were included into the wider American society, at least a generation before there was a similar inclusion of blacks into the post-industrial society. Now the American-born Chinese are among the best educated and most middle class of the nation's ethnic groups. Another point that distinguishes them from African Americans is that there has been significant immigration of Chinese into the country since 1965.

The study of Asian Americans is important for students of American ethnicity. It forces us to examine closely the contention that color prejudice and racial discrimination have made the histories of people of color

FIGURE 12.1 Chinese Americans and Change in American Society

Agrarian Society c. 1600–1865		Industrial Society c. 1865–1945		Post-Industrial Society c. 1945–Present
Immigration and contact	→ Early accommodation	→ Competition, conflict, ethnic stratification, and exclusion	→ Middleman minority	→ Present situation and new immigration

in this country similar and uniquely different from those of other ethnic groups. Asian Americans do not conform to the rule that racial groups face permanent exclusion to the bottom strata of American society.

CONTACT

Asian immigration into the United States started with the Chinese in the last century. About 360,000 Chinese immigrated into the United States between 1820 and 1892, although not all these immigrants were permanent settlers. Indeed, 270,000 returned to China (Lyman, 1986). The peak years of early Chinese immigration, 1849 to 1882, began with the gold rush in California, continued with the construction of the transcontinental railroad, and ended with the first Chinese Exclusion Act of 1882. Most of these immigrants were men; almost 97 percent of the Chinese in the United States were men in 1890 (Daniels, 1988; Wong, 1988).

The Chinese had immigrated to Hawaii to work on the islands' sugar plantations prior to their coming to the mainland. Work on the sugar plantations began at five in the morning when a loud siren went off and foremen (*lunas*) and company policemen knocked on barracks' doors, shouting for the workers to get up. "The workers were grouped by the foremen into gangs of twenty to thirty workers and were marched or transported by wagons and trains to the fields" (Takaki, 1989:134). Workers in the fields were constantly watched by the lunas, who swung whips to get their crews to work faster. The social hierarchy on the Hawaiian plantations was evident in the housing; managers lived in mansions "with spacious verandas and white columns overlooking the plantation, ... [while] foremen and the technical employees were housed in handsome bungalow cottages...." (Takaki, 1989:156). Chinese laborers on one plantation lived in a warehouse with bunks "stacked four or five high," and two to three hundred lived in this single building.

This immigration of Chinese into Hawaii and the continental United States was a part of a larger movement of people (Daniels, 1988; Park, 1926/1950). As Europeans settled throughout the world, including the Pacific basin, they used Chinese immigrants, among others, in the building of their settlements. Eventually, the Chinese ringed the Pacific Ocean. Chinese labor immigrated not only to Hawaii and the United States, but also to Canada, Mexico, Central and South America, and the Caribbean in the Western Hemisphere as well as throughout Southeast Asia in the Eastern Hemisphere. In this country, the Chinese joined with blacks, other Asian groups, Mexicans, and the many European nationalities in the building of American society.

Virtually all of the early Chinese immigrants to the United States originated from southeastern China, from the vicinity of the city of Canton, now called Guang Zhou, in the province of Kwangtung (Light, 1972). Most were from the Sze-Yap and Sam-Yap districts south of Canton (Weiss, 1974). These men typically went first down the Pearl River to Hong Kong and then to the United States, many aboard ships of the Pacific Mail Steamship Company (Tsai, 1983). They were peasants whose lives had been woven into a social fabric of clan, village, and dialect groupings. About half of these men were single; those who were married left their wives and families in China. The decision to emigrate from China was usually a family one, and the emigrant was expected to send remittances home and return someday to China. If not the immediate family, then the social network of clan, village, and dialect group was reconstructed by these immigrants on American soil. Virtually every Chinese immigrant was integrated into the Chinese community, an immigrant brotherhood.

Early Chinese immigrants were *sojourners,* who sought work and wages in this country with the intention of returning home to China with their savings (Lyman, 1986). Poverty, wars, natural disasters, and surplus population pushed peasants out of China, and, paradoxically, poverty pulled them back again. Population in Kwangtung province had increased from 16 million in 1787 to 28 million in 1850, but floods in 1847 and a series of wars, including the Opium Wars (1839–1842 and 1856–1860), the Taiping Rebellion (1851–1864), and Hakka-Punti War (1855–1868), were pushing refugees toward emigration (Lyman, 1986; Takaki, 1989; Tsai, 1983; Weiss, 1974). Two and one-half million people left China between 1840 and 1900 (Takaki, 1989).

Emigration was an escape from the political turmoil and poverty of China, but it also meant that emigrants with savings earned elsewhere could return to China and live well. Chinese emigrants also sent money home to their families throughout their stay overseas. As a consequence, Chinese immigrants in the United States suffered hardships at work on the West Coast, at times undercutting the working conditions and wage rates of other ethnic groups in California and invoking their wrath. According to Lyman (1974:75), "Labor tended to identify Chinese immigrants as the tools of a consortium of monopoly capital that would drive the white workingman to utter degradation." At least the actions of Chinese immigrant labor gave the appearance of an alliance with capital. Often Chinese immigrants undercut the economic position of whites unknowingly, however, for they were generally ignorant of the prevailing wage rates on the West Coast, many having contracted the terms of their employment while still in China. Furthermore, neither the Chinese immigrants nor China itself was in any position to complain about the exploitation of Chinese labor by American employers. The poverty and powerlessness of China meant that it and its emigrés were unable to prevent such exploitation in America. These were the conditions when the Chinese first entered the rough-and-ready atmosphere of California during the gold rush.

EARLY ACCOMMODATION

Labor demand was high while its supply was short in nineteenth-century California. This made for an early accommodation between the Chinese and other laboring groups; there was initially little labor competition. Chinese immigrants were welcomed on the West Coast as orderly and industrious citizens who were law-abiding, inoffensive, and tractable (Tsu Wu, 1972). In 1849, 325 Chinese came to California. The number rose to 2,716 in 1851 and more than 20,000 in 1852. By 1870 there were 63,000 Chinese in the United States (Takaki, 1989).

Chinese males were nearly one-quarter of California's work force in the 1870s (Saxton, 1971). Exaggerated stories of the riches of California had spread throughout southern China, and California was known as "golden mountain" among the Chinese. Most of the Chinese initially found their way to the gold fields of northern California. In the census of 1860 for California, more than two-thirds of all Chinese were found in the mining regions of the Sierra Nevada and Trinity Alps (Saxton, 1971:3). While unpopular from the first with white miners (including the American-born and Irish, German, and Scotch-Irish immigrants), the Chinese nonetheless worked claims alongside them. As soon as the good claims became scarce, however, the Chinese were forced to work either abandoned claims or provide personal services for others.

As the good claims petered out, railroad construction picked up, and thousands of Chinese were put to work building the western half of the nation's transcontinental railroad (Box 12.1). Even more Chinese came to California as a consequence. The decision to hire Chinese was taken in 1865 by Charles Crocker, when the Central Pacific found itself far behind schedule, that is, behind the pace of the Union Pacific Railroad, which was laying track from the east. This was a serious problem for the Central Pacific, since Congress in 1862 had made land grants and posted financial bonds for the two railroads on the basis of the miles of track each constructed. Competition between the two railroads in the 1860s was very keen, and the High Sierra was not yet in sight of the Central's construction crew in 1866, while the crews on the Union Pacific were laying a mile of track per day (Saxton, 1971:62).

Not only did the Central Pacific secure Chinese labor from the mining districts of California, it also contracted labor out of China as well. One such labor contractor boasted that he alone had brought 30,000 Chinese into California (Saxton, 1971). The 12,000 Chinese who worked for the Central Pacific were fully 90 percent of the railroad's work force, and the Chinese worked for two-thirds the cost of white labor (Takaki, 1989). There was no competition between Chinese and white workers on the railroad, however. White workers were in short supply, and the mining districts offered them an attractive alternative. Therefore the hiring of Chinese resulted not in the displacement of whites but in their upgrading; whites were foremen, for example. Further, Saxton says, "No man who had any choice would have chosen to be a common laborer on the Central Pacific during the crossing of the High Sierra" (p. 63).

◎◎

BOX 12.1 Workin' on the Railroad

The construction of the Central Pacific Railroad line was a Chinese achievement. Not only did they perform the physical labor required to clear trees and lay tracks; they also provided important technical labor by operating power drills and handling explosives for boring tunnels through the Donner Summit....

The Central Pacific managers forced the Chinese laborers to work through the winter of 1866. The snowdrifts, over sixty feet in height, covered construction operations. The Chinese workers lived and worked in tunnels under the snow, with shafts to give them air and lanterns to light the way. Snowslides occasionally buried camps and crews; in the spring, workers found the thawing corpses, still upright, their cold hands gripping shovels and picks and their mouths twisted in frozen terror.

Source: *From Strangers from a Different Shore: A History of Asian Americans*, pp. 85–86, by Ronald Takaki. Copyright © 1989 by Ronald Takaki. By permission of Little, Brown and Company.

๏๏

After the golden spike was driven into the ground at Promontory, Utah, in 1869, finally linking the Atlantic and Pacific coasts by rail, some Chinese stayed with the railroads and laid track off the trunk line in southern and northern California. Others became wage laborers for California growers and ranchers or began to concentrate in urban trades, domestic services, and manufacturing, particularly in San Francisco. Although competition and conflict between the Chinese and other laboring groups were not totally absent in the early years, this era is best characterized as one of accommodation. Because of the initial shortage of labor on the West Coast there was little reason for labor competition. But the situation soon changed.

COMPETITION, CONFLICT, ETHNIC STRATIFICATION, AND EXCLUSION

Chinese immigrants were initially concentrated in mining, railroad construction, and then agricultural wage labor. So long as there was no labor competition in these endeavors, the Chinese were able to manage an accommodation of sorts with white labor. However, mining became quickly competitive, railroad construction tapered off, and eventually the Chinese even faced competition as field labor from white labor unions and immigrants from Japan and Mexico.

Competition became heated first in the gold fields of California, and in the end the Chinese were virtually excluded from mining. They were relegated to service jobs in the gold fields, such as laundrymen and gatherers of firewood, or they took over from white miners undesirable, worked-over sites. This was the initial stage of the ethnic stratification of Chinese in mining. The Chinese did laundry and cooked in the gold fields, for example, essentially women's work in that era (Li, 1976). A laundry could be started for as little as $75, with a stove, dryroom, trough, sleeping room and business sign. One man washed and another ironed clothes. The laundry business become so popular with Chinese that 69 percent of California's laundry workers were Chinese in 1890 and one of four employed Chinese males throughout the nation in 1900 worked in this business (Takaki, 1989).

As mining evolved from a collection of small operations, primarily placer mining, to the capital-intensive, large-scale endeavor of deep-shaft mining, miners too changed. They became wage laborers instead of independent entrepreneurs working their own small claims. White miners subsequently organized themselves in unions from which they excluded Chinese, thereby forcing them from mining itself, all with the consent of absentee capital. In 1870 there were 27,045 Chinese miners and laborers in the country, but by 1920 only 151 Chinese miners remained (Yuan, 1963).

Chinese were pushed out of mining by a variety of techniques, including local ordinances prohibiting them from working area sites, discriminatory taxation of Chinese miners (e.g., the California Foreign Miners' Tax), closed-shop arrangements, and mob violence. Chinese in the mining regions of California, the Pacific Northwest, and the Rockies were beaten, burned, lynched, and shot by mobs with some frequency in the last half of the nineteenth century. In October of 1880, for example, about 3,000 white men surrounded houses occupied by some 400 Chinese in downtown Denver. The Chinese were beaten, one was killed, and property worth over $53,000 was destroyed (Tsai, 1983). At Rock Springs in Wyoming, 28 Chinese miners were killed in September of 1885, 15 were wounded, and several hundred were driven out of town (Tsai, 1983). The mob also destroyed $147,000 worth of Chinese property. In the same year, residences of the Chinese in Seattle were burned, and the Chinese were told to leave town. In 1887, in Hell's Canyon Gorge, Oregon, 31 Chinese miners were robbed and murdered, their bodies mutilated, in what became known as the Snake River Massacre (Daniels, 1988).

As the Chinese were being forced from mining, railroad construction also fell off after 1869. In May of 1869, 10,000 Chinese were unemployed with the completion of the first transcontinental railroad. As experienced construction workers, great numbers of Chinese began building an agrarian empire in California. They diked, ditched, drained, irrigated, and otherwise made fields in California ready for production, and they also harvested the crops for white growers. Chinese were 18 percent of all farm labor in California in 1870 (Takaki, 1989). In the San Joaquin and Sacramento river valleys, some Chinese became truck farmers, working as tenant farmers.

The Chinese were first welcomed by California growers and ranchers as a source of relatively cheap and experienced labor, in the context of a critical labor shortage in California agriculture. Chinese farm labor was also ten to twenty dollars cheaper per month than white farm labor (Takaki, 1989). Thus, white farm workers were from the start opposed to the Chinese in California agriculture. As the Chinese population grew older and the supply of Chinese labor correspondingly diminished, due to the restrictions on further Chinese immigration with the Chinese Exclusion Acts, Chinese field workers became understandably more militant about wage rates and working conditions. This turned growers cool toward the Chinese, and they began to look elsewhere for labor.

Moreover, "white farmworkers held mass meetings where they demanded the discharge of Chinese labor, and used...coercion such as threatening letters and occasionally setting fire to the barns and fields of those who employed Chinese" (Nee and Nee, 1972:52). Also Chinese living quarters were burned and Chinese workers were murdered. Lyman (1974:74) observed that "a series of racially-based strikes, occurring from 1893 to 1894, dealt the final blow to extensive employment of Chinese in agriculture. ...the Chinese were removed from the agricultural scene by a violent campaign that united independent growers and the thoroughly Sinophobic urban labor unions."

Even before the 1890s, the Chinese had begun to concentrate in urban areas, particularly in San Francisco, taking up work in manufacturing, trade, and domestic service. Twenty-four percent of the Chinese in America lived in San Francisco in 1870, but by 1900, 45 percent were living there (Takaki, 1989). In San Francisco, Chinese found jobs in shoe and woolen manufacturing, cigar-making, and sewing. "...Chinese workers in San Francisco comprised about two-thirds of all garment industry workers and 90% of the cigar makers" (Mangiafico, 1988:114). The city was then the ninth leading manufacturing center in the United States. Chinese workers typically made less money than white workers in these same trades, evidence of a split labor market. The Chinese were ultimately forced out of the skilled trades in industry, however, by white labor unions and relegated to the bottom of the labor hierarchy, in manufacturing (sweatshops) and domestic service (as houseboys). That is, the labor market became segmented. By 1900, 57 percent of the gainfully employed Asians in the United States (including Japanese as well as Chinese, but the bulk of the Japanese immigration came after 1900) were engaged in domestic service, whereas only 40 years before, nearly two-thirds of the Chinese were miners (Light, 1972; Saxton, 1971).

Chinese immigration into the country was being restricted at the same time. The first Chinese Exclusion Act was passed by Congress in 1882 and was renewed twice and made "permanent" between 1904 and 1943. It was through politics, mainly, that the foes of the Chinese managed to force them out of desirable jobs and restrict their entry into the country (Daniels, 1969). In the 1870s, America was in a long postwar depression, and the matter of Chinese labor competition was a serious political issue, especially on the West Coast. Political parties there had anti-Chinese planks in their platforms, and the California Constitutional Convention expressed sentiment for Chinese exclusion in its articles at the insistence of white labor unions. Moreover, California had experimented for more than three decades with immigration restriction, including a number of pieces of legislation known collectively as the passenger acts (Lyman, 1974:63). These acts had little immediate success, since the U.S. Supreme Court declared unconstitutional California's attempt to engage itself unilaterally in international relations.

Ultimately, pressure was felt in Washington, however, and President Chester Arthur signed the first Chinese Exclusion Act into law in May 1882 (Daniels, 1969; Lyman, 1974). This act provided that no skilled or unskilled Chinese laborer or miner could enter the United States for ten years, but it exempted certified merchants, students, and itinerants (Lyman, 1974:66). Wives of alien Chinese laborers were also forbidden entry into the United States. Moreover, Chinese aliens were denied the right to naturalization, and thus American citizenship (Kwang, 1979; Tsai, 1983). They were also denied the due process of law and the right of trial by jury (Tsu, 1972). Nor were Chinese immigrants allowed to give testimony against whites in courts of law on the West Coast.

The Scott Act of 1888 prohibited the re-entry of any Chinese laborer who had previously left the country, and thus Chinese men could not return to China and bring their wives to America (Kwang, 1979). The exclusion of Chinese was extended in 1892 under the Geary Act for another ten years, and this act went so far as to deny bail to Chinese in habeas corpus proceedings and to require all Chinese labor in this country to carry identity cards. The exclusion of Chinese immigration was extended again in 1904, and certain loopholes in the previous acts were closed with the Immigration Act of 1924, which remained essentially in force until 1943. The Exclusion Acts were repealed in 1943 (during the Second World War), and the immigration of Chinese women subsequently rose, especially after the Immigration Act of 1965.

As a consequence of the Exclusion Acts, the Chinese population in the United States declined from 105,000 in 1882 to just over 60,000 in 1920 (Wong, 1988). Chinese immigration fell from a high of over 123,000 between 1871 and 1880 to a low of 20,605 in 1901–1910 (Wong,

1988). Only after 1970 did Chinese immigration return to levels known before 1880. Another consequence of the Exclusion Acts was that the Chinese remained a bachelor society up to 1920 (Nee and Nee, 1972). Almost 97 percent of the Chinese in 1890 were males (Wong, 1988). These homeless men worked long hours and spent their hours off work at gambling, in brothels or opium dens, or visiting in the back rooms of Chinese stores. They were increasingly crowded into Chinatowns; in San Francisco there "were 14,552 bunks for single men in ten blocks of Chinatown" (Takaki, 1989:245).

Although the men sent remittances to their families in China, they could neither bring them here nor marry non-Chinese in the United States because of anti-miscegenation laws. The Chinese family was a *mutilated household*, with the men in America and their women and children in China (Wong, 1988). This exclusion of the Chinese and its consequences prompted protests in the coastal provinces of China. In 1905, there was a large-scale boycott campaign against imported goods from America, such as flour and cigarettes (Tsai, 1983). However, this campaign and other protests both in China and the United States did little to change American immigration policy.

The Exclusion Acts did allow entry of wives of Chinese who were American citizens, and this exemption became important after the 1906 earthquake in San Francisco. Since vital records were destroyed by the earthquake and the fires that followed, many alien Chinese claimed American citizenship to qualify for the exemption under the Exclusion Acts. Between 1910 and 1924, 25 percent of the Chinese immigrants were women, whereas no more than 5 percent of the Chinese community had been women in earlier years (Takaki, 1989). In what was called the *slot system*, some Chinese in America sold family memberships to non-family in China after first claiming American citizenship and thus exemption under the Exclusion Acts. These immigrants were known as paper family members, and they entered the United States at Angel Island near San Francisco (see Box 12.2). Wise to this ruse, immigration officials at Angel Island interrogated new immigrants for months about family details. "The men spent the long days rehearsing what they would say to the Immigration Demon. The forgetful men fingered their risky notes. Those who came back after being examined told what questions they had been asked" (Kingston, 1980). "Me longtime Californ'," they would say to immigration officials (Nee and Nee, 1972:14). The Exclusion Acts had also allowed Chinese merchants to bring immigrant wives to the country, but that loophole was closed by the Quota Act of 1924 (Wong, 1988). However, in 1930 the law was changed to allow Chinese merchants with American citizenship to bring their wives to the United States.

The violence against Chinese Americans in Denver in
October 1880 was only one of many such incidents in
the decades before the 1882 Exclusion Act.

✆

BOX 12.2 ANGEL ISLAND

When the Exclusion Act was passed in 1882, a dilapidated old warehouse on the Pacific Mail Steamship Line's wharf in San Francisco was turned into a processing station for immigrants. Hundreds of Chinese newcomers were held here.... Funds of $200,000 were appropriated to establish an immigrant station and detention facility on Angel Island. Construction began in 1905 but was interrupted by the 1906 earthquake. Angel Island was opened on January 21, 1910, when the first eighty-five Chinese immigrants entered its white-walled buildings.

...presumed guilty of fraud, the exact nature of which was often unspecified, the immigrant had to prove himself innocent while being held in detention on the islet island without bail.... Examinations and interrogations were traumatic events. They usually lasted two or three days but could stretch out interminably. To establish the identity of immigrants, they were asked questions relating to the minutest details of private life and were acutely embarrassing, particularly to Chinese women.

... A Chinese U.S. citizen on returning after a visit to China would report the birth of a son or daughter there.... This created a "slot" which someone in need of offspring could later use to bring in a child. In this way, several thousand "paper sons" were brought in, and when the ruse was exposed it became one of the main aims of the immigration service to catch these paper sons and daughters.

... Some immigrants languished on Angel Island as long as two years before their cases were settled. The poems carved on the walls of the barracks... are poignant witnesses to the anguish endured in these wooden cells....

Angel Island was dubbed the "Ellis Island of the West," or as the Chinese inmates ironically translated the name, "Isle of the Immortals."... In World War II, it was decided to close the station, and on November 4, 1940, the 144 Chinese still held there were moved to temporary facilities in San Francisco.

Source: From *The Chinese of America*, pp. 189–190, by Jack Chen. Copyright ©1981 by Jack Chen. Reprinted by permission of HarperCollins Publishers.

✆

Forced from mining, the railroads, and finally agriculture, the Chinese concentrated in Chinatowns on the West Coast (Kwang, 1979; Takaki, 1989). There was a 343 percent increase in the Chinese population in San Francisco between 1860 and 1870 (Takaki, 1989). The Chinese then moved to other regions of the country as well. In 1880, 83 percent of the Chinese lived on the West Coast, but by 1920 only 55 percent lived in that region. As early as 1870, Chinese immigrants were used as strikebreakers at shoe factories in North Adams, Massachusetts. Others settled in Chinatowns throughout the country, especially in the nation's larger cities, as the percentage of the Chinese population living in California and other western states declined. There were even Chinese in small towns, and the Chinese in the delta region of Mississippi is an intriguing story.

The delta region of Mississippi is in the extreme northwestern part of the state, near the Mississippi River. Between 1866 and 1876 Chinese were brought to the delta region to build plantations by clearing and draining the land (Loewen, 1971). These immigrants came from China as well as California and Chicago, and they were mostly young male sojourners. The Chinese were an alternative to black labor following the Civil War. However, with the end of Reconstruction in 1876, plantation owners again turned to black labor, losing interest in Chinese labor. At this time, the Chinese began to establish themselves in the economic niche of grocery store proprietors in the delta region.

The first Chinese grocery store opened in 1872, offering "meat, meal, and molasses," with an initial $100 investment (Loewen, 1971). The clientele were poor blacks, and the new proprietors often could not speak English, making it necessary for customers to point to what they needed in the store. The Chinese gravitated to these grocery stores for a number of reasons (Loewen, 1971). First, there was little white or black competition in this business niche. Whites avoided doing business with black customers, and most certainly in the black community, because of the implied status loss in the era of Jim Crow. Status loss was not a concern to the Chinese, however, since they were sojourners, intending to make money and return to China. Furthermore, most black business was confined to beauty and barber shops, taverns, cafes, and undertaking. Thus, a niche was open to the Chinese, and the few white grocers in the black community who complained had little standing in the white community since they catered to blacks. The Chinese gravitated into an entrepreneurial niche in other places in the South as well, as laundrymen, cigar-makers, shoe-makers, and cooks in New Orleans, for example (Takaki, 1989).

The question was, of course, where did the Chinese fit into the delta region's status and racial hierarchy? On top of that hierarchy were white planters and old-resident professionals, followed by businessmen and public officials. At the bottom were black manual and farm laborers and domestics (Loewen, 1971). At first, the Chinese were regarded by whites to be blacks, given their close business connection to the black community. Moreover, a few Chinese men had married black women or had black common-law wives. Since the Chinese lived in back of their stores, they also lived in black neighborhoods.

This conception of the Chinese lasted until 1940, according to Loewen (1971). About this time the Chinese began to share the status concerns of local whites, since it was apparent that they would never return to China. When immigration barriers were partially lifted during the Second World War, some of the Chinese men brought Chinese wives to the delta region. The Chinese community put pressure on its members to disassociate with black women, change their residence to white neighborhoods, Americanize their language and names, and otherwise become acceptable to elite whites. The segregation of Chinese children soon ended in the public schools. Although elite whites kept a social distance toward the Chinese, the mental stereotype associating the Chinese with blacks began to dissipate.

The Chinese were historically excluded from American society. They were forced to assume a subordinate position in the nation's system of ethnic stratification, on the one hand, and their entry into the country was restricted on the other. Their rights to naturalization and in the courts were also curtailed. Competition between the Chinese and white workers, demands of the Chinese on white growers in California, the superior political power of their Sinophobic foes, especially on the West Coast—all these set into motion the forces for Chinese exclusion. Furthermore, politicians from California allied in Congress with those from the South to legalize the racial stratification of all non-whites, Asian or African. This history is obviously consistent with ethnic conflict theory. The foes of the Chinese controlled the political process, and through it they got the upper hand in their conflict with the Chinese. The Chinese were virtually powerless in politics; Chinese aliens in the United States could not vote, and China, because of its weakness in world politics, was unable to protect its nationals in this country. China's notes of protest simply went unanswered.

MIDDLEMAN MINORITY

Excluded from the wider society, the Chinese became a middleman minority by building their own ethnic subeconomies in America, and thus Chinese labor could now work for themselves or for Chinese employers. This gave them an alternative to facing the discrimination and prejudice of others, at least on the job. Bonacich (1973:583) wrote that middleman minorities "tend to concentrate in certain occupations, notably trade and commerce, but also other 'middleman' lines such as agent, labor contractor, rent collector, money lender, and broker. They play the role of middlemen between producer and consumer, ... elite and masses." She suggested that the common denominator to middleman minority status is the liquidity of the occupations such groups choose. They concentrate in jobs consistent with sojourning motives, which provide a portable or easily liquidated livelihood, as personified by the trader, truck farmer, and independent professional. That is, their assets can be quickly liquidated, and assets as well as skills can be carried on the return home.

The Chinese began to concentrate in commercial trades and services late in the nineteenth century. They went into "middleman" businesses and became segregated in Chinatowns, withdrawing from mining, railroad construction, and wage labor in agriculture. Lee (1960) referred to this historical period of Chinese Americans as one of reconcentration in which the Chinese moved to the nation's larger cities and there established their subeconomies and Chinatowns. Between 1870 and 1920 there was a 280 percentage increase of Chinese in domestic and service work and a phenomenal 960 percent increase in the number of Chinese traders and dealers (Yuan, 1963). Between 1850 and 1880, the Chinese concentrated in cities on the West Coast; between 1880 and 1910 they dispersed to other regions of the United States, and after 1910 they concentrated in the cities of other regions (Li, 1976). To illustrate, 83 percent of the Chinese lived on the West Coast in 1880, 66 percent were there in 1900, but by 1920 only 55 percent of the Chinese lived on the West Coast (Kwang, 1979). Over 90 percent of the Chinese were urban in 1940, in contrast to 55 percent of the total population (Takaki, 1989). According to the 1940 Census, 61 percent of the Chinese males were manual laborers, and almost all of them worked in laundries, garment factories, and restaurants (Takaki, 1989). Thirty-six percent were in the service industry, compared to 7 percent for whites. Very few Chinese males (1%) were in the crafts compared to white males (20%). Twenty-nine percent of the Chinese females were in domestic service, 26 percent in clerical and sales jobs, and 26 percent in manufacturing (Takaki, 1989).

In the process, a class of Chinese capital emerged that provided Chinese in America with employment without ethnic prejudice and discrimination. The establishment of an ethnic subeconomy and opportunity structure is an important event in the history of any ethnic group, especially for one facing restricted opportunity in the larger society. An ethnic subeconomy does not necessarily mean any better treatment of employees by employers, however; the legendary exploitation of labor in the sweatshops of this nation's Chinatowns is sad. But it did mean that the Chinese were able to avoid the full impact of anti-Asian prejudice and discrimination.

The Chinese middleman minority position took shape in the nation's Chinatowns around the turn of the century. Self-employed Chinese at this time were concentrated in hand laundries, import outlets, restaurants, and retail grocery stores. The bulk of the salaried Chinese were employed in Chinese firms, including manufacturing as well as commercial outlets. Outside their subeconomy, Chinese laborers were domestic servants and gardeners in the larger labor market. The concentration that marked Chinese participation in the labor force is dramatically illustrated by the fact that fully 50 percent of the nation's salaried and self-employed Chinese in 1920 were in hand laundries or restaurants (Light, 1972).

In one Chinatown in California, there were "125 prostitutes, 25 cigar-makers, 10 grocery stores, two large-size food wholesale establishments, one pawnbroker shop, three eating houses, six drug stores, six barber shops employing a total of 12 barbers, seven physicians, two shoe and slipper manufacturers, two fruit stands and four butcher shops" (Weiss, 1974:50). This Chinatown was a distinct district within the city, and Chinese outside the city were engaged in mining, farming, and various types of gardening. In Box 12.3 you can read a description of a typical Chinatown.

☙☙

BOX 12.3 CHINATOWN

For the people living there, the colony was their home and community—a place where they could live "a warmer, freer, and more human life among their relatives and friends than among strangers." The grocery stores of their *wa fau*, or Chinese market town, stocked familiar foods—Chinese cabbage, dried mushrooms, salted fish (*hom yee*), canned lichees, soy sauce, sea cucumber (*hoy tom*), bamboo shoots, shark fins, "bird's nest," dried boned duck's feet, salted duck eggs (*hom don*), bean sprouts, Chinese roast duck, and fresh ("alive") chicken shipped in daily by Chinese chicken farmers in the country. The clothing stores sold pants and shoes that fit the Chinese. In Chinatown, there were newspapers in Chinese available, herb shops, Chinese theaters, and barbershops where residents could have their hair cut and done properly. Chinatown restaurants served bachelors cheap but tasty food and offered lavish, nine-course dinners to wealthy Chinese families, especially on Sundays. In their community were their temples, Chinese-language schools, and centers for family associations. In Chinatown some of the stores served as post offices.... In the outside world, among whites, the Chinese felt they had to be reserved and silent. But among themselves in Chinatown they could untie their tongues, for they liked to "talk and talk loudly."

Source: From *Strangers from a Different Shore: A History of Asian Americans*, p. 253, by Ronald Takaki. Copyright © 1989 by Ronald Takaki. By permission of Little, Brown and Company.

The occupational concentration and residential segregation of the Chinese meant their effective exclusion from the larger American society. There were no horizontal alliances between the Chinese and their class counterparts in the wider society, capital or labor. Instead, Chinese employers and employees were vertically integrated into their own subeconomy and subsociety, secluded from others. Antagonism toward the Chinese drove them further into their own separate ethnic community:

> One of the accusations frequently made by non-Chinese against their Asiatic fellow workers was that they were too docile, too slavelike, to be able to stand on their own feet in a free society. But the greater the pressure from the outside, the more cohesive became the vertical structure of the Chinese establishment, and the more unlikely any horizontal cleavage within it (Saxton, 1971:10).

Antagonism toward Chinese capital was equally great. Chinese businessmen enjoyed a competitive edge in certain industries, in part due to their access to cheaper Chinese labor, and this created ethnic hostility in business circles. This paralleled hostility in the ranks of labor, because of the refusal of Chinese labor to join the union movement. Both labor and business interests saw the Chinese as foreign and clannish; it was also a culture clash. The ethnic solidarity of the Chinese and the antagonism toward them were merely different sides of the same coin.

Chinatowns were organized along Old World lines, into *fongs*, clans (*tsu*), *hui-guans*, secret societies (*tongs*), and trade guilds. Fongs were composed of close family and village members, and clans were larger groupings of village associations (Takaki, 1989). Clans were surname associations that originated in the lineage communities of southeast China. They enforced endogamy until recently and were typically organized around a leading merchant's store. Fongs and clans also had clubhouses and their own temples. While clans had definite economic functions, their purpose was primarily fraternal and welfare. It was the fongs and clans that reminded the sojourner of his obligations to village and family in China and thus acted *in loco parentis*. "The clans established temples, transmitted letters to the villages in the homeland, and shipped home the bodies or bones of the deceased" (Takaki, 1989:119). Today, for the third- and fourth-generation Chinese Americans these obligations have diminished in saliency, and the functions of clans have been curtailed (Lyman, 1974).

Hui-guans were ethnic divisions within the larger Chinese group, composed of those who spoke the same dialect and hailed from the same region of China. They were similar to the *Landsmannschaft* Louis Wirth observed in the Jewish ghetto of Chicago (see Chapter 2). Lyman (1974) wrote that hui-guans were most important in incorporating immigrants into American Chinatowns, serving as caravansaries, credit and loan societies, and employment agencies. Hui-guans administered the *credit-ticket system*, whereby immigrants were advanced passage money to the United States. Agents of hui-guans met ships as they arrived in San Francisco, for instance, found jobs for new arrivals, and later deducted passage advances from their wages. Hui-guans originated in China as hostelries in big cities that provided lodging for their traveling residents and students preparing for imperial exams (Lyman, 1986).

Members of a hui-guan normally employed only their own kind, as trade guilds and commercial establishments were organized around these dialect groups. Hui-guans exercised control over labor, commerce, debts, and disputes, and thus their communal control over economic exchange in Chinatowns and the integration of immigrants into this subeconomy was virtually absolute. Hui-guans also provided attorneys for members with legal troubles. "In San Francisco during the 1850s, the district associations were the *Sze Yup, Ning Yeung, Sam Yup, Yeong Wo, Hop Wo,* and *Yan Wo*; they later organized themselves into the *Chung Wai Wui Koon*. Known popularly as the Chinese Six Companies, the last organization helped settle interdistrict conflict and provided educational and health services to the community.... They interacted with the city's white business community" (Takaki, 1989:119). The Chinese Six Companies was composed of representatives from local Chinese organizations and acted as an unofficial government, controlling conflict within Chinatown and representing the Chinese community to outsiders (Weiss, 1974).

Membership in both clan and hui-guan was ascriptive, based on birthright. Secret societies, or *tongs*, were voluntary associations in which membership was on the basis of mutual choice rather than birthright. Tongs recruited members from those who were either ineligible or ostracized from Chinatown's more powerful clans and hui-guans. The economic function of these secret societies centered around the provision of illegal goods and services, such as prostitutes for homeless Chinese males. Tongs included professional killers, who were known as hatchetmen for their use of small hatchets in that trade. The first tong (1852) in San Francisco was the *Kwong Duck Tong* (Lyman, 1986). Some observers believed that there were as many as thirty tongs in San Francisco alone in 1900, although a government survey in the same era listed only sixteen tongs across the entire nation (Light, 1972). Regardless of their number, secret societies provided a check on the power of prominent clans and hui-guans and offered opportunity to outcasts from these other organizations in the Chinese community. Tongs originated in China as nationalist organizations fighting different dynasties and evolved into mutual-aid and Mafia-type organizations in the United States (Tsai, 1983).

Trade guilds drew their membership not only from people in the same trade or line of work but also from a particular clan or hui-guan. Trade guilds represented an extension of the economic control of powerful clans and hui-guans. Laundrymen, cigar makers, restaurateurs, clothing manufacturers from one clan, hui-guan, or another—all had their trade guilds. Employers in a trade guild would typically hire their own clansmen or members of their own hui-guan. Internal competition was regulated, rules of location and compensation were enforced, and violators of the rules were punished through the trade guilds. Financing members in new locations was often done through rotating credit associations, *woi*, in which each member made contributions taken out periodically by the members in some rotation. The paternalism between Chinese capital and labor was rooted in these Old World blood ties and communal obligations.

Disputes between individual Chinese in Chinatowns typically escalated into conflicts between clans and hui-guans. Declarations of war between these associations were prominently displayed on posters throughout Chinatown, and soldiers for each side engaged in open street warfare. Peace initiatives followed, and a truce was sealed with a banquet (Lyman, 1986). Such conflict was one reason for the formation of the Chinese Six Companies, so that clan and interdistrict disputes could be settled without open conflict. By 1935, San Francisco's Chinatown began to develop tourism as a major business, possible only with peace on the streets (Takaki, 1989).

This was the state of the Chinese in America up to World War II. They had become a middleman minority, a pattern of ethnic change also common to Chinese emigrants outside this country. The Chinese concentrated in certain businesses and built an ethnic subeconomy in the nation's Chinatowns, where they provided opportunity for their own kind. The result was the further exclusion of the Chinese from American society and their divergence, at least the continuation of a foreign Chinese subculture in America's Chinatowns. The past unification of Chinese capital and labor in a single subeconomy and ethnic community, one separated from the larger society economically and culturally, was reinforced by the fact that there was not a significant American-born generation of adult Chinese until World War II. Because of the restrictions on Chinese immigration and the sojourning motives of Chinese males, Chinese women did not join their men in America, and this delayed the birth of an American-born generation of Chinese until the twentieth century. In short, the inclusion of Chinese into American society was minimal just fifty years ago.

The mutilated Chinese family was gradually replaced by the *small-producer Chinese family* in the first half of the twentieth century (Wong, 1988). The mutilated family meant that Chinese males in the United States had left their wives and families back in China. However, Chinese wives did manage to come to the United States late in the nineteenth century and early in the twentieth. They came through the slot system, through other openings in immigration restrictions, and as wives of Chinese merchants. "It was not until the 1920s, seventy years after the beginning of Chinese life in California, that the reproduction of a visible second generation began. These few families grew up in the midst of a declining bachelor society...." (Nee and Nee, 1972:148). Between 1920 and 1950 the percentage of the total Chinese population born in this country rose from 30 to 50 percent (Wong, 1988). These small-producer families drew no line between work and family, for the whole family worked at a family business. The division of labor was based on the age and sex of family members, and the children often acted as intermediaries between their parents and the outside world. The emphasis in the household and at work was the collective family, rather than any single member.

By the same token, the Chinese were better prepared than many other ethnic groups for the changes in the nation's labor needs following World War II. They as a group possessed the economic base for investments in the education of their young, a prerequisite for mobility into higher levels of white-collar work. Because of the historical solidarity of the Chinese community in this country, there was also a network of mutual aid that distributed economic resources to the American-born generation. Thus this generation of Chinese Americans would carry a sense of ethnic pride and achievement into the nation's universities and great work bureaucracies in the second half of the twentieth century.

THE PRESENT SITUATION

Tables 12.1 and 12.2 indicate how the inclusion of the Chinese into the wider society has progressed during the post-industrial phase of American history. By 1980, 33 percent of the Chinese were employed in managerial and professional work. Corresponding with the increasing number of Chinese in professional and technical work, there has been a decreasing number of Chinese proprietors and household servants. Taken together, this indicates the movement of many Chinese Americans out of the economic niche of a middleman minority and into the professional and technical fields of the post-industrial American society. The occupational composition of the Chinese people in 1990 compares favorably with that of the entire labor force (Table 12.2).

TABLE 12.1 PERCENTAGE DISTRIBUTION OF CHINESE AMERICANS AND ALL EMPLOYED PEOPLE BY OCCUPATIONAL GROUPS, 1940–1970

Occupational Group	Chinese Origin				All People			
	1940	1950	1960	1970	1940	1950	1960	1970
White-collar workers								
Professional and technical	3.0	7.2	19.2	26.5	7.5	8.7	11.1	14.9
Managers, officials, and proprietors except farmers	14.7	20.0	13.6	8.9	8.4	8.7	8.4	8.3
Clerical and sales	12.0	16.2	21.9	21.2	16.8	20.3	18.4	13.7
Blue-collar workers								
Craftsmen and foremen	1.4	2.9	5.5	5.4	11.3	14.3	13.5	13.9
Operators	23.3	17.3	16.1	13.8	18.4	20.3	18.4	13.7
Laborers except farm and mine	2.0	1.7	1.4	2.3	6.8	6.5	4.8	4.5
Service workers								
Private household	7.0	2.6	1.1	0.8	6.2	2.5	2.7	1.5
Other service	31.6	29.2	20.1	19.6	6.2	7.8	8.4	11.3
Farm workers								
Farmers and managers	1.3	1.2	0.7	0.3	11.5	7.6	3.9	1.9
Laborers and foremen	3.0	1.4	0.5	0.3	6.9	4.4	2.2	1.3

Note: Percentages may not total 100 because of rounding.

Sources: 1940 Census, *The Labor Force*, Table 62, p. 90; 1940 Census, *Characteristics of the Nonwhite Population by Race*, Table 32, pp. 95–96; 1950 Census, *Characteristics of the Nonwhite Population by Race*, Table 12, p. 42; 1960 Census, *Characteristics of the Nonwhite Population by Race*, Table 35, p. 111; 1970 Census, *Occupational Characteristics*, Table 39, pp. 593–608.

TABLE 12.2   PERCENTAGE DISTRIBUTION OF CHINESE AMERICANS AND ALL
EMPLOYED PEOPLE BY OCCUPATIONAL GROUPS, 1990

Occupational Group	Chinese Origin 1990	All People 1990
Managerial and professional	33.4%	25.5%
Technical, sales, and administrative support	32.7	31.5
Service occupations	17.4	13.5
Precision production, craft, and repair	5.5	11.5
Operators, fabricators, and laborers	8.9	15.5
Farming, forestry, and fishing	0.5	2.5

Source: Census of Population and Housing, 1990: Public Micromedia Samples U.S., prepared by the Bureau of the Census, 1992.

Only 3 percent of the male Chinese Americans 25 years and older possessed a college education in 1940, while, in 1960, 19 percent of them had at least four years of college. This put them as a group ahead of all other ethnic groups in educational attainment. Four percent of the adult Chinese females in the country had a college education in 1940, and, by 1960, nearly 15 percent of them had at least four years of college, placing them behind only Filipino females among the nation's ethnic groups in educational attainment (Schmid and Nobbe, 1965). In 1970, over 25 percent of the Chinese population 25 years or older had four years of college. These figures attest to a great change in Chinese Americans in a short time span, a change that has brought their greater inclusion into American society, and one that is consistent with our view on the increased potential for ethnic inclusion in modern society (see Chapter 6).

The Chinese became engineers, architects, physicians, dentists, optometrists, pharmacists, accountants, and college teachers. Lyman (1974:137) found that of 1,124 Chinese employed in American colleges and universities in 1960, more than half (648) were teaching engineering and physical or natural science and 108 were in medical science; only 254 were employed in the humanities or social sciences. The Chinese selected a narrow range of white-collar work. They opted for work that gave them prestige, high income, free choice of clientele, independence from professional peers, and jobs that did not demand interpersonal skills and facility in English. The Chinese circumvented many potential competitors and barriers for the better white-collar jobs by selecting fields that were to be the growth occupations after World War II and that required technical expertise rather than skillfulness in Anglo-American cultural styles. These fields also represent portable skills and are reminiscent of the occupational choices made by the earlier Chinese sojourners and middleman merchants. Not every Chinese person could satisfy all of these criteria in job choice, of course, but these were some of the occupational goals sought by the Chinese as a class.

There were other changes in the Chinese community after World War II that were connected with their educational and occupational achievements. Lyman (1974:147) observed that:

> Chinese Americans often wish to ratify their newly acquired middle-class status by moving to better residences, purchasing their own homes, and relocating outside Chinatown.... When Chinese did remove to the suburbs they often reconstituted their community and reestablished an ethnic enclave in the supposedly cosmopolitan and raceless regions of American residences.

Community development by middle-class and suburban Chinese was not unlike that of suburban Jews in the Chicago area (see Chapter 3). Typically, suburban Chinese American communities were organized around a Chinese-language school, and the people's interest in the school fostered a wider form of organization (Lyman, 1974:149). According to Weiss (1974), the Chinese in Valley City formed a civic club composed of business and professional people; recreational groups such as golf groups, bowling clubs, and sports clubs; community service clubs; Christian churches; and youth groups. This suggests a continuation of cultural pluralism among middle-class Chinese Americans.

The recent occupational diversification of Chinese Americans has not been so great as to mean their full assimilation into American society. It does mean, however, that divisions between Chinese ethclasses are greater than ever before. There is a growing class of Chinese poor in this country, due to renewed immigration, as the American-born Chinese are simultaneously included more than ever before into the larger American society. Their inclusion results in partial assimilation that includes citizenship for the American-born Chinese, and the adoption of American residential patterns, language practices, clothing styles, and a certain amount of participation in community affairs (Hsu, 1971).

There were several reasons for the greater inclusion of the Chinese into the larger society after World War II. China was an ally of the United States, and the propaganda about the courageous Chinese peasant meeting the Japanese onslaught moderated domestic prejudice against Chinese Americans (Daniels, 1988). Besides, the country was preoccupied at the time with hatred for another Asian group, the

Japanese. The negative image of the Chinese as sly and superstitious changed around World War ll into a positive image of them as being patient, courteous, and loyal to their families (Li, 1976). Opportunities were made available for the first time to Chinese Americans, as a consequence, and many of the young began to pass through doors previously shut to the Chinese. The concentration of Chinese in urban areas and on the West Coast, where many of these opportunities occurred, also helped. This all coincided with the fact that the first large generation of American-born Chinese came of age during the war years.

However, the roots of the inclusion of the Chinese during the post-industrial phase of American society go back to their exclusion in an earlier era. The Chinese had managed to build an ethnic subeconomy and maintain themselves as a communal group in the course of their exclusion. The formation of this subeconomy was facilitated by the original sojourning motives of the early Chinese immigrants and by the ethnic solidarity within clans and hui-guans. The result was the integration of Chinese capital and labor into a single economic endeavor, tied together economically and socially through the overlapping bonds of economic interdependence, clan, and hui-guan membership. This had the effect of preserving the immigrant brotherhood and simultaneously precluding the assimilation of the Chinese with their class counterparts in the larger society. When it came time to prepare an American-born generation for work in the wider society, however, both the economic resources and the mechanism for their distribution were present. Wealth and its distribution through the mutual obligations of clans and hui-guans provided the means for financing the education of the young and thus their entry into professional and technical fields.

Bonacich (1973:593) speculated on an economic reason that the Chinese turned their attention to the inclusion of their young into the wider American society: "one important factor seems to be changing economic conditions (the development of chain stores, supermarkets, etc.), making the family firm less viable, and driving the younger generations to seek employment in higher-paying non-ethnic firms." That is, the Chinese were forced out of their middleman economic roles by the growing scale of business in this country after World War II, while at the same time opportunities in the larger economy were expanding for the Chinese. Furthermore, China underwent a political revolution after World War II, making the eventual return home of the sojourner now virtually impossible. The second-generation Chinese were Americanized, and among them the Old-World regional societies and ascriptive obligations lost much of their saliency. These patterns were partially replaced by participation in voluntary associations. Recently, ethnic interest groups have grown pan-Asiatic and include both

American-born Chinese and Japanese, along with other Asian Americans. All of this indicates the convergence of the middle class, American-born Chinese in recent years.

Nevertheless, almost 40 percent of the Chinese in the nation's labor force remained in manual work by 1980, and nearly half of these were employed in service work as waiters, busboys, and domestics. This is traditional work for Chinese labor in the country, and many of these workers have stayed in Chinatowns, while the better-educated and more mobile ones have moved to the nation's suburbs. Populations in Chinatowns have been inflated by the Chinese immigration into the country since 1965. Many of these recent immigrants appear to be trapped in menial work, perhaps unable to duplicate the historical course of the earlier Chinese immigrants.

NEW CHINESE IMMIGRATION

Due to changes in immigration laws since World War II, the number of Chinese in America has grown. The Chinese Exclusion Acts were repealed in 1943, a War Brides Act was passed in 1945, and the Walter-McCarran Act, with family reunification as an immigration preference, was passed in 1952. International quotas replaced national ones in 1965, and all of these allowed more Chinese into the United States. Between 1965 and 1984, over 400,000 Chinese immigrants entered the United States, making Chinese immigration the third largest, behind only Mexican and Filipino immigration. The Chinese population in the United States increased from 431,583 in 1970 to 1,079,700 in 1985 (Wong, 1988). In 1980, over 54 percent of the Chinese were foreign-born (Mangiafico, 1988). That is, the number of recent immigrants exceeded that of American-born Chinese in 1980. In 1990, there were 1.26 million Chinese in the country and by the year 2000 there are likely to be over 1.6 million (Kitano and Daniels, 1988).

These recent Chinese immigrants are different from the earlier ones in a number of ways. First, they come from all parts of mainland China, not just southern China, as well as from Taiwan, Hong Kong, other parts of southeast Asia, and even South America (Mangiafico, 1988; Tsai, 1986). The old homogeneity of the Chinese in America is now gone, for the roots of the Chinese today go back to several origins, not only southern China. Secondly, they come as families and as students, meaning that Chinese women as well as men are now coming to the United States. This is very different from the bachelor society of the earlier immigrants, when up to 97 percent of the Chinese in American were men. As a result, the sex ratio of the Chinese has become decidedly more balanced; there were only 102 males per 100 females in 1980 (Mangiafico, 1988).

Compared to the American population, Chinese immigrants since 1960 are more likely to be college graduates (Mangiafico, 1988). This is also true for the entire Chinese population in the United States. In 1980, almost 60 percent of the Chinese aged 20–24 were enrolled in school, while only 23.9 percent of white Americans that age were enrolled. The Chinese are also more likely to be in the work force than the total American population. This is true for Chinese women as well as men. Almost one-half of the American women over 16 years old were in the labor force in 1980, but over 58 percent of Chinese women were working outside the home. This has brought change to the Chinese family.

The new professional Chinese family is still conservative about sex roles and other basic values, avoids public displays of affection, has lower divorce rates, and highly values education (Wong, 1988). By the same token, the role of women in the family has changed. Women were subordinate to men in traditional Chinese society, controlled by the three obediences: to father if unmarried, to husband, or to sons if widowed (Tsai, 1986). However, Chinese women are now better educated, work outside the home, and have challenged male authority on a number of counts. They insist now on the right to fall in love, for example, and marry a mate of their choice with or without parental consent. Thirty-three percent of the Chinese marriages are now intermarriages, and over 73 percent of the third-generation Chinese females marry non-Chinese (Wong, 1988).

About half of the new Chinese immigrants went into professional, technical, and managerial work in the United States. Another 43 percent took jobs as operators and clerks and in the service sector (Takaki, 1989). That is, their occupational distribution is bimodal, with two distinct ethclasses, one in professional and technical white-collar work and another in low-paying manufacturing and service work. This is true for the entire Chinese population as well. In 1980, over half of the nation's Chinese workers were employed in menial service and low-skill blue-collar jobs and another 42 percent were in managerial, professional, and technical work (Takaki, 1989). Both the educational and occupational composition of the Chinese are bipolar, with many on top but some on the bottom (Daniels, 1988; Li, 1976). This clearly reflects the current ethclasses in the Chinese community among both American-born Chinese and recent immigrants.

The poorer ethclass remains in the nation's Chinatowns, which are populated increasingly by the foreign-born. Immigrant women work in the garment industry as operators, for example, and the men work in local restaurants. Twenty-five percent of New York's Chinatown residents now live below the poverty line (Takaki, 1989). Will the recent immigrants follow the course of the earlier Chinese immigrants? While the consumer demand for certain Chinese goods and services still exists among immigrants and in the larger society, the era of small mom-and-pop stores and restaurants has peaked and is on the decline, as they are replaced by supermarkets and fast-food chains. Meanwhile, the immigrants are stuck in the enclave economy of the nation's Chinatowns (Sanders and Nee, 1987; Zhou and Logan, 1989). The rapid inclusion of these new immigrants into white-collar work is also problematic. Some of their children are college-bound while others gravitate to local youth gangs (Box 12.4). Chinatowns are now portrayed as areas of festering resentment, alienation, labor exploitation, unemployment, and nascent rebellion (Light and Wong, 1975; Lyman, 1974). Light and Wong believe that these problems have not been publicized in the wider society because elites in Chinatown fear that social protest will inhibit tourism.

The Chinese in America are now stratified into three ethclasses: those in the American middle class, at least with respect to education, occupation, residence, and forms of secondary association; those who are uneducated and still in domestic service and menial work; and powerful merchants in the nation's Chinatowns. The Chinese in America are now more diversified and dispersed; they are a modern ethnic group stratified into ethclasses.

❧

BOX 12.4 GANGS IN NEW YORK'S CHINATOWN

The dramatic rise in the number of Asian immigrants over the last 20 years has been reflected by an increase in gangs.... More immigrants mean more business, more money, more power. There's more heroin trafficking. And when the gangs in the 90s now send a message, they kill people.

An estimated 300,000 Chinese live in New York, 150,000 in Chinatown. In the 1980s, as new groups from Taiwan and Hong Kong flowed in they settled in Flushing in Queens and along Eighth Avenue in Brooklyn, each area with Chinese populations of over 60,000. More recently, Chinatown has felt the influx of a wave of 30,000 undocumented immigrants, mostly from China's Fukien Province....

A possible indication of increased gang activity is reflected in police statistics for Chinatown. The data for the first six months of 1990 show robberies up by 30 percent over 1989. In the Fifth Precinct, which patrols Chinatown, 13 people have been murdered so far, compared with 12 homicides for all of 1989. This month alone, five gang members were murdered in three separate incidents in lower Manhattan.

Source: Donatella Lorch, "A Traditionally Insular Community Begins to Reach Out." *New York Times*, October 28, 1990. Copyright © 1990 by The New York Times Company. Reprinted by permission.

☺☺

SUMMARY

All three theories of the sociological lore on American ethnicity must be taken into account to understand the history of the Chinese in this country. Labor competition led to the exclusion of the Chinese by more powerful and Sinophobic groups, a direct application of conflict theory. The Chinese evolved then into a middleman minority in the nation's Chinatowns and formed their own subeconomy. This meant the isolation of Chinese capital and labor from their class counterparts in the larger American society, resulting in the cultural and structural pluralism of the Chinese community. It also meant the continuation of intense prejudice against the Chinese, distilled into stereotypes about their clannishness and shrewdness, and made for the social distance other Americans have historically expressed toward the Chinese. Thus the psychology of prejudice helps explain the image of the Chinese in the larger society and how this image contributed in perpetuating the exclusion of the Chinese.

Forces for the inclusion of the Chinese came later, with the post-industrial phase of American society. White-collar work provided opportunity for American-born Chinese in the wider society, while the changing picture of enterprise in America simultaneously meant the reduction of small-scale ethnic businesses. The gains that had been made in these businesses helped, however, in the preparation of the American-born generation for white-collar positions. The result is that Chinese Americans are now a much more diverse group, stratified into ethclasses.

Chinese immigration has increased in recent years, and the immigrants are also stratified into ethclasses, symbolized by the immigrant engineer joining the uptown Chinese and the immigrant dishwasher the downtown Chinese. This immigration has added to the diversity of the Chinese in America in other ways as well. The Chinese are now from diverse origins, not only southern China, and there are now about as many Chinese women as men. The old communal organizations once so powerful in the nation's Chinatowns have lost much of their power and influence over the Chinese in America. Differences in ethclass, origin, generation, and residence now divide the Chinese population more than ever. The Chinese live throughout the country, no longer so concentrated on the West Coast.

JAPANESE AMERICANS AND AMERICAN SOCIETY

T here were 804,000 Japanese Americans in 1990. The history of the Japanese in America, which goes back to the nineteenth century, is similar to that of the Chinese in this country. Both Asian groups were initially laborers, mainly on the West Coast, and then both became middleman minorities. Furthermore, the second-generation Japanese Americans (*Nisei*) were included into the larger society after World War II, like their Chinese counterparts, through college education and white-collar work. Unlike the Chinese, however, the Japanese have also been independent farmers over the years, particularly in California, and the Japanese bachelor society did not last nearly as long. An American-born generation came of adult age sooner than that of the Chinese. In addition, the Japanese were placed in internment camps during World War II, making their history in America unique, not just different from that of the Chinese. The history of the Japanese in America is shown in Figure 13.1.

CONTACT

It is estimated that less than 300,000 Japanese had immigrated to the mainland of the United States by 1924, the year that further Asian immigration virtually stopped. The majority of the Japanese immigrants, about 89 percent, arrived here between 1900 and 1924 (Daniels, 1969; Ima, 1976; Petersen, 1971). Mostly men without families entered the United States up to 1908, and then they were joined by wives from 1908 to 1924. Many of these immigrants to the mainland had immi-

FIGURE 13.1 JAPANESE AMERICANS AND CHANGE IN AMERICAN SOCIETY

Industrial Society c. 1865–1945				Post-Industrial Society c. 1945–Present	
Immigration and contact →	Early accommodation →	Competition, conflict, ethnic stratification, and exclusion →	Middleman minority →	→ Internment →	Present situation

grated earlier to Hawaii, and from Hawaii they later came to the West Coast. The intention was for the Japanese to replace the aging Chinese in the fields of California, although many of the Japanese immigrants also found work on the railroads, in mining, fishing and fish canneries, logging, and as domestic servants. In 1900, the Japanese population on the West Coast was nearly 25,000, but by 1920 it was 110,000 (Kitano and Daniels, 1988). There were 126,948 Japanese in the United States in 1940, just before their internment during the Second World War, and nearly two-thirds were American-born (Daniels, 1988).

After a period of European intrusion into Japan between 1543 and 1639, Japan expelled European traders and forbade the emigration of its citizens. The country was in an era of isolation between 1639 and 1853, but its borders were opened after Commodore Perry's negotiations of 1853 and 1854. Japan subsequently underwent a period of rapid industrialization and military build-up, and Japanese farmers were heavily taxed to finance both these changes. Since the practice in Japan was for the eldest son to inherit the family's land, daughters and younger brothers were forced to migrate elsewhere either in Japan or overseas. Consequently, the Japanese began to emigrate, and by 1884 Japan permitted Hawaiian planters to recruit Japanese nationals for work on their sugar plantations. In 1900, there were eleven emigration companies operating in Japan to facilitate this movement of people (Wilson and Hosokawa, 1980). Before allowing them to emigrate, the Japanese government screened emigrants for health, literacy, and strength of character to uphold the honor of the Japanese nation overseas.

By 1894, 30,000 Japanese had emigrated to Hawaii, where they could make six times the earnings possible in Japanese agriculture (Takaki, 1989). About 200,000 had gone to Hawaii by 1924, and the Japanese population in Hawaii was 139,631 in 1930 (Wilson and

Hosokawa, 1980). The Hawaiian elite of planters, merchants, and missionaries had decided to bring in Japanese to counter the labor militancy of the Chinese field hands on the sugar plantations. At first, the Japanese worked for 50 cents a day compared to the $1.00 per day demanded by the Chinese (Daniels, 1988). The planters recruited Japanese women as well as men, for they saw women as labor, and women would help insure labor discipline on the plantations (Takaki, 1989). Over time, the Japanese moved off the plantations and entered varied occupations in Hawaii.

Most of the Japanese immigrants into mainland United States came from the southern prefectures of Hiroshima, Kumamoto, Wakayama, Fukuoka, and Yamaguchi (Kitano, 1969:10). Others remigrated from Hawaii to the mainland. These immigrants are called *Issei*, the first generation in the United States. Most of the immigrants had been farm laborers or small farmers in Japan. As a class they held the agricultural arts and land ownership in high regard, values that were to prove significant in the history of the Japanese in America. Economic and social conditions in Japan pushed these people out of their homeland, as the labor needs in Hawaii and on the West Coast pulled them here. Not only could Japanese farmers earn six times more income in Hawaii than in Japan, but also the Japanese government was taxing farmers heavily to pay for the country's industialization and military build-up (Takaki, 1989).

Like the Chinese before them, the Japanese immigrants to the United States were sojourners who were willing to suffer severe hardships in this country, working for less than others and sticking to themselves. Many returned to Japan after a short stay in America; about 150,000 of the 300,000 Japanese immigrants (up to 1924) returned to Japan (Wilson and Hosokawa, 1980).

But, on the average, the Japanese immigrants were better prepared than the Chinese for their entry into the United States. First, they were better informed about working conditions on the West Coast and in Hawaii, a state of readiness that the Japanese government nurtured in its émigrés. Furthermore, unlike China, Japan was a powerful enough country to have its notes protesting the mistreatment of its nationals taken seriously in this country. Japan was a power in the Pacific at the turn of the century, and President Roosevelt was not indifferent to Japanese protests about discrimination against its nationals in California (Daniels, 1969). Japan in 1905 even curbed Korean emigration to prevent Koreans from competing with the Japanese overseas (Takaki, 1989). As a consequence, Japanese immigrants were less vulnerable than the Chinese to acts of outright discrimination and unscrupulous exploitation in America.

Agitation in the United States for the restriction of Japanese immigrants began early in the twentieth century, shortly after their arrival on the West Coast. In 1907–08 the United States and Japan signed a Gentlemen's Agreement, stipulating that Japan would issue passports good for the continental United States only to those Japanese who were once residents of this country or who were the parents, wives, or children of U.S. residents. Thereafter, Japanese laborers who were not covered by these exemptions were forbidden entry into the country. The United States meant to restrict significantly further Japanese immigration into the country with this legislation, but its intent was circumvented by the Japanese practice of *picture brides*.

A Japanese man in the United States arranged for a marriage with a woman in Japan by proxy, and the bride and groom knew one another only by the exchange of photographs. Typically, the grooms were about ten years older than their immigrant brides, and thus many men sent to Japan pictures of themselves taken ten years earlier (Glenn, 1986). These brides then could legally enter the United States according to the Gentlemen's Agreement. Actually, a man's family in Japan made these arrangements there and knew much about the prospective bride. The custom for women to marry virtual strangers had a long history in Japan, and the practice of picture brides was simply an extension of it.

The Japanese consulate general in San Francisco regulated the practice on this side through the Japanese Association of America, an organization to which about 12 percent of the Issei belonged in 1924 (Kitano and Daniels, 1988; Wilson and Hosokawa, 1980). The rule was that each immigrant had to have $800 in liquid assets, such as a bank account, a considerable sum of money for most. Thus, many immigrants pooled their money—*show money* it was called—and rotated the same $800 from one individual's account to those of all the others (Daniels, 1988; Kitano and Daniels, 1988). After 1908, there was a net immigration into the United States of 25,000 Japanese women; consequently, while there were 25 Japanese men for every woman in 1900, the sex ratio was reduced to 2 to 1 by 1920 (Glenn, 1986; Kitano and Daniels, 1988). Not all Issei women were picture brides; only about one in four were (Wilson and Hosokawa, 1980). The Japanese population on the West Coast continued to grow, to the horror of anti-Asian factions in the state of California (Daniels, 1969). Although later legislation plugged the loophole of picture brides, American-born Japanese children (Nisei) already outnumbered their parents early in the 1930s. Thus, an American-born generation came sooner to the Japanese than to the Chinese; the mutilated family lasted for a much shorter time for the Japanese immigrants.

Issei marriages were described by Yanagisako (1985) in the following terms. The marriages were arranged by the two families of the partners, and marriages were based on a sense of duty, compassion, and respect rather than romantic love (Box 13.1). The male was dominant in the household, and there was a rigid sexual division of labor in the households. Wives were devoted to child care and duties within the home, and males were responsible for matters outside the home. Relations between husbands and wives were emotionally restrained, and the nuclear unit was enmeshed in extended family relationships. In money matters, the family accumulated savings for mobility into businesses in the United States, for the eventual return to Japan, and for remittances to family members still in Japan.

BOX 13.1 AN ISSEI MARRIAGE

The events leading to Katsumi and Tatsuyo Takitani's wedding were typical of Issei marriages arranged in Japan. By the time he was thirty-five years old, Katsumi had been working in America for twelve years. As he was *chonan* (first son), his widowed mother in Japan was anxious to see him married. Tatsuyo's father's sister lived next door to Katsumi's married sister in Katsumi's village, and thus was one of the first to hear that his mother was seeking a bride for him. She told Tatsuyo's parents about this and they in turn arranged a *miai* (viewing session) in which Katsumi, who was back visiting his family, and his mother (his father was deceased) met Tatsuyo and her family. Katsumi was satisfied enough with what he saw, and as Tatsuyo's response to her parents' query as to whether she would like to go to America was that she "didn't mind," the parents proceeded with the arrangements. Each family already knew enough about the other's history and bloodline, as they lived in adjoining *mura* (villages) separated by only two miles. Consequently, there was little need for either to invest much time investigating the other's background, and the wedding took place one month after the *miai.*

Source: S. J. Yanagisako, *Transforming The Past: Tradition and Kinship Among Japanese Americans.* Copyright © 1985. Stanford: Stanford University Press, p. 30. Reprinted by permission.

Issei women often worked beside the men in the fields of California, and 20 percent were employed outside the home as compared to 9 percent for all married women in the United States (Glenn, 1986). In 1920, 34 percent of the Issei women worked in agriculture, another 17.7 percent were servants, and 21.7 percent were personal service workers (Glenn, 1986). Still others worked as sales clerks, often in family-owned shops, and some were dressmakers, sewing at home for others. Women were economic contributors to Issei households.

EARLY ACCOMMODATION

It seemed that at the turn of the century Japanese immigrants would make a rather easy transition into agriculture labor in California, given the shortage of Chinese labor there. Between 1900 and 1930, the Japanese became more concentrated in California, from 41.7 percent of their population in 1900 to over 70 percent in 1930 (Glenn, 1986). Were not the Japanese simply replacements for the aging Chinese in the fields of California? According to Daniels (1969:8):

> This is an oversimplification. California...was in the throes of the most prolonged panic of the century. The earliest Japanese labor gangs were in direct competition with the remaining Chinese, and had to resort to wage cutting to get employment.... Japanese were working for 50 cents a day.... The normal scale for Chinese had long been established at a dollar a day.

Not everyone would agree with this assessment of the early accommodation of the Japanese in California: "Seldom have other classes been discharged in large numbers to make room for the Japanese; on the contrary, Japanese have usually been employed to fill places vacated by others" (Petersen, 1971:28).

Whatever the level of competition between the Japanese and others in the early days, it would grow greater in succeeding years. Daniels (1969:9) wrote that employers initially welcomed the early Issei recruits to the ranks of American agriculture, particularly since the Chinese were using their rapidly diminishing numbers to try to raise wages. Working at a lower wage scale than the Chinese, Japanese farmhands reduced significantly the labor costs of growers; for example, the sugar beet harvest labor cost was reduced from $1.20 to 70 cents per ton (Daniels, 1969:8).

Early on, the Japanese were concentrated in farm labor, although they were also to be found in urban trades, mining, on the railroads, in general construction, logging and fishing, and domestic service. Fully 40 percent of the Japanese immigrants in the United States were working as farm laborers in 1911 (Petersen, 1971). They were funneled into farm work through their version of the padrone system. In response to the need of California growers for gang labor, clusters of boarding-houses run by Issei who doubled as small-scale labor contractors rapidly developed along the Pacific slope (Daniels, 1969:7). The board-inghouse keepers and hotel managers attracted a clientele of newly ar-rived immigrants from the *ken* (prefecture in Japan) of the owner-pro-prietor, who then became the employment agent of kenjin residing with him (Light, 1972:66). The boardinghouse keepers had connections with the Japanese labor bosses who placed Japanese crews into the fields of California. Other immigrants were placed in the United States by emigration companies and labor contractors in Japan (Wilson and Hosokawa, 1980). These funnels moved immigrant laborers fresh off the boat directly into the fields.

Within a few years, however, many of these immigrant workers had become independent farmers by leasing land, sharecropping, or buying land of their own. The role of the Japanese labor boss in the rise of many Japanese out of agrarian wage labor and into the status of landowners is so important that it is worthwhile to quote Light (1972:71–75) at length on the subject:

> In their contractual relationships with the growers, agricultural boss-es were outspokenly mercenary on behalf of their crews... and un-hesitantly allocated their crew to whichever rancher offered the men the best terms.... The Japanese boss system constituted an embryonic form of trade unionism.... Moreover, boss and crew typically shared a loyalty to ken, dialect, religious sect, and circle of friends.... The boss was thus... induced to take on the role of representative of his crew.... The contract labor system became "the central instrument" of the Japanese rise from agricultural day labor to independent farm-ing. Prefectural control of the labor supply and of the contractor en-abled Japanese farm hands to extract maximally favorable terms from white ranchers and so expedited the development of widespread proprietary status.

The Japanese value commitment to farming and land ownership and their skills at labor-intensive agriculture must also be counted among the reasons for their rapid rise out of field labor. The Japanese typically bought marginal land, often swamps and marshes, which they drained, and cultivated crops from their homeland. This required hard, continuous, intelligent effort. Japanese farmers in California con-centrated in the areas around Vacaville, Florin, the San Joaquin Valley, Fresno, the Pajaro Valley, and later in Imperial and Orange Counties in southern California (Wilson and Hosokawa, 1980). When the Japan-ese immigrants became independent farmers, they continued to use their network of ken ties for their mutual advantage and economic growth. In the process, the Japanese became increasingly competitive with white growers in California, which ushered in the era of inter-group competition, ethnic stratification, and exclusion of the Japanese.

COMPETITION, CONFLICT, ETHNIC STRATIFICATION, AND EXCLUSION

Japanese immigrants were welcomed at first by California growers and ranchers, among other employers, as a source of cheap, reliable labor. The Japanese worked also in mining, logging, fishing and fish canneries, and domestic service up and down the West Coast and even into the mountain states of the West. The Japanese as a group did not remain for long in farm labor, however, at least not for white employers. They soon acquired farms and businesses of their own, which meant competition with their former employers. As a consequence, white growers joined with organized labor, which had mobilized demonstrations on the West Coast against the Japanese as early as 1900, and who had formed the Asiatic Exclusion League in 1905 (Daniels, 1988).

Observers of the Japanese in America are all struck by the rapid rise of the Issei, the first generation, out of wage labor and into entrepreneurship. Japanese immigrants began buying their own land in the agricultural valleys of California within a few years after their arrival in this country. Light (1972:72–73) wrote about this remarkable transition:

> ...Japanese farm laborers began to work and lease land as contract, share, and tenant farmers, and ultimately began to purchase substantial amounts of land outright.... Japanese were exceptionally advantaged by their acquaintance with traditional Japanese methods of intensive cultivation.... They introduced new crops, notably rice, in the cultivation of which by dint of enormous effort they were able to make use of the most barren wastelands. Thus, the Japanese began to branch out of agricultural wage-labor by purchasing small tracts of barren land at very low prices. Since they were able to cultivate this land more successfully than others had anticipated, they began to make money in agriculture.

The Japanese version of the padrone system, the network of field laborers and labor bosses tied to one another by regional affiliations (*kenjinkai*), was critical in this movement into independent farming, as we already know. The unswerving advocacy of the labor bosses for their crews meant favorable wage rates for Japanese farm laborers, but the labor bosses made even faster progress for themselves. Daniels

(1974:219) wrote about the career of one very exceptional labor boss, a Mr. Shima:

> By 1909 the press was referring to him as the "Potato King" of California. By 1913, when a Japanese graduate student surveyed his holdings, Shima controlled nearly 30,000 acres directly, and, through marketing agreements, handled the produce raised by many of his compatriots. By 1920 it was estimated that he controlled 85 percent of California's potato crop, valued at over $18 million that year.

Mr. Shima left an estate valued at $15 million when he died in 1926 (Takaki, 1989).

There were two dimensions to the competition between the increasingly successful Japanese immigrants and their former employers. First, Japanese farmers competed directly with white growers in some of the produce markets of California, and they had a competitive edge in these markets because of their ethnic marketing associations. Light (1972) maintained that this applied to only a few markets, in truck vegetables, berries, and flowers, and in only a few cities in California. On the other hand, Takaki (1989) estimated that the Japanese by 1940 controlled 95 percent of California's snap beans, 67 percent of its tomatoes, 95 percent of its spring and summer celery, 44 percent of its onions, and 40 percent of its fresh green peas. As early as 1919, the Japanese held 10 percent of California's total crop, valued at $67 million, while farming only 1 percent of the state's total acreage (Kitano and Daniels, 1988).

Second, the movement of the Japanese into a class of independent farmers meant a corresponding decline in the supply of cheap Japanese field labor for white growers, and it must be remembered that this occurred before the influx of Mexican farm workers into California. Japanese field labor had never established any ties to white growers because Japanese labor bosses always mediated between Japanese farm labor and white growers. Not only were Japanese farmers no longer field labor for white growers, they also hired additional Japanese labor on their own farms. Light believed that it was this loss in their labor supply that most antagonized white ranchers against the Japanese. In any case, white growers took steps to exclude Japanese from agrarian proprietorship in the form of the alien land laws, and they would eventually find a replacement for the Japanese field hands in the Mexican farm worker.

In 1913, an Alien Land Bill was passed in California, with the objective clearly being "to drive the Japanese out of agriculture, and perhaps out of California" (Kitano, 1969:17). Before 1913, competition with the Japanese took the form of barn burnings, verbal assaults on individual Japanese, and other expressions of hostility. Now the growers had the state on their side, and the 1913 law was to ban alien Issei from owning land in California. The Japanese easily circumvented the intent of the 1913 Alien Land Law, however:

> It was quite simple for the attorneys who represented Japanese interests in California to evade the alleged intent of the law in many ways. The simplest was through incorporation so that control was ostensibly held by whites. For the growing number of Issei who had American-born children, things were even easier; they simply transferred the stock or title to their citizen children whose legal guardianship they naturally assumed (Daniels, 1974:226).

Japanese agriculture in California actually prospered after the passage of the Alien Land Law, due in large measure to the increased demand for farm produce during World War I. After 1913, Japanese leased lands increased from 155,488 to 192,150 acres, and land owned from 26,707 to 74,769 acres (Takaki, 1989). There was also the immigration of 70,000 Japanese aliens into the country between 1910 and 1920, many of whom provided dependable labor for a growing number of Japanese agriculturists. Although the Japanese farmed in states other than California, e.g., in sugar beets in the mountain states, the Japanese were concentrated in California between 1900 and 1930.

The Alien Land Law of 1913 was amended in 1920, in an act "designed to prevent the Issei from acting as guardians for the property of a native-born minor if the property could not be held legally by the alien himself" (Kitano, 1969:17–18). The law was hinged to the fact that Japanese aliens (Issei) were ineligible for American citizenship as of 1922, and only citizens had the right to own property under the Alien Land Law. By plugging loopholes in the earlier legislation, it was hoped in exclusionist circles that the Alien Land Law of 1920 would produce the effect intended all along, to drive the Japanese out of farming in California. The Exclusion League was joined by the American Legion, the Native Sons and Daughters of the Golden West, and the Hearst Press in pushing for this legislation (Wilson and Hosokawa, 1980). Similar land laws were passed in other states on the West Coast and as far east as Missouri, Kansas, and Louisiana (Takaki, 1989).

How much of a hindrance the Alien Land Laws proved to be to the Japanese is a matter of some debate. Petersen (1971:53) said that "According to Iwata (1962), the law 'did much to discourage the Japanese from entering farming or expanding their operation.'" On the other hand, Daniels (1969:88) termed the 1920 law "an empty gesture, an ineffective irritant; it caused much litigation, but in no wise significantly affected land tenure in the state." Light (1972:74) reported that Japanese land holdings declined from 458,026 acres in 1920 to 330,053 in 1923 and 304,966 in 1925. Takaki (1989) also observed a significant decrease in Japanese farm acreage in California between 1920 and 1925. Nevertheless, the value of Japanese farm land and the improvements on it continued to increase, and 40 percent of the Japanese were still in agriculture by 1940 (Daniels, 1988; Takaki, 1989).

Some Japanese were "banished from the soil" and moved to the cities of the West Coast (Light, 1972:74). This was only a trend, however, for many Japanese immigrants had initially settled in cities on the West Coast and many others continued in farming, so that by 1941, they raised 42 percent of California's truck crops (Kitano, 1969:18). Unlike the Chinese, a significant minority of the Japanese remained on the land in the face of anti-Asian agitation on the West Coast. By 1940, only 55 percent of the Japanese, as compared to 91 percent of the Chinese, were urban residents in this country, excluding Alaska and Hawaii (Schmid and Nobbe, 1965).

The Japanese in the cities at first competed with white workers but eventually had to withdraw to noncompetitive positions in the urban labor market, particularly on the West Coast, due to pressures from organized labor. They fell back to jobs in domestic service and gardening, a segmented labor market, or retreated from the larger labor market altogether by folding back into the emerging Japanese urban subeconomy. This subeconomy came to include retailing, wholesaling, and service establishments, such as restaurants, hotels, laundries, barber shops, and shoemakers, not unlike that of the Chinese. In 1935, the ten leading trades of the Japanese in Seattle were hotels, groceries, dye works, market stands, produce houses, gardening, restaurants, barber shops, laundries, and produce peddlers (Daniels, 1988). Thus much of the Japanese labor excluded from the urban labor market found work with Japanese employers. For example, only five percent of the Nisei in Los Angles worked for white employers in 1940 (Takaki, 1989).

Japanese employers would typically hire their own kin or kenjin, even their own family members, which solidified through ties of blood and origin the bond between Japanese capital and labor. The same principle applied to the relationship between Japanese farmers and farmhands. The relations between Japanese capital and labor and their class counterparts in the larger society were kept at a minimum in the process. The social distance between Japanese domestics and gardeners and those they served was also observed at this time, all of which meant the cultural and structural pluralism of the Japanese. It also meant that the Japanese to some extent circumvented economic discrimination and color prejudice.

Japanese sections of cities were known as *Nihonmachi*, or little Tokyos. Seattle's Japanese celebrated *Tenchosetsu*, the Emperor's birthday, shouting "banzai, banzai, banzai" and singing *Kimi gayo*, the Japanese national anthem. When the Japanese community knew a Japanese training ship would be arriving...the Japanese sailors would be invited to dinner in the homes of Issei families. Everyone would attend sumo wrestling matches and performances of Japanese classical plays. Every June Seattle's Japanese held a community gathering—the Niho Gakko picnic, where they played games, sang *naniya bushi* songs, danced, and stuffed themselves with sushi, barbecued teriyaki meats, and *musubi* rice balls (Takaki, 1989:226).

San Francisco's and Seattle's were the first nihonmachis, but the one in Los Angeles began to be the largest by 1910. In 1940, there were 37,000 Japanese in Los Angles, 7,000 in Seattle, and 5,000 in San Francisco (Kitano and Daniels, 1988). Reciprocity governed relations within the community. For example, neighbors gave funeral gifts to a family, and that family was expected to reciprocate (Ima, 1976). If not, they were punished by gossip and at times ostracism. All of this "... resulted in a strong sense of community—them and us" (Ima, 1976:268). Japanese consular officials had important roles in these Japanese communities at first, but their influenced waned after 1924, when they no longer played a role in bringing Japanese wives to the United States (Daniels, 1988).

Agitation for the restriction of further Japanese immigration picked up where that for the exclusion of Chinese had left off. There had been demonstrations against the Japanese in Seattle and San Francisco as early as 1900, and an Asiatic Exclusion League was formed in 1905 with branches in several western states (Daniels, 1988). Earlier, in 1890, the Sailors' Union had protested the employment of Japanese seamen on American ships, and there was lobbying in Washington over the use of Japanese labor on building the Great Northern and Northern Pacific railroads (Wilson and Hosokawa, 1980).

According to most writers, movements against Chinese and Japanese were merely different sides of the same set of anti-Asian sentiments on the West Coast. Nevertheless, the two movements were dissimilar in one important way. In the face of the Asiatic Exclusion League and other quarters of the anti-Asian movement in California, the Theodore Roosevelt administration tried to keep the issue of Japanese immigration cool, having in mind the power of Japan in the Pacific. By contrast, the federal government played only a passive role in the mistreatment of Chinese aliens in California. On its side, the Japanese government had always taken a paternal and protective role over its emigrants in the United States.

On October 11, 1906, during a period of Asiatic phobia in California, the San Francisco School Board issued a directive for the segregation of Japanese children in the schools of that city. This action became front-page news in Japan, and the Japanese government protested against the segregation of its nationals in the United States. The protest greatly disturbed President Roosevelt in Washington, and he dispatched a Cabinet member to California to look into the matter while he privately assured the Japanese government that the school segregation of Japanese children would be corrected. He also publicly denounced the school board decision in his annual message of December 2, 1906.

> Roosevelt thus differentiated sharply between Chinese and Japanese. As we have seen, he signed the Chinese Exclusion Act of 1902, and strongly reiterated his opposition to Chinese immigrants in 1905. The reason Roosevelt discriminated between Orientals was because of the different relative military strengths of China and Japan (Daniels, 1974:223–224).

After the Japanese victory in the Russo-Japanese War of 1905, Japan was a power to be reckoned with in the Pacific, while China was weak. Roosevelt took this into account in his concern for Asian residents of this country.

However, Roosevelt was powerless to truly protect Americans of Japanese ancestry. He therefore attempted to reach an agreement with Japan that would restrict immigration of Japanese into this country and thus assuage anti-Asian sentiments on the West Coast. The outcome of these negotiations with Japan was the Gentlemen's Agreement signed in 1907–08, which was discussed earlier in this chapter. As the practice of picture brides among resident Japanese ensured the continued immigration of Japanese into this country, the Japanese population in California grew, and so did the cry for their exclusion. The practice of picture brides became illegal in 1920, and the Immigration Act of 1924 granted absolutely no quota for Japanese. The Japanese were excluded in two senses. They were forced to assume a subordinate position in the nation's system of ethnic stratification, on the one hand, and their immigration into the country was restricted, on the other. The foes of the Japanese had gotten the upper hand through politics, as they had with the Chinese, for, like the Chinese alien, the Japanese immigrant did not have the franchise.

MIDDLEMAN MINORITY

Facing barriers in the larger economy, the Japanese evolved into a middleman minority, concentrating in retail sales and personal services in the cities on the West Coast. As early as 1909, there were 3,000 to 3,500 Japanese-owned businesses in western states providing jobs for 12,000 Japanese (Takaki, 1989). In this way they followed the Chinese, who also had become a middleman minority in urban areas. Unlike the Chinese, however, many Japanese continued as a class of agrarian entrepreneurs on the West Coast. Bonacich (1973:585) observed that the middleman minorities:

> tend to concentrate in certain occupations, notably, trade and commerce, but ... other easily liquidated or transportable occupations ... are also found among so-called "middleman" groups. Among them are the independent professions, ... *truck farming specializing in crops that have rapid turnover*, found among the Japanese in California; and various skilled trades. In other words, the term "middleman minorities" is really a misnomer. The more general occupational characteristic of these groups is liquidity. (Italics added.)

The search for liquidity in occupations on the part of middleman minorities is tied to their sojourning motives, according to Bonacich. Japanese and Chinese selected such economic positions and established their own ethnic subeconomies with the idea of accumulating portable wealth for their eventual return home.

Ethnic cooperation was evident among Japanese farmers:

> According to the California Board of Control in 1920 there were nineteen local affiliates of the Japanese Agricultural Association of Southern California and thirty-six associations in northern and central California affiliated with the Japanese Agricultural Association and the California Farmers Cooperative Association. Almost every Japanese farmer belonged to some Japanese agricultural organization. These associations were organized along the familiar lines of the trade guild, taking as their purpose the marketing of members' produce, control of prices and wages, regulation of labor disputes and of internal competition, protection of farmers' interests, and guardianship of the social welfare of members' families (Light, 1972:75–76).

This amounts to extensive communal self-regulation among Japanese farmers, which is clearly indicated in their common practice of dumping a portion of their produce to keep prices up. Farmers involved in this practice were reimbursed by the Japanese Cooperative Farm Industry, a marketing mechanism connecting Japanese farmers, wholesalers, and retailers to the point of the consumer. This network of Japanese growers, wholesalers, and retailers was so extensive as to vertically integrate some aspects of the truck farming industry in California before the giant food corporations of our era moved in that direction. Keep in mind that Japanese farmers grew a wide variety of crops, from artichokes and strawberries to nursery stock and cut flowers, and because of refrigerated rail cars this produce could be shipped throughout a national market.

Communal regulation was also evident among urban Japanese businessmen. "Urban self-employment absorbed the energies of Japanese men who faced discriminatory barriers . . . in the urban labor market. By 1919, for example, 47 percent of hotels and 25 percent of grocery stores in Seattle were Japanese owned. The census of 1940 reported that 40 percent of Japanese men in Los Angeles were self-employed" (Light, 1972:10). In 1929, Japanese owned one and one-half times as many businesses per thousand people as did other residents of the United States (Daniels, 1969).

Family and regional ties reinforced the economic interdependence between Japanese businessmen and farmers and their employees and field hands. Because Japanese businessmen typically hired members of their own family or kenjin the relationship between employer and employee was in most cases more than simply economic; it was one of blood and regional loyalty as well. Moral obligations to family and ken tied employers and employees to one another, checking the tendency in a purely economic exchange for each party to seek only self-interest. The mutual loyalty between Japanese capital and labor was further strengthened by the common practice of Japanese employers to set up their employees in businesses of their own after an apprenticeship had been served. Because of the self-regulation among Japanese businessmen, the employer in these cases was assured that he was not launching a competitor. Competition among Japanese in the same business or trade was regulated communally, through trade guilds or other cooperative arrangements, based on ethnic and family loyalty. The infusion of blood ties and ethnic loyalties into economic exchange among the Japanese united capital and labor, rich and poor, into a common economic effort and a single moral community. In this manner the Japanese community evolved as a middleman minority through the industrial phase of American society, protecting its members from prejudice and discrimination as it did. The Japanese were also protected from the effects of the Great Depression, for there were only twenty-five Japanese welfare cases in a population of 37,000 in Los Angeles County (Kitano, 1988).

It was common for members of the same family to run the small farms, grocery stores, restaurants, cleaning establishments, and floral shops of the Japanese Americans. This was similar to the small-producer family of Chinese Americans. In these operations, of course, there is no clear line between labor and capital, employee and employer. Even when employer and employee were not members of the same family, their relationship was understood in fictive family terms (Ima,

1976). Families were also the first source of relief and welfare, since seeking public assistance was a sign of disgrace among the Japanese.

The next level of communal obligations concerning employment and assistance was the prefectural associations, *kenjinkai*, which were ascriptive associations with origins in the provinces of southern Japan. Nearly all the Japanese immigrants to this country were eligible for membership in one of the kenjinkai. When an employer for any reason could not secure sufficient labor from within his own family he would typically turn to his own ken for labor. Kenjinkai functioned as employment agencies for the urban Japanese, just as they had for immigrant Japanese field labor. Moreover, just as the ken affiliations between Japanese field hands and their labor bosses were important in the mobility of both into the ranks of independent farmers, these same affiliations also helped urban Japanese workers into their own businesses. Japanese employers would often help finance employees into businesses of their own, an unusual arrangement made possible by ken affiliations and the mutual obligations they implied. Kenjin would teach each other how to run small businesses, and the Japanese had their own version of the rotating-credit association, the *tanomoshi*. While the exploitation of Japanese employees by Japanese employers was not completely eradicated, ethnic and family ties did bring a mutual commitment and sense of fraternity to their relationship. This meant that Japanese employees often were more loyal to their employers than to the labor movement, and Japanese businessmen with access to cheap and dependable ethnic labor had an important edge over their competitors. This often brings the charge that the middleman minority is clannish and unfair in business competition, a charge that can be used as a rationalization for a direct attack on the group (Bonacich, 1973).

Japanese businessmen in urban areas were also organized in trade guilds. These guilds regulated internal competition between Japanese in the same trade (e.g., shoemakers), while they assisted Japanese in their competition with outsiders. The same principle applied to Japanese farmers, who were organized in ethnic agricultural associations. Membership in these trade associations overlapped with ken and family obligations, integrating the Japanese into an ethnic subeconomy and subsociety.

> In sum, middleman community organizations, combined with thrift, enable middleman firms to cut costs at every turn, so that they can compete effectively with other enterprises in the same line. Add to this a preference for liquidable occupations, and the result is a tremendous degree of concentration in, and domination of, certain lines of endeavor (Bonacich, 1973:587).

The irony is that while communal effort in an ethnic subeconomy can mean the economic advancement of a group, it can also result in competition and conflict with certain interest groups in the wider society. Because of the communal and noneconomic ties between Japanese employers and their employees, Japanese workers generally rejected efforts toward their unionization and willingly worked longer hours for less money. Because of this same ethnic solidarity, Japanese businessmen and farmers, with their reduced labor costs and ethnic marketing associations, could undercut their competitors, in some cases driving them out of the market. This meant in some instances the vertical integration by the Japanese of an entire market, from production to the consumer. The result was hostility toward the Japanese in both business circles and labor unions. According to Bonacich (1973:591), it is labor in the larger society that stands to lose the most from competition with a middleman minority:

> Host management has some interest in opposing middleman cheap labor, as we have seen. But management can use this as a weapon against labor by arguing that, if labor insists on higher wages and better work conditions, both will lose. Labor is caught in a bind: either improve its position and accept the possibility of losing the job altogether, or accept a low standard of living and middleman work conditions.

The solution for organized labor would have been to incorporate Japanese labor into the union movement, reducing the threat of wage undercutting and deterioration in working conditions. However, this was improbable for two reasons. There had been a history of antagonism, ethnocentrism, and forceful exclusion of the Japanese from the broader labor market on the West Coast. Given this history, an alliance of Japanese and white labor under the banner of the union movement was virtually impossible. Japanese labor also rejected unionization because, as members of a middleman minority, they were "more closely tied to their co-ethnic employers than to the working class. Besides, most see their position in the 'working class' as a temporary status; a gateway to a business of their own" (Bonacich, 1973:591).

White customers and clients of Japanese businessmen could also understand the anti-Asian sentiments of some business groups and labor unions, given the suspicions that usually surround transactions between merchants and their customers. Thus the public could unite with certain self-serving interest groups on the issue of presumed Japanese clannishness and unfair business practices, and could even suspect their patriotism. This hostility in the host society can flare up against a middleman minority if some precipitating event ignites it. The war with Japan was that event in American history.

By the same token, the Japanese community in America was changing before World War II. In 1940, the Nisei were 63 percent of the Japanese population in the United States, and their impact was growing with their numbers (Takaki, 1989). Moreover, many Issei had been forced to put family assets in the names of Nisei children, uplifting the relative power of this generation from the very start. There was communal control over the Nisei, on the one hand, in terms of the economic niche of middleman minority, Japanese cultural organizations, and blocked opportunity on the outside. Only 5 percent of the Nisei in Los Angeles worked for white employers in 1940. On the other hand, communal control was declining, symbolized by the declining attendance at Japanese-language schools. Despite the approximately 15 percent of the Nisei who returned to Japan for an education, most of the second generation were culturally oriented toward this country. Nisei established the Japanese American Citizens League (JACL) in 1930, and it had grown to fifty chapters with 56,000 members by 1940 (Takaki, 1989). Its creed, written in 1940, expressed the Nisei orientation:

> I am proud that I am an American citizen of Japanese ancestry, for my very background makes me appreciate more fully the wonderful advantages of this nation. I believe in her institutions, ideas and traditions; I glory in her heritage; I boast of her history; I trust in her future.... She has permitted me to build a home, to earn a livelihood, to worship, think, speak and act as I please—as a free man equal to every other man (Kitano and Daniels, 1988:60).

Aside from the patriotic tone of this creed, the second generation of Japanese were coming of age and moving toward assimilation. Nisei women were concentrated in three lines of work in 1940. Nearly one-quarter were farm workers, many working on Japanese-owned farms. Another 23 percent were clerical workers, and over one-quarter were private household workers (Glenn, 1986). Women as clerical and private household workers were being enculturated on the job, another indication of the assimilationist direction of Japanese Americans prior to the Second World War.

THE INTERNMENT

On Sunday morning, December 7, 1941, the Japanese launched a surprise attack on the U.S. Pacific Fleet at Pearl Harbor, Hawaii. The United States Congress declared war on Japan the following day. The entry of America into a war with Japan began a chain of events within the country that eventually led to the forcible relocation of Japanese aliens and Japanese American citizens from their homes on the West Coast to War Relocation Centers further inland.

The Mochida family was one of many Japanese American families forced
into internment camps as a result of the anti-Japanese hysteria following
the bombing of Pearl Harbor.

Immediately after the attack on Pearl Harbor, the FBI detained aliens throughout the country, Germans and Italians as well as Japanese. About 1,500 Issei were taken into custody (Wilson and Hosokawa, 1980). The backdrop to this roundup of "enemy aliens" was the widespread fear of fifth-column activities in the country. Secretary of the Navy Frank Knox had earlier accused Japanese in Hawaii of fifth-column action in the bombing of Pearl Harbor, accusations that were later disproved. The West Coast was also vulnerable to sabotage. "Nearly half the U.S. military aircraft output was concentrated in the Los Angeles area. Naval yards and port facilities from San Diego on the south to Puget Sound in the north were essential to the launching of any counterattack. The fleet depended heavily on oil pumped from California's coastal fields" (Hosokawa, 1969:258).

Among the Japanese aliens detained in the early weeks following the attack on Pearl Harbor, only one was ever convicted of any wrongdoing, and he was sentenced to a term of two to six months for not having registered as a foreign agent "because one of his customers was the Japanese government" (Petersen, 1971:67). The bank accounts of Japanese aliens were frozen and American branches of Japanese banks were closed (Daniels, 1988). ". . . continuing raids, with or without search warrants, were made throughout Japanese America from the very outbreak of the war" (Daniels, 1988:206). Late in December of 1941 the government terminated Japanese American draftees and volunteers for military service. Japanese were dismissed from their jobs, their insurance policies were canceled, and their checks were not honored by banks (Wilson and Hosokawa, 1980). In March of 1942, a curfew was also imposed on the Japanese on the West Coast, one that lasted from 8 P.M. to 6 A.M.

There was considerable public sentiment for evacuating all Japanese on the West Coast, particularly among certain political interest groups and patriotic organizations in the region. Agricultural interests claimed, for example, that Japanese farmers planted crop rows pointing toward military installations to guide enemy aircraft. The idea of an evacuation of the Japanese was first dismissed as undemocratic and impractical, even by the same officials who would later implement the evacuation order. In December 1941, for instance, Lt. General John L. DeWitt, commander of the Western Defense Command, firmly opposed the evacuation of Japanese and justified his opposition in these words: "An American citizen, after all, is an American citizen. And while they may not be loyal, I think we can weed the disloyal out of the loyal and lock them up if necessary." Later, in 1943, after he had directed the evacuation of the Japanese, General DeWitt said before a Congressional committee: "A Jap's a Jap.... You can't change him by giving him a piece of paper [American citizenship]" (Hosokawa, 1969:259–260).

The relocation of the Japanese on the West Coast, alien and citizen alike, was mandated on February 19, 1942, when President Roosevelt signed Executive Order 9066. The western half of the three Pacific Coast states and the southern third of Arizona were designated as military areas in the order, and the Secretary of War was authorized to remove "any or all" persons from these areas.

All the people removed were of Japanese ancestry, although Japanese east of this boundary were unaffected by the order. On March 2, 1942, General DeWitt issued an order to evacuate all persons of Japanese ancestry. Notices of the evacuation were posted in Japanese neighborhoods, and the people could bring only what they could carry. The Japanese on Terminal Island, near San Pedro, had already been forced from their homes late in February (Wilson and Hosokawa, 1980). More than 110,000 of the 126,000 Japanese in the United States were affected by the evacuation order, and two-thirds of these were U.S. citizens (Kitano, 1969:33). The evacuation proceeded in two phases. People were first taken to temporary assembly centers on the West Coast in the summer of 1942, and later were relocated to more permanent camps inland. These relocation camps in Arizona, Arkansas, California, Colorado, Idaho, Utah, and Wyoming, were administered by a civilian agency, the War Relocation Authority, under the directorship of Milton S. Eisenhower and, later, Dillon S. Myer.

The temporary assembly centers had been hastily converted from other uses: livestock exposition halls, fairgrounds, racetracks. The conditions Japanese families faced in these centers reflected the haste of the conversion. Mine Okubo writes of her first impression of her new home at one of these centers:

> The guide left us at the door of Stall 50. We walked in and dropped our things inside the entrance. The place was in semidarkness; light barely came through the dirty window on either side of the entrance. A swinging half-door divided the 20 by 9 ft. stall into two rooms. ... The rear room had housed the horse and the front room the fodder. Both rooms showed signs of a hurried whitewashing. Spider webs, horse hair, and hay had been whitewashed with the walls. Huge spikes and nails stuck out all over the walls. A two-inch layer of dust covered the floor, but on removing it we discovered that linoleum ... had been placed over the rough manure-covered boards. We opened the folded cots lying on the floor of the rear room and sat on them in the semidarkness. We heard someone crying in the next stall (quoted in Hosokawa, 1969:329–330).

The more permanent relocation centers were in isolated regions of the United States, many in the arid expanse of the western states. One

471

of these camps might be home to as many as 16,000 people. Accommodations consisted of tarpaper-covered barracks, the rooms of which
were furnished with only a stove, one droplight, and Army cots and
mattresses. To each room one family was assigned. Latrines substituted for sanitary facilities in the barrack rooms, and mess halls took the
place of family kitchens. The inmates were fed meals costing only 38
cents per day (Daniels, 1988). The camps were surrounded by barbed-
wire fences and guard towers. Tule Lake was the worst camp, and it
came to be a virtual prison camp where the staff and inmates were po-
larized against each other (Daniels, 1988). Though the residents would
try to beautify the camps by planting shrubs and flowers, anything
that would grow in the arid climate, the centers still gave the appearance of concentration camps despite such amenities. However, forced-
labor and death camps they were not. Thousands of the Japanese, especially the Nisei (second generation), were eventually released
through work programs, resettling in the Midwest and East, and early
in 1943 the Army began to recruit among the Nisei.

> Some 40,000 persons had left camp during 1942–1944. The earliest de-
> partures were made by those furloughed to harvest crops or to attend
> college in 1942. Others had left as a result of enlisting in the military.
> Later, still more were drafted right out of the concentration camps. A
> few hundred were repatriated to Japan, ... 1,900 had died in camp,
> while 6,485 new American citizens were born behind barbed wire
> (Daniels, 1988:241).

Both the work-release program and the Army draft required clear-
ances for loyalty. The loyalty of camp inmates was ascertained in the
form of three clumsily conceived questions: (1) Are you loyal to the
United States, abjuring allegiance to the emperor? (2) Do you hope the
United States wins the war? (3) Would you serve in the combat forces
of the United States wherever ordered? (Haak, 1970:28). As an indication of the insensitivity to the conditions faced by many Japanese evac-
uees, the first question required an alien Issei, ineligible for American
citizenship, to forswear allegiance to the only country wherein his or
her citizenship was assigned. While the wording of this question was
later changed, the manner in which various Japanese people answered
these questions on loyalty divided the camps, often along generational
lines. Between 80 and 90 percent of the eligible camp inmates were
later cleared for loyalty, and Nisei draftees went on to serve their
country with great distinction. The Nisei served in both Europe and
the Pacific. The 442nd Infantry Regiment of Nisei alone "... won forty-
three Division Commendations, thirteen Army Commendations, and
seven Presidential Distinguished Unit Citations" (Wilson and
Hosokawa, 1980:240). In addition, members of the 442nd won more

than 18,000 individual decorations, including a Congressional Medal of Honor (Chan, 1991).

Hosokawa (1969) wrote that before the internment, even before the war, the Issei realized that they had planted roots in this country, a fact they saw in the faces of their children. The Nisei naturally adopted American habits and mannerisms and blended them with the traditional ways. They ate peanut butter and jelly sandwiches as well as fishcakes, celebrated American holidays along with the traditional Japanese New Year's Day, and otherwise combined Japanese and American customs. The Issei saw this and were even willing to send their sons into the service of the United States after hearing of Pearl Harbor.

While the Issei may have encouraged the entry of their offspring into the larger society, the middleman subeconomy might have just as naturally pulled many Nisei toward the old ways if it were not now gone, lost in the evacuation and never to be regained. The Japanese would never be fully compensated for the loss of their businesses, farms, and other economic assets. The parental authority of the Issei also declined, due to their loss of wealth and economic function, and it shrank further in the relocation camps as the Nisei assumed the leadership roles and went off to war or work elsewhere, outside the subeconomy of their parents.

It is understandable that so many Americans have asked who was responsible for the internment of the Japanese. The constitutional rights of 110,000 residents of the country, two-thirds of them U.S. citizens, were unilaterally suspended. This was done in the absence of any substantial evidence as to the disloyalty of Japanese Americans. Mindful of the fact that the Japanese Americans were essentially innocent victims, the nagging feeling that this historical episode leaves is the question: Can it happen again, and could it happen to any of us?

Everybody was responsible for the internment of the Japanese is essentially the answer of Ten Broek, Burnhart, and Matson (1954). They argued that responsibility for evacuation and internment of the Japanese must be shared by many groups. These groups include the various branches of government at both the state and national levels; numerous interest groups; the general public, especially people on the West Coast; and the press (see Box 13.2). Kitano (1969:43) amplified the argument for wholesale responsibility and added that it was racism that united these various groups in the country against the Japanese: "It is difficult to avoid the conclusion that the primary cause of the wartime evacuation was West Coast racism." Petersen (1971:73) chose to focus on the absence of a liberal counterattack and the obvious conservative interests served by the removal of the Japanese from the West Coast: "The most interesting clue to the influence of pressure

groups, as in the Sherlock Holmes story, is the dog that did not bark."
Not only were liberals not barking at the conservative groups over the
issue of Japanese evacuation, but they were in the vanguard of the agitation for the evacuation and internment. The liberal columnist Walter
Lippmann was four days ahead of the conservative columnist West-
brook Pegler in calling for the mass evacuation of Japanese Americans
from the West Coast. Petersen believed that the liberal support for the
evacuation stemmed from the control the Communist Party exercised
at the time over the American political left. Once Nazi Germany broke
the Stalin-Hitler Pact in 1941, the American Communist Party shifted
to all-out support of the war against the Axis powers. Many Japanese
in the camps also blamed the Japanese American Citizens League for
accommodating to governmental pressure for evacuation.

©©

BOX 13.2 HOW TO TELL YOUR FRIENDS FROM THE JAPS

- ... Virtually all Japanese are short.
- Japanese are likely to be stockier and broader-hipped than short Chinese.
- Japanese—except for wrestlers—are seldom fat; they often dry up and grow lean as they age.
- Although both [Chinese and Japanese] have the typical epi-canthic fold of the upper eyelid, ... the Japanese eyes are usu-ally set closer together.
- ... the Chinese expression is likely to be more placid, kindly, open; the Japanese more positive, dogmatic, arrogant.
- Japanese are hesitant, nervous in conversation, laugh loudly at the wrong time.
- Japanese walk stiffly erect, hard heeled. Chinese, more re-laxed, have an easy gait, sometimes shuffle.

Source: *Time* magazine, December 22, 1941. Copyright © 1941 Time, Inc. Reprinted by permission.

©©

Some may still feel that war hysteria united Americans, liberal and
conservative alike, in their support of the mass evacuation and internment of the Japanese. But this "mass panic" thesis has never adequately accounted for the fact that the Japanese of Hawaii were never
interned on such a mass scale, uprooted from their homes, and deprived of their livelihood, though there had also been agitation for the
evacuation of Japanese on Hawaii, and the islands were more vulnera-

ble to Japanese invasion and sabotage because of their location and greater number of Japanese residents. Less than 1,500 Japanese in Hawaii were interned, whereas more than 110,000 on the West Coast were removed to relocation centers (Takaki, 1989). It was primarily the Japanese on the West Coast who were interned for the stated reason of national security.

The Japanese on the West Coast were a middleman minority, largely bereft of political allies. They were in direct competition with white growers and businessmen and indirectly competed with organized labor over the issue of nonunion Japanese labor. Because the Japanese in Hawaii had faced less discrimination than on the mainland, and because they had lived in Hawaii longer, they were more occupationally diversified and politically involved. They had political allies who spoke out against Japanese evacuation there. The Japanese on the West Coast had no such allies, and because of their concentration in middleman economic roles, they were seen as clannish and beyond assimilation by their competitors and by the general public. This brought accusations commonly made against middleman minorities: "middleman minorities are disloyal to the countries in which they reside," and "middleman groups drain the host society of its resources" (Bonacich, 1973:591). On the basis of such fears, people on the West Coast clamored for the evacuation of the Japanese.

The irony is that before the war the Nisei on the mainland had been gradually moving toward inclusion in the larger society, following the pattern of the Japanese in Hawaii. The first generation of any immigrant group typically stays to itself, and the Issei were no exemption. These first-generation Japanese had compounded the effects of their cultural isolation with those of being a middleman minority. The Nisei had begun, however, to make political and social friends in the wider society before the war, as Hosokawa (1969:200) observed:

> The *Nisei* of this period were just beginning to feel their way into the involved world of politics and pressures outside their communities. Of those days, Mary Oyama Mittwer has written: "Between wienie bakes and the beaches and dances *Nisei* would gather at church and JACL meetings to ponder ways of getting out the *Nisei* vote, planning ways of putting up Japanese American candidates for political offices, mixing more into the larger American community...."

But there were simply too few adult Nisei before the war for the Japanese to have accomplished much in the way of political influence on the West Coast. In 1930 fewer than 4,000 Nisei in the entire United States were of voting age (Hosokawa, 1969:152), which suggests that the perceived clannishness of the Japanese also followed from the absence of an adult generation of Nisei. The decision to intern was a political one, which had always been the most successful line of attack on Japanese and Chinese Americans. Their foes used the state to further their interests in excluding Asians, not only in the internment of the Japanese, but also in Alien Land Laws, immigration restrictions, and the denial of citizenship rights for both Chinese and Japanese.

THE PRESENT SITUATION

As the Nisei left the internment camps, a new era for Japanese Americans began, an era that brought their greater inclusion into American society. American society was just entering its post-industrial phase, and the Nisei converged with the larger trend toward college education and professional and technical work. By 1960, 26 percent of the Japanese males in the nation's nonfarm labor force were engaged in technical work and the professions, compared to only 12.5 percent of the white males. In the same period, 1940–60, the percentage of Japanese males in the nonfarm labor force who were proprietors, managers, and officials declined from 23 to 13 percent, and the percentage of the Japanese in farm work declined from 43 to 26 percent (Schmid and Nobbe, 1965). One-half of the Nisei women were in professional, managerial, sales, and clerical work by 1970 (Glenn, 1986). The end had come for the Japanese subeconomy.

Tables 13.1 and 13.2 tell the same story for both Japanese males and females. Note the increase in professional and technical workers in the past decades and the decrease in Japanese proprietors. Also observe the decline in the percentage of Japanese men and women in farming. The occupational composition of the Japanese in 1970 and 1990 compared favorably with that of all employed people and whites in the country. The most common occupational categories for both males and females are technical, sales, and administrative support, and managerial and professional. This indicates that the Nisei and later generations have moved away from a middleman minority in urban commerce and agrarian enterprise and toward technical and professional work in the larger post-industrial society.

A college education was a requisite in this evolution of the Nisei into the technical and professional fields, and for many postgraduate study was necessary. Around 6 percent of the nation's Japanese males and 4 percent of the females (25 years and older) had a college education in 1940. By 1960, over 18 percent of the men and 8 percent of the women had at least a college education. In contrast, just over 10 percent of the nation's white males had a college education in 1960 (Schmid and Nobbe, 1965). In 1970, 30 percent of the Japanese had

476

TABLE 13.1 PERCENTAGE DISTRIBUTION OF JAPANESE AMERICANS AND ALL
EMPLOYED PEOPLE BY OCCUPATIONAL GROUPS, 1940–1970

Occupational Group	Japanese Origin				All People			
	1940	1950	1960	1970	1940	1950	1960	1970
White-collar workers								
Professional and technical	3.0	6.8	14.2	19.0	7.5	8.7	11.1	14.9
Managers, officials, and proprietors except farmers	11.4	7.1	7.7	8.4	8.4	8.7	8.4	8.3
Clerical and sales	11.3	15.4	22.8	26.4	16.8	19.2	21.6	25.0
Blue-collar workers								
Craftsmen and foremen	2.0	5.5	12.9	11.6	11.3	14.3	13.5	13.9
Operators	7.3	13.2	13.5	9.7	18.4	20.3	18.4	13.7
Laborers except farm and mine	18.4	9.5	4.0	6.3	6.8	6.5	4.8	4.5
Service workers								
Private household	7.6	6.5	3.6	1.7	6.2	2.5	2.7	1.5
Other service	7.3	8.7	8.1	11.4	6.2	7.8	8.4	11.3
Farm workers								
Farmers and managers	14.7	11.1	7.9	2.0	11.5	7.6	3.9	1.9
Laborers and foremen	16.3	16.2	5.3	1.9	6.9	4.4	2.2	1.3

Note: Percentages may not total to 100 because of rounding.

Sources: 1940 Census, *The Labor Force*, Table 62, p. 90; 1940 Census, *Characteristics of the Non-white Population by Race*, Table 38, pp. 107–108; 1950 Census, *Occupational Characteristics*, Table 3, pp. 29–36; 1950 Census, *Characteristics of the Nonwhite Population by Race*, Table 11, p. 37; 1960 Census, *Occupational Characteristics*, Table 2, pp. 11–20; 1960 Census, *Characteristics of the Non-white Population by Race*, Table 34, p. 108; 1970 Census, *Occupational Characteristics*, Table 39, pp. 593–608.

some college, as compared to 22 percent of the nation's whites (Ima, 1976). Petersen (1971) studied the files of the Nisei at the University of California's placement bureau for signs of their occupational selection and found that their degrees were almost never in liberal arts, but rather in business administration, optometry, engineering, or some other middle-level profession. For them, "education was obviously a means of acquiring a salable skill that could be used either in the general commercial world or, if that remained closed, in a small personal enterprise" (p. 116).

After the internment experience, the Nisei evolved away from the middleman minority status of their parents, first by going in goodly numbers to college and then by entering the growing technical and

TABLE 13.2   PERCENTAGE DISTRIBUTION OF JAPANESE AMERICANS AND
ALL EMPLOYED PEOPLE BY OCCUPATIONAL GROUPS, 1990

Occupational Group	Japanese Origin 1990	All People 1990
Managerial and professional	34.8%	25.5%
Technical, sales, and administrative support	35.0	31.5
Service occupations	12.2	13.5
Precision production, craft, and repair	7.7	11.5
Operators, fabricators, and laborers	7.8	11.5
Farming, forestry, and fishing	2.8	2.5

Source: Census of Population and Housing, 1990: Public Micromedia Samples U.S., prepared by the Bureau of the Census, 1992.

professional fields. They avoided direct competition with others over white-collar work by steering away from jobs that put a premium on interpersonal skills and language mastery. Instead, they chose the technical fields and independent professions, choices that are also reminiscent of the middleman's gravitation toward portable skills. For this accomplishment, this generation of Japanese Americans has been called America's *model minority*. The Japanese also relocated to different regions of the country and new neighborhoods on the West Coast rather than returning to Little Tokyos.

The role that internment played in the accomplishments of the Nisei is a matter of some debate. One argument is that the internment experience lessened the control of the Issei over the Nisei, allowing the latter to break out of the Japanese subeconomy and the mobility trap of small farming and business. Petersen (1971:126) spoke to this argument:

> The occupational traps of the young *Nisei* tending vegetable stands in Los Angeles, the seemingly unreasonable control that *Issei* exerted in their families, the restrictive life in a Little Tokyo—these elements of prewar existence were reduced in importance or eliminated, together with the agricultural economy, the Japanese Association, consular authority, and much of the informal community solidarity. This is what is meant by the preposterous statement that, in one version or another, is found in several accounts of the internment—that today many Japanese "are grateful for the evacuation experience."

Petersen agreed that the internment experience and the subsequent collapse of the Japanese subeconomy forced the Nisei on the mainland out into the mainstream of society. The demise of the Japanese subeconomy was due to both the evacuation of the Japanese on the West Coast and the increasing scale of business and agriculture in this country after World War II. Many small Japanese firms and farms were made obsolete. Moreover, many Japanese farms were converted after the war into tracts for suburban housing in California. The Japanese in Hawaii, on the other hand, could and did continue in their parents' businesses after the war, or could go into the lower and middle rungs of the state's civil service:

> In Hawaii…the impetus to rise was to some degree countered by the pressure to take over one's father's retail store, to follow one's father in his skilled trade. And if, as has been hypothesized, the electoral gains in the islands were accompanied by similar increases in the proportion of Japanese in the lower and middle ranks of the state's civil service, this was another relatively easy route to modest financial security. On the mainland, the postwar rule had to be the famous slogan of the 442nd, "Go for broke"—all or nothing; for there were no easy routes to middle-level status (Petersen, 1971:126).

A second argument is that the mobility of the Nisei into white-collar work was a direct application of traditional Japanese values for success, the transmission of which was uninterrupted, even intensified, by the internment experience. Haak (1970:30–31) wrote they responded with:

> an ancestral reflex pattern of self-sacrifice and cooperation with no reward in sight…. What helped them most…was the way they chose to earn recognition by performance…. They simply worked and endured until their performance overwhelmed, without contentiousness, society's negative definitions of their worth…. The *Nisei* with whom I spoke were all active Buddhists. The more articulate spoke of resolving conflict through cooperation, invoking the higher synthesis of yin and yang, rather than savage partisan duels to the social death.

The traditional communal network of Japanese helped translate the equally traditional values into new forms of success. Petersen (1971) noted that the Nisei students at the University of California often had letters of reference from Japanese professors in unrelated fields and frequently had part-time jobs in Japanese-owned establishments. The historical solidarity of the Japanese continued to play a role in the evolution of the Japanese, it appears, even after the loss of much of their property and wealth.

It is estimated that the Japanese lost nearly $400,000,000 in property due to their internment (Daniels, 1988). In 1948, the U.S. government authorized the payment of $38 million to interned Japanese for their financial losses, or 10 cents on the dollar (Daniels, 1988; Wilson and Hosokawa, 1980). In 1952, the California Supreme Court declared the Alien Land Laws to be unconstitutional. The Walter-McCarran Act of 1952 allowed Japan an immigration quota, and this quota was expanded in 1965. After 1953, the Issei could apply for citizenship, and 46,000 had become citizens by 1965 (Wilson and Hosokawa, 1980). President Ford repealed in 1976 Roosevelt's Executive Order 9066 that began the internment. Then, in 1980, Congress created a Commission on Wartime Relocation and Internment of Civilians. A grave injustice was admitted by Congress for the internment, and Congress formally apologized and authorized the payment of $20,000 to each survivor (Kitano and Daniels, 1988).

Nisei views on marriage and family were different from those of the Issei. First, the Nisei engaged in an American pattern of dating in conjunction with dances, retreats, and outings (Kitano, 1988). There was the freedom to choose one's spouse, a choice based on romantic love, and Nisei wedding ceremonies blended American and Japanese traditions (Glenn, 1986). In Nisei marriages, priority was placed on the conjugal bond, and there were greater equality between the sexes, more flexible sex roles, high emotional intensity, greater verbal communication between the partners, and also greater instability (Yanagisako, 1985:122). According to Yanagisako (1985), Nisei marriages evolved away from Issei ones through a sequence of stages, from the pre-war period, through the war years, and to the post-resettlement period. Over the years, the Nisei gained increasing independence from the first generation, deviating from Issei patterns as they did.

After the Second World War and with the occupation of Japan by American forces, a number of U. S. servicemen married Japanese women and returned home with their Japanese wives. About 45,000 Japanese war brides came to the United States between 1947 and 1975 (Glenn, 1986). These women were isolated not only from friends and family in Japan, but also the Japanese community in America. Most did not speak English well, and were thus employed as operators and service workers in 1960. They were disproportionately waitresses, for example, deviating significantly from the Nisei after the Second World War. Their marriages were unstable, and because of their social isolation in America their close ties were almost exclusively with their children (Glenn, 1986).

The success of Nisei after the Second World War can be exaggerated. Like most Asians, Japanese Americans are concentrated in urban areas, in California and Hawaii, for example, with high costs of living. By 1970, 90 percent of the Japanese population was already in metropolitan areas, as compared to 73 percent of the entire population. Thus the incomes of Japanese are offset in part by higher living costs (Takaki, 1989). Moreover, while the earnings of Japanese and white men in California are comparable, "... they [the Japanese] did so only by acquiring more education (17.7 years compared to 16.8 years for white men twenty-four to forty-five years old) and by working more hours (2,160 hours compared to 2,120 hours for white men isn the same age category)" (Takaki, 1989:475).

The third generation, *Sansei*, has continued in the same direction as the Nisei and now is something of an elite among the later native-born generations of the nation's immigrant groups. From data on a national sample of three generations of Japanese in the country, Levine and Montero (1973:45) observed, "Whereas 57% of the Nisei respondents have at least some college training, 88% of the Sansei had as much.... Further, fully 92% of the Sansei intend to become professionals." Upwardly mobile Japanese tend to live in mostly white neighborhoods and have frequent, even intimate, contact with whites. This generation has little direct experience with prejudice and discrimination and little in the way of close ethnic ties (Kitano and Daniels, 1988). Kikumura and Kitano (1973:79) concluded that the Japanese in this country "are no longer a group that marries their own." The rate of out-group marriage among the Sansei reached 50 percent in many parts of the country in the 1970s. Among younger Sansei, seven in ten marry non-Japanese (Wilson and Hosokawa, 1980). Kikumura and Kitano (1973:79) speculated that "this rate will continue to grow with each new successive generation, so that in time there may no longer be a pure Japanese American group." Additionally, studies show that most attitudes and behaviors of each succeeding generation of Japanese have converged with those of white Americans. This most likely means continued convergence with and inclusion in the larger society for the *Yonsei*, the next generation of Japanese Americans.

Nevertheless, this process varies by ethclass among the Japanese. White-collar Japanese are more likely to live in primarily white neighborhoods and be less involved in their ethnic community, less fluent in the Japanese language, and more accepting of out-group marriage than are the blue-collar (Ima, 1976). In other words, "the higher the occupational and educational achievement, the more likely that Nisei and Sansei will move out of the ethnic orbit" (Wilson and Hosokawa, 1980:298). By the same token, the international ascendancy of Japan, the ethnic revival in the last decade, the growing acceptance of ethnic pluralism in the United States, and other trends suggest a certain continuation of Japanese America.

Unlike the Chinese, there has been no significant immigration of Japanese in recent decades. In 1970, the Japanese were the largest Asian group in the country, but in 1980 the Japanese population was smaller than both the Chinese and Filipino populations in the United States. While the Japanese increased by over 18 percent in this decade, the Chinese population had increased over 85 percent and the Filipino population by over 125 percent (Daniels, 1988).

A COMPARISON OF ASIAN AND AFRICAN AMERICANS

Asian American and African American history run along similar lines up to a point and then diverge. Africans, Chinese, and Japanese are immigrant groups whose histories have been implicated in the nation's changing labor needs. Asian and African Americans are also racial minorities in the United States, and both have been objects of racial discrimination and color prejudice. They competed with other immigrant groups and were forced in the course of this competition to the bottom of the labor hierarchy, where they were expected to work at menial jobs, in field labor and domestic service, for example. The immigration of Chinese and Japanese was also restricted, nearly to the point of complete exclusion. While Asians were not brought to this country as slaves, many came as contract laborers, perhaps a difference of degree rather than kind. Moreover, Asians and blacks alike have been prohibited from owning land and other forms of capital necessary for their mobility out of menial wage labor. In short, Chinese, Japanese, and African Americans have faced racial stratification and color prejudice in this country.

However, this is where the similarities end. The two Asian groups became middleman minorities, circumventing racial barriers and building subeconomies of their own. African Americans did not do this, remaining employed instead in domestic service and agriculture. Moreover, Asian Americans converged shortly after World War II with the trend toward a post-industrial society, while African Americans only more recently have made significant steps toward their inclusion into society.

There have been several attempts to explain the differences between these two racial minorities. Racism alone cannot account for these differences, since both African Americans and Asian Americans have been objects of color prejudice and discrimination in this country. Some writers point out that special consumer demands among Chinese and Japanese helped establish Asian businessmen, and no comparable special needs existed among African Americans. Chinese and Japanese immigrants were restricted by language barriers and ethnic preferences to certain consumption patterns, to be sure, and this resulted in a ready-made clientele for Chinese and Japanese business-men. African American shopkeepers have always had to compete with the better financed operations in the larger society, since African American customers have not been restricted in this manner, either by language barriers or foreign preferences.

While this is all true, it is an inadequate explanation. Light (1972) noted that non-Asians apparently consumed one-half of the food and one-quarter of the dry goods sold by Asian businesses. He concluded that the consumer-demands explanation is but one part of a larger, so-ciological explanation (p. 108). This explanation begins by emphasiz-ing the sojourning motives of the Chinese and Japanese immigrants in this country. According to Bonacich (1973:585), "Sojourning is not a sufficient condition of the middleman form in that there are sojourners who do not become middlemen; but it is a necessary one, with impor-tant economic and social consequences directly related to the pattern." These consequences include a "tendency toward thrift" and a "concen-tration in certain occupations." Black slaves were never sojourners, of course; they neither elected to come to this country nor could hope to accumulate savings here and return to Africa.

Sojourners concentrate in occupations that provide a portable or easily liquidated livelihood, intending all along to return home with their savings. In addition, since they plan to return, "sojourners have little reason to develop lasting relationships with members of the sur-rounding host society" (Bonacich, 1973:586). This enhances the cohe-sion of the middleman minority, a solidarity that for the two Asian im-migrant groups was rooted in their transplantation of Old-World familial and regional loyalties to the United States. Ethnic solidarity, communal regulation of internal competition, and cooperation be-tween Asian capital and labor provided them with a competitive edge in urban commerce and farming. It gave Chinese and Japanese busi-nessmen access to cheap and dependable labor from within their own groups, and it gave them access to internal sources of credit, making possible the establishment of businesses and the purchase of property. Ethnic solidarity also facilitated the marketing of goods and services. Bonacich (1973:586) observed:

> Solidarity is interjected into economic affairs in two ways: it plays a part in the efficient distribution of resources, and helps to control in-ternal competition. Resources distributed within the ethnic commu-nity include capital ... , credit and easier terms to purchasers, infor-mation and training, and jobs and labor.

Bonacich (1973:586) also suggested the mechanism for the transla-tion of sojourning motives and ethnic solidarity into collective economic action: "The 'primordial tie' of blood provides a basis for trust, and is reinforced by multi-purpose formal and informal associations." The role of blood ties and communal associations in the Asian sub-economies and immigrant brotherhoods has already been noted. Primordial ties have specific, direct roles in the accumulation of capital and ownership of land by both the Chinese and Japanese. In the movement of a group from the bottom of society to a position of middleman minority, it must accumulate savings and effectively distribute this capital to members of the group. Asians accomplished this pooling of capital largely through rotating credit associations. Members of such an association agree to make regular contributions to a common fund, to be given in total or in some fixed proportion to each contributor in rotation. For example, ten Chinese immigrants might agree to contribute $10 monthly to a common fund, to be distributed to one of the members each year until each contributor had received a share. This is a general model of a rotating credit association; there were many variations on this common theme. For instance, while the Japanese rotating credit associations in this country included unrelated persons, the Chinese *hui* did not (Light, 1972). The importance of rotating credit associations is that they serve to capitalize small business people who, for many reasons, including racism in the case of minority groups, cannot readily turn to banks or other financial institutions in the larger society for funding. Moreover, banks and other formal financial institutions owned by racial minorities have been notoriously unstable in the history of this country, an observation that applies to both Asian and African Americans. Immigrant Chinese and Japanese engaged in rotating credit arrangements on an informal basis, however, while African Americans did not, at least not to the same degree.

Chinese and Japanese brought their rotating credit associations with them to the United States and transplanted these "Old-World traits" in this country. Light (1972) noted that the Japanese had probably adopted this tradition from the Chinese back in the thirteenth century. The risk involved in rotating credit associations is that members may default on their obligations to one another, but the high level of interpersonal trust and communal control among immigrant Chinese and Japanese eliminated much of this risk. For instance, extended kin often honored the financial obligations of someone who might have otherwise failed to meet his or her obligation to other members. Overlapping primordial ties took much of the risk out of these transactions, without which the Chinese and Japanese could not have accumulated capital and property to the extent that they did at a time when they were denied credit in the larger society.

Amid the wreckage of Leghorn, Italy, in August 1944,
General Mark Clark and Secretary of the Navy James Forrestal
inspect Nisei troops of the 100th Infantry Battalion.

There is no positive evidence for the existence of such practices among African Americans. Evidence does indicate, however, that a tradition of rotating credit associations did exist in West Africa. Among the Yoruba, the rotating credit association was known as *esusu*, and it existed among them as early as 1843. Thrift clubs were also in practice in Sierra Leone as early as 1794. Moreover, Africans brought this tradition to the New World, at least to the West Indies. It was called *asu* in the Bahamas, *susu* in Trinidad, and *partners* by Jamaicans; West Indians imported the practice into Harlem in the twentieth century (Light, 1972). But there is no evidence for the existence of some variant on *esusu* among American-born blacks. Light (1972:36) concluded that "lack of reference to rotating credit associations among Negroes in the United States may be taken as prima facie evidence that such practices were not, in fact, employed. Students of the question have thus far been unable to locate any instance of rotating credit practices among American-born Negroes."

How do we account for the disappearance of this African tradition among African Americans? First, there is a possibility that the tradition of rotating credit associations began in West Africa after most slaves had already arrived in the United States. Free African labor might have introduced the tradition into the West Indies after emancipation there in 1838, and no such immigration into the United States occurred, at least not until West Indians brought the tradition to Harlem in the twentieth century. Partly because of this practice, West Indians stand out as entrepreneurs among the nation's blacks and are known among American-born blacks as "Black Jews." There is also reason to believe that the tradition of rotating credit associations was indeed brought by slaves to the United States, but somehow the practice disappeared here while it survived among West Indian slaves. In the West Indies, black slaves were a numerical majority who worked for absentee landlords and, most importantly, were allowed to install their own subeconomy and market system there, from production through distribution. After emancipation, blacks in the West Indies moved into the interior of those islands, removed almost completely from the political and economic domination of the white planters. The rotating credit association had almost daily relevance in this environment, and it survived.

In the United States, by contrast, blacks did not have the same measure of economic autonomy. Except for a small class of freed blacks in the North, African Americans never were able to establish a subeconomy of their own, as had Africans in the West Indies and Asians in the United States. African Americans have been historically deprived of economic independence. Indeed, it was once illegal for them to own property, as they themselves were virtually nothing more than the property of others. Nor were slaves in the United States ever permitted to pursue entrepreneurial activity on their own terms. Unlike the pattern in the West Indies, plantation owners and small white farmers managed the local markets and subsistence economy of the South. After emancipation, black labor in this country remained under the economic domination of white landowners. No room was ever made for black entrepreneurial activity in the South, a critical difference from both the Asian American and West Indian patterns. This alone might have led to the disappearance of rotating credit associations among American-born blacks.

Tribal bonds among slaves in the South had largely disappeared by the time of their emancipation, making them bereft of those human bonds that meant so much in the rise of Asian Americans to a position of a middleman minority. Gone with these primordial ties was the degree of interpersonal trust and internal self-regulation that made such practices as rotating credit associations work for the Chinese and Japanese. Although there was always trust and love within black families, family units were too small for the effective pooling of resources, and black voluntary associations could not compensate for the absence of ascriptive solidarity among African Americans (Light, 1972). Certain entrepreneurial practices and skills and the cohesion that make them work were gone by the time African Americans had the chance to evolve as free people. Tribal integrity had been better maintained in the West Indies, due to the larger plantations there and the more frequent influx of African immigrants into those islands. Moreover, slaves in the West Indies had greater economic autonomy, and they evolved into subsistence farmers with land of their own after their emancipation. When they immigrated to this country in the twentieth century, West Indians became something of a middleman minority among the nation's blacks. Thus the history of African Americans is significantly different from that of their West Indian counterparts, as well as from that of Asians in this country.

It appears that their internal structure affects how minority groups fare in their competition with others for land, labor, and capital. Asian and African Americans share prejudice and discrimination as a common experience, yet because of their different internal organizations they are very different in how they have coped with this experience. This does not deny or in any way diminish the fact that minority groups have faced restricted opportunity in American society. Indeed, it is assumed that lack of opportunity is the common denominator in the minority experience in America. What makes the histories of minority groups variable is how they cope with prejudice and discrimination, which is at least in part affected by their internal solidarity. The Chinese and Japanese transplanted their tribal ties to American soil and then translated these loyalties into economic advancement in spite of intense prejudice and discrimination against them. This principle can been seen in the mobility of immigrant field hands into independent farmers, through a padrone system, in the placing of ken into urban enterprises of their own, and in the practice of rotating credit associations. Blacks had lost their tribal bonds in slavery, however, and were thereby disadvantaged in their fight against prejudice and discrimination as free people.

This comparison of Asian and African Americans also illustrates the role of capital in ethnic change. Their accumulation of capital was critical in the movement of the Chinese and Japanese out of menial wage labor and economic subordination. The internal organization of these groups enabled them to accumulate capital within their own ranks and with it build their own subeconomies, which offered their members an alternative to the prejudice and discrimination in the larger society.

The emphasis up to now has been on the relationship between societal and ethnic change. The modernization of American society brought changes to the nation's ethnic and racial groups that were articulated through their exchange of land, labor, and capital. Ethnic groups have both converged with and diverged from this process of societal change, a view that expands on assimilationism, pluralism, and conflict theory. The nation's more powerful ethnic groups have excluded the weaker ones from full participation in modern society, causing the divergence of the latter. Prejudice was generated to justify the exclusion, and it, too, helped perpetuate the divergence. Exclusion and divergence mean different things for different minority groups, however, a point made in this comparison of Asian and African Americans.

SUMMARY

All three sociological theories of American ethnicity must be used to understand the Japanese in America. Competition led to ethnic stratification, or at least attempts to keep the Japanese on the bottom, and their exclusion from the country. This is consistent with conflict theory. As a result, the Japanese built an ethnic subeconomy and became a middleman minority, much like the Chinese before them. The Japanese subeconomy and middleman community was different, however, composed of families rather than homeless males, and it was rooted on the land as well as in urban commerce. It was at this point that the histories of both the Japanese and Chinese Americans diverged from that of African Americans.

Competition continued between the Japanese and their ethnic rivals, and stereotypical images of the clannish and unpatriotic Japanese had a reception in the wider society. Their rivals got the upper hand at the start of World War II, an attack that seemingly supported already-held stereotypes. The result was the internment of the West Coast Japanese, citizen and alien alike. The ethnic subeconomy destroyed, and with the coming of the post-industrial phase of American history, the Nisei and later generations have moved into the larger society.

OTHER ASIAN AMERICANS AND AMERICAN SOCIETY

hile the history of Chinese and Japanese Americans goes back to the nineteenth century, Koreans, Filipinos, and Vietnamese are more recent Asian immigrant groups to the United States. Their history in America is limited to the twentieth century, and they are just beginning to establish themselves in this country (Box 14.1), although their immigration was preceded by military or economic ties between their homelands and the United States. These groups share with Chinese and Japanese Americans a history of labor in America, experience with prejudice and discrimination against Asians, and a role in business enterprise.

BOX 14.1 ASIAN AMERICANS TODAY

Although Asian-Americans were once largely confined to a few states, like California and Hawaii, and clustered in urban centers like the Chinatowns of New York and San Francisco, they have now spread to virtually every part of the nation.

...[A]round the country the Asian population increased by 79.5 percent in the 1980's, rising to 6.88 million from 3.83 million. That is seven times faster than the general population and makes them far and away the most rapidly growing ethnic group in the country....

In some states, the growth of the Asian-American population is stunning: New Jersey, up 162 percent,...Texas, up 165.5 percent, ...Rhode Island, up 245 percent....

The flow of immigrants has changed the ethnic balance radically. Whereas in 1970, Japanese formed the largest group, in 1980 Chinese surpassed them, and in 1990 Filipinos jumped over them....in 1990 there were 1.4 million Filipinos, 1.26 million Chinese, 859,000 Vietnamese, 814,000 Koreans, 804,000 Japanese, 684,000 Asian-Indians and 706,000 others, including Cambodians, Laotians and Pacific Islanders.

Given this diversity of national origins—and perhaps an even greater diversity in social classes among the immigrants between peasants and nuclear physicists—some Asian-American leaders say it is misleading to use the term "Asian-American" at all.

Source: Fox Butterfield, "Asians Spread Across a Land, and Help Change It." *New York Times*, February 24, 1991. Copyright © 1991 by the New York Times Company. Reprinted by permission.

◎◎

KOREAN AMERICANS

CONTACT

There was a small Korean immigration to the United States early in the twentieth century. Korean men immigrated between 1902 and 1907, after which Korean picture brides joined their husbands in the United States through the Gentlemen's Agreement with Japan (Mangiafico, 1988). Korea was annexed by Japan in 1910, and a small number of Korean political refugees fled to the United Sates between 1910 and 1924. After passage of the Quota Act of 1924, Korean immigration virtually stopped. There were only 1,677 Koreans on the mainland of the United States in 1920, 1,860 in 1930, and 1,711 in 1940, with another 6,851 in Hawaii in 1940. Koreans were an invisible minority at this time and were often mistaken for Japanese and Chinese Americans.

During the 1950s, 600 Koreans immigrated per year, many of them war brides of U.S. servicemen stationed in Korea (Mangiafico, 1988). Over 28,000 war brides eventually came to the United States, as did another 6,293 war orphans (Kitano and Daniels, 1988). The Korean population in the United States increased from 70,000 in 1970 to 814,000 in 1990, an increase of 1,062 percent.

Much of this increase is due to the recent immigration of Koreans, especially since the 1965 Immigration Act. A total of 267,638 Koreans immigrated to the United States during the 1970s, and about 30,000 were coming each year during the 1980s (Mangiafico, 1988). A majori-

FIGURE 14.1   KOREAN AMERICANS AND CHANGE IN AMERICAN SOCIETY

Industrial Society c. 1865–1945		Post-Industrial Society c. 1945–Present	
Early immigration and contact	Accommodation, → competition, and conflict	Community and → the independence movement	Recent → immigration	Middleman → minority?

ty of these immigrants have been women; there were only 67 males per 100 females in the Korean-born population in 1980. In that same year, almost 82 percent of the Koreans in the country were foreign-born, and two-thirds had been U.S. residents for less than ten years (Mangiafico, 1988). Thus a majority of Koreans in the country are female and either first or second generation.

Korea, a 600-mile-long peninsula that points southeastward from the Manchurian border to Japan, is a bit larger than Minnesota. The land is largely mountainous and hilly, with narrow river valleys and wider coastal plains, especially in the west and south. The Korean peninsula divides the Yellow Sea from the Sea of Japan, and is surrounded by three world powers, China, Japan, and Russia. Much of its history is a story of these powers competing for and dominating the Korean peninsula.

By legend, the Korean tribal state was founded in 2333 B.C. by the spirit King *Tan'gun* (Choy, 1979). From 57 B.C. to 668 A.D, there were three separate kingdoms on the peninsula, which were then unified into a single kingdom by the Silla. The Yi dynasty began in 1392 and lasted until 1910 with the annexation of Korea by Japan. Korea was a feudal society during the Yi dynasty, with the king on top of the social hierarchy, followed by the aristocracy (*Yangban*), who were hereditary landlords. Access to the *Yangban* began with passing the state civil service exams, but titles were then inherited by succeeding generations of a family. Below the aristocracy were middlemen (*Kung-in*), or skilled professionals, followed by commoners (*Sang-min*), most of whom were farmers but also including merchants, artisans, and fishermen. Slaves were at the bottom of the hierarchy.

Korean families were traditionally headed by the oldest male, and families were clustered in small villages and organized into clans (Melendy, 1977). The indigenous religion in Korea was a mixture of ancestor worship, totemism, and shamanism (Dearman, 1982). However, both Buddhism and Confucianism have dominated Korean life for the last ten centuries. Christianity came to Korea as early as 1784, and its impact on Korean culture spread in the nineteenth century, due primarily to an American missionary movement (Kim, 1977b). By late in the nineteenth century, the isolation of Korea and its historical dependency on China had been broken.

The Sino-Japanese War of 1894–95 overturned the Chinese influence in Korea. Following the war, there was a period (1895–1904) of Russian and Japanese rivalry over the country (Choy, 1979). Russian influence ascended for a time, but the Japanese took control of Korea after winning the Russo-Japanese War of 1904–05. The Japanese became landlords in Korea and controlled import-export trade as well as banking and construction. In 1910, Japan annexed Korea. These events increased taxes on the peasants and food shortages forced Koreans to emigrate (Choy, 1979; Hatada, 1969; Hurh and Kim, 1984; Kim, 1971; Kim, 1977a; Yang, 1982). Along with a smaller number of political exiles, Korean peasants emigrated to Manchuria, Japan, Russia, and Mexico, as well as to Hawaii and the mainland of the United States. In 1961, there were 1.25 million Koreans in Manchuria, 600,000 in Japan, and 300,000 in Siberia (Mangiafico, 1988).

The Japanese plan was to make Korea a granary for an industrializing home country, which led to an expansion of Japanese landholdings in Korea, Japanese control over imports and exports, and increased tenancy among Korea peasants. Forced off the land, Korean peasants began to immigrate to Japan and took low-level jobs there in industry (Lee and De Vos, 1981; Weiner, 1989). They were miners, workers in textile mills, and generally were relegated to the worst jobs and paid at lower wages than Japanese workers. After 1939, Koreans were involuntarily brought to Japan as both military conscripts and civilian workers (Lee and De Vos, 1981). There were over 2 million Koreans in Japan at the end of the Second World War. Japanese stereotypes of Koreans centered on their being lazy, dirty, emotional, and unintelligent. Not only did these stereotypes justify the stratification and segregation of Koreans in Japan, they also led to violent attacks on Koreans (see Box 14.2).

❦

BOX 14.2 THE KANTO EARTHQUAKE

[An earthquake shook the Tokyo area on September 1, 1923.] During the week after the earthquake, the Japanese in Tokyo went berserk hunting Koreans. They used bamboo spears to stab, clubs to beat, and bare hands to choke Koreans to death.... [A] "Korean accent" marked a person for extermination. On the evening of the earthquake...one hundred Korean manual laborers on their way home had been killed around Shibuya station. On 3 September Ueno police captured seventy Koreans. They chopped off their arms and threw the bodies into a fire. In Kanda, Tokyo, several Korean female students were raped and killed. The Japanese stripped them, tore their legs apart, cut their sexual organs, and stabbed them to death. On 7 September Japanese soldiers arrested 368 Korean students and machine-gunned them on the bank of the Sumida River in Tokyo. During this week, 2,000 or more Koreans in Haneda, 400 in Samida and Honjo, 200 in Kameido, 150 in Ueno, and 1,000 or more in Saitama, Gunma, and Ibaragi were tortured and killed....

Source: Changsoo Lee and George De Vos, *Koreans in Japan: Ethnic Conflict and Accommodation.* Berkeley: University of California Press, p. 23. Copyright © 1981 The Regents of the University of California. Reprinted by permission.

Other estimates put the number of Korean dead following the Kanto Earthquake as high as 6,000 (Weiner, 1989).

Korea experienced a bad grain crop in 1901, and there was a threat of famine (Kim, 1977a). At the same time, there were growing labor needs in Hawaii, particularly on the sugar plantations. Once sugar had replaced coffee production as Hawaii's main crop by 1835, the need for plantation workers escalated (Patterson, 1977). Eventually, 400,000 workers migrated to Hawaii from 33 countries. The islands' planters had previously imported both Chinese and Japanese workers, as well as others, but when Japanese workers on the sugar plantations staged 34 strikes between 1900 and 1905, the planters looked for an alternative labor supply (Choy, 1979). Between 1902 and 1905, over 7,000 Koreans were imported into Hawaii; over 6,000 of these immigrants were adult males and 40 percent were Christian (Yang, 1982). Representatives of the Hawaiian planters lobbied the Korean emperor for this labor emigration, and Koreans were then recruited for work on Hawaii through American Christian missionaries in Korea (Patterson, 1988). These immigrants were young men with semi- and unskilled jobs, who had been exposed to the missionaries. Japan halted this immigration to Hawaii in 1905, except for a few hundred picture brides, in order to better protect Japanese labor in Hawaii and keep needed labor in Korea (Choy, 1979; Patterson, 1988; Yun, 1977).

Korean workers were paid $15 per month on the sugar plantations for ten hours of work per day, six days a week (see Box 14.3). They were not allowed to talk nor stand up straight during working hours and were addressed by numbers rather than names. Virtually all their provisions came from company stores. The Koreans established village councils (*Tonghoe*) on the plantations, each with a head man (*Dong Jang*), who arbitrated disputes, levied fines and punishments, and who was a camp's ceremonial leader for Korean workers (Melendy, 1977). The immigrants also built Christian churches and formed ethnic associations, such as Korean schools, newspapers, and mutual-aid societies. After 1905, and with the coming of picture brides, Koreans in Hawaii began to move into urban trades—shoemakers, tailors, apartment and rooming house proprietors, grocers and other retail shopkeepers, skilled dock laborers, and workers at pineapple canneries and for the American military (Choy, 1979; Melendy, 1977).

☺☺

BOX 14.3 LIFE OF MRS. KIM

Mrs. Kim prepared meals for twenty bachelors and her husband. To stretch her limited budget took resolve and imagination. She planted watercress along a nearby stream and cultivated pepper bushes to provide seasoning necessary for kim chee. She discovered that beef innards were free for the asking at a nearby slaughterhouse, and these became part of the Kim larder. Every morning at five o'clock her boarders received a breakfast of rice, kim chee, and broth. Six days a week she packed twenty-one lunch tins with rice and dried salt fish. Dinner consisted of soup, rice, and either a soy seasoned dish of vegetables, meat, or fish, or a dish of corned beef and onions. "Burned rice tea," brewed from rice burned to the bottom of the pot, was the beverage. Every Saturday fresh beef or pork was served at dinner.

In addition to preparing the meals, Mrs. Kim, then but eighteen years of age, did the men's laundry. Each paid her one dollar a month for this service. A wood fire heated the water in her galvanized tub, which also contained brown soap and an endless pile of denim work pants and shirts. She boiled the clothes to clean them of red dirt and sweat. Each article was scrubbed on a washboard, beaten with a wooden rod, rinsed, and hung to dry. The entire wash was then starched with flour and water to be ironed with a charcoal-heated iron.

Source: Reprinted with permission of Twayne Publishers, an imprint of Macmillan Publishing Company, from *Asians in America: Filipinos, Koreans, and East Indians* by H. Brett Melendy. Copyright © 1977 by G. K. Hall & Co.

☺☺

In 1904, over a thousand Koreans immigrated to Mexico to work on the Yucatan's henequen farms and its mines (Kim, 1971). Conditions were exploitive and deplorable, and Korean associations charged that these contract laborers had been defrauded. Later some of the workers migrated again to Cuba to work on that island's sugar plantations. After 1905, Koreans came to the United States mainland. Between 1905 and 1916, over 1,000 Koreans emigrated from Hawaii into the United States, and in 1920 there were over 1,600 Koreans living in the continental United States (Melendy, 1977).

ACCOMMODATION, COMPETITION, AND CONFLICT

As they had done in Hawaii, most Koreans on the mainland worked in agriculture. Throughout California, they became farm laborers, typically working under a Korean labor boss, a pattern similar to that of the earlier Japanese farm workers in California. Eighty percent of the Koreans in the continental United States between 1910 and 1920 resided in rural California (Yim, 1984). Since farm work was seasonal, these immigrants also took up other jobs, especially during the slack seasons (Yang, 1982). In the cities, they were dishwashers and busboys, janitors, gardeners, and domestic servants. They also were employed in railroad maintenance, and some found jobs in the fish canneries of Alaska. Living in labor camps in rural areas and boarding houses in the cities, the society of the early Korean immigrants was essentially a bachelor one. Their settlement resembled the earlier bachelor societies of the Chinese and Japanese, and Koreans faced the same anti-Asian prejudice and discrimination.

The decision of the San Francisco Board of Education in 1906 to segregate Japanese students applied to Korean students as well. Along with other Asians, they experienced a form of Jim Crow on the West Coast, as well as housing discrimination. The Alien Land Laws in California and other states excluded alien Koreans as well as Japanese from owning land (Choy, 1979; Melendy, 1977; Takaki, 1989). In 26 states they were denied old-age pensions (Melendy, 1977). After the Quota Act of 1924, only Korean students were allowed into the country, and Korean aliens were denied naturalization until 1952. The stereotype of Koreans was that they were loud, dirty, oddly dressed, and ate foreign food. Korean workers were also seen as competitors by others, and this occasionally led to conflict. For example, one California grower, Mary Steward, employed Koreans as orange-pickers in Upland, California, and these workers were attacked one night: "... white farmers and workers attacked the Korean camp with stones and rocks, threatening to kill the Koreans if they did not leave the camp at once. The frightened Koreans had no other place to go.... They stayed at the camp site, afraid to move for fear of being killed by the rioting white mob... " (Choy, 1979:109). Because Mrs. Steward took a firm stand in favor of the Korean workers, hostility subsided and Koreans were later accepted by other growers in the area.

KOREAN COMMUNITY AND THE INDEPENDENCE MOVEMENT

As did the Chinese and Japanese before them, Koreans established an ethnic community in America. Some Koreans began businesses of their own, often employing other Koreans, building an ethnic sub-economy. It was the Korean church that was the center of the Korean community, however, and more often than not, these were Christian churches. What truly distinguished Koreans from Chinese and Japanese Americans was their independence movement to free the homeland from Japanese control. Let us first look into the Korean subeconomy.

The Korean subeconomy was found in urban trades as well as agriculture. In cities on the West Coast, Koreans moved into self-employment as barbers, restaurant owners, and proprietors of laundries and rooming houses (Yim, 1984). In Los Angeles, for example, Korean small businesses between 1910 and 1920 included grocer, wholesale produce, horse market, fish counter, cigar maker, restaurant owner, florist, barber, brewer, laundry, and jeweler (Yim, 1984). To start their own small businesses, Koreans invested their own savings and pooled money, sometimes through Korean rotating-credit associations (*Kae* or *Kye*). The hours were long, and there were many business failures.

Some Korean firms were larger corporations doing business in the United States, Hawaii, and Korea. Investment capital was raised through the sale of stock certificates in many of these cases. One example of Korean business in California agriculture was the Kim Brothers.

> As early as 1921, a partnership was formed between Charles Kim and Harry Kim...in Reedley, California. The business began as a trucking wholesaler of fruit. As the years went by, it expanded into large orchards, fruit-packing sheds, and nurseries. It was called the Kim Brothers Company. The Kim brothers tried to develop new varieties of fruit trees, working mainly with peaches and nectarines. Eventually, they developed a "fuzzless peach." Today it is sold on the market as "Le Grand" and "Sun Grand," and saplings from the orchards are shipped throughout the United States. The Kim brothers developed more than a dozen other hybrid fruits for which they obtained patents from the government. They continued their business for thirty years, retiring in 1965. They owned six farms containing five hundred acres. The farms, packing plants, and nursery facilities were worth about $1.5 million. Every year they grossed more than $1 million... (Choy, 1979:130).

Other examples of Korean corporations in the country, some of which did business in the United States and others in Korea, are shown in Box 14.4. Kim (1977d) added the Prospering Business Company (1910), Tongji Investment Company (1924), and the Oriental Food Products of California (1926) to the list.

☯☯

BOX 14.4 KOREAN CORPORATIONS IN CALIFORNIA, 1903–1920

Asian Industrial Corporation: Established in 1908 by thirty-one Koreans, all of whom were members of the United Association of California. The purpose was to develop industry in Korea and help to liberate Korea from Japanese rule. The capital was $20,000, raised by selling 800 shares at $25 each.

Kwon-Up Industrial League Corporation: Set up in 1908 by several Koreans in Los Angeles to purchase land in Korea for agricultural and industrial purposes. There were thirty-six stockholders in 1908, and the capital was $2,200. By 1911 the capital had increased to $6,000. They bought some land in Korea.

Tae-Dong (Great Eastern) Industrial Corporation: Established in San Francisco in 1909 with $25,000 in capital. A year later there was still a balance of $5,000 to be raised.

Hung-Up Corporation: Started in Redlands in 1909 to purchase land for cultivation. The corporation raised $4,000 from fifty Koreans. Work was started on orange fields, but the corporation went out of business in 1911.

The Korean American Trading Company: Started in San Francisco in 1910 to import Korean paintings and antiques and to export American goods. The shares were priced at $15.

The Industrial League: Organized in 1911 in Los Angeles for agricultural and industrial purposes. By 1914, $33,000 was raised by thirty-three shareholders, each of whom contributed $1,000. The league planned to open businesses in trees, vegetables, restaurants, stores, hotels, and the like.

Source: Sun Bin Yim, 1984. "The Social Structure of Korean Communities in California, 1903–1920," in Lucie Cheng and Edna Bonacich (eds.), *Labor Immigration Under Capitalism: Asian Workers in the United States Before World War II*, Berkeley: University of California Press, p. 536. Copyright © 1984 The Regents of the University of California. Reprinted by permission.

☯☯

Korean immigrants had established thirty-one Christian churches in Hawaii and seven on the mainland within a decade of their arrival

(Kim, 1971). Churches were centers of worship, to be sure, but also they were places for contact with one's own kind that promoted Korean nationalism against the Japanese and offered important social and educational services. Although most of the early Korean immigrants were illiterate when they left the homeland, Koreans had the highest literacy rate of all Asian immigrants in the United States by 1920, due for the most part to the educational services provided by Korean churches (Takaki, 1989). Virtually all the leaders of the Korean independence movement were connected at one time or another to the Korean Christian churches in America and Hawaii. The Korean community consisted also of schools, newspapers and other periodicals, and cultural centers. For example, the *New Korea* was a weekly newspaper from Los Angeles, and the *Korean National Herald* was published in Honolulu (Kim, 1971).

In a later period, 1960–1972, Lee (1977) studied two small Korean communities in Georgia, one in Atlanta and another in a university town, where he found four stages in Korean community formation. The first was the *initiative stage*, during which Koreans came together because of common interests and nationality. The second was the *formative stage*, in which subgroups of Koreans emerged based on regional and educational ties, etc. The third was the *institutionalized stage*, during which specific churches and alumni groups, for example, were established. The last was the *stage of segmentation*, when interaction was more and more confined within the subgroups of the larger Korean community. The fragmentation of the Korean community into subgroups was also evident in the earlier Korean independence movement.

There were a multitude of organizations for Korean independence, each promoting different tactics to gain that independence (Choy, 1979; Kim, 1971; Kim, 1977c; Melendy, 1977; Takaki, 1989). Throughout its history, the movement was fragmented, as illustrated by three leaders and their followers.

Park Yong-man established a military corps in 1914 to train a paramilitary force to liberate Korea from the Japanese. This represented the militant wing of the independence movement. Syngman Rhee advocated persuasion and diplomacy with western nations as the route to eventual Korean independence. He gained control of the Korean National Association in Hawaii in 1918 after a bitter rivalry with Park Yong-man, and he later formed the Comrade Society in 1920. Park died in 1928, while Rhee became the first president of South Korea after the Second World War. The third leader was Ahn Chang-ho, who established the Corps for the Advancement of Individuals in 1913. His tactics were to educate Koreans as the best method to insure the national integrity of Korea.

The independence movement peaked with the 1919 independence demonstrations in Korea itself and shortly thereafter, but the movement stagnated after the 1930s and until Korean independence following World War II (Choy, 1979). By the same token, political protest still occurs in the Korean community, evident in the political rallies in Los Angeles that followed the 1980 Kwangju uprising in Korea (Chang, 1988). The student demonstrations in Kwangju, a city southwest of Seoul, resulted in at least 174 deaths.

RECENT IMMIGRATION

There were 70,000 Koreans in the United States in 1970, but the population grew to 814,000 in 1990 due largely to immigration. Almost 30 percent of the Koreans lived in California in 1980, but there were also Korean concentrations in New York, Illinois, Washington, and Maryland, for example. By the year 2000, there are likely to be 1 million Koreans in the United States (Mangiafico, 1988).

The Immigration Act of 1965 instituted international quotas and gave preferences in immigration for family reunification. After this act, Asian immigration, including that from Korea, increased. Not only family reunification, but also war brides and orphans account for the flow of Korean immigrants in recent decades. In the past two decades, Korean immigration has been triple that of the 1960s. Additional reasons for Korean immigration include educational opportunity and a better standard of living in America, as well as political unrest in Korea and the threat of war there (Light and Bonacich, 1988; Choy, 1979; Melendy, 1977).

Recent immigration is different than earlier Korean immigration. For one thing, these newcomers "... are literate. Eighty percent of the immigrants between 1965 and 1972 were high school graduates: 50 percent were college graduates and classified professionals. In 1980, over 33 percent of the Koreans in the United States (foreign- or native-born) aged 25 or older had four or more years of college, whereas only 16.2 percent of the entire U.S. population did" (Mangiafico, 1988). Professional and technical workers made up over 67 percent of the Korean immigrants in 1964 and almost 66 percent in 1969 (Ishi, 1988). The recent Korean immigrants were the Westernized middle and upper classes in Korea, seen in the high number of educated and professional immigrants. In 1980, over 92 percent of the Koreans lived in standard statistical metropolitan areas as defined by the U.S. Census. Earlier in the century, by contrast, Korean immigrants were largely uneducated, semi- and unskilled workers in agriculture and marginal urban jobs.

Korean immigration changed recently, however: "the profession-al-preference immigrants have decreased from 25 percent in 1972 to 19 percent in 1974, while the non-preference immigrants increased from 1 percent in 1968 to 28 percent in 1974" (Choy, 1979:217). Only 25.5 per-cent of the Korean immigrants in 1979 were professional and technical workers (Ishi, 1988). It has been a chain immigration, meaning that family members who settled first in the United States, largely edu-cated professionals, then brought their relatives here as non-quota im-migrants to reunify their families. In 1981, 92 percent of the Korean immigration was to unite families, and thus the occupational composi-tion of Korean immigrants has changed over this period (Light and Bonacich, 1988; Hurh and Kim, 1984). There has been a decreasing number of Korean professionals immigrating into the country as fami-ly reunification has taken over as a primary reason for immigration. Ten percent of world's Koreans resided abroad in 1982 (Light and Bonacich, 1988).

Recent Korean immigrants often experienced initial downward mobility in the United States (Kitano and Daniels, 1988; Yu, 1982). They had better occupations in Korea than their first jobs in the Unit-ed States. Recall that over 67 percent of Korean immigrants in 1964 and almost 66 percent in 1969 were professional and technical work-ers, and among these workers were significant numbers of nurses, doctors, engineers, and teachers (Ishi, 1988). This downward mobili-ty is illustrated by Korean professionals, such as physicians, taking jobs in the United States on the periphery of their profession, for ex-ample, family and general practice (Shin and Chang, 1988). Another illustration is Korean teachers who have gone into small businesses in the United States. In one sample of Korean household heads and their spouses in southern California in 1978, Yu (1982) found that al-most 40 percent of the household heads and 34 percent of their spouses were business proprietors. About 25 percent of the house-hold heads and 12.4 percent of their spouses were professional work-ers. Table 14.1 shows the occupational composition of Korean Ameri-cans (employed persons 16 years and over) across the country in 1990. As the table shows, Korean Americans compare favorably with all Americans.

MIDDLEMAN MINORITY?

Korean Americans are concentrated in the nation's cities, particu-larly those on the two coasts. In 1980, over 47 percent of the nation's Korean population lived in seven metropolitan areas. Los Angeles–Long Beach was home to over 17 percent of the nation's Ko-

TABLE 14.1   PERCENTAGE DISTRIBUTION OF KOREAN AMERICANS AND ALL
EMPLOYED PEOPLE BY OCCUPATIONAL GROUPS, 1990

Occupational Group	Korean Origin 1990	All People 1990
Managerial and professional	24.0%	25.5%
Technical, sales, and administrative support	37.9	31.5
Service occupations	16.6	13.5
Precision production, craft, and repair	8.3	11.5
Operators, fabricators, and laborers	13.0	15.5
Farming, forestry, and fishing	0.7	2.5

Source: Census of Population and Housing, 1990: Public Micromedia Samples U.S., prepared by the
Bureau of the Census, 1992.

reans, New York City was home for 8 percent, almost 6 percent lived
in Chicago, nearly 5 percent were in Washington, D.C., another 5 percent lived in Honolulu, and Anaheim and San Francisco–Oakland
each had a little over 3 percent of the nation's Koreans (Light and
Bonacich, 1988). It has been found in several studies that Koreans disproportionately go into their own businesses in these cities (Bonacich
and Jung, 1982; Choy, 1979; Kim 1977d; Light and Bonacich, 1988).

For example, Light and Bonacich (1988) found that 60 percent of
the Koreans in Los Angeles County were self-employed or employed
in Korean firms. The business lines of these Korean firms included retail outlets, such as grocery stores, gas stations, wig and apparel shops,
and liquor stores. Korean firms also provided services, such as auto repair, restaurants, travel agencies, janitorial services, and professional
services (Bonacich and Jung, 1982; Choy, 1979). Korean immigrants
usually go into their own businesses within the first three years of
their residence in the United States (Kim, 1977d). Does this mean that
Korean Americans are becoming a middleman minority, as did Chinese and Japanese Americans?

To some extent they are, since they use ethnic ties as a route to
business enterprise, Korean businesses serve disproportionately a minority clientele, and this creates friction between Korean business people and the larger society (Bonacich and Jung, 1982). They also use Korean rotating credit associations for business capital (Light, et al.,
1990). In other ways, Koreans are not a middleman minority. Light

and Bonacich (1988) argued that Koreans are actually cheap labor in America under the guise of entrepreneurs in small businesses. The typical Korean firm in Los Angeles is small, has low receipts, and few employees, and thus low payrolls, and it pays low wages to co-ethnics and family members. Owners and employees work long hours. Either as franchises or subcontractors, these Korean firms assume high risks for larger companies, exploit their labor with low wages and long hours, and earn profits that tend to move up to parent companies in the case of franchises. Many of their owners are blocked by professional licensing standards from getting jobs in America comparable to those they had in Korea, and thus starting a small business of their own in America is a case of downward mobility.

The Korean community in America has grown larger and more diverse because of the recent immigration. There are distinct ethclasses, for example, with 25 percent of the Korean population in professional and managerial positions in 1980 and another 20 percent working as operatives. The diversity is also seen in Korean churches and associations. Choy (1979) estimated that there were 121 Korean Christian churches in Los Angeles alone, and one out of every 240 Koreans is a clergyman. In addition, "there are hundreds, if not thousands, of Korean community groups in this country" (Choy, 1979:229). Among the associations are the Korean-American Political Association, the Korean Medical Association in America, the Korean Scientists and Engineers Association in America, the Korean Chamber of Commerce in Los Angeles, and the Korean Christian Businessmen's Association; and the list goes on (Choy, 1979).

Over 78 percent of the Koreans in America consider themselves Korean, not American or Korean American, and 62 percent would like to return to Korea for good at a suitable time (Yung-Hwan, 1982). Hurh and Kim (1984) found that Koreans in Los Angeles typically speak Korean at home, read Korean rather than American newspapers, and have a strong attachment to their ethnic group. Korean language use and media exposure, but not ethnic attachment, declined with length of residence and education. Moreover, Koreans maintain contact with Korean kin, friends, and neighbors, and this is true for even those with non-Korean friends and neighbors. Koreans in great numbers also join Korean associations and go to Korean churches. By the same token, Yu (1977) found that acculturation of Koreans in America is related to length of residence, education, occupation, religion, and English proficiency. Being Christian, fluent in English, and high in educational and occupational status were positively associated with acculturation.

FIGURE 14.2   FILIPINO AMERICANS AND CHANGE IN AMERICAN SOCIETY

Industrial Society c. 1865–1945		Post-Industrial Society c. 1945–Present
Early immigration and contact →	Accommodation, competition and conflict →	Recent immigration

FILIPINO AMERICANS

CONTACT

Contact between Americans and Filipinos began not in the United States but in the Philippines with the Spanish-American War of 1898. Magellan landed in the Philippines in 1521, Cebu was the first Spanish settlement, and the Spanish colonial capital became Manila in 1571. The Spanish ruled the Philippines until the Spanish-American War of 1898, after which the Philippines were an American possession until Philippine Independence in 1946.

The Philippines are an archipelago of more than 7,000 islands in the Pacific off the coast of Asia. To the north is Taiwan, to the south are Malaysia and Indonesia, and to the west is Vietnam. The island of Luzon is in the north and Mindanao in the south; a third section consists of smaller islands around the Visayan Sea, and a fourth section is a cluster of islands running southwesterly to Borneo (Melendy, 1977; Richardson, 1989). The eleven largest islands have about 94 percent of the land area and population.

Even before the coming of the Spanish, successive waves of immigrants from Indonesia and Malaysia had pushed the first people of the Philippines into remote areas of the archipelago (Cady, 1964). These people were called *Negritos* by the Spanish. The stated mission of Spanish colonial policy was to bring Christianity to the Philippines, and thus religious orders had as much power there as the Spanish colonial government. The monastic orders were also big landholders, especially around Manila on Luzon, and thus economic interests were part of Spanish colonial policy. Up to 1815 the Philippines were also Spain's trading link between China and Mexico.

The stratification of Filipino society under Spanish rule had Spanish aristocrats and clergy on top; Chinese in retail trade, crafts, and services in the middle; and Filipino peasants and servants on the bottom (Cady, 1964). The Spanish received land grants and rights to tax and impress Filipino labor, who were essentially landless sharecroppers under this *cacique* system.

On May 1, 1898, less than a week after Congress declared war against Spain, an American fleet under Commodore George Dewey sailed into Manila Bay and easily defeated a small Spanish squadron there. American ground forces later accepted the surrender of the Philippines, and Spain ceded the islands to the United States with the Treaty of Paris in December. Spain received a payment of $20,000,000 and some other concessions from the United States for the Philippines. There had been open revolt against the Spanish before American forces arrived in the Philippines, and rebellion continued against the American administration up to 1907 (Cady, 1964). This nationalist movement was led by elite Filipinos, and its base of support also included landowners and peasants in Luzon who stood to gain from the end of Spanish rule.

At first, the United States imposed a military government on the Philippines, but it ended in 1901. With the subsequent civilian government, the United States appointed the chief executive of the Philippines, the governor-general, and a commission that had both legislative and administrative functions. In 1907 the Filipinos elected a lower house, the Philippine Assembly. The Jones Act of 1916 promised eventual independence and hastened the Filipinization of the civil service, so that by 1936 there were 22,555 Filipinos and only 160 Americans in the Philippine civil service (Taylor, 1964). The Philippine Independence Act of 1934 established a commonwealth government in 1936 and set a target date for independence ten years later. The islands were occupied by the Japanese in 1942 (during World War II), but they were later retaken by American and Filipino forces, and the country finally became independent in 1946.

The American administration liquidated the Spanish friar landholdings, separated church and state in the government, and provided improved health and educational services. For example, 37 percent of the Filipinos were literate in English by 1946 (Taylor, 1964). By the same token, the economic position of the peasants and the entire Philippines improved little under American rule. Peasants remained as cash renters in the transition to commercial agriculture for export crops of sugar, copra, and tobacco under American administration (Taylor, 1964). American imports undermined the Filipino handicrafts, and there was virtually no development of an industrial sector in the country. The economic relation between the Philippines and the United States was one of economic dependency, whereby the Philippines exported agricultural products and imported manufactured goods from the United States.

Filipinos began to emigrate about 1907 to work on the sugar plantations in Hawaii, where the rise of sugar production necessitated the importation of labor, especially from Asia. The planters turned increasingly to both Filipino and Korean labor after a series of strikes by Japanese workers on the Hawaiian plantations. In 1915, Filipinos made up 19 percent of the Hawaiian plantation work force and the Japanese 54 percent. By 1932, however, Filipinos were 70 percent of the work force and the Japanese 19 percent (Sharma, 1984b). Between 1906 and 1946, over 125,000 Filipinos immigrated to Hawaii; most came from Ilocos in northeast Luzon (Sharma, 1984a). Other areas of the Philippines, also in sugar and other cash-crop production, had labor shortages, but this was not the case in Ilocos (Sharma, 1984a). Émigrés from Ilocos had the prospect of returning home from Hawaii with savings to buy small farms.

Early Filipino migration to Hawaii consisted mainly of single men, who were joined after 1920 by women. Nevertheless, the migration to Hawaii was predominately male; there was fewer than one woman for each ten Filipino males (Mangiafico, 1988). Filipinos were a bachelor society on the bottom of the plantations' labor hierarchy, facing a segmented and split labor market, and living in segregated housing. Conditions for plantation workers dramatically improved, however, after the International Longshoremen and Warehousemen's Union organized all plantation workers by 1946. In 1950 Hawaiian plantation workers were the best-paid agricultural labor in the world. Later, as the plantations increasingly mechanized, Filipino workers were pushed into other lines of work in Hawaii (Anderson, 1984; Sharma, 1984b). The second generation found jobs in the canneries and in the tourist industry in Hawaiian cities (Anderson, 1984). The development of a Filipino subeconomy was limited in Hawaii to only a few businesses (Sharma, 1984b).

In the 1970s, Filipinos were still living in villages near the sugar plantations, although the plantations were closing or in decline (Anderson, 1984). Residents relied on their *compadres,* ritual kin who formed *compadrazgo* alliance systems used in times of need and for rites of passage. The system is an elaboration on godparents, a custom in several cultures. Compadres helped each other for social occasions, baby sitting, and transportation and shared time and other resources. The respective alliance systems divided villages into different factions, and there was still a division between Ilocanos and Visayans. The older residents especially depended on village notables, usually union officials who were also enmeshed into the compadrazgo system, in dealing with outsiders such as government officials. In 1980, Hawaii was the only state that still had a significant Filipino rural population, 25 percent of the total Filipino population in that state.

Filipino immigration to the United States mainland followed that to Hawaii, and many (up to 45%) who ultimately came to the United States had first migrated to Hawaii (Rabaya, 1971). In 1910 there were only 406 Filipinos in the United States, but by 1930 there were over 45,000 (Takaki, 1989). Early Filipino immigrants were primarily students who studied in the United States and then returned home. They were called *pensionados,* and their migration commenced shortly after the turn of the century.

The next wave were laborers to the West Coast; most of these came after 1920 (McWilliams, 1964). They were mostly men meant to replace the Japanese as farm labor in California, but this immigration dropped off in the 1930s. The third wave, 1946–1964, were mostly women (70.9%), many of them spouses, children, or other family members of U.S. servicemen stationed in the Philippines after the Second World War (Mangiafico, 1988). The last wave, the most recent Filipino immigration since 1965, is described below.

ACCOMMODATION, COMPETITION, AND CONFLICT

In 1930, 60 percent of the Filipinos in the United States were agriculture workers, 25 percent were service workers, and 9 percent worked in the Alaska fishing industry (Takaki, 1989). Filipinos were migratory labor in California agriculture who also worked in the cities during the off seasons (Melendy, 1977). They were the majority of the farm labor in asparagus, lettuce, strawberries, sugar beets, and potatoes (Melendy, 1977). Like other Asian groups, Filipino farm workers were organized by labor bosses under their version of the *padrone* system. In the cities, Filipinos were service workers, e.g., dishwashers, busboys, waiters, cooks, houseboys, janitors, porters, and bellboys (Rabaya, 1971). They also worked in the sawmills of Oregon, the salmon canneries in Alaska, as section hands on the railroads, as seaman in the merchant marine, and as mess boys for the U.S. Navy (Buaken, 1948).

The initial accommodation of Filipino workers was soon replaced by competition and conflict. Filipino workers engaged in work strikes, union organizing, and other forms of labor agitation, which antagonized their employers. In addition, white workers began to react to the labor competition posed by Filipino workers (McWilliams, 1964; Melendy, 1977; Rabaya, 1971). Riots against Filipino workers on the West Coast began in Yakima, Washington, in 1928 and continued into the

1930s up and down the Pacific Coast. In October 1929, a mob of 300 attacked Filipinos on a ranch near Exeter, California, and a riot in Watsonville, California, in January of 1930 left one Filipino dead and others badly beaten (Rabaya, 1971). "And when a group of Filipino field workers migrated to Florida to work in the vegetable fields, riots were reported there in July 1932. Even after Filipino immigration was barred, a few riots were reported, as in Lake County, California, in June 1939" (McWilliams, 1964:242).

୧୭

BOX 14.5 THE WATSONVILLE, CALIFORNIA, RIOT
AGAINST FILIPINOS

First the mob of some one hundred and fifty went to the beach and raided the Filipino club where social dances were staged nightly, clubbing and bludgeoning the Filipinos who resisted. When Filipinos passed through the streets in automobiles they were targets for bullets shot at them from every angle. Places where Filipinos lived in Watsonville were raided and all those who could not escape were severely beaten....

These series of assaults continuing for two weeks....

Finally, to quench the thirst of this mob, a carload of some one hundred and fifty men went at night to the camp occupied by Filipinos. It was at a time when the boys were thought to be in bed. The mob came armed with machine guns and rifles and surprised the sleeping Filipinos.... There were seventy Filipinos housed in the shack. At the surprise raid, however, the boys fought their way out of the trap. Fifty were wounded with clubs and by the flying volley of bullets. Fermin Tovera ran to the attic to hide, but he was pursued there and was shot in the heart. He died....

Source: Manuel Buaken, 1948. *I Have Lived with the American People.* Caldwell, Idaho: The Caxton Printers, Ltd. Pp. 102–103. Copyright © 1948 by The Caxton Printers, Ltd. Reprinted by permission.

୧୭

When the body of Fermin Tovera was returned to the Philippines, "a National Humiliation Day was proclaimed, and 10,000 Filipinos attended the funeral service..." (McWilliams, 1964:242).

One intent behind the conflict was to keep Filipinos at the bottom of the labor hierarchy and to exclude them from the country if necessary. The Alien Land Laws in California and other states applied to

509

Filipinos as well as other Asians, and thus were also meant to exclude Filipinos from land ownership (Takaki, 1989). The Philippine Independence Act of 1934 defined Filipinos as aliens ineligible for U.S. citizenship and granted them only a token immigration quota of 50 per year (Kim and Mejia, 1976; McWilliams, 1964). Exemptions to this quota were made, however, for Hawaiian planters. In 1935, Congress passed the Filipino Repatriation Act, and between 1935 and 1940 over 2,000 agreed to be repatriated to the Philippines and over 7,000 of the 45,000 Filipinos in the United States actually returned (Thernstrom, 1980). Those repatriated could not return to the United States, and Filipinos in Hawaii could not remigrate to the mainland. Thousands of Filipinos were discharged from the merchant marine in 1937 with legislation that reserved most of those jobs to American citizens (McWilliams, 1964).

The stereotypes that were used to justify this conflict and eventual exclusion included the old anti-Asian sentiments on the West Coast and the threat of over-sexed young Filipino men to white womanhood. "Famous in this respect were the dance halls in which young, single, Filipino males had the opportunity to mix with Caucasian girls. Such dance halls were the starting point of innumerable fights. ... Filipinos were characterized as unreliable, hot-tempered gigolos who loved to show off and have sexual relations with white women and who were prone to violence and crime" (Mangiafico, 1988:36). Antimiscegenation laws forbade marriages between Filipinos and whites up to 1948. At the base of these stereotypes was the image that Filipinos were primitive, and the men were known as "brown monkeys" in those days.

Unlike the Chinese and Japanese, Filipinos did not build an ethnic subeconomy. For one thing, the Chinese had virtually monopolized retail trade in the Philippines, and thus the immigrants brought with them to the United States little business experience. According to Takaki (1989), another reason was that the Chinese and Japanese in the United States were already entrenched in businesses that Filipinos could have taken up. Of course, these explanations hardly help us understand why Koreans did follow Chinese and Japanese into an ethnic subeconomy of their own in the United States. However, Filipinos did establish an ethnic community in America. The first Filipino newspaper, *The Philippine Independent News*, began publication in Salinas, California, in 1921 (Kim and Mejia, 1976). The Filipino Christian Youth Movement was organized in 1923, and Filipino churches were built throughout the country.

After World War II, Filipinos began to move out of agriculture and into urban factories, trades, and retail businesses (Melendy, 1977).

TABLE 14.2 PERCENTAGE DISTRIBUTION OF FILIPINO AMERICANS AND ALL
EMPLOYED PEOPLE BY OCCUPATIONAL GROUPS, 1990

Occupational Group	Philippine Origin 1990	All People 1990
Managerial and professional	24.7%	25.5%
Technical, sales, and administrative support	37.0	31.5
Service occupations	17.8	13.5
Precision production, craft, and repair	7.8	11.5
Operators, fabricators, and laborers	11.6	15.5
Farming, forestry, and fishing	1.9	2.5

Source: Census of Population and Housing, 1990: Public Micromedia Samples U.S., prepared by the
Bureau of the Census, 1992.

Nevertheless, 31 percent of the Filipinos in California were still employed in agriculture by 1960. Many California farm workers were
unionized in the 1960s, separately by the Agriculture Workers Organizing Committee, led by Larry Itlion, a Filipino, and the Farm Workers Organization, led by Cesar Chavez, a Chicano. These two unions
later merged into the United Farm Workers Organizing Committee
(Thernstrom, 1980).

The 1990 occupational composition of Filipino Americans is
shown in Table 14.2. There has been a great change in the occupational status of Filipino Americans since their early years in the country.
The 1990 occupational composition of Filipinos compared favorably
with that of all Americans. Over 50 percent of the Filipino American
labor force was in white-collar work in 1990, and nearly 25 percent
were in managerial and professional positions. This is a significant
change since the early days of Filipino farm labor. By 1990, only 2 percent of the Filipinos in the work force were still in agriculture, and Filipinos were still overrepresented in service jobs compared to all
Americans.

RECENT IMMIGRATION

The improvement in the occupational status of Filipinos is due in
part to the recent immigration of Filipinos into the country. Since the
Immigration Act of 1965, Asian immigration into the United States has
greatly increased, and this increase includes immigrants from the
Philippines. To illustrate, there were 101,500 Filipino immigrants into

the country in the decade 1961–1970; 360,200 in the following decade; and 431,500 between 1981 and 1989. There were 774,640 Filipinos in the United States in 1980—501,440 of them born in the Philippines (Mangiafico, 1988). Four-fifths of the Filipino population in 1980 had lived in the United States less than fifteen years. There were 1.4 million Filipinos in 1990, and the Filipino population in the United States is expected to exceed 2 million by the year 2000 (Kitano and Daniels, 1988). Filipinos are now the largest Asian ethnic group in the country; and Filipino emigrants can be found elsewhere in the world—the Mideast, Hong Kong, Japan, Singapore, and southern Europe—as well as the United States.

These new immigrants to the United States are different than the earlier Filipino immigrants. First, most of the recent immigrants are women. In 1980, there were only 86 men for every 100 women in the Filipino-born population in the United States (Mangiafico, 1988). Second, two-thirds of these recent immigrants are professional and technical and kindred workers (Thernstrom, 1980). By contrast, 60 percent of the Filipino workers in the United States were in agriculture in 1930. These professional people do not necessarily take up professional work in the United States immediately; many are forced into lower-level jobs while they prepare for licensing exams. Nevertheless, over 20 percent of the Filipino-born in 1980 were professionals, compared to 12.3 percent for the total U.S. labor force.

Whereas the earlier Filipino immigrants earned less than white Americans, recent Filipino immigrants earn at least as much when matched on occupational skills and education (Mangiafico, 1988). This recent immigration represents a brain drain from the Philippines into the United States; over 43 percent of the Filipino-born women in the United States in 1980 were college graduates.

In recent years, however, the education and occupations of Filipino immigrants have been declining as family reunification begins to play a role in immigration to the United States. Filipino immigrants have concentrated in the larger cities throughout the country, which distinguishes them from the settlement of earlier Filipinos in California agriculture. Recent Filipino immigrants are similar to earlier ones in at least one respect; they have not established an ethnic subeconomy in the United States. In 1980, only 2.3 percent of the Filipino-born population were self-employed, compared to 6.3 percent for the total work force in the United States.

The diversity of Filipinos in the United States has increased with the immigration in the past two or three decades. The old timers are largely uneducated and clannish and have low-paying jobs. The new arrivals are educated, cosmopolitan, and concentrated in white-collar

---

FIGURE 14.3   VIETNAMESE AMERICANS AND CHANGE IN AMERICAN SOCIETY

Post-Industrial Society
c. 1945–Present

| Immigration and contact | → | Accommodation | → | Competition and conflict |

---

work. The prospects for the assimilation of professional and middle-class Filipinos appears good, although loyalty to family and region of the home country is still evident.

VIETNAMESE AMERICANS

CONTACT

There were only 603 Vietnamese living in the United States in 1964, but by 1990 there were 859,000. There may be more than 1.5 million Vietnamese in America by the year 2000, which will make the Vietnamese the third largest Asian group in the country, behind only Filipinos and Chinese (Kitano and Daniels, 1988). In 1980, almost half of the Vietnamese lived in the West, particularly California, another 31 percent resided in the South, and the remainder lived in the Midwest and the Northeast (Kitano and Daniels, 1988).

Virtually all of the Vietnamese came to America after the Vietnam War. The first wave of 130,000 people came at the time of the American evacuation of Vietnam because they had been connected with the American government in Vietnam during the war and thus at risk after the fall of Saigon in 1975. They were educated, and two-thirds could speak English. Most came from urban South Vietnam, especially Saigon, and one-half were Christians, although only 10 percent of the Vietnam population was Christian (Takaki, 1989). The second wave began in 1978, due to the nationalization of private businesses, the establishment of "reeducation" camps, and the ordering of urban residents to New Economic Zones in rural Vietnam by the communist government of Vietnam. These immigrants were more diverse than those in the first wave and included farmers, fishermen, and many ethnic Chinese, as well as professional and educated classes (Kelly, 1977; Sutter, 1990; Takaki, 1989).

513

Vietnam lies along the coast of mainland Southeast Asia, with China to the north and the Mekong Delta to the south. The *Truong Son* mountain chain runs the full length of the country, dividing it from Laos and Cambodia to the west. The north of Vietnam was a Chinese colony from 111 B.C. to 939 A.D. and was then independent except for brief periods during the next 900 years (Beresford, 1988; Grant, 1979; Montero, 1979; Rutledge, 1985). While repelling Chinese invaders from the north, the Vietnamese also expanded southward into the Champa kingdom. Saigon was taken in 1672, followed by Vietnamese control over the Mekong Delta as well. Vietnam was united in 1802 with three regions: Tonkin in the north, with the capital at Hanoi; Annam in the center, with the capital at Hue; and Cochinchina in the south, with Saigon as its capital (Grant, 1979).

Vietnam has been a rural society, and more than 80 percent of the people still lived in the countryside in 1960 (Beresford, 1988; Burling, 1965; Wiegersma, 1988). The rural Vietnamese family was patriarchal and practiced ancestor worship. Land was held by both individual families and communally by entire villages, and villages also controlled the water supply for cultivation. The lowland people in Vietnam were sedentary farmers, while the highland people engaged in slash and burn agriculture, moving periodically to new locations because of soil exhaustion. The hierarchy of the larger society was the imperial court at the top, village notables and family patriarchs in the middle, and the peasants at the bottom. This hierarchy reflected the Confucian legacy in the country.

Land ownership and control over water for farming was a circular process in Vietnamese history, according to Wiegersma (1988). With the ascendancy of a strong central government, land was redistributed to poor peasants from the holdings of supporters of a previous dynasty. When that newer dynasty went into decline, the upkeep of the water-control system slackened and communal land fell again into the hands of fewer families. Peasant resentment grew, and emerging elites, with the support of the peasantry, overturned the existing dynasty, and the process began again.

Vietnam became a French colony in 1883, following the French navy's seizure of Saigon in 1861, control over the Mekong Delta by 1867, and finally French control over central and northern Vietnam (Beresford, 1988; Montero, 1979). Laos and Cambodia were also French colonies, and the entire region was known as French Indochina. The top posts in the French colonial administration went to French naval officers and the intermediate posts to the French civil service (Cady, 1964). The relation between Vietnam and France was one of a colony providing agricultural products to the industrial metropole. Traditional agriculture in Vietnam became commercialized in order to export rice, rubber, corn, and minerals to France (Beresford, 1988; Cady, 1964). By taxing Vietnamese peasants, the French built an infrastructure of roads and railroads to facilitate export agriculture.

French colonial policy caused a great change in the social structure of Vietnamese society. Most Vietnamese peasants became landless sharecroppers or farm labor under French administration, as the family and communal land holdings fell into the hands of the few and large estates and plantations replaced village agriculture. By 1939, 2 percent of the population owned 45 percent of the land. No industrial sector was built by the French, so landless peasants had no choice but to become sharecroppers or laborers for typically absentee landlords, both Vietnamese and French. Ethnic Chinese and Indians became merchants and money lenders to the Vietnamese peasants. Thus, the French were on top, economically as well as politically, the Vietnamese peasants were on the bottom, and the Chinese and Indians were middleman minorities.

During World War II, Vietnam was occupied by Japanese troops, but the administration of the country remained in the hands of the Vichy French government. After the war, the Democratic Republic of Vietnam, or North Vietnam, was formed in 1945 under the leadership of Ho Chi Minh. The French returned to Vietnam and attacked North Vietnam, thus beginning the French-Indochina War. The French were defeated in 1954 at the decisive battle of Dien Bien Phu, and the country was split at the seventeenth parallel into the Democratic Republic of Vietnam in the north and the Republic of Vietnam in the south.

The United States then entered into the political history of Vietnam. American military advisors were sent to South Vietnam in the early 1960s, and American troops in the Vietnam War numbered over a half million by late in the 1960s. The American policy in South Vietnam was to contain communism, represented by the National Liberation Front (NLF), also known as the Viet Minh or Viet Cong (Provencher, 1975). Ngo Dinh Diem was installed as the head of South Vietnam, and his government embarked on a policy of creating strategic hamlets in rural Vietnam in order to isolate the rural population from the Viet Minh. Eight million people were relocated to these hamlets by the time of Diem's assassination in 1963 (Beresford, 1988; Strand and Jones, 1985). The Diem regime also continued the agrarian policy of the French: absentee landlords of large estates and plantations worked by landless peasant sharecroppers and laborers. Officials of the Diem government even collected rents from sharecroppers in the rural areas for absentee landlords in the cities (Wiegersma, 1988).

515

The policy of the Viet Minh was land reform, and land confiscated by the NLF was returned to the peasants. The American military withdrew from Vietnam in 1975 with the fall of Saigon, and the Socialist Republic of Vietnam was formed in 1976, unifying North and South Vietnam.

In 1975, 130,000 Vietnamese refugees fled the country with the American evacuation. This was the first wave of Vietnamese immigrants into the United States. The second wave started in late 1978 after American evacuation (Beresford, 1988; Grant, 1979; Strand and Jones, 1985). Once Americans left Vietnam, the new government undertook domestic policies and engaged in international conflict that pushed people out of Vietnam and the rest of Indochina. The government began a campaign against black marketeering, and eventually all private business. It forced the migration of urban residents to the countryside in New Economic Zones and the collectivization of agriculture. Productivity fell and there were food shortages. Vietnam invaded Kampuchea (Cambodia) in 1978 and replaced the infamous Pol Pot with a new leader under Vietnamese control. In 1979, there was a brief war with China, and this led to an internal campaign against ethnic Chinese at home. Together with the damage left by the Vietnam War, these conditions forced people out of Vietnam. Members of this second wave of refugees are known as the *boat people* (Box 14.6). In the late 1970s, 4 million people left Indochina—Laos and Cambodia (Kampuchea) as well as Vietnam (Grant, 1979).

൭൭

BOX 14.6 THE VIETNAMESE BOAT PEOPLE

The boat was maybe ten meters long with an engine and thirty-seven people on board. We spent four days and nights on the sea and we were robbed three times by pirates. I think they were all Thai fishermen....

They destroyed our engine, too, so we had to sew some mats together to make a sail. The weather was very fine and there was no wind, but eventually we came near the coast of Thailand and there was enough wind for us to sail until we were washed up onto the shore.

We arrived in the south of Thailand very near the Malaysian border in a district named Saiburi in Pattani Province. We came to the beach at midnight and stayed there three or four hours waiting for daylight....

After two or three weeks there in Saiburi we were sent to Songkhla camp, still in the south of Thailand. We stayed there

about three months.... Then we were transferred to Sikiew camp
which is north and east of Bangkok....

I was accepted by the United States delegation on July 22,
1985, and on August 14 I was transferred to the Panat Nikhom
transit center near Bangkok. Then, on September 17, I was transferred to Manila and the next day I came here to the Philippine
Refugee Processing Center.

When I reach my destination in the United States I will try
my best to reunite my family.

Source: Joanna C. Scott, 1989. *Indochina's Refugees: Oral Histories from Laos,
Cambodia and Vietnam*. Jefferson, NC: McFarland & Company, Inc., Publishers, pp.
38–39. Reprinted by permission.

☺☺

Traveling by small boats, the Indochinese refugees set out for nearby countries that would become their first asylum, be the country Thailand, Malaysia, Singapore, Indonesia, or Hong Kong. About one-quarter of a million ethnic Chinese also emigrated to south China. Risks in
passage were great, and some estimates have the number dying in
transit as high as 50 percent (Grant, 1979). While at the refugee camps
in these countries of first asylum, the refugees would apply for entry
into a country of final destination. Between April 1975 and June 1981,
1,370,113 Indochinese refugees reached a country of final destination,
503,906 of them arriving in the United States (Strand and Jones, 1985).
The other countries of final destination included France, Britain,
Australia, the Scandinavian countries, Japan, and India.

The American government established reception centers in the
United States for Indochinese refugees at Camp Pendleton, California;
Fort Indiantown Gap, Pennsylvania; Elgin Air Force Base, Florida; and
Fort Chaffee, Arkansas. The average stay at these centers was seven
months (Strand and Jones, 1985). There were four ways in which
refugees could leave these centers. A refugee could go to another
country for resettlement, repatriate to Vietnam, prove financial self-
support and be released in the United States, or have an American
sponsor (Montero, 1979). The sponsors were expected to provide "...
food, clothing, and shelter; assistance in finding employment; help
with school enrollment; and coverage of ordinary medical costs until
the refugee becomes self-sufficient" (Stand and Jones, 1985:40). Almost
all refugees left by means of an American sponsor. Agencies that
helped with resettlement in the United States included the United
States Catholic Conference, American Fund for Czechoslovak
Refugees, and Church World Services. The process is described below:

Cambodian immigrants, like this family, shared with the
Vietnamese a difficult adaptation period in America.

First, the U.S. embassy and INS [Immigration and Naturalization Service] review the cases of refugees who are residing in first asylum camps. If these refugees are approved for resettlement in the United States, their files are sent to the American Council of Voluntary Agencies (ACVA), in New York, which serves as a clearinghouse for voluntary agencies, Refugees without sponsors are divided among ACVA members according to their capacity to provide needed services. When the ACVA has secured voluntary agency sponsorships, it sends its assurances to representatives in Southeast Asia. The voluntary agencies and the Intergovernmental Committee for Migration ... are responsible for the processing of refugees out of the first asylum countries. The voluntary agencies handle legal documentation and airport reception. When a refugee arrives at the final destination, the local voluntary agency office counsels the refugee regarding health, employment, social, and vocational services.... Sponsors provide the initial resettlement needs for food, clothing, and housing... (Strand and Jones, 1985:40).

ACCOMMODATION, COMPETITION, AND CONFLICT

Vietnamese refugees faced problems in adjusting to life in the United States. Most experienced language and other cultural barriers, found initially only low-level jobs, and were often psychologically depressed because of these problems and family separation (Rumbaut, 1989). Difficulty in finding employment was due to deficiency in the English language and the lack of an automobile to commute from home to work (Strand and Jones, 1985). Many experienced downward mobility upon entering the American labor market. This was especially the case for those who had professional and managerial jobs in Vietnam, less so for clerical and sales workers, and least for blue-collar workers. Vietnamese professionals had relatively long waits before obtaining U.S. licenses, and former managers in Vietnam often did not have the requisite interpersonal and language skills to land comparable jobs in this country (Montero, 1975). Among the Vietnamese in San Diego, their most pressing problems, in rank order, were the English language, family separation, war memories and being away from home, not having enough money, and little help in getting a job (Strand and Jones, 1985).

Social and economic conditions tended to improve for the immigrants with their length of residence in the United States (Montero, 1979; Strand and Jones, 1985). Over time, most found employment, and they worked more hours per week and had higher incomes. The 1990 occupational composition of Vietnamese Americans is shown in Table 14.3. Vietnamese were underrepresented in managerial and professional work but overrepresented as operators and laborers in blue-collar work. In a 1984 sample of employed Vietnamese refugees, al-

TABLE 14.3   PERCENTAGE DISTRIBUTION OF VIETNAMESE AMERICANS AND ALL
EMPLOYED PEOPLE BY OCCUPATIONAL GROUPS, 1990

Occupational Group	Vietnamese Origin 1990	All People 1990
Managerial and professional	15.9%	25.5%
Technical, sales, and administrative support	29.7	31.5
Service occupations	16.3	13.5
Precision production, craft, and repair	14.9	11.5
Operators, fabricators, and laborers	21.8	15.5
Farming, forestry, and fishing	1.9	2.5

Source: Census of Population and Housing, 1990: Public Micromedia Samples U.S., prepared by the
Bureau of the Census, 1992.

most one-half had jobs in manufacturing plants (Rumbaut, 1989). The Vietnamese are comparable to all Americans in the other occupational categories shown in Table 14.3.

Since leaving the reception centers, the Vietnamese have concentrated in urban areas, especially in California, Texas, Louisiana, and Washington, D.C. Thus, many Vietnamese migrated three times, first from Vietnam to countries of first asylum, then to reception centers in the United States, and finally to American cities. In some locales, there have been competition and open conflict between Vietnamese and other Americans. For example:

> ...a 1979 conflict between Vietnamese Americans and local fish catchers in Seadrift, Texas, culminated in the shooting death of a white fish catcher. Two Vietnamese refugees were arrested for the shooting, which followed an argument over the placement of crab traps. Within hours of the death, three Vietnamese boats were burned, one house was fire-bombed, and an attempt was made to bomb a packing plant where many Vietnamese Americans worked, causing most of the refugees to flee to another town. The Vietnamese American crabbers were eventually acquitted of the shooting. In response to this verdict, some white fish catchers turned to the local Ku Klux Klan for protection of their industrial interest (Feagin, 1989:347).

In other locales, Vietnamese have begun their own businesses with considerable success. In southern California (Los Angeles and Orange counties), Vietnamese businesses and professional offices are thriving. "Vietnamese professionals are in abundance as doctors and dentists, and ethnic-Chinese Vietnamese are almost ubiquitous in restaurants and grocery stores. Their businesses are not just mom-and-pop stores. In fact, many of the retailers had been big merchants in Vietnam . . . [and] here they own supermarket chains like Wai Wai Supermarkets and Man Wah Supermarkets" (Takaki, 1989:459). In northern California, the Vietnamese own nearly half of the retail businesses in downtown San Jose. Outside Washington, D.C., in Falls Church, Virginia, there are more than sixty Vietnamese businesses in the Eden Center, a shopping center named after one in Saigon.

Nevertheless, the adaptation process for Vietnamese, as well as other Indochinese refugees, has been difficult. Psychological depression has been common among the refugees, greatest for those who had lost family members in Vietnam and those who are now separated from family members still in Vietnam. "Depression scores were also significantly higher for the least acculturated, those most desirous of returning to the homeland, the least English proficient, the unemployed, those below the poverty line and dependent on welfare assistance... " (Rumbaut, 1989:166).

The adaptation process takes at least three years. The first year is a relatively euphoric one for refugees, but their depression scores go up and measures of well-being go down in the second year (Rumbaut, 1989). The refugees rebound and stabilize during the third year. Over these years, depression is first affected by the gap between the refugees' earlier lives in Vietnam and current experiences in the United States, e.g., rural background, family separation, and lack of American acculturation while still in Vietnam. Later, depression and well-being are more affected by current experiences in this country, being employed or not, for example. Women play important roles in the adjustment of refugee families. They can provide enough income to lift the family above the poverty line, and their financial and psychological resources are critical for the adjustment of their children to American schools.

Barriers to the inclusion of the first-generation Vietnamese are the match between their cultural skills and the requirements for the better jobs in the labor market. Obviously, English language skills are paramount in this regard. Indicators of enculturation for the Vietnamese, such as outmarriage rates, are well below those for more established Asian groups in the country, but they should approach the higher rates of others over time.

SUMMARY

Koreans, Filipinos, and Vietnamese come from countries that were traditional agricultural societies that became colonial possessions by early in the twentieth century. Their homelands became economic colonies as well, supplying agricultural exports to an industrial colonial power and importing manufactured goods from that power. The economies remained underdeveloped during the colonial period, symbolized by the lack of an industrial sector. Along with wars, other political upheavals, and natural disasters, changes in agriculture back home pushed these people off the land and into international migration. This emigration brought them to the United States in the twentieth century.

Two distinct waves of Korean and Filipino immigration are evident, one earlier in the century and one in recent decades. The first wave gravitated toward jobs in agriculture and urban services, and the second wave found white-collar jobs in post-industrial America. Both waves met the nation's labor needs, whatever they were at the time of immigration. Family reunification is now playing a more significant role in Korean and Filipino immigration. Virtually all Vietnamese immigrants have come to the United States since the end of the Vietnam War, and the waves of Vietnamese immigration, although evident, are less distinct. The populations of all three groups in America have increased significantly in recent years because of immigration.

The common pattern was for these immigrants to find jobs in the United States either similar to or below their former occupations in Korea, the Philippines, and Vietnam. This was their accommodation, but it was punctuated by competition and even open conflict with other Americans. The results varied by group and included acts of violence and exclusion for a time from the country. One response was to build an ethnic subeconomy, as had the Chinese and Japanese, and this was particularly true for Koreans. In all three cases, however, there is evidence for their greater inclusion into American society over time. If not assimilation, this will mean a changing pattern of pluralism between these Asian groups and the larger American society.

@

CONCLUSIONS

C H A P T E R
15
๑/๑

MINORITY COMMUNITY: PATHOLOGY OR COMMUNALISM?

I n the social sciences there are two very different depictions of American minority groups: social pathology and ethnic communalism. According to the first, members of minority groups become psychologically damaged, and the group itself becomes disorganized in the course of its exclusion from the larger society. Psychological damage and community deterioration can be mutually reinforcing, and thus minority-group members may be trapped in a vicious circle and downward spiral. This is what is meant by the metaphor of minority groups' being caught in a tangle of pathology.

The second depiction is that minority groups evolve as communal groups when excluded from the larger society. There is no necessary psychological damage to minority-group members, nor is the social disorganization of the group itself inevitable. Members of the minority group can pull together, build their own community, and become strong in the face of externally imposed hardships. They can find their sense of self-worth in their own community, from their own kind, quite apart from the surrounding prejudice and discrimination. In short, prejudice and discrimination lead to neither the collapse of the minority group as a community nor the demoralization of its members. This depiction accentuates the communalism, consciousness, and solidarity of the minority group.

Changing ethnic groups in the course of societal change have been the principal topic of this book. Some ethnic groups have been included into American society, and they have converged with the course of the national history. Other groups have been excluded from American society, and they have diverged. There are different versions of what happens to groups that are included into the larger society. One disagreement is over whether they lose their ethnic community. Social scientists disagree at least as much about minority groups, those excluded from society. The debate is over the exact nature of the social and psychological consequences of exclusion. One version is that minority groups become entangled in pathology, and another has it that they evolve as communal groups. This debate is the topic of the chapter.

It must be remembered that theories on American ethnicity are, as a rule, only partial explanations of ethnic history, and social pathology and ethnic communalism as perspectives are no exception. While it is true that prejudice and discrimination can result in psychological damage of minority-group members and the social disorganization of the group itself, it is equally true that minority groups can endure as communal groups whose members draw together and, by dint of collective effort, overcome the barriers of prejudice and discrimination. Both types of adjustment to exclusion have occurred in American history, and pathology and communalism as perspectives show these two sides of the same coin.

The chapter begins with key terms; then the basic assumptions of both pathology and communalism are identified. Samples of the pathology and communalism perspectives are then surveyed. The chapter ends with an analysis of the communalism that often follows from ethnic group subeconomies and political mobilization.

DEFINITIONS AND ASSUMPTIONS

KEY TERMS

ETHNIC EXCLUSION AND DIVERGENCE: In Chapter 5 ethnic exclusion was defined as being evident *when an ethnic group does not share with others a common culture, similar socioeconomic characteristics, and societal resources because of its exclusive participation in the secondary institutions of the larger society, and by virtue of its ethnically restrictive social participation.* Exclusion is typically a product of ethnic competition and conflict, a direct result of discrimination, and excluded groups have been traditionally called *minority groups*. Minority groups follow a course of divergence, *evident when the history of an ethnic or racial group does not flow into the historical trend of the larger society*. This means that an ethnic group lags behind a societal change such as the shift from an industrial to a post-industrial society. Two forms of divergence have been identified in the social sciences: social pathology and ethnic communalism.

PATHOLOGY: Pathology can be evident in the psychological states and life-styles of minority-group members and in the social condition of the minority community. *Pathology includes personality disorganization, self-debilitating behavior, and community deterioration. These conditions make a minority group appear to be so deviant or divergent from others that it impedes its inclusion into society and can make prejudice against the minority group appear to be justified.* The various manifestations of pathology might be considered instances of self-alienation, where self-alienation is a process "in which individual selves may lose contact with any inclinations or desires that are not in agreement with prevailing social patterns, manipulate their selves in accordance with apparent social demands, and/or feel incapable of controlling their own actions" (Taviss, 1969:47). This self-alienation results in self-debilitating behavior and ultimately leads to the deterioration of the minority community.

ETHNIC COMMUNALISM AND CONSCIOUSNESS: *A minority is a communal group when its members have a consciousness of kind and a sense of their societal position.* A communal group provides its members with their own set of standards, a subculture, and a context in which their exclusion from the larger society is understood. There is no necessary psychological damage, self-debilitating behavior, or community deterioration. Rather, communalism brings about the social alienation of minority group members, not their self-alienation, a process "in which individual selves may find the social system in which they live to be oppressive or incompatible with some of their own desires and feel estranged from it" (Taviss, 1969:46).

Consciousness of kind refers to the self-consciousness of group members, to their realization that they belong to the same group and have a loyalty to each other. Thus they draw a distinction between themselves and others. While consciousness of kind is most certainly rooted in members' sense of historical continuity of the group, it is made continuously current by the persistent struggle with others for wealth, power, and status or, from our own conflict perspective, by the competition over land, labor, and capital. To the extent that minority groups are party to this struggle, they should manifest a consciousness of kind.

Ethnic consciousness also includes a sense among minority group members of their position in society or their rank in the system of ethnic stratification. Consciousness of kind is self-reflexive, and the object of contemplation is one's own group. *Consciousness of societal position is the awareness of the relation of one's group to other groups in the larger soci-*

ety, particularly within the context of ethnic stratification. A sense of societal position by minority-group members combines their social comparison to the majority group with a sense of injustice about their deprivation within the system of ethnic stratification. Consciousness of kind and societal position refer to a shared definition of their situation by minority-group members, and both lie behind their collective action with respect to that situation. Once undertaken, communal action tends to intensify consciousness of kind and societal position.

Minority groups can and do preserve their communalism in the face of their exclusion from the larger society. Ethnic communalism represents the preservation of the group, whether the group is converging into or diverging away from society. It is the continuance of certain traditions by group members, their sense of historical continuity, and, in a phrase, their consciousness of kind. It is also their awareness of the ethnic hierarchy and their relation in it—that is, their sense of societal position. These ideas and feelings are structured and given organizational expression through newspapers, fraternal societies, churches, and the informal relationships among members of the group. The communalism and consciousness of minority-group members are also reinforced by the very fact of their exclusion from the larger society, as prejudice and discrimination remind them almost daily that they are different from others and share the same fate. Exclusion can mean the preservation of the group, and it is in the ethnic community that prejudice and discrimination are comprehended and coped with.

BASIC ASSUMPTIONS ABOUT THE MINORITY COMMUNITY

1. Some of the nation's ethnic groups have been included and have converged with the changing American society. These groups are now considered the nation's majority group. Other ethnic groups have been excluded and have diverged from societal change, and these groups are now known as the nation's minority groups.

2. Minority groups can be caught in a tangle of pathology in the course of their exclusion and divergence. Minority groups also can retain their community, even under the pressures of prejudice and discrimination, and evolve as communal groups in their struggle with others for wealth, power, and prestige.

3. Both pathology and communalism are evident to some degree in all minority groups. The ability of a minority group to accumulate capital, develop a subeconomy, or accomplish the political mobilization of its membership, among other factors, is critical in determining which course of divergence it will take.

PATHOLOGY

Pathology can be found in the psychological states of minority-group members, their debilitating life-styles, and the deterioration of their community. It has been said that minority-group members deviate from certain psychological states considered normal and healthy in American society, experiencing a crisis of identity and exhibiting low self-esteem, for example. Minority-group members may feel a sense of low self-worth, and some may even become self-prejudiced by internalizing the racial ethnocentrism of the majority group. Such pathological consequences of prejudice and discrimination were called the "mark of oppression" by Kardiner and Ovesey (1951). Pathological psychological states can lead to self-debilitating behavior, exemplified by crime and the abuse of drugs and alcohol.

Comparing the black ghetto on Chicago's South Side today with what it was in the 1940s, Lemann (1986:31) painted a picture of minority community deterioration as well:

> There's hardly ever any bustle at Forty-seventh and King Drive (as South Parkway is now called), especially during the day. The shopping strip still exists, though as a shadow of what it obviously once was, and there are heavy metal grates on virtually every storefront that has not been abandoned. Many of the landmarks of the neighborhood...are boarded up or gone entirely.... Prostitutes cruise Forty-seventh Street in the late afternoon. In cold weather middle-aged men stand in knots around fires built in garbage cans....

Thus, not only can the personalities of minority-group members be damaged because of prejudice and discrimination, but also the community itself can deteriorate under the same pressures. The minority community can become abnormal and impede assimilation. One example is: "The gangs are the real authorities, the most powerful force, in the worst parts of the Chicago ghetto.... Gang recruitment...forces kids, through physical terror, to give up school and work, and become professional criminals" (Lehmann, 1986:39).

Studies of and commentaries about the minority family provide a good example of this point of view. A high incidence of female-headed households among the Irish in the nineteenth century, along with their troubled marriages and frequent desertions, were seen as signs of social pathology (Diner, 1983). Generational conflict between immigrant Polish parents and their children was also construed as pathological early in the twentieth century.

> But the most complete break between parents and children—one presenting itself every day in our juvenile courts—comes with the emigration of the family as a whole to America.... there frequently re-

sults a complete and painful antagonism between children and parents…. The mutual hate, the hardness, unreasonableness, and brutality of the parents, the contempt and ridicule of the child—ridicule of the speech and old-country habits and views of the parents—become almost incredible. The parents…resort to the juvenile court not as a means of reform but as an instrument of vengeance; they will swear away the character of their girl, call her a "whore" and a "thief," when there is not the slightest ground for it (Thomas and Znaniecki, 1984:78–79).

Later in the twentieth century, a score of writers analyzed the low-income African American family in pathological terms (e.g., Frazier, 1939; Liebow, 1967; Moynihan, 1965; Rainwater, 1966; Shulz, 1969). The pathological characteristics of the African American family are said to include marital instability, matriarchy, the absence of fathers (and thus the lack of masculine identification for boys), and early sexual experiences for children. Such characteristics, it is further argued, hinder the inclusion of low-income African Americans into the larger American society.

In essence, the Negro community has been forced into a matriarchal structure which, because it is so out of line with the rest of the American society, seriously retards the progress of the group as a whole, and imposes a crushing burden on the Negro male and, in consequence, on a great many Negro women as well (Moynihan, 1972:197).

The fact is overlooked that some of these same practices in groups who have assimilated are seen as experiments in family living.

Commentary on pathology is not confined to a single class or ethnic group. Nearly all minorities in American history have been considered pathological at one time or another. Earlier in the century it was a common belief, even in official circles, that the new European immigrants—Italians, Jews, and Slavs, among others—had innumerable pathologies. Harry Laughlin wrote that these new European immigrants had high incidences of feeblemindedness, insanity, crime, epilepsy, tuberculosis, and dependency on welfare (cited in Handlin, 1957). Laughlin concluded that these tendencies were hereditary rather than the effects of prejudice and discrimination, using committals to public institutions as his measure of hereditary traits. Handlin (1957) remarked that groups, old and new immigrants alike, varied so much across these indicators of pathology that there was no consistent pattern of overall pathology, a point that Laughlin, in the heat of the politics of immigration restriction, apparently chose to ignore. A work like Laughlin's seemed to use science as a vindication for racism against the new immigrants, a racism that ultimately resulted in the restriction of immigrants from southern and eastern Europe into our country. Nevertheless, social pathology continued to be a popular perspective on the American minority community.

One can read today about the current pathology not only of African Americans, but also other groups. With respect to Mexican Americans, McWilliams (1968:206–207) observed:

> The data "proved" that Mexicans lacked leadership, discipline, and organization; that they segregated themselves; that they were lacking in thrift and enterprise and so forth. A mountainous collection of masters' theses "proved" conclusively that Spanish-speaking children were "retarded" because, on the basis of various so-called intelligence tests, they did not measure up to the intellectual calibre of Anglo-American students.... Paradoxically, the more sympathetic the writer, the greater seems to have been the implied condescension. All in all, the conclusion is unavoidable that Mexicans have been regarded as the essence of "the Mexican Problem."

Research today continues to paint a picture of pathology in the black ghetto (e.g., Anderson, 1990; Wilson, 1987). Drugs have moved in as the African American middle class has moved out. Now, with the crack houses and drug dealing on the streets, the role models are the criminals, and drug hustlers in particular. The model is for men to evade family responsibility toward women and children, resulting in ever more women raising children without the help of men, as well as a life in crime and violence. Indeed, violence seems to hang in the air, and the middle class go so far as to cross a street when they see ahead on the sidewalk a group of young, black males.

The ultimate cause of pathology is thought to be prejudice and discrimination, and the process of becoming pathological commences in childhood. Minority-group children learn that their own group is devalued by others and deviates significantly from others in the larger society, and they frequently become self-prejudiced or self-alienated at a very early age. Thus begins a cycle of human development that is impaired from the very start.

THE EVIDENCE

Clark and Clark (1947) found in 1939 that black children (3–7 years old) preferred white dolls and rejected black dolls when asked to choose which dolls they would like to play with, which were nice, which were bad, and which were the nice color. These observations also have been made in subsequent studies utilizing a variety of testing methods and in various geographical and social settings (Asher and Allen, 1969; Brown, 1986; Frenkel-Brunswik, 1948; Goodman, 1952; Greenwald and Oppenheim, 1968; Landreth and Johnson, 1953;

Morland, 1958, 1966; Radke, Trager, and Davis, 1949; Trager and Yarrow, 1952). When white children have been used as a control group, they generally have made responses favorable to the dolls of their own race. The results of the Clark and Clark study are shown in Table 15.1 (see p. 542).

This long tradition of research showing a preference among African American children for white dolls implies a history of self-prejudice on the part of black children in this country. At least this has been a common interpretation of these findings. Morland (1969:360) offered this generalization on the basis of these findings: "In a multi-racial society in which there is a dominant and subordinate race, young children of the subordinate race tend to prefer and identify with members of the dominant race, while children of the dominant race tend to prefer and identify with members of their own race."

From a bad start, matters get worse for minority-group children, according to social pathologists. These children soon enter school, where many do not do well. Reasons for this "failure" are many, obviously, but the inadequacies of the home in preparing and supporting children in serious school work are the ones emphasized by social pathologists. Instead of academic success and preparation for careers in the professions and technical fields, there is a pattern of early pregnancy for girls, and for boys there is life on the streets.

By the time they are adults, many members of minority groups are unprepared for entry into all but the most menial work. They lack the necessary credentials for better jobs, and this, combined with the prejudice and discrimination they face, means more exclusion and divergence for the group as a whole. The lack of educational preparation or vocational training of adolescents eventually translates into their economic and social marginality as adults—lives that are spent either at the bottom of a split and segmented labor market, in unskilled and occasional work, or on welfare. In this way, generation after generation, the cycle of poverty and pathology continues.

Liebow (1967) wrote about low-income African American men, street-corner men, they were called, who hung out at a carry-out restaurant somewhere in Washington, D.C. These men despised their own fathers for not having lived up to the mainstream model of an adult male. Their dilemma was that they themselves were fast becoming what their fathers had been, men with marginal jobs, drifters, men on street corners. The mainstream model of manhood was the ideal for these street-corner men, Liebow said, as it was for those around them, especially their women. Men and women alike sought the mainstream ideals—for men to be good providers, husbands, and fathers—but this was impossible.

The reasons for the "failures" of the street-corner men Liebow studied go back to their childhood. These men had not prepared themselves for vocations that put a premium on cultural and technical skills—in a word, on schooling. They came into adulthood with skills qualifying them for only marginal jobs, in food service and unskilled construction work, for instance. The extremely low pay or the seasonal nature of the work meant no more than a marginal economic existence for these men and their families. Money for them was always in short supply. The result was that these men found it increasingly impossible to live by the mainstream model of the adult male, and thus they eventually turned away from their families and toward the street corner.

At home, the wives of these men appeared always ready to point to the gap between the mainstream ideals and what the men really were, undoubtedly reminding each man of the conflict between his mother and father in the previous generation. These men saw in themselves their own fathers, something they had wished to avoid. Children also jogged unpleasant memories, reminding them that the cycle of poverty had been perpetuated through their own generation and would probably continue into the next. These men were not prepared for anything but a low-level entry into the occupational structure of our post-industrial society, and the result was the formation of certain personal pathologies and the disruption of family life.

The roots of the pathology of the African American family go back to slavery, according to E. Franklin Frazier (1939). African family forms were lost by the masses of black people under slavery. Stable family life was disrupted during slavery by the selling of family members separately, particularly the fathers, and by forced mating of slaves at the whim of the master. In other words, African Americans lost the principal elements of their ethnic community under slavery. This theory is not supported, however, by historical evidence (Chapter 10).

According to Frazier, in the tradition of the social pathologists, the disintegration of the African American family, and thus of the African American community, continued with the twentieth-century migration of African Americans into the industrial cities of America. While sturdy African American women found work readily as domestics and service workers in the cities, many African American men took up a migratory career of living off these women, moving from woman to woman until their luck ran out or age caught up with them. This made for promiscuity, desertion, female-headed households, and the delinquency of children.

Has the current welfare system encouraged female-headed households among poor African Americans, one specific instance of the supposed pathology on the part of minorities? It has, according to the conservative writer Charles Murray (1984). Murray contended that welfare benefits discourage the poor from working and encourage female-headed households on welfare. Specifically, Aid for Dependent Children (AFDC) enables poor women to stay at home and continue on welfare, and the more children they have, the more welfare benefits they get. His solution was to scrap the entire federal welfare system.

Murray's critics argued that poverty persists because of the national economy, not welfare. Unemployment increased and real wages fell in the 1970s, and the same was true in the 1980s. "The fact that poverty was no higher in 1980 than in 1968, despite the doubling of the unemployment rate, actually provides strong evidence that these [welfare] programs were helping people who would have been otherwise impoverished by the sluggish economy" (Greentein, 1985:15). Greentein also noted that welfare benefits have sharply declined since the 1970s, hardly making them a disincentive to work. Moreover, research has found no connection between welfare and out-of-wedlock births, and the recent rise in the numbers of African American children in female-headed households is not due to the number of children on AFDC.

Observers have found pathology in the Irish, the eastern and southern Europeans, and Asians, and today they find it in American Indians, Hispanics, and African Americans. There must be hundreds of academic articles and research reports on Indian alcoholism, for example. The pathology of Native American drinking patterns is not that Indians drink so much more than anyone else; it lies in the manner in which they consume alcohol, drinking to extreme intoxication, together, and in public. The result is that police are often summoned, and arrests and incarceration follow. The reasons given for Indian alcoholism center around their material circumstances and the loss of their communal traditions (Dozier, 1966). Alcohol provides a temporary release from poverty and deprivation and can sometimes capture, if only temporarily, the old communal solidarity lost in conquest. Levy and Kunitz (1974:174) saw the Navajo use of alcohol in a different light: "The level of acculturation stands in an inverse relationship to the level of involvement with alcohol. This and the nature of the difference between Navajo and white patterns of drinking raise questions concerning the definition of alcoholism as a pathology and the notion that problem drinking is the result of strains attendant upon the acculturative process."

Pathology as a perspective is one portrait of exclusion and divergence, reminiscent of a passage describing African societies from the perspective of white colonists (Fanon, 1963:41):

Native society is not simply described as a society lacking in values. It is not enough for the colonist to affirm that those values have disappeared from, or still better never existed in, the colonial world. The native is declared insensible to ethics; he represents not only the absence of values, but also the negation of values.

REASONS FOR PATHOLOGY

There are, in the social sciences, two different explanations for social pathology. One explanation is that minority groups live by a culture of poverty, one that is passed down from generation to generation, and it is this culture of poverty that prevents each generation from evolving toward its inclusion in the larger society. A second explanation is that pathology is a direct and immediate consequence of exclusion, or prejudice and discrimination. This is the blocked-opportunity theory.

THE CULTURE OF POVERTY: *"A culture of poverty is thus a design for living within the constraints of poverty, passed down from generation to generation, thereby achieving stability and persistence"* (Lewis, 1961:xxiv). The culture of poverty can become the culture of groups excluded from society, minority groups. Pathological conditions, personal and social, can become ingrained in this culture and thus be passed from one generation to the next. It is this culture of poverty, separate from prejudice and discrimination, that prohibits the inclusion of the minority group.

Lemann (1986:35 and 47) put African American ghetto life and outlook in Chicago into a culture of poverty context:

> The black underclass did not just spring into being over the past twenty years. Every aspect of the underclass culture in the ghettos is traceable to roots in the South—and not the South of slavery but the South of a generation ago.... The similarities between sharecropping and welfare are eerie: dependency on "the man"; more money for having more children; little value placed on education; no home ownership; an informal attitude toward marriage and childbearing.

In this view, the underclass culture began in the South with sharecropping and has been transmitted across the generations. With the migration of black families from the South that culture is observable now among welfare families in northern ghettos. The underclass culture includes, in the abstract, peculiarities in psychological make-up, debilitating life-styles, and certain abnormalities in social organization, illustrated by childbearing outside of marriage and welfare dependency. Because this culture is considered to be out of line with the norms of the larger society, the assimilation of this or any other minority group that shows signs of it can be seriously impeded. Remember that these same traits in the majority group would not often be considered pathological.

However, Ball (1968) applied this analysis even to white Americans, specifically the folk subculture of the Southern Appalachians. There are two fundamentally different designs for living, one that is motivation instigated and another that is frustration instigated. We see motivation-instigated action when people take steps in a rational manner to attain their goals, and this is presumably characteristic of most Americans. But the poor of Southern Appalachia are characterized by a different mode of behavior, one that is frustration instigated. Frustration-instigated behavior is neither rational nor goal oriented in any ordinary sense: "there is no apparent goal in frustration-instigated behavior, such behavior appears senseless.... Behavior resulting from extreme frustration may represent a terminal response to the frustration itself rather than a means to any end" (Ball 1968:887). Frustration originates in the hardships of life among the poor in this region, and its release has been institutionalized into the region's folk culture. Ball termed this folk subculture the *analgesic subculture* of the Southern Appalachians and likened it to a downward spiral, a descending cycle of frustration and its irrational release without any attempt to remove the sources of frustration.

The principal components of this analgesic subculture include fixation, regression, aggression, and resignation, all of which have been observed by experimental psychologists to be among the responses of animals to extreme frustration. These responses have been codified in the folk culture of Southern Appalachia, so that "the young learn to anticipate defeat and to perform subcultural rituals which reduce its impact" (Ball, 1968:890). Ball found fixation in "the obstinate tradition of the Southern Appalachian folk subculture" and institutionalized regression in "the lack of aesthetic appreciation, anti-intellectualism, the preference of anecdote over abstraction, the insistence upon a literal interpretation of the Bible, the entanglement of religious fundamentalism with deep superstition, the improvident squandering which often accompanies 'pay day' or a welfare check." Moreover, "resignation, apathy, and fatalism are rarely so prominent as among the members of the mountain folk subculture" (Ball, 1968:892).

Like the culture of poverty the world over, the analgesic subculture of the Southern Appalachians is seen as a design for living with the frustrations of poverty. It is passed down from generation to generation, which incapacitates these mountain folk even more from moving toward their inclusion into the larger American society. Like so many other instances of the culture of poverty in this country, it provides only for the irrational release of frustrations, without doing anything about ameliorating the conditions that cause those frustrations in the first place.

BLOCKED-OPPORTUNITY THEORY: Those who subscribe to the blocked-opportunity theory take exception to the notion that a culture of poverty was formed long ago and has been transmitted over the generations to the young, so that "the young learn to anticipate defeat." For instance, Liebow (1967) maintained that black street-corner men shared with other Americans the national culture, both its goals and prescribed means, but could not live by those standards due to their lack of opportunity. This resulted in their behavioral deviation from the larger cultural standards, as seen in the desertion of their wives and children. In search of some aid and comfort after such failures, these men found one another on street corners and there spun myths about their manly flaws.

The magic of the street corner was that vices were turned into virtues, and a man's failures became signs of a more basic and truer masculinity; failures become manly flaws. To explain the desertion of his wife and nonsupport of his children, the man on the street corner, with the consent and approval of the others, turned to the theory of manly flaws, that men have too much dog in them: "Men are just dogs! We shouldn't call ourselves human, we're just dogs, dogs, dogs! They call me a dog, 'cause that's what I am, but so is everybody else—hopping around from woman to woman, just like a dog" (Liebow, 1967:120–121). Street-corner mythmaking is dialectical; out of failure arises its opposite, success; a man fails at manhood by being too much of a man.

It was Liebow's conclusion that such street-corner mythmaking was an ex post facto rationalization of a painful reality, the fact that these men could not live by common standards expected of adult males in the larger American society at the time. There was no intergenerational transmission of these myths; for each generation they were ex post facto rationalizations for failure to live by the cultural standards of the larger society.

Minority group members share in the cultural values of the larger society, especially in an era of mass education and communication, and their behavioral deviations from those values cannot in any way be attributed to some culture of poverty. This latter view appears to square with Gordon's (1964) contention that ethnic groups in American society have usually been enculturated into the national ethos long before they have attained full structural assimilation into American society.

Merton (1957) observed that American culture contains prescriptions for the legitimate goals of life and the means of attaining those goals. One should not only strive for success but do it in a respectable way by becoming a doctor or lawyer, for instance, not a pimp. Using only legitimate means in the pursuit of success is not always possible for members of minority groups, however; because of prejudice and discrimination they often must take deviant paths to success. Political machines, crime, prostitution, street-corner life, and drug hustling are among the many illustrations of this phenomenon in American history. The point is that these deviations are not necessarily evidence for a culture of poverty; they may represent alternative ways to realize goals that the poor share with the rich.

Other versions of blocked-opportunity theory are evident in Hannerz (1969), Rodman (1969), and Moore (1978). Hannerz (1969:182) located psychological states, behavioral styles, and patterns of social organization of minority poor in the hardships of poverty, not in a culture of poverty. The culture of poverty, if it does exist, is the result of poverty, not its cause. In other words, characteristics of minority poor are due to the lack of opportunity, which results in poverty. This is a conclusion reached in several critiques of the culture of poverty as an explanation of poverty (e.g., Roach and Gursslin, 1967; Valentine, 1968). This view is consistent with our own, which is that social pathology is one form of divergence and a consequence of exclusion, not a product of the motivational peculiarities of the poor.

The behavioral deviations from the standards of the larger culture among minority poor represent what Hyman Rodman (1968:301) called the lower-class value stretch:

> By the value stretch I mean that the lower-class person, without abandoning the general values of the society, develops an alternative set of values. Without abandoning the values placed on success, such as high income and high educational and occupational attainment, he stretches the values so that lesser degrees of success also become desirable. Without abandoning the values of marriage and legitimate childbirth he stretches these values so that a nonlegal union and legally illegitimate children are also desirable. The result is that the members of the lower class, in many areas, have a wider range of values than others within the society. They share the general values of the society with members of other classes, but in addition they have stretched these values, or developed alternative values, which help them to adjust to their deprived circumstances.

Because of blocked opportunity, minority poor engage in a value stretch, according to Rodman.

The value stretch can be illustrated in the economic strategies of low-income Mexican Americans in Los Angeles (Moore, 1978). Many of these people are barred from the primary labor market of Los Angeles, one that requires educational credentials for jobs with good pay, security, and a career ladder. Instead, they are confined to the secondary labor market, welfare, or the illegal, underground economy of the barrio. Because the secondary labor market provides only unstable, part-time, low-paying jobs with no chance of advancement, some residents turn to the alternatives of crime or welfare. Uzzell (1980) called such tactics mixed economic strategies, which include moonlighting, mixing welfare with low wages, home production, and crime. Good strategies are having jobs that bring in income without taking all of one's time, cutting deals on the side, and getting an entire family into money-making. The values embedded in the American dream are stretched to include strategies, legal and illegal, that at least allow for survival.

According to social pathology, the relative impoverishment of the minority community and its low standing in the nation's ethnic hierarchy somehow impacts the self-worth of minority-group members, and they engage in self-debilitating behavior that merely adds to the downward spiral of the minority community. The psychological process that connects the condition of the minority community to the self-worth of its members is a combination of Festinger's (1954) social comparison theory and the social identity theory of Tajfel (1982) and Tajfel and Turner (1979). Apparently, minority-group members first compare their own group to the majority group, realizing that their group is below the majority group in what counts in American society. This is social comparison, and it can result in a negative social identity and, ultimately, low self-esteem. Minority-group members can accept the invidious comparison, resulting in social and psychological pathology. According to Tajfel, and Tajfel and Turner, however, minority-group members can do other things as well. If possible, members can exit from the devalued group, enhancing their self-worth in the process. They also can undertake joint action to raise the social identity of the minority group, either within the minority community itself or on the outside among other groups, and thus scale up their own sense of self-worth. This last alternative comes close to ethnic communalism and consciousness.

SOME NEGATIVE EVIDENCE

Although the preceding evidence seems to support social pathology, a number of studies have cast doubt on relying exclusively on the pathological perspective as a depiction of American minority groups. To conclude that patterns of behavior and social organization of a minority group are pathological is ultimately a value judgment. Because members of a minority group may deviate in certain respects from the styles of the majority group does not necessarily mean that they are pathological. Is it not possible that the way of life of the majority group is pathological, and, by deviating from it, the life-style of the minority group is more normal and wholesome? Observers also often forget that members of a minority group are not homogenous and that there is significant diversity of life-styles within all minority communities. Another issue raised in research is to what degree members of minority groups actually deviate from mainstream standards of psychological well-being and social organizational integrity. There is a growing body of evidence that pathology in minority groups is not as widespread as once supposed and that the traditional view, social pathology, distorts the situation beyond recognition (Heiss and Owens, 1972; Hughes and Demo, 1989).

Several studies show that blacks have self-esteem at least equal to that of whites (Gordon, 1969; Hughes and Demo, 1989; Rosenberg and Simmons, 1972; Simmons, et al., 1978; Taylor and Walsh, 1979). For negative attitudes of whites to impact the self-esteem of blacks, blacks must be aware of these attitudes, accept them as legitimate, think them significant, and find them personally relevant. According to Rosenberg (1979), these conditions are not often met, and black self-esteem is largely independent of white attitudes. Rather, it is related, for black adolescents, to the appraisals of parents, friends, and teachers within their own community. Hughes and Demo (1989) found that the self-esteem of a national sample of African Americans was indeed rooted in relations with family and friends in the minority community. Minority members do not necessarily compare themselves with the majority and find themselves deficient as a consequence.

The findings of African American children's preference for and misidentification with white dolls have been traditionally interpreted as evidence of rampant self-prejudice on the part of black children, and the start of identity problems for millions of African Americans. McCarthy and Yancey (1971:658) suggested that this might be an impetuous conclusion: "It is a rather long jump in our opinion, however, from racial awareness, preference for white dolls, and assignment of inferior roles to brown dolls to self-hatred."

The interpretation that for black children interracial contact engenders preference for whites since it facilitates social comparison with whites stands out in this traditional literature. Some have been advocates of this position (e.g., Armstrong and Gregor, 1964; Asher and Allen, 1969; Gregor, 1963; Gregor and McPherson, 1966). Asher and Allen (1969:164) put it this way: "Enhanced status will not necessarily lead to greater racial pride, but may instead contribute, through more frequent comparison with whites, to increased feelings of inferiority." Gregor and McPherson (1966:103) phrased it in another way: "Negro children tend to be more out-group oriented the more systematically they are exposed to white contact."

Hraba and Grant (1970) tested this thesis by duplicating the Clark and Clark (1947) doll study in an interracial setting. This study was done in Lincoln, Nebraska, a city where black children went to predominately white schools. The percentage of black children in the elementary schools of this city in which the study was done ranged from 3 to 18 percent. Moreover, the sample of school children studied, both black and white, demonstrated friendship patterns which substantiated the interracial nature of this setting. Sociometric choices confirmed by teachers indicated that 70 percent of the black children had white friends and 59 percent of the white children had black friends. In short, these black children could not and did not avoid systematic contact with whites.

Did they show self-prejudice as a consequence? No. On the contrary, these black children demonstrated a belief in "black is beautiful," generally preferring and identifying with the black dolls. White children also preferred and identified with the dolls of their own race. Children of both races also made responses favorable to the other race, reflecting the interracial nature of their friendships (Hraba, 1972). The racial preferences of these children, black and white, and a comparison with the Clark and Clark data are shown in Table 15.1. More recent studies find a mix of preferences for white and black dolls on the part of black children (cf., Brown, 1986).

In the traditional view, black children develop into psychologically damaged adults, beginning with early self-hatred, doubt, and identity crises. But often there was no explicit and formal comparison of the psychological states of African Americans with those of whites. Handlin (1957) noted that the comparative mental health of old and new immigrant groups was studied earlier in the century by comparing only their committals to public institutions. The newer immigrants, being overrepresented among the poor, would certainly be overrepresented among the committals to public institutions, even if their mental health was identical to that of the older immigrant groups. In this case, as is so often in the case of African Americans, assessments of the supposed pathology of minority groups lack systematic and unbiased comparisons between minority and majority groups.

Moynihan's (1972:199) statement that "at the center of the tangle of pathology is the weakness of the family structure," written in 1965, is his controversial conclusion on the role of the black family in the

TABLE 15.1 COMPARISON OF DATA IN HRABA AND GRANT (1970) AND CLARK AND CLARK (1947)

Item	Clark & Clark (1939 data) Blacks		Hraba & Grant (1969 data) Blacks		χ^2 (1939–1969) Blacks	Hraba & Grant (1969 data) Whites	
1. (Play with)							
White doll	67%	(169)	30%	(27)	36.2%**	83%	(59)
Black doll	32	(83)	70	(62)		16	(11)
Don't know/ no response						1	(1)
2. (Nice doll)							
White doll	59	(150)	46	(41)	57*	70	(50)
Black doll	38	(97)	54	(48)		30	(21)
3. (Looks bad)							
White doll	17	(42)	61	(54)	43.5**	34	(24)
Black doll	59	(149)	36	(32)		63	(45)
Don't know/ no response			3	(3)		3	(2)
4. (Nice color)							
White doll	60	(151)	31	(28)	23.1**	48	(34)
Black doll	38	(96)	69	(61)		49	(35)
Don't know/ no response						3	(2)

*p ≤ .02
**p ≤ .001

Note: Data in percentage. Nos. in parentheses. Individuals failing to make either choice not included; hence some percentages add to less than 100.

Source: Joseph Hraba and Geoffrey Grant, "Black Is Beautiful: A Reexamination of Racial Preference and Identification." *Journal of Personality and Social Psychology* 16 (November): 398-402. Copyright © 1970 by the American Psychological Association. Reprinted by permission of the publisher.

pathology of the black community as a whole. One year later, Rainwater (1966:200) expressed the same sentiment:

> The impact of the system of victimization is transmitted through the family; the child cannot be expected to have the sophistication an outside observer has for seeing exactly where the villains are. From the child's point of view, if he is hungry, it is his parents' fault; if he experiences frustrations in the streets or in the school it is his parents'

fault; if that world seems incomprehensible to him it is his parents' fault; if people are aggressive or destructive toward each other it is his parents' fault, not that of a system of race relations.

While the problems of low-income black families might begin in the system of ethnic stratification, those problems are perpetuated through the weaknesses of these families. This is the essence of Rainwater's position: there is a cycle that for each maturing generation begins with early pregnancy and proceeds through illegitimate births, the economic instability of adult males, female-headed households, the trap of public dependency, and inability to keep the next generation off the streets. The cycle continues with entrapment of the next generation. Rainwater (1966:205–206) was specific about the impact of this cycle for each generation of African American children:

> In sum, we are suggesting that Negro slum children as they grow up in their families and in their neighborhoods are exposed to a set of experiences—and a rhetoric which conceptualizes them—that brings home to the child an understanding of his essence as a weak and debased person who can expect only partial gratification of his needs, and who must seek even this level of gratification by less than straightforward means.

This is the pathological view on the minority family.

The reaction of some African American intellectuals to this version of the African American family was swift. Moynihan's report was claimed to be racist, for it seemed to imply that the problems of poor blacks were largely their own doing. Books and articles soon followed that emphasized the strengths of African American families. Billingsley (1968:21) found a wide variety of family structures in every African American neighborhood of any size in the country:

> This range and variety does not suggest, as some commentaries hold, that the Negro family is falling apart, but rather that these families are fully capable of surviving by adapting to the historical and contemporary social and economic conditions facing the Negro people. How does a people survive in the face of oppression and sharply restricted economic and social support? One way is to adapt the most basic of its institutions, the family, to meet the often conflicting demands placed on it. In this context, then, the Negro family has proved to be an amazingly resilient institution.

Hill (1972), in an essay on the strengths of the African American family, wrote that many of the beliefs that underlie the pathological conception of the African American family have been uncritically accepted as true but actually are false. This applies to the widespread belief about black matriarchy. Matriarchy in African American families is not so prevalent as supposed, according to Hill (1972:281), who reported findings that "most black families, whether low-income or not, are characterized by an 'equalitarian' pattern in which neither spouse dominates, but [they] share decision making and the performance of expected tasks." Another traditional image of the black family is that of the black male who is weak, often irresponsible, and unable to measure up to the mainstream model of husband and father. This is clearly the image projected in Liebow's (1967) study of street-corner men. Contrary to this image, Hill (1972:281) noted that "in 85 percent of the black families with incomes under $3,000, the husband's earnings surpassed the wife's." Moreover, the desertion of the family by the male hardly characterizes the majority of AFDC families; "only one-fifth of the black families receiving AFDC in 1969 were so described" (Hill, 1972:282). Nor are all women who do head black families on welfare, contrary to the traditional view; rather, "two-thirds of the women heading black families work—most of them full-time" (Hill, 1972:281).

It is the contention of Robert Hill that the African American family has several strengths, most of which have been overlooked in the collective works of the social pathologists. As to what he means by family strength, Hill (1972:264) wrote that "we . . . define as family strengths those traits which facilitate the ability of the family to meet the needs of its members and the demands made upon it by systems outside the family unit." Hill indicated three major sources of strength in African American families: strong kinship bonds, strong work orientation, and the adaptability of family roles. The strength of kinship bonds in African American families is evident in their practice of taking in the children of other family members, the historical existence of African American extended families, and the informal adoption of babies born out of wedlock. The practice of the informal adoption of dependent children is positively functional for the African American community as a whole, for it "helps to minimize the number of new black families headed by a single woman" (Hill, 1972:266).

As evidence for the existence of a strong work orientation among African Americans, Hill cites the fact that the black poor are more likely to work than the white poor. Moreover, black women are more likely to work to help keep their families above the poverty line than are white women. This certainly appears to be a positive adaptation to social and economic reality, as black women experience it, and in no way does it seem to further disable people from being included into the larger society. Furthermore, the finding that black families are equalitarian at home appears to follow from the fact that both partners are typically in the work force outside of the home. Thus, the adaptability of family roles seems to be a functional adaptation for most black families and should not be mistaken for some sort of pathology that hinders the progress of the race.

Shimkin, Louie, and Frate (1973) found that a fundamental strength of the African American community in Holmes County, Mississippi, has been the extended African American family. Familial bonds among extended kin have been stable and durable, reinforced by patterns of residential propinquity and common church affiliation. The network of extended kin enforces the obligations of family members toward one another, especially the responsibility of adults for children. These networks originating in Holmes County have acted as mechanisms for the migration of some family members to other areas of the country, mostly to the cities of the South and Midwest. Family members already located in urban areas have been important sources of job information for later migrants, have provided them an initial place to stay in the city, and generally have helped their own kin in the transition from rural to urban life, from an agrarian peasantry to a class of industrial workers. Shimkin et al. in no way overlooked the economic marginality of most African American families in Holmes County, particularly the absence of land proprietorship, but still concluded that the African American family has been resilient and typically self-sufficient.

In his classical study of the African American family, Frazier (1939) sounded the hopeful note that with economic progress the weakness he saw in the African American family would be overcome. John Scanzoni (1971) initiated on that note a study of the overlooked majority (67 percent) of urban African American families in which both husband and wife are present and that are above the poverty level. The sample consisted of 400 African American households with both partners present in Indianapolis, Indiana, in 1968. Both spouses had to be African American and married for at least five years to be in the sampling frame. Data collected on these families were compared with those on other families, black and white.

The major finding of the work is that most of the families in this sample had broken the cycle of economic deprivation and marital dissolution. Urban residence was important while not vital to this economic and social evolution, as were the resources passed to these people by their parents. Religious involvement was found to reinforce mainstream occupational and conjugal values and practices. Both husbands and wives in this sample of the "broad middle class of blacks" reported that their parents had been active in their preparation for participation in the larger society by providing certain class resources and stressing the values of that society. Even though middle-class blacks remain deprived relative to their white counterparts, Scanzoni observed that as blacks enter the larger society economically, they enter it conjugally as well. In other words, the divergence evident in minority-group family patterns, whatever their degree, is due to exclusion and discrimination. As the inclusion of a minority group proceeds, and as discrimination lessens, family patterns begin to converge with those of their class counterparts in the larger society.

Meanwhile, the number of female-headed household among poor African Americans has continued to increase since the 1960s and 1970s. In 1960, 42 percent of the African American teenagers who had babies were unmarried, but by 1983 it was 89 percent. One explanation for female-headed households is that slavery had torn apart the African American family. However, the historical evidence does not support this theory.

> As recently as the early 1960's, 75 percent of black households were husband-and-wife families. The figure represents remarkable continuity—it is about the same as those reported in census records from the late nineteenth century. Indeed, the evidence suggests that most slaves grew up in two-parent families reinforced by ties to larger extended families (Norton, 1985:93).

The rise of the black female-headed household is a recent phenomenon, not an historical one (see Chapters 10 and 11).

Another explanation is the high unemployment rates for young, African American males in the post-industrial economy since World War II. Unable to find well-paying jobs, these men cannot support a family. Unemployment rates for young, African American males range from 50 to 90 percent in some ghettos. Since 1960, African American males have lost their labor niche in agriculture due to mechanization, and more recently in blue-collar industrial jobs due to the de-industrialization of America (see Chapter 11). White-collar jobs have expanded since 1945, but they have not been filled by African American men.

"The [family] breakdown begins with working-class black men, whose loss of function in the post–World War II economy has led directly to their loss of function in the family" (Norton, 1985:93). These black men cannot maintain a stable family because of their underemployment and unemployment. Moreover, Guttentag and Secord (1983:201) reported that "...it appears that in 1970, for the age cohorts most eligible for marriage, there were almost two black women for every man." The reasons were the relatively high death rates of young black males, their imprisonment, and their disproportionate presence in the American armed forces stationed overseas. The odds are stacked against marriage and stable family life.

A final explanation begins with the migration of rural southern blacks to northern ghettos in recent decades. Middle-class blacks simultaneously moved out of these same ghettos as better housing became available. The middle class personified and promoted middle-class values, including two-parent family life. However, the middle class is now gone. The black poor became separated from the black middle class as well as from the larger society, and they transplanted their southern subculture in the nation's ghettos. Underclass culture in ghettos is traceable to southern roots—the South of a generation ago, not slavery (Lemann, 1986).

Some evidence refutes the allegation that members of minority groups show what are considered to be signs of pathology. Black children are not necessarily self-prejudiced, for example. Other evidence acknowledges the fact of female-headed households but refutes the interpretation that these households are pathological. Rather, the households may simply be sensible reactions to current economic realities.

ETHNIC COMMUNALISM AND CONSCIOUSNESS

The evidence contrary to minority pathology has always suggested a second conceptualization of the American minority community. This view, ethnic communalism and consciousness, posits that the minority group can and does maintain its community in the course of its exclusion from the larger society, and its members find psychological succor among their own kind and in their own community. There is no necessary psychological damage and community deterioration in the course of exclusion and divergence. Instead, a minority group always has the potential of engaging in communal action, or action "which is oriented to the feelings of the actors that they belong together" (Weber, 1966:22). This can lead to the building of the ethnic community, exemplified by ethnic subeconomies and protest movements.

This position stands in sharp contrast to social pathology. From the perspective of minority communalism, any deviation from mainstream standards is due to the persistence of the ethnic community in the course of divergence, not to its disintegration and the pathology of its members. There is no necessary loss of the ethnic community in societal change, for either the majority or the minority group. Ethnic competition and conflict continuously make current ethnic boundaries and consciousness of kind, while the persistence of ethnic stratification keeps alive a minority group's sense of its societal position. According to the social identity theory of Tajfel (1982) and Tajfel and Turner (1979) a minority group can engage in social action to raise its social identity and thus the self-worth of its members. Ethnic movements in this country are an example.

COMMUNALISM

Most immigrant groups to this country initially settled near where they worked, either in urban ghettos or ethnic clusters in the country-side. At the time of their initial settlement, nearly all of these groups were minority groups, at the bottom of the labor hierarchy. The ethnic enclave of the immigrants represented their economic adaptation to the New World. They adapted to the economy and ecology of their lo-cale, which was often in the low-rent districts alongside factories, foundries, mines, and stockyards. Of course, the initial concentration of immigrants was due to other reasons, including language barriers, the need to seek help from one's own kind, and the industrial ecology of the era. George Homans (1950) termed this process of adapting to an environment the *external system* of a group, those relations among group members that are initially conditioned by their need to adapt to a particular environment. Out of this external system a new set of rela-tionships will emerge, however, that are not conditioned by economic adaptation and that represent an elaboration on economic necessity. This is the *internal system*.

In her excellent survey of the writings on the American minority community, Judith Kramer (1970:52–53) turned primarily to Robin Williams, Jr. (1964) for an account of the emergence of the internal sys-tem, the communalization of the minority ghetto:

> ...[T]he ability to impose such categories on others is part of the domi-nant group's power to subordinate.... As a result, members of a cate-gory acquire a sense of common identity, which tends to increase in-teraction among themselves and to reduce contacts with others. Such social closure makes it even more likely that others will treat them as a unit; this treatment further enhances the new collectivity's cultural distinctiveness and social separation. It is not a completely closed so-cial system since it is economically and politically dependent on the larger society. As as subordinate group, it must not only maintain re-lationships with others, it must accept the dominant rules of the game.

There have been several examples of ethnic communalism in pre-ceding chapters. For example, Wirth (1928/1956:193) pointed out (see Chapter 2) that:

> In its initial stages the Jewish community is scarcely distinguishable from the rest of the city. As the numbers increase, however, the typi-cal communal organization of the European ghetto gradually emerges. The addition of diverse elements to the population results in diversification and differentiation....

In subsequent chapters, we learned about ethnic subeconomies of Asian Americans; independence movements on the part of Irish, Polish, and Korean Americans; and the various ethnic organizations of other groups as well.

Wirth described in abstract terms the emergence of an internal system of one ethnic community, a process that includes both the *elaboration* of the external system into an internal community and the *differentiation* of that community. Elaboration itself is a complex process, including the formation of a network of ethnic formal associations, such as lodges, hospitals, even civil rights groups, and of informal networks of family and friends. Wirth provided some detail as to the elaboration of the Jewish ghetto in Chicago. By 1900 there were 50 congregations, 39 charities, 60 lodges, 11 social clubs, 4 Zionist organizations, and hospitals, cafes, and theaters in the Jewish community. As the Jewish community elaborated, it became more diversified as well, differentiated into various trades, functions, and activities, of course, but more importantly, it became differentiated into nationality and locality groups. Chinatowns were internally differentiated into clans, *huiguans,* tongs, and trade guilds, and the Japanese were internally divided into *kenjinkai.* Nearly all groups have become differentiated into ethclasses and have often become geographically dispersed as well. This is as true for minority groups as for majority groups. Communalism does not imply a static group, stuck in time and preserved by custom. The ethnic community is an evolving entity, undergoing the dual phenomena of elaboration and differentiation. Communalism as an internal system simply means that a group maintains enough of its organizational integrity to give structure and meaning to its members' lives.

Hannerz (1969) offered an example of the differentiation of a minority community. He observed that residents of a black ghetto tended to dichotomize each other into respectables and undesirables. The respectables saw themselves as the "good people," "model citizens," and the "middle class." They described their opposites, the undesirables, as "no good," "the rowdy bunch," and "trash." The self-named respectables characterized the undesirables collectively as exhibiting "drinking and drunkenness in public, spontaneous brawls, unwillingness to work, sexual license, and occasional trouble with police" (Hannerz, 1969:35).

Hannerz believed that the actual picture of differentiation within this ghetto was not nearly so simple. Instead of two status groups in the area, he discerned four: mainstreamers, swingers, street families, and the street-corner men described in Liebow's *Talley's Corner* (1967). The mainstreamers are the respectables by another name; they are steadily employed, often own their homes, and have stable family lives: "It is usually not very hard to detect from the outside which houses are the homes of mainstreamers. The new metal screen doors, the venetian blinds, and the flower pots in the windows are usually absent from other people's houses" (Hannerz, 1969:39). Inside these homes, Hannerz reported finding paneled walls, stylish furniture, new TV and stereo sets, and wedding and graduation pictures of the family hanging on the walls. Outside, in the yards, Hannerz found aluminum garden chairs and a barbecue grill or two. Any middle-class American would immediately recognize such a home and feel comfortable in it.

The swingers are the young socialites of the neighborhood, from their late teens to their thirties. Their interest is in a good time. They buy stylish clothing and cars in a narcissistic celebration of self. These young men and women are usually where the action is, typically keep night hours, and are always cool. While mainstreamers and swingers are obviously different, there is little antagonism between them, and as they grow older swingers usually become mainstreamers.

However, antagonism between mainstreamers and street families and street-corner men does exist: "It is often the members of street families who are conspicuously engaging in affairs with the other sex outside marriage, whose children are born out of wedlock and engage in juvenile delinquency as they grow up, and who drink and fight in public" (Hannerz, 1969:46). This prompts the mainstreamers to regard street families as "trash." Street families, not mainstreamers and swingers, are characterized by the pathologies discussed earlier, including early pregnancy, conflict-ridden relationships between the sexes, the segregation of male and female social lives, flexible household composition, delinquency of the kids, and all the rest. Mainstreamers try to avoid contact with members of street families. A social distance is maintained between members of these two different status groups within the neighborhood.

Recent studies of African American low-income neighborhoods paint a more distressing picture (e.g., Anderson, 1990; Lemann, 1986; Wilson, 1987). There have been changes in American society in the last fifteen years, and for the ghetto this has brought declining employment prospects for ghetto youth, the rise of illegitimate births and female-headed households, the exodus of the middle class to the suburbs, and the infusion of drugs into these neighborhoods, along with rising crime rates. As a symbol of the change, crack houses now dot the neighborhoods, and the drug dealer has become an attractive role model for the young (Anderson, 1990). The young male hipster now avoids the mainstream roles of husband, father, and provider, and girls raise babies without husbands. More than ever before, the mainstreamers, black and white, make every effort to avoid trouble on the street. Some try to ingratiate themselves with petty criminals, some buy dogs for protection, and all closely watch strangers on the block.

We see evidence of both ghetto pathology and ethnic communalism in this outline of the differentiation of a black ghetto. Drunkenness and abstinence, crime and concern for law and order, shacks and well-kept homes—all of these contrasts can be seen in a single African American neighborhood, and they seem to vary by ethclass. This suggests that communalism characterizes the American minority community as much as does social pathology, and the center of gravity for ethnic communalism is the ethclass.

Communalism serves a variety of psychological and social functions for members of a minority group. The ethnic community is often an agency of socialization; its members come to share a common set of values and traditions, a subculture through which the larger national ethos is translated (Gordon, 1964). In the process, subcultural standards for self-worth are passed from generation to generation (Hughes and Demo, 1989). Often minority-group members are socialized into a shared definition of their minority situation, a sense of their societal position. This definition, more often than not, attributes minority poverty and deprivation to dominant-group oppression, not to the shortcomings of minority-group members. It expresses social alienation, not self-alienation. There is no necessary weakening of the self-image, since the system rather than the self is blamed. All of this protects the minority-group members from the prejudice in the larger society, acting as a counter ideology to that prejudice. The subcultural values of a minority group serve as standards against which members of the minority group compare the competence of one another. In effect, "it is the minority community that offers its members criteria for self-validation that are independent of the categorical criteria of the dominant group" (Kramer, 1970:66).

In their own communities, members of minority groups can see themselves as whole people, competent or incompetent, good or bad, in accord with their own criteria. Communalism of this sort can be a basis for social improvement "when there is a strong family at the core of the community" (Kramer, 1970:66). Communalism may hinder inclusion into the larger society, however, as the isolation of members of a minority group from outsiders may reinforce the existing pattern of social distance between themselves and others. Psychological relief from prejudice and oppression found within the confines of their own community may also cool out minority discontent about their circumstances. The "circle of lament" among members of a minority group about prejudice and discrimination "neither discharges the onus nor distracts from it" (Kramer, 1970:71).

Other functions of ethnic communalism include sustaining and giving structure to the lives of group members and maintaining the boundary exchange of the group with the outside world. With respect to the first function, Gordon (1964:34) wrote:

> Within the ethnic group there develops a network of organizations and informal social relationships which permits and encourages the members of the ethnic group to remain within the confines of the group for all of their primary relationships and some of their secondary relationships throughout all the stages of the life-cycle.

Kramer (1970:56), on the other hand, looked to the boundary maintenance of the minority group:

> It permits the self-sufficiency and the segregation that the family alone is unable to provide. The minority community formed by the ethnic group practices self-exclusion as a protection against the social exclusion of the dominant group. Its institutions and ideologies provide a way of life that is independent of the categorical status of its members. Their social honor is thereby secured against dominant derogation.

The degree to which minority communities can maintain their boundaries and thus regulate their exchange with the larger society varies from group to group, however, and the degree to which any given group can do this is a matter of debate. No ethnic subsociety can be an entirely closed system, having boundaries impermeable to all the pressures from the outside. Minority communities are from the start open systems permeable to pressures from the outside, a fact to which their subordination attests. No minority group can protect its members fully from the effects of prejudice and discrimination, encasing them economically, politically and socially, as if in quarantine. Williams (1964:18) offered these criteria for a fully developed communal group:

> (1) a distinctive culture, (2) tests or criteria of membership, (3) a set of constitutive norms regulating social relations both within the collectivity and with outsiders, (4) an awareness of a distinct identity by both members and nonmembers, (5) obligations of solidarity, such as enforced requirements to help members in need and to resist derogation by outsiders, and (6) a high capacity for continued action on behalf of its members or of itself as a unit. In its most comprehensive development such a collectivity may become a potentially self-sufficient society, able to meet all internal needs from its own resources and to perpetuate itself as a functioning system from generation to generation.

To illustrate, the Chinese immigrant brotherhood had a distinctive culture; the Chinese surely distinguished members from non-members by language and physical appearance; they followed collective norms in relations with each other, in rotating credit associations for example, as well as with outsiders; and their huiguans helped members in need.

CONSCIOUSNESS OF KIND AND SOCIETAL POSITION

It is within the minority community that minority-group children experience their early and most important socializing influences, according to the perspective of ethnic communalism. The communal group is a socialization agency, in other words, and through its internal network of communication, members, young and old, are socialized into a consciousness of their ethnic identity and an awareness of their position in the larger society. This is one of the more important functions of the ethnic community. Consciousness of kind is the realization that one belongs with others by birthright to some particular group in a larger society and thus shares with them a common past, present, and future. Consciousness of kind means "a sense of us" among members of an ethnic group, and it enhances the solidarity of the group. While consciousness of kind is not fully dependent on ghetto experience—that is, on subordination, segregation, and occupational concentration—it is nevertheless rooted in human action as that occurs day in and day out. And when people see each other through the reflections of having the same jobs, living in the same neighborhoods, sharing experiences, engaging in similar customs and rituals, and being excluded from the larger society, their consciousness of kind is more apparent and likely to be more prevalent.

Consciousness of societal position is the other side of the same coin. Consciousness of kind is self-reflexive, as members of a minority group see themselves reflected in the group's history and in their current "place" in society. Consciousness of societal position is the awareness of that "place" in society, which for a minority group usually means the realization that they face discrimination and have an inferior position in the system of ethnic stratification. You will recall from Chapter 5 that Blumer (1958) located the prejudice of the majority group in their sense of social position, their superior status in the system of ethnic stratification. Minority groups are just as aware of their social position in the larger society. A minority group's sense of societal position is transmitted through the channels of communication in the minority community, as is its consciousness of kind, and it serves as a counter ideology to the prejudice of others (Hraba and Siegman, 1974). The more developed and comprehensive is this network, the more control the minority community can exercise over its participants.

EXCLUSION AND DIVERGENCE:
SOCIAL PATHOLOGY OR ETHNIC COMMUNALISM?

All minority groups by definition share the experience of having been excluded at one time or another from the larger American society. Many ethnic groups in American history have been excluded by their more powerful competitors from land and capital and from the better positions in the labor market. That is, systems of ethnic stratification have been established around ethnic exchange, and these systems have been persistent phenomena, running through all three historical phases of American society. Illustrations of ethnic stratification abound in American history; only some of these historical instances have been presented in this book (Chapters 7–14).

More often than not, a minority group follows a course of divergence, one that is somewhere on the continuum between the extremes of social pathology and ethnic communalism. A minority group may evolve either toward a state of social pathology, becoming as it does less able to work toward its inclusion into the larger society, or it can evolve as a communal group in the face of prejudice and discrimination, maintaining its solidarity. In the one case the ethnic community disintegrates in the course of divergence, while in the other it is conserved. It cannot be said that the history of any one minority group exemplifies either extreme, for the historical course of most minority groups falls somewhere between these two extremes. Minority groups generally show a mixture of pathology and communalism in the course of their divergence. Some minority groups, however, have shown more signs of pathology than have others, and by the same token, some groups more than others appear to have conserved their communalism in the face of prejudice and discrimination.

What explains these different courses of divergence? Why have some groups when excluded from the larger society evolved toward a state of pathology, meaning the loss of their ethnic community, while other minority groups have evolved as communal groups, preserving their ethnic community? The answer we propose lies in the degree to which a minority group is oppressed, and by the same token, its ability to control its own boundaries, to internally regulate to some degree its boundary exchange with the larger society and thus to shelter its members to some extent from the debilitating effects of prejudice and discrimination. Boundary maintenance is rooted in the capacity of a minority group to provide to its members, within their own community, alternatives to the prejudice and discrimination in the larger society. Such an alternative can be provided by an ethnic subeconomy or its functional equivalents.

THE ETHNIC SUBECONOMY

Historically, the ethnic subeconomy has offered opportunity to members of a minority group unavailable in the larger American society, protecting participants from extreme hardships, preserving group boundaries, and conserving in-group cohesion and consciousness. This is a major role for capital accumulation on the part of minority groups; it can, by building a subeconomy, help buffer members of such groups from the full impact of prejudice and discrimination.

If fully functioning, a subeconomy can offer to members of a minority group opportunity that is not restricted by the ethnic barriers and ethnocentrism in the wider society. If the ethnic subeconomy as an opportunity structure is at all broad, then members of a minority group can truly circumvent the discrimination imposed on them by others. Perhaps no ethnic subeconomy has ever been so complete and without disadvantages, but Jews in Europe and Asians in America have made real, practical gains against discrimination in this way. Although it falls short of a subeconomy in providing alternatives to prejudice and discrimination, a viable social system and subculture can help minority group members who face restricted opportunities without realistic alternatives cope with the effects of such a life. It soothes the soul from the wear and tear of racism. It does not, however, preclude racism or the effects of it. Such a system can only maintain folks in the face of racism.

Members of a minority group without a subeconomy have no alternative but to seek opportunity on the outside, in the larger society, however limited those opportunities may be. Because of the power of their competitors, they face persistent discrimination and material deprivation, exclusion, and divergence. It also means that members of the minority group must face, day in and day out, the prejudice of others and the stigma that their ethnicity has in the larger society. Hope often contracts under such circumstances, serious ambitions sound absurd, and aspirations are scaled downward. This is the crucible for merely coping, if not pathology.

A minority group without an opportunity structure of its own is, to phrase it abstractly, an open subsystem within a wider society. Its boundaries are so permeable to the forces of prejudice and discrimination in that wider society, its domination by others so complete, that little in the way of internal communalism is possible. Virtually nothing buffers members of such a minority group from the hardships of their exclusion, from prejudice, discrimination, and poverty, and the ghetto provides little more than a "circle of lament" over circumstances no one can change. There is no internal opportunity so that members of the group can practice their skills, workmanship, professional expertise, and so on, on their own terms, in their own communities, away from the degrading and impeding ethnocentrism of others. Instead, they must face that degradation on a daily basis. Communalism, and thus the sheltering of minority-group members from prejudice and discrimination, is severely limited when the life chances of minority-group members are solely at the discretion of dominant outsiders, that is, when there is no ethnic subeconomy or internal opportunity structure of some kind. Pathology is an expected outcome in this minority situation. Rainwater (1966:200) expressed it this way:

> ...[I]f a subculture could exist which provided comfort and security within its limited world and the individual experienced frustration only when he moved out into the larger society, the family might not be thought so much to blame. The effect of the caste system, however, is to bring home through a chain of cause and effect all of the victimization processes, and to bring them home in such a way that it is often difficult even for adults in the system to see the connection between the pain they feel at the moment and the structured patterns of the caste system.

We would argue that a subeconomy is more important in this regard than is a subculture. An ethnic subeconomy can provide internal opportunity and can prevent in large measure the social and psychological disorganization associated with minority status in America. Some minority groups, through communal effort, have overcome the barriers to their mobility and have built subeconomies in which their own kind have worked unencumbered by prejudice and discrimination. The Asian American case illustrates this course of action, at least among Chinese and Japanese Americans, who became middleman minorities. The role of the internal formation of capital through rotating credit associations and communal associations in the Asian communities were vital in the establishment of Asian subeconomies. The ties of kenjinkai between Japanese labor bosses and their crews were also important in the mobility of Japanese immigrants out of field labor and into a class of independent farmers and land owners. This movement was executed despite systematic attempts to exclude Japanese from land proprietorship. The infusion of blood and regional loyalties into the economic activity of urban Asian immigrants also resulted in the practice of businessmen's financing their apprentices into businesses of their own. Asian labor and capital were integrated into a common ethnic community, which was a mutually reinforcing social entity and subeconomy, and both classes were thereby sheltered in a significant way from racism in the larger society. Asian labor benefited from a much better alternative to their categorical discrimination in the larger society, and Asian capital benefited from reduced labor costs. In the entire process, the Asian communal groups maintained their boundaries and buffered their members from the full impact of prejudice and discrimination.

A minority group with an opportunity structure of its own is a somewhat closed subsystem within a larger society. Its boundaries are to some extent impermeable to many of the pathological consequences of minority status in a society, since internal opportunities act as an alternative to poverty, prejudice, and discrimination on the outside. Group members do not necessarily have to exchange land, labor, and capital with outsiders when it is to their disadvantage. Away from the ethnocentrism of others, members of the group can practice their skills and workmanship and can be whole people on their own terms and among their own kind. They are sheltered from the self-debilitating effects of their exclusion from opportunity in the larger society by having, within their own community, opportunities of their own. Hope does not contract under these circumstances, serious ambition need not sound absurd, and aspirations do not have to be scaled downward. On the contrary, advancement is possible and likely. This is the crucible of communalism and consciousness, the conservation of the sense and substance of the ethnic community in the face of prejudice and discrimination.

The cornerstone to an ethnic subeconomy is the communal solidarity of a minority group. Communal solidarity is a cause as well as an effect of the ethnic subeconomy. For instance, the Chinese and Japanese had cohesive immigrant communities because of their Old-World regional loyalties and their homogeneity with respect to age, gender, and generation. Many were sojourners, with little incentive for permanent residence in the United States, and they tended to settle in the same part of the country. Thus they stuck together in the face of prejudice and discrimination and established their own opportunity structure. By contrast, other immigrant groups were heterogeneous, reflecting the full regional, social, and economic diversity of their homelands. They also dispersed themselves across the entire country and more quickly conformed to the Anglo-American culture, due in part to their intention of permanent settlement. As the homogeneity and sojourning motives of the Asian immigrants engendered their communal solidarity and ethnic subeconomy, the heterogeneity and motives for permanent settlement of others precluded to some degree the same type of adjustment to prejudice and discrimination. Once established, the Asian subeconomy reinforced the broader Asian communalism.

It is equally important to note that Asian Americans were allowed to transplant their immigrant brotherhoods in this country while they were being excluded from the larger society. By contrast, African Americans were unable, under slavery, to conserve their tribal communalism in the South. A critical mass of a single West African tribe was seldom reached on the small plantations in this country, and black slaves were systematically denied the right of assembly without the presence of a white. Both these factors hindered the transplantation of West African tribal communalism. Nor could slaves develop any semblance of a subeconomy of their own, since virtually all entrepreneurial activity in the Old South was dominated by whites. Another instance is the case of Native Americans. The communalism of many Indian tribes disintegrated in the conquest, particularly as the ecological and economic base of Indian life was destroyed with the expropriation of their land. The deterioration of Indian communalism continued in the course of the several governmental programs that kept Indians in a state of economic and political dependence, all of which had the effect of undermining traditions within the tribes. The boundaries of many Indian tribes thus became porous to pressures that make for social pathology. All of this suggests that we might modify our definition of a minority group in line with that of Barth (1969): a group that faces both prejudice and discrimination in the larger society and is unable to provide its members an internal system sufficient for their access to desired ends.

While the ethnic subeconomy is here emphasized as one means of preventing minority pathology, it perhaps was possible in only a limited period of American history. The ethnic subeconomy is not as realistic an undertaking as it once was, now that the scale of business in this country has grown so great. Giant corporations, such as supermarket chains and fast-food franchises, have since taken over much of the economic niche once filled by small-scale ethnic enterprises (Bonacich, 1973). Programs for black capitalism, for instance, cannot duplicate today the ethnic subeconomy of the past.

Nevertheless, recent immigrants from Asia have moved into their own businesses (Chapter 14). Light and Bonacich (1988) interpreted Korean businesses, however, as merely a disguised form of cheap labor in America. Korean firms in Los Angeles are typically small, have low receipts, and exploit the labor of co-ethnics with long hours and low wages, and profits tend to rise up to parent companies in the case of franchises. However small ethnic businesses are seen, either as capital or labor, they still provide a refuge to prejudice and discrimination on the outside, limited by their size and economic viability.

AN EYE TO POLITICS

There are other ways in which a minority group can protect itself, and the political mobilization of minority groups appears to be increasingly important in this regard. Politics has always been important in a way; the Irish used political machines as a mobility route. Political mobilization can protect minority-group members to some extent from prejudice and discrimination, and thus from some of the pathological consequences of minority status. An ideology counter to racism often emerges in the course of ethnic political movements, providing its participants with an alternative to self-prejudice and other forms of pathology. Activism of this kind can pull a group together and restore its communalism.

The symbolism of ethnic consciousness and communalism has certainly been coupled with the rise of minority protest in this country. If real political gains accompany mobilization, then discrimination against a minority might also be reduced. African Americans have become an important voting bloc and political interest group in recent years and have consequently made some progress against prejudice and discrimination in American society. This opened opportunity for some members through affirmative action, for example, as it made for organizational growth in the African American community. During the civil rights era, African American organizations turned to the state in their rivalry with the white majority. To better deal with both state bureaucracy and the organizations of their rivals, civil rights organizations became bureaucratized as well, with paid managerial staffs and boards of directors. There was organizational growth within the group as it made progress against its rivals. It would appear that an eye to politics is critical in forecasting the future of ethnicity in this country.

BIBLIOGRAPHY

Abramson, H. J.
  1973 *Ethnic Diversity in Catholic America*. New York: John Wiley and Sons, Inc.
Adorno, T. W., E. Frenkel-Brunswik, D. J. Leyinson, and R. N. Sanford
  1950 *The Authoritarian Personality*. New York: Harper & Row, Publisher.
Alba, R. D.
  1976 "Social Assimilation among American Catholic National-Origin
    Groups." *American Sociological Review* 41:1030–1046.
  1985 *Italian Americans: Into the Twilight of Ethnicity*. Englewood Cliffs, NJ:
    Prentice-Hall, Inc.
Alba, R. D. and G. Moore
  1982 "Ethnicity in the American Elite." *American Sociological Review* 47:373–383.
Alba, R. D. and M. B. Chamlin
  1983 "A Preliminary Examination of Ethnic Identification among Whites."
    American Sociological Review 48:240–247.
Allen, P. G.
  1986 *The Sacred Hoop: Recovering the Feminine in American Indian Traditions*.
    Boston: Beacon Press.
Allen, R. L.
  1970 *Black Awakening in Capitalist America*. Garden City, New York:
    Doubleday and Company, Inc.
Allport, G. W.
  1935 "Attitudes." Pp. 798–844 in C. Murchinson (ed.), *A Handbook of Social
    Psychology*. Worcester, MA: Clark University Press.
  1954 *The Nature of Prejudice*. Reading, MA: Addison-Wesley Publishing
    Company, Inc.
  1962 "Prejudice: Is It Societal or Personal." *Journal of Social Issues* 18:120–134.
  1968 "The Historical Background of Modern Social Psychology." Pp. 1–80 in
    Gardner Lindzey and Elliot Aranson (eds.), *The Handbook of Social
    Psychology*. Reading, MA: Addison-Wesley Publishing Company, Inc.
Alvarez, R.
  1985 "The Psycho-Historical and Socioeconomic Development of the
    Chicano Community in the United States. Pp. 33–56 in R. O. De La Garza,
    F. D. Bean, C. M. Bonjean, R. Romo, and R. Alvarez (eds.), *The Mexican
    American Experience: An Interdisciplinary Anthology*. Austin: University of
    Texas Press.

Amir, Y.

  1976 "The Role of Intergroup Contact in Change of Prejudice and Ethnic Relations." In P. A. Katz (ed.), *Towards the Elimination of Racism*. New York: Pergamon Press.

Anderson, E.

  1990 *Streetwise*. Chicago: University of Chicago Press.

Anderson, R. N.

  1984 *Filipinos in Rural Hawaii*. Honolulu: University of Hawaii Press.

Aptheker, H.

  1939 *Negro Slave Revolts in the United States, 1526–1860*. New York: International Publishers.

Armstrong, C. P. and A. J. Gregor

  1964 "Integrated Schools and Negro Character Development." *Psychiatry* 27:69–72.

Asher, S. R. and V. L. Allen

  1969 "Racial Preference and Social Comparison Processes." *Journal of Social Issues* 25:157–165.

Ashmore, R. D.

  1981 "Sex Stereotypes and Implicit Personality Theory." In D. L. Hamilton (ed.), *Cognitive Processes in Stereotyping and Intergroup Behavior*. Hillsdale, NJ: Lawrence Erlbaum Associates.

Axelrod, M.

  1956 "Urban Structure and Social Participation." *American Sociological Review* 21:13–18.

Babchuk, N. and A. Booth

  1969 "Voluntary Association Membership: A Longitudinal Analysis." *American Sociological Review* 34:31–45.

Bagehot, W.

  1869/1948 *Physics and Politics*. New York: Alfred A. Knopf, Inc.

Ball, R. A.

  1968 "A Poverty Case: The Analgesic Subculture of the Southern Appalachians." *American Sociological Review* 33:885–895.

Bandura, A.

  1962 "Social Learning through Imitation." Pp. 211–269 in M. R. Jones (ed.), *Nebraska Symposium on Motivation*. Lincoln: University of Nebraska Press.

Bane, M. J.

  1986 "Household Composition and Poverty." Pp. 207–231 in S. H. Danziger and D. H. Weinberg (eds.), *Fighting Poverty: What Works and What Doesn't*. Cambridge, MA: Harvard University Press.

Banton, M.

  1967 *Race Relations*. New York: Basic Books, Inc., Publishers.

Barker, M.

  1981 *The New Racism*. London: Junction Books Ltd.

Barnes, P.

  1971 "The Great American Land Grab." *The New Republic* 164(June):19–24.

Baron, H.

  1971 "The Demands for Black Labor: Historical Notes on the Political

Economy of Racism." *Radical America* 5:34–38.

Barrera, M.

1979 *Race and Class in the Southwest: A Theory of Racial Inequality*. Notre Dame: University of Notre Dame Press.

1988 *Beyond Aztlan: Ethnic Autonomy in Comparative Perspective*. New York: Praeger.

Barth, F. (ed.)

1969 *Ethnic Groups and Boundaries: The Social Organization of Culture Difference*. London: George Allen & Unwin.

Barth, E. A. T. and D. L. Noel

1972 "Conceptual Frameworks for the Analysis of Race Relations: An Evaluation." *Social Forces* 50 (March):333–348.

Bash, H. H.

1979 *Sociology, Race and Ethnicity: A Critique of American Ideological Intrusions upon Sociological Theory*. New York: Gordon and Breach.

Bass, B. M.

1955 "Authoritarianism of Acquiescence." *Journal of Abnormal and Social Psychology* 51:616–623.

Beales, D.

1971 *The Resorgimento and the Unification of Italy*. London: George Allen & Unwin.

Bean, F. D. and M. Tienda

1987 *The Hispanic Population of the United States*. New York: Russell Sage Foundation.

Bean, F. D., E. H. Stephen, and W. Opitz

1985 "The Mexican Origin Population in the United States: A Demographic Overview." Pp. 57–75 in R. O. De La Garza, F. D. Bean, C. M. Bonjean, R. Romo, and R. Alvarez (eds.), *The Mexican American Experience: An Interdisciplinary Anthology*. Austin: University of Texas Press.

Bean, F. D., G. Vernez, and C. B. Keely

1989 *Opening and Closing the Doors: Evaluating Immigration Reform and Control*. Washington, D.C.: The Urban Institute Press.

Becker, G. S.

1957/1971 *The Economics of Discrimination*. Chicago: University of Chicago Press.

Beckett, J. C.

1966 *The Making of Modern Ireland, 1603–1923*. New York: Alfred A. Knopf.

Bennett, J. W. (ed.)

1975 *The New Ethnicity: Perspectives from Ethnology*. St. Paul, MN: West Publishing Company.

Bennett, M. T.

1963 *American Immigration Policies*. Washington, DC: Public Affairs Press.

Beresford, M.

1988 *Vietnam: Politics, Economics and Society*. London: Pinter Publishers.

Bernard, J.

1951 "The Conceptualization of Intergroup Relations with Special Reference to Conflict." *Social Forces* 29:243–251.

Berndt, T. J. and K. A. Heller
  1986 "Gender Stereotypes and Social Inferences: A Developmental Study."
  Journal of Personality and Social Psychology 50:889–898.
Berreman, G. D.
  1960 "Caste in India and the United States." *The American Journal of Sociology*
  66:120–127.
Billig, M.
  1985 "Prejudice, Categorization and Particularization: From a Perceptual to
  a Rhetorical Approach." *European Journal of Social Psychology* 15:79–103.
Billingsley, A.
  1968 *Black Families in White America.* Englewood Cliffs, NJ: Prentice-Hall, Inc.
Birmingham, S.
  1973 *Real Lace: America's Irish Rich.* New York: Harper & Row.
Blalock, H. M., Jr.
  1967 *Toward a Theory of Minority Group Relations.* New York: John Wiley and
  Sons, Inc.
Blassingame, J. W.
  1972 *The Slave Community: Plantation Life in the Antebellum South.* New York:
  Oxford University Press.
Blau, P. M.
  1965 "The Flow of Occupational Supply and Recruitment." *American
  Sociological Review* 30:475–490.
Blauner, R.
  1969 "Internal Colonialism and Ghetto Revolt." *Social Problems* 16:393–409.
Blum, J.
  1957 "The Rise of Serfdom in Eastern Europe." *American Historical Review*
  62:807–835.
Blumer, H.
  1958a "Race Prejudice as a Sense of Group Position." *Pacific Sociological
  Review* 1:3–7.
  1958b "Research on Racial Relations: The United States of America."
  International Social Science Bulletin 10:403–447.
  1965 "Industrialization and Race Relations." Pp. 220–253 in G. Hunter (ed.),
  Industrialization and Race Relations: A Symposium. London: Oxford
  University Press.
Bobo, L.
  1983 "Whites' Opposition to Busing: Symbolic Racism Ordeal Group
  Conflict" *Journal of Personality and Social Psychology* 45:1196–1210.
Bodenhausen, G. V. and R. S. Wyer, Jr.
  1985 "Effects of Stereotypes on Decision Making and Information-
  Processing Strategies." *Journal of Personality and Social Psychology*
  48:267–282.
Bodnar, J.
  1977 *Immigration and Industrialization: Ethnicity in an American Mill Town,
  1870–1940.* Pittsburgh: University of Pittsburgh Press.
  1985 *The Transplanted: A History of Immigrants in Urban America.*
  Bloomington: Indiana University Press.

Bodnar, J., R. Simon, and M. Weber
1982 *Lives of Their Own: Blacks, Italians, and Poles in Pittsburgh, 1900–1960.*
Urbana: University of Illinois Press.
Bogardus, E. S.
1928 *Immigration and Race Attitudes.* Boston: D. C. Heath and Company.
1930 "A Race-Relations Cycle." *American Journal of Sociology* 35:612–617.
1958 "Racial Distance Changes in the United States During the Past Thirty
Years." *Sociology and Social Research* 43:127–135.
1967 *A Forty-Year Racial Distance Study.* Los Angeles: University of Southern
California Press.
1968 "Comparing Racial Distance in Ethiopia, South Africa, and the United
States." *Sociology and Social Research* 52:149–156.
Bonacich, E.
1972 "A Theory of Ethnic Antagonism: The Split-Labor Market." *American
Sociological Review* 37(October):547–559.
1973 "A Theory of Middleman Minorities." *American Sociological Review*
38(October):583–594.
1975 "Abolition, the Extension of Slavery, and the Position of Free Blacks: A
Study of Split Labor Markets in the United States, 1830–1863." *American
Journal of Sociology* 81:601–628.
1976 "Advanced Capitalism and Black/White Relations in the United States:
A Split-Labor Market Interpretation." *American Sociological Review* 41
(February):34–51.
Bonacich, E. and T. H. Jung
1982 "A Portrait of Korean Small Businesses in Los Angeles: 1977." Pp.
75–98 in E. Y. Yu, E. H. Phillips, and E. S. Yang (eds.), *Koreans in Los
Angeles: Prospects and Promises.* Los Angeles: Koryo Research Institute,
California State University, Los Angeles.
Borjas, G. J. and M. Tienda
1987 "The Economic Consequences of Immigration." *Science*, February 6,
1987.
Boswell, T. D. and J. R. Curtis
1983 *The Cuban-American Experience: Culture, Images, and Perspectives.*
Totowa, NJ: Rowman and Allanheld, Publishers.
Boyd, M.
1989 "Family and Personal Networks in International Migration: Recent
Developments and New Agendas." *International Migration Review*
23:638–670.
Braudel, F.
1984 *Civilization and Capitalism.* Volume III, The Perspective of the World.
(Translated by Siân Reynolds.) London: Collins.
Breton, R.
1964 "Institutional Completeness of Ethnic Communities and the
Personal Relations of Immigrants." *American Journal of Sociology*
70:193–205.
Broom, L. and N. Glenn
1965 *Transformation of the Negro American.* New York: Harper & Row.

565

Brown, H.

1985 *People, Groups and Society.* Milton Keynes: UK: Open University Press.

Brown, R.

1986 *Social Psychology.* The Second Edition. New York: The Free Press.

Brown, T. N.

1966 *Irish-American Nationalism, 1870–1890.* Philadelphia: J. B. Lippincott Company.

Brown, W. O.

1931 "The Nature of Race Consciousness." *Social Forces* 10:90–97.

1934 "Culture Contact and Race Conflict." Pp. 34–37 in E. B. Reuter (ed.), *Race and Culture Contacts.* New York: McGraw-Hill Publishing Company.

Browning, H. L. and N. Rodriquez

1985 "Chapter 9: The Migration of Mexican Indocumentos as a Settlement Process: Implications for Work." Pp. 277–297 in G. J. Borjas and M. Tienda (eds.), *Hispanics in the U. S. Economy.* Orlando, FL: Academic Press.

Buaken, M.

1948 *I Have Lived with the American People.* Caldwell, ID: The Caxton Printers, Ltd.

Buckley, W.

1967 *Sociology and Modern Systems Theory.* Englewood Cliffs, NJ: Prentice-Hall, Inc.

Bukowczyk, J. J.

1987 *And My Children Did Not Know Me: A History of Polish-Americans.* Bloomington: Indiana University Press.

Burling, R.

1965 *Hill Farms and Paddie Fields: Life in Mainland Southeast Asia.* Englewood Cliffs, NJ: Prentice-Hall, Inc.

Byington, M.

1910 *Homestead: The Households of a Mill Town.* New York: The Russell Sage Foundation.

Cady, J. F.

1964 *Southeast Asia: Its Historical Development.* New York: McGraw-Hill Book Company.

Campbell, D. T.

1963 "Social Attitudes and Other Acquired Behavioral Dispositions." Pp. 94–172 in S. Koch (ed.), *Psychology: A Study of a Science.* New York: McGraw-Hill Book Company.

Cantor, N. and W. Mischel

1977 "Traits as Prototypes: Effects of Recognition Memory." *Journal of Personality and Social Psychology* 35:38–48.

1979 "Prototypicality and Personality: Effect on Free Recall and Personality Impressions." *Journal of Research in Personality* 13:187–205.

Carmichael, S. and C. V. Hamilton

1967 *Black Power: The Politics of Liberation in America.* New York: Random House, Inc.

Cash, W. J.

1960 *The Mind of the South.* New York: Vintage Books.

Chamberlain, H.S.
 1911 *Foundations of the Nineteenth Century.* (Translated by John Lees.)
    London: John Lane.
Chan, S.
 1991 *Asian Americans: An Interpretive History.* Boston: Twayne Publishers.
Chang, E.
 1988 "Korean Community Politics in Los Angeles: The Impact of the
    Kwangju Uprising." *Amerasia* 14:51–67.
Chapman, L. J. and D. T. Campbell
 1957 "Response Set in the F Scale." *Journal of Abnormal and Social Psychology*
    54:129–132.
Chein, I.
 1948 "Behavior Theory and the Behavior of Attitudes: Some Critical
    Comments." *Psychological Review* 55:175–188.
Child, I. L.
 1943 *Italian or American? The Second Generation in Conflict.* New Haven: Yale
    University Press.
Choy, B.
 1979 *Koreans in America.* Chicago: Nelson-Hall.
Clark, K. B. and M. K. Clark
 1947 "Racial Identification and Preference in Negro Children." In T.
    Newcomb and E. Hartley (eds.), *Readings in Social Psychology.* New York:
    Holt.
Cohen, E. G. and S. S. Roper
 1972 "Modification of Interracial Interaction Disability: An Application of
    Status Characteristic Theory." *American Sociological Review* 37:643–657.
Cohen, S. M.
 1988 *American Assimilation or Jewish Revival?* Bloomington: Indiana
    University Press.
Coleman, J. S.
 1974 *Power and the Structure of Society.* New York: W. W. Norton &
    Company, Inc.
Coleman, J. S., E. Q. Campbell, C. J. Hobson, J. McPartland, A. Mood, F. D.
    Weinfeld, and R. L. York
 1966 *Equality of Educational Opportunity.* Washington, D.C.: Government
    Printing Office.
Collins, O.
 1946 "Ethnic Behavior in Industry: Sponsorship and Rejection in a New
    England Factory." *American Journal of Sociology* 51:293–298.
Collins, R.
 1971 "Functional and Conflict Theories of Educational Stratification."
    American Sociological Review 36:1002–1019.
 1975 *Conflict Sociology: Toward an Explanatory Science.* New York: Academic
    Press, Inc.
Columbus, C.
 1906 "Letter from Columbus to Luis Santangel." Pp. 264–270 in Julius E.
    Olson and Edward Gaylord Bourne (eds.), *The Northmen, Columbus and*

Cabot, 985–1503. Early Narratives of American History Series. New York: Charles Scribners Sons.

Connery, D. S.

1970 *The Irish*. Revised Edition. New York: Simon and Schuster.

Connor, W.

1985 "Who Are the Mexican-Americans?" Pp. 3–28 in W. Connor (ed.), *Americans in Comparative Perspective*. Washington, DC: The Urban Institute Press.

Cordasco, F.

1980 *Italian Mass Emigration*. Totowa, NJ: Rowman and Littlefield.

Cornelius, W. A. and R. A. Montoya (eds.)

1983 *America's New Immigration Law: Origins, Rationales and Potential Consequences*. Center for U.S.-Mexican Studies, University of California, San Diego.

Coser, L.

1956 *The Functions of Social Conflict*. Glencoe, IL: Free Press.

Couch, A. and K. Keniston

1960 "Yeasayers and Naysayers: Agreeing Response Set as a Personality Variable." *Journal of Abnormal and Social Psychology* 60:151–174.

Cox, O. C.

1948 *Caste, Class, and Race*. Garden City, NY: Doubleday and Company Inc.

Cravens, H.

1971 "The Abandonment of Evolutionary Social Theory in America: The Impact of Academic Professionalization upon American Sociological Theory 1890–1920." *American Studies* 12(Fall):5–20.

Crow Dog, M. and R. Erodes

1990 *Lakota Woman*. New York: Grove Weidenfeld.

Cruse, H.

1967 *The Crisis of the Negro Intellectual*. New York: William Morrow and Company, Inc.

Curtis, J.

1971 "Voluntary Association Joining: A Cross-National Comparative Note." *American Sociological Review* 36:872–880.

Dahrendorf, R.

1959 *Class and Class Conflict in Industrial Society*. Stanford: Stanford University Press.

D'Andrade, R.

1987 "A Folk Model of the Mind." Pp. 112–148 in D. Holland and N. Quinn (eds.), *Cultural Models in Language and Thought*. Cambridge: Cambridge University Press.

Daniels, R.

1969 *The Politics of Prejudice*. New York: Atheneum Publishers.

1971 *Concentration Camps USA, Japanese Americans and World War II*. New York: Holt, Rinehart and Winston, Inc.

1974 "The Japanese American Experience 1890–1940." Pp. 214–235 in R. Gomez, C. Cottinghan, Jr., R. Endo and K. Jackson (eds.), *The Social Reality of Ethnic America*. Lexington, MA: D. C. Heath and Company.

1988 *Asian Americans: Chinese and Japanese in the United States Since 1850.*
Seattle: University of Washington Press.

Darwin, C.
1859 *On the Origin of the Species by Means of Natural Selection.* London: J.
Murray.

Davie, M. R.
1936 *World Immigration.* New York: The Macmillan Company.

Davis, A. and J. Dollard
1940 *Children of Bondage.* Washington, DC: American Council on Education.

Davis, A., B. B. Gardner, and M. R. Gardner
1941 *Deep South.* Chicago: University of Chicago Press.

Davis, K. and W. Moore
1945 "Some Principles of Stratification." *American Sociological Review*
10:242–249.

Dearman, M.
1982 "Structure and Function of Religion in the Los Angeles Korean
Community: Some Aspects." Pp. 163–183 in E. Y. Yu, E. H. Phillips, and E.
S. Yang (eds.), *Koreans in Los Angeles: Prospects and Promises.* Los Angeles:
Koryo Research Institute, California State University, Los Angeles.

Deaux, K. and L. L. Lewis
1984 "Structure of Gender Stereotypes: Interrelationships among Components
and Gender Level." *Journal of Personality and Social Psychology* 46:991–1004.

DeFleur, M. L. and F. R. Westie
1963 "Attitude as a Scientific Concept." *Social Forces* 42:17–31.

de Gobineau, A.
1854/1915 *The Inequality of Human Races.* (Translated by Adrian Collins.)
New York: G. P. Putnam.

DeGre, G.
1964 "Freedom and Social Structure." *American Sociological Review* 11:529–536.

De La Garza, R.
1985 "As American as Tamale Pie: Mexican-American Political Mobilization
and the Loyalty Question." Pp. 227–244 in W. Connor (ed.), *Mexican-
Americans in Comparative Perspective.* Washington, DC: The Urban Institute
Press.

de Lapouge, G. V.
1896 *Les Selections Sociales.* Paris: A. Fontemoing.

Despres, L. A.
1975 "Toward a Theory of Ethnic Phenomena." Pp. 187–207 in L. A. Despres
(ed.), *Ethnicity and Resource Competition in Plural Societies.* The Hague:
Mouton Publishers.

DeVos, G.
1975 "Ethnic Pluralism: Conflict and Accommodation." Pp. 5–41 in G.
DeVos and L. Romanucci-Ross (eds.), *Ethnic Identity: Cultural Continuities
and Change.* Palo Alto, CA: Mayfield Publishing Company.

Diner, H. R.
1983 *Erin's Daughters in America: Irish Immigrant Women in the Nineteenth
Century.* Baltimore: The Johns Hopkins University Press.

Doise, W.
  1986 *Levels of Explanation in Social Psychology*. Cambridge: Cambridge
    University Press.
Dollard, J.
  1957 *Caste and Class in a Southern Town*. Third Edition. New York: Double-
    day and Company, Inc.
Donato, K. M. and A. Tyree
  1986 "Family Reunification, Health Professionals, and the Sex Composition
    of Immigrants to the United States." *Sociology and Social Research* 70:226–230.
Doob, L. W.
  1947 "The Behavior of Attitudes." *Psychological Review* 54:135–156.
Dorris, M. A.
  1981 "The Grass Still Grows, the Rivers Still Flow: Contemporary Native
    Americans." *Daedulus* 110 (Spring):43–69.
Dotson, F.
  1951 "Patterns of Voluntary Associations among Urban Working-Class
    Families." *American Sociological Review* 16:687–693.
Dozier, E. P.
  1966 "Problem Drinking among American Indians—the Role of
    Sociocultural Deprivation." *Quarterly Journal Studies on Alcohol* 27:72–78.
Drake, S. C. and H. R. Cayton
  1945 *Black Metropolis: A Study of Negro Life in a Northern City*. New York:
    Harcourt, Brace and Company.
Driedger, L. and G. Church
  1974 "Residential Segregation and Institutional Completeness: A Compari-
    son of Ethnic Minorities." *Canadian Review of Sociology and Anthropology*
    2:30–52.
Du Bois, W. E. B.
  1935 *Black Reconstruction*. New York: Harcourt, Brace and Company.
Durkheim, E.
  1893/1947 *The Division of Labor in Society*. (Translated by George Simpson.)
    Glencoe, IL: Free Press.
Dworkin, A. G. and R. J. Dworkin.
  1976 *The Minority Report*. New York: Praeger Publishers.
Edwards, H.
  1969 *The Revolt of the Black Athlete*. New York: The Free Press.
Eggebeen, D. J. and D. T. Lichter
  1991 "Race, Family Structure and Changing Poverty among American
    Children." *American Sociological Review* 56:801–817.
Eitzen, I. S. and G. H. Sage
  1982 *Sociology of American Sport*. Second Edition. Dubuque, IA: Wm C.
    Brown Company Publishers.
Ellison, R.
  1953/1964 *Shadow and Act*. New York: Random House. 1964.
Essien-Udom, E. U.
  1962 *Black Nationalism: A Search for an Identity in America*. Chicago:
    University of Chicago Press.

Etzioni, A.
 1959 "The Ghetto—A Re-evaluation." *Social Forces* 37:255–262.
Fagen, R. R., R. A. Brody, and T. J. O'Leary
 1968 *Cubans in Exile: Disaffection and the Revolution*. Stanford: Stanford
  University Press.
Falcon, A.
 1984 "A History of Puerto Rican Politics in New York City: 1860s to 1945."
  Pp. 15–42 in J. Jennings and M. Rivera, (eds.), *Puerto Rican Politics in Urban
  America*. Westport, CT: Greenwood Press.
Fallows, M. R.
 1979 *Irish Americans: Identity and Assimilation*. Englewood Cliffs, NJ: Prentice-
  Hall, Inc.
Fanon, F.
 1963 *The Wretched of the Earth*. New York: Grove Press, Inc.
Farley, R.
 1977 "Trends in Racial Inequalities: Have the Gains of the 1960s Disappeared in the 1970s?" *American Sociological Review* 42:189–208.
Feagin, J. R.
 1989 *Racial and Ethnic Relations*. Third Edition. Englewood Cliffs, NJ:
  Prentice-Hall, Inc.
Fein, R.
 1965 "An Economic and Social Profile of the Negro American." *Daedalus*
  94:815–846.
Fenton, W. N.
 1978 "Northern Iroquoian Culture Patterns." Pp. 296–321 in B. C. Trigger
  (ed.), *Handbook of North American Indians*, Volume 15: Northeast. Washington, DC: Smithsonian Institution.
Festinger, L.
 1954 "A Theory of Social Comparison." *Human Relations* 7:117–140.
 1957 *A Theory of Cognitive Dissonance*. Evanston, IL: Row, Peterson.
 1964 *Conflict, Decision, and Dissonance*. Stanford: Stanford University Press.
Fishbein, M. (ed.)
 1967 *Readings in Attitude Theory and Measurement*. New York: John Wiley and
  Sons, Inc.
Fitzpatrick, J. P.
 1971/1987 *Puerto Rican Americans*. Englewood Cliffs, NJ: Prentice-Hall, Inc.
Flavell, J. H.
 1963 *The Developmental Psychology of Jean Piaget*. New York: Van Nostrand
  Reinhold Company.
Fogel, R. W.
 1989 *Without Consent or Contract: The Rise and Fall of American Slavery*.
  New York: W. W. Norton and Company.
Fogel, R. W. and S. L. Engerman
 1974 *Time on the Cross: The Economics of American Negro Slavery*. Boston:
  Little, Brown and Company.
Foley, D. E.
 1988 *From Peones to Politicos: Class and Ethnicity in a South Texas Town,*

1900–1987. Revised and Enlarged Edition. Austin: University of Texas Press.

Forbes, J. D. (ed.)

1964 *The Indian in America's Past*. Englewood Cliffs, NJ: Prentice-Hall, Inc.

Foskett, J. M.

1955 "Social Structure and Social Participation." *American Sociological Review* 20:431–438.

Fox, P.

1970 *The Poles in America*. New York: Arno Press.

Frazier, E. F.

1939 *The Negro Family in the United States*. Chicago: University of Chicago Press.

1947 "Sociological Theory and Race Relations." *American Sociological Review* 12(June):265–271.

1949 *The Negro in the United States*. New York: Macmillan Company.

1957 *Black Bourgeoisie*. Glencoe, IL: Free Press.

Frenkel-Brunswik, E.

1948 "A Study of Prejudice in Children." *Human Relations* 1:295–306.

Frisby, D.

1986 *Fragments of Modernity*. Cambridge, MA: The MIT Press.

Fuchs, E. and R. J. Havighurst

1972 *To Live on This Earth: American Indian Education*. Garden City, NY: Doubleday and Company, Inc.

Galbraith, J. K.

1971 *The New Industrial State*. Boston: Houghton Mifflin.

Gans, H. J.

1959 "Park Forest: Birth of a Jewish Community." *Commentary* 21:330–339.

1979 "Symbolic Ethnicity: The Future of Ethnic Groups and Cultures in America." *Ethnic and Racial Studies* 2:1–20.

Geschwender, J.

1978 *Racial Stratification in America*. Dubuque, IA: Wm C. Brown Company Publishers.

Glazer, N.

1954 "Ethnic Groups in America: From National Culture to Ideology." Pp. 158–173 in M. Berger (ed.), *Freedom and Control in Modern Society*. New York: Octagon Books, Inc.

1957 *American Judaism*. Chicago: University of Chicago Press.

1971 "Blacks and Ethnic Groups: The Difference and the Political Difference It Makes." *Social Problems* 18:444–461.

Glazer, N. and D. P. Moynihan

1963/1970 *Beyond the Melting Pot: The Negroes, Puerto Ricans, Jews, Italians, and Irish of New York City*. Cambridge, MA: The M.I.T. Press.

1975 "Introduction." Pp. 1–26 in N. Glazer and D. P. Moynihan (eds.), *Ethnicity: Theory and Experience*. Cambridge, MA: Harvard University Press.

Glenn, E. N.

1986 *Issei, Nisei, War Bride: Three Generations of Japanese American Women in Domestic Service*. Philadelphia: Temple University Press.

Glenn, N. D.
  1965 "The Role of White Resistance and Facilitation in the Negro Struggle
    for Equality." *Phylon* 26:105–116.
Goffman, E.
  1961 *Asylums*. Garden City, New York: Doubleday and Company, Inc.
Gooch, J.
  1986 *The Unification of Italy*. London: Methuen.
Goodman, M. E.
  1946 "Evidence Concerning the Genesis of Interracial Attitudes." *American
    Anthropologist* 48:624–630.
  1952 *Racial Awareness in Young Children*. Reading, MA: Addison-Wesley
    Publishing Company.
Gordon, C.
  1969 *Looking Ahead*. Washington, D.C.: American Sociological Association.
Gordon, M.
  1964 *Assimilation in American Life*. New York: Oxford University Press.
Grant, B.
  1979 *The Boat People*. New York: Penguin Books.
Grant, M.
  1916 *The Passing of the Great Race*. New York: C. Scribner's Sons.
Grant, P. R. and J. G. Holmes
  1981 "The Integration of Implicit Personality Theory Schemas and Stereo-
    type Images." *Social Psychology Quarterly* 44:107–115.
  1982 "The Influence of Stereotypes in Impression Formations: A Reply to
    Locksley, Hepburn, and Ortz." *Social Psychology Quarterly* 45:274–276.
Grebler, L., J. W. Moore, and R. C. Guzman
  1970 *The Mexican-American People: The Nation's Second Largest Minority*. New
    York: Free Press.
Greeley, A.
  1970 "Religious Intermarriage in a Denominational Society." *American
    Journal of Sociology* 75:949–952.
Greeley, A. M.
  1974 *Ethnicity in the United States: A Preliminary Reconnaissance*. New York:
    John Wiley and Sons, Inc.
  1981 *The Irish Americans: The Rise to Money and Power*. New York: Harper &
    Row.
Greenstein, R. L.
  1985 "Losing Faith in 'Losing Ground'." *The New Republic*, March 25.
Greenwald, H. J. and D. P. Oppenheim
  1968 "Reported Magnitude of Self-Misidentification among Negro Child-
    ren—Artifact?" *Journal of Personality and Social Psychology* 8:49–52.
Gregor, A. J.
  1963 "Science and Social Change: A Review of K. B. Clark's 'Prejudice and
    Your Child.'" *Mankind Quarterly* 3:229–237.
Gregor, A. J. and D. A. McPherson
  1966 "Racial Attitudes among White and Negro Children in a Deep South
    Standard Metropolitan Area." *Journal of Social Psychology* 68:95–106.

Grenier, G.
  1985 "Shifts to English As Usual Language by Americans of Spanish Mother Tongue." Pp. 346–358 in R. O. De La Garza, F. E Bean, C. M. Bonjean, R. Romo, and R. Alvarez (eds.), *The Mexican American Experience: An Interdisciplinary Anthology*. Austin: University of Texas Press.
Griffin, W. D.
  1973 *The Irish in America, 550–1972: A Chronology and Fact Book*. Dobbs Ferry, NY: Oceana Publications, Inc.
Griswold Del Castillo, R.
  1984 *La Familia: Chicano Families in the Urban Southwest: 1848 to the Present*. Notre Dame: University of Notre Dame Press.
Gross, E. R.
  1989 *Contemporary Federal Policy toward American Indians*. New York: Greenwood Press.
Grzelonski, B.
  1976 *Poles in the United States of America, 1776–1865*. Warsaw: Interpress.
Guest, A. M. and J. A. Weed
  1976 "Ethnic Residential Segregation: Patterns of Change." *American Journal of Sociology* 81:1088–1111.
Gumplowicz, L.
  1899 *The Outlines of Sociology*. (Translated by Frederick W. Moore.) Philadelphia: American Academy of Political and Social Science.
Gurak, D. T. and J. P. Fitzpatrick
  1982 "Intermarriage among Hispanic Ethnic Groups in New York City." *American Journal of Sociology* 87:921–934.
Gutman, H. L. G.
  1975 *Slavery and the Numbers Game*. Urbana: University of Illinois Press.
  1976 *The Black Family in Slavery and Freedom, 1750–1925*. New York: Pantheon Books.
Guttentag, M. and P. F. Secord
  1983 *Too Many Women?* Beverly Hills, CA: Sage Publications.
Haak, R. O.
  1970 "Co-opting the Oppressors: The Case of Japanese Americans." *Society* 7:23–31.
Hagendoorn, L. and J. Hraba
  1987 "Social Distance toward Holland's Minorities: Discrimination against and among Ethnic Outgroups." *Ethnic and Racial Studies* 10:317–333.
  1989 "Foreign, Different, Deviant, Seclusive and Working Class: Anchors to an Ethnic Hierarchy in Holland." *Ethnic and Racial Studies* 12:441–468.
Hamilton, D. L. (ed.)
  1981 *Cognitive Processes in Stereotyping and Intergroup Behavior*. Hillsdale, NJ: Lawrence Erlbaum Associates.
Hammerback, J. C., R. J. Jensen, and J. A. Guitierrez
  1985 *A War of Words: Chicano Protest in the 1960s and 1970s*. Westport, CT: Greenwood Press.
Handlin, O.
  1957 *Race and Nationality in American Life*. Boston: Little, Brown and Company.
  1973 *The Uprooted*. Second Edition. Boston: Little, Brown and Company.

Hannan, M.
   1979 "The Dynamics of Ethnic Boundaries in Modern States." Pp. 253–275 in
       J. Meyer and M. Hannan (eds.), *National Development and the World System:*
       Educational, Economic, and Political Change, 1950–1970. Chicago: University
       of Chicago Press.
Hannerz, U.
   1969 *Soulside.* New York: Columbia University Press.
Hansen, M. L.
   1940 *The Immigrant in American History.* New York: Harper & Row.
Harding, J., H. Proshansky, B. Kutner, and I. Chen
   1969 "Prejudice and Ethnic Relations." Pp. 1–76 in G. Lindzey and E.
       Aronson (eds.), *The Handbook of Social Psychology.* Second Edition. Reading,
       MA: Addison-Wesley Publishing Company, Inc.
Harris, M.
   1964/1974 *Patterns of Race in the Americas.* New York: W. W. Norton and
       Company, Inc.
Hatada, T.
   1969 *A History of Korea.* (Translated and edited by W. W. Smith, Jr., and B. H.
       Hazard.) Santa Barbara, CA: ABC-Clio, Inc.
Hauser, P.
   1964 "Labor Force." Pp. 160–190 in Robert E. L. Faris (ed.), *Handbook of*
       Modern Sociology. Chicago: Rand McNally and Company.
Havighurst, R. J.
   1977 "Indian Education Since 1960." Paper presented at the Meeting of the
       American Sociological Association, Chicago, September 5, 1977.
Hawk, E. T.
   1934 *Economic History of the South.* New York: Prentice-Hall, Inc.
Hechter, M.
   1974 "The Political Economy of Ethnic Change." *American Journal of Sociology*
       79:1151–1178.
Heiss, J, and S. Owens
   1972 "Self-Evaluations of Blacks and Whites." *American Journal of Sociology*
       78:360–370.
Henri, F.
   1975 *Black Migration: Movement North, 1900–1920.* Garden City, NY: Anchor
       Press/Doubleday.
Herberg, W.
   1955 *Protestant-Catholic-Jew.* Garden City, New York: Doubleday and
       Company, Inc.
   1964 "The Triple Melting Pot in the Third Generation: From Ethnic to Reli-
       gious Diversity." Pp. 99–104 in R. L. Simpson and I. Harper Simpson
       (eds.), *Social Organization and Behavior.* New York: John Wiley & Sons, Inc.
Herbert, D. T. and H. Tritt
   1984 *Corporations of Corruption.* Springfield, IL: Charles C Thomas, Publisher.
Herbst, A.
   1932 *The Negro in the Slaughtering and Meat-Packing Industry in Chicago.*
       Boston: Houghton Mifflin Company.

575

Hill, R. B.
  1972 "The Strengths of Black Families." Pp. 262–290 in D. G. Bromley and C.
    F. Longino, Jr., (eds.), *White Racism and Black Americans.* Cambridge, MA:
    Schenkman Publishing Company, Inc.
Himes, J. S.
  1966 "The Functions of Racial Conflict." *Social Forces* 45(September):1–16.
Hirschman, C.
  1983 "America's Melting Pot Reconsidered." *Annual Review of Sociology*
    9:397–423.
Hirschman, C. and M. G. Wong
  1984 "Socioeconomic Gains of Asian Americans, Blacks, and Hispanics."
    American Journal of Sociology 90:584–607.
Hofstadter, R.
  1944 *Social Darwinism in American Thought, 1860–1915.* Philadelphia:
    University of Pennsylvania Press.
Hollingshead, A. B.
  1950 "Cultural Factors in the Selection of Marriage Mates." *American
    Sociological Review* 15:619–677.
  1961 "A Re-examination of Ecological Theory." In George A. Theodorson
    (ed.), *Studies in Human Ecology.* New York: Harper & Row.
Holt, G. S.
  1972 "Stylin' Outta the Black Pulpit." Pp. 189–204 in T. Kochman (ed.),
    Rappin' and Stylin' Out. Urbana: University of Illinois Press.
Homans, G. C.
  1950 *The Human Group.* New York: Harcourt, Brace.
Horowitz, D. L.
  1985a "Conflict and Accommodation: Mexican-Americans in the
    Cosmopolis." Pp. 58–103 in W. Connor (ed.), *Mexican-Americans in
    Comparative Perspective.* Washington, DC: The Urban Institute Press.
  1985b *Ethnic Groups in Conflict.* Berkeley: University of California Press.
Horton, J.
  1966 "Order and Conflict Theories of Social Problems as Competing
    Ideologies." *American Journal of Sociology* 71(May):701–713.
Hosokawa, B.
  1969 *Nisei: The Quiet Americans.* New York: William Morrow and Company.
Houstoun, M. F., R. G. Kramer, and J. M. Barrett
  1984 "Female Predominance in Immigration to the United States since 1930:
    A First Look." *International Migration Review* 18:908–963.
Hout, M.
  1984 "Occupational Mobility of Black Men: 1962 to 1973." *American
    Sociological Review* 49:308–322.
Hraba, J.
  1972 "The Doll Technique: A Measure of Racial Ethnocentrism?" *Social
    Forces* 50:522–527.
Hraba, J. and G. Grant
  1970 "Black Is Beautiful: A Reexamination of Racial Preference and Iden-
    tification." *Journal of Personality and Social Psychology* 16:398–402.

Hraba, J. and W. Mok
1990 "Ethnic Hierarchies as Social Representations: The Netherlands and the United States." Unpublished paper.
Hraba, J. and J. Siegman
1974 "Black Consciousness." *Youth and Society* 6:63–90.
Hraba, J., L. Hagendoorn, and R. Hagendoorn
1989 "The Ethnic Hierarchy in the Netherlands: Social Distance and Social Representation." *British Journal of Social Psychology* 28:57–69.
Hsu, F. L. K.
1971 *The Challenge of the American Dream: The Chinese in the United States.* Belmont, CA: Wadsworth Publishing Co.
Hughes, L.
1958 *The Langston Hughes Reader.* New York: George Brazier, Inc.
Hughes, M. and D. H. Demo
1989 "Self-Perceptions of Black Americans: Self-Esteem and Personal Efficacy." *American Journal of Sociology* 95:132–159.
Humfreville, J. L.
1964 "A Letter." Pp. 18–19 in Jack D. Forbes (ed.), *The Indian in America's Past.* Englewood Cliffs, NJ: Prentice-Hall, Inc.
Hurh, W. M. and K. C. Kim
1984 *Korean Immigrants in America: A Structural Analysis of Ethnic Confinement and Adhesive Adaptation.* London: Associated University Presses.
Hyman, H. H.
1954 "Inconsistencies as a Problem in Attitude Measurement." *Journal of Social Issues* 5:38–42.
Hyman, H. H. and P. B. Sheatsley
1954 "The Authoritarian Personality: A Methodological Critique." Pp. 50–122 in R. Christie and M. Jahoda (eds.), *Studies in the Scope and Method of the Authoritarian Personality.* Glencoe, IL: Free Press.
Ianni, F. A. J.
1972 *A Family Business: Kinship and Social Control in Organized Crime.* New York: Russell Sage Foundation.
Ima, K.
1976 "Japanese Americans: The Making of 'Good' People." Pp. 254–296 in A. G. Dworkin and R. J. Dworkin (eds.), *The Minority Report: An Introduction to Racial, Ethnic, and Gender Relations.* New York: Praeger Publishers.
Insko, C. A.
1967 *Theories of Attitude Change.* New York: Appleton-Century-Crofts.
Institute for Government Research.
1928 *The Problem of Indian Administration.* Under the technical direction of Lewis Meriam. Baltimore: Johns Hopkins Press.
Iorizzo, L. J. and S. Mondello
1971 *The Italian Americans.* New York: Twayne Publishers, Inc.
Ishi, T.
1988 "International Linkage and National Class Conflict: the Migration of Korean Nurses to the United States." *Amerasia* 14:23–50.

Iwata, M.
  1962 "The Japanese Immigrants in California Agriculture." *Agricultural History* 36:25–37.
Jaynes, G. D. and R. M. Williams, Jr.
  1989 *A Common Destiny: Blacks and American Society*. Washington, DC: National Academy Press.
Jerome, H.
  1926/1973 *Migration and the Business Cycle*. New York: National Bureau of Economic Research, Inc.
Johnson, C. S.
  1934 *Shadow of the Plantation*. Chicago: University of Chicago Press.
  1939 "Race Relations and Social Change." Pp. 271–303 in E. I. Thompson (ed.), *Race Relations and the Race Problem: A Definition and Analysis*. Durham, NC: Duke University Press.
Johnson, D. M. and R. R. Campbell
  1981 *Black Migration in America: A Social Demographic History*. Durham, NC: Duke University Press.
Jones, J.
  1985 *Labor of Love, Labor of Sorrow: Black Women, Work, and the Family from Slavery to the Present*. New York: Basic Books.
Jones, L. R.
  1963 *Blues People*. New York: William Morrow and Company.
Jones, M. A.
  1960 *American Immigration*. Chicago: University of Chicago Press.
Josephy, A. M., Jr.
  1969 *The Indian Heritage of America*. New York: Alfred A. Knopf, Inc.
  1982 *Now That the Buffalo's Gone: A Study of Today's American Indians*. New York: Alfred A. Knopf.
Kan, S.
  1989 *Symbolic Immortality: The Tlingit Potlatch of the Nineteenth Century*. Washington, D.C. : Smithsonian Institution Press.
Kane, R. L. and R. A. Kane
  1972 *Federal Health Care (with Reservations!)*. New York: Springer Publishing Company, Inc.
Kantrowitz, N.
  1969 "Segregation in New York City, 1960." *American Journal of Sociology* 74:685–695.
Kardiner, A. and L. Ovesey
  1951 *The Mark of Oppression: Explorations in the Personality of the American Negro*. New York: Norton.
Katz, D.
  1960 "The Functional Approach to the Study of Attitudes." *Public Opinion Quarterly* 24:163–204.
Kaufman, R. L.
  1983 "A Structural Decomposition of Black-White Earnings Differentials." *American Journal of Sociology* 89:585–611.

Keefe, S. E. and A. M. Padilla
  1987 *Chicano Ethnicity*. Albuquerque: University of New Mexico Press.
Kelly, G. P.
  1977 *From Vietnam to America*. Boulder, CO: Westview Press.
Kennedy, R. E., Jr.
  1973 *The Irish: Emigration, Marriage, and Fertility*. Berkeley: University of
    California Press.
Kennedy, R. J. R.
  1944 "Single or Triple Melting Pot? Intermarriage Trends in New Haven,
    1870–1940." *American Journal of Sociology* 49:331–339.
  1952 "Single or Triple Melting Pot? Intermarriage in New Haven,
    1870–1950." *American Journal of Sociology* 58:56–59.
Key, V. O., Jr.
  1949 *Southern Politics: In State and Nation*. New York: Alfred A. Knopf,
    Inc.
Kidd, B.
  1894/1921 *Social Evolution*. New York: G. P. Putnam's Sons.
Kiesler, C. A., B. E. Collins, and N. Miller
  1969 *Attitude Change*. New York: John Wiley and Sons, Inc.
Kikumura, A. and H. H. L. Kitano
  1973 "Interracial Marriage: A Picture of the Japanese Americans." *The
    Journal of Social Issues* 29:67–81.
Killian, L. M.
  1953 "The Adjustment of Southern White Migrants to Northern Urban
    Norms." *Social Forces* 33:66–69.
Kim, H.
  1977a "Introduction." Pp. 3–8 in H. Kim (ed.), *The Korean Diaspora: Historical
    and Sociological Studies of Korean Immigration and Assimilation in North
    America*. Santa Barbara, CA: ABC-Clio.
  1977b "The History and Role of the Church in the Korean American
    Community." Pp. 47–63 in H. Kim (ed.), *The Korean Diaspora: Historical and
    Sociological Studies of Korean Immigration and Assimilation in North America*.
    Santa Barbara, CA: ABC-Clio.
  1977c "Korean Community Organizations in America: Their Characteristics
    and Problems." Pp. 65–83 in H. Kim (ed.), *The Korean Diaspora: Historical
    and Sociological Studies of Korean Immigration and Assimilation in North
    America*. Santa Barbara, CA: ABC-Clio.
  1977d "Ethnic Enterprises among Korean Immigrants in America." Pp.
    85–107 in H. Kim (ed.), *The Korean Diaspora: Historical and Sociological
    Studies of Korean Immigration and Assimilation in North America*. Santa
    Barbara: ABC-Clio.
Kim, H. and C. C. Mejia (eds.)
  1976 *The Filipinos in America, 1898–1974, A Chronology and Fact Book*. Dobbs
    Ferry, NY: Oceana Publications, Inc.
Kim, W. Y.
  1971 *Koreans in America*. Seoul: Po Chin Chai Printing Co., Ltd.

579

Kinder, D.
1986 "The Continuing American Dilemma: White Resistance to Racial Change 40 Years After Myrdal." *Journal of Social Issues* 42:151–171.
Kinder, D. and D. Sears
1981 "Prejudice and Politics: Symbolic Racism Versus Racial Threats to the Good Life." *Journal of Personality and Social Psychology* 40:414–431.
Kingston, M. H.
1980 *China Men*. New York: Alfred A. Knopf.
Kinlock, G. C.
1974 *The Dynamics of Race Relations: A Sociological Analysis*. New York: McGraw-Hill Book Company.
Kitano, H. H. L.
1969 *Japanese Americans: The Evolution of a Subculture*. Englewood Cliffs, NJ: Prentice-Hall, Inc.
1988 "The Japanese American Family." Pp. 258–275 in C. H. Mindel, R. W. Habenstein, and R. Wright, Jr. (eds.), *Ethnic Families in America: Patterns and Variations*. Third Edition. New York: Elsevier.
Kitano, H. H. L. and R. Daniels
1988 *Asian Americans: Emerging Minorities*. Englewood Cliffs, NJ: Prentice-Hall, Inc.
Kleinpenning, G. and L. Hagendoorn
1993 "Forms of Racism and the Cumulative Dimension of Ethnic Attitudes." *Social Psychology Quarterly* 56:21–36.
Knowles, L. L. and K. Prewitt (eds.)
1969 *Institutional Racism in America*. Englewood Cliffs, NJ: Prentice-Hall, Inc.
Kohlberg, L.
1968 "Stage and Sequence: The Cognitive-Developmental Approach to Socialization." Pp. 347–80 in D. A. Goslin (ed.), *Handbook of Socialization Theory and Research*. Chicago: Rand McNally and Company.
Kramer, J. R.
1970 *The American Minority Community*. New York: Thomas Y. Crowell Company.
Kwang, P.
1979 *Chinatown, New York: Labor and Politics, 1930–1950*. New York: Monthly Review Press.
Lamphere, L.
1987 *From Working Daughters to Working Mothers: Immigrant Women in a New England Industrial Community*. Ithaca: Cornell University Press.
Landale, N. S. and A. M. Guest
1990 "Generation, Ethnicity, and Occupational Opportunity in Late 19th Century America." *American Sociological Review* 55:280–296.
Landreth, C. and B. C. Johnson
1953 "Young Children's Responses to a Picture and Inset Test Designed to Reveal Reactions to Persons of Different Skin Color." *Child Development* 24:63–80.
Landry, B.
1977 "The Economic Position of Black Americans." Pp. 50–108 in H. R.

Kaplan (ed.), *American Minorities and Economic Opportunity*. ltasca, IL: F. E. Peacock Publishers, Inc.

1987 *The New Black Middle Class*. Berkeley: University of California Press.

LaPiere, R. T.

1934 "Attitudes vs. Actions." *Social Forces* 13:230–237.

Larzelere, A.

1988 *The 1980 Cuban Boatlift*. Washington, DC: National Defense University Press.

Lawrence, R. Z.

1985 "The Middle Class is Alive and Well." *The New York Times*, June 23.

Lee, C. and G. De Vos

1981 *Koreans in Japan: Ethnic Conflict and Accommodation*. Berkeley: University of California Press.

Lee, D.

1977 "A Study of Social Networks within Two Korean Communities in America." Pp. 155–166 in H. Kim (ed.), *The Korean Diaspora: Historical and Sociological Studies of Korean Immigration and Assimilation in North America*. Santa Barbara, CA: ABC-Clio.

Lee, R. H.

1960 *The Chinese in the United States*. Hong Kong: Hong Kong University Press.

Lemann, N.

1986 "The Origins of the Underclass." *The Atlantic Monthly*, June:31–55.

1991 *The Promised Land: The Great Black Migration and How It Changed America*. New York: Alfred A. Knopf.

Lenski, G.

1966 *Power and Privilege: A Theory of Social Stratification*. New York: McGraw-Hill Book Company.

Levine, G. N. and D. M. Montero

1973 "Socioeconomic Mobility among Three Generations of Japanese Americans." *Journal of Social Issues* 29:33–48.

LeVine, R. A. and D. T. Campbell

1972 *Ethnocentrism: Theories of Conflict, Ethnic Attitudes and Group Behavior*. New York: John Wiley and Sons, Inc.

Levitan, S. A., W. B. Johnston, and R. Taggart

1975 *Still a Dream: The Changing Status of Blacks Since 1960*. Cambridge, MA: Harvard University Press.

Levy, J. E. and S. J. Kunitz

1974 *Indian Drinking: Navajo Practices and Anglo-American Theories*. New York: John Wiley and Sons, Inc.

Lewis, O.

1961 *The Children of Sanchez*. New York: Random House.

Li, W. L.

1976 "Chinese Americans: Exclusion from the Melting Pot." Pp. 297–324 in A. G. Dworkin and R. J. Dworkin (eds.), *The Minority Report: An Introduction to Racial, Ethnic, and Gender Relations*. New York: Praeger Publishers.

Lichter, D. T.
  1988 "Racial Differences in Underemployment in American Cities."
    American Journal of Sociology 93:771–792.
Lieberson, S.
  1961 "A Societal Theory of Race and Ethnic Relations." *American Sociological
    Review* 26(December):902–910.
  1980 *A Piece of the Pie: Blacks and White Immigrants since 1880*. Berkeley:
    University of California Press.
Lieberson, S. and D. K. Carter
  1979 "Making It in America: Difference between Eminent Blacks and White
    Ethnic Groups." *American Sociological Review* 44:347–366.
Lieberson, S. and G. V. Fuguitt
  1967 "Negro-White Occupational Differences in the Absence of Discrim-
    ination." *American Journal of Sociology* 73: 188–200.
Lieberson, S. and M. C. Waters
  1985 "Ethnic Mixtures in the United States." *Sociology and Social Research*
    70:43–52.
  1988 *From Many Strands: Ethnic and Racial Groups in Contemporary America*.
    New York: Russell Sage Foundation.
Liebow, E.
  1967 *Talley's Corner*. Boston: Little, Brown and Company.
Light, I. J.
  1972 *Ethnic Enterprise in America*. Berkeley: University of California Press.
Light, I. and C. C. Wong
  1975 "Protest or Work: Dilemmas of the Tourist Industry in American
    Chinatowns." *American Journal of Sociology* 80:1342–1368.
Light, I. and E. Bonacich
  1988 *Immigrant Entrepreneurs: Koreans in Los Angeles, 1965–1982*. Berkeley:
    University of California Press.
Light, I., I. J. Kwuon, and D. Zhong
  1990 "Korean Rotating Credit Associations in Los Angeles." *Amerasia* 16:35–54.
Linden, F.
  1940 "Repercussions of Manufacturing in the AnteBellum South." *North
    Carolina Review* 17:313–331.
Lipmann, W.
  1922 *Public Opinion*. New York: Harcourt, Brace, Jovanovich, Inc.
Littlefield, D. F.
  1979 *Africans and Creeks: From the Colonial Period to the Civil War*. Westport,
    CT: Greenwood Press.
Llanes, Jose
  1982 *Cuban Americans: Masters of Survival*. Cambridge, MA: Abt Books.
Locksley, A., C. Hepburn, and V. Ortiz
  1982a "Social Stereotypes and Judgments of Individuals: An Instance of the
    Base-Rate Fallacy." *Journal of Experimental Social Psychology* 18:23–42.
  1982b "On Effects of Social Stereotypes on Judgments of Individuals: A
    Comment on Grant and Holmes's 'The Integration of Implicit Personality
    Schemas and Stereotype Images.'" *Social Psychology Quarterly* 45:270–273.

Loewen, J. W.
 1971 *The Mississippi Chinese: Between Black and White*. Cambridge, MA: Harvard University Press.
Lopata, H. Z.
 1976 *Polish Americans: Status, Competition in an Ethnic Community*. Englewood Cliffs, NJ: Prentice-Hall, Inc.
Lopreato, J.
 1970 *Italian Americans*. New York: Random House.
Lord, E., J. J. D. Trenor, and S. J. Barrows
 1970 *The Italian in America*. Freeport, NY: Books for Libraries Press.
Lyman, S. M.
 1972 *The Black American in Sociological Thought: A Failure of Perspective*. New York: Capricorn Books.
 1974 *Chinese Americans*. New York: Random House, Inc.
 1986 *Chinatown and Little Tokyo: Power, Conflict, and Community among Chinese and Japanese Immigrants in America*. Milwood, NY: Associated Faculty Press, Inc.
Maccoby, E. E., T. M. Newcomb, and E. L. Hartley (eds.)
 1958 *Readings in Social Psychology*. Third Edition. New York: Henry Holt and Co.
Malcolm X.
 1966 *The Autobiography of Malcolm X*. New York: Grove Press, Inc.
Mandle, J. R.
 1978 *The Roots of Black Poverty: The Southern Plantation Economy after the Civil War*. Durham: Duke University Press.
Mangiafico, L.
 1988 *Contemporary American Immigrants: Patterns of Filipino, Korean, and Chinese Settlement in the United States*. New York: Praeger.
Maril, R. L.
 1989 *Poorest of Americans: The Mexican Americans of the Lower Rio Grande Valley of Texas*. Notre Dame: University of Notre Dame Press.
Marshall, T. H.
 1950 *Citizenship and Social Class and Other Essays*. Cambridge, England: Cambridge University Press.
Martin, T.
 1983 *Marcus Garvey, Hero: A First Biography*. Dover, MA: The Majority Press.
Massey, D. S.
 1981 "Dimensions of the New Immigration to the United States and the Prospects for Assimilation." *Annual Review of Sociology* 7:57–85.
Massey, D. S. and B. P. Mullan
 1984 "Process of Hispanic and Black Assimilation." *American Journal of Sociology* 89:836–873.
Massey, D. S. and N. A. Denton
 1985 "Spatial Assimilation as a Socioeconomic Outcome." *American Sociological Review* 50:94–106.
 1988 "Suburbanization and Segregation in U.S. Metropolitan Areas." *American Journal of Sociology* 94:592–626.

583

Massey, D. S., R. Alacron, J. Durand, and H. Gonzalez
  1987 *Return to Aztlan*. Berkeley: University of California Press.
Matson, F. W.
  1966 *The Broken Image*. New York: Anchor Books.
Matthews, G.
  1987 *"Just A Housewife": The Rise and Fall of Domesticity in America*. New York: Oxford University Press.
McArthur, L. Z.
  1982 "Judging a Book by Its Cover: A Cognitive Analysis of the Relationship between Physical Appearance and Stereotyping." In A. H. Hastorf and A. M. Isen (eds.), *Cognitive Psychology*. New York: Elsevier.
McCaffrey, L. J.
  1976 *The Irish Diaspora in America*. Bloomington: Indiana University Press.
McCarthy, J. D. and W. L. Yancey
  1971 "Uncle Tom and Mr. Charlie: Metaphysical Pathos in the Study of Racism and Personal Disorganization." *American Journal of Sociology* 76:648–671.
McConahay, J. B. and J. Hough
  1976 "Symbolic Racism." *Journal of Social Issues* 32:23–45.
McConahay, J. B., B. B. Hardee, and V. Batts
  1981 "Has Racism Declined in America? It Depends on Who Is Asking and What Is Asked." *Journal of Conflict Resolution* 25:563–579.
McFee, M.
  1972 *Modern Blackfeet: Montanans on a Reservation*. New York: Holt, Rinehart, and Winston, Inc.
McLemore, S. D. and R. Romo
  1985 "The Origins and Development of the Mexican American People." Pp. 3–32 in R. O. De La Garza, F. D. Bean, C. M. Bonjean, R. Romo, and R. Alvarez (eds.), *The Mexican American Experience: An Interdisciplinary Anthology*. Austin: University of Texas Press.
McNickle, D.
  1962 *The Indian Tribes of the United States: Ethnic and Cultural Survival*. London: Oxford University Press.
  1972 "Indian and European: Indian-White Relations from Discovery to 1887." Pp. 75–86 in Deward E. Walker, Jr. (ed.), *The Emergent Native Americans*. Boston: Little, Brown and Company.
  1973 *Native American Tribalism: Indian Survivals and Renewals*. New York: Oxford University Press.
McPherson, J. M.
  1991 *Abraham Lincoln and the Second American Revolution*. New York: Oxford University Press.
McWilliams, C.
  1964 *Brothers under the Skin*. Revised Edition. Boston: Little, Brown and Company.
  1968 *North from Mexico: The Spanish-Speaking People of the United States*. New York: Greenwood Press, Inc.

Meier, A. and E. Rudwick
  1970 *From Plantation to Ghetto*. Revised Edition. New York: Hill and Wang, Inc.
Melendy, H. B.
  1977 *Asians in America: Filipinos, Koreans, and East Indians*. Boston: Twayne
    Publishers.
Merton, R. K.
  1949 "Discrimination and the American Creed." Pp. 99–126 in R. M. MacIver
    (ed.), *Discrimination and National Welfare*. New York: Harper & Row.
  1957 *Social Theory and Social Structure*. Revised Edition. Glencoe, IL: Free
    Press.
Messick, S. and D. Jackson
  1957 "Authoritarianism or Acquiescence in Bass's Data." *Journal of Abnormal
    and Social Psychology* 54:424–427.
Metzger, L. P.
  1971 "American Sociology and Black Assimilation: Conflicting Perspec-
    tives." *American Journal of Sociology* 76(January):627–647.
Mill, J. S.
  1859/1956 *On Liberty*. Indianapolis, IN: The Liberal Arts Press.
Miller, L.
  1967 *The Petitioners: The Story of the Supreme Court of the United States and the
    Negro*. New York: World Publishing Company.
Mills, C. W.
  1951 *White Collar*. New York: Oxford University Press.
  1957 *The Puerto Rican Journey*. New York: Russell and Russell.
  1963 *Power, Politics, and People*. New York: Oxford University Press.
Minard, R. D.
  1952 "Race Relationships in the Pocahontas Coal Fields." *Journal of Social
    Issues* 8(1):29–44.
Mirande, A.
  1985 *The Chicano Experience: An Alternative Perspective*. Notre Dame:
    University of Notre Dame Press.
  1987 *Gringo Justice*. Notre Dame: University of Notre Dame Press.
Mitchell, J. C.
  1956 *The Kalela Dance*. Manchester: Manchester University Press.
Molotch, H.
  1969 "Racial Integration in a Transition Community." *American Sociological
    Review* 34:878–893.
Montero, D.
  1979 *Vietnamese Americans: Patterns of Resettlement and Socioeconomic
    Adaptation in the United States*. Boulder, CO: Westview Press.
Moore, B., Jr.
  1970 "Progress, Revolution and Freedom." In M. Olson (ed.), *Power in
    Societies*. London: Macmillan.
Moore, J. W.
  1970a "Colonialism: The Case of the Mexican Americans." *Social Problems*
    17:463–472.

1970b *Mexican Americans*. Englewood Cliffs, NJ: Prentice-Hall, Inc.

1978 *Homeboys: Gangs, Drugs, and Prisons in the Barrios of Los Angeles*. Philadelphia: Temple University Press.

Moore, J. W. and H. Pachon

1985 *Hispanics in the United States*. Englewood Cliffs, NJ: Prentice-Hall, Inc.

Moraga, C.

1986 "From a Long Line of Vendidas: Chicanas and Feminism." Pp. 173–189 in T. de Hauretes (ed.), *Feminist Studies: Critical Studies*. Bloomington: Indiana University Press.

Morawska, E.

1985 *For Bread with Butter: The Life-Worlds of East Central Europeans in Johnstown, Pennsylvania, 1890–1940*. Cambridge, England: Cambridge University Press.

Morland, K. J.

1958 "Racial Recognition by Nursery School Children in Lynchburg, Virginia." *Social Forces* 37:132–137.

1963 "The Development of Racial Bias in Young Children." *Theory into Practice* 2:120–127.

1966 "A Comparison of Race Awareness in Northern and Southern Children." *American Journal of Orthopsychiatry* 36:22–31.

1969 "Racial Awareness among American and Hong Kong Chinese Children." *American Journal of Sociology* 75:360–375.

Moquin, W. and C. Van Doren (eds.)

1974 *Documentary History of the Italian Americans*. New York: Praeger Publishers.

Moynihan, D. P.

1965 *The Negro Family: The Case for National Action*. Washington, DC: Office of Policy Planning and Research, United States Department of Labor.

1972 "The Tangle of Pathology." Pp. 197–218 in D. G. Bromley and C. F. Longino (eds.), *White Racism and Black Americans*. Cambridge, MA: Schenkman Publishing Company, Inc.

Muller, T. and T. J. Espenshade

1985 *The Fourth Wave: California's Newest Immigrants*. Washington, DC: The Urban Institute.

Munoz, A. N.

1971 *The Filipinos in America*. Los Angeles: Mountainview Publishers, Inc.

Murray, C.

1984 *Losing Ground: American Social Policy, 1950–1980*. New York: Basic Books.

Myrdal, G.

1944 *An American Dilemma: The Negro Problem and Modern Democracy*. New York: Harper & Row.

National Advisory Commission on Civil Disorders

1968 *Report of the National Advisory Commission on Civil Disorders*. New York: Bantam Books, Inc.

Nee, V. G. and B. B. Nee

1972 *Longtime Californ': A Documentary Study of an American Chinatown*. New York: Pantheon Books.

Neihardt, J. G.
  1961 *Black Elk Speaks, Being the Life Story of a Holy Man of the Oglala Sioux.*
  Lincoln: University of Nebraska Press.
Nelli, H. S.
  1983 *From Immigrants to Ethnics: The Italian Americans.* Oxford: Oxford
  University Press.
Newcomer, M.
  1955 *The Big Business Executive: The Factors That Made Him, 1900–1950.* New
  York: Columbia University Press.
Newman, W. M.
  1973 *American Pluralism.* New York: Harper & Row.
Nisbet, R.
  1975 *Twilight of Authority.* New York: Oxford University Press.
Noel, D. L.
  1968 "A Theory of the Origin of Ethnic Stratification." *Social Problems*
  16(Fall):157–172.
Norton, E. H.
  1985 "Restoring the Traditional Black Family." *The New York Times Magazine,*
  June 2, pp. 43–98.
Novak, M.
  1971 *The Rise of the Unmeltable Ethnics.* New York: Macmillan Publishing Co., Inc.
Oberg, K.
  1973 *The Social Economy of the Tlingit Indians.* Seattle: University of
  Washington Press.
Oberschall, A.
  1972 "The Institutionalization of American Sociology." Pp. 187–251 in A.
  Oberschall (ed.), *The Establishment of Empirical Sociology.* New York: Harper
  & Row.
O'Hare, W. P., K. M. Pollard, T. L. Mann, and M. M. Kent
  1991 "African Americans in the 1990s." *PRB Population Bulletin.* Washington,
  DC: Population Reference Bureau, Inc.
O'Kane, J. M.
  1969 "Ethnic Mobility and the Lower-Income Negro: A Socio-Historical
  Perspective." *Social Problems* 16:302–311.
Olmsted, F. L.
  1857 *A Journey through Texas.* New York: Dix, Edwards & Company.
  1970 *The Cotton Kingdom: A Traveller's Observations on Cotton and Slavery in
  the American Slave States.* (Edited by A. M. Schlesinger.) New York: Alfred
  A. Knopf.
Olsen, M. E.
  1968 *The Process of Social Organization.* New York: Holt, Rinehart and Winston, Inc.
Olson, J. S. and R. Wilson
  1984 *Native Americans in the Twentieth Century.* Provo: Brigham Young
  University Press.
Olzak, S.
  1983 "Contemporary Ethnic Mobilization." *Annual Review of Sociology*
  9:355–374.

Owen, C. A., H. C. Eisner, and T. R. McPaul
 1981 "A Half-Century of Social Distance Research: National Replication of
 the Bogardus' Studies." *Sociology and Social Research* 66:80–98.
Oxendine, J. B.
 1988 *American Indian Sports Heritage*. Champaign, IL: Human Kinetics Books.
Palmer, D. H.
 1967 "Moving North: Migration of Negroes during World War I." *Phylon*
 28:52–62
Park, R.
 1924 "The Concept of Social Distance." *Journal of Applied Sociology* 8:339–344.
Park, R. E.
 1915 "The City: Suggestions for the Investigation of Human Behavior in the
 City Environment." *American Journal of Sociology* 20:577–612.
 1926/1950 *Race and Culture*. New York: Free Press.
 1939 "The Nature of Race Relations." In Edgar T. Thompson (ed.), *Race
 Relations and the Race Problem: A Definition and Analysis*. Durham: Duke
 University Press.
Park, R. E. and E. W. Burgess
 1921 *Introduction to the Science of Sociology*. Chicago: University of Chicago
 Press.
Passel, J. S.
 1986 "Undocumented Immigration." *The Annals of the American Academy of
 Political and Social Sciences* 487:181–200.
Patterson, L.
 1989 *Martin Luther King, Jr., and the Freedom Movement*. New York: Facts on
 File.
Patterson, W.
 1977 "The First Attempt to Obtain Korean Laborers for Hawaii, 1896–1897."
 Pp. 9–31 in H. Kim (ed.), *The Korean Diaspora: Historical and Sociological
 Studies of Korean Immigration and Assimilation in North America*. Santa
 Barbara, CA: ABC-Clio.
 1988 *The Korean Frontier in America: Immigration to Hawaii, 1896–1910*.
 Honolulu: University of Hawaii Press.
Pavalko, R. M.
 1977 "Racism and the New Immigration: Toward a Re-interpretation of the
 Experiences of White Ethnics in American Society." Paper read at the
 annual meeting of the American Sociological Association, Chicago.
Peabody, D.
 1961 "Attitude Content and Agreement Set in Scales of Authoritarianism,
 Dogmatism and Anti-Semitism, and Economic Conservatism." *Journal of
 Abnormal and Social Psychology* 63:1–11.
Peach, C.
 1980 "Which Triple Melting Pot? A re-examination of ethnic intermarriage
 in New Haven, 1900–1950." *Ethnic and Racial Studies* 3:1–16.
Pedraza, S.
 1991 "Women and Migration: The Social Consequences of Gender." *Annual
 Review of Sociology* 17:303–325.

Petersen, W.
  1971 *Japanese Americans*. New York: Random House, Inc.
Pettigrew, T. F.
  1967 "Social Evaluation Theory: Convergence and Applications." Pp.
    241–310 in *Nebraska Symposium on Motivation*, Vol. 15. Lincoln: University
    of Nebraska Press.
  1969 "Racially Separate or Together?" *Journal of Social Issues* 25:43–69.
  1988 "Integration and Pluralism." In P. A. Katz and D. A. Taylor (eds.),
    Eliminating Racism: Profiles in Controversy. New York: Plenum Press.
  1989 "The Nature of Modern Racism in the United States." Unpublished
    Paper. University of Amsterdam.
Piaget, J.
  1932 *The Moral Judgment of the Child*. London: Kegan Paul.
Polanyi, K.
  1944 *The Great Transformation*. New York: Farrar and Rinehart, Inc.
Portes, A.
  1984 "The Rise of Ethnicity: Determinants of Ethnic Perceptions among
    Cuban Exiles in Miami." *American Sociological Review* 49:383–397.
Portes, A. and A. Stepick
  1985 "Unwelcomed Immigrants: The Labor Market Experiences of the 1980
    (Mariel) Cuban and Haitian Refugees in South Florida." *American
    Sociological Review* 50:493–514.
Portes, A. and C. Truelove
  1987 "Making Sense of Diversity: Recent Research on Hispanic Minorities in
    the United States." *Annual Review of Sociology* 13:359–385.
Portes, A. and R. G. Rumbaut
  1990 *Immigrant America: A Portrait*. Berkeley: University of California Press.
Portes, A. and J. Walton
  1981 *Labor, Class, and the International System*. New York: Academic Press.
Powers, M. N.
  1986 *Oglala Women: Myth, Ritual, and Reality*. Chicago: University of Chicago
    Press.
Provencher, R.
  1975 *Mainland Southeast Asia: An Anthropological Perspective*. Pacific
    Palisades, CA: Goodyear Publishing Company, Inc.
Prucha, F. P.
  1962 *American Indian Policy in the Formative Years*. Cambridge, MA: Harvard
    University Press.
Quadagno, J.
  1990 "Race, Class, Gender and the U.S. Welfare State: Nixon's Failed Family
    Assistance Plan." *American Sociological Review* 55:11–28.
Quadagno, J. S.
  1984 "Welfare Capitalism and the Social Security Act of 1935." *American
    Sociological Review* 49:632–647.
Raab, S.
  1989 "John Gotti Running the Mob." *The New York Times Magazine*, April 2,
    1989.

Rabaya, V.
  1971 "Filipino Immigration: The Creation of a New Social Problem." Pp.
    188–200 in A. Tachiki, E. Wong, and F. Odo (eds.), *Roots: An Asian
    American Reader*. Los Angeles: The UCLA Asian American Studies Center.
Radke, M. J., H. Trager, and H. Davis
  1949 "Social Perception and Attitudes of Children." *Genetic Psychology
    Monographs* 19:327–347.
Rainwater, L.
  1966 "Crucible of Identity: The Negro Lower-Class Family." *Daedalus*
    95:172–216.
  1970 *Behind Ghetto Walls*. Chicago: Aldine-Atherton.
Ransom, R. L. and R. Sutch
  1977 *One Kind of Freedom: The Economic Consequences of Emancipation*.
    Cambridge: Cambridge University Press.
Rasinski, K. A., J. Crocker, and R. Hastie
  1985 "Another Look at Sex Stereotypes and Social Judgments: An Analysis
    of the Social Perceiver's Use of Subjective Probabilities." *Journal of
    Personality and Social Psychology* 49:317–326.
Rawley, J. A.
  1981 *The Transatlantic Slave Trade: A History*. New York: W. W. Norton and
    Company.
Reddaway, W. F., J. H. Penson, O. Holecki, and R. Dyboski (eds.)
  1941 *The Cambridge History of Poland, 1697–1935*. Cambridge, England:
    Cambridge University Press.
  1950 *The Cambridge History of Poland*. Volume I. Cambridge, England:
    Cambridge University Press.
Reisler, M.
  1976 *By the Sweat of Their Brow: Mexican Immigrant Labor in the United States,
    1900–1940*. Westport, CT: Greenwood Press.
Reuter, E. B.
  1945 "Racial Theory." *American Journal of Sociology* 50:452–461.
Richardson, J.
  1989 *Philippines*. Volume 106. World Bibliographical Series. Oxford: Clio Press.
Riesman, D.
  1950 *The Lonely Crowd*. New Haven: Yale University Press.
Ringer, B. B. and E. R. Lawless
  1989 *Race-Ethnicity and Society*. New York: Routledge.
Rivera, M.
  1984 "Organizational Politics of the East Harlem Barrio in the 1970s." Pp.
    61–72 in J. Jennings and M. Rivera (eds.), *Puerto Rican Politics in Urban
    America*. Westport, CT: Greenwood Press.
Roach, J. L. and O. R. Gursslin
  1967 "An Evaluation of the Concept 'Culture of Poverty'." *Social Forces*
    45:383–392.
Robinson, P. A.
  1969 *The Freudian Left*. New York: Harper & Row.

Rodman, H.
  1968 "The Lower-Class Value Stretch." Pp. 296–310 in R. W. Mack (ed.),
    Race, Class, and Power. New York: Van Nostrand Reinhold Company.
Rodriguez, C. E.
  1989 *Puerto Ricans: Born in the USA*. Boston: Unwin Hyman.
Rodriguez, N. and R. T. Nunez
  1986 "An Exploration of Factors That Contribute to Differentiation between
    Chicanos and Indocumentados." Pp. 138–156 in H. L. Browning and R. O.
    de la Garza (eds.), *Mexican Americans and Mexican Immigrants: An Evolving
    Relation*. Austin, TX: CMAS Publications.
Rokeach, M.
  1956 "Political and Religious Dogmatism: An Alternate to the Authoritarian
    Personality." *Psychological Monographs* 70:1–43.
  1960 *The Open and Closed Mind*. New York: Basic Books, Inc., Publishers.
Rolle, A. F.
  1968 *The Immigrants Upraised: Italian Adventurers and Colonists in Expanding
    America*. Norman: University of Oklahoma Press.
  1980 *The Italian Americans: Troubled Roots*. New York: The Free Press.
Romo, R.
  1983 *East Los Angeles: History of a Barrio*. Austin: University of Texas Press.
Rose, P. M.
  1922 *The Italians in America*. New York: George H. Doran Company.
Rosenbaum, R. J.
  1981 *Mexicano Resistance in the Southwest*. Austin: University of Texas Press.
Rosenberg, M.
  1979 *Conceiving the Self*. New York: Basic Books.
Rosenberg, M. and R. G. Simmons
  1972 *Black and White Self-Esteem: The Urban School Child*. Rose Monograph
    series. Washington, DC: American Sociological Association.
Rosenthal, E.
  1960 "Acculturation without Assimilation? The Jewish Community of
    Chicago, Illinois." *American Journal of Sociology* 66:275–288.
Rumbaut, R. G.
  1989 "Portraits, Patterns, and Predictors of the Refugee Adaptation Process:
    Results and Reflections from the IHARP Panel Study." Pp. 138–190 in
    D. W. Haines (ed.), *Refugees as Immigrants: Cambodians, Laotians and
    Vietnamese in America*. Totowa, NJ: Rowman and Littlefield Publishers,
    Inc.
Rutledge, P.
  1985 *The Role of Religion in Ethnic Self-Identity: A Vietnamese Community*.
    Lanham, MD: University Press of America.
Samora, J. and P. V. Simon
  1977 *A History of the Mexican American People*. Notre Dame: University of
    Notre Dame Press.
Sanchez-Ayendez, M.
  1988 "The Puerto Rican American Family." Pp. 173–198 in C. H. Mindel, R.

W. Habenstein, and R. Wright, Jr. (eds.), *Ethnic Families in America*. Third Edition. New York: Elsevier.

Sandberg, N. C.
1974 *Ethnic Identity and Assimilation: The Polish-American Community*. New York: Praeger Publishers.

Sanders, J. M. and V. Nee
1987 "Limits of Ethnic Solidarity in the Enclave Economy." *American Sociological Review* 52:745–773.

Saxton, A.
1971 *The Indispensable Enemy: Labor and the Anti-Chinese Movement in California*. Berkeley: University of California Press.

Scanzoni, J. H.
1971 *The Black Family in Modern Society*. Boston: Allyn and Bacon, Inc.

Schaefer, R. T.
1990 *Racial and Ethnic Groups*. Fourth Edition. Glenview, IL: Scott, Foresman/Little, Brown.

Schmid, C. F. and C. E. Nobbe
1965 "Socioeconomic Differentials among Nonwhite Races." *American Sociological Review* 30(December):909–922.

Schneider, E. V.
1969 *Industrial Sociology: The Social Relations of Industry and the Community*. Second Edition. New York: McGraw-Hill Book Company.

Schulz, D. A.
1969 *Coming up Black: Patterns of Ghetto Socialization*. Englewood Cliffs, NJ: Prentice-Hall, Inc.

Schwieder, D., J. Hraba, and E. Schwieder
1987 *Buxton: Work and Racial Equality in a Coal Mining Community*. Ames: Iowa State University Press.

Scott, J. W.
1976 *The Black Revolts: Racial Stratification in the U.S.A.* Cambridge, MA: Schenkman Publishing Company, Inc.

Seller, M. S.
1975 "Beyond the Stereotype: A New Look at the Immigrant Woman." *Journal of Ethnic Studies* 3:59–68.

Sexton, P. C.
1965 *Spanish Harlem*. New York: Harper & Row.

Shannon, W. V.
1963/1966 *The American Irish: A Political and Social Portrait*. Amherst: University of Massachusetts Press.

Sharma, M.
1984a "The Philippines: A Case of Migration to Hawaii, 1906–1946." Pp. 337–358 in L. Cheng and E. Bonacich (eds.), *Labor Immigration under Capitalism: Asian Workers in the United States before World War II*. Berkeley: University of California Press.
1984b "Labor Migration and Class Formation among the Filipinos in Hawaii, 1906–1946." Pp. 579–616 in L. Cheng and E. Bonacich (eds.), *Labor*

Immigration under Capitalism: Asian Workers in the United States before World War II. Berkeley: University of California Press.

Shibutani, T. and K. M. Kwan

  1965 *Ethnic Stratification*. New York: Macmillan Company.

Shimkin, D., G. J. Louie, and D. Frate

  1973 "The Black Extended Family: A Basic Rural Institution and a Mechanism of Urban Adaptation." Paper prepared for the Ninth International Congress of Anthropological and Ethnological Sciences.

Shin, E. H. and K. Chang

  1988 "Peripherization of Immigrant Professionals: Korean Physicians in the United States." *International Migration Review* 22:609–629.

Simcox, D. E.

  1988a "Mexico's Dilemma: Finding a Million Jobs a Year." Pp. 201–213 in D. E. Simcox (ed.), *U.S. Immigration in the 1980s: Reappraisal and Reform*. Boulder, CO: Westview Press.

  1988b "Overview—A Time of Reform and Reappraisal." Pp. 1–63 in D. E. Simcox (ed.), *U.S. Immigration in the 1980s: Reappraisal and Reform*. Boulder, CO: Westview Press.

Simmel, G.

  1955 *Conflict: The Web of Group-Affiliation*. (Translated By Kurt H. Wolff and R. Bendix.) Glencoe, IL: Free Press.

Simmons, R. G., L. Brown, D. M. Bush, and D. A. Blyth

  1978 "Self-Esteem and Achievement of Black and White Adolescents." *Social Problems* 26:86–96.

Simon, J. L.

  1986 "Basic Data Concerning Immigration into the United States." *The Annals of the American Academy of Political and Social Sciences* 487:12–56.

Simpson, G. E. and J. M. Yinger

  1972 *Racial and Cultural Minorities: An Analysis of Prejudice and Discrimination*. Fourth Edition. New York: Harper & Row.

Smith, A.

  1776/1896 *An Inquiry into the Nature and Causes of the Wealth of Nations*. Oxford: Clarendon Press.

Smith, T. W. and G. R. Dempsey

  1983 "The Polls: Ethnic Social Distance and Prejudice." *Public Opinion Quarterly* 47:584–600.

Sniderman, P. M. and P. E. Tetlock

  1986 "Symbolic Racism: Problems of Political Motive Attribution." *Journal of Social Issues* 42:129–150.

Snipp, C. M.

  1989 *American Indians: The First of This Land*. New York: Russell Sage Foundation.

Sorkin, A. L.

  1971 *American Indians and Federal Aid*. Washington, DC: Brookings Institution.

Sowell, T.

  1975 *Race and Economics*. New York: David McKay Company, Inc.

1981 *Ethnic America: A History*. Basic Books, Inc.

Spencer, R. F. and J. D. Jennings, et al.
1977 *The Native Americans*. Second Edition. New York: Harper & Row.

Spero, S. D. and A. L. Harris
1931 *The Black Worker: The Negro and the Labor Movement*. New York: Columbia University Press.

Spicer, E. H.
1962 *Cycles of Conquest: The Impact of Spain, Mexico, and the United States on the Indians of the Southwest*. Tucson: University of Arizona Press.
1969 *A Short History of the Indians of the United States*. New York: Van Nostrand Reinhold Company.
1972 "Indigenismo in the United States, 1870–1960." Pp. 159–160 in Seward E. Walker, Jr. (ed.), *The Emergent Native Americans*. Boston: Little, Brown and Company.

Squires, G. S.
1977 "Education, Jobs and Inequality: Functional and Conflict Models of Social Stratification in the United States." *Social Problems* 24:436–450.

Staats, A. W. and C. K. Staats
1958 "Attitudes Established by Classical Conditioning." *Journal of Abnormal and Social Psychology* 57:37–40.

Stampp, K. M.
1968 *The Peculiar Institution: Slavery in the Ante-Bellum South*. New York: Alfred A. Knopf.

Stein, D. D., J. A. Hardyck, and M. B. Smith
1965 "Race and Belief: An Open and Shut Case." *Journal of Personality and Social Psychology* 1:281–289.

Stephan, W. G.
1985 "Intergroup Relations." Pp. 599–658 in G. Lindzey and E. Aronson (eds.), *Handbook of Social Psychology*. Third Edition. New York: Random House.

Stevens, G.
1985 "Nativity, Intermarriage, and Mother-Tongue Shift." *American Sociological Review* 50:74–83.

Stoddard, E. R.
1973 *Mexican Americans*. New York: Random House, Inc.

Stoddard, L.
1922 *The Revolt against Civilization*. New York: Scribner's.

Stolzenberg, R. M.
1990 "Ethnicity, Geography and Occupational Achievement of Hispanic Men in the United States." *American Sociological Review* 55:143–154.

Strand, P. J. and W. Jones, Jr.
1985 *Indochinese Refugees in America: Problems of Adaptation and Assimilation*. Durham: Duke University Press.

Stuart, P.
1987 *Nations within a Nation: Historical Statistics of American Indians*. New York: Greenwood Press.

Sullivan, T. A.
  1986 "Stratification of the Chicano Labor Market under Conditions
    of Continuing Mexican Immigration." Pp. 53–73 in H. L. Browning
    and R. O. de la Garza (eds.), *Mexican Immigrants and Mexican
    Americans: An Evolving Relation.* Austin, TX: CMAS
    Publications.
Sutter, V. O.
  1990 *The Indochinese Refugee Dilemma.* Baton Rouge: Louisiana State
    University Press.
Suttles, G. S.
  1968 *The Social Order of the Slum: Ethnicity and Territory in the Inner City.*
    Chicago: University of Chicago Press.
Szapocznik, J. and R. Hernandez
  1988 "The Cuban American Family." Pp. 160–172 in C. H. Mindel, R. W.
    Habenstein, and R. Wright, Jr. (eds.), *Ethnic Families in America: Patterns
    and Variations.* New York: Elsevier.
Szczepanski, J.
  1970 *Polish Society.* New York: Random House.
Tajfel, H.
  1969 "Cognitive Aspects of Prejudice." *Journal of Social Issues* 25:79–99.
  1981 *Human Groups and Social Categories.* Cambridge, England: Cambridge
    University Press.
  1982 *Social Identity and Intergroup Relations.* Cambridge, England: Cambridge
    University Press.
Tajfel, H. (ed.)
  1978 *Differentiation between Social Groups.* London: Academic Press.
Tajfel, H. and J. C. Turner
  1979 "An Interpretative Theory of Social Conflict." Pp. 33–47 in W. Austin
    and S. Worchel (eds.), *The Social Psychology of Intergroup Relations.*
    Monterey, CA: Brooks/Cole.
  1986 "The Social Identity Theory of Intergroup Behavior." Pp. 7–24 in
    S. Worchel and W. G. Austin (eds.), *Psychology of Intergroup Relations.*
    Second Edition. Chicago: Nelson-Hall Publishers.
Takaki, R.
  1989 *Strangers from a Different Shore: A History of Asian Americans.* Boston:
    Little, Brown and Company.
Taussig, F. W. and C. S. Joslyn
  1932 *American Business Leaders.* New York: Macmillan Company.
Taviss, I.
  1969 "Changes in the Form of Alienation: The 1900s vs. the 1950s." *American
    Sociological Review* 32:46–57.
Taylor, G. E.
  1964 *The Philippines and the United States: Problems of Partnership.* New York:
    Frederick A. Praeger, Publisher.
Taylor, M. C. and E. J. Walsh
  1979 "Explanations of Black Self-Esteem: Some Empirical Tests." *Social
    Psychology Quarterly* 42:242–253.

Ten Broek, J., E. N. Burnhart, and F. W. Matson
  1954 *Prejudice, War, and the Constitution.* Berkeley: University of California
    Press.
Theodorson, G. A.
  1961 *Studies in Human Ecology.* New York: Harper & Row.
Thernstrom, S.
  1966 "Class and Mobility in a Nineteenth-Century City: A Study of Unskilled
    Laborers." Pp. 602–615 in R. Bendix and S. M. Lipset (eds.), *Class, Status,
    and Power.* Second Edition. New York: Free Press.
Thernstrom, S. (ed.)
  1980 *Harvard Encyclopedia of American Ethnic Groups.* Cambridge: The
    Belknap Press of Harvard University Press.
Thomas, J. L.
  1951 "The Factor of Religion in the Selection of Marriage Mates." *American
    Sociological Review* 16:487–491.
Thomas, W. I.
  1931 *The Unadjusted Girl.* Boston: Little, Brown and Company.
Thomas, W. I. and F. Znaniecki
  1918/1920 *The Polish Peasant in Europe and America.* Chicago: University of
    Chicago Press.
  1984 *The Polish Peasant in Europe and America.* (Edited and abridged by E.
    Zaretsky.) Urbana: University of Illinois Press.
Tienda, M., L. Jensen, and R. L. Bach
  1984 "Immigration, Gender and the Process of Occupational Changes in the
    United States, 1970–80." *International Migration Review* XVIII:1021–1044.
Tolnay, S. E.
  1984 "Black Family Formation and Tenancy in the Farm South, 1900."
    American Journal of Sociology 90:305–325.
Tooker, E.
  1978 "The League of the Iroquois: Its History, Politics, and Ritual." Pp.
    418–441 in B. C. Trigger (ed.), *Handbook of North American Indians*, Volume
    15: Northeast. Washington, DC: Smithsonian Institution.
Trager, J. and M. Yarrow
  1952 *They Live What They Learn.* New York: Harper & Row.
Treudley, M. B.
  1949 "Formal Organization and the Americanization Process, with Special
    Reference to the Greeks of Boston." *American Sociological Review* 14:44–53.
Triandis, H. C.
  1961 "A Note on Rokeach's Theory of Prejudice." *Journal of Abnormal and
    Social Psychology* 62:184–186.
Triandis, H. C. and E. E. Davis
  1965 "Race and Belief as Determinants of Behavioral Intentions." *Journal of
    Personality and Social Psychology* 2:715–725.
Trigger, B. G.
  1978 "Early Iroquoian Contact with Europeans." Pp. 344–356 in B. C. Trigger
    (ed.), *Handbook of North American Indians*, Volume 15: Northeast.
    Washington, DC: Smithsonian Institution.

Trow, M.
  1966 "The Second Transformation of American Secondary Education." Pp.
    437–448 in R. Bendix and S. M. Lipset (eds.), *Class, Status, and Power.*
    Second Edition. New York: Free Press.
Tsai, S. H.
  1983 *China and the Overseas Chinese in the United States, 1868–1911.*
    Fayetteville: University of Arkansas Press.
  1986 *The Chinese Experience in America.* Bloomington: Indiana University
    Press.
Tsu Wu, C. (ed.)
  1972 *Chink.* New York: World Publishing.
Turner, J. C.
  1975 "Social Comparison and Social Identity: Some Prospects for Intergroup
    Behavior." *European Journal of Social Psychology* 5:5–34.
Uzzell, O. J.
  1980 "Mixed Strategies in the Formal Sector." *Human Organization* 39:40–49.
Valdez, L. and S. Steiner (eds.)
  1972 *Aztlan: An Anthology of Mexican American Literature.* New York: Alfred
    A. Knopf.
Valentine, C. A.
  1968 *Culture and Poverty: Critique and Counter-Proposals.* Chicago: University
    of Chicago Press.
Vance, R. B.
  1939 "Racial Competition for the Land." Pp. 97–124 in E. T. Thompson (ed.),
    Race Relations and the Race Problem: A Definition and Analysis. Durham:
    Duke University Press.
Van den Berghe, P.
  1967 *Race and Racism: A Comparative Perspective.* New York: John Wiley and
    Sons, Inc.
  1976 "The African Diaspora in Mexico, Brazil, and the United States." *Social
    Forces* 54:530–545.
Vander Zanden, J. W.
  1972 *American Minority Relations.* Third Edition. New York: Ronald Press
    Company.
  1973 "Sociological Studies of Black Americans." *Sociological Quarterly*
    14:32–52.
Vecoli, R. J.
  1970 "Contadini in Chicago: A Critique of *The Uprooted.*" Pp. 216–228 in
    L. Dinnerstein and F. C. Jaher (eds.), *The Aliens: A History of Ethnic
    Minorities in America.* New York: Appleton-Century-Crofts.
Vogel, V. J.
  1972 *This Country Was Ours.* New York: Harper & Row.
Wade, R. C.
  1964 *Slavery in the Cities: The South, 1820–1860.* New York: Oxford University
    Press.
Ware, C. F.
  1935 *Greenwich Village.* Boston: Houghton Mifflin Company.

597

Warner, W. L.
  1959 *The Living and the Dead*. New Haven: Yale University Press.
Warner, W. L. and J. C. Abegglen
  1955 *Occupational Mobility in American Business and Industry, 1928–1952*. Minneapolis: University of Minnesota Press.
Warner, W. L. and Associates
  1949 *Democracy in Jonesville*. New York: Harper & Row, Publishers
Warner, W. L. and J. O. Low
  1947 *The Social System of Modern Factory*. New Haven: Yale University Press.
Warner, W. L. and P. S. Lunt
  1941 *The Social Life of a Modern Community*. New Haven: Yale University Press.
  1942 *The Status System of a Modern Community*. New Haven: Yale University Press.
Warner, W. L. and L. Srole
  1945 *The Social Systems of American Ethnic Groups*. New Haven: Yale University Press.
Weatherford, D.
  1986 *Foreign and Female: Immigrant Women in America, 1840–1930*. New York: Schocken Books.
Weber, M.
  1966 "Class, Status, and Party." Pp. 21–28 in R. Bendix and S. M. Lipset (eds.), *Class, Status, and Power*. Second Edition. New York: Free Press.
Weiner, M.
  1985 "Transborder Peoples." Pp. 130–158 in W. Connor (ed.), *Mexican-Americans in Comparative Perspective*. Washington, DC: The Urban Institute Press.
  1989 *The Origins of the Korean Community in Japan, 1910–1923*. Manchester: Manchester University Press.
Weiss, M. S.
  1974 *Valley City: A Chinese Community in America*. Cambridge, MA: Schenkman Publishing Company.
Whitlow, R.
  1973 *Black American Literature: A Critical History*. Chicago: Nelson Hall.
Whyte, W. F.
  1955 *Street Corner Society*. Second Edition. Chicago: University of Chicago Press.
Wicker, A. W.
  1969 "Attitudes Versus Actions: The Relationship of Verbal and Overt Behavioral Response to Attitude Objects." *Journal of Social Issues* 25:41–78.
Wiegersma, N.
  1988 *Vietnam: Peasant Land, Peasant Revolution: Patriarchy and Collectivity in the Rural Economy*. New York: St. Martin's Press.
Wilensky, H. L.
  1961 "Orderly Careers and Social Participation: The Impact of Work History on Social Integration in the Middle Class." *American Sociological Review* 26:521–539.

Wilhelm, S. M.
1971 *Who Needs the Negro?* Garden City, NY: Doubleday and Company Inc.
Williams, E.
1966 *Capitalism and Slavery*. New York: Capricorn Books.
Williams, J. A., Jr., N. Bahchuk, and D. R. Johnson
1973 "Voluntary Association and Minority Status: A Comparative Analysis of Anglo, Black, and Mexican Americans." *American Sociological Review* 38:637–646.
Williams, R. M., Jr.
1964 *Strangers Next Door*. Englewood Cliffs, NJ: Prentice-Hall, Inc.
Wilson, K. L. and W. A. Martin
1982 "Ethnic Enclaves: A Comparison of the Cuban and Black Economies in Miami." *American Journal of Sociology* 88:135–160.
Wilson, K. L. and A. Portes
1980 "Immigrant Enclaves: An Analysis of the Labor Market Experiences of Cubans in Miami." *American Journal of Sociology* 86:295–319.
Wilson, R. A and B. Hosokawa
1980 *East to America: A History of the Japanese in the United States*. New York: William Morrow and Company.
Wilson, W. J.
1973 *Power, Racism and Privilege: Race Relations in Theoretical and Socio-historical Perspectives*. New York: Macmillan Company.
1978 *The Declining Significance of Race: Blacks and Changing American Institutions*. Chicago: University of Chicago Press.
1987 *The Truly Disadvantaged: The Inner City, the Underclass, and Public Policy*. Chicago: University of Chicago Press.
Wirth, L.
1928/1956 *The Ghetto*. Chicago: University of Chicago Press.
Wittke, C.
1970 *The Irish in America*. New York: Russell and Russell.
Wong, M. G.
1988 "The Chinese American Family." Pp. 230–257 in C. H. Mindel, R. W. Habenstein, and R. Wright, Jr. (eds.), *Ethnic Families in America: Patterns and Variations*. New York: Elsevier.
Wood, A. E.
1955 *Hamtramck: Then and Now*. New York: Bookman Associates.
Woodward, C. V.
1966 *The Strange Career of Jim Crow*. Second Revised Edition. New York: Oxford University Press.
1974 *The Strange Career of Jim Crow*. Third Revised Edition. New York: Oxford University Press.
Woolf, S.
1979 *A History of Italy 1700–1860*. London: Methuen.
Wrobel, P.
1979 *Our Way: Family, Parish, and Neighborhood in a Polish-American Community*. Notre Dame: University of Notre Dame Press.

Wytrwal, J. A.
1961 *America's Polish Heritage: A Social History of Poles in America*. Detroit:
Endurance Press.
Yanagisako, S. J.
1985 *Transforming the Past: Tradition and Kinship among Japanese Americans*.
Stanford: Stanford University Press.
Yancey, W. L., E. P. Erickson, and R. N. Julian
1976 "Emergent Ethnicity: A Review and Reformation." *American Sociological
Review* 41:391–402.
Yang, E. S.
1982 "Koreans in America, 1903–1945." Pp. 5–22 in E. Y. Yu, E. H. Phillips,
and E. S. Yang (eds.), *Koreans in Los Angeles: Prospects and Promises*. Los
Angeles: Koryo Research Institute, California State University, Los
Angeles.
Yetman, N. R.
1970 *Life under the "Peculiar Institution."* New York: Holt, Rinehart and
Winston, Inc.
Yim, S. B.
1984 "The Social Structure of Korean Communities in California,
1903–1920." Pp. 515–548 in L. Cheng and E. Bonacich (eds.), *Labor
Immigration under Capitalism: Asian Workers in the United States before World
War II*. Berkeley: University of California Press.
Yu, C.
1977 "The Correlates of Cultural Assimilation of Korean Immigrants in the
United States." Pp. 167–176 in H. Kim (ed.), *The Korean Diaspora: Historical
and Sociological Studies of Korean Immigration and Assimilation in North
America*. Santa Barbara, CA: ABC-Clio.
Yu, E. Y.
1982 "Occupation and Work Patterns of Korean Immigrants." Pp. 49–74 in E.
Y. Yu, E. H. Phillips, and E. S. Yang (eds.), *Koreans in Los Angeles: Prospects
and Promises*. Los Angeles: Koryo Research Institute, California State
University, Los Angeles.
Yuan, D. Y.
1963 "Voluntary Segregation: A Study of New York Chinatown." *Phylon*
24:255–265.
Yun, Y.
1977 "Early History of Korean Immigration to America." Pp. 33–46 in H.
Kim (ed.), *The Korean Diaspora: Historical and Sociological Studies of Korean
Immigration and Assimilation in North America*. Santa Barbara, CA: ABC-
Clio.
Yung-Hwan, J.
1982 "Problems and Strategies of Participation in American Politics." Pp.
203–218 in E. Y. Yu, E. H. Phillips, and E. S. Yang (eds.), *Koreans in Los
Angeles: Prospects and Promises*. Los Angeles: Koryo Research Institute,
California State University, Los Angeles.

Zeul, C. and C. R. Humphrey
  1971 "The Integration of Blacks in Suburban Neighborhoods: A
    Reexamination of the Contact Hypothesis." *Social Problems* 18:462–474.
Zhou, M. and J. R. Logan
  1989 "Returns on Human Capital in Ethnic Enclaves: New York City's
    Chinatown." *American Sociological Review* 54:809–820.

INDEX

AMERICAN ETHNICITY
Edited by Norm Mysliwiec
Photographs compiled by Cheryl Kucharzak
Production supervision by Kim Vander Steen
Designed by Lesiak/Crampton Design, Inc., Chicago, Illinois
Composition by Point West Inc., Carol Stream, Illinois
Paper, Glatfelter
Printed and bound by Braun-Brumfield, Ann Arbor, Michigan